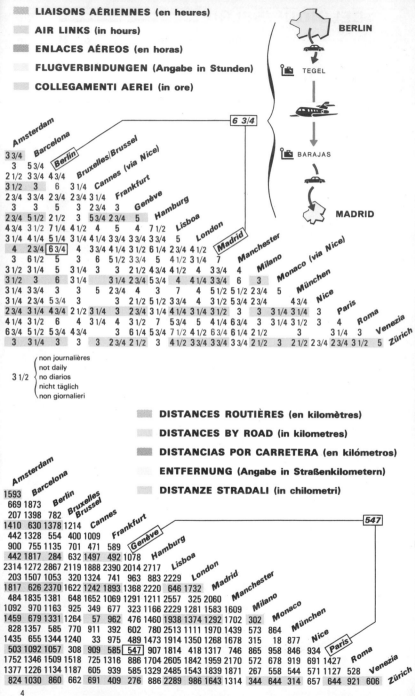

LIAISONS AÉRIENNES (en heures)
AIR LINKS (in hours)
ENLACES AÉREOS (en horas)
FLUGVERBINDUNGEN (Angabe in Stunden)
COLLEGAMENTI AEREI (in ore)

BERLIN
TEGEL
6 3/4
BARAJAS
MADRID

	Amsterdam	Barcelona	Berlin	Bruxelles/Brussel	Cannes (via Nice)	Frankfurt	Genève	Hamburg	Lisboa	London	Madrid	Manchester	Milano	Monaco (via Nice)	München	Nice	Paris	Roma	Venezia
Barcelona	3 3/4																		
Berlin	3	5 3/4																	
Bruxelles/Brussel	2 1/2	3 3/4	4 3/4																
Cannes (via Nice)	3 1/2	3	6	3 1/4															
Frankfurt	2 3/4	3 3/4	2 3/4	2 3/4	3 1/4														
Genève	3	3	5	3	2 3/4	3													
Hamburg	2 3/4	5 1/2	2 1/2	3	5 3/4	2 3/4	5												
Lisboa	4 3/4	3 1/2	7 1/4	4 1/2	4	5	4	7 1/2											
London	3 1/4	4 1/4	5 1/4	3 1/4	4 1/4	3 3/4	3 3/4	3 3/4	5										
Madrid	4	2 3/4	6 3/4	4	3 3/4	4 1/4	3 1/2	6 1/4	2 3/4	4 1/2									
Manchester	3	6 1/2	5	3	6	5 1/2	3 3/4	5	4 1/2	3 1/4	7								
Milano	3 1/2	3 1/4	5	3 1/4	3	2 1/2	4 3/4	4 1/2	2	4 3/4	3 3/4	4							
Monaco (via Nice)	3 1/2	3	6	3 1/4		3 1/4	2 3/4	5 3/4	4	4 1/4	3 3/4	6	3						
München	3 1/4	3 3/4	3	3	5	2 3/4	4	3	7	4	5 1/2	5 1/2	2 3/4	5					
Nice	3 1/4	2 3/4	5 3/4	3		3	2 1/2	5 1/2	3 3/4	4	3 1/2	5 3/4	2 3/4		4 3/4				
Paris	2 3/4	3 1/4	3 3/4	2 1/2	3 1/4	3	2 3/4	3 1/4	4 1/4	3 1/2	3	3	3 1/4	3 1/4	3				
Roma	4 1/4	3 1/2	6	4	3 1/4	4	3 1/2	7	5 3/4	4	6 3/4	3	3 1/4	3 1/2	3	4			
Venezia	6 3/4	5 1/2	5 3/4	4 3/4	3	6 1/4	5 3/4	7 1/2	4 1/2	6 3/4	6 1/4	2 1/2	3		3 1/4	3			
Zürich	3	3 1/4	3	3	3	2 3/4	2 1/2	3	4 1/2	3 3/4	3 3/4	3 3/4	2 1/2	3	2 1/2	2 3/4	2 3/4	3 1/2	5

3 1/2 { non journalières / not daily / no diarios / nicht täglich / non giornalieri

DISTANCES ROUTIÈRES (en kilomètres)
DISTANCES BY ROAD (in kilometres)
DISTANCIAS POR CARRETERA (en kilómetros)
ENTFERNUNG (Angabe in Straßenkilometern)
DISTANZE STRADALI (in chilometri)

547

	Amsterdam	Barcelona	Berlin	Bruxelles/Brussel	Cannes	Frankfurt	Genève	Hamburg	Lisboa	London	Madrid	Manchester	Milano	Monaco	München	Nice	Paris	Roma	Venezia
Barcelona	1593																		
Berlin	669	1873																	
Bruxelles/Brussel	207	1398	782																
Cannes	1410	630	1378	1214															
Frankfurt	442	1328	554	400	1009														
Genève	900	755	1135	701	471	589													
Hamburg	442	1817	284	632	1497	492	1078												
Lisboa	2314	1272	2867	2119	1888	2390	2014	2717											
London	203	1507	1053	320	1324	741	963	883	2229										
Madrid	1817	626	2370	1622	1242	1893	1368	2220	646	1732									
Manchester	484	1835	1381	648	1652	1069	1291	1211	2557	325	2060								
Milano	1092	970	1163	925	349	677	323	1166	2229	1281	1583	1609							
Monaco	1459	679	1331	1264	57	962	476	1460	1938	1374	1292	1702	302						
München	828	1357	585	770	911	392	602	780	2513	1111	1970	1439	573	864					
Nice	1435	655	1344	1240	33	975	489	1473	1914	1350	1268	1678	315	18	877				
Paris	503	1092	1057	308	909	585	547	907	1814	418	1317	746	865	958	846	934			
Roma	1752	1346	1509	1518	725	1316	886	1704	2605	1842	1959	2170	572	678	919	691	1427		
Venezia	1377	1226	1134	1187	605	939	585	1329	2485	1543	1839	1871	267	558	544	571	1127	528	
Zürich	824	1030	860	662	691	409	276	886	2289	986	1643	1314	344	644	314	657	644	921	606

VILLES SÉLECTIONNÉES DANS CE GUIDE

TOWNS LISTED IN THIS GUIDE

CIUDADES QUE APARECEN EN ESTA GUÍA

AUSGEWÄHLTE STÄDTE IM FÜHRER

CITTÀ SELEZIONATE IN QUESTA GUIDA

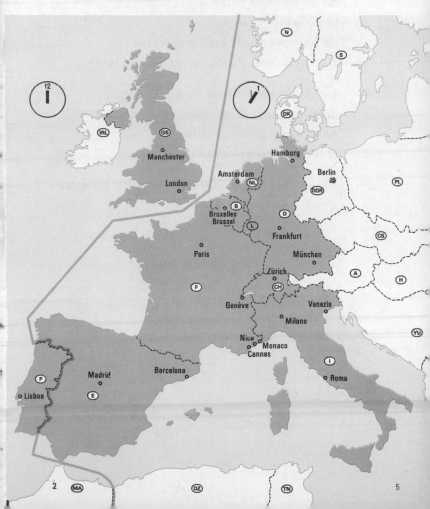

Avec cette nouvelle publication,
les Services de Tourisme Michelin
vous proposent une sélection
de 20 villes d'Europe,
choisies en raison
de leur vocation internationale
sur le plan des affaires et du tourisme.

Ce guide est destiné à vous aider
dans le choix d'un hôtel, d'un restaurant,
pour la visite de la ville
et de ses principales curiosités.

Nous vous souhaitons d'agréables séjours.

Signes
et
symboles

HOTELS ET RESTAURANTS

CLASSE ET CONFORT

Grand luxe et tradition	🏰 XXXXX
Grand confort	🏯 XXXX
Très confortable	🏛 XXX
Confortable	🏠 XX
Assez confortable	🏡 X
Simple mais convenable	🏚
Autre ressource hôtelière conseillée	↑
Dans sa catégorie, hôtel d'équipement moderne	M

L'AGRÉMENT

Hôtels agréables	🏰 ... 🏡
Restaurants agréables	XXXXX ... X
Élément particulièrement agréable	« Parc Fleuri »
Hôtel très tranquille, ou isolé et tranquille	⑤
Hôtel tranquille	⑤
Vue exceptionnelle, panorama	⩽ mer, ❄
Vue intéressante ou étendue	⩽

LA TABLE

Une des meilleures tables du pays, vaut le voyage	✿ ✿ ✿
Table excellente, mérite un détour	✿ ✿
Une très bonne table dans sa catégorie	✿
Autre table soignée	Karte, **R, M,** Pas

7

L'INSTALLATION

🛗 📺	Ascenseur, Télévision dans la chambre
🌡 ▭	Chauffage central, air conditionné
🛁wc 🛁	Bain et wc privés, bain sans wc
🚿wc 🚿	Douche et wc privés, douche privée sans wc
☎	Téléphone dans la chambre direct avec l'extérieur
☏	Téléphone dans la chambre relié par standard
✂ ⚒ ⬛	Tennis — Piscine : de plein air ou couverte
⬦s ⬟ ⬤ ⛰s	Sauna — Jardin — Pelouse ou terrasse — Plage aménagée
🚗 🚗 Ⓟ	Garage gratuit — Garage payant — Parc à voitures
♿	Chambres accessibles aux handicapés physiques
⛺	L'hôtel reçoit les séminaires
🐕̸	Accès interdit aux chiens
garni	L'hôtel n'a pas de restaurant

LES PRIX

Les prix sont indiqués dans la monnaie du pays. Ils ont été établis en fin d'année 1981 et peuvent être modifiés en fonction de l'évolution du coût de la vie.

Au restaurant

Karte	Com	Pas
M	Ref	**R** 40/85

Prix minimum et maximum des repas

A l'hôtel

30 hab	**cam**	**qto**
Z	**rm**	**ch** 60/120

Prix minimum 60 pour une chambre d'une personne et maximum 120 pour la plus belle chambre occupée par deux personnes

34 Z : 55 B 23/45

Nombre de chambres et de lits avec prix minimum et maximum pour une nuit et par personne, petit déjeuner inclus.

Petit déjeuner

🛏 12   🍽 10

Prix du petit déjeuner servi dans la chambre ; servi en salle.

Fb

petit déjeuner buffet

Service et taxes

s.   t.

Service compris   T.V.A. comprise

stc SC st.

prix tout compris ou prix nets.

En Allemagne, Italie, Suisse, Espagne et Portugal, les prix indiqués sont nets.

8

LES CURIOSITÉS

Vaut le voyage

Mérite un détour

Intéressante

★★★
★★
★

LES PLANS

Principaux signes conventionnels

Information touristique ....

Hôtel, restaurant — Lettre les repérant sur le plan ....

Monument intéressant et entrée principale ⎫
Église ou chapelle intéressante .... ⎬ Lettre les repérant sur le plan ......

Rue commerçante — Parc de stationnement public ....

Tramway-Trolleybus ....

Station de métro ....

Sens unique ....

Église ou chapelle — Poste restante, télégraphe — Téléphone ....

Édifices publics repérés par des lettres :

Police (dans les grandes villes commissariat central) — Théâtre — Musée ....

Gare routière — Aéroport — Hôpital — Marché couvert ....

Ruines — Monument, statue — Fontaine ....

Jardin, parc, bois — Cimetière, cimetière israélite ....

Piscine de plein air, couverte — Hippodrome — Golf ....

Téléphérique — Funiculaire ....

Stade — Vue — Panorama ....

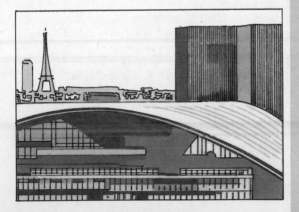

This latest publication from the Michelin Tourism Department offers you a selection of 20 European towns chosen for their business or tourist interest.
The aim of this guide is to help you choose a hotel or restaurant for your visit to the town and its sights.
We hope you enjoy your stay.

HOTELS AND RESTAURANTS

CLASS, STANDARD OF COMFORT

Luxury in the traditional style
Top class
Very comfortable
Comfortable
Good average
Plain but adequate
Other recommended accommodation
In its class, hotel with modern amenities

AMENITY

$\hat{\underline{\text{舟舟舟}}}$ ... 🏠
🗙🗙🗙🗙🗙 ... 🗙
« Park »
🦢
🦢
≤ sea, ☀
≤

Pleasant hotels
Pleasant restaurants
Particularly attractive feature
Very quiet or quiet secluded hotel
Quiet hotel
Exceptional view — Panoramic view
Interesting or extensive view

CUISINE

❀❀❀
❀❀
❀
Karte, **R, M,** Pas

Exceptional cuisine in the country, worth a special journey
Excellent cooking : worth a detour
An especially good restaurant in its class
Other recommended carefully prepared meals

HOTEL FACILITIES

Lift (elevator) — Television in room

Central heating, air conditioning

Private bathroom with toilet, private bathroom without toilet

Private shower with toilet, private shower without toilet

Telephone in room : direct dialling for outside calls

Telephone in room : outside calls connected by operator

Hotel tennis court(s) — Outdoor or indoor swimming pool

Sauna — Garden — Lawns — Beach with bathing facilities

Free garage — Charge made for garage — Car park

Bedrooms accessible to the physically handicapped

Equipped conference hall

Dogs are not allowed

The hotel has no restaurant

garni

PRICES

Prices are given in local currency. Valid for late 1981, they may be revised if the cost of living changes to any great extent.

Meals

Lowest 40 and highest 85 prices for meals

Karte Com Pas
M Ref **R** 40/85

Hotels

Lowest price 60 for a comfortable single and highest price 120 for the best double room

30 hab cam qto
Z rm ch 60/120

Number of rooms and beds with lowest and highest price for one night per person, breakfast included

34 Z : 55 B 23/45

Breakfast

Price of breakfast served in the bedroom ; in the dining room

⊑12 ⚏10

Breakfast with choice from buffet

Fb

Service and taxes

Service only included.   V.A.T. only included.

s.   t.

Service and V.A.T. included (net prices).

stc SC st.

In Germany, Italy, Switzerland, Spain and Portugal, prices shown are inclusive, that is to say service and V.A.T. included.

SIGHTS

★★★ Worth a journey
★★ Worth a detour
★ Interesting

TOWN PLANS

Main conventional signs

Tourist Information Centre

Hotel, restaurant — Reference letter on the town plan

Place of interest and its main entrance }
Interesting church or chapel .... } Reference letter on the town plan

Shopping street — Public car park

Tram, trolleybus route

Underground station

One-way street

Church or chapel — Poste restante, telegraph — Telephone

Public buildings located by letters :

Police (in large towns police headquarters) — Theatre — Museum

Coach station — Airport — Hospital — Covered market

Ruins — Monument, statue — Fountain

Garden, park, wood — Cemetery, Jewish cemetery

Outdoor or indoor swimming pool — Racecourse — Golf course

Cable-car — Funicular

Sports ground, stadium — View — Panorama

12

Mit dieser neuen Veröffentlichung stellen Ihnen die Michelin-Touristikabteilungen eine Auswahl von 20 europäischen Großstädten vor, die von internationaler Bedeutung für Geschäftsreisende und Touristen sind.

Dieser Führer soll Ihnen helfen bei der Wahl eines Hotels, eines Restaurants, beim Besuch der Stadt und ihrer wichtigsten Sehenswürdigkeiten.

Wir wünschen Ihnen einen angenehmen Aufenthalt.

HOTELS UND RESTAURANTS

KLASSENEINTEILUNG UND KOMFORT

Großer Luxus	🏨	XXXXX
Luxus	🏨	XXXX
Sehr komfortabel	🏨	XXX
Mit gutem Komfort	🏨	XX
Bürgerlich	🏠	X
Einfach, ordentlich	🏠	
Preiswerte, empfehlenswerte Gasthäuser	⌂	
Moderne Einrichtung	Ⓜ	

ANNEHMLICHKEITEN

Angenehme Hotels	🏨 ... 🏠
Angenehme Restaurants	XXXXX ... X
Besondere Annehmlichkeit	« Park »
Sehr ruhiges oder abgelegenes und ruhiges Hotel	🖎
Ruhiges Hotel	🖎
Reizvolle Aussicht, Rundblick	≤ Rhein, ⁂
Interessante oder weite Sicht	≤

KÜCHE

Eine der besten Küchen des Landes : eine Reise wert	✿✿✿
Eine hervorragende Küche : verdient einen Umweg	✿✿
Eine sehr gute Küche : verdient Ihre besondere Beachtung	✿
Andere sorgfältig zubereitete Mahlzeiten	Karte, **R, M,** Pas

EINRICHTUNG

🛗 📺	Fahrstuhl — Fernsehen im Zimmer
♨ 🗔	Zentralheizung, Klimaanlage
🛁wc 🛁	Privatbad mit wc, Privatbad ohne wc
🚿wc 🚿	Privatdusche mit wc, Privatdusche ohne wc
☎	Zimmertelefon mit direkter Außenverbindung
✆	Zimmertelefon mit Außenverbindung über Telefonzentrale
✂ ⌇ 🏊	Tennis — Freibad, Hallenbad
🜻s 🌳 ⛱ 🏖	Sauna — Garten — Liegewiese, -terrasse — Strandbad
🚗 🚗 Ⓟ	Garage kostenlos — Garage wird berechnet — Parkplatz
♿	Für Körperbehinderte leicht zugängliche Zimmer
🏛	Konferenzraum
🐕̸	Das Mitführen von Hunden ist unerwünscht
garni	Hotel ohne Restaurant

DIE PREISE

Die Preise sind in der Landeswährung angegeben. Sie wurden uns Ende 1981 angegeben und können sich entsprechend der Steigerung der Lebenshaltungskosten erhöhen.

Im Restaurant

Karte Com Pas
M Ref **R** 40/85

Mindest- und Höchstpreis für die Mahlzeiten

Im Hotel

30 hab cam qto
Z rm ch 60/120

Mindestpreis 60 für ein Einzelzimmer und Höchstpreis 120 für das schönste Doppelzimmer für zwei Personen

34 Z : 55 B 23/45

Zimmer- und Bettenzahl mit Mindest- und Höchstpreis pro Person für eine Übernachtung mit Frühstück

Frühstück

🛏 12 🍽 10

Frühstückspreis (im Zimmer serviert) — Preis des Frühstücks, im Frühstücksraum serviert

Fb

Frühstücksbuffet

Bedienungsgeld und Gebühren

s. t.

Bedienung inbegriffen — MWSt inbegriffen.

stc SC st.

Bedienung und MWSt inbegriffen (Inklusivpreise).

In Deutschland, Italien, Schweiz, Spanien und Portugal sind die angegebenen Preise Inklusivpreise.

SEHENSWÜRDIGKEITEN

Eine Reise wert
Verdient einen Umweg
Sehenswert

STADTPLÄNE

Erklärung der wichtigsten Zeichen

Informationsstelle . . . .

Hotel, Restaurant – Referenzbuchstabe auf dem Plan . . . .

Sehenswertes Gebäude mit Haupteingang ⎫
Sehenswerte Kirche oder Kapelle . . . . ⎬ Referenzbuchstabe auf dem Plan . . .

Einkaufsstraße – Öffentlicher Parkplatz, Parkhaus

Straßenbahn oder O-Bus . . . .

U-Bahnstation . . . .

Einbahnstraße . . . .

Kirche oder Kapelle – Postlagernde Sendungen, Telegraph – Telefon . . . .

Öffentliche Gebäude, durch Buchstaben gekennzeichnet:

Polizei (in größeren Städten Polizeipräsidium) – Theater – Museum . . . .

Autobusbahnhof – Flughafen – Krankenhaus – Markthalle . . . .

Ruine – Denkmal, Statue – Brunnen . . . .

Garten, Park, Wald – Friedhof, Jüd. Friedhof . . . .

Freibad – Hallenbad – Pferderennbahn – Golfplatz und Lochzahl . . . .

Seilschwebebahn – Standseilbahn . . . .

Sportplatz – Aussicht – Rundblick . . . .

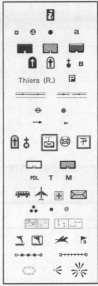

Con esta nueva publicación, los Servicios de Turismo Michelin presentan una selección de 20 ciudades de Europa, escogidas por su carácter internacional en el campo de los negocios y el turismo.
Esta guía está destinada a facilitar la elección de un hotel, de un restaurante, la visita de la ciudad y sus principales curiosidades.
Le deseamos una feliz estancia.

HOTELES Y RESTAURANTES

CLASE Y CONFORT

🏨	🏨	Gran lujo y tradición
🏨	🏨	Gran confort
🏨	🏨	Muy confortable
🏨		Confortable
🏨		Bastante confortable
🏛		Sencillo pero decoroso
⋔		Otros alojamientos aconsejados
M		Dentro de su categoria, hotel con instalaciones modernas

EL ATRACTIVO

🏨 ... 🏛	Hoteles agradables
... ✕	Restaurantes agradables
« Parque »	Elemento particularmente agradable
⬥	Hotel muy tranquilo, o aislado y tranquilo
⬥	Hotel tranquilo
⩽ mar, ☀	Vista exceptional, Panorama
⩽	Vista interesante o extensa

LA MESA

❀ ❀ ❀	Una de las mejores mesas del país : justifica el viaje
❀ ❀	Mesa excelente, merece un rodeo
❀	Una muy buena mesa en su categoría
Karte, **R, M,** Pas	Otra buena mesa

LA INSTALACIÓN

Ascensor, televisión
Calefacción central, aire acondicionado
Baño privado con wc, baño privado sin wc
Ducha privada con wc, ducha privada sin wc
Teléfono en la habitación, directo con el exterior
Teléfono en la habitación (exterior tras centralita)
Tenis, Piscina al aire libre o cubierta
Sauna, jardín, césped, playa
Garaje gratuito, Garaje de pago, Aparcamiento
Habitaciones accessibles a los minusválidos
El hotel dispone de una o varias salas de congresos
Prohibidos los perros
El hotel no tiene restaurante

garni

LOS PRECIOS

Los precios están indicados en la moneda del país. Han sido fijados a finales de 1981 y pueden sufrir variaciones según la evolución del coste de vida.

Comidas

Precios mínimo y máximo de las comidas

Karte Com Pas
M Ref **R** 40/85

Habitaciones

Precio mínimo 60 de una habitación individual y precio máximo 120 de la mejor habitación ocupada por dos personas

**30 hab cam qto
Z rm ch** 60/120

Número de habitaciones y de camas con precios mínimo y máximo por noche y por persona con desayuno incluido

34 Z : 55 B 23/45

Desayuno

Precio del desayuno : servido en la habitación, en el comedor

Desayuno al "buffet".

🍽12 ☕10
Fb

El servicio y los impuestos

Servicio incluido ; impuestos incluidos

Precios con servicio e impuestos incluidos

En Alemania, Italia, Suiza, España y Portugal, los precios indicados son netos.

s.   t.
stc SC st.

17

LAS CURIOSIDADES

Justifica el viaje
Merece un rodeo
Interesante

LOS PLANOS

Principales signos convencionales

Oficina de Información de Turismo

Hotel, restaurante — Letra de referencia en el plano

Monumento interesante con la entrada principal ⎫

Iglesia o capilla interesante .... ⎬ Letra de referencia en el plano

Calle comercial — Aparcamiento público

Tranvía o trolebús

Boca de metro

Calle de sentido único

Iglesia o capilla — Lista de correos, telégrafos — Teléfonos

Edificios públicos localizados con letras :

Policía (en las grandes ciudades : Jefatura) — Teatro — Museo

Estación de autobuses — Aeropuerto — Hospital — Mercado cubierto

Ruinas — Monumento, estatua — Fuente

Jardín, parque, bosque — Cementerio, cementerio israelita

Piscina al aire libre, cubierta — Hipódromo — Golf

Teleférico — Funicular

Estadio — Vista — Panorama

Con questa nuova pubblicazione, i Servizi Turismo Michelin vi propongono una selezione di 20 città europee, scelte per la loro importanza internazionale sul piano economico e turistico.
Questa guida è destinata a facilitarVi sia la scelta di un albergo o di un ristorante, sia la visita della città e delle sue principali curiosità.
Vi auguriamo un piacevole soggiorno.

ALBERGHI E RISTORANTI

CLASSE E CONFORT

Gran lusso e tradizione	🏰	XXXXX
Gran confort	🏯	XXXX
Molto confortevole	🏠	XXX
Confortevole	🏠	XX
Abbastanza confortevole	🏠	X
Semplice, ma conveniente	🏠	
Altra risorsa, consigliata per prezzi contenuti	🏠	
Nella sua categoria, albergo con attrezzatura moderna	M	

AMENITÀ

Alberghi ameni	🏰 ... 🏠
Ristoranti ameni	XXXXX ... X
Un particolare ameno	« Parco fiorito »
Albergo molto tranquillo o isolato e tranquillo	🦢
Albergo tranquillo	🦢
Vista eccezionale, panorama	⇐ mare, ✲
Vista interessante o estesa	⇐

LA TAVOLA

Una delle migliori tavole del paese : vale il viaggio	❀❀❀
Tavola eccellente : merita una deviazione	❀❀
Un'ottima tavola nella sua categoria	❀
Altri pasti accurati	Karte, **R, M,** Pas

INSTALLAZIONI

	Ascensore — Televisione in camera
	Riscaldamento centrale, aria condizionata
wc	Bagno e wc privati, bagno privato senza wc
wc	Doccia e wc privati, doccia privata senza wc
	Telefono in camera comunicante direttamente con l'esterno
	Telefono in camera collegato con il centralino
	Tennis — Piscina : all'aperto, coperta
S	Sauna — Giardino — Prato per il riposo — Spiaggia attrezzata
P	Garage gratuito — Garage a pagamento — Parcheggio per auto
	Camere d'agevole accesso per i minorati fisici
	L'albergo dispone di una o più sale per conferenze
	E' vietato l'accesso ai cani
garni	L'albergo non ha ristorante

I PREZZI

I prezzi, indicati nella valuta del paese sono stati stabiliti alla fine del 1981, per cui possono subire delle variazioni in funzione dell' aumento del costo della vita.

Al ristorante

Karte Com Pas **M** Ref **R** 40/85	Prezzi minimo e massimo per pasti

All'albergo

30 hab cam qto Z rm ch 60/120	Prezzo minimo 60 per una camera singola e prezzo massimo 120 per la camera più bella per due persone
34 Z : 55 B 23/45	Numero di camere e di letti con prezzo minimo e massimo per notte e per persona, compresa la prima colazione.

Prima colazione

12 10	Prezzo della prima colazione servita in camera, non servita in camera
Fb	Prima colazione servita al buffet

Servizio e tasse

s. t.	Servizio compreso. — I.V.A. compresa.
stc SC **st.**	Servizio ed I.V.A. compresi (prezzi netti).
	In Germania, Italia, Svizzera, Spagna e Portogallo i prezzi indicati sono netti.

LE CURIOSITÀ

Vale il viaggio
Merita una deviazione
Interessante

LE PIANTE

Principali segni convenzionali

Ufficio informazioni turistiche . . . .

Albergo-Ristorante — Lettera di riferimento sulla pianta . . . .

Monumento interessante ed entrata principale ⎱ Lettera di riferimento sulla pianta
Chiesa o cappella interessante . . . . ⎰

Via commerciale — Parcheggio pubblico . . . .

Tranvia-Filovia . . . .

Stazione della Metropolitana . . . .

Via a senso unico . . . .

Chiesa o cappella — Fermo posta, telegrafo — Telefono . . . .

Edifici pubblici indicati con lettere :

Polizia (Questura, nelle grandi città) — Teatro — Museo . . . .

Autostazione — Aeroporto — Ospedale — Mercato coperto . . . .

Ruderi — Monumento, statua — Fontana . . . .

Giardino, parco, bosco — Cimitero, cimitero ebreo . . . .

Piscina : all'aperto, coperta — Ippodromo — Golf . . . .

Funivia — Funicolare . . . .

Stadio — Vista — Panorama . . . .

3

21

Belgique
België

Bruxelles

Brussel

BRUXELLES
BRUSSEL

BRUXELLES (BRUSSEL) 1000 🅿 Brabant 🄸 ⑱ et 🄌🄌🄌 ⑬ – 1 008 715 h. agglomération – ✿ 02.

Voir Grand-Place★★★ (p. 12) LZ – Manneken Pis★★ (p. 12) KZ – Rue des Bouchers (p. 12) LZ – Cathédrale St-Michel★★ (p. 8) FU – Place du Grand Sablon★ et église N.-D. du Sablon★ (p. 8) FV – Anderlecht : maison d'Erasme★ (p. 6) AB **B**.
Musées : d'Art ancien★★★ (Brueghel) p. 8 FV –Royaux d'Art et d'Histoire★★★ (antiquités, arts décoratifs belges) p. 5 CQ **M7** – Instrumental★★ (p. 8) FV.
Env. Forêt de Soignes★★ (p. 7) CDS – Tervuren : Musée Royal de l'Afrique Centrale★ par ⑥ : 13 km – Beersel : château fort★ S : 11 km (p. 6) AS **C** – Gaasbeek : domaine★ SO : 12 km par rue de Lennick (p. 6) AR – Meise : domaine de Bouchout★ : Palais des Plantes★★ par ① : 13 km – Grimbergen : confessionnaux★ dans l'église St-Servais (St. Servaaskerk) par ① : 18 km – Vilvoorde : stalles★ dans l'église Notre-Dame (O.L.-Vrouwkerk) p. 5 CN.

🖼🖼 Château de Ravenstein à Tervuren par ⑥ : 13 km ☎ 7675801.
✈ **National** NE : 12 km (p. 5) DN ☎ 7518080 – **Aérogare** : Air Terminus, r. du Cardinal-Mercier 35 (p. 12) LZ ☎ 5119060.
🚗 ☎ 2186050 ext. 4106.
🛈 r. du Marché-aux-Herbes 61 ☎ 5138940 – Fédération provinciale de tourisme r. Marché-aux-Herbes 61 ☎ 5130750.
Paris 308 ⑨ –◆Amsterdam 207 ① – Düsseldorf 222 ⑤ – Lille 116 ⑫ –◆Luxembourg 213 ⑦.

HOTELS

et RESTAURANTS

Liste alphabétique : Bruxelles p. 10 et 11

Les prix de chambres risquent d'être majorés d'une taxe locale de 6 %

Centre

Nord (Place Rogier, Jardin Botanique) *plan p. 8 et 9*

🏨🏨 **Brussels-Sheraton** M, pl. Rogier 3, ⊠ 1000, 𝔗 2193400, Télex 26887, ⬚ – 🛗 ☰ 📺 ☎ ᵫ ☞ – 🛆
476 ch et 33 appartements.
FT **e**

🏨🏨 **Hyatt Regency Brussels** M, r. Royale 250, ⊠ 1030, 𝔗 2194640, Télex 61871 – 🛗 ☰ 📺 ᵫ ☞ – 🛆. AE ⓞ. 🛠 rest
R 585/990 **stc** – 😅 275 – **320 ch** 2100/3200 **stc** – P 2755/3030 **stc**.
GT **r**

🏨 **Queen Anne** sans rest, bd Émile-Jacqmain 110, ⊠ 1000, 𝔗 2171600, Télex 63840 – 🛗 ⌷wc ☎. AE ⓞ E.
59 ch 😅 995/1425 **stc**.
plan p. 12 LY **y**

🏨 **Siru** sans rest, pl. Rogier 1, ⊠ 1000, 𝔗 2177580, Télex 21722 – 🛗 ⌷wc ☎
100 ch 😅 890/1530 **stc**.
FT **f**

XX **Den Botaniek,** r. Royale 328, ⊠ 1030, 𝔗 2184838, « Jardin-terrasse, repas en plein-air » – AE ⓞ
fermé sam. midi, dim. et jours fériés – **R** carte 1025 à 1525 **stc**.
GT **n**

XX **Gousse d'Ail,** pl. Rogier 1, ⊠ 1000, 𝔗 2177580
R (déjeuner seult en juil.-août) 750 **stc**.
FT **f**

Centre Ville (Bourse, Grand'Place, Pl. de Brouckère, Ste-Catherine) *plan p. 12*

🏨🏨 **Amigo,** r. Amigo 1, ⊠ 1000, 𝔗 5115910, Télex 21618, « Bel aménagement intérieur » – 🛗 ☰ rest. 📺 ☎ ᵫ – 🛆. AE ⓞ E. 🛠 rest
R carte 600 à 1010 **stc** – **183 ch** 😅 1650/3400 **stc**.
KZ **h**

🏨🏨 **Royal Windsor** M, r. Duquesnoy 5, ⊠ 1000, 𝔗 5114215, Télex 62905 – 🛗 ☰ 📺 ☎ ᵫ – 🛆. AE ⓞ E. 🛠
R carte 1025 à 1425 **stc** – **270 ch** 😅 3100/3710 **stc**.
LZ **k**

🏨🏨 **Atlanta,** bd A.-Max 7, ⊠ 1000, 𝔗 2170120, Télex 21475 – 🛗 ☰ rest. ☎ ᵫ ☞ – 🛆. AE ⓞ E. 🛠 rest
R carte 435 à 1090 **stc** – **239 ch**.
LY **a**

🏨🏨 **Président Nord** M sans rest, bd A.-Max 107, ⊠ 1000, 𝔗 2190060, Télex 61417 – 🛗 📺 ☎. AE ⓞ E
63 ch 😅 1760/2240 **stc**.
LY **b**

🏨🏨 **Bedford,** r. Midi 135, ⊠ 1000, 𝔗 5127840, Télex 24059 – 🛗 ☰ rest. ☎ ᵫ – 🛆. AE ⓞ E. 🛠
R 550 **stc** – **250 ch** 😅 1330/2370 **stc** – P 2360/2870 **stc**.
KZ **r**

🏨 **Arenberg** M sans rest, r. d'Assaut 15, ⊠ 1000, 𝔗 5110770, Télex 25660 – 🛗 ⌷wc ⌷wc ☎
158 ch.
LZ **p**

🏨 **Scheers,** bd A.-Max 132, ⊠ 1000, 𝔗 2177760, Télex 21675 – 🛗 ☰ rest. ⌷wc ⌷wc ᵫ. AE ⓞ E. 🛠 rest
R carte 630 à 930 **stc** – **62 ch** 😅 1400/1715 **stc**.
LY **d**

🏨 **La Légende,** r. Etuve 33, ⊠ 1000, 𝔗 5128290 – 🛗 ⌷wc ᵫ. 🛠
fermé 15 déc.-14 janv. – **R** *(fermé merc. et 15 déc.-29 janv.)* carte 435 à 585 **stc** – **32 ch** 😅 880/1180 **stc**.
KZ **p**

XXXX ⊛⊛ **Maison du Cygne,** Grand'Place 9, ⊠ 1000, 𝔗 5118244, « Belle demeure ancienne, intérieur élégant » – AE ⓞ E. 🛠
fermé sam., dim., 3e sem. août et Noël-Nouvel An – **R** carte 1275 à 1850 **stc**
Spéc. Foie aux épinards, Selle de chevreuil, Carré d'agneau.
LZ **q**

XXX ⊛ **Huîtrière,** quai aux Briques 20, ⊠ 1000, 𝔗 5120866, Produits de la mer – AE ⓞ
R carte 1020 à 1630 **stc**
Spéc. Homard grillé au beurre de corail, Rôti de turbot aux trois parfums, Langouste au basilic (en saison).
KY **v**

XXX **Tête d'Or,** r. Tête d'Or 9, ⊠ 1000, 𝔗 5110201, « Décor vieux Bruxelles » – AE ⓞ
fermé sam. et dim. – **R** carte 1170 à 1610 **stc**.
KZ **t**

XXX **Cheval Marin,** Marché-aux-Porcs 25, ⊠ 1000, 𝔗 5130287, « Décor ancien » – AE ⓞ E
fermé dim. soir – **R** carte env. 1300 **stc**.
KY **u**

BRUXELLES
BRUSSEL
AGGLOMÉRATION NORD

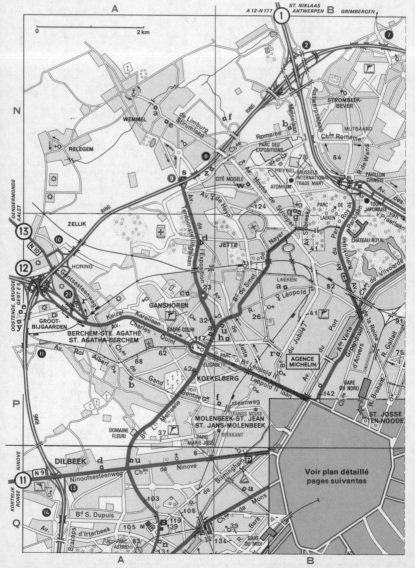

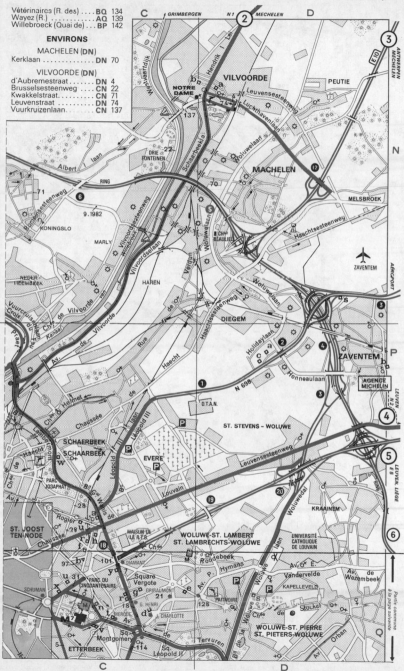

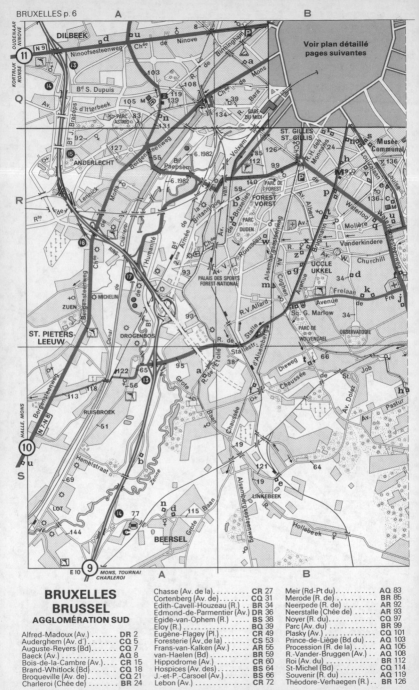

BRUXELLES
BRUSSEL
AGGLOMÉRATION SUD

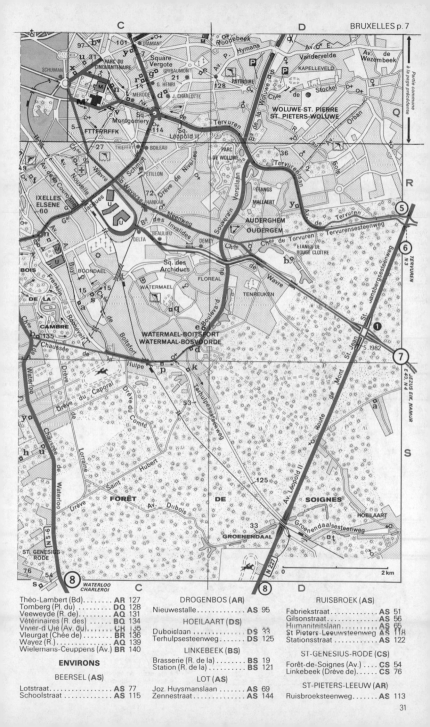

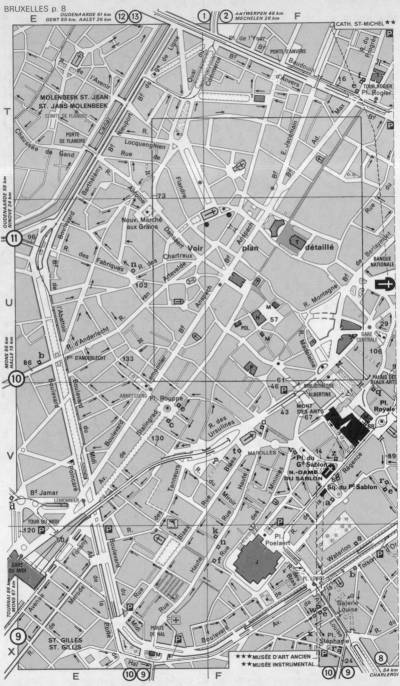

BRUXELLES
BRUSSEL
CENTRE

LISTE ALPHABÉTIQUE HOTELS ET RESTAURANTS

LES BONNES TABLES... A ÉTOILES

GERENOMMEERDE KEUKENS... MET STERREN

DIE GUTEN RESTAURANTS... UND DIE STERNE

OUTSTANDING CUISINE... AND STARS

Les Bonnes Tables (voir page 15)

Gourmets...

Nous distinguons à votre intention
certains restaurants par ❀, ❀❀ ou ❀❀❀.

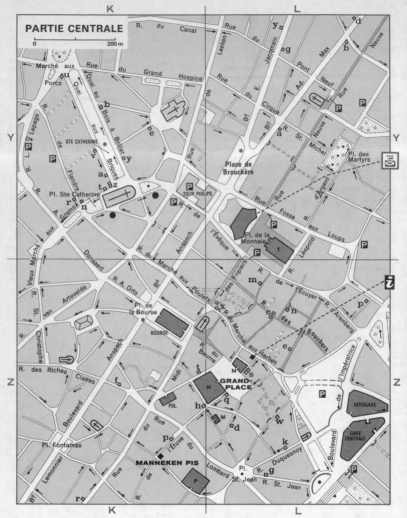

XXX **Perraudin,** r. St-Jean 49, ⊠ 1000, ☎ 5111388 – AE ⓞ E   LZ **g**
fermé dim. soir, lundi et août – **R** 825 **stc**.

XXX **Filet de Boeuf,** r. Harengs 8, ⊠ 1000, ☎ 5119559, « Décor vieux Bruxelles » – AE ⓞ E
fermé sam., dim. et août – **R** carte 1150 à 1830 **stc**.   LZ **s**

XXX **Éperon d'Or,** r. Éperonniers 8, ⊠ 1000, ☎ 5125239, Classique – AE ⓞ E   LZ **w**
fermé sam. et 21 juil.-14 août – **R** carte 770 à 1150 **stc**.

XXX **Bon Vieux Temps,** 1er étage, r. Marché-aux-Herbes 12 (dans l'impasse St-Nicolas 4), ⊠
1000, ☎ 2181546, « Ancienne demeure bruxelloise » – AE E   LZ **x**
fermé dim., jours fériés et juil. – **R** 950/1125 **stc**.

XX ❀ **Sirène d'Or,** pl. Ste-Catherine 1 a, ⊠ 1000, ☎ 5135198 – AE ⓞ   KY **n**
fermé dim. et août – **R** 470/900 **stc**.

XX **Épaule de Mouton,** r. Harengs 16, ⊠ 1000, ☎ 5110594, Décor vieux Bruxelles – AE ⓞ E
fermé dim. et 21 juil.-15 août – **R** 1150 **stc**.   LZ **s**

XX **Serge et Anne,** r. Peuplier 23, ⊠ 1000, ☎ 2181662   KY **e**
fermé merc. et août – **R** carte 560 à 800 **stc**.

XX **Rôtiss. Au Cochon d'Or,** quai Bois-à-Brûler 15, ⊠ 1000, ☎ 2180771 – AE ⓞ E   KY **y**
fermé dim. et 14 sept. – **R** 610/1085 **stc**.

XX **Belle Maraîchère,** pl. Ste-Catherine 11, ⊠ 1000, ☎ 5129759 – AE ⓞ E   KY **t**
fermé merc. soir et jeudi – **R** 525/1190 **stc**.

XX **Armes de Bruxelles,** r. Bouchers 13, ⊠ 1000, ☎ 5115598, Ambiance bruxelloise – AE ⓞ E
fermé lundi et juin – **R** carte 715 à 1150 **stc**.   LZ **c**

XX **Chapon Fin,** r. Chapeliers 16, ⊠ 1000, ☎ 5120717 – AE ⓞ E   LZ **d**
fermé lundi soir, mardi et du 15 au 30 sept. – **R** carte 535 à 1075 **stc**.

XX **Passage,** galerie de la Reine 30, ⊠ 1000, ☎ 5123731, Taverne-restaurant, Ambiance bruxelloise – AE ⓞ E   LZ **e**
R carte 480 à 800 **stc**.

XX **Le Chablis,** r.Flandre 6, ⊠ 1000, ☎ 5124631 – ⓞ E   KY **r**
fermé lundi et août – **R** carte 925 à 1580 **stc**.

X **Maggi,** r. Teinturiers 6, ⊠ 1000, ☎ 5114792   KZ **f**
fermé jeudi, vend. et juil. – **R** 495/670 **stc**.

X **Marie-Joseph,** quai au Bois-à-Brûler 47, ⊠ 1000, ☎ 2180596, Produits de la mer – AE ⓞ
R carte 700 à 1280 **stc**.   KY **b**

X **Maison Lejeune.** r. Fourche 48, ⊠ 1000, ☎ 2181842, Produits de la mer – AE E   LZ **m**
fermé dim., lundi et juil.-août – **R** carte 515 à 1047 **stc**.

X **Léon,** r. Dominicains 2, ⊠ 1000, ☎ 5111415, Ambiance bruxelloise – AE ⓞ E   LZ **c**
fermé juin – **R** carte 690 à 1170 **stc**.

X **Ogenblik,** Galerie des Princes 1, ⊠ 1000, ☎ 5116151, Ouvert jusqu'à 24 h – AE ⓞ E   LZ **n**
fermé dim. – **R** carte 640 à 1200 **stc**.

X **Rugbyman,** quai aux Briques 4, ⊠ 1000, ☎ 5125640, Produits de la mer – ▤ AE ⓞ E
R 1130 **stc**.   KY **z**

X **Crustacés,** quai aux Briques 8, ⊠ 1000, ☎ 5131493, Produits de la mer – ▤ AE ⓞ E. ✖
R carte 1050 à 1510 **stc**.   KY **a**

X **Al Buco,** bd E.-Jacqmain 89, ⊠ 1000, ☎ 2171172, Cuisine italienne – E   LY **g**
fermé sam. – **R** carte 400 à 650 **stc**.

X **In 't Spinnekopke,** pl. Jardin aux Fleurs, ⊠ 1000, ☎ 5118695, Dans une maison du 18e s.
fermé sam. et août – **R** carte env. 450 **stc**.   plan p. 8 EU **n**

Centre Sud

Quartier Place Rouppe : plan p. 8 :

🏠 **Windsor** sans rest, pl. Rouppe 13, ⊠ 1000, ☎ 5112014 – 🕮 🕮   EV **e**
24 ch ⊇ 840/1380 **stc**.

XXX ❀❀❀ **Comme Chez Soi** (Wynants), pl. Rouppe 23, ⊠ 1000, ☎ 5122921 – ▤ AE   EV **c**
fermé dim., lundi, juil. et Noël-Nouvel An – **R** (nombre de couverts limité - prévenir) carte 1365
à 2145 **stc**.
Spéc. Les mousses Wynants, La nage de saumon à la vapeur en verdure sauvage (avril-sept.), Le pigeonneau
farci diamant noir (janv.-août).

Quartier Sablon : plan p. 8 :

XXX ❀❀ **L'Écailler du Palais Royal,** r. Bodenbroek 18, ⊠ 1000, ☎ 5128751, Produits de la mer
– AE ⓞ E   FV **z**
fermé dim., jours fériés et 29 juil.-août – **R** (nombre de couverts limité - prévenir) carte 1460 à
2020 **stc**.
Spéc. Cassolette d'écrevisses aux fines herbes, Petite langouste rôtie, Turbot au four.

XXX **En Provence,** pl. Petit-Sablon 1, ⊠ 1000, ☎ 5122789, Intérieur rustique – ▤ AE ⓞ E
fermé dim. – **R** carte 1150 à 1870 **stc**.   FV **s**

XXX **Debussy,** pl. Petit Sablon 2, ⊠ 1000, ☎ 5128041 – AE ⓞ E   FV **s**
fermé sam. midi, dim., jours fériés, 24 déc., 2 janv. et 17 juil.-15 août – **R** carte 1170 à 1720 **stc**.

4

XX **Chez Christopher,** pl. Chapelle 5, ✉ 1000, ☏ 5126891, Décor rétro – 🆎 ⓪ **E**   FV **t**
fermé sam., dim., jours fériés et Noël-Nouvel An – **R** carte 1080 à 1580 **stc**.

XX **Au Duc d'Arenberg,** pl. Petit-Sablon 9, ✉ 1000, ☏ 5111475, Taverne-restaurant rustique –
🆎 ⓪   FV **a**
R carte 920 à 1650 **stc**.

XX **La Sainte Famille,** Petite rue des Minimes 5, ✉ 1000, ☏ 5127138   FV **v**
fermé dim. soir et lundi – **R** carte env. 1200 **stc**.

X **Les Années Folles,** r. Haute 17, ✉ 1000, ☏ 5135858 – 🆎   FV **c**
fermé sam. midi et dim. – **R** 595/760 **stc**.

Quartier Palais de Justice : plan p. 8 :

XX **Cheval Blanc,** r. Haute 204, ✉ 1000, ☏ 5123771, Ouvert jusqu'à 23 h 30 – ⓟ 🆎 ⓪ **E**
fermé dim. soir – **R** 600 **stc**.   FX **n**

X **Au Beurre Blanc,** r.Faucon 2a, ✉ 1000, ☏ 5130111 – 🆎 ⓪ **E**   FX **f**
fermé sam. midi, dim., 13 août-1er sept. et 24 déc.-3 janv. – **R** carte env. 1100 **stc**.

X **La Marée Haute,** r. Haute 189, ✉ 1000, ☏ 5126976 – 🆎 ⓪ **E**   FX **k**
fermé sam. midi et mardi – **R** 600 **stc**.

Quartier Gare du Midi : plan p. 8 :

XXX ✿ **Da Gesuino,** r. Fiennes 3, ✉ 1070, ☏ 5215163, Avec cuisine italienne – 🆎 ⓪ **E**   EV **d**
fermé sam., dim. et 20 juil.-17 août – **R** carte 1060 à 1555 **stc**.

Quartier Porte Louise : plans p. 6 et 8 :

🏨 **Ramada-Brussels** Ⓜ, chaussée de Charleroi 38, ✉ 1060, ☏ 5393000, Télex 25539 – 🛗 🖺
📺 ☎ – 🔒 🆎 ⓪ **E**. ≉ rest   BR **n**
R carte 1100 à 1380 **stc** – ☲ 320 – **201 ch** 2660/3085 **stc**.

🏨 **La Cascade** sans rest, r. Source 14, ✉ 1060, ☏ 5388830, Télex 26637 – 🛗 📺 ☎ 🚗 ⓟ –
🔒. 🆎 ⓪ **E**   BR **r**
42 ch ☲ 1840/2285 **stc**.

🏨 **Ascot** sans rest, pl. Loix 1, ✉ 1060, ☏ 5388835, Télex 25010 – 🛗 ☎. 🆎 ⓪ **E**. ≉   BR **r**
58 ch ☲ 1410/1775 **stc**.

🏨 **L'Agenda** Ⓜ sans rest, r. Florence 6, ✉ 1050, ☏ 5390031, Télex 63947 – 🛗 📺 ☎ 🚗. 🆎 ⓪
E   BR **n**
☲ 185 – **38 ch** 1465/1695 **stc**.

🏨 **Diplomat** Ⓜ sans rest, r. Jean-Stas 32, ✉ 1060, ☏ 5374250, Télex 61012 – 🛗 📺 ⌴wc ☎
68 ch.   FX **x**

🏨 **Delta** Ⓜ, chaussée de Charleroi 17, ✉ 1060, ☏ 5390160, Télex 63225 – 🛗 ⌴wc ☎ – 🔒
225 ch.   FX **r**

🏨 **Alfa Louise** Ⓜ sans rest, r. Blanche 4, ✉ 1050, ☏ 5379210, Télex 62434 – 🛗 ⌴wc 🚗   BR **n**
55 ch.

🏨 **Richmond House** sans rest, r. Concorde 21, ✉ 1050, ☏ 5124824 – 🛗 ⌴wc 🚗. 🆎 ⓪ **E**.
≉   plan p. 9 GX **a**
27 ch ☲ 600/1000 **stc**.

XX **Meo Patacca,** r. Jourdan 20, ✉ 1060, ☏ 5381546, Ouvert jusqu'à 1 h. – 🆎 ⓪ **E**   FX **w**
fermé 20 juil.-16 août – **R** carte 820 à 1235 **stc**.

XX **La Closerie,** r. Jourdan 15, ✉ 1060, ☏ 5381448 – 🆎 ⓪ **E**   FX **w**
fermé sam. midi, dim., jours fériés, 27 fév.-6 mars et 18 juil.-1er août.

X **Uncle Joe's,** r. Jourdan 12, ✉ 1060, ☏ 5382525, Ouvert jusqu'à minuit – 🆎 ⓪ **E**. ≉ FX **e**
fermé dim. et 15 mai-14 juin – **R** carte 515 à 950 **stc**.

X **La Mer,** r. Jourdan 2, ✉ 1060, ☏ 5391230, Produits de la mer, ouvert jusqu'à 23 h. – 🖺. 🆎
⓪ **E**   FX **e**
fermé sam. midi, dim. et 15 juil.-15 août – **R** 470/940 **stc**.

Quartier Porte de Namur : plans p. 8 et 9 :

🏨 **Brussels Hilton** Ⓜ, bd Waterloo 38, ✉ 1000, ☏ 5138877, Télex 22744, « Rest. au 27ᵉ étage
avec ≤ sur ville » – 🛗 🖺 📺 🔒 🚗. 🆎 ⓪ **E**. ≉ rest   FX **s**
R carte 1025 à 1475 **stc** – ☲ 315 – **373 ch** 2475/3875 **stc**.

XXX **Bernard,** 1ᵉʳ étage, r. Namur 93, ✉ 1000, ☏ 5128821, Produits de la mer – 🆎   GV **c**
fermé dim., lundi soir, jours fériés et juil. – **R** carte 1080 à 1520 **stc**.

XXX **Old Mario,** r. Alsace Lorraine 44, ✉ 1050, ☏ 5116162, Cuisine italienne – ⓟ. 🆎 ⓪ **E**
fermé sam. et dim. – **R** carte 760 à 1250 **stc**.   GX **e**

XX **Charles-Joseph,** r. E. Solvay 9, ✉ 1050, ☏ 5134390 – 🆎 ⓪   GX **r**
fermé sam. midi, dim. et 15 juil.-14 août – **R** 615/1110 **stc**.

XX **J. et B.,** r. Baudet 5, ✉ 1000, ☏ 5120484, Rustique, ouvert jusqu'à 23 h. – 🆎 ⓪ **E** FV **r**
fermé sam. midi, dim. et 21 juil.-14 août – **R** 560/815 **stc**.

XX **Chez Adrienne,** r. Capitaine Crespel 1a, ✉ 1050, ☏ 5119339, Rustique, Hors d'oeuvre – 🆎
⓪ **E**   FX **b**
fermé sam., dim., 3 sem. en juil., Noël-Nouvel An et après 20 h. – **R** 550 **stc**.

XX **Pimm's,** r. Baudet 2, ⊠ 1000, ℡ 5111704, Ouvert jusqu'à 0 h 30 – 🆎 ⓞ 🅴. ⚅   FV **e**
fermé sam. midi, dim. et 1ʳᵉ quinz. sept. – **R** 560/1025 **stc**.

XX **Maison d'Allemagne,** 1ᵉʳ étage, av. Toison-d'Or 10, ⊠ 1060, ℡ 5123354, Cuisine allemande
– 🍽 🆎 ⓞ 🅴   GX **x**
fermé dim. – **R** carte 715 à 1180 **stc**.

X **Yser,** r. Edimbourg 9, ⊠ 1050, ℡ 5117459   GX **y**
fermé dim. soir, lundi et 15 juil.-15 août – **R** 400/535 **stc**.

Centre Est (Pl. Royale, Cité administrative, Cité Européenne, Arts-Loi, Madou, Luxembourg)
plans p. 8 et 9 :

🏨 **Brussels Europa H.** Ⓜ, r. de la Loi 107, ⊠ 1040, ℡ 2301333, Télex 25121 – 🛗 🍽 📺 ☎ ⊖ –
🅰 🆎 🅴. ⚅ rest   HV **s**
R *(fermé sam. et août)* carte env. 1240 **stc** – **245 ch** ⊃ 2255/2960 **stc**.

🏨 **Astoria et Rest. Palais Royal,** r. Royale 103, ⊠ 1000, ℡ 2176290, Télex 25040 – 🛗 – 🅰.
🆎 ⓞ. ⚅ rest   GTU **b**
R *(fermé sam. et dim.)* 860 **stc** – **125 ch** ⊃ 2550/3300 **stc** – P 2600/3300 **stc**.

🏨 **Président Centre** Ⓜ sans rest, r. Royale 160, ⊠ 1000, ℡ 2190065, Télex 26784 – 🛗 🍽 📺.
🆎 ⓞ 🅴   GU **a**
73 ch ⊃ 1980/2600 **stc**.

🏨 **Charlemagne** Ⓜ sans rest, bd Charlemagne 25-27, ⊠ 1040, ℡ 2302135, Télex 22772 – 🛗 📺
☎ ⇌ – 🅰. 🆎 ⓞ 🅴   HU **a**
62 ch ⊃ 1800/1900 **stc**.

🏠 **Congrès et Rest. Le Carrousel,** r. Congrès 42, ⊠ 1000, ℡ 2171890 – 🛗 ⊟wc 🚿 ☎. 🆎
ⓞ 🅴   GU **c**
R *(fermé sam. et dim.)* carte 600 à 980 **stc** – **38 ch** ⊃ 500/970 **stc** – P 1250/1540 **stc**.

XXXX ✿ **Ravenstein,** r. Ravenstein 1, ⊠ 1000, ℡ 5127768, « Ancienne demeure seigneuriale du
16ᵉ s. » – 🆎 ⓞ 🅴   FV **q**
fermé sam. midi, dim. et août – **R** carte 1155 à 1935 **stc**
Spéc. Soufflé de homard, Huîtres au champagne (15 sept.-15 avril), Canard au sang (oct.-janv.).

XXX **Astrid "Chez Pierrot",** r. de la Presse 21, ⊠ 1000, ℡ 2173831, Classique – 🍽. ⓞ   GU **d**
fermé dim., Pâques et 15 juil.-14 août – **R** 700/1100 **stc**.

XX **Marie-José "Chez Callens"** avec ch, r. Commerce 73, ⊠ 1040, ℡ 5120843 – 🛗 ⊟wc
🚿wc ☎. 🆎 ⓞ 🅴   GV **x**
fermé sam. en juil.-août – **R** *(fermé sam. soir, dim. et jours fériés)* (ouvert jusqu'à 23 h) carte
700 à 1420 **stc** – ⊃ 120 – **17 ch** 700/1335 **stc**.

X **Chambertin,** r. Cultes 36, ⊠ 1000, ℡ 2187047, Taverne-restaurant   GU **s**
fermé sam. soir, dim. et jours fériés.

X **Maxevil,** r. de Trèves 66, ⊠ 1040, ℡ 2301632 – 🆎   HV **a**
fermé sam., dim. et 17 juil.-16 août – **R** (déjeuner seult) carte 750 à 1125 **stc**.

Agglomération

Nord

Quartier Basilique (Koekelberg, Ganshoren, Jette) *plan p.4 :*

XXX ✿✿ **Dupont,** av. Vital-Riethuisen 46, ⊠ 1080, ℡ 4275450, Classique - élégant – 🆎 ⓞ
fermé lundi, mardi et 12 juil.-17 août – **R** carte 1095 à 1720 **stc**   AP **a**
Spéc. Filet de merlan en écailles de St-Jacques (oct. à mai), Langouste chaude, Caneton aux pêches de vigne
(avril à sept.).

XXX ✿✿ **Bruneau,** av. Broustin 73, ⊠ 1080, ℡ 4276978, Classique-élégant – 🆎 ⓞ 🅴   BP **h**
fermé mardi soir, merc., 24 juin-16 juil. et 22 déc.-4 janv. – **R** carte 1160 à 1780 **stc**
Spéc. Salade de filets de truite grillée aux pignons de pin, Pot-au-feu de saumon aux tomates et basilic, Pomme
de ris de veau au vinaigre.

XXX **Pannenhuis,** r. Léopold-1ᵉʳ 317, ⊠ 1090, ℡ 4258373, Ancien relais du 17ᵉ s. – 🆎 ⓞ 🅴
fermé vend. saint – **R** carte 840 à 1185 **stc**.   BP **a**

XXX **Au Chaudron d'Or,** Drève du Château 71, ⊠ 1080, ℡ 4283737, « Fermette aménagée avec
recherche » – 🆎 ⓞ 🅴   AP **c**
fermé dim., lundi et août – **R** carte env. 1260 **stc**.

XX ✿ **Le Sermon** (Kobs), av. Jacques-Sermon 91, ⊠ 1090, ℡ 4268935 – 🆎   BP **u**
fermé dim., lundi et 26 juin-2 août – **R** carte 750 à 1230 **stc**.
Spéc. Moules au champagne (sept.-avril), Sole sermon, Ris de veau aux primeurs.

XX **Ancienne Barrière,** chaussée de Dieleghem 154, ⊠ 1090, ℡ 4780253, Relais de style
flamand   AP **d**
fermé merc. soir, jeudi et juil. – **R** carte 520 à 1000 **stc**.

X **Le Téléphone,** 1ᵉʳ étage, bd Jubilé 106, ⊠ 1020, ℡ 4269037, Avec restauration rapide – ⓞ
🅴   BP **r**
fermé dim., lundi soir et jours fériés – **R** carte 605 à 1090 **stc**.

tourner →

Quartier Centenaire et Atomium (Laeken, Wemmel, Strombeek-Bever) *plan p. 4 :*

XXX **De Kam,** chaussée de Bruxelles 7, ⊠ 1810, ☏ 4792020, Rustique – **Ⓟ**. 🆎 ⓪   AN **a**
fermé dim. soir, lundi, merc. soir et août – **R** 775/1250 **stc**.

XXX ✿✿ **Eddie Van Maele,** chaussée Romaine 964, ⊠ 1810, ☏ 4785445, Élégant, Jardin-terrasse
– 🆎. ✀   AN **z**
fermé dim. soir, lundi, jeudi soir, juil. et du 15 au 30 janv. – **R** carte 1255 à 1425 **stc**.
Spéc. Blanc de turbot au biscuit de homard et vert de poireaux, Canette et ris de veau aux pêches et poivre vert (juil.-oct.), Caramel de framboises (juil.-sept.).

XXX **Centenaire,** av. J.-Sobieski 84, ⊠ 1020, ☏ 4786623 – 🆎 ⓪ **E**   BNP **g**
fermé du 5 au 31 juil., du 20 au 31 déc., dim. soir et lundi – **R** 550/1150 **stc**.

XXX **Castel,** av. Houba-de-Strooper 96, ⊠ 1020, ☏ 4784392, Classique – 🆎 ⓪ **E**   BN**w**
fermé mardi soir et du 15 au 30 juil. – **R** 640/1020 **stc**.

XX **Aub. Arbre Ballon,** chaussée de Bruxelles 416, ⊠ 1810, ☏ 4789759 – **Ⓟ**. 🆎 ⓪   AN **s**
fermé du 1er au 20 juil. et lundis non fériés – **R** carte 615 à 900 **stc**.

XX **Val Joli,** r. Leestbeek 16, ⊠ 1820, ☏ 4783443, «Jardin-terrasse» – **Ⓟ**. 🆎   BN **f**
fermé lundi soir, mardi et du 1er au 20 nov. – **R** carte 800 à 1070 **stc**.

XX **Figaro,** r. Émile-Wauters 137, ⊠ 1020, ☏ 4786529   BNP **q**
fermé dim. soir, lundi et juil. – **R** carte 675 à 1200 **stc**.

X **Balcaen,** av. Limburg-Stirum 19, ⊠ 1810, ☏ 4789564 – **Ⓟ**   AN **e**
fermé lundi soir, mardi, merc. soir et 28 juin-29 juil. – **R** 400/875 **stc**.

X **Aub. de Strombeek** avec ch, Temselaan 6, ⊠ 1820, ☏ 4788367   BN **b**
fermé juil. et 15 déc.-1er janv. – **R** *(fermé dim.)* 400/510 **stc** – **10 ch** � 600/1000 **stc**.

Ouest

Anderlecht : *plan p. 6 :*

🏠 **Van Belle,** chaussée de Mons 39, ⊠ 1070, ☏ 5213516 – |≡| ⌂wc 🛁wc 🕾. 🆎 **E**. ✀ rest
R 400 **stc** – **84 ch** ⊠ 675/1350 **stc**.   *plan p. 8* EU **b**

XX **La Réserve,** chaussée de Ninove 675, ⊠ 1080, ☏ 5222653, Cadre rustique – 🆎 ⓪ **E**. ✀   AQ **d**
fermé sam. midi, mardi et 15 juil.-4 août – **R** carte 890 à 1525 **stc**.

X **La Paix,** r. Ropsy-Chaudron 49 (face Abattoirs), ⊠ 1070, ☏ 5230958, Taverne-restaurant
fermé sam. et dim. – **R** (déjeuner seult) carte 450 à 800 **stc**.   BQ **a**

X **Sporting,** r. Veeweyde 22, ⊠ 1070, ☏ 5236003 – ⓪   AQ **n**
fermé dim. soir, lundi et 5 juil.-2 août – **R** carte 500 à 1055 **stc**.

Berchem Ste Agathe (Sint-Agatha Berchem) : *plan p. 4 :*

XX **Saule,** chaussée de Gand 1110, ⊠ 1080, ☏ 4656682 – 🆎 ⓪   AP **b**
fermé dim. soir, lundi et juil. – **R** carte 720 à 1050 **stc**.

Molenbeek St-Jean (Sint-Jans Molenbeek) : *plan p. 4 :*

XXX ✿ **Béarnais,** bd Mettewie 318, ⊠ 1080, ☏ 5231151, Classique – ≡. 🆎 ⓪ **E**   AQ **u**
R 1350/1650 **stc**.

XX **Michel Haquin,** chaussée de Gand 395, ⊠ 1080, ☏ 4283961 – 🆎 ⓪ **E**   BP **f**
fermé mardi soir, merc. et juil. – **R** 950/1350 **stc**.

Sud

Bois de la Cambre : *plan p. 7 :*

XXXX ✿✿✿ **Villa Lorraine,** av. Vivier-d'Oie 75, ⊠ 1180, ☏ 3743163, Classique élégant – **Ⓟ**. 🆎 ⓪ **E**   CR **b**
fermé dim., lundi et du 6 au 27 juil. – **R** (réservation souhaitable) carte 1630 à 3120 **stc**.
Spéc. Terrine de foie gras truffé au vin de Malvoisie, Selle de chevreuil Cumberland aux grains de muscat (oct.-déc.), Soufflé au chocolat et jus de noix vertes.

Quartier "Ma Campagne" (Ixelles, St-Gilles) *plan p. 6 :*

🏨 Forum Ⓜ sans rest, avec snack-bar, av. Haut-Pont 2, ⊠ 1060, ☏ 3430100, Télex 62311 – |≡|
⌂wc 🕾 – 🛗   BR **p**
78 ch.

XXX ✿ **Chouan** (Fleuvy), av. Brugmann 100, ⊠ 1060, ☏ 3440999, Classique-Produits de la mer –
≡. 🆎 ⓪ **E**   BR **t**
fermé dim. en mai-juin, sam. midi et juil.-22 août – **R** carte 1060 à 1355 **stc**.
Spéc. Huîtres et coquillages (oct.-mars), Sole aux quatre légumes, Ballottine d'anguilles à la crème de courgettes.

XX **France,** chaussée de Charleroi 132, ⊠ 1060, ☏ 5385975 – 🆎 ⓪   BR **h**
fermé dim. et 3 juil.-2 août – **R** (déjeuner seult) 760 **stc**.

XX **Ecailler Jean-Pierre,** av. Haut-Pont 25, ⊠ 1050, ☏ 3457118, Produits de la mer   BR **p**
fermé dim., lundi et juil. – **R** carte 730 à 1175 **stc**.

Quartier Avenue Louise et Bascule (Ixelles) *plan p. 6* :

🏨 **Mayfair** sans rest, av. Louise 381, ⌧ 1050, ℡ 6499800, Télex 24821 – 🛗 📺 ☎ 🚗 – 🏬 ⬛ 🔺
ⓞ E. 🍽
100 ch ⌸ 3250/4100 **stc**
BR **c**

🏨 **Brussels,** av. Louise 315, ⌧ 1050, ℡ 6402415 – 🛗 📺 ☎ 🚗. 🔺 ⓞ
R *(fermé dim.)* carte 780 à 1130 **stc** – **40 ch** ⌸ 2320/2635 **stc**
BR **e**

XXXX **Parc Savoy,** r. Emile Claus 3, ⌧ 1050, ℡ 6401522 – ▤. 🔺 ⓞ E
fermé sam., dim. et juil. – **R** carte 1045 à 1700 **stc**
BR **u**

XXX ❁❁ **Cravache d'Or,** pl. A.-Leemans 10, ⌧ 1050, ℡ 5383746 – ▤. 🔺 ⓞ E
fermé août et sam. midi en juin-juil. – **R** carte 2000 à 2275 **stc**
Spéc. Foie gras d'oie chaud, Loup de mer frais fumé, Canard au vinaigre de framboises.
BR **v**

XX **Chez Adrienne,** av. Louise 124, ⌧ 1050, ℡ 6495441, Hors-d'œuvre – 🔺 ⓞ E
fermé sam., dim., 3 sem. en juil. et Noël-Nouvel An – **R** (déjeuner seult) 450/550 **stc**.
BR **s**

XX **Comme Ça,** r. Châtelain 61, ⌧ 1050, ℡ 6496290 – 🔺 ⓞ E
fermé dim., lundi soir et juil. – **R** carte 720 à 1130 **stc**.
BR **v**

XX **Armagnac,** chaussée de Waterloo 591, ⌧ 1060, ℡ 3459279 – 🔺 ⓞ
fermé sam. midi, dim. et août – **R** 600/900 **stc**.
BR **q**

XX **Arche de Noé,** r. Beau-Site 27, ⌧ 1050, ℡ 6475383
fermé sam. soir, dim. et 2ᵉ quinz. août – **R** carte 600 à 1145 **stc**.
BR **s**

Forest (Vorst) : *plan p. 6* :

XX ❁ **De Reu,** chaussée de Bruxelles 226, ⌧ 1190, ℡ 3435460 – 🔺. 🍽
fermé mardi, sam. midi, 17 août-14 sept. et 2 fév.-1ᵉʳ mars – **R** (nombre de couverts limité
prévenir) carte 800 à 2145 **stc**
Spéc. Foie d'oie frais au naturel, Agneau sarladaise, Mousse glacée au marc de Gewurztraminer.
BR **y**

XX **César,** bd G.-Van-Haelen 109, ⌧ 1190, ℡ 3431560 – 🔺 ⓞ E
fermé merc. soir, sam. midi et juil. – **R** carte 620 à 1075 **stc**.
BR **b**

X **Au Saucier,** av. des Armures 53, ⌧ 1190, ℡ 3448725 – 🔺 E
fermé dim., lundi et 15 juil.-14 août – **R** 550 **stc**.
BR **w**

Quartier Boondael (Ixelles) *plan p. 7* :

XXX ❁ **La Pomme Cannelle,** av. F.-Roosevelt 6, ⌧ 1050, ℡ 6407788 – 🔺 ⓞ E. 🍽
fermé sam., midi, lundi et août – **R** carte 900 à 1660 **stc**.
CR **v**

XXX **Aub. de Boendael,** square du Vieux-Tilleul 12, ⌧ 1050, ℡ 6727055, «Intérieur rustique » –
🅿. 🔺 ⓞ E
fermé sam. – **R** carte 645 à 1085 **stc**.
CR **s**

XX **Relais,** av. Jeanne 7, ⌧ 1050, ℡ 6496107 – 🔺 ⓞ E
fermé 15 juil.-15 août – **R** 800 **stc**.
CR **n**

Uccle (Ukkel) : *plans p. 6 et 7* :

XXX ❁ **Kolmer,** Drève de Carloo 18, ⌧ 1180, ℡ 3755653, ≼, «Élégante installation avec jardin-
terrasse » – 🔺 ⓞ
fermé dim., lundi, 17 août 7 sept. et 9 fév. 2 mars – **R** carte 1425 à 1750 **stc**
Spéc. Feuilleté de cuisses de grenouilles au cresson, Éminoé de volaille alsacienne-truffes et nouilles fraîches,
Homard chiffonnade de laitues et tomates.
BS **h**

XXX **Prince d'Orange,** av. Prince-d'Orange 1, ⌧ 1180, ℡ 3744871, Classique – 🅿. 🔺 ⓞ E
fermé lundi – **R** 675/1020 **stc**.
CS **u**

XXX **Le Taillis,** av. Floréal 47, ⌧ 1180, ℡ 3455731, Classique élégant – 🔺 ⓞ
fermé 31 août-26 sept., du 23 au 28 fév., dim. soir et lundi – **R** 990/1290 **stc**.
BR **g**

XXX ❁ **Arcades,** chaussée de Waterloo 1441, ⌧ 1180, ℡ 3743516 – 🔺 ⓞ E
fermé lundi soir, dim. et août – **R** carte 850 à 1350 **stc**
Spéc. Feuilleté d'écrevisses Magenta, Ris de veau Orloff, Selle d'agneau Porte-Maillot.
CS **y**

XX **Villa d'Este,** r. Etoile 142, ⌧ 1180, ℡ 3778646, Repas en plein air – 🅿. ⓞ
fermé lundi et 28 juin-26 juil. – **R** 580 **stc**.
AS **a**

XX **Le Brasier,** chemin du Crabbegat 2, ⌧ 1180, ℡ 3749730, Auberge rustique – 🔺 ⓞ E
fermé sam. midi, dim. et jours fériés – **R** 690/1200 **stc**.
BR **a**

XX **Les Pélerins,** av. de Fré 190, ⌧ 1180, ℡ 3742046 – 🅿. 🔺 ⓞ E
fermé sam. et dim.
BR **k**

XX **Dikenek,** chaussée de Waterloo 830, ⌧ 1180, ℡ 3748346, Rustique – 🔺 ⓞ E
fermé dim. – **R** carte 1070 à 1575 **stc**.
BR **f**

XX **Marronniers,** chaussée d'Alsemberg 1084, ⌧ 1180, ℡ 3767071, Rustique – 🅿. 🔺 ⓞ
fermé dim. soir, lundi et juil. – **R** 755 **stc**.
BS **f**

XX **Paroisse,** chaussée de Waterloo 1035, ⌧ 1180, ℡ 3743616, «Intérieur typique suisse » – 🔺
ⓞ
fermé lundi.
BR **j**

XX **Coin-Coin,** chaussée d'Alsemberg 572, ⌧ 1180, ℡ 3444794, Rustique, ouvert jusqu'à 22 h 30
– 🔺
fermé sam. midi, dim. et jours fériés – **R** 580 **stc**.
BR **m**

XX **Ventre-Saint-Gris,** r. Basse 10, ⊠ 1180, ℡ 3752755 – 🅰🅴 ⓪   BS **t**
fermé dim. – **R** carte 870 à 1075 **stc**.

XX **Le Brugmann,** av. Brugmann 261, ⊠ 1180, ℡ 3448430 – 🅰🅴 ⓪ 🇪   BR **x**
fermé dim. soir, lundi et juil. – **R** carte 645 à 1080 **stc**.

XX **Le Calvados,** av. de Fré 182, ⊠ 1180, ℡ 3747098 – 🅰🅴 ⓪ 🇪   BR **k**
fermé sam. midi, lundi et août – **R** carte 955 à 1355 **stc**.

X **De Hoef,** r. Edith-Cavell 218, ⊠ 1180, ℡ 3743417, Ancien relais du 17ᵉ s., Repas en plein air
– 🅰🅴 ⓪   BR **d**
fermé du 10 au 31 juil. – **R** carte 530 à 800 **stc**.

X **Henri I,** av. Messidor 183, ⊠ 1180, ℡ 3452629, Rustique, Grillades   BR **g**
fermé lundi et sept. – **R** 475/570 **stc**.

X **Le Baluchon,** pl. Ste Alliance 16, ⊠ 1180, ℡ 3745281 – 🅰🅴 ⓪   CS **h**
fermé lundi, 2 sem. en janv. et 2 sem. en sept. – **R** (dîner seult) carte 760 à 890 **stc**.

X **Petits Pères,** r.Carmélites 149, ⊠ 1180, ℡ 3456671   BR **z**
fermé dim., lundi et du 1ᵉʳ au 15 août – **R** carte 500 à 850 **stc**.

Est

Quartier Cinquantenaire (Etterbeek) *plans p. 5 et 7 :*

🏨 **Park H.** sans rest, av. Yser 21, ⊠ 1040, ℡ 7344991, 🌳 – 🛗. 🅰🅴 ⓪ 🇪   CQ **n**
46 ch ⌷ 1480/2240 **stc**.

🏨 **Chelton Concorde** Ⓜ sans rest, r. Véronèse 48, ⊠ 1040, ℡ 7364095, Télex 64253 – 🛗 📺 ☎
🚗. 🅰🅴 ⓪ 🇪. 🦞   CQ **u**
⌷ 160 – **41 ch** 2295/2495 **stc**.

🏨 **Derby** sans rest, av. Tervuren 24, ⊠ 1040, ℡ 7337581 – 🛗 ⌷wc 🛁wc 🚗. 🅰🅴 ⓪ 🇪   CQ **t**
⌷ 100 – **28 ch** 850/1150 **stc**.

XX **Fontaine de Jade,** av. Tervuren 5, ⊠ 1040, ℡ 7363210, Cuisine chinoise – 🍽. 🅰🅴 ⓪ 🇪
fermé mardi – **R** 550/815 **stc**.   CQ **v**

XX **Casse-Dalle,** av. Celtes 37, ⊠ 1040, ℡ 7336625   CQ **v**
fermé 1 sem. en mai, du 24 au 31 déc., sam. midi d'oct. à juin, sam. de juin à oct. et dim. –
R carte 485 à 1045 **stc**.

XX **Charolais,** av. Cortenberg 30, ⊠ 1040, ℡ 7347040 – 🅰🅴 ⓪ 🇪   CQ **x**
fermé 21 juil.- août et week-ends – **R** carte 500 à 800 **stc**.

Quartier Place Eugène-Flagey (Ixelles) *plan p. 7 :*

XX **Piano à Bretelles,** r. A.-Dewitte 40, ⊠ 1050, ℡ 6476105   CR **f**
fermé sam. midi, dim. et août – **R** carte 750 à 1730 **stc**.

Quartier Place Meiser (Schaerbeek) *plan p. 5 :*

🏨 **Lambermont** Ⓜ sans rest, bd Lambermont 322, ⊠ 1030, ℡ 2425595, Télex 62220 – 🛗 📺.
🅰🅴 ⓪ 🇪   CP **w**
45 ch ⌷ 1500/2000 **stc**.

🏨 **Plasky** sans rest, av. Eugène-Plasky 212, ⊠ 1040, ℡ 7337518 – 🛗 ⌷wc 🛁 🚗. 🅰🅴 ⓪ 🇪
⌷ 105 – **30 ch** 690/1170 **stc**.   CP **h**

XXX **Le Meiser,** bd Gén.-Wahis 55, ⊠ 1030, ℡ 7353769, Classique – 🅰🅴 ⓪ 🇪   CP **a**
fermé sam., dim. et 15 juil.-14 août – **R** carte 790 à 1270 **stc**.

XX **L'Armor,** av. Milcamps 126, ⊠ 1040, ℡ 7331981 – 🅰🅴 ⓪ 🇪. 🦞   CPQ **f**
fermé sam. midi, dim. et du 5 au 30 juil. – **R** 680/1250 **stc**.

XX **Anak Timoer,** av. Rogier 357, ⊠ 1030, ℡ 7338987, Cuisine indonésienne et chinoise   CP **u**
fermé dim. soir, merc., Pâques, juil.-août et 18 déc.-5 janv. – **R** carte 480 à 785 **stc**.

XX **Mayfair,** av. Émile-Max 81, ⊠ 1040, ℡ 7357021, Taverne-restaurant – ⓪   CQ **b**
fermé sam., dim., jours fériés et juin-juil. – **R** carte 470 à 1200 **stc**.

XX **La Sole,** bd Aug. Reyers 165, ⊠ 1040, ℡ 7364138 – 🅰🅴 ⓪ 🇪   CQ **y**
fermé sam. soir, dim. et 21 juil.-août – **R** carte 770 à 1285 **stc**.

X **Au Cadre Noir,** av. Milcamps 158, ⊠ 1040, ℡ 7341445 – 🅰🅴 ⓪ 🇪   CP **r**
fermé sam. midi, lundi et du 1ᵉʳ au 21 juil. – **R** carte 610 à 840 **stc**.

Auderghem (Oudergem) : *plan p. 7 :*

XX **L'Abbaye de Rouge Cloître,** Rouge Cloître 8, ⊠ 1160, ℡ 6724525, ≼, Repas en plein air,
« Cadre de verdure » – 🅿. 🅰🅴 ⓪   DR **b**
fermé fév. – **R** 690/925 **stc**.

Woluwé-St-Lambert (Sint-Lambrechts-Woluwé) : *plans p. 5 et 7 :*

🏨 **Résidence Armorial** sans rest, bd Brand-Whitlock 101, ⊠ 1200, ℡ 7345636 – 📺 ⌷wc 🛁
🚗. 🅰🅴 ⓪   CQ **r**
15 ch ⌷ 690/1400 **stc**.

🏨 **Résidence Lambeau** sans rest, av. Lambeau 150, ⊠ 1200, ℡ 7338414 – ⌷ 🚗   CQ **g**
12 ch ⚎ 810/1060 **stc**.

🏨 **Léopold III,** sans rest, square Jos.-Charlotte 11, ⊠ 1200, ℡ 7706540 – ⌷ 🛁 🦞   CQ **d**
15 ch.

XXXX **Moulin de Lindekemale,** av. J.-F.-Debecker 6, ⊠ 1200, ☏ 7709057, « Aménagé dans un moulin du 15ᵉ s. » – 🅟 🆀 🄓 🄴 ⚘
fermé dim. et lundi – **R** 400/700 **stc**.   DQ **s**

XXX **Coq en Pâte,** r. Tomberg 259, ⊠ 1200, ☏ 7621971 – 🄰🄴 🄓 🄴   CQ **e**
fermé lundi et 20 juil.-19 août – **R** carte 820 à 1125 **stc**.

XXX **Sugito,** 1ᵉʳ étage, bd Brand-Whitlock 107, ⊠ 1200, ☏ 7335045, Cuisine indonésienne – 🄰🄴 🄓
🄴   CQ **r**
fermé lundi.

Woluwé-St-Pierre (Sint-Pieters Woluwé) : *plan p. 7* :

XX **Des 3 Couleurs,** av. Tervuren 453, ⊠ 1150, ☏ 7703321 – ⚘   DR **y**
fermé dim. soir, lundi, sept. et 1ʳᵉ sem. fév. – **R** carte 1045 à 1265 **stc**.

Watermael-Boitsfort (Watermael-Bosvoorde) : *plan p. 7* :

🏛 **Aub. du Souverain** sans rest, av. Fauconnerie 1, ⊠ 1170, ☏ 6721601 – 🄣🄥 🔏 🄰🄴   CR **e**
fermé 15 juil. -14 août – **12 ch** ☛ 1000/1300 **stc**.

XXX **Aub. Bécasse Blanche,** bd du Souverain 1, ⊠ 1170, ☏ 6722761 – 🅟 🄰🄴 🄓 🄴   CR **d**
fermé dim. – **R** 575/1075 **stc**.

XXX **Trois Tilleuls** ⚘ avec ch, Berensheide 8, ⊠ 1170, ☏ 6723014 – 🄣🄥 🖒wc ☎. 🄰🄴 🄓 🄴.
⚘ ch   CR **q**
R *(fermé dim.)* carte 900 à 1765 **stc** – **8 ch** � 785/1565 **stc**.

XX **Samambaia,** r. Philippe Dewolfs 7, ⊠ 1170, ☏ 6728720, Cuisine brésilienne, « Intérieur bien aménagé » – 🄰🄴 🄓 🄴   CS **p**
fermé dim., lundi et 18 juil.-17 août – **R** carte 860 à 1400 **stc**.

X **Le Middelbourg,** r. Middelbourg 21, ⊠ 1170, ☏ 6724565 – 🄰🄴 🄓 🄴   CS **k**
fermé mardi, merc. et juil. – **R** carte 400 à 575 **stc**.

Environs de Bruxelles

à Beersel : *plan p. 6* – 20 839 h. – ⊠ 1650 Beersel – ✆ 02 :

🏛 **Du Centre** ⚘, Steenweg op Ukkel 11, ☏ 3762615, 🐎 – 🖒wc 🅟 – 🏛
R *(fermé dim.)* carte 640 à 1040 **stc** – **6 ch** ⊻ 1000/1600 **stc**.   AS **n**

XX **New-Castle,** Schoolstraat 1, ☏ 3769933 – 🄰🄴 🄓 🄴   AS **d**
fermé lundi soir, mardi et juil. – **R** 650/850 **stc**.

à Diegem *plan p. 5* 🄲 Machelen – 11 132 h. – ⊠ 1920 Diegem – ✆ 02 :

🏨 **Sofitel** 🅼, Bessenveldstraat 15, autoroute Bruxelles-Zaventem sortie Diegem, ☏ 7206050,
Télex 26595, ⌸, 🏊 – 🄰🄴 🄓 🄴 ⚘ rest   DP **c**
R *(fermé sam. en juil.-août)* carte 810 à 1380 **stc** – ⊻ 250 – **125 ch** 2400/2800 **stc**.

🏨 **Holiday Inn** 🅼, Holidaystraat 7, près de l'autoroute Bruxelles-Zaventem, ☏ 7205865, Télex
24286, ⌸, ✂ – 🖒 🅟 🄳 🏛 🄰🄴 🄓 🄴 ⚘ rest   DP **a**
R carte 780 à 1140 **stc** – **288 ch** ☛ 2600/3550 **stc**.

🏨 **Novotel** 🅼, Olmenstraat (près de l'autoroute Bruxelles-Zaventem), ☏ 7205830, Télex 26751,
⌸ chauffée, 🐎 – 🚲 🍽 rest. 🄣🄥 🖒wc 🅟 – 🏛 🄰🄴 🄓 🄴   DN **s**
R carte 400 à 810 **stc** – ⊻ 150 – **158 ch** 1750/1900 **stc**.

à Dilbeek par ⑪ : 7 km – 34 932 h. – ⊠ 1710 Dilbeek – ✆ 02 :

XXX **Host. d'Arconati** ⚘ avec ch, d'Arconatistraat 77, ☏ 5693500, ≤, 🐎 – 🄣🄥 🖒wc ☎ 🚗
🅟. 🄰🄴 ⚘ ch
fermé fév. – **R** *(fermé dim. soir et lundi)* 580/1010 **stc** – **8 ch** ⊻ 670/1495 **stc**.

à Essene 🄲 Hekelgem, par ⑫ : 18 km, par E 5 sortie Ternat – 11 165 h. – ⊠ 1705 Essene –
✆ 053 :

XXXX ✿✿ **Host. Bellemolen** ⚘ avec ch, Statiestraat 9, SO : 1,5 km, ☏ 666238, ≤, « Ancien moulin du 12ᵉ s. aménagé avec recherche » – 🖒wc 🅟 🏛. 🄰🄴. ⚘
fermé du 4 au 29 juil., 23 déc.- 1ᵉʳ janv., dim. soir et lundi – **R** carte 1210 à 1760 **stc** – 6 ch ⊻
1850/2500 **stc**
Spéc. Terrine de foie d'oie frais, Blanc de turbot, Émincé de ris de veau au salpicon de homard.

à Grimbergen : *plan p. 4* – 31 137 h. – ⊠ 1850 Grimbergen – ✆ 02 :

🏨 **Tower Bridge** ⚘, Heidebaan 98 (près du Canal, Est : 3 km), ☏ 2520240, Télex 22398 – 🄣🄥
🖒wc ☎ 🅟 🄰🄴 🄴   BN
R *(fermé 3 sem. en juil.)* carte 570 à 950 **stc** – **12 ch** ⊻ 790/1210 **stc**.

XX **El Gaucho,** Rijkenhoekstraat 67, ☏ 2696448, Grillades, « Cadre rustique » – 🅟. 🄰🄴 🄓
fermé sam. midi, dim. soir, lundi et 5 juil.-5 août – **R** carte 1075 à 1560 **stc**.   BN

à Groenendaal : *plan p. 7* – ⊠ 1990 Hoeilaart – ✆ 02 :

XXXX ✿✿ **Romeyer,** chaussée de Groenendaal 109, ☏ 6570581, « Belle demeure, ≤ jardin avec pièce d'eau » – 🅟. 🄰🄴 🄓 🄴   DS **t**
fermé dim. soir, lundis non fériés, fév. et août – **R** 1490/1900 **stc**
Spéc. Boudin de homard, Ecrevisses farcies Nantua, Caneton au Chambertin.

à Groot-Bijgaarden (Grand-Bigard) : *plan p. 4* Ⓒ Dilbeek, par ⑫ : 7 km – 34 932 h. – ✉ 1720 Groot-Bijgaarden – ✿ 02 :

🏠 **Victory,** Nieuwe Gentse Steenweg 6, ☎ 4657234 – 🛏 🖨 🎬. **E**　　　　　　　AP **r**
R *(fermé sam. et dim.)* (dîner seult) 400 **stc** – **18 ch** ⚌ 755/1305 **stc**.

XXXX ❀ **De Bijgaarden,** I. Van Beverenstraat 20 (près du château), ☎ 4664485, ≼, Classique
élégant – 🆔 ⓪①　　　　　　　　　　　　　　　　　　　　　　　　　　　　　　　AP **e**
fermé dim. – **R** carte 1360 à 2210 **stc**
Spéc. Saumon mariné à l'aneth, Faisan rôti aux witloof-mousse de céleri (15 oct.-déc.), Gratin d'amandes aux poires caramélisées.

XXX ❀ **Michel,** Schepen Gossetlaan 31, ☎ 4666591, « Villa aménagée » – **Ⓟ**. 🆔 ⓪①　AP **y**
fermé dim. et lundi – **R** 1020/1290 **stc**
Spéc. Coquilles St-Jacques "Michel" (oct.-avril), Blanc de turbot aux fines herbes en papillote, Faisan rôti braban-çonne (oct.-fév.).

à Hoeilaart par ⑦ et N 227 : 15 km – 8 758 h. – ✉ 1990 Hoeilaart – ✿ 02 :

XX **Fol Atre,** Gemeenteplaats 24, ☎ 6571363 – ▥
fermé dim. soir, lundis non fériés, jeudi soir et 2e quinz. août – **R** 495/675 **stc**

à Huizingen Ⓒ Beersel, par ⑨ : 14 km – 20 839 h. – ✉ 1511 Huizingen – ✿ 02 :

XXX **Terborght,** Oud Dorp 16 (près de l'E 10), ☎ 3563996 – **Ⓟ**
fermé dim. soir, lundi et du 2 au 16 fév. – **R** carte 870 à 1055 **stc**

à Jezus-Eik par ⑦ : 12 km – ✉ 1900 Overijse – ✿ 02 :

XXXX ❀❀ **Barbizon** (Deluc), Welriekendedreef 95, à la lisière de la forêt de Soignes, ☎ 6570462 –
Ⓟ. 🆔　　　　　　　　　　　　　　　　　　　　　　　　　　　　　　　　　　　　　DS **a**
fermé mardi, merc., 20 juil.-4 août et fév. – **R** (nombre de couverts limité - prévenir) 1500/2500
stc
Spéc. Petites mousses légères de saison, Homard en chemise-beurre Barbizon, Chariot de gourmandises.

XX **Aub. Bretonne,** Steenweg op Brussel 670, ☎ 6571111
fermé merc. et août – **R** 535/1150 **stc**

XX **Denaeyer,** Steenweg op Brussel 649, ☎ 6570509 – **Ⓟ**. 🆔 ⓪①
fermé jeudi, vend. et du 1er au 28 août – **R** carte 900 à 1500 **stc**

à Kobbegem Ⓒ Asse, par ⑬ : 12 km – 26 393 h. – ✉ 1703 Kobbegem – ✿ 02 :

XXX Chalet Rose, Gentsesteenweg 1, ☎ 4526041 – **Ⓟ**. 🆔 ⓪① **E**
fermé dim. soir et lundi.

à Kortenberg par ④ : 15 km – 14 510 h. – ✉ 3070 Kortenberg – ✿ 02 :

XXX **Hof te Linderghem,** Leuvensesteenweg 346, ☎ 7597264 – **Ⓟ**. 🆔
fermé lundi soir, mardi et du 1er au 28 juil. – **R** carte 925 à 1225 **stc**.

à Linkebeek : *plan p. 6* – 4 776 h. – ✉ 1630 Linkebeek – ✿ 02 :

XX **Café de la Gare,** r. Station 90 (face à la gare), ☎ 3745490 – 🆔 ⓪①, **E**　　　　BS **e**
fermé dim. soir et lundi – **R** carte 1060 à 1500 **stc**.

à Meise par ① : 13 km – 15 003 h. – ✉ 1860 Meise – ✿ 02 :

XX **Aub. Napoléon,** Bouchoutlaan 1, ☎ 2693078, Rustique – **Ⓟ**. 🆔 **E**
fermé août et dern. sem. juil. – **R** carte 895 à 1470 **stc**.

à Overijse par ⑦ : 14 km – 20 576 h. – ✉ 1900 Overijse – ✿ 02 :

🏩 **Panorama** Ⓜ, Hengstenberg 73 (près de l'E 40), ☎ 6877198 – 🛏 🖨wc 🎬wc ☎ **Ⓟ** – 🛗. 🆔
⓪①
R 510 **stc** – **54 ch** ⚌ 830/1950 **stc**.

à Ruisbroek *plan p. 6* Ⓒ Sint-Pieters Leeuw – 28 068 h. – ✉ 1610 Ruisbroek – ✿ 02 :

🏠 **AC Relais Ruisbroek,** sur autoroute E 10, ☎ 3771156, Télex 62740 – ▥ rest. 📺 🖨wc 🎬wc
☎ **Ⓟ** – 🛗. 🆔 ⓪① **E**　　　　　　　　　　　　　　　　　　　　　　　　　　　　　　AS **b**
R 400 **stc** – **60 ch** ⚌ 870/1265 **stc** – P 1235/1570 **stc**.

à Sint-Genesius-Rode (Rhode St-Genèse) par ⑧ : 10 km – 16 831 h. – ✉ 1640 Sint-Genesius-Rode – ✿ 02 :

XXX **L'Orée de la Forêt,** av. Forêt-de-Soignes 361, ☎ 3581321, « Jardin, repas en plein air » –
🆔 ⓪① **E**
fermé merc. et fév. – **R** carte 1010 à 1360 **stc**.

à Sint-Pieters-Leeuw par ⑩ : 12 km – 28 068 h. – ✉ 1600 Sint-Pieters-Leeuw – ✿ 02 :

XXX **Ten Brukom,** Steenweg op Bergen 711, ☎ 3562337, « Aménagé dans une ancienne ferme »
– **Ⓟ**. 🆔 ⓪① **E**　　　　　　　　　　　　　　　　　　　　　　　　　　　　　　　AS **u**
fermé lundi soir et mardi – **R** 750 **stc**.

X **De Witte Hoeve,** J. Calloensstraat 10, ☎ 3774789, ≼, « Ancienne ferme brabançonne dans
un cadre champêtre » – **Ⓟ** – 🛗. 🆔 ⓪① **E**
fermé lundi, 2e quinz. fév. et 2e quinz. juil; d'oct. à avril fermé mardi, merc. et jeudi soir –
R carte 435 à 805 **stc**.

à Sterrebeek Ⓒ Zaventem, par ⑤ : 14 km – 25 337 h. – ⊠ 1960 Sterrebeek – ✪ 02 :

XX **Chasse des Princes,** av. Hippodrome 141, ☎ 7311964 – 🆎 ⓪
fermé lundis et mardis non fériés – **R** carte 900 à 1320 **stc**.

à Vilvoorde : plan p. 5 – 33 239 h. – ⊠ 1800 Vilvoorde – ✪ 02 :

XXX **Hertog Jan,** Grote Markt 37, ☎ 2518943 – 🆎 E. ⋙   CDN **b**
fermé merc. soir, dim., 15 juil.-16 août et du 25 au 30 déc. – **R** 595/1350 **stc**.

XX **'t Riddershof,** Riddersstraat 33, ☎ 2512379 – 🆎 ⓪ E   DN **a**
fermé dim. soir, lundi et 29 juin-2 août – **R** carte 880 à 1320 **stc**.

à Vlezenbeek Ⓒ Sint-Pieters-Leeuw, par ⑩ : 11 km – 28 068 h. – ⊠ 1712 Vlezenbeek –
✪ 02 :

XX **Aub. St-Esprit,** Postweg 250, rte du Château de Gaasbeek, ☎ 5324218 – ⋙
fermé dim. soir, lundi, sept. et 1re quinz. mars – **R** carte 830 à 1500 **stc**

à Wezembeek-Oppem par ⑤ : 11 km – 11 732 h. – ⊠ 1970 Wezembeek-Oppem – ✪ 02 :

XXX **Aub. St-Pierre,** Parvis St-Pierre 8, ☎ 7312179, « Intérieur rustique » – 🆎 ⓪
fermé sam. midi, dim. et 18 juil.-18 août – **R** carte 710 à 1155 **stc**.

à Zaventem : plan p. 5 25 337 h. – ⊠ 1930 Zaventem – ✪ 02 :

🏨 **Résidence Z** sans rest, Kerkplein 19, ☎ 7206391 – 🛏 🛎   DP **b**
8 ch ⇌ 950/1190 **stc**.

à Zellik Ⓒ Asse par ⑬ : 10 km – 26 393 h. – ⊠ 1730 Zellik – ✪ 02 :

X **Sandy,** Steenweg op Gent 527, ☎ 4651376 – 🅿. ⓪
fermé mardi, dim. soir et 15 juin-1er juil. – **R** carte 670 à 1000 **stc**.

Nederland

Amsterdam

AMSTERDAM

AMSTERDAM Noord-Holland 🄶 ③ et 🄸🄾🄸 ⑩ ㉗ ㉘ – 718 577 h. – ✪ 0 20.

Voir Le vieil Amsterdam★★★ (p. 6 et 7) : les Canaux★★★ (Grachten) : Singel, Herengracht, Reguliersgracht, Keizersgracht, promenade en bateau★ (Rondvaart) – Béguinage★★ (Begijnhof) p. 7 LY – Dam : Nouvelle église★ (Nieuwe Kerk) p. 7 LX – Marché aux fleurs★ (Bloemenmarkt) p. 7 LY – Rembrandtsplein (place Rembrandt) p. 7 MY – Pont Maigre★ (Magere Brug) p. 7 MZ.

Musées : Rijksmuseum★★★ (p. 6) KZ – Rijksmuseum Vincent van Gogh★★★ (p. 4) FV – Municipal★★ (Stedelijk Museum) : art moderne (p. 4) FV – Historique d'Amsterdam★★ (Amsterdams Historisch Museum) p. 7 LY – Madame Tussaud★ : musée de cires (p. 7) LY **M1** – ''Le Bon dieu au grenier''★ (Museum Amstelkring Ons'Lieve Heer op Solder) : ancienne chapelle clandestine (p. 7) MX **M4** – Maison de Rembrandt★ (Rembrandthuis) : œuvres graphiques du maître (p. 7) MY **M5** – Histoire maritime des Pays-Bas★ (Nederlands Scheepvaart Museum) p. 5 HU **M6** – des Tropiques★ (Tropenmuseum) p. 5 HU **M7** – Allard Pierson★ : collections archéologiques (p. 5) LY **M8**.

🏌 Zwarte Laantje 4 à Duivendrecht (p. 3 DS) ☎ (0 20) 943650.

🏇 Sportpark Overamstel (p. 3 CS) ☎ (0 20) 413584.

✈ à Schiphol (p. 2 AS) : 9,5 km ☎ (0 20) 5110432 (renseignements) et (0 20) 434242 (réservations) – **Aérogare** : Gare Centrale (p. 5 GT) ☎ (0 20) 495575.

🚗 (départs de 's-Hertogenbosch et de Hoek van Holland) ☎ (0 20) 238383.

⚓ et ⚓ vers Gothenburg (Suède). Liaison de bateaux de la Cie Tor Line, Suezhaven (au départ des bateaux) ☎ (0 20) 117005.

🛈 Stationsplein (Koffiehuis), ✉ 1012 AB ☎ 266444 – Fédération provinciale Rokin 9-15, ✉ 1012 KK, ☎ 221016, Télex 12324.

Bruxelles 207 ③ – Düsseldorf 227 ③ – Den Haag 63 ④ – Luxembourg 412 ③ – Rotterdam 76 ④ .

LISTE ALPHABÉTIQUE HOTELS ET RESTAURANTS

AMSTERDAM
AGGLOMÉRATION

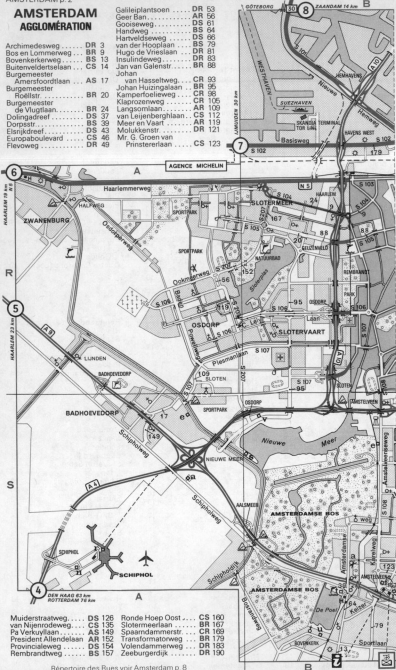

Répertoire des Rues voir Amsterdam p. 8

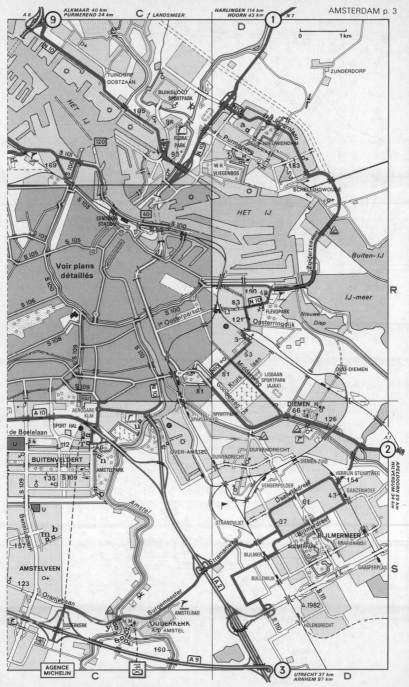

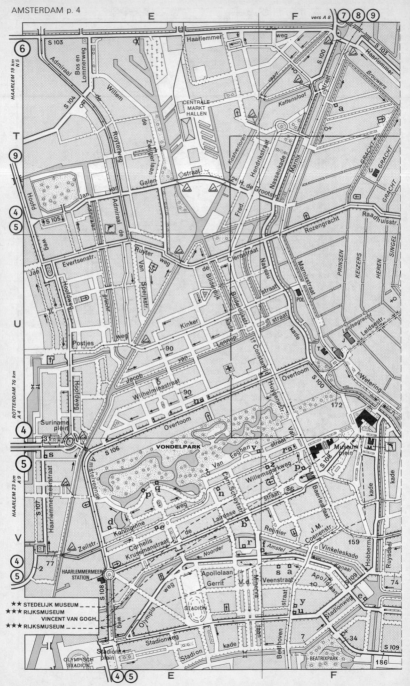

STEDELIJK MUSEUM ★★
RIJKSMUSEUM ★★★
VINCENT VAN GOGH
RIJKSMUSEUM ★★★

AMSTERDAM

Répertoire des Rues
voir Amsterdam p. 8

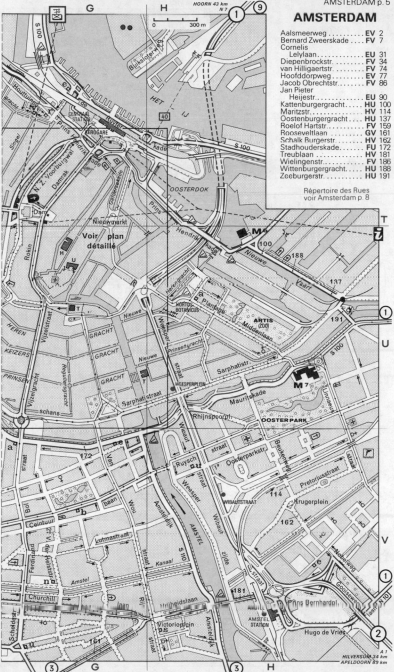

AMSTERDAM
CENTRE

Répertoire des Rues
voir Amsterdam p. 8

***RIJKSMUSEUM

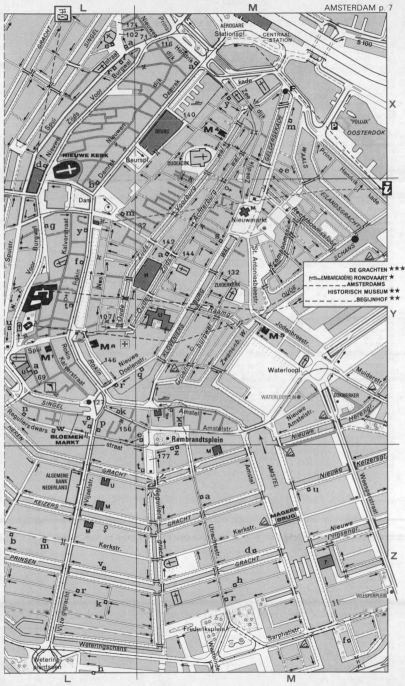

DE GRACHTEN ★★★
(⌐EMBARCADÈRE) RONDVAART ★
AMSTERDAMS
HISTORISCH MUSEUM ★★
BEGIJNHOF ★★

55

RÉPERTOIRE GÉNÉRAL DES RUES D'AMSTERDAM

HOTELS et RESTAURANTS

Liste alphabétique : Amsterdam p. 1 bis

Quartiers du Centre - plans p. 6 et 7 sauf indication spéciale :

Amstel et Rest. La Rive, Professor Tulpplein 1, ⊠ 1018 GX, ☎ 226060, Télex 11004, « Terrasse ombragée avec ≤ l'Amstel » – |$| ▤ rest. TV ☎ Ⓟ – 🏛. AE ⓞ E. ✻ MZ **f**
R 70/98 **stc** – ☕ 16 – **111 ch** 180/295 **stc** – P 258/336 **stc**.

Sonesta et Rest. Rib Room Ⓜ, Kattengat 1, ⊠ 1012 SZ, ☎ 212223, Télex 17149 – |$| ▤ rest. TV ☎ ♿ 🚗 – 🏛. AE ⓞ E. ✻ rest LX **a**
R carte 48 à 85 **stc** – ☕ 17 – **425 ch** 165/270 **stc**.

Amsterdam Marriott et Rest. Port O'Amsterdam Ⓜ, Stadhouderskade 21, ⊠ 1054 ES, ☎ 835151, Télex 15087 – |$| ▤ TV ☎ ♿ 🚗 – 🏛. AE ⓞ E. ✻ rest JZ **p**
R carte 30 à 60 **stc** – ☕ 22 – **395 ch** 200/275 **stc**.

Europe et Rest. Excelsior, Nieuwe Doelenstraat 2, ⊠ 1012 CP, ☎ 234836, Télex 12081, ≤ – |$| ▤ rest. TV ☎ – 🏛. AE ⓞ E LY **r**
R 65 **stc** – ☕ 13 – **81 ch** 145/240 **stc**.

Carlton sans rest, Vijzelstraat 2, ⊠ 1017 HK, ☎ 222266, Télex 11670 – |$| TV 🚗 – 🏛. AE ⓞ LY **v**
156 ch ☕ 130/218 **stc**.

Victoria, Damrak 1, ⊠ 1012 LG, ☎ 234255, Télex 16625 – |$| ▤ rest. – 🏛. AE ⓞ E MX **a**
R *(fermé dim.)* 33/85 **stc** – **160 ch** ☕ 145/210 **stc**.

Caransa et Rest. Le Petit Café Ⓜ, Rembrandtsplein 19, ⊠ 1017 CT, ☎ 229455, Télex 13342 – |$| ▤ TV – 🏛. AE ⓞ E MY **x**
R carte 30 à 39 **stc** – **66 ch** ☕ 148/190 **stc**.

Doelen et Rest. Café Savarin, Nieuwe Doelenstraat 24, ⊠ 1012 CP, ☎ 220722, Télex 14399 – |$| ▤ rest. TV ☎. AE ⓞ MY **q**
R 25 **stc** – **84 ch** ☕ 155/200 **stc**.

American, Leidsekade 97, ⊠ 1017 PN, ☎ 245322, Télex 11379 – |$| – 🏛. AE ⓞ. ✻ ch
R (Café Américain) 15/45 **stc** – **185 ch** ☕ 138/215 **stc** – P 185/200 **stc**. JKZ **v**

Gd H. Krasnapolsky et Rest. Le Reflet d'Or, Dam 9, ⊠ 1012 JS, ☎ 263163, Télex 12262 – |$| ▤ rest. TV ♿ 🚗 – 🏛. AE ⓞ E LY **m**
R carte 45 à 66 **stc** – **250 ch** ☕ 130/280 **stc**.

Pulitzer et Rest. Goudsbloem, Prinsengracht 323, ⊠ 1016 GZ, ☎ 228333, Télex 16508 – |$| ▤ rest. TV ☎ – 🏛. AE ⓞ E. ✻ rest KY **r**
R carte 30 à 81 **stc** – ☕ 17 – **195 ch** 148/221 **stc**.

Port van Cleve, Nieuwe Zijds Voorburgwal 178, ⊠ 1012 SJ, ☎ 244860, Télex 13129 – |$| TV – 🏛. AE ⓞ E. ✻ LX **d**
R carte 42 à 59 **stc** – **110 ch** ☕ 118/210 **stc** – P 165/175 **stc**.

Arthur Frommer et Rest. Oranjehof, Noorderstraat 46, ⊠ 1017 TV, ☎ 220328, Télex 14047 – |$| Ⓟ. AE ⓞ E LZ **k**
R (dîner seult) 27 **stc** – **90 ch** ☕ 113/148 **stc**.

Centraal, Stadhouderskade 7, ⊠ 1054 ES, ☎ 185765, Télex 12601 – |$| TV ☎ – 🏛. AE ⓞ E. ✻ ch JZ **p**
R (Travellers Grill) 26/50 **stc** – **116 ch** ☕ 122/184 **stc**.

Ambassade sans rest, Herengracht 341, ⊠ 1016 AZ, ☎ 262333, Télex 10158 – 🛁wc ☎. AE KY **f**
34 ch ☕ 58/130 **stc**.

Parkhotel, Stadhouderskade 25, ⊠ 1071 ZD, ☎ 717474, Télex 11412 – |$| ▤ rest. 🛁wc ☎ 🚗 – 🏛. AE ⓞ E. ✻ KZ **f**
R 23/60 **stc** – **184 ch** ☕ 134/192 **stc** – P 140/178 **stc**.

Schiller, Rembrandtsplein 26, ⊠ 1017 CV, ☎ 231660, Télex 14058 – |$| 🛁wc 🚿wc ☎. AE ⓞ E MZ **t**
R carte 30 à 58 **stc** – **96 ch** ☕ 115/168 **stc** – P 161 **stc**.

Amster Centre, Herengracht 255, ⊠ 1016 BJ, ☎ 221727, Télex 15424 – |$| – 🏛 KY **a**
110 ch.

Aalborg sans rest, Sarphatipark 106, ⊠ 1073 EC, ☎ 799057 – |$| 🛁wc plan p. 5 GV **b**
33 ch ☕ 70/120 **stc**.

tourner →

🏨 **Owl Hotel** sans rest, Roemer Visscherstraat 1, ✉ 1054 EV, ☏ 189484, Télex 13360 – 🛗
🖴wc 🛁wc 🅿. 🆎   JZ **e**
34 ch ⛔ 75/112 **stc**.

🏨 **Choura** sans rest, Marnixstraat 372, ✉ 1016 XX, ☏ 237524, Télex 15362 – 🛗 📺 🖴wc 🛁wc
🅿. 🆎 🇪   JY **a**
22 ch ⛔ 78/165 **stc**.

🏨 **Asterisk** sans rest, Den Texstraat 16, ✉ 1017 ZA, ☏ 262396 – 🖴wc 🛁wc. 🇪   LZ **h**
19 ch 🍴 43/95 **stc**.

🏨 **Parklane** sans rest, Plantage Parklaan 16, ✉ 1018 ST, ☏ 224804 – 🛁wc. 🌿
8 ch ⛔ 45/100 **stc**.   plan p. 5 HU **a**

🏨 **Linda** sans rest, Stadhouderskade 131, ✉ 1074 AW, ☏ 725668 – 🖴 🛁. 🌿
mars-oct. – **17 ch** 🍴 40/95 **stc**.   plan p. 5 GV **e**

🏨 **Roode Leeuw,** Damrak 93, ✉ 1012 LP, ☏ 240396 – 🛗 🖴wc 🅿 🕭 – 🔒 🆎   LXY **b**
R carte 27 à 37 **stc** – **80 ch** ⛔ 65/133 **stc**.

🏨 **Estheréa** sans rest, Singel 305, ✉ 1012 WJ, ☏ 245147, Télex 14019 – 🛗 🖴wc 🛁wc. 🆎. 🌿
70 ch 🍴 70/128 **stc**.   KY **t**

🏨 **Atlanta** sans rest, Rembrandtsplein 8, ✉ 1017 CV, ☏ 253585, Télex 15528 – 🖴wc 🛁wc. 🆎
⓿ 🇪   LMY **e**
24 ch ⛔ 73/125 **stc**.

🏨 **Stadhouder** sans rest, Stadhouderskade 76, ✉ 1072 AE, ☏ 718428 – 🛗 🛁wc. 🌿
20 ch 🍴 50/80 **stc**.   plan p. 5 GV **a**

🏨 **Fantasia** sans rest, Nieuwe Keizersgracht 16, ✉ 1018 DR, ☏ 238259 – 🛁wc   MZ **u**
fermé 15 nov.-15 déc. – **19 ch** 🍴 40/80 **stc**.

🏨 **Engeland** sans rest, Roemer Visscherstraat 30a, ✉ 1054 EZ, ☏ 180862 – 🛁wc   JZ **g**
mars-nov. – **28 ch** 🍴 55/100 **stc**.

🏨 **Parkzicht** sans rest, Roemer Visscherstraat 33, ✉ 1054 EW, ☏ 180897 – 🖴 🛁wc   JZ **b**
15 ch 🍴 45/95 **stc**.

🏨 **Sipermann** sans rest, Roemer Visscherstraat 35, ✉ 1054 EW, ☏ 161866 – 🛁wc 🕭   JZ **b**
fermé 18 déc. - 5 janv. – **13 ch** 🍴 45/90 **stc**.

🏨 **Vondel** sans rest, Vondelstraat 28, ✉ 1054 GE, ☏ 120120 – 🖴wc 🛁wc 🕭   JZ **s**
35 ch ⛔ 52/133 **stc**.

🍴🍴🍴🍴 **Dikker en Thijs et Alexander H.** avec ch, Prinsengracht 444, ✉ 1017 KE, angle Leidsestraat, ☏ 267721, Télex 13161 – 🛗 📺 🖴wc 🛁wc 🅿. 🆎 ⓿ 🇪. 🌿   KZ **s**
R *(fermé dim.)* (dîner seult) carte 58 à 85 **stc** – ⛔ 15 – **25 ch** 120/165 **stc**.

🍴🍴🍴 ❀ **Boerderij** (Wunneberg), Korte Leidsedwarsstraat 69, ✉ 1017 PW, ☏ 236929, Rôtisserie
dans un cadre rustique – 🆎 ⓿ 🇪. 🌿   KZ **k**
fermé sam.midi, dim., 17 juil.-1er août et 24 déc.-2 janv. – **R** 65/88 **stc**
Spéc. Caille farcie à l'Armagnac, Filets de sole soufflés au fumet de homard.

🍴🍴🍴 **Martinn,** 12e étage, De Ruyterkade 7 (havengebouw), ✉ 1013 AA, ☏ 256277, ≤ – 🍽. 🆎 ⓿
🇪   plan p. 5 GT **e**
fermé sam., dim. et jours fériés – **R** carte 47 à 78 **stc**.

🍴🍴🍴 **Swarte Schaep,** 1er étage, Korte Leidsedwarsstraat 24, ✉ 1017 RC, ☏ 223021, « Intérieur
17e s. » – 🍽. 🆎 ⓿ 🇪   KZ **d**
fermé 5 déc., Noël et Nouvel An – **R** 73/105 **stc**.

🍴🍴🍴 **Lido,** Leidsekade 105, ✉ 1017 PP, ☏ 263300 – 🍽. 🆎 ⓿   KZ **t**
15 mars- 15 oct. – **R** 38/95 **stc**.

🍴🍴🍴 **Bali,** 1er étage, Leidsestraat 89, ✉ 1017 NZ, ☏ 227878, Rest. indonésien – 🍽. 🆎 🇪   KZ **a**
fermé dim., 5, 24, 31 déc. et 1er janv. – **R** 38/49 **stc**.

🍴🍴 **Prinsenkelder,** Prinsengracht 438, ✉ 1017 KE, ☏ 267721 – 🆎 ⓿ 🇪. 🌿   KZ **s**
fermé sam. et dim. midi – **R** 40/58 **stc**.

🍴🍴 **Les Quatre Canetons,** Prinsengracht 1111, ✉ 1017 JJ, ☏ 246307 – 🆎 ⓿ 🇪   MZ **d**
fermé sam. midi et dim. – **R** carte 62 à 79 **stc**.

🍴🍴 **Les Trois Neufs,** Prinsengracht 999, ✉ 1017 KM, ☏ 229044 – ⓿   LZ **v**
fermé sam.midi, dim.midi, lundi et août – **R** carte 37 à 54 **stc**.

🍴🍴 **Oesterbar,** Leidseplein 10, ✉ 1017 PT, ☏ 232988, Produits de la mer – 🍽   KZ **y**
fermé 1er au 22 juil. et 24 déc. - 1er janv. – **R** 30/65 **stc**.

🍴🍴 **Indonesia,** 1er étage, Singel 550, ✉ 1017 AZ, ☏ 232035, Rest. indonésien – 🍽. 🆎 ⓿ 🇪
R 25/35 **stc**.   LY **v**

🍴🍴 **Le Rêve,** Kerkstraat 148, ✉ 1017 GR, ☏ 241394, Exposition de peintures – 🆎 ⓿   LZ **b**
fermé mardi, 30 avril, du 2 au 18 août, 5 déc. et 20 déc.-11 janv. – **R** (dîner seult) carte 41 à
59 **stc**.

🍴🍴 **The Guru of India,** Lange Leidsedwarsstraat 56, ✉ 1017 NM, ☏ 246966, Rest. indien – 🍽.
🆎 ⓿. 🌿   KZ **p**
R carte 29 à 50 **stc**.

🍴🍴 **Den Duvelshoeck,** 1er étage, Vijzelstraat 37, ✉ 1017 HD, ☏ 247615 – 🍽. 🆎 ⓿ 🇪   LY **p**
fermé dim. – **R** carte 36 à 68 **stc**.

XX **Le Musicien,** Amstel 100, ⊠ 1017 AC, ✆ 228945 – 🅰🅴 🅞 🅴   MY **f**
fermé merc. et du 1er au 22 août – **R** (dîner seult) carte 62 à 78 **stc**.

XX **Bon Retour,** Oude Zijds Achterburgwal 160, ⊠ 1012 DW, ✆ 236634 – 🅰🅴 🅞 🅴   MY **a**
R carte 32 à 70 **stc**.

XX **Da Canova,** Warmoesstraat 9, ⊠ 1012 HT, ✆ 266725, Cuisine italienne – 🅰🅴 🅞   MX **y**
fermé dim. et 2e quinz. juin – **R** (dîner seult) carte 44 à 57 **stc**.

XX **Camargue,** Reguliersdwarsstraat 7, ⊠ 1017 BJ, ✆ 239352 – 🅴. 🅰🅴 🅞 🅴   LY **n**
fermé du 3 au 18 juil., 23 déc.-7 janv., sam.midi, dim.midi et lundi midi – **R** carte 55 à 73 **stc**.

XX **Ardjuna,** 1er étage, Reguliersbreestraat 21, ⊠ 1017 CL, ✆ 220204, Rest. indonésien   LY **k**
R 20/33 **stc**.

XX **Lotus,** Binnen Bantammerstraat 5, ⊠ 1011 CH, ✆ 242614, Rest. chinois – 🅴. 🅰🅴 🅞 🅴   MX **e**
fermé 5, 24, 25, 26 et 31 déc. – **R** carte 40 à 55 **stc**.

XX **Sancerre,** Reestraat 28, ⊠ 1016 DN, ✆ 278794 – 🅴. 🕸   KY **d**
fermé Pâques, Pentecôte et Noël – **R** 38/70 **stc**.

XX **Vijff Vlieghen,** Spuistraat 294, ⊠ 1012 VX, ✆ 248369, « Intérieur vieil hollandais » – 🅴. 🅰🅴
🅞 🅴   KY **h**
R (dîner seult) carte 55 à 85 **stc**.

XX **Kopenhagen,** Rokin 84, ⊠ 1012 KX, ✆ 249376, Avec cuisine danoise – 🅴. 🅰🅴 🅞 🅴   LY **t**
fermé dim. – **R** 17/55 **stc**.

XX **Cave Internationale,** avec ch, Herengracht 561, ⊠ 1017 BW, ✆ 234371 – 🛏wc   MZ **t**
R (dîner seult) – 8 ch.

XX **Djawa,** 1er étage, Korte Leidsedwarsstraat 18, ⊠ 1017 RC, ✆ 246016, Rest. indonésien – 🅴.
🅰🅴 🅞 🕸   KZ **n**
fermé 31 janv. - 14 fév. – **R** 25/40 **stc**.

XX **Opatija,** Weteringschans 93, ⊠ 1017 RZ, ✆ 225184, Cuisine balkanique   KZ **b**
R (dîner seult) 23/40 **stc**.

XX **Dorrius,** Nieuwe Zijds Voorburgwal 336, ⊠ 1012 RX, ✆ 235675, Cuisine hollandaise – 🅰🅴
🅞 🅴   LY **u**
fermé 25 et 26 déc. – **R** carte 30 à 60 **stc**.

X **L'Enfant Terrible,** Binnen Wieringerstraat 28, ⊠ 1013 GX, ✆ 253316 – 🅰🅴
fermé dim. – **R** (dîner seult) carte 58 à 77 **stc**.   plan p. 5   GT **v**

X **Provençal,** Weteringschans 91, ⊠ 1017 RZ, ✆ 239619 – 🅰🅴 🅞 🅴. 🕸   KZ **b**
fermé sam.midi, dim. et lundi – **R** carte 47 à 62 **stc**.

X **Roma,** Rokin 18, ⊠ 1012 KR, ✆ 245873, Cuisine italienne – 🅰🅴   LY **y**
fermé lundi – **R** carte 20 à 39 **stc**.

X **Groene Lanteerne,** Haarlemmerstraat 43, ⊠ 1013 EJ, ✆ 241952, Intérieur vieil hollandais –
🅰🅴 🅞   plan p. 5   GT **r**
fermé sam. midi, dim. midi, lundi, mardi et 2e quinz. juin – **R** carte 29 à 58 **stc**.

X **Bistro La Forge,** Korte Leidsedwarsstraat 26, ⊠ 1017 RC, ✆ 240095 – 🅰🅴 🅴   KZ **d**
fermé jours fériés – **R** carte 41 à 64 **stc**.

X **Mandarijn,** Rokin 26, ⊠ 1012 KS, ✆ 230885, Rest. chinois – 🅴. 🅰🅴 🅞   LY **f**
R 19/25 **stc**.

X **Claes Claesz,** Egelantiersstraat 24, ⊠ 1015 PM, ✆ 255306 – 🅰🅴 🅞 🅴   KX **u**
fermé mardi – **R** (dîner seult) carte 40 à 64 **stc**.

X **Cartouche,** Anjeliersstraat 177, ⊠ 1015 NG, ✆ 227438 – 🅴. 🅰🅴 🅞 🅴   JX **x**
fermé dim., lundi et juin – **R** (dîner seult) carte 46 à 67 **stc**.

X **'t Seepaerd,** 1er étage, Rembrandtsplein 22, ⊠ 1017 CV, ✆ 221759, Avec produits de la mer
– 🅰🅴 🅞 🅴   MZ **z**
fermé 31 déc. – **R** carte 35 à 67 **stc**.

X **La Gaieté,** Utrechtsestraat 141, ⊠ 1017 VM, ✆ 257977 – 🅰🅴 🅞 🅴   MZ **r**
fermé sam. midi et dim. midi – **R** carte 33 à 59 **stc**.

X **Valentijn,** Kloveniersburgwal 6, ⊠ 1012 CT, ✆ 242028 – 🅴. 🅰🅴 🅞   MY **s**
fermé dim. et du 1er au 20 juil. – **R** (dîner seult) carte 46 à 84 **stc**.

X **Piaf,** Handboogstraat 19, ⊠ 1012 XM, ✆ 226266 – 🅰🅴   LY **a**
fermé mardi et 6 juil.-1er août – **R** (dîner seult) carte 42 à 69 **stc**.

X **Manchurian,** Leidseplein 10a, ⊠ 1017 PT, ✆ 231330, Rest. chinois – 🅰🅴 🅞 🅴   KZ **y**
fermé 20 déc.-1er fév. – **R** 22/31 **stc**.

X **Bacchus,** Spuistraat 3 e, ⊠ 1012 SP, ✆ 230051 – 🅴. 🅰🅴 🅞   LX **r**
R (dîner seult) carte 40 à 55 **stc**.

X **Pinang,** Reguliersdwarsstraat 30, ⊠ 1017 BM, ✆ 268400, Cuisine orientale – 🅰🅴 🅞   LY **w**
fermé sam. midi, dim. midi et lundi – **R** 27/53 **stc**.

X **Türkiye,** Nieuwe Zijds Voorburgwal 169, ⊠ 1012 RK, ✆ 239919, Rest. ture 🅴. 🅰🅴 🅞   LY **g**
R (dîner seult) 28/55 **stc**.

X **Entresol,** Geldersekade 29, ⊠ 1011 EJ, ✆ 237912 – 🅴   MX **m**
fermé mardi, merc. et juil. – **R** (dîner seult) carte 42 à 79 **stc**.

X **Gijsbrecht van Aemstel,** Herengracht 435, ⊠ 1017 BR, ✆ 235330, Taverne rustique – 🅴.
🅰🅴 🅞   KY **x**
fermé dim., 25 et 26 déc. – **R** carte 43 à 90 **stc**.

tourner →

XX **Pied de Cochon,** Noorderstraat 19, ☒ 1017 TR, ℡ 237677   LZ **r**
R (dîner seult).

XX **Little Hungary,** Utrechtsedwarsstraat 85, ☒ 1017 WD, ℡ 228389, Rest. hongrois   MZ **h**
fermé lundi, merc. et 22 juil. -12 août – **R** (dîner seult) carte 30 à 58 **stc**.

XX **Albatros,** Westerstraat 264, ☒ 1015 MT, ℡ 279932, Produits de la mer – ▤. 𝔸𝔼 ⓘ 𝔼
fermé dim. – **R** (dîner seult) carte 40 à 69 **stc**.   JX **w**

XX **Mangerie,** Spuistraat 3b, ☒ 1012 SP, ℡ 252218   LX **f**
R (dîner seult) carte 33 à 48 **stc**.

XX **Fleur d'Or,** Goudsbloemstraat 207, ☒ 1015 JN, ℡ 252470 – ⓘ   plan p. 4   FT **a**
fermé lundi, mardi, 12 juil.-4 août et 27 déc.-7 janv. – **R** (dîner seult) carte 28 à 54 **stc**.

XX **Mirafiori,** Hobbemastraat 2, ☒ 1071 ZA, ℡ 723013, Cuisine italienne   KZ **r**
fermé mardi et du 5 au 14 juil. – **R** 15/35 **stc**.

XX **Holland's Glorie,** Kerkstraat 222, ☒ 1017 GV, ℡ 244764   LZ **m**
R (dîner seult) carte 22 à 47 **stc**.

XX **Sluizer,** Utrechtsestraat 45, ☒ 1017 VH, ℡ 263557, Poisson seult – 𝔸𝔼 ⓘ   MZ **a**
R (dîner seult) 28/61 **stc**.

XX **Cacerola,** Weteringstraat 41, ☒ 1017 SM, ℡ 265397, Cuisine espagnole   KZ **k**
fermé dim., 19 juil.-8 août et 2ᵉ quinz. déc. – **R** (dîner seult) carte 31 à 72 **stc**.

XX **Silveren Spiegel,** 1ᵉʳ étage, Kattengat 4, ☒ 1012 SZ, ℡ 246589 – 𝔸𝔼 ⓘ   LX **e**
fermé dim. – **R** (dîner seult) 31 à 61 **stc**.

Quartiers Sud et Ouest - plans p. 4 et 5 sauf indication spéciale :

🏨 **Amsterdam Hilton** Ⓜ, Appollolaan 138, ☒ 1077 BG, ℡ 780780, Télex 11025 – |📶| ▤ rest.
📺 ☎ & 🄿 – 🏊 𝔸𝔼 ⓘ. ⅏ rest   EV **r**
R 22/86 **stc** – ⛱ 17 – **276 ch** 205/305 **stc**.

🏨 **Dikker en Thijs Garden Hotel et Rest. De Kersentuin** Ⓜ, Dijsselhofplantsoen 7, ☒
1077 BJ, ℡ 642121, Télex 15453 – |📶| ▤ 📺 ☎ 🄿 – 🏊 𝔸𝔼 ⓘ 𝔼   EFV **f**
R *(fermé dim. et 25 déc.-2 janv.)* 50/85 **stc** – **98 ch** ⛱ 164/217 **stc**.

🏨 **Okura et Rest. Ciel Bleu** Ⓜ avec rest. japonais Yamazato, Ferdinand Bolstraat 175, ☒
1072 LH, ℡ 787111, Télex 16182, ⩻ – |📶| ▤ 📺 ☎ ⇌ 🄿 – 🏊 𝔸𝔼 ⓘ 𝔼. ⅏   GV **n**
R (Ciel Bleu) (dîner seult) 68/130 **stc** – ⛱ 18 – **402 ch** 120/250 **stc**.

🏨 **Apollohotel,** Apollolaan 2, ☒ 1077 BA, ℡ 735922, Télex 14084, « Terrasse avec ⩻ canal » –
|📶| 📺 ☎ & 🄿 – 🏊 𝔸𝔼 ⓘ 𝔼. ⅏   FV **e**
R carte 48 à 89 **stc** – ⛱ 20 – **230 ch** 165/270 **stc**.

🏨 **Crest H. Amsterdam** Ⓜ, De Boelelaan 2, ☒ 1083 HJ, ℡ 429855, Télex 13647 – |📶| ▤ 📺 🄿
– 🏊. 𝔸𝔼 ⓘ 𝔼   plan p. 3   CS **a**
R carte 34 à 69 **stc** – **260 ch** ⛟ 149/189 **stc**.

🏨 **Novotel Amsterdam** Ⓜ, Europaboulevard 10, ☒ 1083 AD, ℡ 442851, Télex 13375 – |📶|
▤ rest. 📺 🄿 – 🏊   plan p. 3   CS **r**
R carte 27 à 64 **stc** – ⛱ 14 – **600 ch** 120/150 **stc**.

🏨 **Jan Luyken** sans rest, Jan Luykenstraat 58, ☒ 1071 CS, ℡ 764111, Télex 16254 – |📶| 📺 ☎.
𝔸𝔼 ⓘ 𝔼   plan p. 6   JZ **x**
63 ch ⛱ 123/155 **stc**.

🏨 **Memphis,** De Lairessestraat 87, ☒ 1071 NX, ℡ 733141, Télex 12450 – |📶|. 𝔸𝔼 ⓘ 𝔼. ⅏
R 25/55 **stc** – **81 ch** ⛱ 142/204 **stc** – P 146/186 **stc**.   EV **b**

🏨 **Delphi** sans rest, Apollolaan 105, ☒ 1077 AN, ℡ 795152, Télex 16659 – |📶| 📺 ⌂wc 🚿wc ☎.
𝔸𝔼 ⓘ 𝔼   FV **a**
50 ch ⛱ 100/145 **stc**.

🏨 **Apollofirst** sans rest, Apollolaan 123, ☒ 1077 AP, ℡ 730333, Télex 13446 – |📶| 📺 ⌂wc 🚿.
𝔸𝔼 ⓘ 𝔼   FV **s**
33 ch ⛱ 101/148 **stc**.

🏨 **Atlas H.,** Van Eeghenstraat 64, ☒ 1017 GK, ℡ 766336, Télex 17081 – |📶| 📺 ⌂wc 🚿. 𝔸𝔼 ⓘ
𝔼. ⅏ rest   EV **v**
R 20/35 **stc** – **24 ch** ⛱ 100/130 **stc**.

🏨 **Casa 400,** James Wattstraat 75, ☒ 1097 DL, ℡ 651171, Télex 14677 – |📶| 🚿wc 🚿. 𝔸𝔼   HV **e**
juin-sept. – **R** carte 35 à 42 **stc** – **400 ch** ⛟ 81/142 **stc** – P 84/135 **stc**.

🏠 **Zandbergen** sans rest, Willemsparkweg 205, ☒ 1071 HB, ℡ 769321, Télex 16443 – 📺
⌂wc 🚿wc 🚿. 𝔸𝔼 𝔼   EV **n**
17 ch ⛱ 73/120 **stc**.

🏠 **Borgmann** ⛵ sans rest, Koningslaan 48, ☒ 1075 AE, ℡ 735252 – |📶| ⌂wc 🚿wc 🚿. 𝔸𝔼 ⓘ
𝔼   EV **q**
fermé 20 déc.- 3 janv. – **15 ch** ⛱ 48/105 **stc**.

🏠 **Koningshof** sans rest, Koninginneweg 169, ☒ 1075 CN, ℡ 793526 – 🚿wc 🚿. 𝔸𝔼 ⓘ   EV **e**
15 ch ⛟ 45/90 **stc**.

🏠 **Toro** ⛵ sans rest, Koningslaan 64, ☒ 1075 AG, ℡ 737223 – ⌂wc 🚿 🚿. 𝔸𝔼 ⓘ 𝔼   EV **p**
12 ch ⛱ 48/105 **stc**.

🏠 **Fita** sans rest, Jan Luykenstraat 37, ☒ 1071 CL, ℡ 790976 – 🚿wc. ⅏   plan p. 6   JZ **z**
fermé 15 janv.-14 fév. – **20 ch** ⛟ 40/95 **stc**.

🏠 Belfort, Surinameplein 53, ☒ 1058 GN, ℡ 174333 – ▤ rest. 📺 🚿wc – 20 ch   EV **s**

XXX **Parkrest. Rosarium,** Europa boulevard, Amstelpark 1, ⊠ 1083 HZ, ☏ 444085, « Au milieu
d'un parc fleuri » – 🍴 ◪ ⓪ Ε   plan p. 3 **CS** **n**
fermé dim. d'oct. à mars – **R** carte 46 à 87 **stc**.

XX **Fong Lie,** P.C. Hooftstraat 80, ⊠ 1071 CB, ☏ 716404, Rest. chinois – ▤. ⚘
fermé dim.midi, lundi, jours fériés et du 5 au 31 juil. – **R** carte 42 à 61 **stc**.   plan p. 6 **JZ** **w**

XX **Entre Nous,** Sophialaan 36, ⊠ 1075 BS, ☏ 724343 – ◪ ⓪ Ε   **EV** **d**
R (dîner seult) 50/70 **stc**.

XX **Hamilcar,** Overtoom 306, ⊠ 1054 JC, ☏ 837981, Rest. tunisien – Ε   **EU** **n**
fermé lundi – **R** (dîner seult) carte 34 à 44 **stc**.

XX **Henri Smits,** 1er étage, Beethovenstraat 55, ⊠ 1077 HN, ☏ 791715 – ▤. ◪ ⓪ Ε **FV** **y**
fermé dim. midi et 25-26 déc. – **R** 30/45 **stc**.

XX **Bistro Lapin,** 1er étage, Scheldeplein 3, ⊠ 1078 GR, ☏ 642211 – ▤. ⚘   **GV** **u**
R (dîner seult) carte 30 à 53 **stc**

XX **Miranda Paviljoen,** Amsteldijk 223, ⊠ 1079 LK, ☏ 445768 – Ⓟ. ◪ ⓪ Ε plan p. 3 **CS** **u**
fermé 1er janv. – **R** 55/83 **stc**.

XX **Keijzer,** Van Baerlestraat 96, ⊠ 1071 BB, ☏ 711441 – ◪ ⓪. ⚘   **FV** **p**
fermé dim. – **R** carte 40 à 52 **stc**.

X **L'Entrecôte,** P.C. Hooftstraat 70, ⊠ 1071 CB, ☏ 737776, Style 1920, Grillades
fermé dim., lundi, jours fériés et juil. – **R** carte 31 à 41 **stc**.   plan p. 6 **JZ** **w**

X **Hoffman,** Van Baerlestraat 17a, ⊠ 1071 AM, ☏ 733991   plan p. 6 **JZ** **q**

X **Rembrandt,** P.C. Hooftstraat 31, ⊠ 1071 BM, ☏ 729011 – ▤. ◪ ⓪ Ε plan p. 6 **KZ** **h**
fermé lundi et 24 déc.- 1er janv. – **R** 23/55 **stc**.

X **Bistro Bonheur,** De Clercqstraat 18, ⊠ 1052 ND, ☏ 128827 – ◪. ⓪ Ε plan p. 6 **JY** **f**
fermé mardi, merc. et 1re quinz. juil. – **R** (dîner seult) 25/55 **stc**.

X **Les Frères,** Bosboom Toussaintstraat 70, ⊠ 1054 AV, ☏ 187905   plan p. 6 **JZ** **u**
fermé dim. et jours fériés – **R** (dîner seult) carte 30 à 43 **stc**.

X **Sama Sebo,** P.C. Hooftstraat 27, ⊠ 1071 BL, ☏ 728146, Rest. indonésien – ▤. ◪ 🄶 **KZ** **m**
fermé dim., jours fériés, 15 juil.-1er août et 20 déc.-2 janv. – **R** carte 21 à 38 **stc**.

X **La Taverna Da Bruno,** 1er Oosterparkstraat 69, ⊠ 1091 GW, ☏ 927800, Cuisine italienne **HV** **u**
R carte 29 à 56 **stc**.

X **Merapi,** Rijnstraat 67, ⊠ 1079 GW, ☏ 445377, Rest. indonésien   **HV** **s**
fermé lundi et 15 déc.- janv. – **R** carte 20 à 40 **stc**.

X **Croq-O-Vin,** Stadionweg 100, ⊠ 1077 SR, ☏ 711119 – ▤   **FV** **u**
R carte 27 à 58 **stc**.

X **Swart,** Willemsparkweg 87, ⊠ 1071 GT, ☏ 760700, Cuisine juive – ◪ ⓪ Ε   **FV** **z**
fermé lundi, mardi et 27 déc.- 14 janv. – **R** (dîner seult) carte env. 37 **stc**.

Environs - plans p. 2 et 3

à Amsterdam-Nord :

X Dirckshof, Bulkslotermeerplein 164, ⊠ 1025 EZ, ☏ 327591   **DR** **a**

à Amsterdam-Sud par Amstelveenseweg :

X **Bosrand,** Amstelveenseweg 764, ⊠ 1081 JK, ☏ 445814 – ▤ Ⓟ   **BS** **e**
fermé 5, 24 et 31 déc. – **R** carte 23 à 33 **stc**.

à l'entrée de l'autoroute d'Utrecht A 2 :

🏨 **Euromotel E 9,** Joan Muyskenweg 10, ⊠ 1096 CJ, ☏ 658181, Télex 13382 – 🛁wc 🕿 Ⓟ –
🍴 ◪ ⓪ Ε   **CS** **e**
R carte 23 à 45 **stc** – **140 ch** 🛏 74/114 **stc** – P 97 **stc**.

à Badhoevedorp – 🕿 0 2968 :

🏨 **Ibis Amsterdam,** Schipholweg 181, ⊠ 1171 PK, ☏ 1234, Télex 16491 – 🛗 ▤ 📺 🛁wc 🕿
Ⓟ – 🍴. ◪ ⓪ Ε   **AS** **a**
R carte 28 à 53 **stc** – **392 ch** 🛏 100/137 **stc**.

XX **Rôtiss. Schuilhoeve,** Nieuwe Meerdijk 98, ⊠ 1171 NE, ☏ 5500, Intérieur rustique – Ⓟ. ◪
⓪ Ε   **AS** **e**
fermé sam. midi, dim. midi et 21 déc.-1er janv. – **R** carte 44 à 81 **stc**.

à Landsmeer N : 6 km – 🕿 0 2908 :

XX **Meerpaal,** Noordeinde 78a, ⊠ 1121 AG, ☏ 3381 – Ⓟ. ◪ ⓪ Ε. ⚘   **CR**
fermé merc. et 19 juin-5 août – **R** 40/75 **stc**.

à Schiphol – 🕿 0 20 :

🅱 Aéroport, hall d'arrivée ☏ 175667.

🏨 **Hilton International Schiphol** Ⓜ, Herbergierstraat 1, ⊠ 1118 ZK (près de l'aéroport), ☏
5115911, Télex 15186, 🖫 – 🛗 ▤ 📺 🕿 🕭 Ⓟ – 🍴. ◪ ⓪. ⚘ rest   **AS** **n**
R carte 29 à 83 **stc** – 🖵 18 – **204 ch** 195/225 **stc**.

XXX **Aviorama,** 3e étage, à l'aéroport, ⊠ 1118 AA, ☏ 152150, ≤ – ▤. ◪ ⓪. ⚘   **AS** **r**
R carte 40 à 66 **stc**.

près de l'autoroute de Den Haag A 4 :

Euromotel Amsterdam M, Oude Haagseweg 20, ✉ 1066 BW, ☎ 179005, Télex 15524 – ♿ P – 🏛. AE ⓓ E BS **v**
R 15 **stc** – **157 ch** ☕ 82/118 **stc**.

De Boekanier, Oude Haagseweg 49, ✉ 1066 BV, ☎ 173525 – P. AE ⓓ E BS **s**
fermé sam. midi et dim. – **R** 65/125 **stc**.

sur l'autoroute de Den Haag A 4 : par ④ : 12 km – ☎ 0 2526 :

Rick's Brugrestaurant, Rijksweg A4, ✉ 2130 AG Hoofddorp, ☎ 86841, ← – P. AE ⓓ E
R (Polderrestaurant) 15/50 **stc**.

sur l'autoroute de Den Haag A 4 par ④ : 15 km – ☎ 0 2503 :

Sheraton Schiphol Inn M, Kruisweg 495, ✉ 2132 NA, ☎ 15851, Télex 41646 – TV ☎ ♿ P – 🏛. AE ⓓ. ✂ rest
R *(fermé sam. midi et dim. midi)* 35/93 **stc** – ☕ 13 – **166 ch** 150/185 **stc**.

Deutschland

Berlin

Frankfurt am Main

Hamburg

München

BERLIN

BERLIN Berlin-West 1000. 987 ⑰ — 1 964 000 Ew — Höhe 40 m — ✆ 030.

Frühere Reichshauptstadt, seit 1945 Viersektorenstadt unter Verwaltung des Alliierten Kontrollrates. Seit 1948 durch den Auszug der Sowjets aus dem Kontrollrat Spaltung in Berlin-Ost und Berlin-West.

Im Vertrag von 1972 zwischen der Bundesrepublik Deutschland und der DDR wurde die Zugehörigkeit von West-Berlin zur Rechts-, Wirtschafts- und Finanzordnung der Bundesrepublik Deutschland bestätigt.

Als Kultur- und Wissenschaftszentrum, Theater- und Konzertstadt (Deutsche Oper, Schiller-Theater, Philharmonie, Staatliche Museen) aber auch als Kongreß-, Messe- und Ausstellungsstadt (Messegelände, Internationales Congress-Centrum) ist Berlin weltbekannt.

Berlin ist aber auch eine « grüne » Stadt (ein Drittel des Stadtgebiets besteht aus Grün-, Wald- und Wiesenfläche) : keine andere deutsche Stadt hat so viele Seen (Havelseen) mit solcher Uferlänge (290 km), so ausgedehnte Wälder (Grunewald, Tegeler Forst), Park- und Grünanlagen (Botanischer Garten, Tiergarten) wie West-Berlin.

HAUPTSEHENSWÜRDIGKEITEN

Berlin-West

Kurfürstendamm★★ und Kaiser-Wilhelm-Gedächtniskirche DEV **A** — Brandenburger Tor★★ (Berlin-Ost) — Zoologischer Garten★★.

Museum Dahlem★★★ (Gemäldegalerie★★, Museum für Völkerkunde★★) MT — Schloß Charlottenburg★★ (im Knobelsdorff-Flügel : Gemäldesammlung★★, Goldene Galerie★★, Kunstgewerbemuseum★ mit Welfenschatz★★) — Antikenmuseum★ (Schatzkammer★★★) BU **M3** — Ägyptisches Museum★ (Büste der Königin Nofretete★) BU **M4** — Nationalgalerie★ FV **M6**.

Olympia-Stadion★★ LS **F** — Funkturm (❄★) AV — Botanischer Garten★★ MT.

Havel★ und Pfaueninsel★ LT — Wannsee★★ LT.

Maria-Regina-Martyrum-Kirche★ BU **D** und Gedenkstätte von Plötzensee DU **E**.

Berlin-Ost

Brandenburger Tor★★ — Unter den Linden★ GUV (Deutsche Staatsoper★ GHU **C**, Neue Wache★ HU **D**, Zeughaus★★) — Platz der Akademie★ GV.

Museumsinsel (Pergamon-Museum★★★ mit Pergamon-Altar, Nationalgalerie★★).

Alexanderplatz★★ — Fernsehturm (❄) — Karl-Marx-Allee★ HU — Sowjetisches Ehrenmal★ NS.

🛫 Tegel, ☏ 4 10 01 (Berlin S. 5 MS). — 🚗 Berlin - Wannsee, ☏ 3 13 81 30.

Messegelände (Berlin S. 6 AV), ☏ 3 03 81, Telex 0182908.

🅱 Berlin Tourist-Information im Europa-Center (Budapester Straße), ☏ 7 82 30 31, Telex 018 3356 ;

🅱 Verkehrsamt im Flughafen Tegel, ☏ 41 01 31 45.

ADAC, Berlin-Wilmersdorf, Bundesallee 29 (B 31), ☏ 8 68 61, Telex 0183513 ; Notruf ☏ 86 86 86.

ZUGÄNGE NACH BERLIN

Diese Angaben erfolgen ohne Gewähr.

Übergänge (alle sind Tag und Nacht geöffnet) - siehe nebenstehenden Plan.

Erforderliche Papiere : Gültiger Reisepaß (auch für Jugendliche ab 15 Jahre), Führerschein, Kraftfahrzeugschein. Das benötigte Transitvisum wird am Grenzübergang ausgestellt.

Geld : DM-West und Devisen dürfen unbeschränkt mitgeführt werden. Die Mitnahme von DM-Ost ist nicht gestattet.

Straßenbenutzungsgebühren und Visagebühren sind nur noch von Ausländern zu entrichten.

Benzin : Benzin kann in ausreichender Menge mitgeführt werden.
Im übrigen stehen an den Transitstrecken besondere Tankstellen zur Verfügung.

Geschwindigkeitsbeschränkung : Auf den Autobahnen der DDR ist die Geschwindigkeit auf 100 km/h begrenzt.

Auf dem Luftweg : Für die Flugreise nach Berlin gelten für ausländische Staatsangehörige die gleichen Reisepapiere wie für Reisen in die Bundesrepublik.
Zahlreiche Flugverbindungen bestehen täglich zwischen Berlin und den Flughäfen der Bundesrepublik : Köln - Bonn, Bremen, Düsseldorf, Frankfurt am Main, Hamburg, Hannover, München, Nürnberg, Saarbrücken und Stuttgart mit Anschlüssen an das internationale Flugnetz. Direktflüge auch nach Glasgow, London, New York, Paris, Washington und Zürich.

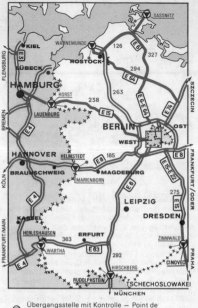

Übergangsstelle mit Kontrolle — Point de passage contrôlé — Check-entrance Punto di transito (Controllo)

185 Entfernung nach Berlin (West)
Distance entre ce point et Berlin-Ouest
Distance from this point to West Berlin
Distanza tra questo punto e Berlino-Ovest

ACCÈS A BERLIN

Les recommandations ci-dessous sont données sous toute réserve.

Points de transit (tous sont ouverts jour et nuit) — Voir ci-dessus.

Papiers : Passeport en cours de validité (même pour les jeunes à partir de 15 ans), visa de transit en République Démocratique Allemande délivré aux points de contrôle. Permis de conduire national, papiers nationaux de la voiture (carte grise ou certificat de propriété...), carte de contrôle remise au point de passage de la RDA. Carte Verte (assurance internationale), plaque de nationalité apposée sur la voiture.

Monnaie : Les étrangers peuvent avoir sur eux une somme illimitée de DM-Ouest et d'argent étranger (à l'exclusion de DM-Est).

Taxes : Péage et visa de transit 10,- DM (aller et retour).

Essence : En RDA, en cas de nécessité seulement, il est possible de s'approvisionner aux « postes d'essence internationaux ».

Limitation de vitesse sur les autoroutes de la RDA : 100 km/h.

Par avion : Pour les voyages aériens à destination de Berlin-Ouest, les papiers nécessaires à l'entrée en Allemagne fédérale suffisent.
Tous les jours, de nombreux avions assurent la liaison entre Berlin et les aérodromes de l'Allemagne fédérale : Cologne - Bonn, Brême, Düsseldorf, Francfort-sur-le-Main, Hambourg, Hanovre, Munich, Nuremberg, Sarrebruck, Stuttgart, et permettent la correspondance avec les réseaux aériens internationaux. Vols directs vers Glasgow, Londres, New York, Paris, Washington et Zurich.

Passage à Berlin-Est : Les étrangers (non ressortissants de l'Allemagne fédérale) qui ont l'intention de se rendre à Berlin-Est, doivent emprunter le point de contrôle de la Friedrichstraße. Ce seul point de passage est connu sous le nom de « Checkpoint Charlie » (Visa 5,- DM, valable de 0^{00} à 24^{00} h). Le passage est ouvert jour et nuit. Il n'est pas nécessaire d'avoir de laisser-passer, mais il faut présenter le passeport, le permis de conduire, la carte grise et la carte verte d'assurance internationale.

ACCESS TO BERLIN

The following information must be re-checked before travelling.

Transit Points (these are open day and night) — See Berlin p. 2.

Papers : Valid passport (separate one necessary for all children over 15), transit visa for the German Democratic Republic issued at checkpoints, current driving licence (for country of origin), vehicle documents (i.e. : registration book), control card issued at the crossing into the GDR, Green Card (international insurance), nationality plate fixed to the car.

Currency : Foreigners may carry an unlimited amount of West DM and foreign currencies (except East DM).

Taxes : Toll and transit visa (10 DM Rtn).

Petrol : In the GDR, « International filling stations » should be used in cases of emergency only.

Speed limit on motorways in GDR : 100 km/h (60 mph).

By air : To fly to West Berlin, the papers required for entering the Federal Republic are sufficient. Planes from international lines link Berlin daily with airports in the Federal Republic and elsewhere. Cologne - Bonn, Bremen, Düsseldorf, Frankfurt am Main, Hamburg, Hannover, Munich, Nuremberg, Saarbrücken, Stuttgart, Glasgow, London, New York, Paris, Washington and Zürich.

Entering East Berlin : Foreigners (non-nationals of the Federal Republic) planning to go to East Berlin must go through the checkpoint located on Friedrichstraße. This is the only access, known as « Checkpoint Charlie » (visa 5 DM, expires at midnight), and is open day and night. A pass is not required but passport, driving licence, registration book and international insurance Green Card have to be produced.

ACCESSI A BERLINO

Le raccomandazioni seguenti sono date con riserva.

Punti di transito (questi passaggi sono aperti giorno e notte) — Vedere Berlin p. 2.

Documenti : Passaporto non scaduto (anche per i giovani di età superiore ai 15 anni), visto di transito nella Repubblica Democratica Tedesca rilasciato ai posti di controllo. Patente di guida del proprio Paese, documento nazionale d'immatricolazione dell'automobile (libretto di circolazione), carta di controllo rilasciata ai punti di passaggio dalla RDT. Carta Verde (certificato di assicurazione internazionale), targa di nazionalità applicata all'automobile.

Moneta : Gli stranieri possono portare indosso una somma illimitata in DM-Occidentali ed in denaro straniero (esclusi i DM Orientali).

Tasse : Pedaggio e visto di transito (10 DM andata e ritorno).

Benzina : Nella RDT, soltanto in caso di necessità è possible rifornirsi ai « distributori internazionali ».

Nella RDT, sulle autostrade, velocità limitata a 100 chilometri orari.

Via aerea : Per i viaggi aerei diretti a Berlino-Ovest, sono sufficienti i documenti necessari per l'ingresso nella Germania Federale.
Ogni giorno, numerosi aerei effettuano il collegamento tra Berlino e gli aeroporti della Germania Federale : Amburgo, Colonia - Bonn, Brema, Düsseldorf, Francoforte sul Meno, Hannover, Monaco di Baviera, Norimberga, Saarbrücken, Stoccarda, che consentono le coincidenze con le reti aeree internazionali. Collegamenti aerei diretti con Glasgow, Londra, New-York, Parigi, Washington e Zurich.

Passaggio a Berlino-Est : Gli stranieri (non originari della Germania Federale) che intendono recarsi a Berlino-Est, devono passare dal punto di controllo della Friedrichstraße. Quest' unico punto di transito è noto con il nome di « Checkpoint Charlie » (visto 5 DM, valido dalle ore 0 alle 24). Il passaggio è aperto giorno e notte. Non occorre avere un lasciapassare, ma bisogna presentare il passaporto, la patente, il libretto di circolazione e la carta verde di assicurazione internazionale.

Straßenverzeichnis
siehe Berlin S.9 und S.12

····· Grenze zw. Berlin-West
und Berlin-Ost
Ligne de séparation entre
Berlin-Ouest et Berlin-
Est
Partition line between
West-Berlin and East-
Berlin
Linea di separazione tra
Berlino-Ovest e Berlino-
Est

🚩 Übergangsstelle mit
Kontrolle.
Point de passage
contrôlé.
Check-entrance.
Punto di transito
(controllo)

◐ Nur für Einwohner
der Bundesrepublik
Deutschland.
Réservé aux ressor-
tissants de la Répu-
blique Fédérale.
For the nationals of the
Federal Republic only.
Riservato ai cittadini della
Repubblica Federale.

◓ Nur für Ausländer.
Réservé aux étrangers.
For Foreigners only.
Solamente per gli stranieri

◒ Nur für Westberliner.
Réservé aux Berlinois de
l'Ouest.
For West Berliners only.
Solo per i Berlinesi della
zona Ovest

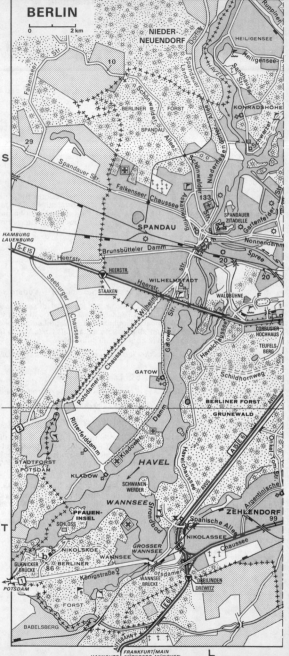

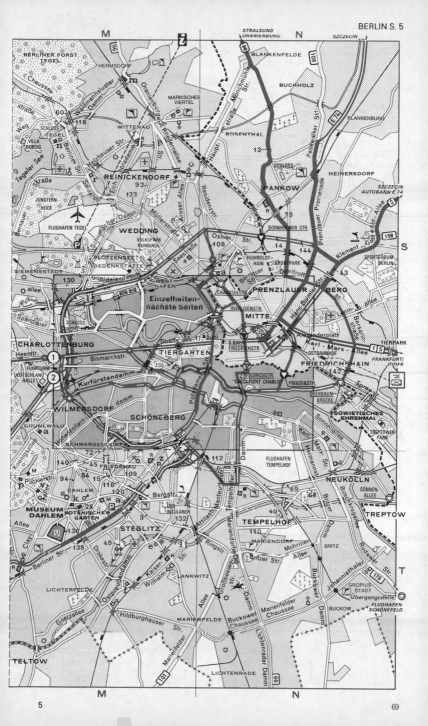

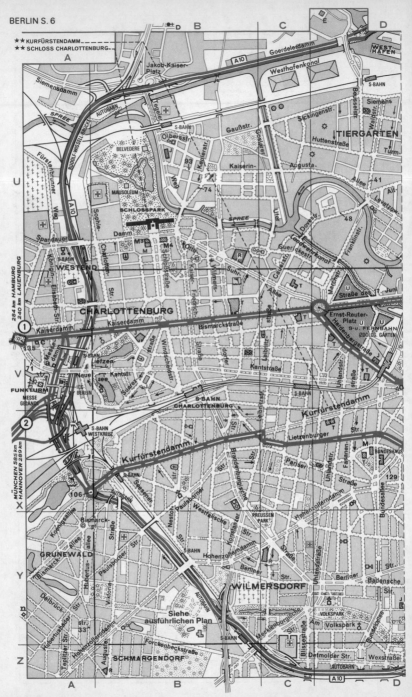

★★ KURFÜRSTENDAMM
★★ SCHLOSS CHARLOTTENBURG

Goerdelerdamm

A 10

Westhafenkanal

WEST-
HAFEN

Jakob-Kaiser-
Platz

Siemensdamm

Tegeler

S-BAHN

Siemens

Sickingenstr.

TIERGARTEN

Gaußstr.

Olbersstr.

Goslarer

Kaiserin-

Augusta-

Huttenstraße

Turm

Fürstenbrunner

BELVEDERE

93

Kaiserin-

Allee — 41

Weg

74

MAUSOLEUM

SPREE

Dovestr.

48

SCHLOSSPARK

Sophie-

Damm

Uferstr.

Landwehrkanal

Frankl.str.

Spandauer

Charlotten

M3

M4

Otto-

Suhr-

Kaiser-

Guerickestr.

Cauerstr.

Marchstr.

WESTEND

M

Schloßstr.

Wintersteinstr.

Allee

R

T

Königin-Elisabeth-Str.

Str.

Friedrich-

Suhr-

Allee

Straße des 17. Juni

CHARLOTTENBURG

Kaiserdamm

Kaiserdamm

Bismarckstraße

straße

Hardenbergstraße

Ernst-Reuter-
Platz

S-U-FERNBAHN
(ZOOLOG. GARTEN)

Kaiserdamm

35

Masuren

Lietzen-

Windscheidstr.

Straße

dorfer

Kantstraße

Uhlandstr.

straße

71

Neue

Kantstr.

Suarez-

see

FUNKTURM

ICC
BERLIN

S-BAHN
CHARLOTTENBURG

MESSE
GELÄNDE

Leibnizstr.

S-BAHN

Kurfürstendamm

2

S-BAHN
WESTKREUZ

Kurfürstendamm

Lietzenburger

Str.

Pariser

Fasanen

BUNDESHAUS

Kurfürstendamm

S-BAHN

Brandenburgische

Uhlandstr.

Straße

M

129

106

Nestor-

Paulsborn.

Westfälische

Str.

Hohenzollerndamm

PREUSSEN
PARK

AUTOBAHN

Königsallee

Bismarck-
pl.

Str.

Berliner

Str.

GRUNEWALD

Bismarck

Paulsborn.

Hohenzollerndamm

S-BAHN

Berliner

Str.

Badensche

allee

allee

Viktoria-

Str.

WILMERSDORF

Uhlandstraße

Str.

Delbrück-

Str.

Am

Hubertus

str.

33

Hohenzollerndamm

Siehe
ausführlichen Plan

VOLKSPARK

Volkspark

Str.

Teplitzer

Auguste-

SCHMARGENDORF

Forckenbeckstraße

S-BAHN

Mecklenburgische

Blissestraße

Detmolder Str.

AUTOBAHN

Wexstraße

A 10

284 km HAMBURG
240 km LAUENBURG

MÜNCHEN 585 km
HANNOVER 289 km

BERLIN
INNENSTADT-WEST

0 — 500 m

★★ BRANDENBURGER TOR
★★ ZOOLOGISCHER GARTEN

Franzensbader Str.	AY 33
Friedrich-List-Ufer	FU 34
Goebenstraße	FX 39
Gotzkowskystraße	DU 41
Helmholtzstraße	DU 48
Innsbrucker Platz	EZ 54
Klingelhöferstraße	EV 61
Masurenallee	AV 71
Mierendorffstraße	BU 74
Moltkestraße	FU 77
Neue Wilhelmstraße	GU 85
Oldenburger Straße	EU 90
Osnabrücker Straße	BU 93
Pallasstraße	FX 96
Rathenauplatz	AX 106
Spichernstraße	DX 129
Theodor-Heuss-Platz	AV 135

Straßenverzeichnis
siehe Berlin S. 9 u. 12.

← Gleicher Teil des Planes, →
auch auf der folgenden Seite

östl. Teil, siehe
nächste Seite

71

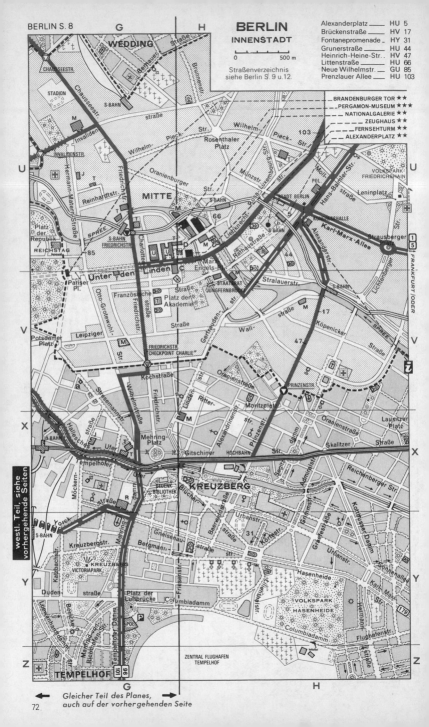

Fortsetzung
siehe Berlin S. 12

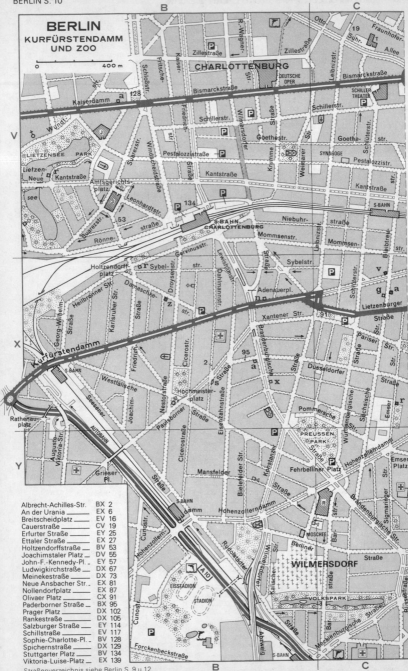

BERLIN
KURFÜRSTENDAMM UND ZOO

0 ———— 400 m

Straßenverzeichnis siehe Berlin S. 9 u. 12.

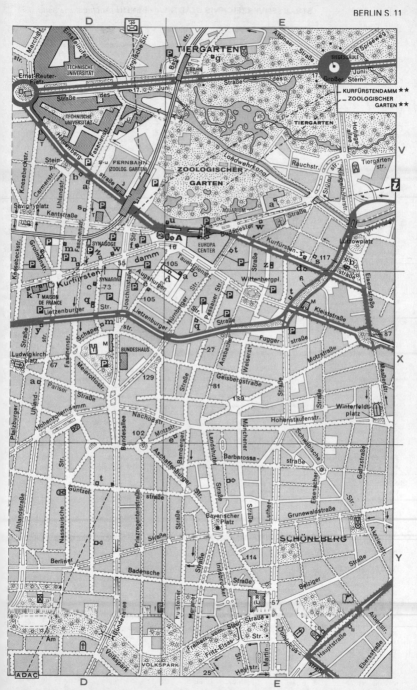

HOTELS UND

RESTAURANTS

Am Kurfürstendamm und Nähe Kurfürstendamm Stadtplan Berlin : S. 10-11 :

Bristol-H. Kempinski, Kurfürstendamm 27 (B 15), 88 10 91, Telex 0183553, Massage, — (mit), Rest
Karte 35/85 — **358 Z : 645 B** 162/262. DV n

Steigenberger Berlin, Rankestr. 30 (B 30), 2 10 80, Telex 0181444, — Rest
— **Berliner Stube** *(Sonntag gooohl.)* Karte 25/49 — **Park-Rest.** Karte 41/66 — **396 Z : 600 B** EX d
139/199 Fb.

Parkhotel Zellermayer, Meinekestr. 15 (B 15), 88 20 51, Telex 0184200 —
(Rest. nur für Hausgäste) — **140 Z : 250 B** Fb. DX m

Am Zoo garni, Kurfürstendamm 25 (B 15), 88 30 91, Telex 0183835 —
145 Z : 200 B Fb. DV z

Henry's Place garni, Meinekestr. 10 (B 15), 88 28 11 — wc wc . DX q
60 Z : 120 B 89/104 Fb.

Bremen garni, Bleibtreustr. 25 (B 15), 8 81 40 76, Telex 0184892 — wc . CX g
48 Z : 72 B.

Kurfürstendamm, Kurfürstendamm 68 (B 15), 88 28 41, Telex 0184630 — wc wc . Rest BX n
Karte 18,50/44 *(nur Abendessen)* — **33 Z : 55 B** 70/90.

Arosa-Berlin-Aparthotel, Lietzenburger Str. 79 (B 15), 88 20 11, Telex 0183397, (geheizt) — wc wc . DX y
Karte 24/50 *(Sonntag geschl., Okt.- Mai nur Abendessen)* — **199 Z : 347 B** 85/110 Fb.

Hecker's Deele, Grolmanstr. 35 (B 12), 8 89 01, Telex 0184954 — Rest wc . DV e
Karte 26/54 — **60 Z : 120 B** 104.

Domus garni, Uhlandstr. 49 (B 15), 88 20 41, Telex 0185975 — wc . DX a
76 Z : 100 B.

XXX **Maître**, Meinekestr. 10 (B 15), 8 83 84 85 — . DX q
19. Juli - 9. Aug. und Sonntag geschl., Montag und Dienstag nur Abendessen — Karte 52/140
(Tischbestellung erforderlich)
Spez. Tartar von Wildlachs, Lammrücken mit kleinen Gemüsen, Blätterteig mit Orangen und Caramel.

XXX **Ristorante Anselmo**, Damaschkestr. 17 (B 31), 3 23 30 94, « Modernes ital. Restaurant » BX z
10. Juli - 9. Aug. und Montag geschl. — Karte 36/70.

XX **Tessiner Stuben**, Bleibtreustr. 33 (B 15), 8 81 36 11 — CX a
ab 18 Uhr geöffnet — Karte 35/68 (Tischbestellung ratsam).

XX **Alexander**, Kurfürstendamm 46 (B 15), 8 83 34 60, Straßenterrasse — . CX v
Karte 20/64.

XX **Zlata Praha - Pilsner Urquell-Stuben**, Meinekestr. 4 (B 15), 8 81 97 50 — DX c
Sonntag geschl. — Karte 19/44.

XX **Kopenhagen** (Dänische Smörrebröds), Kurfürstendamm 203 (B 15), 8 83 25 03 — DX k
Karte 23/45.

XX **Hongkong** (China-Rest.), Kurfürstendamm 210 (2. Etage,) (B 15), 8 81 57 56 — DX T
Karte 22/35. DX e

X **Drei Bären**, Kurfürstendamm 22 (1. Etage) (B 15), 8 82 10 76, Terrassen — DV w
Karte 19,50/44.

X **Friesenhof**, Uhlandstr. 185 (B 12), 8 83 60 79 — . DV m
Karte 18,50/37.

Nähe Gedächtniskirche und Zoo Stadtplan Berlin : S. 10-11 :

🏨🏨 **Inter-Continental**, Budapester Str. 2 (B 30), ☏ 2 60 20, Telex 0184380, Bade- und Massageabteilung, 🚗, 🔲 – 🗄 📺 🕭 🅿 🚲, 🖭 🕦 **E**. ❦ Rest   EV **a**
Karte 28/70 – **600 Z : 1 100 B** 141/191 Fb.

🏨🏨 **Schweizerhof**, Budapester Str. 25 (B 30), ☏ 2 69 61, Telex 0185501, Bade- und Massageabteilung, 🚗, 🔲 – 🗄 Rest 📺 🕭 ⇔ 🅿 🚲 (mit 🖵). 🖭 🕦 **E**. ❦ Rest   EV **w**
Karte 30/65 – **431 Z : 876 B** 122/177.

🏨🏨 **Berlin Penta H.** Ⓜ 🕭, Nürnberger Str. 65 (B 30), ☏ 24 00 11, Telex 0182877, Massage, 🚗,
🔲 – 🗄 📺 🕭 🅿 🚲, 🖭 🕦 **E**   EV **t**
Karte 30/49 – **425 Z : 850 B** 111/145 Fb.

🏨🏨 **Palace**, Budapester Str. 42 (im Europa-Center) (B 30), ☏ 26 20 11, Telex 0184825 – 🖵 Rest
📺 🅿 🚲 (mit 🖵). 🖭 🕦 **E**. ❦ Rest   EV **k**
Karte 28,50/59 – **175 Z : 250 B** 75/160.

🏨🏨 **Berlin Excelsior H.** Ⓜ, Hardenbergstr. 14 (B 12), ☏ 3 19 91, Telex 0184781 – 🖵 Rest 📺 🅿
🚲 (mit 🖵). 🖭 🕦 **E**. ❦ Rest   DV **b**
Karte 22,50/47 – **320 Z : 556 B** 115/135 Fb.

🏨🏨 **Hotel Berlin**, Kurfürstenstr. 62 (B 30), ☏ 26 92 91, Telex 0184332 – 🖵 Rest 📺 🅿 🚲 (mit
🖵). 🖭 🕦 **E**. ❦ Rest   EV **b**
Karte 25/59 (siehe auch **Berlin Grill**) – **255 Z : 400 B** 96/118 Fb.

🏨🏨 **Ambassador**, Bayreuther Str. 42 (B 30), ☏ 24 01 01, Telex 0184259, Massage, 🚗, 🔲 – 🖵 Rest
📺 ⇔ 🅿 🚲. 🖭 🕦 **E** – **120 Z : 180 B** Fb   EV **z**

🏨🏨 **Savoy**, Fasanenstr. 9 (B 12), ☏ 31 06 54, Telex 0184292 – 🖭 🕦 **E**. ❦ Rest   DV **s**
Karte 21/50 – **115 Z : 180 B** 110/180 Fb.

🏨 **Alsterhof - Rest. Hanseaten Grill**, Augsburger Str. 5 (B 30), ☏ 2 13 70 01, Telex 0183484
– 🖨 📺 ⌷wc 🚿wc ☎ 🅿 🚲, 🖭 🕦 **E**   EX **q**
Karte 23/56 – **139 Z : 256 B** 73/93.

🏨 **Hamburg**, Landgrafenstr. 4 (B 30), ☏ 26 91 61, Telex 0184974 – 🖨 📺 ⌷wc ☎ ⇔ 🅿 🚲.
🖭 🕦 **E**   EV **s**
Karte 18,50/50 – **240 Z : 330 B** 92/110 Fb.

🏨 **Sylter Hof**, Kurfürstenstr. 116 (B 30), ☏ 2 12 00, Telex 0183317 – 🖨 📺 ⌷wc ☎ 🅿 🚲. 🖭
🕦 **E**. ❦ Rest   EV **d**
Karte 20,50/56 *(Sonntag ab 15 Uhr geschl.)* – **147 Z : 200 B** 96/140 Fb.

🏨 **President**, An der Urania 16 (B 30), ☏ 2 13 80 61, Telex 0184018, 🚗 – 🖨 📺 ⌷wc 🚿wc
🅿. 🖭 🕦 **E**   EX **t**
(Rest. nur für Hausgäste) – **90 Z : 170 B** 100/140.

🏨 **Remter** garni, Marburger Str. 17 (B 30), ☏ 24 60 61, Telex 0183497 – 🖨 📺 ⌷wc 🚿wc ☎. **E**
33 Z : 51 B 80/90 Fb.   EVX **c**

🏨 **Astoria** garni, Fasanenstr. 2 (B 12), ☏ 3 12 40 67, Telex 181745 – 🖨 ⌷wc ☎. 🖭 🕦 **E**
32 Z : 51 B 48/80.   DV **a**

XXX 🕸 **Berlin-Grill**, Kurfürstenstr. 62 (im Hotel Berlin) (B 30), ☏ 26 92 91 – 🖵 🅿. 🖭 🕦 **E**.
Juli, Samstag bis 18 Uhr und Sonntag geschl. – Karte 33/75 (Tischbestellung ratsam)   EV **b**
Spez. Hummer mit Gemüse in Sauce Nantua, Rinderfilet in Quittensauce, Kalbsnieren "Rivioli" in Estragonsauce.

XXX 🕸 **Conti-Fischstuben**, Bayreuther Str. 42 (im Hotel Ambassador) (B 30), ☏ 24 01 01 – 🖵. 🖭
🕦 **E**. ❦   EV **z**
(Tischbestellung ratsam).
Spez. Feinschmeckersalat, Steinbuttfilets "Diplomaten Art", Lachsschnitte in Sauerampfer.

XXX **Ritz**, Rankestr. 26 (B 30), ☏ 24 72 50 – 🖭 🕦 **E**   DX **e**
Mitte Juli - Mitte Aug. sowie Samstag, Sonn- und Feiertage geschl. – Karte 35/68 (Tischbestellung ratsam).

XX **Ristorante Bacco** (Italienische Küche), Marburger Str. 5 (B 30), ☏ 2 11 86 87 – 🖭 🕦 **E**
Sonntag bis 18 Uhr geschl. – Karte 25/57.   EX **a**

XX **Mampes Gute Stube**, Kurfürstendamm 14 (B 15), ☏ 8 81 71 01 – 🖭 🕦 **E**. ❦   DV **f**
Karte 25/49.

XX **Tai-Tung** (China-Rest.), Budapester Str. 50 (1. Etage, 🖨) (B 30), ☏ 2 61 30 91 – 🖭 🕦 **E**
Karte 17,50/35.   EV **u**

X Il Sorriso (Italienische Küche), Kurfürstenstr. 76 (B 30), ☏ 2 62 13 13 – ❦   EV **r**

In Berlin-Charlottenburg Stadtplan Berlin : S. 4, 6 und 10-11 :

🏨🏨 **Seehof** 🕭, Lietzensee-Ufer 11 (B 19), ☏ 32 10 51, Telex 0182943, ≤, « Terrasse am See »,
🔲 – 🅿 ⇔ 🚲. 🖭 🕦 **E**. ❦ Rest   BV **r**
Karte 31/61 – **77 Z : 100 B** 92,50/180 Fb.

🏨 **Europäischer Hof** garni, Messedamm 10 (B 19), ☏ 30 20 11, Telex 0182882 – 🖨 ⌷wc 🚿wc
🅿. 🖭 **E**   AV **a**
180 Z : 250 B 90/105 Fb.

🏨 **Apartment-H. Heerstraße**, Heerstr. 80 (B 19), ☏ 3 05 50 51, 🚗, 🔲 – 🖨 📺 ⌷wc ☎ ⇔
🅿   LS **t**
Karte 25/47 – **38 Appart. : 70 B** 98,50/160.

🏨 **Am Studio** garni, Kaiserdamm 80 (B 19), ☏ 30 20 81, Telex 0182825 – 🖨 📺 ⌷wc ☎. 🖭 🕦
E   AV **c**
78 Z : 94 B 69/76.

🏨 **Kardell**, Gervinusstr. 24 (B 12), 🕿 3 24 10 66 — 🛗 ⌸wc 🚿wc 🕿 🅿. 🖭 🕦 🖿. 🐾   BX **r**
30 Z : 43 B Fb.

🏨 **Excellent** garni, Kaiserdamm 3 (B 19), 🕿 3 22 10 11, Telex 0182835 — 🛗 🖭 ⌸wc 🕿 🅿. 🖭
🕦 🖿   BV **a**
44 Z : 89 B 89/119 Fb.

XX **Pullmann**, Messedamm 11 (Im Congress-Center) (B 19), 🕿 30 38 39 46 — 🛗 🖩 🕭. 🖭 🕦 🖿
Karte 25/54 (auch Self-service - Rest. Nipkow).   AV **s**

XX **Funkturm**, Messegelände (auf dem Funkturm, 🛗 DM 1.-) (B 19), 🕿 30 38 29 96, ≤ Berlin
🖭 🕦 🖿. 🐾   AV
Karte 21/49.

In Berlin-Dahlem Stadtplan Berlin : S. 5 :

X **Forsthaus Paulsborn** 🦌 mit Zim (B 33), 🕿 8 13 81 29, « Gartenterrasse » — 🖭 🕿 🅿. 🕦
🖿   MT **p**
Karte 21,50/46 *(Okt.- April Dienstag geschl.)* — **8 Z : 18 B** 45/55.

X **Alter Krug**, Königin-Luise-Str. 52 (B 33), 🕿 8 32 50 89, Gartenterrasse — 🅿   MT **k**
Donnerstag geschl. — Karte 17,50/49.

In Berlin-Friedenau Stadtplan Berlin : S. 5 :

🏨 **Hospiz Friedenau** 🦌 garni, Fregestr. 68 (B 41), 🕿 8 51 90 17 — ⌸wc 🚿 🕿 🅿. 🐾   MT **z**
16 Z : 25 B 50/60.

In Berlin-Grunewald Stadtplan Berlin : S. 4-6 :

🏨 **Belvedere** 🦌 (ehem. Villa), Seebergsteig 4 (B 33), 🕿 8 26 10 77, 🍽 — 🖭 ⌸wc 🚿 🕿. 🕦
(Rest. nur für Hausgäste) — **17 Z : 31 B** 50/75.   AY **n**

X **Castel Sardo** (Italienische Küche), Hagenstr. 2 (B 33), 🕿 8 25 60 14, Gartenterrasse   MS **a**

X **Chalet Suisse**, Im Jagen 5 (B 33), 🕿 8 32 63 62, Terrasse — 🅿. 🖭   MT **v**
Karte 22/52.

In Berlin-Hermsdorf Stadtplan Berlin : S. 5 :

XX **Rockendorf**, Düsterhauptstr. 1 (B 28), 🕿 4 02 30 99   MS **m**
Feb. und Aug. je 2 Wochen, Sonntag - Montag sowie Feiertage geschl. — Karte 44/78 (Tischbestellung ratsam).

In Berlin-Kreuzberg Stadtplan Berlin : S. 7-8 :

🏨 **Hervis International** garni, Stresemannstr. 97 (B 61), 🕿 2 61 14 44, Telex 0184063 — 🛗 🖭
⌸wc 🚿wc 🕿 🅿. 🖭 🕦 🖿   GV **a**
71 Z : 118 B 80/120.

In Berlin-Lankwitz Stadtplan Berlin : S. 5 :

🏨 **Pichlers Viktoriagarten**, Leonorenstr. 18 (B 46), 🕿 7 71 60 88, Terrasse — 🚿 🕿 🅿   MT **e**
5. Juli - 1. Aug. geschl. — Karte 14/38 *(Montag bis 17 Uhr geschl.)* — **24 Z : 31 B** 48/88.

In Berlin-Lichterfelde Stadtplan Berlin : S. 5 :

🏨 **Haus Franken** 🦌 garni (ehem. Villa), Hochbergplatz 7 (B 45), 🕿 7 72 40 16, 🛏, 🏖 — 🚿wc
🕿 🅿   MT **f**
11 Z : 18 B 65/87.

In Berlin-Reinickendorf Stadtplan Berlin : S. 5 :

🏨 **Rheinsberg am See**, Finsterwalder Str. 64 (B 26), 🕿 4 02 10 92, Telex 0185972, Terrasse mit
≤, Bade- und Massageabteilung, 🛏, 🏊, 🖎, 🍽 — 🛗 🖭 ⌸wc 🚿wc 🕿 🅿   MS **e**
Karte 21,50/50 — **55 Z : 110 B** 58/86 Fb.

In Berlin - Steglitz Stadtplan Berlin S. 5 :

🏨 **Tourotel** 🅼, Albrechtstr. 2 (Ecke Schloßstr.) (B 41), 🕿 79 10 61, Telex 0183545, Massage, 🛏
— 🖭 🖎 🕭. 🖭 🕦 🖿. 🐾 Rest   MT **a**
Restaurants — **Schloßpark-Rest.** Karte 27,50/57 — **Wienerwald** Karte 14/26 — **220 Z : 440 B**
95/125 Fb.

In Berlin-Tegel Stadtplan Berlin : S. 5 :

🏨 **Gästehaus am Tegeler See**, Wilkestr. 2 (B 27), 🕿 4 38 40 — 🛗 🖭 🚿wc 🕿 🚗 🅿   MS **n**
39 Z : 70 B 58/78 Fb.

🏨 **Central**, Holzhauser Str. 2 (B 27), 🕿 4 32 10 77 — 🚿wc 🅿   MS **r**
Karte 17/41 *(nur Abendessen, Samstag, Sonn- und Feiertage geschl.)* — **42 Z : 64 B** 48/75.

X **Seeterrasse**, Wilkestr. 1 (B 27), 🕿 4 33 80 01, « Terrasse mit ≤ » — 🖩 🅿. 🕦   MS **n**
Okt.- März Montag geschl. — Karte 16/43.

In Berlin-Tegelort Stadtplan Berlin : S. 4 :

🏨 **Igel** 🦌, Friederikestr. 33 (B 27), 🕿 4 33 90 67, « Terrasse mit ≤ » — ⌸wc 🚿wc 🕿 🅿. 🖭
Karte 15,50/38 *(Freitag geschl.)* — **43 Z : 84 B** 40/65.   LS **u**

In Berlin-Tiergarten Stadtplan Berlin : S. 11 :

XX **Giraffe**, Klopstockstr. 2 (B 21), 🕿 3 91 47 17, « Terrasse » — 🅿. 🖭 🕦 🖿   EV **g**

Fortsetzung →

In Berlin-Wedding Stadtplan Berlin : S. 5 :

🏨 **Pückler-Hospiz** 🦢 garni, Schönwalder Str. 21 (B 65), ☏ 46 10 21 — |≢| 🏠wc ☎ 🄿   NS a
54 Z : 67 B 42/68.

In Berlin-Wilmersdorf Stadtplan Berlin : S. 10-11 :

🏨 **Crest.-H.** garni, Güntzelstr. 14 (B 31), ☏ 87 02 41, Telex 0182948 — |≢| 📺 🛏wc 🏠wc ☎ 🚗.
🆎 🄾 🗉   DY t
110 Z : 150 B 108/140 Fb.

🏨 **Franke**, Albrecht-Achilles-Str. 57 (B 31), ☏ 8 92 10 97, Telex 0184857 — |≢| 🛏wc ☎ 🄿. 🆎 🄾
🗉   BX s
Karte 17,50/34 — **67 Z : 90 B** 76,50/89.

🏨 **Atrium-H.** garni, Motzstr. 87 (B 30), ☏ 24 40 57 — |≢| 🏠wc ☎   EX e
22 Z : 40 B 48/65.

🏨 **Lichtburg**, Paderborner Str. 10 (B 15), ☏ 8 91 80 41, Telex 0184208 — |≢| 🛏wc ☎ 🄿. 🆎 🄾
🗉. 🍴 Rest   BX a
Karte 16/34 — **62 Z : 100 B** 70/89.

🏨 **Savigny** garni, Brandenburgische Str. 21 (B 31), ☏ 8 81 30 01, Telex 0184053 — |≢| 🛏wc
🏠wc ☎   BX x
60 Z : 90 B 44/66.

XX **Rest. im Logenhaus**, Emser Str. 13 (B 31), ☏ 87 63 26 — 🔔. 🆎 🄾   CX r
Sonntag und Aug. geschl. — Karte 20/40.

Am Wannsee und an der Havel Stadtplan Berlin : S. 4 :

X **Blockhaus Nikolskoe**, Nikolskoer Weg (B 39), ☏ 8 05 29 14, « Blockhaus a.d.J. 1819, Terrasse mit ≤ » — 🄿   LT b
Donnerstag geschl. — Karte 15/40.

An der Avus Stadtplan Berlin : S. 4 :

🏨 **Raststätte-Motel Grunewald**, Spanische Allee 177 (B 38), ☏ 8 03 10 11, Terrasse — |≢|
🏠wc ☎ 🄿   LT x
Karte 17/46 — **36 Z : 76 B** 57/65.

FRANKFURT AM MAIN

FRANKFURT AM MAIN 6000. Hessen 987 ㉙. 204 ⑤ − 631 200 Ew − Höhe 91 m − ✆ 0611.

Sehenswert : Zoo*** − Goethehaus** und Goethemuseum* CY **M1** − Dom* (Turm**, Domschatz*, Chorgestühl*) − Palmengarten* AV − Senckenberg-Museum* (Paläonthologie**) AX **M** − Städelsches Kunstinstitut* (Gemäldesammlung ** altniederländischer und deutscher Maler des 16. Jh.) BY **M2** − Museum für Kunsthandwerk* CY **M4** − Evangelische Katharinenkirche (Glasfenster*) CX **A**.

🛬 Rhein-Main (⑤ ; 12 km, S). 🎫 6 98 91.

🚄 in Neu-Isenburg, 🎫 (06102) 85 75.

Messegelände (AY), 🎫 7 57 51, Telex 0411558.

🅱 Verkehrsverein, Im Hauptbahnhof (Nordseite), 🎫 23 11 08 und 23 22 18.

🅱 U-Bahnstation Hauptwache, B-Ebene, 🎫 28 74 86.

ADAC, Schumannstr. 4, 🎫 7 43 01, Telex 0411855, Notruf 🎫 7 43 06, Wiesbadener Straße, 🎫 77 95 62, Münchener Str. 1, 🎫 23 13 33, Walter-Kolb-Str. 9, 🎫 62 20 03, Telex 0411470.

♦Wiesbaden 38 ⑤ − ♦Bonn 176 ⑤ − ♦Nürnberg 222 ④ − ♦Stuttgart 205 ⑤.

Stadtpläne : siehe Frankfurt am Main Seiten 3 bis 7.

🏨🏨🏨🏨 **Steigenberger-H. Frankfurter Hof**, Am Kaiserplatz 17, 🎫 2 02 51, Telex 0411806 − ▤ Rest 📺 & 🛁 (mit ▤). ⒶⒺ ⓄⒹ Ⓔ. ⅏ Rest   CY e
Karte 31/59 (Samstag geschl.) (siehe auch **Rest. français** und **Frankfurter Stubb**) − **400 Z : 600 B** 149/215.

🏨🏨🏨🏨 **Frankfurt Intercontinental**, Wilhelm-Leuschner-Str. 43, 🎫 23 05 61, Telex 0413639, < Frankfurt, Massage, ⬛, ▦ − ▤ 📺 & 🛁. ⒶⒺ ⓄⒹ Ⓔ. ⅏ Rest   BY s
Restaurants − **Rôtisserie** (Sonntag geschl.) Karte 43/77 − **Brasserie** Karte 26/58 − **Bierstube** (Samstag, sowie Sonn- und Feiertage geschl.) Karte 15/22 − **500 Z : 1000 B** 153/263.

🏨🏨🏨🏨 **Hessischer Hof**, Friedrich-Ebert-Anlage 40, 🎫 7 51 00, Telex 0411776, « Sèvres Porzellansammlung im Restaurant » − 📺 Ⓟ 🛁. ⒶⒺ ⓄⒹ Ⓔ. ⅏ Rest   AY p
Karte 35/83 − **161 Z : 192 B** 139/235.

🏨🏨🏨🏨 **Parkhotel Frankfurt**, Wiesenhüttenplatz 36, 🎫 2 69 70, Telex 0412808 − ▤ 📺 & 🚘 Ⓟ 🛁. ⒶⒺ ⓄⒹ Ⓔ. ⅏   AY k
Karte 38/68 (Tischbestellung ratsam) − **280 Z : 420 B** 163/293 Fb.

🏨🏨🏨🏨 **CP Frankfurt Plaza H.** Ⓜ, Hamburger Allee 2, 🎫 77 07 21, Telex 0416745, < Frankfurt, ⬛ − ▤ 📺 & 🛁. ⒶⒺ ⓄⒹ Ⓔ. ⅏ Rest   AX a
Restaurants − **Geheimratsstube** (Sonntag geschl.) Karte 40/75 − **Bäckerei** Karte 20/43 − **596 Z : 1192 B** 178/228 Fb.

🏨🏨🏨 **National**, Baseler Str. 50, 🎫 23 48 41, Telex 0412570 − 📺 🛁. ⒶⒺ ⓄⒹ Ⓔ. ⅏ Rest   AY x
Karte 23,50/40 − **95 Z : 130 B** 65/120 Fb.

🏨🏨🏨 **Savoy**, Wiesenhüttenstr. 42, 🎫 23 05 11, Telex 0416394, Massage, ⬛, ▦ − ▤ Rest 📺 🚘 🛁 (mit ▤). ⒶⒺ ⓄⒹ Ⓔ. ⅏ Rest   AY s
Karte 23/64 − **151 Z : 200 B** 115/180.

🏨🏨🏨 **Savigny**, Savignystr. 14, 🎫 74 04 81, Telex 0412061 − 📺 🛁. ⒶⒺ ⓄⒹ Ⓔ. ⅏ Rest   AY f
122 Z : 176 B.

🏨🏨 **Continental**, Baseler Str. 56, 🎫 23 03 41, Telex 0412502 − ▤ 📺 ➿wc 🕿 🛁. ⒶⒺ ⓄⒹ Ⓔ. ⅏ Rest   AY y
Karte 22,50/34 (Sonn- und Feiertage geschl.) − **80 Z : 140 B** 62/85.

🏨🏨 **Turm-Hotel** garni (siehe auch Rest. Sudpfanne), Eschersheimer Landstr. 20, 🎫 55 00 01 − ▤ 📺 ➿wc 🕿 Ⓟ. ⒶⒺ ⓄⒹ Ⓔ   CX b
75 Z : 130 B.

🏨🏨 **Mozart** garni, Parkstr. 17, 🎫 55 08 31 − ▤ ➿wc ⫿wc 🕿. ⒶⒺ ⓄⒹ   BV p
37 Z : 60 B.

🏨🏨 **An der Messe** garni, Westendstr. 102, 🎫 74 79 79, Telex 04189009 − ▤ 📺 ➿wc ⫿wc 🕿 🛁. ⒶⒺ Ⓔ   AX e
46 Z : 88 B 89.

🏨🏨 **Jaguar** garni, Theobald-Christ Str. 17, 🎫 43 93 01 − ▤ ⫿wc 🕿 🚘. ⒶⒺ   EX y
37 Z : 56 B 62,50/72,50.

🏨🏨 **Falk** garni, Falkstr. 38 a, 🎫 70 80 94 − ▤ ➿wc ⫿wc 🕿 Ⓟ 🛁   AV n
32 Z : 50 B 68/75.

🏨 **Wolff-Astor** garni, Kreuznacher Str. 37, 🎫 77 20 71 − ▤ ➿wc ⫿wc 🕿. ⒶⒺ ⓄⒹ Ⓔ   AX u
25 Z : 40 B 85/90 Fb.

🏨 **Ebel** garni, Taunusstr. 26, 🎫 25 28 42 − ▤ ➿wc ⫿wc 🕿. ⒶⒺ ⓄⒹ Ⓔ   BY r
32 Z : 55 B 50/80.

🏨 **Meyn** garni, Grüneburgweg 4, 🎫 59 01 79, 🚘 − ▤ 📺 ➿wc ⫿wc 🕿 Ⓟ. ⓄⒹ Ⓔ   CX u
28 Z : 32 B.

🏨 **Am Zoo** garni, Alfred-Brehm-Platz 6, 🎫 49 07 71 − ▤ ➿wc ⫿wc 🕿 Ⓟ. ⒶⒺ ⓄⒹ Ⓔ   EX q
85 Z : 140 B.

🏨 **Luxor** garni, Allerheiligentor 2, 🎫 29 30 67, Telex 0414136 − ▤ 📺 ➿wc 🕿. ⒶⒺ ⓄⒹ Ⓔ   DX x
46 Z : 80 B 62/79.

🏠 **Admiral** garni, Hölderlinstr. 25, ℱ 44 80 21 – 🛗 🛁wc 🛁wc ☎ 🅿. 🆎 ⓪ 🇪   EX w
52 Z : 75 B 55/80.

🏠 **Am Dom** garni, Kannengießergasse 3, ℱ 28 21 41, Telex 0414955 – 🛗 📺 🛁wc 🛁wc ☎. 🆎
⓪ 🇪   CY s
36 Z : 58 B 75/85 Fb.

🏠 **Henninger Hof**, Hanauer Landstr. 127, ℱ 43 91 15, Telex 0411091 – 🛗 📺 🛁wc 🛁 ☎. 🆎
⓪ 🇪   EY m
24.-31. Dez. geschl. – Karte 18,50/36 *(nur Abendessen, außerhalb der Messezeiten Sonntag
geschl.)* – **64 Z : 80 B** 60/90 Fb.

🏠 **Corona** garni, Hamburger Allee 48, ℱ 77 90 77 – 🛗 🛁 ☎ 🅿. 🆎   AX n
27 Z : 52 B 50/60.

🏠 **Kolpinghaus**, Lange Str. 26, ℱ 28 85 41 – 🛗 🛁wc ☎ 🅿 🛠   DX k
44 Z : 57 B.

🏠 **Westfälinger Hof** garni, Düsseldorfer Str. 10, ℱ 23 47 17 – 🛗 🛁wc ☎. 🎀   AY u
23. Dez.- 2. Jan. geschl. – **61 Z : 82 B** 44/65.

🏠 **Palmenhof** garni, Bockenheimer Landstr. 91, ℱ 75 10 26 – 🛁wc 🛁wc ☎. 🆎 ⓪ 🇪   AX f
54 Z : 80 B 44/96.

🏠 **Neue Kräme** garni, Neue Kräme 23, ℱ 28 40 46 – 🛗 📺 🛁wc 🛁wc ☎. 🆎 ⓪ 🇪   CY w
21 Z : 30 B 75/80.

🏠 **Rhein-Main** garni, Mainluststr. 15, ℱ 25 00 35, Telex 0416365 – 🛗 🛁wc 🛁wc ☎. 🆎 ⓪ 🇪.
🎀   BY a
37 Z : 56 B 75/110.

🏠 **Landgraf**, Böhmerstr. 20, ℱ 59 00 89 – 🛗 🛁wc ☎ 🅿. 🆎 ⓪ 🇪   BV a
Karte 19/53 *(außerhalb der Messezeiten Samstag - Sonntag geschl.)* – **16 Z : 24 B** 51/90.

🏠 **Diana** garni, Westendstr. 83, ℱ 74 70 07 – 🛁wc 🛁 ☎. 🆎 ⓪ 🇪   AX d
24 Z : 33 B 52/65.

🏠 **Sophienhotel Schwille** garni, Sophienstr. 36, ℱ 70 20 34 – 🛗 🛁wc 🛁 ☎ 🛠   AV a
50 Z : 70 B.

🏠 **Palmengarten** garni, Palmengartenstr. 8, ℱ 75 20 41 – 🛗 📺 🛁wc 🛁 ☎   AX r
11. Dez.- 10. Jan. geschl. – **20 Z : 28 B** 45/80.

🏠 **Balmoral** garni, Emil-Sulzbach-Str. 14, ℱ 77 50 04 – 🛁 ☎ 🚗   AX c
16 Z : 25 B 45/50.

🏠 **Württemberger Hof**, Karlstr. 14, ℱ 23 31 06 – 🛗 🛁wc 🛁 ☎   AY z
23. Dez.-2. Jan. geschl. – Karte 12,50/36 *(Sonntag geschl.)* – **67 Z : 95 B** 42/75.

🏠 **Café Schwille** garni, Große Bockenheimer Str. 50, ℱ 28 30 54 – 🛗 🛁wc 🛁wc ☎ 🅿. 🆎 ⓪
🇪   BX e
62 Z : 90 B 52/90.

🏠 **Terminus** garni, Münchener Str. 59, ℱ 23 40 84 – 🛗 🛁 ☎ 🚗. 🆎 ⓪ 🇪   AY q
49 Z : 62 B 37/50.

XXXX ✿ **Rest. français**, Kaiserplatz (im Steigenberger-H. Frankfurter Hof), ℱ 2 02 51 – 🍽. 🆎 ⓪
🇪. 🎀   CY e
Karte 47/81 (Tischbestellung ratsam)
Spez. Scampi et chanterelles frâiches dans ses jus, Filet de boeuf mariné, La selle de chevreuil ¨Baden-Baden¨.

XXX **Weinhaus Brückenkeller**, Schützenstr. 6, ℱ 28 42 38, « Alte Kellergewölbe mit kostbaren
Antiquitäten » – 🅿. 🆎 ⓪ 🇪   DY a
ab 18 Uhr geöffnet, außerhalb der Messezeiten Sonn- und Feiertage geschl. – Karte 30/65
(Tischbestellung ratsam).

XXX **Mövenpick-Baron de la Mouette**, Opernplatz 1, ℱ 28 78 57, Terrasse – 🍽. 🆎 ⓪ 🇪
Karte 31/61 – **Orangerie** : Karte 19/39.   BX f

XXX **Rest.H.Segschneider**, Am Leonhardsbrunn 12 (im Union-International-Club), ℱ 70 30 33,
« Terrasse » – 🆎 ⓪ 🇪   AV v
Juni - Juli 4 Wochen und Samstag geschl. – Karte 34,50/80.

XXX **Rest. Français Jacques Offenbach**, Opernplatz 1, ℱ 28 48 20 – 🍽. 🆎 ⓪ 🇪. 🎀   BX c
Juli geschl. – Karte 31/65.

XX **Da Bruno** (Italienische Küche), Elbestr. 15, ℱ 23 34 16 – 🍽. 🆎 ⓪ 🇪   BY t
außerhalb der Messezeiten Sonn- und Feiertage sowie Mitte Juli - Mitte Aug. geschl. – Karte
28/56.

XX **Frankfurter Stubb** (Rest. im Kellergewölbe des Hotel Frankfurter Hof), Kaiserplatz,
ℱ 21 56 41 – 🍽. 🆎 ⓪ 🇪. 🎀   CY e
außerhalb der Messezeiten Sonn- und Feiertage sowie 21. Dez.- 6. Jan. geschl. – Karte 21/50
(Tischbestellung ratsam).

XX **La Galleria** (Italienische Küche), Theaterplatz 2 (BfG-Haus), ℱ 23 56 80 – 🍽. 🆎 ⓪ 🇪
Sonntag geschl. – Karte 29/60 (Tischbestellung ratsam).   BY u

XX **Heyland's Weinstube**, Kaiserhofstr. 7, ℱ 28 48 40, Straßenterrasse – 🆎 ⓪ 🇪   CX a
Samstag ab 16 Uhr sowie Sonn- und Feiertage geschl. – Karte 22/60.

XX **Maison Pierre**, Junghofstr. 14, ℱ 28 22 33 – 🆎 ⓪ 🇪   CX n
Samstag bis 19 Uhr, Sonntag und Jan. 2 Wochen geschl. – Karte 40/80 (Tischbestellung
ratsam).

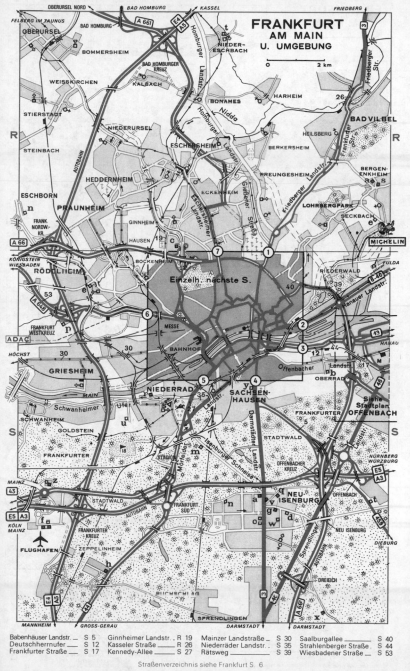

FRANKFURT
AM MAIN
U. UMGEBUNG

0   2 km

Babenhäuser Landstr.	S 5	Ginnheimer Landstr.	R 19
Deutschherrnufer	S 12	Kasseler Straße	R 26
Frankfurter Straße	S 17	Kennedy-Allee	S 27

Mainzer Landstraße	S 30	Saalburgallee	S 40
Niederräder Landstr.	S 35	Strahlenberger Straße	S 44
Rätsweg	S 39	Wiesbadener Straße	S 53

Straßenverzeichnis siehe Frankfurt S. 6

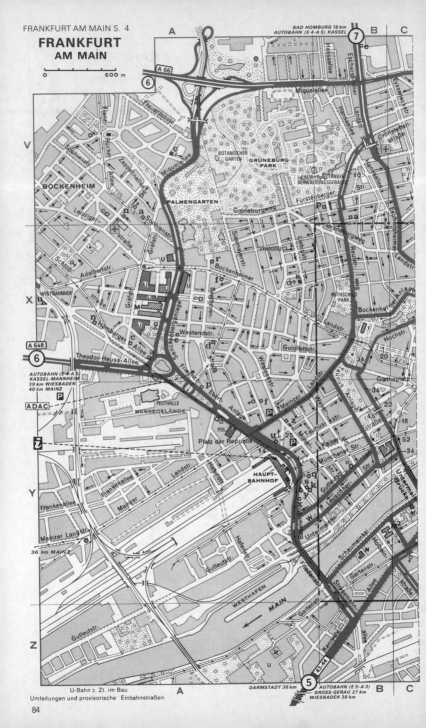

FRANKFURT
AM MAIN

BAD HOMBURG 18 km
AUTOBAHN (E 4-A 5) KASSEL

A 66

BOTANISCHER
GARTEN

GRÜNEBURG-
PARK

PALMENGARTEN

BOCKENHEIM

Miquelallee

Grüneburgweg

EHEM. I.G.-FARBEN
VERWALTUNGSGEBÄUDE

Fürstenberger

SYNAGOGE

Bockenheimer

ROTHSCHILD-
PARK

WESTBAHNHOF

Adalbertstr.

Westendstr.

Guiollettstr.

Bockenheimer Anlage

A 648

Theodor-Heuss-Allee

AUTOBAHN (E 4-A 5)
KASSEL-MANNHEIM
39 km WIESBADEN
40 km MAINZ

ADAC

Goetheplatz

Friedrich-Ebert-

PESTHALLE

MESSEGELÄNDE

POL.

Platz der Republik

Kaiser-

Münchener Str.

HAUPT-
BAHNHOF

Frankenallee

Mainzer

Landstr.

Hafenstr.

Gutleutstr.

Baseler Str.

Untermainkai

Untermain-
brücke

36 km MAINZ

Gutleutstr.

Mainzer Landstr.

WESTHAFEN

MAIN

Kennedy-

Schaumainkai

Gartenstr.

U-Bahn z. Zt. im Bau
Umleitungen und provisorische Einbahnstraßen

DARMSTADT 36 km
AUTOBAHN (E 5-A 3)
GROSS-GERAU 27 km
WIESBADEN 38 km

84

BAD HOMBURG 17 km — FRIEDBERG 32 km

GÜNTHERSBURG
PARK

BORNHEIM

ZOO ★★

ZOO

FULDA 104 km
HANAU 20 km

OSTBAHNHOF

Danziger
Platz

MAIN

OFFENBACH 6 km

Deutschherrnufer

DOM ★
GOETHEHAUS ★★

SACHSENHAUSEN

Einzelheiten
nächste Seiten

SÜDBAHNHOF

HENNINGER TURM

OFFENBACH 7 km

AUTOBAHN (E 5-A 3)
WÜRZBURG 117 km
NÜRNBERG 222 km

Straßenverzeichnis siehe Frankfurt S. 6

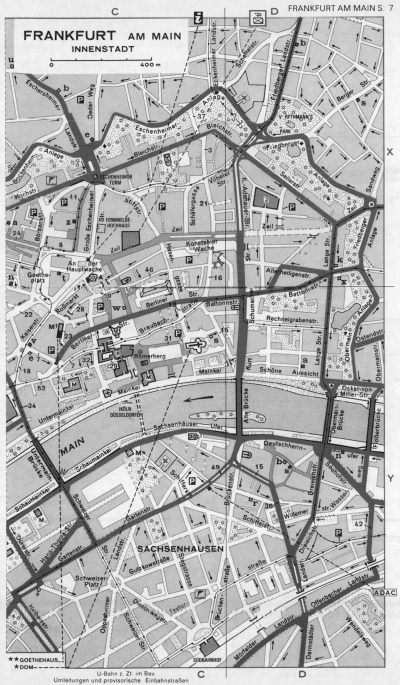

FRANKFURT AM MAIN
INNENSTADT

0   400 m

★★ GOETHEHAUS
★ DOM

U-Bahn z. Zt. im Bau
Umleitungen und provisorische Einbahnstraßen

87

XX **Firenze** (Italienische Küche), Berger Str. 30, ☎ 43 39 56 — 🖹. ⒶⒺ ⓸ Ⓔ. 🛇   DX **s**
Montag geschl. — Karte 35/65 (Tischbestellung ratsam).

XX **Börsenkeller**, Schillerstr. 11, ☎ 28 11 15 — 🖹 🕭. ⒶⒺ ⓸ Ⓔ   CX **z**
außerhalb der Messezeiten Samstag 15 Uhr - Sonntag geschl. — Karte 17/52.

XX **Peking** (Chinesische Küche), Kaiserstr. 15 (1. Etage 🛗), ☎ 28 85 72 — 🖹. 🛇   CY **v**

XX **Les Halles**, Ostendstr. 61, ☎ 44 64 34 — ⒶⒺ ⓸ Ⓔ   EY **u**
ab 19 Uhr geöffnet, Montag und Mitte Juli - Mitte Aug. geschl. — Karte 38/58 (Tischbestellung ratsam).

X ⚘ **Ernos Bistro** (Französische Küche), Liebigstr. 15, ☎ 72 19 97, Straßenterrasse — ⒶⒺ ⓸ Ⓔ
15. Juni - 15. Juli und Samstag - Sonntag geschl. — Karte 45/77 (Tischbestellung erforderlich)
Spez. Foie d'oie frais, Sandre au pinot noir, Carré d'agneau rôti au four.   AX **s**

X **San Remo** (Italienische Küche), Steinweg 7 (Passage), ☎ 28 54 77 — ⒶⒺ ⓸ Ⓔ   CX **t**
Karte 25/55.

X **Sudpfanne**, Eschersheimer Landstr. 20, ☎ 55 21 22 — ⒶⒺ ⓸ Ⓔ   CX **b**
Karte 18,50/50.

X **Intercity Rest.**, im Hauptbahnhof (1. Etage), ☎ 23 19 56 — 🛇   AY
Karte 19/44.

X **Dippegucker**, Eschenheimer Anlage 40, ☎ 55 19 65, Straßenterrasse — 🕭. ⒶⒺ ⓸ Ⓔ   CX **e**
Karte 17/45.

In Frankfurt 50-Ginnheim Stadtplan Frankfurt : S. 3 :

XX **Skyline-Turm-Rest.** (Drehrestaurant in 218 m Höhe, 🛗 DM 3,50), Wilh.-Epstein-Str. 20,
☎ 53 20 81, ☀ Frankfurt — 🖹 Ⓟ. ⒶⒺ ⓸ Ⓔ. 🛇   R **c**
Karte 29/66 (Tischbestellung ratsam).

In Frankfurt 80-Griesheim Stadtplan Frankfurt : S. 3 :

🏨 **Ramada-Caravelle**, Oeserstr. 180, ☎ 3 90 51, Telex 0416812, 🖚, 🖾 — 🕐 Ⓟ 🕭 (mit 🖹). ⒶⒺ
⓸ Ⓔ. 🛇 Rest   S **p**
Karte 33/67 — **236 Z : 400 B** 120/195 Fb.

In Frankfurt 56 - Nieder-Eschbach Stadtplan Frankfurt : S. 3 :

🏠 **Schaller** 🛇, Deuil-La-Barre-Str. 103, ☎ 5 07 57 67 — 🕳wc ☎ Ⓟ. 🛇 Rest   R **t**
Karte 18/41 *(Freitag 14 Uhr - Samstag geschl.)* — **13 Z : 16 B** 57/67.

In Frankfurt 71-Niederrad Stadtplan Frankfurt : S. 3 :

🏨 **Crest-H. Frankfurt** 🛇, Isenburger Schneise 40, ☎ 67 80 51, Telex 0416717 — 🖹 🕐 🕭 Ⓟ 🕭.
ⒶⒺ ⓸ Ⓔ. 🛇 Rest
300 Z : 500 B Fb   S **m**

🏨 **Arabella-H. Frankfurt**, Lyoner Str. 44, ☎ 66 80 41, Telex 0416760, 🖚, 🖾 — 🖹 🕐 🕭 Ⓟ
🕭. ⒶⒺ ⓸ Ⓔ. 🛇 Rest   S **u**
Karte 27/52 — **400 Z : 600 B** 130/150 Fb.

🏠 **Schilff** garni, Triftstr. 33, ☎ 67 70 12 — 🛗 🕳wc ☎ Ⓟ
52 Z : 61 B 65/75 Fb   S **s**

X **Weidemann**, Kelsterbacher Str. 66, ☎ 67 59 96, Gartenterrasse — Ⓟ. Ⓔ   S **r**
(Tischbestellung ratsam).

In Frankfurt 70-Sachsenhausen Stadtplan Frankfurt : S. 4-5 :

🏨 **Holidy Inn-City Tower** Ⓜ, Mailänder-Str. 1, ☎ 68 00 11, Telex 0411805 — 🖹 🕐 Ⓟ 🕭. ⒶⒺ
⓸ Ⓔ. 🛇 Rest   Frankfurt S. 3   S **y**
Karte 26/54 — **187 Z : 279 B** 155/198 Fb.

🏠 **Mühlberg** garni, Offenbacher Landstr. 56, ☎ 61 30 63 — 🛗 🕳wc ☎ ⇔. ⒶⒺ ⓸   EY **h**
23. Dez.- 4. Jan. geschl. — **69 Z : 93 B** 42/70.

🏠 **Royal** garni, Wallstr. 17, ☎ 62 30 26 — 🛗 🕳wc ☎. ⒶⒺ ⓸ Ⓔ   Frankfurt S. 7   DY **r**
35 Z : 50 B 55/80.

🏠 **Hübler** garni, Große Rittergasse 91, ☎ 61 60 38, 🖾 — 🕳wc 🕳wc ☎. 🛇
2. Juli - 22. Aug. und 3. Dez.- 4. Jan. geschl. — **46 Z : 58 B** 45/70.   Frankfurt S. 7   DY **b**

XXX ⚘ **Le caveau**, Deutschherrnufer 29, ☎ 61 41 61 — ⒶⒺ ⓸ Ⓔ   DY **n**
Juni - Juli 4 Wochen Betriebsferien, außerhalb der Messezeiten Samstag-Sonntag geschl. —
Karte 40/120 (Tischbestellung ratsam)
Spez. Hummer mit warmer Schnittlauchcrème (für 2 Pers.), Gefüllte Poulardenbrust in Ingwersauce, Wildhasen
rückenroulade auf Pumpernickelsauce.

XX **Bistro M**, Wendelsweg 79, ☎ 62 71 92 — ⒶⒺ ⓸ Ⓔ   EZ **b**
Samstag geschl. — Karte 29/70.

XX **Bistrot 77** (modernes Bistro-Restaurant), Ziegelhüttenweg 1, ☎ 61 40 40 — ⒶⒺ ⓸ Ⓔ   CZ **a**
Sonntag und 15. Juli - 15. Aug. geschl. — Karte 47/70.

XX **Henninger Turm-Panorama** Drehrestaurant (Höhe 101 m, 🛗 DM 2), Hainer Weg 60, ☎ 61 04 71,
☀ Frankfurt — 🖹 Ⓟ. ⒶⒺ ⓸ Ⓔ   DZ

X **Straßburger Haus**, Große Rittergasse 79, ☎ 61 05 05 — ⒶⒺ ⓸ Ⓔ   DY **s**
nur Abendessen — Karte 29/60 (Tischbestellung ratsam).

Beim Main-Taunus-Einkaufszentrum W : 14 km über ⑥ :

🏨 **Holiday Inn**, Am Main-Taunus-Zentrum 1, ⊠ 6231 Sulzbach, ☏ (06196) 78 78, Telex 0410373, ⇄, ⬛ – ⊟ 📺 🍴 🅿 🛗 🖧. ᴬᴱ ⓪ 🅴
291 Z : 566 B Fb.

In Neu-Isenburg 6078 S : 7 km (Stadtplan Frankfurt : S. 3) – ⓩ 06102.
🚗 ☏ 85 75.

🏨 **Isabella-H.**, Herzogstr. 61, ☏ 35 71, Telex 04185651, ⇄ – 📺 🅿 🛗. ᴬᴱ ⓪ 🅴. ⅀⅀ Rest
Karte 21/50 *(Samstag geschl.)* – **230 Z : 400 B** 110/170 Fb.   S w

🏨 **Wessinger am Wald**, Alicestr. 2, ☏ 2 70 79, Telex 04185654, « Gartenterrasse » – 🛗 ⬛ Zim
📺 🚿wc ☎ 🅿. ᴬᴱ. ⅀⅀   S n
Karte 22,50/61 *(Montag geschl.)* – **42 Z : 60 B** 53/109.

🏨 **Alfa** garni, Frankfurter Str. 123, ☏ 2 26 09 – 🚪🚿wc 🚿wc ☎   S c
18 Z : 32 B 30/55.

🏨 **Linde**, Frankfurter Str. 111, ☏ 40 75 – 🛗 🚪🚿wc 🚿wc ☎ 🅿   S c
Karte 11/26 – **34 Z : 60 B** 30/60.

🏨 **Sauer** garni, Offenbacher Str. 83, ☏ 3 68 79 – 🚪🚿wc 🚿wc 🅿   S d
15 Z : 25 B 38/48.

XX **Ammerländer Schinkenkrug**, Frankfurter Str. 1, ☏ 42 76 – 🅿   S a

X **Grüner Baum** (traditionelles Äppelwoilokal), Marktplatz 4, ☏ 3 83 18, « Innenhof » – 🅿. ᴬᴱ
⓪ 🅴   S q
außerhalb der Messezeiten Montag geschl. – Karte 16,50/39 *(auch Diät)* (Tischbestellung ratsam).

X **Isenburger Hof** mit Zim, Frankfurter Str. 40, ☏ 3 53 20 – 🚿 🅿
11 Z : 18 B   S v

X **Alt-Isenburg**, Offenbacher Str. 21, ☏ 3 63 08 – ⬛. ᴬᴱ ⓪ 🅴   S g
Karte 21/48.

In Neu-Isenburg 2-Gravenbruch 6078 SO . 11 km, Nähe Autokino .

🏨 **Gravenbruch-Kempinski-Frankfurt** Ⓜ, ☏ (06102) 50 50, Telex 0417673, Massage, ⇄,
🔺, ⬛, ⅀⅀ – ⊟ 📺 🍴 🖧 ⟵ 🅿 🛗. ᴬᴱ ⓪ 🅴. ⅀⅀ Rest   S t
Restaurants: – **Gourmet-Rest.** Karte 45/95 – **Forsthaus-Rest.** Karte 30/65 – **317 Z : 520 B**
175/235.

In Neu-Isenburg - Zeppelinheim 6078 ⑤ : 11 km an der B 44 :

X **Forsthaus Mitteldick**, Forsthausweg 1, ☏ (0611) 69 18 01, Gartenterrasse – 🅿. ᴬᴱ ⓪ 🅴.
⅀⅀   S h
Samstag geschl. – Karte 19/50.

Beim Rhein-Main Flughafen SW : 12 km (Nähe BAB-Ausfahrt Flughafen) – ⓩ 0611 :

🏨 **Sheraton** Ⓜ ♨, Am Flughafen (Terminal Mitte), ⊠ 6000 Frankfurt 75, ☏ 6 98 11,
Telex 04189294, ⇔, ⬛ – ⊟ 📺 🍴 🛗 🖧. ᴬᴱ ⓪ 🅴. ⅀⅀ Rest   S f
Karte 26/71 – **555 Z : 1 110 B** 204/264.

🏨 **Steigenberger Airporthotel** ♨, Flughafenstr. 300, ⊠ 6000 Frankfurt 75, ☏ 6 98 51,
Telex 0413112, ⇄, ⬛ – ⊟ 📺 🍴 🅿 🛗. ᴬᴱ ⓪ 🅴   S z
Restaurants: – **Grill-Rest.** Karte 33/63 – **Pergola** Karte 23/48 – **350 Z : 500 B** 129/189.

XX **Waldrestaurant Unterschweinstiege**, Flughafenstraße, ⊠ 6000 Frankfurt 75, ☏ 69 25 03,
« Gartenterrasse, rustikale Einrichtung » – ⬛ 🅿. ᴬᴱ ⓪ 🅴. ⅀⅀   S z
Karte 30/59 (Tischbestellung ratsam).

Im Rhein-Main Flughafen SW : 12 km :

XXX **Rôtisserie 5 Continents**, Ankunft Ausland B 3 (Besucherhalle), ⊠ 6000 Frankfurt 75,
☏ (0611)6 90 57 06, ⇐ – ⬛. ᴬᴱ ⓪ 🅴   S f
Karte 31,50/61.

X **Quo Vadis** (Italienische Küche), Ankunft B (Treffpunkt), ⊠ 6000 Frankfurt 75,
☏ (0011) 0 90 34 54   S f
Karte 23/40.

HAMBURG

HAMBURG 2000. 🔲 Stadtstaat Hamburg 9̲8̲7̲ ⑤ — 1 698 000 Ew — Höhe 10 m — 🕐 040.

Sehenswert : Rathausmarkt★ und Jungfernstieg★ DY — Außenalster★★★ (Rundfahrt★★★) — Tierpark Hagenbeck★★ T — Fernsehturm★★ (🔭★★) BX — Kunsthalle★★ (Deutsche Malerei des 19. Jh.) EY **M** — St. Michaelis★ (Turm 🔭★) — Stintfang (≤★) BZ — Hafen★★ (Rundfahrt★★).

Ausflugsziele : Norddeutsches Landesmuseum★★ AV **M** — Altonaer Balkon ≤★ AV **S** — Wedel : Willkomm-Höft (Schiffsbegrüssungsanlage beim Schulauer Fährhaus ≤★) **W** : 23 km über die B 431 U.

🛫 Hamburg-Fuhlsbüttel (N : 15 km T), 🕾 50 81, City-Center Airport (Air Terminal), Brockesstraße (im ZOB FY), 🕾 50 85 57 — 🚌 🕾 39 18 65 56.

Messegelände (BX), 🕾 3 56 91, Telex 0212609.

🖪 Tourist-Information, Fremdenverkehrszentrale, Hachmannplatz 1 (am Hbf), 🕾 24 87 00, Telex 02163036 und Hotelnachweis im Hbf, 🕾 24 12 34 und 32 69 17.

🖪 Zimmernachweis im Flughafen (Ankunftshalle), 🕾 50 84 57.

ADAC, Amsinckstr. 39 (H 1), 🕾 2 39 91, Telex 02162190, Notruf 🕾 2 39 99, 2000 Hamburg 60, Kapstadtring 5,🕾 6 31 01 41, 2050 Hamburg 80, Kampchaussee 66, 🕾 7 21 55 65,🕾 77 15 51 und 2080 Pinneberg, Saarlandstr. 18, 🕾 (04101) 2 22 23.

♦Berlin 284 ③ — ♦Bremen 119 ④ — ♦Hannover 152 ④.

Die Angabe (H 15) nach der Anschrift gibt den Postzustellbezirk an : Hamburg 15
L'indication (H 15) à la suite de l'adresse désigne l'arrondissement : Hamburg 15
The reference (H 15) at the end of the address is the postal district : Hamburg 15
L'indicazione (H 15) posta dopo l'indirizzo, precisa il quartiere urbano : Hamburg 15

Stadtpläne : siehe Hamburg Seiten 2 bis 7.

Beim Hauptbahnhof, in St. Georg, östlich der Außenalster Stadtplan : S. 5 und 7 :

🏨 **Atlantic** 🏊, An der Alster 72 (H 1), 🕾 24 80 01, Telex 02163297, ≤ Außenalster, Massage, ≘, 🔲 — 📺 Rest 📺 🚗 🅿 🏋(mit 🍴). 🆎 ⓪ **E**. 🞿 Rest — EX **a**
Restaurant — **Brücke** *(Samstag - Sonntag geschl.)* Karte 32/65 (siehe auch **Atlantic-Grill**) —
320 Z : 410 B 192/227.

🏨 **Europäischer Hof,** Kirchenallee 45 (H 1), 🕾 24 81 71, Telex 02162493 — 📺 Rest 📺 🚗 🏋(mit 🍴). 🆎 ⓪ **E** — FY **e**
Karte 22,50/56 — **295 Z : 450 B** 108/160 Fb.

🏨 **Prem,** An der Alster 9 (H 1), 🕾 24 22 11, Telex 02163115, « Garten » — 📺. 🆎 ⓪ **E**. 🞿 Rest — FX **c**
Karte 29/67 *(Sonntag geschl.)* — **48 Z : 75 B** 89/149.

🏨 **Reichshof,** Kirchenallee 34 (H 1), 🕾 24 83 30, Telex 02163396 — 📺 🚗 🏋. 🆎 ⓪ **E**. 🞿 Rest — FY **d**
Karte 25/58 — **343 Z : 466 B** 125/155 Fb.

🏨 **Ambassador,** Heidenkampsweg 34 (H 1), 🕾 24 98 44, Telex 02162398, Massage, ≘, 🔲 — 📺 🚗 🅿 🏋(mit 🍴). 🆎 ⓪ **E**. 🞿 Rest — GY **c**
Karte 29/53 — **123 Z : 200 B** 80/125 Fb.

🏨 **Senator** Ⓜ, Lange Reihe 18 (H 1), 🕾 24 12 03, Telex 02174002 — 🛗 📺 ⌂wc 🚿wc 🕾 🅿. ⓪ — FY **r**
(nur Abendessen für Hausgäste) — **56 Z : 120 B** 90/110 Fb.

🏨 **St. Raphael,** Adenauer-Allee 41 (H 1), 🕾 24 11 91, Telex 02174733 — 🛗 📺 🚿wc 🕾 🅿 🏋. 🆎. 🞿 Rest — FY **m**
Karte 19/41 *(nur Abendessen, Samstag, Sonn- und Feiertage geschl.)* — **120 Z : 160 B** 75/95 Fb.

🏨 **Berlin,** Borgfelder Str. 1 (H 26), 🕾 25 72 11, Telex 0213939 — 📺 Rest 📺 ⌂wc 🚿wc 🕾 🚗 🅿 🏋(mit 🍴). 🆎 ⓪ **E**. 🞿 Rest — **96 Z : 121 B** — GY **a**

🏨 **Fürst Bismarck** garni, Kirchenallee 49 (H 1), 🕾 2 80 10 91, Telex 02162980 — 🛗 📺 ⌂wc 🚿wc 🕾. 🆎 ⓪ **E**. 🞿 — 23. Dez.- 1. Jan. geschl. — **59 Z : 92 B** 85/95 — FY **x**

🏨 **Kronprinz-Rest. Schiffer-Börse,** Kirchenallee 46 (H 1), 🕾 24 32 58 (Hotel) 24 52 40 (Rest.), Telex 02161005 — 📺 📺 ⌂wc 🚿wc 🅿. 🆎 ⓪ **E**. 🞿 — **73 Z : 103 B** — FY **e**

🏨 **Alte Wache** garni, Adenauer-Allee 25 (H 1), 🕾 24 12 91, Telex 02162254 — 🛗 📺 🚿wc 🕾 🅿 🏋. 🞿 — 20.-31. Dez. geschl. — **72 Z : 80 B** 82/98 — FY **s**

🏠 **Dänischer Hof** garni, Holzdamm 4 (H 1), 🕾 24 55 56, Telex 02162760 — 🛗 ⌂wc 🚿wc 🕾 🅿. 🆎 ⓪ — **50 Z : 70 B** 55/95 — EX **b**

🏠 **Merkur** garni, Bremer Reihe 12 (H 1), 🕾 24 33 83 — 🛗 ⌂wc 🚿wc 🕾. 🆎 ⓪ **E** — FY **z**
57 Z : 83 B 55/95.

🏠 **Metro** garni, Bremer Reihe 14 (H 1), 🕾 24 72 66, Telex 02162683 — 🛗 ⌂wc 🚿wc 🕾 🚗 — FY **z**
56 Z : 85 B.

🏠 **Eden-H.** garni, Ellmenreichstr. 20 (H 1), 🕾 24 15 21 — 🛗 ⌂wc 🚿 🕾. 🆎 ⓪ **E**. 🞿 — FY **g**
110 Z : 185 B.

🏠 **Alt Nürnberg** garni, Steintorweg 15 (H 1), 🕾 24 60 24 — ⌂wc 🚿wc 🕾 — FY **a**
19 Z : 29 B 45/90.

🏠 **Wedina** 🏊 garni, Gurlittstr. 23 (H 1), 🕾 24 30 11, ≘, 🔲 (geheizt), 🕿 — ⌂ 🚿wc 🕾. 🆎 ⓪ **E** — 17. Dez.- 5. Feb. geschl. — **23 Z : 40 B** 46/85 — FX **n**

XXXX ❀ **Atlantic-Grill**, An der Alster 72 (im Hotel Atlantic) (H 1), ☎ 24 80 01 — ▤ 🅿. 🆎 ◉ 🇪. 🛇
Montag geschl. — Karte 48/90   EX **a**
Spez. Cassolette von Langostinos, Gefülltes Stubenküken, Sülze von Lammfilet und Auberginen.

XX **Peter Lembcke**, Holzdamm 49 (H 1), ☎ 24 32 90 — ◉   FY **t**
9.- 31. Juli sowie Sonn- und Feiertage geschl. — Karte 34/70.

XX ❀ **Le Delice** (modernes Rest. in einem Kommunikationszentrum), Klosterwall 9 (Markthalle)
(H 1), ☎ 32 77 27   FYZ **n**
Samstag bis 18 Uhr, Sonntag und Juli geschl. — Karte 45/95 (Tischbestellung ratsam)
Spez. Gebeizter Lachs in warmer Limonenjus, Gebackene Rehzunge in Majoran, Pot au feu vom Hirschschinken.

Binnenalster, Altstadt, Neustadt Stadtplan Hamburg : S. 6 und 7 :

🏨🏨 ❀ **Vier Jahreszeiten - Rest. Haerlin**, Neuer Jungfernstieg 9 (H 36), ☎ 3 49 41,
Telex 0211629, ≤ Binnenalster — 📺 ⇔. 🆎 ◉ 🇪. 🛇   DY **v**
Karte 39/92 — **200 Z : 300 B** 175/280
Spez. Savarin von Hummer, Seezunge "Americaine", Lammrücken "Matignon".

🏨🏨 **Inter-Continental**, Fontenay 10 (H 36), ☎ 44 10 81, Telex 0211099, ≤ Hamburg und Alster,
« Gartenterrasse », Massage, ≦, ☒, – ▤ 🅿 🚗 🆎 ◉ 🇪. 🛇 Rest   EX **r**
Restaurants — **Hulk-Brasserie** Karte 28,50/58 (siehe auch Rest. **Fontenay-Grill**) — **300 Z : 600 B**
193/233 Fb.

🏨🏨 **CP Hamburg Plaza** Ⓜ, Marseiller Str. 2 (H 36), ☎ 35 10 35, Telex 0214400, ≤ Hamburg, ≦,
☒, 🛁 – ▤ 📺 ⇔ 🅰 🆎 ◉ 🇪. 🛇 Rest   CX **a**
Restaurants — **Englischer Grill** *(Samstag bis 18 Uhr und Sonntag geschl.)* Karte 37/75 —
Vierländerstube Karte 25/57 — **570 Z : 1 180 B** 166/186 Fb.

🏨🏨 **Ramada-Renaissance-H.**, Große Bleichen (H 36), ☎ 34 28 96, Telex 02162983, Massage,
≦ — ▤ 📺 🅿 🅰 🆎 ◉ 🇪. 🛇 Rest   CY **e**
Karte 38/74 — **211 Z : 297 B** 190/225 Fb.

🏨 **Hafen Hamburg**, Seewartenstr. 9 (H 11), ☎ 31 15 25, Telex 02161319, ≤ — 🛗 ⌷wc ☎ 🅿. 🆎
◉ 🇪   BZ **y**
Karte 24/57 — **92 Z : 191 B** 77/90 Fb.

🏨 Alsterhof garni, Esplanade 12 (H 36), ☎ 34 17 01, Telex 0213043 — 🛗 ⌷wc ⌷wc ☎. ◉
78 Z : 138 B.   DX **x**

🏨 **Baseler Hospiz**, Esplanade 11 (H 36), ☎ 34 19 21, Telex 02163707 — 🛗 ⌷wc ⌷wc 🅿.
🛇   DX **x**
Karte 20/46 *(Sonn- und Feiertage geschl.)* — **160 Z : 202 B** 44/72.

XXXX **Fontenay Grill**, Fontenay 10 (9. Etage, im Hotel Inter-Continental) (H 36), ☎ 44 10 81, ≤
Hamburg und Binnenalster — ▤ 🅿 🆎 ◉ 🇪   EX **r**
Samstag bis 18 Uhr geschl. — Karte 48/82 (Tischbestellung ratsam).

XXX **Ratsweinkeller**, Gr. Johannisstr. 2 (H 11), ☎ 36 41 53, « Hanseatisches Rest. a.d.J. 1896 »
— 🅰 🆎 ◉ 🇪   DY **R**
Sonn- und Feiertage geschl. — Karte 21/66.

XXX **Ehmke**, Grimm 14 (H 11), ☎ 32 71 32 — 🆎 🇪. 🛇   DZ **a**
Samstag bis 18 Uhr und Sonntag geschl. — Karte 33/62.

XXX **Alt-Hamburger Bürgerhaus**, Deichstr. 37 (H 11), ☎ 36 56 31 — 🆎 ◉ 🇪   CZ **e**
Sonn- und Feiertage geschl. — Karte 24/60.

XX **Mövenpick im Hanseviertel**, Große Bleichen 36 (H 36), ☎ 35 16 35 — 🛗. 🆎 ◉ 🇪   CY **r**
Karte 19/36 — Café des Artistes Karte 25,50/60.

XX **Harmonie**, Ost-West-Str. 12 (H 1), ☎ 32 71 91   EZ **d**
Sonn- u. Feiertage geschl. — Karte 44/85 (Tischbestellung ratsam).

XX **Überseebrücke**, Vorsetzen (H 11), ☎ 31 33 33, ≤ Hafen und Werften — ▤ 🆎 ◉ 🇪   BZ **x**
Karte 25/68.

XX **Rest. Im Finnlandhaus**, Esplanade 41 (12. Etage, 🛗) (H 36), ☎ 34 41 33, ≤ Hamburg — ▤.
🆎 ◉ 🇪. 🛇   DX **b**
Samstag, Sonn- und Feiertage geschl. — Karte 28/67.

XX **Schümann's Austernkeller** (Rest. aus der Zeit der Jahrhundertwende mit Séparées und
Salons), Jungfernstieg 34 (H 36), ☎ 34 62 65 — 🛇   CY **a**
Sonn- und Feiertage geschl. — Karte 40/90.

XX **Kranzler-Grill**, Im Congress-Centrum (H 36), ☎ 3 59 24 52 — ▤ 🅿. 🆎 ◉ 🇪. 🛇   CX **e**
Karte 24/42 (auch Self-service).

XX Alsterpavillon (Konzert-Café), Jungfernstieg 54 (H 36), ☎ 34 50 52, ≤ Binnenalster, Terrasse
— 🛇   DY **d**

XX **Deichgraf**, Deichstr. 23 (H 11), ☎ 36 42 08 — 🆎 ◉ 🇪   CZ **a**
Samstag bis 18 Uhr, Sonn- und Feiertage geschl. — Karte 35/74.

XX **Viking** (im Chilehaus), Depenau 3 (H 1), ☎ 32 71 71 — 🆎 ◉ 🇪   F7 **t**
Sonn- und Feiertage geschl. — Karte 32/58.

XX **Johann Cölln-Austernstuben**, Brodschrangen 1 (H 11), ☎ 33 07 22 — 🆎 ◉ 🇪   DZ **z**
Sonn- und Feiertage geschl. — Karte 33/89 (Tischbestellung ratsam).

XX **Valentin's Rest.**, Neuer Wall 30 (H 36), ☎ 36 52 80 — 🆎 ◉   CY **s**
Sonn- und Feiertage geschl. — Karte 20/55.

X **Martini Osteria** (Italienische Küche), Badestr. 4 (H 13), ☎ 4 10 16 51 — 🆎 ◉ 🇪   DX **t**
Sonntag geschl. — Karte 28,50/50 (Tischbestellung ratsam).

STRASSENVERZEICHNIS STADTPLAN HAMBURG

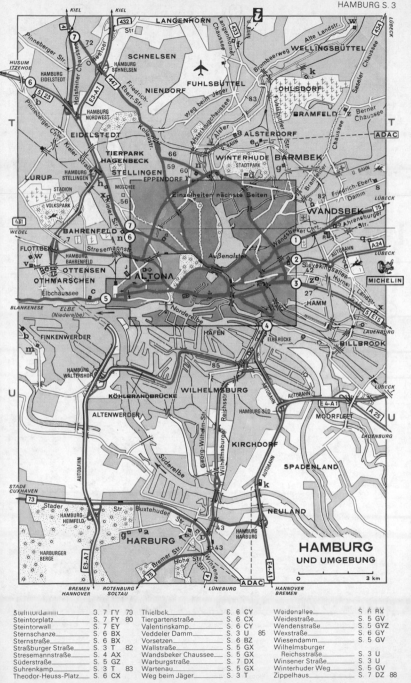

HAMBURG
UND UMGEBUNG

0   3 km

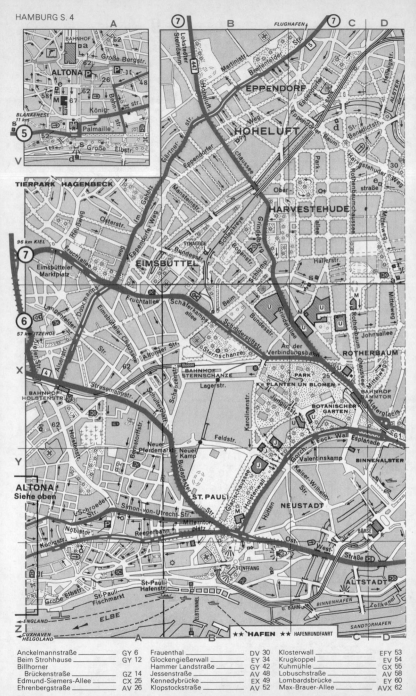

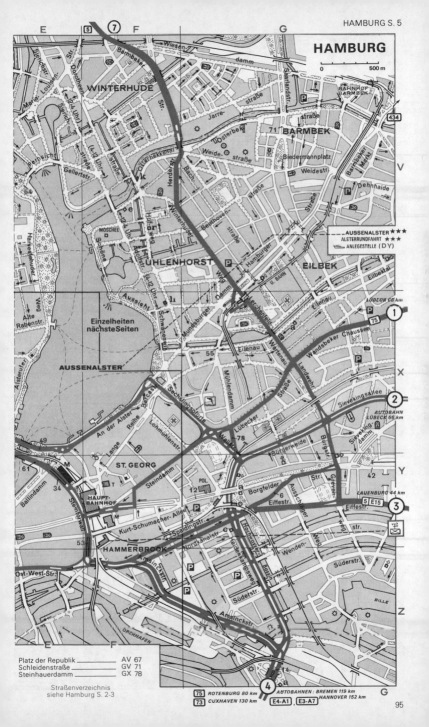

HAMBURG

0   500 m

WINTERHUDE

BARMBEK

BAHNHOF
BARMBEK

Biedermannplatz

UHLENHORST

EILBEK

AUSSENALSTER ★★★
ALSTERRUNDFAHRT ★★★
ANLEGESTELLE (DY)

Einzelheiten
nächste Seiten

AUSSENALSTER

Alte
Rabenstr.

An der Alster

ST. GEORG

HAUPT-
BAHNHOF

Kurt-Schumacher-Allee

HAMMERBROCK

Ost-West-Str.

Platz der Republik _____ AV 67
Schleidenstraße _____ GV 71
Steinhauerdamm _____ GX 78

Straßenverzeichnis
siehe Hamburg S. 2-3

75 ROTENBURG 80 km   AUTOBAHNEN : BREMEN 119 km
73 CUXHAVEN 130 km   HANNOVER 152 km
E4-A1   E3-A7

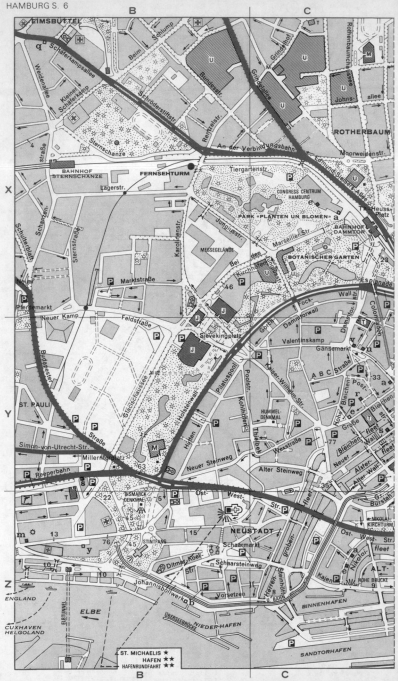

EIMSBÜTTEL

Schäferkampsallee
Weidenallee
Kleiner Schäferkamp
Schröderstiftstr.
Beim Schlump
Rentzelstr.
Bundesstr.
ROTHERBAUM
Grindelhof
Grindelallee
Rothenbaumchaussee
Johns allee
Moorweidenstr.

Straße
Sternschanze
An der Verbindungsbahn
Edmund-Siemers-Allee

BAHNHOF STERNSCHANZE
FERNSEHTURM
Lagerstr.
Tiergartenstr.
CONGRESS CENTRUM HAMBURG
Th.-Heuss-Platz

X
Schanzen
Sternstraße
Karolinenstr.
Jungiusstr.
PARK "PLANTEN UN BLOMEN"
BAHNHOF DAMMTOR
BOTANISCHER GARTEN
23

Schulterblatt
MESSEGELÄNDE
Marseiller Str.
Esplanade

Neuer
Marktstraße
Bei den
Kirchen
Mühlen
46
Wall str.
Colonnaden

Pferdemarkt
Neuer Kamp
Feldstraße
Sievekingplatz
Brock
Dammtorwall
Valentinskamp
Gänsemarkt

Budapester
Glacischaussee
Platauspool
Gorch
Kohlhofen
Kaiser-Wilhelm-Str.
A B C Straße
Hohe Bleichen
Post
33

ST. PAULI
Y
Holstenwall
Thielbek
HUMMEL-DENKMAL
Wexstraße
Große Bleichen
Alster fleet
Bleichen fleet

Simon-von-Utrecht-Str.
Straße
Hütten
Neuer Steinweg
77
Neuer
Alster-Wall

Reeperbahn
Millerntorplatz
63
Alter Steinweg
35
Alter Wall

BISMARCK-DENKMAL
22
5
Ost-
West-
Str.
NEUSTADT
Gr. Bursah
NIKOLAI-KIRCHTURM

m
13
76
45
STINTFANG
15
Schaarmarkt
Ost-
West-
Str.
fleet
ALT

y
45
Ditmar-Koel
Schaarsteinweg
Str.
Nikolai
HOHE BRÜCKE

Z
10
10
Johannisbollwerk
Vorsetzen
U-BAHN
BINNENHAFEN
Kajen

ENGLAND
ELBTUNNEL
ELBE
ÜBERSEEBRÜCKE
NIEDER-HAFEN

CUXHAVEN
HELGOLAND
SANDTORHAFEN

ST. MICHAELIS ★
HAFEN ★★
HAFENRUNDFAHRT ★★

B
C

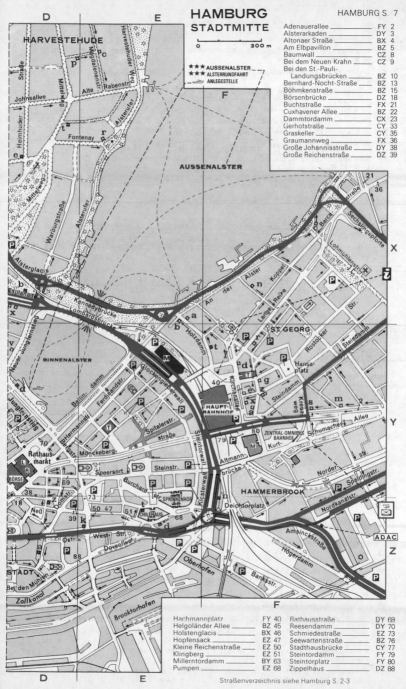

HAMBURG
STADTMITTE

0   300 m

★★★ AUSSENALSTER
★★★ ALSTERRUNDFAHRT
⚓ ANLEGESTELLE

Straßenverzeichnis siehe Hamburg S. 2-3

In den Außenbezirken :

In Hamburg-Altona :

🏛 **Am Bahnhof** garni, Präsident-Krahn-Str. 13 (H 50), ☏ 38 12 39 − 🛗 🛁wc ☎ 🅿 ⑩ 🄴
60 Z : 90 B 52/78.   AV **a**

🏛 **Commerz** garni, Lobuschstr. 26 (H 50), ☏ 39 13 87 − 🛁wc ☎. 🄰🄴 ⑩ 🄴
20 Z : 36 B 52/70.   AV **e**

XXXX ❀ **Landhaus Scherrer**, Elbchaussee 130 (H 50), ☏ 8 80 13 25 − 🅿   U **c**
Sonntag geschl. − Karte 47/93 (Tischbestellung erforderlich)
Spez. Seeteufel auf Gemüsenudeln, Kalbsleber mit Pfefferkirschen, Kohlroulade mit Lammrücken gefüllt.

XXX Fischereihafen-Rest. Hamburg, Große Elbstr. 143 (H 50), ☏ 38 18 16, ≼ − 🅿. ⑩   AV **d**

XX Hanse-Grill, Elbchaussee 94 (H 50), ☏ 39 46 11 − 🅿   AV **s**

In Hamburg-Blankenese W : 16 km über ⑤ und Elbchaussee U :

🏨 **Strandhotel** ⌚ garni, Strandweg 13 (H 55), ☏ 86 09 93, ≼ − 🛁wc 🛁wc ☎ 🅿
11 Z : 20 B.

🏛 **Behrmann** garni, Elbchaussee 528 (H 55), ☏ 86 36 73 − 🛁wc 🛁wc ☎ 🅿. ❄
23 Z : 38 B 55/85.

XXX **Süllberg**, Süllbergsterrasse 2 (H 55), ☏ 86 16 86, « Gartenterrasse mit ≼ » − 🅿 🏔. 🄰🄴 ⑩
🄴
Karte 36/76.

XXX **Sagebiels Fährhaus**, Blankeneser Hauptstr. 107 (H 55), ☏ 86 15 14, « Gartenterrasse mit ≼ »
− 🅿. 🄰🄴 ⑩ 🄴. ❄.

X **Strandhof** (Französische Küche), Strandweg 27 (H 55), ☏ 86 52 36, ≼, Terrasse − 🄰🄴 ⑩ 🄴
Mittwoch geschl. − Karte 38/61.

In Hamburg-Bramfeld :

X **Don Camillo e Peppone** (Italienische Küche), Im Soll 50 (H 71), ☏ 6 42 90 21   T **z**
nur Abendessen, Dienstag und Mitte Juli - Mitte Aug. geschl. − Karte **25,50**/48 (Tischbestellung
ratsam).

In Hamburg-Eppendorf :

XXX ❀ **Le canard**, Martinistr. 11 (H 20), ☏ 4 60 48 30 − ⑩. ❄   T **r**
Jan., 1.- 21. Aug. und Sonntag geschl. − Karte 50/143 (Tischbestellung erforderlich)
Spez. Salat von Kaninchen und Gemüsen, Forellenfilet auf Dillbutter, Wachtelbrüstchen mit Gänsestopfleber.

XX **Fisch Sellmer**, Ludolfstr. 50 (H 20), ☏ 47 30 57 − 🅿. ❄   T **n**
Karte 25/62.

In Hamburg-Geschäftsstadt Nord :

🏨 **Crest-H. Hamburg**, Mexicoring 1 (H 60), ☏ 6 30 50 51, Telex 02174155 − 🍽 Rest 📺 🚗 🅿
🏔 (mit 🍽). 🄰🄴 ⑩ 🄴. ❄ Rest   T **e**
Karte 27/69 − **185 Z : 270 B** 138/144 Fb.

In Hamburg-Harvestehude :

🏨 **Smolka**, Isestr. 98 (H 13), ☏ 47 50 57, Telex 0215275 − 📺. 🄰🄴 ⑩ 🄴. ❄ Rest   CV **d**
Karte 23,50/63 *(Sonn- und Feiertage geschl.)* − **40 Z : 65 B** 75/145 Fb.

🏨 **Mittelweg** garni, Mittelweg 59 (H 13), ☏ 45 32 51 − 📺 🛁wc 🛁wc ☎   DV **e**
38 Z : 51 B 85/100.

🏨 **Greve** ⌚ garni, Magdalenenstr. 60 (H 13), ☏ 44 99 58, Telex 0212621, « Kleine Terrasse » −
📺 🛁wc 🛁wc ☎. 🄰🄴   EX **c**
30 Z : 50 B 90/110.

🏨 **Pöseldorf** ⌚ garni, Böttgerstr. 3 (H 13), ☏ 41 80 87, Telex 0212621, ☏ − 📺 🛁wc 🛁wc ☎.
🄰🄴   DX **p**
23 Z : 40 B 90/130.

XX Daitokai (Japanisches Rest.), Milchstr. 1 (H 13), ☏ 4 10 10 61 − 🍽. ❄   DV **a**
(Tischbestellung ratsam).

XX **La vite** (Italienische Küche), Heimhuder Str. 5 (H 13), ☏ 45 84 01 − 🄰🄴 ⑩ 🄴   DX **e**
Mai - Sept. Samstag geschl. − Karte 33/52 (Tischbestellung ratsam).

X **Block-House** (Steakhaus), Mittelweg 122 (H 13), ☏ 44 31 30   DV **r**
Samstag, Sonn- und Feiertage nur Abendessen − Karte 19/45.

In Hamburg-Rotherbaum :

XX ❀ **L'auberge française** (Französische Küche), Rutschbahn 34 (H 13), ☏ 4 10 25 32 − 🄰🄴 ⑩
🄴. ❄   CVX **r**
Juli und Sonntag geschl. − Karte 34/65 (Tischbestellung erforderlich)
Spez. Schottischer Lachs mit Schnittlauchsauce, Fischteller mit Basilikum, Flugente in Champagnersauce.

XX **Skyline-Turm-Rest.**, Lagerstr. 2 (🛗, Gebühr 3 DM) (H 6), ☏ 44 16 41, ❄ Hamburg,
« Rotierendes Restaurant in 132 m Höhe » − 🍽 🚗. 🄰🄴 ⑩ 🄴. ❄   BX
Karte 29/64 (Tischbestellung ratsam).

X **Block-House** (Steakhaus), Grindelhof 73 (H 13), ☏ 45 90 22   CV **s**
Samstag, Sonn- und Feiertage nur Abendessen − Karte 19/45.

MÜNCHEN

MÜNCHEN 8000. 🗓️ Bayern 🄈🄉🄀 🄴 – 1 297 000 Ew – Höhe 520 m – 🄰 089.

Sehenswert : Marienplatz★ KLY – Frauenkirche★★ (Turm ☀★) KY – Alte Pinakothek★★★ KY – Deutsches Museum★ LZ **M1** – Residenz★ (Schatzkammer★★, Altes Residenztheater★) LY – Asamkirche★ KZ **A** – Bayerisches Nationalmuseum★★ HV – Neue Pinakothek★★ GU – Staatsgalerie Moderner Kunst★ LY **M3** – Lenbachhaus★ KY **M5** – Antikensammlungen★★ KY **M6** – Glyptothek★★ KY **M7** – Deutsches Jagdmuseum ★ KY **M8** – Olympia-Park (Olympia-Turm ☀★★★) CR.

Ausflugsziel : Nymphenburg★★ (Schloß★, Park★, Amalienburg★★, Botanischer Garten ★★) BS.

🛫 München-Riem (③ : 11 km), 🕾 4 46 02 27.

🚗 🕾 12 88 44 05.

Messegelände (EX), 🕾 5 10 71, Telex 05212086.

🄑 Verkehrsamt, im Hauptbahnhof (gegenüber Gleis 11), 🕾 2 39 11, Telex 0524801.

🄑 Verkehrsamt im Flughafen München-Riem, 🕾 2 39 12 66.

ADAC, Hauptverwaltung, Baumgartnerstr. 53, 🕾 7 67 61, Telex 0529231, Sendlinger-Tor-Platz 9, 🕾 5 17 11, Telex 0523120, Frankfurter Ring 30, 🕾 3 59 78 91, Telex 0523694, Laplacestr. 2, 🕾 98 79 19, Telex 0524010, Ossinger Str. 2, 🕾 7 14 52 51, Telex 0523606, Rosenheimer Str. 250, 🕾 49 17 46, Telex 0522331, Flisabethstr. 39, 🕾 37 10 50, Telex 0523961 und Irmonherstr. 7, 🕾 83 83 38, Telex 0528390.

DTC, Amalienburgstr. 23 BS, 🕾 8 11 10 48, Telex 0524508.

Innsbruck 162 ④ – ✦Nürnberg 165 ⑦ – Salzburg 140 ④ – ✦Stuttgart 220 ⑦.

Die Angabe (M 15) nach der Anschrift gibt den Postzustellbezirk an : München 15
L'indication (M 15) à la suite de l'adresse désigne l'arrondissement : München 15
The reference (M 15) at the end of the address is the postal district : München 15
L'indicazione (M 15) posta dopo l'indirizzo, precisa il quartiere urbano : München 15

Stadtpläne : siehe München Seiten 2 bis 7.

🏨 **Vier Jahreszeiten** ⌘, Maximilianstr. 17 (M 22), 🕾 22 88 21, Telex 0523859, Massage, 🄴, ▣ – 🔲 🄣🄥 🍽️ 🄰🄔 🄾
🄴. 🍽️ Rest
LY **a**
Karte 25/50 *(Sonntag ab 15 Uhr geschl.)* (siehe auch Rest. **Walterspiel**) – **365 Z : 550 B** 160/230.

🏨 ✿ **Der Königshof** ⌘, Karlsplatz 25 (M 2), 🕾 55 84 12, Telex 0523616 – ▣ 🔲 🄟 🄖. 🄰🄔 🄾
🄴. 🍽️ Rest
KY **s**
Karte 38/98 – **120 Z : 200 B** 150/165
Spez. Le foie gras du chef, Langouste au beurre vanillé, Carré d'agneau aux fines herbes.

🏨 **Bayerischer Hof - Montgelas-Palais**, Promenadeplatz 6 (M 2), 🕾 2 12 00, Telex 0523409, Massage, 🄴, ▣ – ▣ Rest 🔲 🄖 🄰 🄰🄔 🄾
KY **y**
421 Z : 633 B.

🏨 **Eden-Hotel-Wolff**, Arnulfstr. 4 (M 2), 🕾 55 82 81, Telex 0523564 – 🔲 🄰 🄰🄔 🄾
Karte 20/48 – **214 Z : 320 B** 104/150 Fb.
JY **p**

🏨 **Excelsior**, Schützenstr. 11 (M 2), 🕾 55 79 06, Telex 0522419 – ▣ Rest 🔲 🄟 🄰 🄰🄔 🄾
Karte 24/54 – **118 Z : 170 B** 140/150.
JY **z**

🏨 **Drei Löwen - Rest. Strawberry**, Schillerstr. 8 (M 2), 🕾 59 55 21, Telex 0523867 – 🄰 🄟
🄰. 🄰🄔 🄾 🄴. 🍽️ Rest
JY **e**
Karte 21/43 *(Sonntag geschl.)* – **145 Z : 230 B** 89/110 Fb.

🏨 **Deutscher Kaiser**, Arnulfstr. 2 (M 2), 🕾 55 83 21, Telex 0522650, Rest. in der 15. Etage mit ⬱ München – 🄖 🄟 🄰. 🄰🄔 🄾. 🍽️ Rest
JY **s**
Karte 28/56 – **165 Z : 300 B** 78/112 Fb.

🏨 **Metropol**, Bayerstr. 43, (Eingang Goethestr.) (M 2), 🕾 53 07 64, Telex 0522816 – 🔲 🄖 🄰.
🄰🄔 🄾
JY **k**
Karte 17,50/48 *(außerhalb der Messezeiten Sonntag geschl.)* – **272 Z : 364 B** 59/119.

🏨 **Bundesbahnhotel**, Bahnhofplatz 2 (M 2), 🕾 55 85 71, Telex 0523174 – 🄍 🔲 🛁wc 🚿wc 🕾
228 Z : 276 B.
JY **u**

🏨 **Reinbold** garni, Adolf-Kolping-Str. 11 (M 2), 🕾 59 79 45, Telex 0522539 – 🄍 ▣ 🔲 🛁wc 🕾
🄰🄔 🄾
JY **t**
56 Z : 84 B 55/137.

🏨 **Central-H.** 🄼 garni, Schwanthalerstr. 111 (M 2), 🕾 50 60 81 – 🄍 🛁wc 🕾 🄖 🄰 🄰. 🄰🄔
🄾
EV **s**
69 Z : 120 B 89/149 Fb.

🏨 **Splendid** garni, Maximilianstr. 54 (M 22), 🕾 29 66 06, Telex 0522427 – 🄍 🛁wc 🕾. 🄰🄔
40 Z : 60 B 90/165 Fb.
HV **d**

🏨 **Adria** garni, Liebigstr. 8 a (M 22), 🕾 29 30 81 – 🄍 🔲 🛁wc 🚿wc 🕾. 🄰🄔 🄾 🄾
24. Dez.- 7. Jan. geschl. – **54 Z : 76 B** 50/90.
HV **a**

🏨 **Ariston** garni, Unsöldstr. 10 (M 22), 🕾 22 26 91, Telex 0522437 – 🄍 🛁wc 🚿wc 🕾 🄖 🄰 🄟.
🄰🄔 🄾
LY **c**
63 Z : 112 B 75/100 Fb.

99

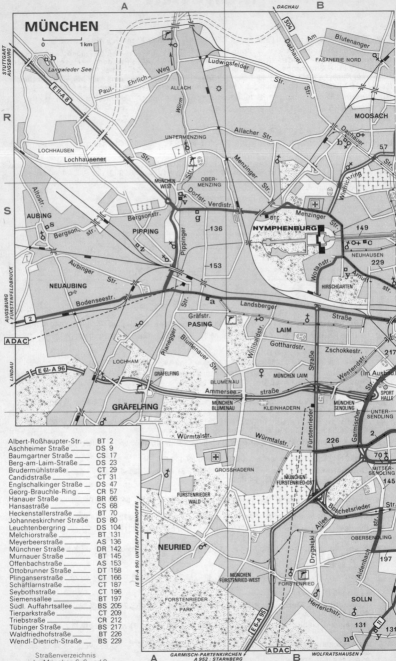

MÜNCHEN

0   1 km

Straßenverzeichnis
siehe München S. 6 und 8

100

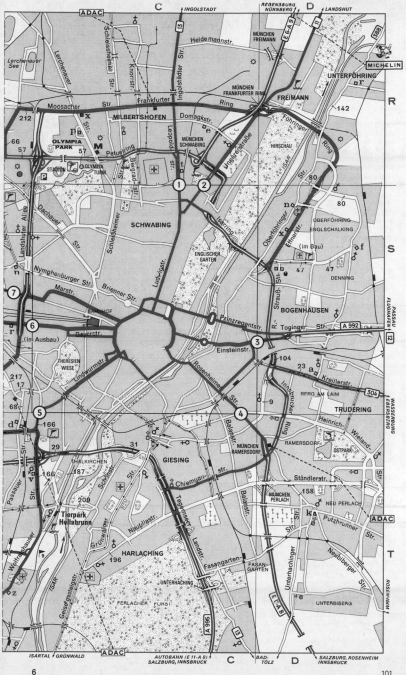

Straßenverzeichnis
siehe München S. 6 und 8

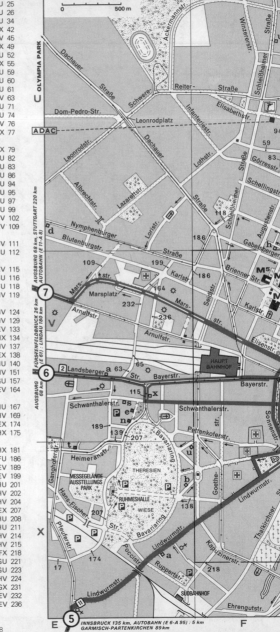

MÜNCHEN

0   500 m

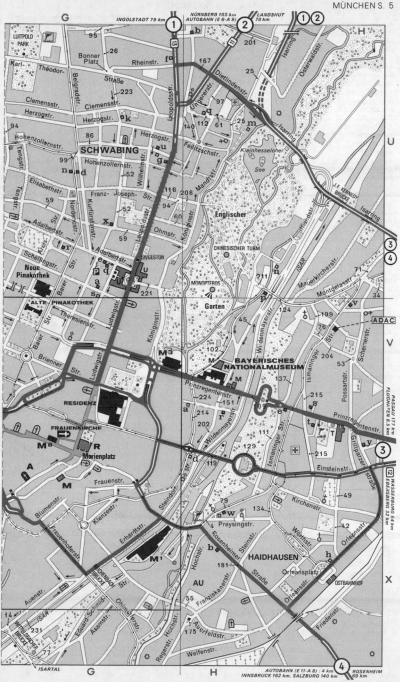

Fortsetzung
siehe München S. 8

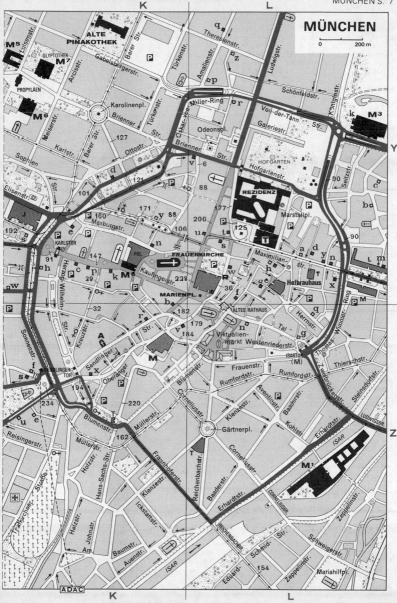

105

🏛 **Domus** garni, St.-Anna-Str. 31 (M 22), ☎ 22 17 04, Telex 0529835 — 🛗 📺 🖵wc ☎ ⬅ 🛁.
🏧 ⓘ 🇪
                                                                     LY **b**
23.- 27. Dez. geschl. — **45 Z : 82 B** 85/140 Fb.

🏛 **Concorde** garni, Herrnstr. 38 (M 22), ☎ 22 45 15, Telex 0522002 — 🛗 📺 🖵wc 🖳wc ☎ ⬅
🛁 🏧 ⓘ 🇪
                                                                LZ **q**
45 Z : 90 B Fb.

🏛 **An der Oper** garni (siehe auch Rest. **Bouillabaisse**), Falkenturmstr. 10 (M 2), ☎ 22 87 11,
Telex 0522588 — 🛗 🖵wc 🖳wc ☎. 🏧 ⓘ 🇪
                                                                  LY **h**
54 Z : 99 B 76/100.

🏛 **Europäischer Hof** (Hospiz, garni), Bayerstr. 31 (M 2), ☎ 55 46 21, Telex 0522642 — 🛗 🖵wc
🖳wc ☎ ⬅ 🛁 🏧 ⓘ 🇪 ✦
                                                                    JY **b**
160 Z : 230 B Fb.

🏛 **Wapler** garni, Schwanthalerstr. 8 (M 2), ☎ 59 16 64, Telex 0523165 — 🛗 📺 🖵wc ☎. 🏧 ⓘ
🇪
                                                                  KY **w**
52 Z : 100 B 95/145 Fb.

🏛 **Bristol** garni, Pettenkoferstr. 2 (M 2), ☎ 59 51 51, Telex 0524767 — 🛗 📺 🖵wc ☎ ⬅ 🏧
ⓘ 🇪
                                                                  KZ **f**
23. Dez.- 6. Jan. geschl. — **57 Z : 100 B** 85/155.

🏛 **Königswache**, Steinheilstr. 7 (M 2), ☎ 52 20 01, Telex 0529161 — 🛗 📺 🖵wc ☎ ⬅ 🏧 ⓘ
🇪
                                                                  FU **h**
Karte 26/70 *(Samstag geschl.)* — **40 Z : 60 B** 75/95 Fb.

🏛 **Senator** garni, Martin-Greif-Str. 11 (M 2), ☎ 53 04 68 — 🛗 📺 🖵wc ☎ ⬅ 🏧 ⓘ 🇪 EV **x**
28 Z : 48 B 85/125 Fb.

🏛 **Germania**, Schwanthalerstr. 28 (M 2), ☎ 59 77 03, Telex 0523790 — 🛗 🖵wc 🖳 ☎ ⬅ ⓟ
🛁 🏧 ⓘ 🇪
                                                                  JY **q**
100 Z : 150 B.

🏛 **Arnulf** garni, Arnulfstr. 12 (M 2), ☎ 59 86 41, Telex 0529975 — 🛗 🖵wc ☎ ⬅   JY **m**
128 Z : 186 B 55/100.

🏛 **Mark**, Senefelderstr. 12 (M 2), ☎ 59 28 01, Telex 0522721 — 🛗 📺 🖵wc 🖳wc ☎ ⬅ 🛁 🏧
ⓘ 🇪
                                                                  JY **v**
Karte 20/50 *(Sonn- und Feiertage geschl.)* — **104 Z : 145 B** 44/70.

🏛 **City-H.** garni, Schillerstr. 3a (M 2), ☎ 55 80 91, Telex 0522602 — 🛗 🖵 🖵wc ☎ ⬅ ⓘ 🇪
23. Dez.- 8. Jan. geschl. — **65 Z : 120 B** 98/150 Fb.   JY **r**

🏛 **Carlton** garni, Fürstenstr. 12 (M 2), ☎ 28 20 61, Telex 0524918 — 🛗 🖵wc 🖳wc ☎. 🏧 ⓘ 🇪
42 Z : 59 B.   LY **z**

🏠 Torbräu, Tal 37 (M 2), ☎ 22 50 16, Telex 0522212 — 🛗 🖵wc 🖳wc ☎ ⬅ ⓟ   LZ **g**
102 Z : 165 B.

🏠 **Platzl**, Münzstr. 8 (M 2), ☎ 29 31 01, Telex 0522910 — 🛗 🖵wc 🖳wc ☎. 🏧 🇪   LY **e**
Karte 15/37 — **100 Z : 162 B** 55/77.

🏠 **Drei Mohren** garni, Schubertstr. 6 (M 2), ☎ 53 47 28 — 🖵wc 🖳wc ☎ ⬅ ⓟ 🏧 ⓘ 🇪
20. Dez.- 10. Jan. geschl. — **34 Z : 53 B** 65/75.   EX **b**

🏠 **Uhland** garni, Uhlandstr. 1 (M 2), ☎ 53 92 77 — 🛗 🖵wc 🖳wc ☎ ⓟ. 🏧 ⓘ   EX **u**
7.- 18. Jan. geschl. — **25 Z : 50 B** 45/85 Fb.

🏠 **Alfa** garni, Hirtenstr. 22 (M 2), ☎ 59 23 77 — 🛗 🖵wc 🖳wc ☎ ⓟ. 🏧 ⓘ 🇪   JY **n**
80 Z : 130 B 42/95.

🏠 **Amba** garni, Arnulfstr. 20 (M 2), ☎ 59 29 21, Telex 0523389 — 🛗 🖵wc 🖳wc ☎ ⬅ ⓟ. 🏧
                                                                  JY **d**
90 Z : 130 B 50/90.

🏠 **Kraft** garni, Schillerstr. 49 (M 2), ☎ 59 48 23 — 🛗 🖵wc 🖳wc ☎. 🏧 ⓘ   JZ **y**
39 Z : 60 B 49/90.

🏠 **Daniel** garni, Sonnenstr. 5 (M 2), ☎ 55 49 45, Telex 0523863 — 🛗 🖵wc 🖳wc ☎. 🏧 ⓘ
80 Z : 120 B 51/85.   KY **h**

🏠 **Brack** garni, Lindwurmstr. 153 (M 2), ☎ 77 10 52, Telex 0524416   🛗 🖵wc 🖳wc ☎. 🏧 ⓘ 🇪
54 Z : 80 B 50/75.   EX **a**

🏠 **Dachs** garni, Amalienstr. 12 (M 2), ☎ 28 20 86 — 🛗 🖳wc ☎ ⓟ. 🏧 🇪   LY **p**
23. Dez.- 6. Jan. geschl. — **50 Z : 90 B** 40/75.

🏠 **Stachus** garni, Bayerstr. 7 (M 2), ☎ 59 28 81, Telex 0523696 — 🛗 🖵wc 🖳wc ☎. 🏧 ⓘ 🇪
65 Z : 110 B 55/95.   JY **g**

🏠 **Schlicker** garni, Tal 74 (M 2), ☎ 22 79 41 — 🛗 🖵wc 🖳wc ☎ ⓟ. 🏧 ⓘ 🇪   LZ **n**
23. Dez.- 3. Jan. geschl. — **70 Z : 120 B** 48/64.

🏠 **Müller** garni, Fliegenstr. 1 (M 2), ☎ 26 60 63 — 🛗 🖵wc 🖳wc ☎ ⓟ   KZ **e**
24. Dez.-7. Jan. geschl. — **40 Z : 60 B** 50/70.

🏠 **Präsident** garni, Lindwurmstr. 13 (M 2), ☎ 26 30 11, Telex 0529468 — 🛗 🖵wc 🖳wc ☎ ⬅. 🏧
ⓘ 🇪
                                                                  KZ **u**
75 Z : 150 B Fb.

🏠 **Meier** garni, Schützenstr. 12 (M 2), ☎ 59 56 23, Telex 0529126 — 🛗 🖵wc 🖳wc ☎. 🏧 ⓘ 🇪
59 Z : 120 B 54/115.   JY **x**

🏠 **Luitpold** garni, Schützenstr. 14 (Eingang Luitpoldstr.) (M 2), ℡ 59 44 61 — 📷 🛁wc 🛏 ☎. 🆔
　🅿 🅴　　　　　　　　　　　　　　　　　　　　　　　　　　　　　　　　JY x
　48 Z : 72 B 45/69.

🏠 **Westend** garni, Landsberger Str. 20 (5. Etage) (M 2), ℡ 50 40 04 — 📷 🛁wc ☎ 🅿. 🆔 🅾 🅴
　31 Z : 54 B 45/70.　　　　　　　　　　　　　　　　　　　　　　　　　　EV a

🏠 Das Blaue Haus garni, Fürstenstr. 15 (M 2), ℡ 28 20 28 — 📷 🛁wc 🛏 ☎. 🅴　　　　LY r
　32 Z : 50 B.

🏠 **Hahn** garni, Landsberger Str. 117, ℡ 50 11 58, Telex 05213322 — 🛁wc ☎. 🆔 🅾 🅴　　CS r
　40 Z : 80 B 65/85.

🏮 ⊗ **Walterspiel**, Maximilianstr. 17 (im Hotel Vier Jahreszeiten) (M 22), ℡ 22 88 21 — 🍽. 🆔
　🅾 🅴. 🕸　　　　　　　　　　　　　　　　　　　　　　　　　　　　　　LY a
　Montag und Samstag jeweils bis 18 Uhr geschl. — Karte 53/97
　Spez. Parfait von Kalbsleber und Bries mit rotem Pfeffer, Loup de mer mit Kerbel, Kalbsbries in Schnittlauchcrème.

🏮 ⊗⊗⊗ **Aubergine**, Maximiliansplatz 5 (M 2), ℡ 59 81 71 — 🅴　　　　　　　　KY d
　1.- 22. Aug. sowie Sonn- und Feiertage geschl., Montag und Samstag nur Abendessen — Karte
　51/150 (Tischbestellung erforderlich)
　Spez. Salade de pigeon aux artichauts, Fricassée de carpe au piment doux, Râble de lapin farci aux cêpes.

🏮 ⊗ **Sabitzer**, Reitmorstr. 21 (M 22), ℡ 29 85 84 — 🅾 🅴. 🕸　　　　　　　HV r
　Samstag - Sonntag geschl. — Karte 44/98 (Tischbestellung ratsam)
　Spez. Fischtopf ″maison″, Gefüllter Lammrücken, Käsestrudel.

🏮 **Weinhaus Schwarzwälder** (altes Münchener Weinrestaurant), Hartmannstr. 8 (M 2),
　℡ 22 72 16 — 🍴. 🆔 🅾 🅴　　　　　　　　　　　　　　　　　　　　　　KY n
　Karte 30/85.

🏮 ⊗ **Le Gourmet**, Ligsalzstr. 46 (M 2), ℡ 50 35 97 — 🅾 🅴　　　　　　　　EX t
　Dienstag, Freitag und Samstag nur Abendessen. Sonntag und Mai - Okt. auch Montag geschl.,
　1.- 8. Jan. und über Pfingsten 3 Wochen Betriebsferien — Karte 53/92 (Tischbestellung ratsam)
　Spez. Entenschinken mit Kartoffelsalat, Marinierter Lachs mit Trüffeln, Lammcarré mit Senfkörnern paniert.

🏮 **Maximilianstuben**, Maximilianstr. 27 (M 22), ℡ 22 90 44 — 🍽 🆔 🅾 🅴　　　LY y
　Sonn- und Feiertage geschl. — Karte 37/93 (Tischbestellung ratsam).

🏮 ⊗ **Boettner**, Theatinerstr. 8 (M 2), ℡ 22 12 10 — 🍽. 🅴　　　　　　　　　LY u
　Samstag ab 15 Uhr sowie Sonn- und Feiertage geschl. — Karte 46/107 (Tischbestellung ratsam)
　Spez. Hechtsoufflé mit Sauce Nantua, Hummereintopf ″Hartung″, Rote Grütze.

🏮 El Toula (Italienische Küche), Sparkassenstr. 5 (M 2), ℡ 29 28 69 — 🆔 🅾 🅴　　LY f
　(abends Tischbestellung ratsam).

🏮 Belle Epoque, Maximilianstr. 29 (M 22), ℡ 29 33 11 — 🆔 🅴　　　　　　　　LY n
　nur Abendessen (Tischbestellung erforderlich).

🏠 Zum Bürgerhaus, Pettenkoferstr. 1 (M 2), ℡ 59 79 09 — 🅾 🅴　　　　　　　KZ s

🏠 **Chesa Rüegg**, Wurzerstr. 18 (M 22), ℡ 29 71 14, « Rustikale Einrichtung im Schweizer Stil »
　— 🍽. 🆔 🅾 🅴　　　　　　　　　　　　　　　　　　　　　　　　　　　LY d
　Samstag, Sonn- und Feiertage geschl. — Karte 28/63 (Tischbestellung ratsam).

🏠 Zur Kanne, Maximilianstr. 36 (M 22), ℡ 22 12 36 — 🆔 🅾 🅴　　　　　　　LY x
　(abends Tischbestellung ratsam).

🏠 **Dallmayr**, Dienerstr. 14 (1. Etage) (M 2), ℡ 2 13 51 00 — 🆔 🅾　　　　　　LY w
　Samstag 15 Uhr-Sonntag geschl. — Karte 27/63.

🏠 Tivoli (Italienische Küche), Widenmayerstr. 52 (M 22), ℡ 22 12 74, Terrasse — 🅾 🅴. 🕸
　23. Dez.- 2. Jan. und Samstag geschl. — Karte 24/62 (Tischbestellung ratsam).　　HU p

🏠 **Mövenpick im Künstlerhaus**, Lenbachplatz 8 (M 2), ℡ 55 78 65, Terrasse — 🆔 🅾 🅴
　Karte 24,50/52.　　　　　　　　　　　　　　　　　　　　　　　　　　　KY e

🏠 Bouillabaisse, Falkenturmstr. 10 (im Hotel An der Oper) (M 2), ℡ 29 79 09 — 🆔 🅾 🅴　LY h

🏚 **Csarda Piroschka** (Ungarisches Rest. mit Zigeunermusik), Prinzregentenstr. 1 (M 22),
　℡ 29 54 25 — 🅿. 🆔 🅾 🅴　　　　　　　　　　　　　　　　　　　　　　LY k
　ab 18,30 Uhr geöffnet, Sonntag geschl. — Karte 25,50/53 (Tischbestellung ratsam).

🏚 **Goldene Stadt** (Böhmische Spez.), Oberanger 44 (M 2), ℡ 26 43 82 — 🅾 🅴　　KZ x
　Samstag geschl. — Karte 22/42.

🏚 Spatenhaus-Bräustuben, Residenzstr. 12 (M 2), ℡ 22 78 41, Terrasse — 🍴. 🆔 🅾 🅴　LY t

🏚 Opatija (Jugoslawische Küche), Brienner Str. 41 (M 2), ℡ 59 12 02 — 🍽　　　　JY a

🏚 Zum Klösterl, St.-Anna-Str. 2 (M 22), ℡ 22 50 86　　　　　　　　　　　　LY m
　nur Abendessen, 25. Aug.- 5. Sept. sowie Samstag und Feiertage geschl. — Karte 19/44.

🏚 **Haxnbauer**, Münzstr. 2 (M 2), ℡ 22 19 22, « Rustikale Einrichtung » — 🅴　　　LY e
　Karte 16,50/43.

🏚 **Scheck-Alm**, Sendlinger Str. 85 (M 2), ℡ 2 16 62 01　　　　　　　　　　KZ r
　Sonn- und Feiertage geschl. — Karte 15/39.

🏚 **Ratskeller**, Marienplatz 8 (M 2), ℡ 22 03 13 — 🍴. 🆔 🅾 🅴　　　　　　　LY R
　Karte 18/46.

🏚 **Grill-Rest. im Café Luitpold**, Brienner Str. 11 (M 2), ℡ 29 28 65, Boulevard-Terrasse — 🍽
　♿.　　　　　　　　　　　　　　　　　　　　　　　　　　　　　　　　LY v
　24. Dez.-1. Jan. sowie Sonn- und Feiertage geschl. — Karte 18,50/56.

Brauerei-Gaststätten :

✗ Spatenhof, Neuhauser Str. 26 (M 2), ☎ 2 60 31 54   KY **c**

✗ **Augustiner-G.**, Neuhauser Str. 16 (M 2), ☎ 2 60 41 06, « Biergarten »   KY **p**
Sonntag geschl. − Karte 14/40.

✗ Franziskaner-Fuchsenstuben, Perusastr. 5 (M 2), ☎ 22 50 02, Terrasse − ⬛   LY **s**

✗ **Spöckmeier**, Rosenstr. 9 (M 2), ☎ 26 80 88   KY **b**
Sonn- und Feiertage ab 17 Uhr geschl. − Karte 15/38.

✗ Drei Rosen, Rindermarkt 5 (M 2), ☎ 26 84 08 − ⓞ **E**   KZ **v**

✗ **Zum Pschorrbräu**, Neuhauser Str. 11 (M 2), ☎ 2 60 30 01, Terrasse − ⚖. ⬛ ⓞ **E**   KY **k**
Karte 15/40.

✗ **Pschorr-Keller**, Theresienhöhe 7 (M 2), ☎ 50 10 88, Biergarten − ⚖   EV **n**
Karte 13,50/34,50.

✗ **Hackerkeller**, Theresienhöhe 4 (M 2), ☎ 50 70 04, Biergarten − ⬛ ⓞ **E**   EV **e**
Karte 14,50/37.

Beim Englischen Garten :

🏨 Hilton Ⓜ, Am Tucherpark 7 (M 22), ☎ 34 00 51, Telex 05215740, Massage, ≘, 🔲 − ▤ 📺 ♿
Ⓟ ⚖. ⬛ ⓞ **E**   HU **n**
Karte 33/70 − **485 Z : 900 B** 148/208.

In München-Bogenhausen :

🏨 Sheraton Ⓜ ⚘, Arabellastr. 6 (M 81), ☎ 92 40 11, Telex 0522391, ≼ München, Biergarten,
Massage, ≘, 🔲, ⌄ − ▤ 📺 ♿ ♿ ⚖. ⚘   DS **e**
Karte 29/73 − **650 Z : 1 300 B** 126/196.

🏨 Arabella-H. Ⓜ, Arabellastr. 5 (M 81), ☎ 9 23 21, Telex 0529987, ≼ München, Massage, ≘,
🔲 − 📺 ♿ ⚖. ⬛ ⓞ **E**   DS **o**
Karte 24,50/60 − **275 Z : 430 B** 110/180 Fb.

🏨 Crest-H., Effnerstr. 99 (M 81), ☎ 98 25 41, Telex 0524757 − ▤ 📺 Ⓟ ⚖. ⬛ ⓞ **E**. ⁂ Rest
Karte 23,50/46 − **155 Z : 240 B** 105/135 Fb.   DS **x**

✗✗✗ ❀ **Käfer-Schänke**, Schumannstr. 1 (M 80), ☎ 4 16 81, Telex 0523073 − ⓞ **E**. ⁂   HV **s**
Sonn- und Feiertage geschl. − Karte 33/74 (Tischbestellung erforderlich)
Spez. Vorspeisen vom Schaubuffet, Babylanguste im Basilikumgewürzsud, Gerichte von Bresse-Geflügel.

✗✗ Tai Tung (China-Rest.), Prinzregentenstr. 60 (Villa Stuck) (M 80), ☎ 47 11 00 − ⓞ **E**   HV **e**

✗✗ **Mifune** (Japanisches Rest.), Ismaninger Str. 136 (M 80), ☎ 98 75 72, Telex 0529344 − ⬛ ⓞ
E ⁂   HV **v**
Karte 26/57.

✗ Ischia (Italienische Küche), Neherstr. 9 (M 80), ☎ 47 19 83, Terrasse   HV **t**

✗ **Zum Klösterl**, Schneckenburger Str. 31 (M 80), ☎ 47 61 98   HV **y**
Samstag geschl. − Karte 15,50/44.

In München 80-Haidhausen :

🏨 Preysing Ⓜ garni (siehe auch Rest. Preysing-Keller), Preysingstr. 1, ☎ 48 10 11,
Telex 0529044, ≘, 🔲 − ▤ ♿ ⚖.   HX **w**
23. Dez.-7. Jan. geschl. − **73 Z : 92 B** 90/160.

🏨 Stadt Rosenheim, Orleansplatz 6a, ☎ 4 48 24 24 − 🛗 ⌂wc 🚿wc ☎ ♿ ⬛ ⓞ **E**   HX **h**
Karte 16/27 (nur Abendessen, Samstag-Sonntag geschl.) − **61 Z : 90 B** 47/65.

✗✗ ❀ **Preysing-Keller**, Innere-Wiener-Str. 6, ☎ 48 10 15, « Gewölbe mit rustikaler Einrichtung »
− ⓞ   HX **w**
nur Abendessen, 23. Dez.- 7. Jan. sowie Sonn- und Feiertage geschl. − Karte 34/59
Spez. Hummer in Buttersauce, Rehfilet im Blätterteigmantel.

✗ **Ile de France**, Rosenheimer Str. 32, ☎ 4 48 13 66 − ⬛ ⓞ   HX **b**
Sonntag geschl. − Karte 25,50/55.

In München 40-Oberwiesenfeld :

🏨 Olympiapark-H., Helene-Mayer-Ring 12, ☎ 3 51 60 71, Telex 05215231, freier Zugang zum
🔲 in den Thermen − Ⓟ ⚖. ⬛ ⓞ **E**. ⁂ Rest   CR **p**
20. Dez.- 4. Jan. geschl. − Karte 20/38 (Sonntag geschl.) − **100 Z : 194 B** 95/118 Fb.

✗✗ Im Olymp (Drehrestaurant im Olympiaturm, Höhe 182 m, 🛗 DM 3), Spiridon-Louis-Ring 7,
☎ 3 08 10 39, ❅ München − Ⓟ. ⬛ ⓞ **E**   CR
Karte 22/58.

✗ Ischia (Italienische Küche), Moosacher Str. 81, ☎ 3 51 49 45, Terrasse − Ⓟ   CR **x**

In München 87-Riem ③ : 11 km :

✗ **Flughafen-Rest.**, Töginger Str. 400, ☎ 92 11 88 41
Karte 19,50/48.

In München 40-Schwabing :

🏨 **Holiday Inn**, Leopoldstr. 200, ℡ 34 09 71, Telex 05215439, Massage, ⇔, ▨ – ▤ ▣ ⇦
▵. ᴁ ◉ **E**　　　　　　　　　　　　　　　　　　　　　　　　　　　　CR **t**
Restaurants — **Almstuben-Grill** *(nur Abendessen, Sonntag geschl.)* : Karte 35/75 — **Schwabing-Klause** : Karte 23/42 — **360 Z : 720 B** 140/165 Fb.

🏨 **Residence**, Artur-Kutscher-Platz 4, ℡ 39 90 41, Telex 0529788, Terrasse, ▨ – ▣ ⇦ ▵.
ᴁ ◉ **E**. ✀ Rest　　　　　　　　　　　　　　　　　　　　　　　　　　HU **q**
Karte 26/57 — **150 Z : 300 B** 118/152.

🏨 **Holiday Inn Olympic**, Schleißheimer Str. 188, ℡ 30 90 10, Telex 05215370, ⇔, ▨ – ▤ ▣
▵ ⇦ ❷ ▵. ᴁ ◉ **E**. ✀ Rest　　　　　　　　　　　　　　　　　　　　FU **u**
Karte 25/48 — **151 Z : 220 B** 140 Fb.

🏛 **Leopold**, Leopoldstr. 119, ℡ 36 70 61, Telex 05215160 – ▮ ▣ ⊟wc ⟍wc ☎ ▵ ⇦ ❷. ᴁ
◉ **E**　　　　　　　　　　　　　　　　　　　　　　　　　　　　　　　GU **f**
Karte 19/37,50 *(Samstag geschl.)* — **85 Z : 120 B** 60/100 Fb.

🏛 **Biederstein** ▩ garni, Keferstr. 18, ℡ 39 50 72, ⬘ – ▮ ⊟wc ❷ ⇦. ᴁ　　HU **m**
31 Z : 39 B 74/90.

🏛 **International-H. Auer** garni, Hohenzollernstr. 5, ℡ 33 30 43, Telex 0529148 – ▮ ▣ ⊟wc
☎ ⇦. ᴁ　　　　　　　　　　　　　　　　　　　　　　　　　　　　　　GU **g**
70 Z : 140 B 78/108.

🏛 **Tourotel**, Domagkstr. 26, ℡ 38 10 00, Telex 05215533, Massage, ⇔, ▨ – ▮ ▣ ⊟wc ☎
⇦ ❷ ▵. ᴁ ◉ **E**. ✀ Rest　　　　　　　　　　　　　　　　　　　　　CR **e**
Karte 17/49 — **230 Z : 320 B** 77/115 Fb.

🏛 **Consul** garni, Viktoriastr. 10, ℡ 33 40 35 – ▮ ▣ ⊟wc ☎ ❷　　　　　GU **k**
30 Z : 60 B Fb.

🏛 **Lettl** ▩ garni, Amalienstr. 53, ℡ 28 30 26 – ▮ ▣ ⊟wc ⟍wc ☎ ❷　　GU **s**
26 Z : 45 B 42/64.

XXXX ❀❀❀ **Tantris**, Johann-Fichte-Str. 7, ℡ 36 20 61, « Moderner Restaurant-Bau mit eleganter
Einrichtung » – ▤ ❷. ᴁ ◉ **E**. ✀　　　　　　　　　　　　　　　　　HU **b**
Montag und Samstag jeweils bis 18 Uhr sowie Sonn- und Feiertage geschl. — Karte 54/142
(Tischbestellung ratsam)
Spez. Königskrabbenterrine auf Courgettensalat, Navarin vom Hummer, Lammnüßchen mit glacierten Zwiebeln.

XXX ❀ **La mer**, Schraudolphstr. 24, ℡ 2 72 24 39 – ᴁ ◉ **E**. ✀　　　　　GU **r**
nur Abendessen, Ende Juli - Ende Aug. und Sonntag - Montag geschl. — Karte 49/95 (Tisch-bestellung erforderlich)
Spez. Entenleberparfait, Steinbutt in Champagner, Feinschmecker - Menu.

XX **Aquitaine-La maison de Bordeaux** (Französische Küche), Amalienstr. 39, ℡ 28 40 28 –
ᴁ ◉ **E**　　　　　　　　　　　　　　　　　　　　　　　　　　　　　LY **q**
Sonn- und Feiertage geschl. — Karte 35/70 (Tischbestellung ratsam).

XX **Daitokai** (Japanisches Rest.), Nordendstr. 64, ℡ 2 71 14 21 – ᴁ ◉ **E**. ✀　GU **d**
Samstag-Sonntag und an Feiertagen nur Abendessen — Karte 33/59.

XX **Walliser Stuben**, Leopoldstr. 33, ℡ 34 80 00 – ᴁ ◉ **E**　　　　　　GU **g**
ab 17 Uhr geöffnet, Sonn- und Feiertag geschl. — Karte 26/52.

XX ❀ **Bistro Terrine** (Französische Küche), Amalienstr. 89, ℡ 28 68 41 – ✀　GU **q**
Montag und Samstag nur Abendessen, Sonn- und Feiertage geschl. — Karte 38/69 (Tischbes-tellung ratsam)
Spez. Geflügelleberparfait, Fischgerichte, Lammrücken mit Estragon.

XX **Schwabinger Grillroom**, Friedrichstr. 1, ℡ 39 31 01, Terrasse – ▤　　　GU **x**
20. Dez.-10. Jan. geschl. — Karte 19/58.

XX **Le Bazar**, Bauerstr. 2, ℡ 2 71 30 66 – ᴁ ◉ **E**　　　　　　　　　　GU **n**
nur Abendessen, Sonntag geschl. — Karte 34/59 (Tischbestellung ratsam).

XX **Rauchfang**, Hohenzollernstr. 14, ℡ 34 22 71 – ᴁ ◉ **E**　　　　　　GU **u**

X **Bei Mario** (Italienische Küche), Adalbertstr. 15, ℡ 2 80 04 60, Terrasse　　GU **e**

X **Rodella** (Italienische Küche), Schellingstr. 24, ℡ 28 15 04　　　　　　GU **a**

España

Madrid

Barcelona

MADRID

MADRID ℗ 990 ⑮ y ㉟ – 3 201 234 h. alt. 646 – ⚙ 91 – Plaza de toros.

Ver : Museo del Prado★★★ (p. 9) NZ – Paseo del Prado (Plaza de la Cibeles) (p. 9) NXYZ – Paseo de Recoletos (p. 9) NVX – Paseo de la Castellana (p. 9) NV – Puerta del Sol (p. 8) y Calle de Alcalá (p. 9) LMNY – Plaza Mayor★ (p. 8) KYZ – Palacio Real★★ (p. 8) KY – Convento de las Descalzas Reales★★ (p. 8) KY L – San Antonio de la Florida (frescos de Goya★) (p. 6) DX R.

Otros museos : Arqueológico Nacional★★ (p. 9) NV M22 – de America★ (p. 6) DV M8 – Español de Arte Contemporáneo★ (p. 2) AL M9 – del Ejército (p. 9) NY M2.

Alred. : El Pardo★ NO : 13 km por C 601 AL

Hipódromo de la Zarzuela AL.

🛆₁₈, 🛆₁₈ Puerta de Hierro ℡ 216 17 45 AL – 🛆, 🛆₁₈ Club de Campo ℡ 207 03 95 AL – 🛆₁₈ La Moraleja por ① : 11 km ℡ 650 07 00 – 🛆 Club Barberán por ⑥ : 10 km ℡ 218 85 05 – 🛆, 🛆₁₈ Las Lomas – El Bosque por ⑥ : 18 km ℡ 464 32 15 – 🛆₁₈ Real Automóvil Club de España por ① : 28 km ℡ 652 26 00 – 🛆₁₈ Nuevo Club de Madrid, Las Matas por ⑦ : 26 km ℡ 630 08 20 – 🛆 de Somosaguas O : 10 km por Casa de Campo ℡ 212 16 47.

✈ de Madrid-Barajas por ② : 13 km ℡ 222 11 65 – Iberia : pl. de Cánovas 4, ⊠ 14, ℡ 261 91 00 y Aviaco, Maudes 51, ⊠ 3, ℡ 254 36 00.

🚉 Atocha ℡ 228 52 37 – Chamartín ℡ 733 11 22 – Príncipe Pío ℡ 248 87 16.

🚢 Cia Aucona, Alcalá 63, ⊠ 14, ℡ 225 51 10, Telex 23189.

🛈 Princesa 1, ⊠ 8, ℡ 241 23 25, Castelló 117, ⊠ 6, ℡ 441 40 14, pl. Mayor 3, ⊠ 12, ℡ 266 48 74, estación Chamartín ℡ 733 10 20 y aeropuerto de Barajas ℡ 205 86 56 – **R.A.C.E.** José Abascal 10, ⊠ 3, ℡ 447 32 00, Telex 27341.

Paris (por Irún) 1317 ① – ♦Barcelona 626 ② – ♦Bilbao 400 ① – ♦La Coruña 601 ⑦ – ♦Lisboa 646 ⑥ – ♦Málaga 546 ④ – ♦Porto 598 ⑦ – ♦Sevilla 536 ④ – ♦Valencia 348 ③ – ♦Zaragoza 321 ②.

113

MADRID

0   2 km

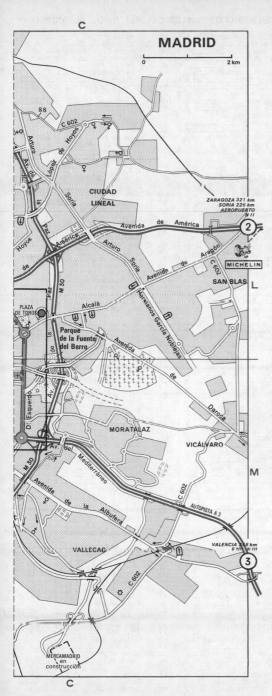

Continuación Madrid p. 4

115

REPERTORIO DE CALLES DEL PLANO DE MADRID (fin)

MADRID
NORTE

Parte común con
la página siguiente

117

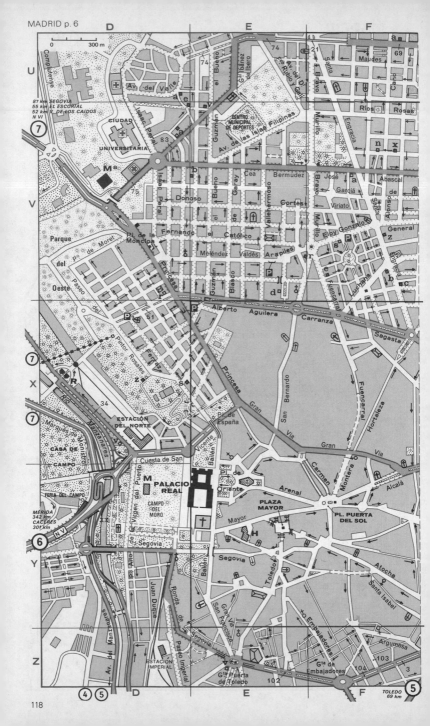

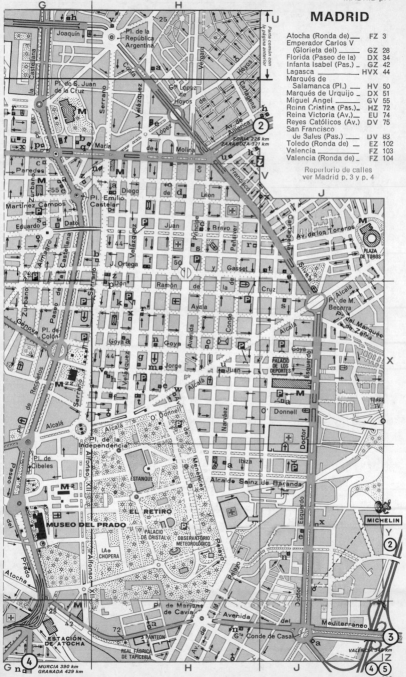

MADRID

Repertorio de calles
ver Madrid p. 3 y p. 4

MICHELIN

119

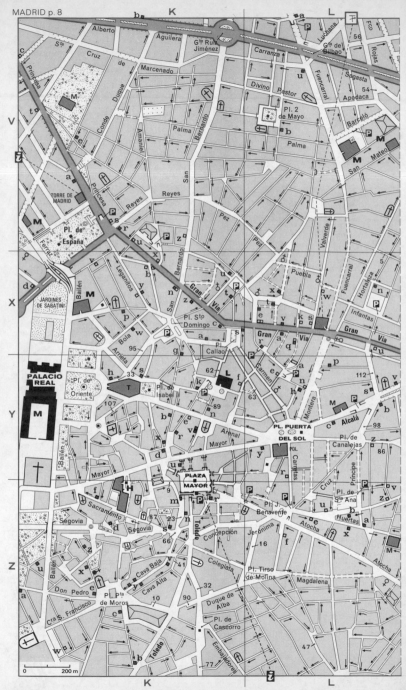

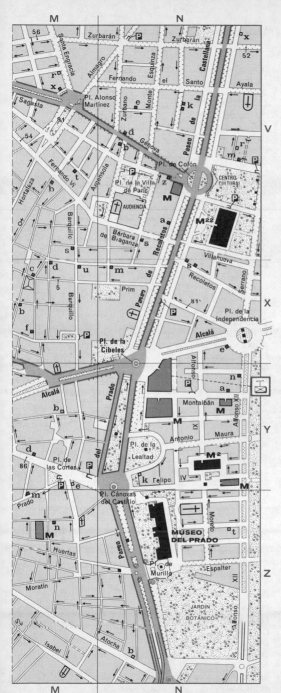

MADRID

Repertorio de Calles
ver Madrid p. 3 y p. 4

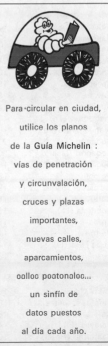

Para circular en ciudad,

utilice los planos

de la **Guía Michelin** :

vías de penetración

y circunvalación,

cruces y plazas

importantes,

nuevas calles,

aparcamientos,

calles peatonales...

un sinfín de

datos puestos

al día cada año.

LISTA ALFABÉTICA DE HOTELES Y RESTAURANTES

1° Centro : Paseo del Prado, Puerta del Sol, Gran Vía, Cibeles, Alcalá, Paseo de Recoletos, Plaza de Colón, Plaza Mayor, Palacio Real, Plaza de España, Serrano, (planos p. 8 a 9).

🏨 **Ritz,** pl. de la Lealtad 5, ⊠ 14, ⟐ 221 28 57, Telex 43 986 – ▤ ⇐⇒ (del Hotel Palace). 🆎 VISA. ❄️ rest   NY **k**
Com 2 750 – � 550 – **170 hab** 8 800/12 500.

🏨 **Villá Magna** Ⓜ, paseo de la Castellana 22, ⊠ 1, ⟐ 261 49 00, Telex 22914 – ▤ ⇐⇒ Ⓟ –
🅰. 🆎.   NV **x**
Com 2 900 – � 610 – **200 hab** 11 500/16 000.

🏨 **Palace,** pl. de las Cortes 7, ⊠ 14, ⟐ 429 75 51, Telex 22272 y 27704 – ▤ ⇐⇒ – 🅰. 🆎 VISA. ❄️ rest   MY **e**
Com 2 200 – � 440 – **515 hab** 6 250/7 850 – P 8 040/10 365.

🏨 **Meliá Madrid** Ⓜ, Princesa 27, ⊠ 8, ⟐ 241 82 00, Telex 22537 – ▤ – 🅰. 🆎 Ⓞ 🇪 VISA. ❄️
Com 2 100 – � 450 – **250 hab** 5 300/7 900.   KV **t**

🏨 **Plaza** sin rest, con cafetería, pl. España 2, ⊠ 13, ⟐ 247 12 00, Telex 27383, ≤, ⒔, – ▤. 🆎 Ⓞ
🇪 VISA. ❄️   KV. **s**
� 360 – **306 hab** 4 760/5 960.

🏨 **Sideral,** Casado del Alisal 14, ⊠ 14, ⟐ 467 12 00 – ▤ ⇐⇒. 🆎 Ⓞ. ❄️   NZ **t**
Com 1 050 – � 250 – **50 hab** 2 900/4 900 – P 4 445/4 895.

🏨 **Sanvy** sin rest, con cafetería, Goya 3, ⊠ 1, ⟐ 276 08 00, ⒔ – ▤ ⇐⇒. 🆎 Ⓞ 🇪 VISA. ❄️   NV **r**
� 250 – **108 hab** 3 700/4 700.

🏨 **Emperador** sin rest, Gran Vía 53, ⊠ 13, ⟐ 247 28 00, Telex 27521, ⒔ – ▤ ⇐⇒. 🆎 Ⓞ 🇪 VISA. ❄️
� 250 – **231 hab** 3 600/4 500.   KX **n**

🏨 **Menfis** sin rest, con cafetería, Gran Vía 74, ⊠ 13, ⟐ 247 09 00 – ▤ – **122 hab**   KV **u**

🏨 **Liabeny,** Salud 3, ⊠ 13, ⟐ 232 53 06 – ▤ ⇐⇒. 🆎. ❄️   LY **e**
Com 700 – � 220 – **158 hab** 2 800/4 200.

🏨 **Suecia y Rest. Bellman,** Marqués de Casa Riera 4, ⊠ 14, ⟐ 231 69 00, Telex 22313 – ▤.
🆎 Ⓞ 🇪 VISA. ❄️   MY **b**
Com 1 400 – � 300 – **64 hab** 4 200/5 300 – P 5 750/7 300.

🏨 **G. H. Victoria,** pl. del Angel 7, ⊠ 12, ⟐ 231 45 00 – ▤. 🆎 Ⓞ VISA. ❄️   LZ **u**
Com 900 – � 155 – **110 hab** 1 840/3 130 – P 3 265/3 540.

🏨 **El Prado** sin rest, con cafetería, calle del Prado 11, ⊠ 14, ⟐ 429 35 68 – ▤ ⇐⇒. 🆎 VISA. ❄️
� 200 – **45 hab** 3 500/5 000.   LZ **z**

🏨 **Mayorazgo** sin rest, con cafetería, Flor Baja 3, ⊠ 13, ⟐ 247 26 00, Telex 45647 – ▤ ⇐⇒.
🆎 Ⓞ VISA. ❄️   KX **b**
� 200 – **200 hab** 2 300/3 800.

🏨 El Coloso sin rest, con cafetería, Leganitos 13, ⊠ 13, ⟐ 248 76 00 – ▤ ⇐⇒ – **69 hab**   KX **y**

🏨 **Arosa** sin rest, con cafetería, Salud 21, ⊠ 13, ⟐ 232 16 00, Telex 43618 – ▤. 🆎 Ⓞ 🇪 VISA
� 260 – **121 hab** 3 120/4 670.   LX **q**

🏨 **Casón del Tormes** sin rest, Río 7, ⊠ 13, ⟐ 241 97 45 – ⧄ ▥ ▤ ⌂wc ☎. VISA. ❄️   KX **v**
� 165 – **61 hab** 2 980/4 970.

🏨 **Mercator** sin rest, con cafetería, Atocha 123, ⊠ 12, ⟐ 429 05 00, Telex 46129 – ⧄ ▥ ▤
⌂wc ⓟ. 🆎 Ⓞ 🇪 VISA   NZ **b**
� 175 – **90 hab** 1 675/2 635.

🏨 **Atlántico** piso 3°, sin rest, Gran Vía 38, ⊠ 13, ⟐ 222 64 80 – ⧄ ▥ ▤ ⌂wc ☎. Ⓞ VISA. ❄️
51 hab � 2 000/3 100.   LX **e**

🏨 **Lope de Vega** piso 9°, sin rest, Gran Vía 59, ⊠ 13, ⟐ 247 70 00, ≤ – ⧄ ▥ ▤ ⌂wc ☎. Ⓞ. ❄️
� 130 – **50 hab** 1 200/2 100.   KX **b**

🏨 **Carlos V** sin rest, Maestro Vitoria 5, ⊠ 13, ⟐ 231 41 00, Telex 48547 – ⧄ ▥ ▤ ⌂wc ▥wc
☎. 🆎 🇪 VISA. ❄️   KY **f**
� 165 – **67 hab** 2 300/3 160.

🏨 **Reyes Católicos** sin rest, Angel 18, ⊠ 5, ⟐ 265 86 00, Telex 44474 – ⧄ ▥ ▤ ⌂wc ☎. 🆎.
❄️   KZ **w**
� 150 – **38 hab** 3 850/5 750.

🏨 Montesol sin rest, Montera 25, ⊠ 14, ⟐ 231 76 00 – ⧄ ▥ ⌂wc ☎ – **52 hab**   LY **n**

🏨 **Embajada** sin rest, Santa Engracia 5, ⊠ 10, ⟐ 447 33 00 – ⧄ ▥ ⌂wc ☎. ❄️   MV **r**
� 200 – **84 hab** 2 150/3 750.

🏨 **Madrid** sin rest, Carretas 10, ⊠ 12, ⟐ 221 65 20 – ⧄ ▥ ▤ ⌂wc ▥wc ☎. 🆎 Ⓞ VISA. ❄️
� 175 – **71 hab** 1 850/3 050.   LY **r**

🏨 **Cortezo** sin rest, con cafetería, Dr Cortezo 3, ⊠ 12, ⟐ 239 38 00 – ⧄ ▥ ▤ ⌂wc ☎ ⇐⇒. 🆎
VISA. ❄️   LZ **f**
� 150 – **90 hab** 1 750/2 750.

🏨 **Francisco I,** Arenal 15, ⊠ 13, ⟐ 248 02 04 – ⧄ ▥ ▤ ⌂wc ☎. VISA. ❄️   KY **e**
Com 740 – � 150 – **57 hab** 1 600/2 300 – P 2 530/2 980.

🏨 **Italia** piso 2°, Gonzalo Jiménez de Quesada 2, ⊠ 13, ⟐ 222 47 90 – ▥ ⌂wc ☎. 🆎 Ⓞ VISA.
❄️   LX **k**
Com 500/650 – � 150 – **50 hab** 1 500/2 000 – P 2 160/2 660.

🏨 **Alexandra** sin rest, San Bernardo 29, ⊠ 8, ⟐ 242 04 00 – ⧄ ▥ ⌂wc ▥wc ☎. ❄️   KV **z**
� 130 – **69 hab** 1 570/2 540.

🏠 **Lar** sin rest, Valverde 14, 🖂 13, ☏ 221 65 92 – 🛗 🏭 🗏 📶wc 📺 ⇦. 🖭 ⓞ 🇪 𝙑𝙄𝙎𝘼. 🍴
⚱ 160 – **80 hab** 1 600/2 400. LX **w**

🏠 **Anaco** sin rest, Tres Cruces 3, 🖂 13, ☏ 222 46 04 – 🛗 🏭 🗏 📶wc 📶wc 📺. 🖭 ⓞ 🇪 𝙑𝙄𝙎𝘼. 🍴
⚱ 170 – **37 hab** 1 975/3 400. LY **a**

🏠 **Fontela** piso 2°, sin rest, Gran Via 11, 🖂 14, ☏ 221 64 00 – 🛗 🏭 🗏 📶wc 📶 📺. 🖭 🇪.
⚱ 120 – **64 hab** 1 120/1 685. LX **u**

🏠 **California** piso 1°, sin rest, Gran Via 38, 🖂 13, ☏ 222 47 02 – 🛗 🏭 📶wc 📶wc 📺. 🖭 🇪 𝙑𝙄𝙎𝘼
⚱ 145 – **27 hab** 1 425/2 360. LX **e**

🏠 **Amberes** piso 7°, sin rest, Gran Via 68, 🖂 13, ☏ 247 61 00 – 🛗 🏭 📶wc 📺. 🖭 ⓞ 𝙑𝙄𝙎𝘼. 🍴
⚱ 140 – **48 hab** 1 900/2 300. KX **x**

🏠 **Galicia** piso 4°, sin rest, Valverde 1, 🖂 13, ☏ 222 10 13 – 🛗 🏭 📶wc 📺. 🇪 𝙑𝙄𝙎𝘼. 🍴
⚱ 250 – **39 hab** 1 400/2 800. LX **s**

🏠 **Santander** sin rest, Echegaray 1, 🖂 14, ☏ 429 95 51 – 🛗 🏭 📶wc 📺
⚱ 130 – **38 hab** 1 500/2 200. LY **z**

🏠 **Persal** piso 1°, sin rest, pl. del Angel 12, 🖂 12, ☏ 230 31 08 – 🛗 🏭 📶wc 📺. 🖭 𝙑𝙄𝙎𝘼. 🍴
⚱ 160 – **80 hab** 1 600/2 000. LZ **e**

🏠 **Lisboa** sin rest y sin ⚱, Ventura de la Vega 17, 🖂 14, ☏ 429 46 76 – 🛗 🏭 📶wc 📶wc 📺
25 hab 635/2 760. LZ **v**

Restaurantes de lujo.

XXXX ✿✿ **Jockey**, Amador de los Ríos 6, 🖂 4, ☏ 419 24 35, « Decoración elegante » – 🍽. 🖭 ⓞ
𝙑𝙄𝙎𝘼. 🍴 NV **k**
cerrado domingos y agosto – Com carta 2 200 a 3 200
Espec. Tuétano y trufa en bollo de leche, Anguila ahumada del Tajo al basílico, Pato deshuesado macerado con
higos al vino añejo.

XXXX ✿✿ **Horcher**, Alfonso XII - 6, 🖂 14, ☏ 222 07 31, « Decoración clásica elegante » – 🍽. 🍴
cerrado domingos – Com carta 2 495 a 4 175 NY **n**
Espec. Macedonia de pescado, Emince de ternera al estragón, Becada flambeada.

Restaurantes clásicos o modernos.

XXX **Clara's**, Arrieta 2, 🖂 13, ☏ 242 09 45, « Decoración elegante » – 🍽 𝙑𝙄𝙎𝘼. 🍴 KY **s**
cerrado domingos y festivos – Com carta 1 800 a 2 930.

XXX ✿ **Club 31**, Alcalá 58, 🖂 14, ☏ 231 00 92, Decoración moderna – 🍽. 🖭 ⓞ 𝙑𝙄𝙎𝘼. 🍴 NX **e**
cerrado agosto – Com carta 1 300 a 2 275.

XXX **Korynto**, Preciados 36, 🖂 13, ☏ 221 59 65, Pescados y mariscos – 🍽. 🖭 ⓞ 🇪 𝙑𝙄𝙎𝘼. 🍴
Com carta 1 425 a 2 300. KX **a**

XXX **Bajamar**, Gran Via 78, 🖂 13, ☏ 248 48 18, Telex 22818, Pescados y mariscos – 🍽. 🖭 ⓞ 🇪
𝙑𝙄𝙎𝘼. 🍴 KV **r**
Com carta 1 950 a 3 070

XXX **El Escuadrón**, Tamayo y Baus 8, 🖂 4, ☏ 419 28 30 – 🍽. 🖭 ⓞ 🇪 𝙑𝙄𝙎𝘼. 🍴 NV **s**
Com carta 1 500 a 2 400.

XXX **Luis XIII**, carrera de San Jerónimo 29, 🖂 14, ☏ 429 81 04, Cocina francesa – 🍽. 🖭 ⓞ 𝙑𝙄𝙎𝘼.
🍴 – *cerrado domingos y agosto* – Com carta 1 200 a 2 300 MY **d**

XXX **Medinaceli**, calle del Prado 27, 🖂 14, ☏ 429 13 92 – 🍽. 🖭 𝙑𝙄𝙎𝘼. 🍴 MZ **m**
cerrado domingos – Com carta 1 700 a 2 850.

XXX Pinto, Montalbán 9, 🖂 14, ☏ 231 75 45 – 🍽 NY **a**

XX **Las Reses**, Orfila 3, 🖂 4, ☏ 419 33 15, Carnes – 🍽. 🖭 𝙑𝙄𝙎𝘼. 🍴 NV **e**
cerrado domingos, festivos y agosto – Com carta 1 220 a 2 000.

XX **El Espejo**, paseo de Recoletos 31, 🖂 4, ☏ 410 25 25, « Evocación de un antiguo café
parisino » – 🍽. 🖭 ⓞ 🇪 𝙑𝙄𝙎𝘼. 🍴 NY **a**
cerrado sábados mediodía y domingos – Com carta 1 335 a 2 275.

XX El Barón, Recoletos 1, 🖂 1, ☏ 275 00 47, Carnes a la parrilla – 🍽 NVX **s**

XX **Platerías**, pl. de Santa Ana 11, 🖂 12, ☏ 429 70 48, Evocación de un café de principio de
siglo 🍽. 🍴 LZ **b**
cerrado domingos y agosto – Com (es necesario reservar) carta 1 230 a 1 980.

XX **La Grillade**, Jardines 3, 🖂 13, ☏ 221 22 17 – 🍽. 🖭 ⓞ 🇪 𝙑𝙄𝙎𝘼. 🍴 LY **p**
Com carta 855 a 1 590.

XX **Valentín**, piso 1°, San Alberto 3, 🖂 13, ☏ 221 16 38 – 🍽. 🖭 ⓞ 🇪 𝙑𝙄𝙎𝘼. 🍴 LY **h**
Com carta 1 305 a 2 455.

XX **Baviera**, Alcalá 33, 🖂 14, ☏ 221 55 39 – 🍽. 🖭 ⓞ 🇪 𝙑𝙄𝙎𝘼. 🍴 LY **v**
Com carta 1 350 a 2 125.

XX Kweilin, Manuela Malasaña 5, 🖂 10, ☏ 446 58 88, Cocina china 🍽 LV **u**

XX **Yakarta** piso 1°, General Castaño 15, 🖂 4, ☏ 419 04 39 – 🍽 ℗. 🖭 ⓞ 🇪 𝙑𝙄𝙎𝘼. 🍴 NV **b**
cerrado domingos – Com carta 1 100 a 2 075.

XX **Horno de Santa Teresa**, Santa Teresa 12, 🖂 4, ☏ 419 02 45 – 🍽. 🍴 MV **t**
cerrado sábados, domingos y agosto – Com carta 1 820 a 2 410.

XX **Moaña**, Hileras 4, 🖂 13, ☏ 248 29 14, Cocina gallega – 🍽 ℗. ⓞ 𝙑𝙄𝙎𝘼. 🍴 KY **r**
cerrado domingos y 10 agosto-15 septiembre – Com carta 1 125 a 2 500.

XX **Casablanca,** Barquillo 29, ✉ 4, ☎ 221 15 68 – ▤. 𝐀𝐄 ① 𝑽𝑰𝑺𝑨   MV s
cerrado lunes y 14 agosto-15 septiembre – Com carta 1 500 a 2 150.

XX **Trabuco,** Mesonero Romanos 19, ✉ 13, ☎ 231 01 25 – ▤. 𝐀𝐄 ① E 𝑽𝑰𝑺𝑨   LX t
cerrado domingos noche – Com carta 1 305 a 2 190.

XX **La Rioja,** Las Negras 8, ✉ 8, ☎ 248 06 68, Decoración rústica – ▤. 𝐀𝐄 ① E 𝑽𝑰𝑺𝑨   KV e
cerrado domingos – Com carta 1 400 a 1 500.

XX **Kulixka,** Fuencarral 124, ✉ 10, ☎ 447 25 38, Pescados y mariscos – ▤ 𝐏. 𝐀𝐄 ① 𝑽𝑰𝑺𝑨. 𝕊𝕩   LV a
cerrado 15 agosto-14 septiembre – Com carta 1 700 a 3 100.

XX **La Toja,** Siete de Julio 3, ✉ 12, ☎ 266 46 64, Cocina gallega – ▤. ① 𝑽𝑰𝑺𝑨. 𝕊𝕩   KY u
cerrado 15 julio-15 agosto – Com carta 1 525 a 2 750.

XX **Casa Gallega,** Bordadores 11, ✉ 13, ☎ 241 90 55, Cocina gallega – ▤. 𝐀𝐄 𝑽𝑰𝑺𝑨. 𝕊𝕩   KY v
Com carta 1 125 a 2 050.

XX **Pazo de Gondomar,** San Martín 2, ✉ 13, ☎ 232 31 63, Cocina gallega – ▤. 𝐀𝐄 ① E 𝑽𝑰𝑺𝑨
KY n
Com carta 900 a 1 730.

XX **El Caldero,** Huertas 15, ✉ 12, ☎ 429 50 44 – ▤. 𝐀𝐄 ① E 𝑽𝑰𝑺𝑨. 𝕊𝕩   LZ a
cerrado domingos, lunes noche y 15 agosto-15 septiembre – Com carta 855 a 1 640.

XX ✿ **Gure-Etxea,** pl. de la Paja 12, ✉ 5, ☎ 265 61 49, Cocina vasca – ▤. ① 𝑽𝑰𝑺𝑨. 𝕊𝕩   KZ x
cerrado domingos y agosto – Com carta 1 500 a 2 535
Espec. Bacalao al pil-pil, Merluza Gure-Etxea, Xangurro a la donostiarra.

XX **Le Chateaubriand,** Virgen de los Peligros 1, ✉ 14, ☎ 232 33 41, Decoración inspirada de
los clásicos Bistro franceses, Carnes – ▤. 𝕊𝕩   LY s
cerrado domingos – Com carta 975 a 1 505.

XX **Zarauz,** Fuentes 13, ✉ 13, ☎ 247 30 66, Cocina vasca – ▤. 𝐀𝐄 ① E 𝑽𝑰𝑺𝑨. 𝕊𝕩   KY b
cerrado domingos noche, lunes y 15 julio-10 septiembre – Com carta 900 a 1 275.

XX **Torolla,** Amador de los Ríos 8, ✉ 4, ☎ 410 28 88, Cocina gallega – ▤. ① 𝑽𝑰𝑺𝑨. 𝕊𝕩   NV k
cerrado domingos – Com carta 725 a 1 500.

XX **El Buda Feliz,** Tudescos 5, ✉ 13, ☎ 232 44 75, Cocina china – ▤. 𝐀𝐄 ① E 𝑽𝑰𝑺𝑨. 𝕊𝕩   KX t

XX **Pipo,** Augusto Figueroa 37, ✉ 4, ☎ 221 71 18 – ▤. E 𝑽𝑰𝑺𝑨. 𝕊𝕩   MX c
cerrado domingos y agosto – Com carta 725 a 1 400.

XX **La Lechuza,** Alberto Aguilera 26, ✉ 15, ☎ 447 36 13 – ▤   KV b
cerrado domingos noche – Com carta 800 a 1 650.

XX **Solchaga** en entresuelo, pl. Alonso Martínez 2, ✉ 4, ☎ 447 14 96 – ▤. 𝐀𝐄 ① E 𝑽𝑰𝑺𝑨. 𝕊𝕩   MV x
cerrado sábados mediodía y domingos – Com carta 1 150 a 2 170.

XX Pepe Botella, San Andrés 12, ✉ 10, ☎ 222 52 78, Cocina francesa – ▤   LV b

X Pazo de Monterrey, Alcalá 4, ✉ 14, ☎ 232 82 80, Cocina gallega – ▤   LY c

X Casa Lucio, Cava Baja 35, ✉ 5, ☎ 265 32 52, Decoración castellana – ▤   KZ y

X **Gran Tasca,** Ballesta 1, ✉ 13, ☎ 231 00 44 – 𝐀𝐄 ① E 𝑽𝑰𝑺𝑨. 𝕊𝕩   LX x
cerrado domingos y julio-1 septiembre – Com carta 975 a 1 800.

X **Tropezón,** Toledo 78, ✉ 5, ☎ 266 77 39 – ▤. 𝑽𝑰𝑺𝑨. 𝕊𝕩   KZ b
cerrado domingos – Com carta 1 325 a 2 300.

X Berrio, costanilla de los Capuchinos 4, ✉ 4, ☎ 221 20 35 – ▤   LX n

X **El Schotis,** Cava Baja 11, ✉ 5, ☎ 265 32 30 – ▤. 𝕊𝕩   KZ v
cerrado domingos, festivos noche y agosto – Com carta 1 300 a 2 100.

X Guria, Huertas 12, ✉ 12, ☎ 239 16 36, Cocina vasca – ▤   LZ x

X Esteban 2, Humilladero 4, ✉ 5, ☎ 266 93 91 – ▤   KZ c

X **Hostería Piamontesa,** costanilla de los Angeles 18, ✉ 13, ☎ 248 34 14, Cocina italiana –
▤. 𝐀𝐄 ① E 𝑽𝑰𝑺𝑨   KX g
cerrado lunes no festivos y agosto – Com carta 820 a 1 225.

X La Mesa de Mio Cid, Bola 8, ✉ 13, ☎ 242 51 47 – ▤   KX w

X La Quintana, Bordadores 7, ✉ 13, ☎ 242 04 88 – ▤   KY v

X **Aroca,** pl. de los Carros 3, ✉ 5, ☎ 265 26 26 – 𝕊𝕩   KZ e
cerrado domingos y 25 julio-5 septiembre – Com carta 730 a 1 475.

X **Casa Paco,** Puerta Cerrada 11, ✉ 5, ☎ 266 31 66 – ▤. ① 𝑽𝑰𝑺𝑨. 𝕊𝕩   KZ s
cerrado domingos y agosto – Com carta 1 300 a 2 200.

X **Hogar Gallego,** pl. Comandante Las Morenas 3, ✉ 13, ☎ 248 64 04, Cocina gallega – ▤.
𝕊𝕩   KY d
cerrado domingos noche y agosto – Com carta 860 a 1 780.

X Salvador, Barbieri 12, ✉ 4, ☎ 221 45 24, Cuadros y fotos del mundo taurino – ▤   MX b

X **Los Galayos,** Botoneras 5, ✉ 12, ☎ 201 79 33 – ▤. 𝐀𝐄 𝑽𝑰𝑺𝑨. 𝕊𝕩   KZ r
Com carta 1 120 a 1 895.

X Maitetxu Asador, Almirante 2, ✉ 4, ☎ 231 01 09 – ▤   MX u

X **Casa Valdés,** Libertad 3, ✉ 4, ☎ 232 20 52 – ▤. 𝑽𝑰𝑺𝑨. 𝕊𝕩   MX f
cerrado miércoles y domingos noche – Com carta 1 000 a 1 300.

X El Pajar, Luna 15, ✉ 13, ☎ 222 48 01 – ▤   KX u

X La Argentina, Gravina 18, ✉ 4, ☎ 221 37 63 – ▤   MX d

X Le Bistroquet, Conde 4, ⊠ 12, ☎ 247 10 75, Cocina francesa – 🍽 KZ **d**

X Lucas'o, Cava Baja 38, ⊠ 5, ☎ 266 16 14 – 🍽 KZ **y**

X **Quinta del Sordo,** Sacramento 10, ⊠ 12, ☎ 248 18 52 – ✻ KZ **f**
   cerrado domingos noche – Com carta 690 a 1 300.

X Mesón del Conde, Pelayo 82, ⊠ 4, ☎ 419 10 82 – 🍽 MV **b**

X **Mi Pueblo,** Costanilla de Santiago 2, ⊠ 13, ☎ 248 20 73 – 🍽. ✻ KY **x**
   cerrado domingos noche y lunes – Com carta 700 a 1 245.

X Casa Gades, Conde de Xiquena 4, ⊠ 4, ☎ 232 30 51, Cocina italiana – 🍽 NX **m**

X **Alejandro,** Mesonero Romanos 7, ⊠ 13, ☎ 231 51 04 – 🍽 LX **r**
   cerrado domingos – Com carta 760 a 1 385.

X Villa de Luarca, Concepción Arenal 6, ⊠ 13, ☎ 231 91 89 – 🍽 LX **e**

X **Ingenio,** Leganitos 10, ⊠ 13, ☎ 247 35 34 – 🍽. ⁂ ⓪ ⋿ 𝘝𝘐𝘚𝘈. ✻ KX **y**
   Com carta 695 a 1 350.

Ambiente típico.

XXX **Café de Chinitas,** Torija 7, ⊠ 13, ☎ 248 51 35, Tablao flamenco – 🍽. ⁂ ⋿. ✻ KX **p**
   cerrado domingos, Jueves Santo, Viernes Santo y 24 diciembre – Com (sólo cena) carta 2 150
   a 3 100 (suplemento espectáculo 1 350).

XX **Sixto Gran Mesón** piso 1°, Cervantes 28, ⊠ 14, ☎ 429 22 55, Decoración castellana – 🍽.
   ⁂ ⓪ ⋿ 𝘝𝘐𝘚𝘈. ✻ MZ **n**
   cerrado domingos noche – Com carta 1 250 a 1 800.

XX **Botín,** Cuchilleros 17, ⊠ 12, ☎ 266 42 17, Decoración viejo Madrid, bodega típica 🍽. ⁂
   ⓪ ⋿ 𝘝𝘐𝘚𝘈 KZ **n**
   cerrado 24 diciembre noche – Com carta 1 140 a 1 695.

XX **Al Mounia,** Recoletos 5, ⊠ 1, ☎ 435 08 28, « Ambiente oriental », Cocina maghrebi – 🍽.
   ⁂ ⓪. ✻ NX **s**
   cerrado domingos mediodía, lunes y 2 agosto-2 septiembre – Com carta 1 300 a 1 990.

XX Corral de la Morería, Morería 17, ⊠ 5, ☎ 265 84 46, Tablao flamenco – 🍽 KZ **u**

XX **Las Cuevas de Luis Candelas,** Cuchilleros 1, ⊠ 12, ☎ 266 54 28, Decoración viejo Madrid
   - Camareros vestidos como los antiguos bandoleros – 🍽. ⁂ ⓪ ⋿ 𝘝𝘐𝘚𝘈. ✻ KZ **m**
   Com carta 1 480 a 2 225.

XX Fado, pl. San Martin 2, ⊠ 13, ☎ 231 89 24, Cocina portuguesa, Fados – 🍽 KY **k**

X **Taberna del Alabardero,** Felipe V - 6, ⊠ 13, ☎ 241 51 92, Taberna típica – 🍽. ⁂ ⓪ ⋿
   𝘝𝘐𝘚𝘈. ✻ KY **h**
   Com carta 1 350 a 2 500.

X **El Cosaco,** Alfonso VI - 4, ⊠ 5, ☎ 265 35 48, Rest. ruso – ⁂ KZ **z**
   cerrado mediodía excepto domingos y festivos – Com carta 590 a 1 030.

X Esteban, Cava Baja 36, ⊠ 5, ☎ 265 90 91, Decoración viejo Madrid – 🍽 KZ **y**

Cafeterías, Restaurantes rápidos.

XX **Manila,** Montera 25, ⊠ 14, ☎ 232 47 09 – 🍽. ⁂ ⓪ ⋿ 𝘝𝘐𝘚𝘈. ✻ LY **n**
   Com carta 955 a 1 740.

XX **Nebraska** piso 1°, Mayor 1, ⊠ 13, ☎ 404 68 50 – 🍽. ⁂ ⓪ ⋿ 𝘝𝘐𝘚𝘈. ✻ LY **y**
   Com aprox. 500.

XX **Zahara,** Gran Vía 31, ⊠ 13, ☎ 221 84 24 – 🍽. ⁂ ⓪ ⋿ 𝘝𝘐𝘚𝘈. ✻ LX **a**
   Com carta 920 a 1 220.

XX **Nebraska,** Gran Vía 55, ⊠ 13, ☎ 247 16 35 – 🍽. ⓪ ⋿ 𝘝𝘐𝘚𝘈. ✻ KX **n**
   Com aprox. 500.

XX **Riofrío,** pl. Colón 1, ⊠ 4, ☎ 419 29 77 – 🍽 ✻ NV **z**
   Com carta 1 330 a 2 120.

XX **Vips,** Princesa 5, ⊠ 26, ☎ 241 16 22 – 🍽. ⁂ ⓪ ⋿ 𝘝𝘐𝘚𝘈. ✻ KV **a**
   Com carta 695 a 1 295.

XX **Manila,** Gran Vía 41, ⊠ 13, ☎ 221 71 37 – 🍽. ⁂ ⓪ ⋿ 𝘝𝘐𝘚𝘈. ✻ KX **c**
   Com carta 955 a 1 740.

XX **Nebraska,** Gran Vía 32, ⊠ 13, ☎ 222 63 08 – 🍽. ⓪ ⋿ 𝘝𝘐𝘚𝘈. ✻ LX **v**
   Com aprox 500.

X **Manila,** Génova 21, ⊠ 4, ☎ 419 38 96 – 🍽. ⁂ ⓪ ⋿ 𝘝𝘐𝘚𝘈. ✻ NV **d**
   Com carta 955 a 1 740.

X **Nebraska,** Alcalá 18, ⊠ 14, ☎ 221 19 27 – 🍽. ⓪ ⋿ 𝘝𝘐𝘚𝘈. ✻ LY **b**
   Com aprox. 500.

X **California,** Gran Vía 49, ⊠ 13, ☎ 247 27 30 – 🍽. ⓪ ⋿ 𝘝𝘐𝘚𝘈. ✻ KX **z**
   Com carta 950 a 1 770.

X **Manila** piso 1°, Goya 5, ⊠ 1, ☎ 275 38 68 – 🍽. ⁂ ⓪ ⋿ 𝘝𝘐𝘚𝘈. ✻ NV **m**
   Com carta 955 a 1 740.

X **California 39,** Gran Vía 39, ⊠ 13, ☎ 232 35 72 – 🍽. ⓪ ⋿ 𝘝𝘐𝘚𝘈. ✻ KX **s**
   Com carta 950 a 1 770.

X **California,** Salud 21, ⊠ 13, ☎ 222 61 60 – 🍽. ⓪ ⋿ 𝘝𝘐𝘚𝘈. ✻ LX **q**
   Com carta 950 a 1 770.

Fuera del Centro : Paseo de la Castellana, El Retiro, Plaza República Argentina, Plaza de Manuel Becerra, Ciudad Universitaria, Casa de Campo, Estación de Atocha (planos p. 2 a 7).

🏨 **Eurobuilding** Ⓜ, Padre Damián 23, ✉ 16, ☏ 457 17 00, Telex 22548, « Bonito jardín con ⊒ »
– 🗏 🚗 – 🛦. 🝙 ⓘ 🖃 *VISA*. ⬥
Com (ver **Rest. Balthasar y La Taberna**) – ⌲ 400 – **555 hab** 6 820/8 480.
HS **a**

🏨 **Miguel Angel** Ⓜ, Miguel Angel 31, ✉ 10, ☏ 442 00 22, Telex 44235, 🔳 – 🗏 🚗 🛦. 🝙 ⓘ 🖃
VISA. ⬥
Com 2 000 – ⌲ 425 – **305 hab** 7 200/9 000 – P 8 200/10 900.
GV **c**

🏨 **Mindanao,** paseo San Francisco de Sales 15, ✉ 3, ☏ 449 55 00, Telex 22631, ⊒, 🔳 – 🗏
– 🝙 ⓟ – 🛦. 🝙 ⓘ 🖃 ⬥
Com 1 700 – ⌲ 350 – **300 hab** 5 600/7 000 – P 6 500/8 600.
DV **a**

🏨 **Mélia Castilla** Ⓜ, Capitán Haya 43, ✉ 20, ☏ 270 80 00, Telex 23142, ⊒ – 🗏 – 🛦. 🝙 🖃
VISA. ⬥
Com 1 975 – ⌲ 450 – **1 000 hab** 8 280.
GS **c**

🏨 **Wellington,** Velázquez 8, ✉ 1, ☏ 275 44 00, Telex 22700, ⊒ – 🗏 🚗 🛦. 🝙 ⓘ 🖃 *VISA*. ⬥
Com (ver **Rest. Fogón**) – ⌲ 325 – **261 hab** 4 200/6 700.
HX **t**

🏨 **Princesa Plaza** Ⓜ, Princesa 40, ✉ 8, ☏ 242 21 00, Telex 44378 – 🗏 – 🛦. 🝙 ⓘ 🖃 *VISA*. ⬥
Com 2 100 – ⌲ 450 – **406 hab** 6 400/7 990.
KV **c**

🏨 **Luz Palacio,** paseo de la Castellana 57, ✉ 1, ☏ 442·51 00, Telex 27207 – 🗏 🚗 – 🛦. 🝙
ⓘ 🖃 *VISA*. ⬥
Com 1 800 – ⌲ 380 – **182 hab** 5 500/8 000 – P 7 380/8 880.
GV **p**

🏨 **Castellana** sin rest, con cafetería, paseo de la Castellana 49, ✉ 1, ☏ 410 02 00, Telex 27686
– 🗏 🚗 – 🛦. 🝙 ⓘ 🖃 *VISA*
⌲ 295 – **281 hab** 4 510/5 650.
GV **a**

🏨 **Convención** sin rest, con cafetería, O'Donnell 53, ✉ 9, ☏ 274 68 00, Telex 23944 – 🗏 🚗 –
🛦.
790 hab.
JX **a**

🏨 **Cuzco** sin rest, con cafetería, paseo de la Castellana 133, ✉ 16, ☏ 456 06 00, Telex 22464 –
🗏 ⓟ – 🛦. 🝙 ⓘ 🖃 *VISA*. ⬥
⌲ 250 – **330 hab** 4 150/5 400.
GS **a**

🏨 **Los Galgos y Rest. La Almoraima,** Claudio Coello 139, ✉ 6, ☏ 262 42 27, Telex 43957 –
🗏 🚗 – 🛦. 🝙 🖃 *VISA*
Com 1 200 – ⌲ 380 – **361 hab** 3 280/5 640 – P 4 720/5 120.
HV **a**

🏨 **Florida Norte** Ⓜ, paseo de la Florida 5, ✉ 8, ☏ 241 61 90, Telex 23675 – 🗏 🚗 – 🛦. 🝙 ⓘ
VISA. ⬥ rest
Com 850 – ⌲ 200 – **399 hab** 2 500/3 600 – P 3 500/4 400.
DX **v**

🏨 **G. H. Colón,** av. Doctor Esquerdo 119, ✉ 30, ☏ 273 08 00, Telex 22984, ⊒, 🚋 – 🗏 🚗 –
🛦. 🝙 ⓘ 🖃 ⬥ rest
Com 1 000 – ⌲ 185 – **389 hab** 2 350/3 430 – P 3 900/4 535.
JY **x**

🏨 **Escultor,** Miguel Angel 3, ✉ 10, ☏ 410 42 03, Telex 44285 – 🗏 🚗 🛦. 🝙 ⓘ 🖃 *VISA*. ⬥ rest
Com 1 000/2 500 – ⌲ 325 – **82 apartamentos** 3 700/5 900.
GV **s**

🏨 **El Gran Atlanta** Ⓜ sin rest, con cafetería, Comandante Zorita 34, ✉ 20, ☏ 253 59 00, ⊒,
🗏 🚗 – 🛦. 🝙 ⓘ 🖃 *VISA*
⌲ 250 – **180 hab** 2 800/4 000.
FT **p**

🏨 **Pintor** sin rest, con cafetería, Goya 79, ✉ 1, ☏ 435 75 45, Telex 23281 – 🗏 🚗 🛦. ⬥
⌲ 250 – **176 hab** 2 950/4 250.
HX **c**

🏨 **Emperatriz,** López de Hoyos 4, ✉ 6, ☏ 413 65 11, Telex 43640 – 🗏 🝙 ⓘ 🖃 *VISA*. ⬥
Com 925 – ⌲ 240 – **170 hab** 3 030/4 925.
GV **a**

🏨 **Príncipe Pío,** cuesta de San Vicente 16, ✉ 8, ☏ 247 80 00, Telex 42183 – 🗏
157 hab.
KX **d**

🏨 **Alcalá y Rest. Basque,** Alcalá 66, ✉ 9, ☏ 435 16 50 – 🗏 🚗 🝙 🖃 *VISA*. ⬥
Com *(cerrado domingos)* 1 450 – ⌲ 250 – **153 hab** 2 600/4 250.
HX **w**

🏨 **Agumar** sin rest, con cafetería, paseo Reina Cristina 9, ✉ 7, ☏ 52 69 00, Telex 22814 – 🗏
🚗 – 🛦. 🝙 ⓘ 🖃 *VISA*. ⬥
⌲ 230 – **252 hab** 2 510/3 550.
HZ **a**

🏨 **Carlton,** paseo de las Delicias 26, ✉ 7, ☏ 239 71 00 – 🗏. 🝙 ⓘ *VISA*. ⬥
Com 1 000 – ⌲ 225 – **133 hab** 1 960/3 200 – P 3 490/3 860.
GZ **n**

🏨 **Centro Norte** sin rest, Mauricio Ravel 10, ✉ 16, ☏ 733 34 00, Telex 42598, ⊒, 🚋 – 🗏
🚗 – 🛦. 🝙 ⓘ *VISA*. ⬥
⌲ 200 – **202 hab** 2 700/3 525.
HR **b**

🏨 **Aitana** sin rest, con cafetería, paseo de la Castellana 42, ✉ 16, ☏ 250 71 07 – 🗏
111 hab.
GT **c**

🏨 **Aramo** sin rest, con cafetería, paseo Santa Maria de la Cabeza 73, ✉ 5, ☏ 473 91 11, Telex
45885 – 🗏 🚗. 🝙 ⓘ 🖃 *VISA*
⌲ 200 – **105 hab** 2 075/3 400.
BM **e**

🏨 **Sace** sin rest, con cafetería, José Abascal 8, ✉ 3, ☏ 447 40 00 – 🗏. 🝙 ⓘ 🖃 *VISA*. ⬥
⌲ 200 – **72 hab** 2 300/3 980.
FV **a**

🏨 **Serrano** sin rest, Marqués de Villamejor 8, ✉ 6, ☏ 435 52 00 – 🗏. 🝙 ⓘ 🖃 *VISA*. ⬥
⌲ 250 – **34 hab** 3 280/4 100.
HV **b**

🏨 **Puerta de Toledo,** glorieta Puerta de Toledo 2, ⊠ 5, ☏ 4/4 /1 00, Telex 22291 – 🖳 🚗. 🖭
 E 🎫 EZ **v**
 Com (ver **Rest. Urvi**) – 🍽 150 – **152 hab** 1 750/3 200.

🏨 **Bretón** sin rest, con cafetería, Bretón de los Herreros 29, ⊠ 3, ☏ 442 83 00 – 🖳. 🖭 ⓪ **E**
 🎫. 🛎 FV **n**
 🍽 210 – **57 hab** 2 360/3 865.

🏨 **Claridge** sin rest, con cafetería, pl. del Conde de Casal 6, ⊠ 30, ☏ 251 94 00 – 🛗 🖳 🛁wc
 🛢wc 🐾 🚗 JZ **a**
 150 hab.

🏨 **Abeda** sin rest, Alcántara 63, ⊠ 6, ☏ 401 16 50 – 🛗 🚿 🖳 🛁wc 🐾 🚗. **E** 🎫. 🛎 HV **r**
 🍽 150 – **90 hab.**

🏨 **Conde Duque** sin rest, con cafetería, pl. Conde Valle de Suchil 5, ⊠ 15, ☏ 447 70 00, Telex
 22058 – 🛗 🚿 🛁wc 🐾. 🖭 ⓪ **E** 🎫. 🛎 EV **d**
 🍽 170 – **138 hab** 1 680/2 500.

🏨 **Zurbano,** Zurbano 79, ⊠ 3, ☏ 441 55 00, Telex 27578 – 🛗 🚿 🖳 🛁wc 🐾 🚗. 🖭 **E** 🎫
 🛎 rest GV **x**
 Com 900 🍽 200 – **261 hab** 3 000/5 700 – P 3 500/4 500.

🏨 **Tirol** sin rest, con cafetería, Marqués de Urquijo 4, ⊠ 8, ☏ 248 19 00 – 🛗 🚿 🖳 🛁wc 🐾
 🚗. 🎫. 🛎 DV **r**
 🍽 140 – **93 hab** 1 800/2 640.

🏨 **Aristos** sin rest, con cafetería, av. Pío XII-34, ⊠ 16, ☏ 457 04 50 – 🛗 🚿 🖳 🛁wc 🐾. ⓪. 🛎 HS **d**
 🍽 160 – **25 hab** 2 105/3 490.

🏨 **Trafalgar** sin rest, Trafalgar 35, ⊠ 10, ☏ 445 62 00 – 🛗 🖳 🛁wc 🛢wc 🐾. 🖭 🎫. 🛎 FV **s**
 🍽 110 – **45 hab** 1 600/2 750.

🏨 **Don Diego** piso 5°, sin rest, Velázquez 45, ⊠ 1, ☏ 435 07 60 – 🛗 🚿 🖳 🛁wc 🐾. 🛎 HX **x**
 🍽 180 – **58 hab** 1 900/2 700.

🏠 **Baltimore** sin rest y sin 🍽, Bravo Murillo 160, ⊠ 20, ☏ 234 80 00 – 🛗 🚿 🖳 🛁wc 🛢wc 🐾. 🛎
 25 hab 1 380/2 050. FT **m**

🏢 **Riomiera** sin rest, Antonio López 168, ⊠ 26, ☏ 476 32 11 – 🛗 🚿 🚗 🚗. 🛎 BM **s**
 🍽 125 – **54 hab** 950/1 300.

Restaurantes de lujo.

XXXXX ❀❀ **Zalacaín,** Álvarez de Baena 4, ⊠ 6, ☏ 261 48 40, « Decoración elegante » – 🖳 🚗. 🛎
 cerrado sábados mediodía, domingos y 30 julio-1 septiembre – Com carta 2 225 a 4 025.
 GV **b**

XXXX ❀ **Balthasar,** Juan Ramón Jiménez 8, ⊠ 16, ☏ 457 91 91, « Elegante decoración clásica » –
 🖳. 🛎 HS **a**
 cerrado domingos y agosto-1 septiembre – Com carta 1 950 a 3 150
 Espec. Crepes de cangrejo "Americana", Carre de cordero a la mostaza, Mero al horno con caracoles.

XXXX ❀ **O'Pazo,** Reina Mercedes 20, ⊠ 20, ☏ 234 37 48, Cocina gallega, « Bonita decoración » –
 🖳 🖭 ⓪ **E** 🎫 FT **p**
 cerrado sábados noche, domingos, festivos y agosto – Com carta 1 925 a 2 920.
 Espec. Merluza con vieiras "O Paziño", Lamprea guisada (septiembre-noviembre), Lacón con grelos (febrero-junio).

XXXX **Nuevo Valentín,** Concha Espina 8, ⊠ 16, ☏ 259 75 55 – 🖳. 🖭 ⓪ **E** 🎫. 🛎 GT **n**
 Com carta 1 305 a 2 455.

XXXX **Mayte Commodore,** pl. República Argentina 5, ⊠ 6, ☏ 261 86 06, « Decoración elegante » –
 🖳 HU **v**

XXXX **Comedor Ruperto de Nola** piso 22°, Corazón de María 2, ⊠ 2, ☏ 416 45 21, ⩽ Madrid y
 alrededores, Decoración moderna – 🖳. 🖭 ⓪ **E** 🎫. 🛎 HV **h**
 cerrado domingos y 24 julio-4 septiembre – Com carta 1 650 a 2 700.

XXXX **Valentín Castilla,** paseo de la Castellana 87, ⊠ 16, ☏ 270 39 47 – 🖳. 🖭 ⓪ **E** 🎫. 🛎 GS **n**
 cerrado domingos – Com carta 1 305 a 2 455.

XXXX ❀ **El Bodegón,** Pinar 15, ⊠ 16, ☏ 262 31 37, Decoración de estilo español – 🖳. 🖭 ⓪ **E**
 🎫. 🛎 GV **q**
 cerrado domingos y agosto – Com carta 2 000 a 3 000.
 Espec. Bisque de cangrejos de mar, Rodaballo de roca "Balmoral", Becada sobre canapé (noviembre-enero).

Restaurantes clásicos, modernos o típicos.

XXX **La Fragua,** José Ortega y Gasset 6, ⊠ 6, ☏ 276 40 33 – 🖳. 🖭 ⓪ **E** 🎫. 🛎 HV **z**
 Com carta 1 725 a 2 660.

XXX **Nicolasa,** Velázquez 150, ⊠ 2, ☏ 261 99 85 – 🖳. ⓪ **E** 🎫. 🛎 HU **a**
 cerrado domingos y agosto – Com carta 1 740 a 2 400.

XXX ❀ **El Amparo,** Puigcerdá 8, ⊠ 1, ☏ 431 64 56, Cocina vasca o francesa – 🖳. 🛎 HX **h**
 cerrado sábados mediodía, domingos, Semana Santa y agosto-5 septiembre – Com
 carta 2 100 a 3 300
 Espec. Pastel de verduras naturales, Hojaldre de mollejas con trufa fresca, Terrina de frutas a la mousse de
 almendra.

XXX **José Luis,** Rafael Salgado 11, ⊠ 16, ☏ 457 50 36 – 🖳. 🖭 ⓪ **E** 🎫. 🛎 GT **m**
 cerrado domingos y agosto – Com carta 1 425 a 2 650.

129

XXX **Breda,** paseo de la Castellana 78, ✉ 1, ☎ 261 11 58 – 🍴. 🜇 ⓪ ⋿ 💳. 🕭   GV **f**
Com carta 1 725 a 2 660.

XXX **Café Viena,** Luisa Fernanda 23, ✉ 8, ☎ 248 15 91, Cenas amenizadas al piano, « Evocación
de un antiguo café » – 🍴. 🜇 💳. 🕭   DX **s**
cerrada domingos y agosto – Com carta 1 475 a 2 550.

XXX La Boucade, Capitán Haya 30, ✉ 20, ☎ 456 02 45 – 🍴   GS **a**

XXX Bogavante, Capitán Haya 20, ✉ 20, ☎ 456 26 14 – 🍴   GT **d**

XXX **El Landó,** pl. Gabriel Miró 8, ✉ 5, ☎ 266 76 81, Decoración elegante – 🍴. 🜇 ⓪ 💳. 🕭
cerrado domingos y agosto-1 septiembre – Com carta 1 350 a 1 850.   KZ **a**

XXX ✿ **Príncipe de Viana,** Manuel de Falla 5, ✉ 16, ☎ 259 14 48, Cocina vasca – 🍴. 🕭   GT **c**
cerrado sábados mediodía, domingos y 20 julio-1 septiembre – Com carta 1 525 a 2 675.

XXX **El Circo,** Ortega y Gasset 29, ✉ 6, ☎ 276 01 44, Decoración moderna, cenas amenizadas al
piano – 🍴. 🜇 ⓪ ⋿ 💳. 🕭   HV **f**
Com carta 1 440 a 1 960.

XXX **La Taberna,** av. Alberto Alcocer 18, ✉ 16, ☎ 457 17 00 (ext. 9830) – 🍴. 🜇 ⓪ ⋿ 💳. 🕭
Com carta 1 425 a 2 500.   HS **a**

XXX **Señorío de Bertiz,** Comandante Zorita 6, ✉ 20, ☎ 233 27 57 – 🍴. 🜇 ⓪ 💳   FT **s**
cerrado sábados mediodía, domingos y agosto-1 septiembre – Com carta 1 300 a 2 200.

XXX Los Estribos, av. Alberto Alcocer 46 bis, ✉ 16, ☎ 259 46 66, Carnes a la brasa – 🍴   HS **c**

XXX **Villa y Corte de Madrid,** Serrano 110, ✉ 6, ☎ 261 29 77, Decoración elegante – 🍴. 🜇 ⓪
💳. 🕭   HV **a**
cerrado domingos – Com carta 1 895 a 2 790.

XXX **El Gran Chambelán,** Ayala 46, ✉ 1, ☎ 431 77 45 – 🍴. 🜇 ⓪ 💳. 🕭   HX **r**
cerrado domingos y 3 agosto-2 septiembre – Com carta 1 450 a 2 600.

XXX **Los Porches,** paseo Pintor Rosales 1, ✉ 8, ☎ 247 70 53, Rest. al aire libre – 🍴. 🜇 ⓪ ⋿
💳. 🕭   DX **z**
Com carta 1 305 a 2 455.

XXX Da Renzo, Pedro Muguruza 8, ✉ 16, ☎ 259 10 00, Cocina italiana – 🍴   HS **w**

XXX Hostal Mayte, Príncipe de Vergara 285, ✉ 16, ☎ 259 70 39 – 🍴   HS **e**

XX **Aymar,** Fuencarral 138, ✉ 10, ☎ 445 57 67, Pescados y mariscos – 🍴. 🜇 ⓪ ⋿ 💳. 🕭
Com carta 1 500 a 2 200.   FV **e**

XX El Buscón, Panamá 4, ✉ 16, ☎ 457 30 43 – 🍴   GT **r**

XX Pizzeria Paolo, General Rodrigo 3, ✉ 3, ☎ 254 44 28, Cocina italiana – 🍴 ⓟ   DUV **e**

XX **Gaztelupe,** Comandante Zorita 37, ✉ 20, ☎ 253 51 32, Cocina vasca – 🍴. 🜇 ⓪ 💳. 🕭   FT **a**
cerrado sábados mediodía y domingos – Com carta 1 925 a 2 975.

XX La Dorada, Orense 66, ✉ 20, ☎ 270 20 04, Pescados y mariscos – 🍴   GS **u**

XX **Caruso,** Serrano 70, ✉ 1, ☎ 435 52 62 – 🍴. 🜇 ⓪ 💳. 🕭   HVX **p**
cerrado domingos y festivos – Com carta 820 a 1 555.

XX **Horno de Don Carlos,** Fernández de la Hoz 80, ✉ 3, ☎ 234 38 52 – 🍴. ⓪ 💳. 🕭   GV **r**
cerrado agosto-1 septiembre – Com carta 1 400 a 2 100.

XX **Tattaglia,** paseo de la Habana 17, ✉ 18, ☎ 262 85 90, Cocina italiana – 🍴. 🜇 ⓪ ⋿ 💳. 🕭
Com carta 830 a 2 115.   GT **b**

XX **Parrillón,** Santa Engracia 41, ✉ 10, ☎ 446 02 25 – 🍴. ⓪ ⋿. 🕭   FV **b**
cerrado agosto – Com carta 1 415 a 2 500.

XX **Rugantino,** Velázquez 136, ✉ 6, ☎ 261 02 22, Cocina italiana – 🍴. 🜇 ⓪ ⋿ 💳. 🕭   HV **e**
Com carta 830 a 2 115.

XX **De Funy,** Serrano 213, ✉ 16, ☎ 259 72 25, Rest. libanés – 🍴. 🜇 ⓪ ⋿ 💳. 🕭   HT **z**
cerrado lunes – Com carta 1 275 a 2 025.

XX **Graciano,** Jorge Juan 69, ✉ 9, ☎ 226 60 11 – 🍴. 🜇 ⓪ ⋿ 💳. 🕭   HX **u**
Com carta 750 a 1 500.

XX La Fonda, Lagasca 11, ✉ 1, ☎ 403 83 07, Cocina catalana – 🍴   HX **f**

XX **Cabo Mayor,** Juan Hurtado de Mendoza 11 (posterior), ✉ 16, ☎ 250 87 76 – 🍴. 💳. 🕭
cerrado domingos y agosto – Com carta 1 550 a 2 900.   GHS **r**

XX El Fogón, Villanueva 34, ✉ 1, ☎ 275 44 00, « Estilo rústico español » – 🍴   HX **t**

XX El Invernadero, Jorge Juan 39, ✉ 1, ☎ 276 08 74 – 🍴   HX **m**

XX **House of Ming,** paseo de la Castellana 74, ✉ 1, ☎ 261 98 27, Rest. chino – 🍴. 🜇 ⓪ 💳.
🕭   GV **f**
Com carta 825 a 1 220.

XX Bombín, Rosario Pino 18, ✉ 20, ☎ 270 40 44 – 🍴   GS **d**

XX **La Prensa de Tirgo** con cafetería, av. de Brasil 7, ✉ 20, ☎ 455 08 73 – 🍴. 🜇 ⓪ ⋿ 💳. 🕭
Com carta 650 a 1 375.   GT **a**

XX **Combarro,** Reina Mercedes 12, ✉ 20, ☎ 254 77 84, Pescados y mariscos – 🍴. ⋿ 💳. 🕭   FT **r**
cerrado domingos noche y agosto – Com carta 815 a 1 545.

XX **Antonio,** Santa Engracia 54, ✉ 10, ☎ 447 40 68 – 🍴. ⋿ 💳. 🕭   FV **z**
cerrado lunes y agosto – Com 900.

XX Colony, Alberto Alcocer 43, ✉ 16, ☎ 250 64 99, Cocina francesa – 🍴   HS **v**

XX O'Toxo, Hernanl 60, ⊠ 20, ℡ 234 69 22, Cocina gallega – 🍽 FT s

XX **Jai-Alai,** Balbina Valverde 2, ⊠ 2, ℡ 261 27 42, Cocina vasca – 🍽. 🖭 ⓞ 🛒 𝗩𝗜𝗦𝗔 GU h
cerrado lunes y agosto – Com carta 1 000 a 1 600.

XX **Calycanto,** Velázquez 22, ⊠ 1, ℡ 403 08 11 – 🍽. 🖭 ⓞ 🛒 𝗩𝗜𝗦𝗔. ⋘ HX g
cerrado domingos y agosto – Com carta 1 250 a 2 525.

XX **Aldaba,** Alberto Alcocer 5, ⊠ 16, ℡ 457 21 93 – 🍽. 🖭 ⓞ 𝗩𝗜𝗦𝗔. ⋘ GS e
cerrado sábados mediodía, domingos, festivos y agosto – Com carta 1 050 a 2 075.

XX Sulú, paseo de la Castellana 58, ⊠ 16, ℡ 259 10 40, Rest. filipino – 🍽 GS e

XX **La Ribera del Ebro,** Capitán Haya 51, ⊠ 20, ℡ 279 20 80 – 🍽. 🖭 ⓞ 🛒 𝗩𝗜𝗦𝗔. GS s
Com carta 775 a 1 295.

XX **Ondarreta Felix** en sótano, Doctor Fleming 44, ⊠ 16, ℡ 457 09 88 – 🍽. 🖭 ⓞ 🛒 𝗩𝗜𝗦𝗔. ⋘
cerrado domingos y agosto – Com carta 1 050 a 2 250. GHS r

XX Guten, Orense 70, ⊠ 20, ℡ 270 36 22 – 🍽 GS z

XX **Prost,** Orense 6, ⊠ 20, ℡ 455 28 94 – 🍽. ⋘ FT c
cerrado domingos – Com carta 975 a 1 505.

XX La Mesta, Príncipe de Vergara 60, ⊠ 6, ℡ 226 74 56 – 🍽 HV s

XX **La Marmite,** pl. San Amaro 8, ⊠ 20, ℡ 279 92 61, Cocina francesa – 🍽. ⓞ 𝗩𝗜𝗦𝗔. ⋘ FT v
cerrado domingos y festivos – Com carta 1 200 a 2 100.

XX La Fonda, Príncipe de Vergara 211, ⊠ 13, ℡ 250 14 30, Cocina catalana – 🍽 HT e

XX Darío's, Comandante Zorita 37, ⊠ 20, ℡ 234 82 55, Pescados y mariscos – 🍽 FT a

XX **Fass,** Rodríguez Marín 84, ⊠ 2, ℡ 457 22 02, Cocina alemana – 🍽. 🖭 ⓞ 🛒 𝗩𝗜𝗦𝗔. ⋘ HT t
Com carta 1 160 a 1 830.

XX Gourmet Chaves, paseo de la Castellana 96, ⊠ 16, ℡ 458 07 45 – 🍽 GS b

XX **Urvi,** glorieta Puerta de Toledo 2, ⊠ 5, ℡ 474 12 69 – 🍽. ⓞ 🛒 𝗩𝗜𝗦𝗔. ⋘ EZ v
Com carta 825 a 1 175.

XX **Basarri,** López de Hoyos 16, ⊠ 6, ℡ 413 90 07 – 🍽. ⓞ 🛒 𝗩𝗜𝗦𝗔. ⋘ HV n
cerrado del 10 al 31 agosto Com carta 950 a 1 750.

XX **Toffaneti** con cafetería, paseo de la Castellana 17, ⊠ 16, ℡ 456 42 87, Cocina italiana – 🍽.
🖭 ⓞ 🛒 𝗩𝗜𝗦𝗔. ⋘ GT x
Com carta 775 a 1 955.

XX Mesón Txistu, pl. Ángel Carbajo 6, ⊠ 20, ℡ 270 96 51, Decoración rústica – 🍽 GS d

XX **Las Reses,** pl. General Maroto 2, ⊠ 5, ℡ 473 54 47, Carnes – 🍽. 🖭 𝗩𝗜𝗦𝗔. ⋘ BM v
cerrado domingos, festivos y agosto – Com carta 725 a 1 450.

XX **Alkalde,** Jorge Juan 10, ⊠ 1, ℡ 276 33 59, En una bodega – 🍽. 𝗩𝗜𝗦𝗔. ⋘ HX v
cerrado sábados noche y domingos en julio y agosto – Com carta 1 350 a 2 200.

XX Jeromín, San Bernardo 115, ⊠ 8, ℡ 448 98 43 – 🍽 EFV r

XX **Rafa,** Narváez 68, ⊠ 9, ℡ 273 82 98 – 🍽. 🖭 ⓞ 🛒 𝗩𝗜𝗦𝗔. ⋘ HY a
Com carta 1 300 a 2 200.

XX Blanca de Navarra, av. de Brasil 13, ⊠ 20, ℡ 455 10 29, Cocina navarra – 🍽 GT q

XX **L'Alsace,** Doménico Scarlatti 5, ⊠ 3, ℡ 244 40 75 – 🍽. 🖭 ⓞ 🛒 𝗩𝗜𝗦𝗔 DV a
Com carta 940 a 1 800.

XX **O'Xeito,** paseo de la Castellana 57, ⊠ 1, ℡ 419 83 87, Decoración de estilo gallego, Pescados
y mariscos – 🍽. 🖭 ⓞ 🛒 𝗩𝗜𝗦𝗔. ⋘ GV e
cerrado domingos y del 2 al 31 agosto – Com carta 1 500 a 2 500.

X **Quattrocento,** General Ampudia 18, ⊠ 3, ℡ 234 91 06, Cocina italiana – 🍽. 🖭 ⓞ 🛒 𝗩𝗜𝗦𝗔.
⋘ – *cerrado domingos noche* – Com carta 950 a 1 750 DU a

X **México Lindo,** pl. República del Ecuador 4, ⊠ 16, ℡ 259 48 33, Cocina mejicana – 🍽. 🖭
ⓞ 🛒 𝗩𝗜𝗦𝗔. ⋘ HT y
Com carta 805 a 1 480.

X Chiquito Riz, Coslada 3, ⊠ 28, ℡ 245 18 23 – 🍽 HV u

X Gerardo, D-Ramón de la Cruz 86, ⊠ 8, ℡ 401 83 46 – 🍽 JX x

X El Pajar, Orense 35, ⊠ 20, ℡ 455 00 09 – 🍽 FT b

X **Casa Félix** piso 1°, Bretón de los Herreros 39, ⊠ 3, ℡ 441 24 79 – 🍽. 𝗩𝗜𝗦𝗔. ⋘ FV x
Com carta 1 065 a 2 375.

X ⊛ **El Pescador,** José Ortega y Gasset 75, ⊠ 6, ℡ 402 12 90, Pescados y mariscos – 🍽. ⋘
cerrado domingos y 10 agosto-20 septiembre – Com carta 1 125 a 2 175 JV t
Espec. Sopa El Pescador, Lenguado Evaristo, Langosta a la americana.

X Asador Donostiarra, Pedro Villar 14, ⊠ 20, ℡ 279 73 40, Decoración rústica – 🍽 FS a

X **La Gran Tasca,** Santa Engracia 22, ⊠ 10, ℡ 448 77 79 – 🍽. 🖭 ⓞ 𝗩𝗜𝗦𝗔. ⋘ FV o
cerrado domingos – Com carta 1 050 a 1 950.

X Los Borrachos de Velázquez, Príncipe de Vergara 205, ⊠ 2, ℡ 458 10 76 – 🍽 HT s

X **Tony's,** Menéndez Pidal 27, ⊠ 16, ℡ 457 30 69, Cocina italiana – 🍽. 🖭 ⓞ 𝗩𝗜𝗦𝗔 HS f
cerrado domingos – Com carta 965 a 1 990.

X **Sacha,** Juan Hurtado de Mendoza 11 (Posterior), ⊠ 16, ℡ 457 59 52 – 🍽. 𝗩𝗜𝗦𝗔. ⋘ GHS r
cerrado domingos, festivos y 31 julio-1 septiembre – Com carta 1 500 a 2 600.

X Las Cumbres, av. de América 33, ✉ 2, ☎ 413 08 13 – ▤ HV **h**

X Cesare, Padre Damián 42, ✉ 16, ☎ 458 10 25, Cocina italiana – ▤ HS **u**

X **Sixto,** José Ortega y Gasset 83, ✉ 6, ☎ 402 18 87 – ▤. AE ◑ E VISA. ✗ JV **e**
cerrado domingos noche – Com carta 1 125 a 1 580.

X La Panocha, Alonso Heredia 4, ✉ 28, ☎ 245 10 32 – ▤ JV **x**

X **Bodegón Navarro,** paseo de la Castellana 121, ✉ 16, entrada por Pintor Juan Gris, ☎ 455 30 11, Decoración rústica – ▤. ✗ GS **h**
cerrado domingos y agosto – Com carta 1 275 a 2 125.

X Mesón El Caserío, Capitán Haya 49, ✉ 20, ☎ 270 96 29, Decoración rústica – ▤ GS **k**

X **El Timbal,** Andrés Mellado 69, ✉ 15, ☎ 244 36 15 – ▤. ◑ E VISA. ✗ EV **b**
Com carta 650 a 1 300.

X Samuel, Lagasca 46, ✉ 1, ☎ 276 41 35 – ▤ HX **a**

X Prosit, José Ortega y Gasset 8, ✉ 6, ☎ 276 17 85 – ▤ HV **z**

X Melgar, Antonio López 5, ✉ 19, ☎ 269 51 79 – ▤. AE ◑ VISA BM **a**

X Porto Mouro, Santa María Magdalena 31, ✉ 16, ☎ 250 60 94, Pescados y mariscos – ▤ HS **n**

X ✿ **La Trainera,** Lagasca 60, ✉ 2, ☎ 435 89 54, Pescados y mariscos – ▤. ✗ HX **k**
cerrado domingos y agosto – Com carta 1 625 a 2 250
Espec. Langosta americana, Lenguado plancha, Besugo Trainera.

X Happy Gourmet (Gastrónomo Feliz), av. Nazaret 8, ✉ 7, ☎ 409 12 24, Carnes – ▤. ✗ JY **n**

X Curro's, Coslada 28, ✉ 28, ☎ 246 79 41 – ▤ HV **k**

X Rianxo, Raimundo Fernández Villaverde 49, ✉ 20, ☎ 233 48 18, Pescados y mariscos – ▤ FU **a**

X El Chiscón de Castelló, Castelló 3, ✉ 1, ☎ 275 56 62 – ▤ HX **e**

X **Mesón Auto,** paseo de la Chopera 69, ✉ 5, ☎ 239 66 00, Decoración rústica regional – ▤. ✗ – Com carta 650 a 1 800 BM **c**

X Los Cigarrales, Antonio López 52, ✉ 19, ☎ 469 74 52 – ▤ BM **n**

X Casa Pepe, paseo de la Habana 33, ✉ 16, ☎ 259 66 36 – ▤ HT **k**

X **Don Sancho,** Bretón de los Herreros 58, ✉ 3, ☎ 441 37 94 – ▤. ✗ GV **u**
cerrado domingos, festivos y agosto – Com carta 875 a 1 195.

X Olvido, av. Dr. Esquerdo 82, ✉ 30, ☎ 409 38 13 – ▤ JY **e**

X Mesón del Bierzo, av. del Mediterráneo 22, ✉ 7, ☎ 251 11 41 – ▤ HZ **n**

Cafeterías, Restaurantes rápidos.

XX **California 47,** Goya 47, ✉ 1, ☎ 435 27 17 – ▤. ◑ E VISA. ✗ HX **n**
Com carta 950 a 1 770.

XX **Manila,** Juan Bravo 37, ✉ 6, ☎ 411 14 40 – ▤. AE ◑ E VISA. ✗ HV **c**
Com carta 955 a 1 740.

X **Vips,** Jósé Ortega y Gasset 29, ✉ 6, ☎ 275 64 73 – ▤. AE ◑ E VISA. ✗ HV **f**
Com carta 695 a 1 295.

X **Vips,** paseo de la Habana 17, ✉ 16, ☎ 261 30 59 – ▤. AE ◑ E VISA. ✗ GT **b**
Com carta 695 a 1 295.

X **Manila,** Basílica 17, ✉ 20, ☎ 455 90 31 – ▤. AE ◑ E VISA. ✗ FT **k**
Com carta 955 a 1 740.

X **Manila,** Diego de León 41, ✉ 6, ☎ 262 12 62 – ▤. AE ◑ E VISA. ✗ HV **d**
Com carta 955 a 1 740.

X **Vips,** Velázquez 136, ✉ 6, ☎ 262 84 38 – ▤. AE ◑ E VISA. ✗ HV **e**
Com carta 695 a 1 295.

X **Vips,** Julián Romea 4, ✉ 3, ☎ 233 07 52 – ▤. AE ◑ E VISA. ✗ EV **v**
Com carta 695 a 1 295.

Alrededores

en Ciudad Puerta de Hierro : 8 km par N VI y por carretera de El Pardo – ✉ Madrid 35 – ☏ 91 :

🏨 **Monte Real** ✓, Arroyofresno 19 ☎ 216 21 40, Telex 22089, « Decoración elegante, bonito jardín », ⛱ – ▤ 🚗 🅟 – 🏢. AE ◑ E VISA. ✗ AL **b**
Com 2 220 – ☕ 440 – **79 hab** 5 190/8 485 – P 8 685/9 635.

en El Pardo : 13 km por N VI y por carretera de El Pardo – ✉ El Pardo – ☏ 91 :

XX Menéndez, av. de la Guardia 6 ☎ 736 09 77 – ▤.

X **Pedro's,** av. de la Guardia ☎ 736 08 83 – ▤. ✗
cerrado 7 enero-7 febrero – Com carta 995 a 1 600.

X La Marquesita, av. de la Guardia 4 ☎ 736 03 77 – ▤.

X El Gamo, av. de la Guardia 6 ☎ 736 03 27.

X Montes, pl. Caudillo 1 ☎ 736 03 28 – ▤.

Por la salida ① :

en Fuencarral : 9 km por N I o por Camino Viejo de Alcobendas – HR – ⊠ Madrid 34 – ✪ 91 :

XX **Casa Pedro,** Nuestra Señora de Valverde 119 ℡ 734 02 01 – 🍽. **E** *VISA*. ❄
Com carta 1 150 a 2 050.

en San Sebastián de los Reyes – ⊠ San Sebastian de los Reyes – ✪ 91 :

🏠 Pamplona, carret. N I : 25 km ℡ 652 97 77 – 🏢 ⌷wc ✪ – **16 hab.**

XXX **Mesón Tejas Verdes,** carret. N I : 17,5 km ℡ 652 73 07, « Típico mesón castellano, jardín con arbolado » – 🍽 ✪. 🆔 ⓪ *VISA*
cerrado domingos, festivos noche y agosto – Com carta 1 100 a 1 600.

X Aterpe-Alai, carret. N I : 25 km ℡ 652 78 24, ⬰ – 🍽 ✪.

Por la salida ② :

por la carretera N II y acceso carretera Coslada - San Fernando E : 12 km – ⊠ Madrid 22 – ✪ 91 :

XX **Rancho Texano,** av. Aragón 364 ℡ 747 47 44, Carnes a la brasa, « Agradable terraza » – 🍽. 🆔 ⓪ *VISA*
cerrado domingos noche – Com carta 1 100 a 2 245.

en la carretera del aeropuerto : 12,5 km – ⊠ Madrid 22 – ✪ 91 ·

🏨 **Eurotel Resitur,** Galeón 27 (Alameda de Osuna) ℡ 747 13 55, ⬰ – 🍽 ⬅ ✪ – 🛁. 🆔 ⓪ **E** *VISA*. ❄
Com 950 – ⬕ 200 – **271 apartamentos** 3 360/4 200 – P 4 200/5 560.

en Barajas 15 km por N II – ⊠ Madrid 22 – ✪ 91 :

🏨 **Barajas** Ⓜ, av. de Logroño 305 ℡ 747 77 00, Telex 22255, Cenas amenizadas al piano, ⬰ – 🍽 ✪ – 🛁. 🆔 ⓪ **E** *VISA*. ❄ rest
Com 1 700 – ⬕ 300 – **230 hab** 5 100.

🏨 **Alameda** Ⓜ, av. de Logroño 100 ℡ 747 48 00, Telex 43809, ⬰ – 🍽 ✪ – 🛁. 🆔 ⓪ **E** *VISA*. ❄ rest
Com 1 250/1 700 – ⬕ 650 – **145 hab** 4 250/6 950 – P 6 675/7 450.

X **Mesón Don Fernando,** Canal de Suéz 1 ℡ 747 75 51 – 🍽. 🆔 ⓪ **E** *VISA*. ❄
cerrado sábados y agosto-1 septiembre – Com carta 950 a 1 575.

Por la salida ④ :

en la carretera N IV – ⊠ Getafe – ✪ 91 :

🏨 **Motel Los Olivos** ⬷ 12,5 km, ℡ 695 67 00, ⬰, ⬰ – 🏢 🍽 ⌷wc ☎ ✪. 🆔 ⓪ *VISA*. ❄ rest
Com 500 – ⬕ 130 – **100 hab** 2 300/2 880 – P 2 570/3 430.

🏨 **Motel Los Angeles,** 14,5 km ℡ 696 38 15, ⬰, ⬰, ❀ – 🍽 ⌷wc ☎ ⬅ ✪. 🆔. ❄
Com 700 – ⬕ 250 – **46 hab** 3 900.

Hacia la salida ⑥ :

en Boadilla del Monte : 15 km – ⊠ Boadilla del Monte – ✪ 91 :

XX **La Cañada,** carret. de Madrid ℡ 633 12 83, ⬰, ❀ – 🍽 ✪. ❄
cerrado domingos noche y lunes – Com carta 1 475 a 2 175.

Por la salida ⑦ :

en Aravaca – ⊠ Aravaca – ✪ 91 :

XX **Portonovo,** carret. N VI : 10,5 km ℡ 207 01 73, Cocina gallega – 🍽 ✪. ⓪ *VISA*. ❄
cerrado domingos y festivos noche – Com carta 1 125 a 2 600.

X **El Zaguán,** av. de la Osa Mayor 70 : 9 km ℡ 207 13 12 – 🍽 ✪. *VISA*. ❄
cerrado miércoles y 15 agosto-1 septiembre – Com carta 1 225 a 1 970.

en El Plantío – ⊠ El Plantío – ✪ 91 :

XX ✿ **Los Remos,** carret. N VI : 13 km ℡ 207 72 30, Pescados y mariscos, « Agradable terraza » – 🍽 ✪. ❄
cerrado domingos noche y del 15 al 31 agosto – Com carta 1 625 a 2 250
Espec. Revuelto de salmón ahumado. Lenguado plancha. Dogavante americana.

Por la salida ⑧ :

en la carretera de Colmenar Viejo : – ⊠ Madrid 34 – ✪ 91 :

XX **El Mesón de Fuencarral,** carret. C 607 : 13,5 km ℡ 734 10 19, Decoración rústica en una casa de campo castellana – 🍽 ✪. ⓪
Com carta 1 175 a 2 025.

BARCELONA

BARCELONA P 43 ⑱ y 990 ⑳ – 1 754 714 h. – ✿ 93 – Plaza de toros.

Ver : Barrio Gótico (Barri Gotic)★★ : Catedral★★ MR, Museo Federico Marés (Museu F. Marès)★★ MR, Palau de la Generalitat★ MR – Montjuich (Montjuïc)★ (✎★) : Museo de Arte de Cataluña★★ (colecciones románicas y góticas★★★, museo de Cerámica★) CT M2 – Museo Arqueológico★ CT M3 , Pueblo español★, BT E, Fundación Miró★ CT F – Parque zoológico (Parc zoológic)★ LV – Tibidabo★ (✎★★) AS – Atarazanas y Museo Marítimo★★ KZ M6 – Palacio de la Virreina (colección Cambo★) JX M7 – Museo Picasso★ KV M8 – Templo Expiatorio de la Sagrada Familia★ JU L.

🛫, 🛫 de Prat por ⑤ : 16 km ☏ 379 02 78 – 🛫 de San Cugat por ⑦ : 20 km ☏ 674 39 58 – 🛫 de Vallromanas por ④ : 25 km ☏ 568 03 62.

✈ de Barcelona por ⑤ : 12 km ☏ 317 00 12 – Iberia y Aviaco : pl. Espanya, ✉ 4, ☏ 325 60 00 EZ.

🚂 ☏ 310 00 30.

⛴ para Baleares y Canarias : Cía. Aucona, vía Laietana 2, ✉ 3, ☏ 319 82 12, Telex 54629 KX.

🛈 Gran Vía de les Cortes Catalanes 658, ✉ 10, ☏ 325 58 29 - 218 05 70 - Palacio de Congresos, av. Maria Cristina ☏ 223 31 01 y en el aeropuerto ☏ 325 58 29 – R.A.C.C. Santaló 8, ✉ 6, ☏ 217 05 00, Telex 530 56.

♦Madrid 626 ⑥ – ♦Bilbao 607 ⑥ – ♦Lérida 169 ⑥ – ♦Perpignan 186 ② – Tarragona 108 ⑥ – Toulouse 387 ② – ♦Valencia 360 ⑥ – ♦Zaragoza 307 ⑥.

Planos : Barcelona p. 2 a 7

🏨 **Princesa Sofía** M, pl. del Papa Pius XII, ✉ 28, ☏ 330 71 11, Telex 51032, ✎, 🔲 – 🗐 🚗 ℗ – 🏋. 🏧 ⓘ E VISA. ✾   BT **x**
Com 1 800 – ☐ 375 – **496 hab** 6 400/8 000 – P 7 350/9 750.

🏨 **G. H. Sarriá** M, av. de Sarriá 50, ✉ 29, ☏ 239 11 09, Telex 51638 – 🗐 🚗 – 🏋. 🏧 ⓘ E VISA. ✾   EU **n**
Com 1 500 – ☐ 300 – **309 hab** 5 100/7 500 – P 6 550/7 600.

🏨 **Avenida Palace,** Gran Vía 605, ✉ 7, ☏ 301 96 00, Telex 54734 – 🗐 – 🏋. 🏧 ⓘ E VISA. ✾ rest   GV **r**
Com 1 550 – ☐ 225 – **211 hab** 5 220/6 510 – P 5 855/7 820.

🏨 **Ritz,** Gran Vía de les Corts Catalanes 668, ✉ 10, ☏ 318 52 00, Telex 52 739 – 🗐 – 🏋. 🏧 ⓘ E VISA. ✾ rest   JU **p**
Com 2 000 – ☐ 400 – **203 hab** 5 160/7 040 – P 7 220/8 860.

🏨 **Presidente,** av. de la Diagonal 570, ✉ 21, ☏ 200 21 11, Telex 52180, 🔲 – 🗐 – 🏋. 🏧 ⓘ E VISA. ✾ rest   EU **u**
Com 800/1 000 – ☐ 300 – **161 hab** 5 150/6 435.

🏨 **Majestic,** passeig de Grácia 70, ✉ 28, ☏ 215 45 12, Telex 52211, 🔲 – 🗐 🚗 – 🏋   CU **f**
360 hab.

🏨 **Diplomatic,** Pau Claris 122, ✉ 9, ☏ 317 31 00, Telex 54701, 🔲 – 🗐 🚗 – 🏋. 🏧 ⓘ E VISA. ✾   GU **e**
Com 1 950 Grill carta 1 850 a 3 000 – ☐ 500 – **215 hab** 6 200/7 750 – P 7 615/9 940.

🏨 **G. H. Calderón** sin rest, con cafetería, rambla de Catalunya 26, ✉ 7, ☏ 301 00 00, Telex 51549, 🔲 – 🗐 🚗 – 🏋. 🏧 ⓘ E VISA. ✾   GV **t**
☐ 250 – **244 hab** 4 800/6 000.

🏨 **Colón,** av. de la Catedral 7, ✉ 2, ☏ 301 14 04, Telex 52654 – 🗐. 🏧 ⓘ E VISA   KV **e**
Com 1 075 – ☐ 215 – **161 hab** 2 855/5 105 – P 4 255/4 555.

🏨 **Derby** sin rest, Loreto 21, ✉ 29, ☏ 239 30 07 – 🗐 🚗 – 🏋. 🏧 ⓘ E VISA   EV **v**
☐ 325 – **116 hab** 3 600/5 640.

🏨 **Cristal,** Diputació 257, ✉ 7, ☏ 301 66 00, Telex 54560 – 🗐 🚗 – 🏋. 🏧 ⓘ E VISA. ✾ rest   GV **t**
Com 1 100 – ☐ 200 – **150 hab** 3 600/4 500 – P 4 250/5 600.

🏨 **Núñez Urgel** sin rest, con cafetería, Comte d'Urgell 232, ✉ 36, ☏ 322 41 53 – 🗐 🚗. 🏧 ⓘ VISA – ☐ 300 – **121 hab** 3 000/5 200   EV **a**

🏨 **Royal** M sin rest, Ramblas 117, ✉ 2, ☏ 301 94 00 – 🗐 🚗. 🏧 ⓘ E VISA. ✾   JX **e**
☐ 250 – **107 hab** 2 800/4 500.

🏨 **Balmoral** sin rest, vía Augusta 5, ✉ 6, ☏ 217 87 00 – 🗐 🚗 – 🏋. 🏧 ⓘ E VISA. ✾   FU **n**
☐ 295 – **94 hab** 2 990/4 630.

🏨 **Regente,** rambla de Catalunya 76, ✉ 8, ☏ 215 25 70, Telex 51939, 🔲 – 🗐 🚗. 🏧 ⓘ E VISA. ✾ rest   GU **z**
Com 1 000 – ☐ 220 – **78 hab** 2 900/4 450 – P 4 115/4 790.

🏨 **Condor** sin rest, con cafetería, vía Augusta 127, ✉ 6, ☏ 209 45 11, Telex 52925 – 🗐 🚗. 🏧 ⓘ E VISA   EU **z**
☐ 300 – **75 hab** 3 500/4 700.

🏨 **Arenas** sin rest, con cafetería por la noche, Capitá Arenas 20, ✉ 34, ☏ 204 03 00 – 🗐 🚗 – 🏋. 🏧 ⓘ E VISA. ✾   BT **r**
☐ 250 – **59 hab** 3 760/4 700.

🏨 **Astoria** sin rest, con cafetería, Paris 203, ✉ 36, ☏ 209 83 11 – 🗐. VISA. ✾   FU **a**
☐ 175 – **108 hab** 1 950/3 100.

🏨 **G. H. Cristina** sin rest, con cafetería, av. de la Diagonal 458, ✉ 36, ☏ 217 68 00 – 🗐   FU **y**
127 hab.

🏨 **Dante** sin rest, Mallorca 181, ⊠ 36, ℡ 323 22 54, Telex 52588 – 🖭 🚗 – 🔬. 🖭 ⓞ 🗲 🚾.
🛪 FV **e**
☲ 200 – **81 hab** 2 600 / 4 000.

🏨 **Roma** sin rest, Mallorca 163, ⊠ 36, ℡ 253 35 00 – 🖭 ⓞ 🗲 🚾 FV **u**
☲ 200 – **74 hab** 2 500 / 3 600.

🏨 **Expo H.** sin rest, con cafetería, Mallorca 1, ⊠ 14, ℡ 325 12 12, Telex 54147, ⅃ – 🖭 🚗 –
🔬. 🖭 ⓞ 🗲 🚾. 🛪 EY **m**
☲ 175 – **432 hab** 3 130 / 3 910.

🏨 **Euro-Park** sin rest, con cafetería, Aragó 325, ⊠ 9, ℡ 257 92 05 – 🖭 🚗. ⓞ 🗲 🚾 JU **e**
☲ 250 – **66 hab** 1 900/4 000.

🏨 **Numancia** sin rest, con cafetería, Numáncia 74, ⊠ 29, ℡ 322 44 51 – 🖭 🚗 – 🔬 🖭 ⓞ
🚾. BT **f**
☲ 230 – **140 hab** 1 900/3 500.

🏨 **Gala Placidia**, vía Augusta 112, ⊠ 6, ℡ 217 02 00, Telex 97354 – 🗍 🎟 🖭 rest 🖛wc 🕾, 🖭
ⓞ 🗲 🚾 EU **r**
Com 800 – ☲ 200 – **28 apartamentos** 2 800/4 300 – P 3 500/4 200.

🏨 **Mitre** sin rest, Bertrán 15, ⊠ 23, ℡ 212 11 04 – 🗍 🎟 🖭 🖛wc 🕾 🚗. 🖭 ⓞ 🗲 🚾 BS **t**
☲ 210 – **57 hab** 2 300/3 450.

🏨 Condado, Aribau 201, ⊠ 21, ℡ 200 23 11 – 🗍 🎟 🖭 rest 🖛wc 🎟wc 🕾 – **89 hab** EU **g**

🏨 **Covadonga** sin rest, con cafetería, av. de la Diagonal 596, ⊠ 21, ℡ 209 55 11 – 🗍 🎟 🖛wc
🎟wc 🕾. 🖭 ⓞ 🗲 🚾 EU **v**
☲ 200 – **75 hab** 1 900/3 100.

🏨 **Regencia Colón** sin rest, Sagristans 13, ⊠ 2, ℡ 318 98 58, Telex 52654 – 🗍 🎟 🖭 🖛wc
🎟wc 🕾. 🖭 ⓞ 🗲 🚾. 🛪 KV **r**
55 hab ☲ 1 970/3 265.

🏨 **Terminal** piso 7°, sin rest, con cafetería, Provença 1, ⊠ 29, ℡ 321 53 50 🗍 🎟 🖭 🖛wc
🎟wc 🕾. 🖭 ⓞ 🗲 🚾 EY **a**
☲ 200 – **75 hab** 2 700/3 400.

🏨 **Taber** sin rest, Aragó 256, ⊠ 7, ℡ 318 70 50 – 🗍 🎟 🖛wc 🕾 – 🔬. 🖭 ⓞ 🚾 GV **g**
65 hab ☲ 2 000/3 400.

🏨 **Tres Torres** sin rest, Calatrava 32, ⊠ 17, ℡ 247 73 00 – 🗍 🎟 🖛wc 🕾 🚗. 🗲 🚾. 🛪
☲ 240 – **56 hab** 2 160/3 600. BT **n**

🏨 **Wilson** sin rest, av. de la Diagonal 568, ⊠ 21, ℡ 209 25 11 – 🗍 🖭 🖛wc 🕾. 🖭 ⓞ 🗲 🚾.
🛪 EU **a**
☲ 190 – **52 hab** 2 720/3 400.

🏨 Gótico sin rest, Jaume I 14, ⊠ 2, ℡ 315 22 11, Telex 50065 – 🗍 🎟 🖭 🖛wc 🕾·
72 hab. MR **a**

🏨 **Las Corts** sin rest, con cafetería, Travessera de Les Corts 292, ⊠ 29, ℡ 322 08 11 – 🗍 🎟 🖭
🖛wc 🎟wc 🕾 ⓟ. 🛪 BT **u**
80 hab ☲ 1 950/2 850.

🏨 **Bonanova Park** sin rest, Capitá Arenas 51, ⊠ 34, ℡ 204 09 00 – 🗍 🎟 🖛wc 🎟wc 🕾 🚗. 🗲
🚾. 🛪 BT **b**
☲ 165 – **60 hab** 1 410/2 470.

🏨 **Mesón Castilla** sin rest, Valldoncella 5, ⊠ 1, ℡ 318 21 82 – 🗍 🎟 🖛wc 🎟wc 🕾 🚗
☲ 180 – **56 hab** 1 550/2 300. GX **c**

🏨 **Regina** sin rest, con cafetería, Vergara 2, ⊠ 2, ℡ 301 32 32, Telex 51939 – 🗍 🎟 🖭 🖛wc 🕾.
🖭 ⓞ 🗲 🚾. 🛪 HV **r**
☲ 175 – **102 hab** 1 900/3 100.

🏨 **Habana** sin rest, Gran Via de les Corts Catalanes 647, ⊠ 10, ℡ 301 07 50 – 🗍 🎟 🖭 🖛wc 🕾
🚗. 🖭 ⓞ 🚾 JU **g**
☲ 175 – **65 hab** 1 800/2 900.

🏨 **Montecarlo** sin rest, Rambla dels Estudis 124, ⊠ 2, ℡ 317 58 00 – 🗍 🎟 🖛wc 🕾 🚗. 🚾
☲ 170 – **73 hab** 1 800/2 900. JX **a**

🏨 Suizo, pl. de l'Angel 12, ⊠ 2, ℡ 315 41 11, Telex 97206 – 🗍 🎟 🖛wc 🕾 – **39 hab** MR **p**

🏨 **L'Alguer** sin rest, passeig Pedro Rodriguez 20, ⊠ 28, ℡ 334 60 50 – 🗍 🎟 🎟wc 🕾. 🗲 🚾. 🛪
☲ 145 – **33 hab** 1 000/1 700. AT **b**

🏨 **San Agustín**, pl. Sant Agustín 3, ⊠ 1, ℡ 318 16 62 – 🗍 🎟 🖛wc 🎟wc 🕾. 🚾. 🛪 **u**
Com 600/630 – ☲ 185 – **71 hab** 1 275/2 000 – P 2 115/2 400. JY

🏨 **Lleó** piso 2°, Pelai 24, ⊠ 1, ℡ 318 13 12 – 🗍 🖛wc 🕾. 🛪 rest GV **a**
Com 525 – ☲ 130 – **43 hab** 1 130/1 850 – P 1 925/2 130.

🏨 **Torello** sin rest, Ample 31, ⊠ 2, ℡ 315 40 11 – 🗍 🖛wc 🎟wc 🕾. 🛪 KY **r**
☲ 150 – **74 hab** 1 125/1 875.

🏨 **Rialto** sin rest, Ferràn 42, ⊠ 2, ℡ 318 52 12 – 🗍 🎟 🖛wc 🎟 🕾. 🖭 🚾 MR **s**
☲ 150 – **63 hab** 850/1 850.

🏨 **Continental** piso 2°, sin rest, Rambla de Canaletas 138, ⊠ 2, ℡ 301 25 08 🗍 🎟 🖛wc
🎟wc 🕾. 🚾 JV **n**
☲ 135 – **28 hab** 1 550/1 950.

🏨 **Travesera** piso 1°, sin rest, Travessera de Dalt 121, ⊠ 24, ℡ 213 24 54 – 🗍 🎟 🖛wc 🎟wc
ⓞ. 🛪 CS **u**
☲ 150 – **23 hab** 1 100/1 600.

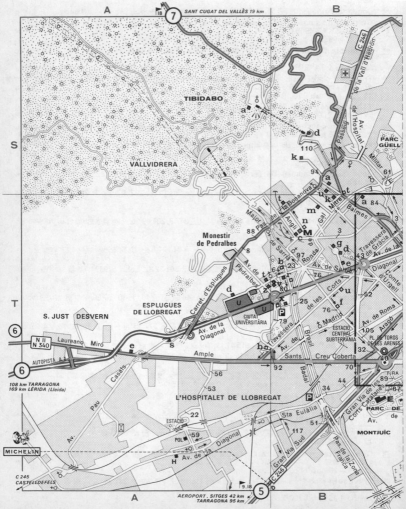

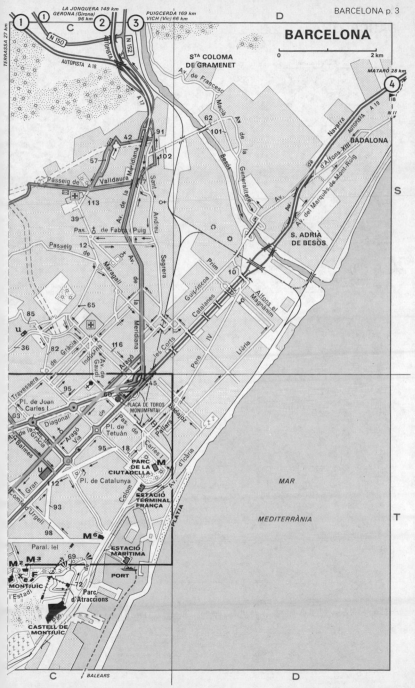

BARCELONA

BARCELONA

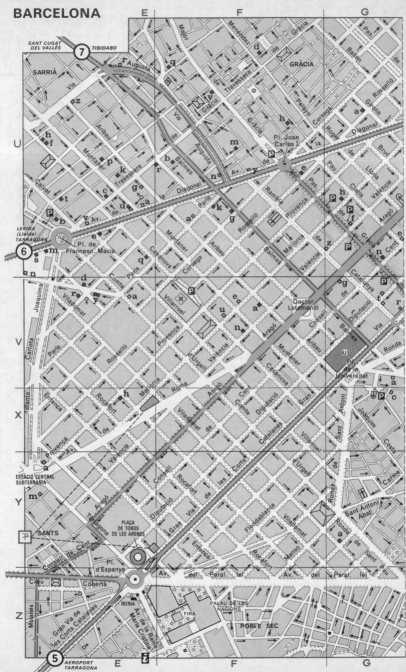

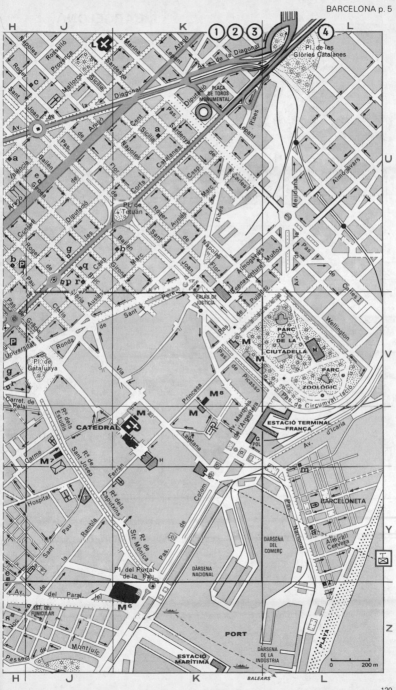

BARCELONA

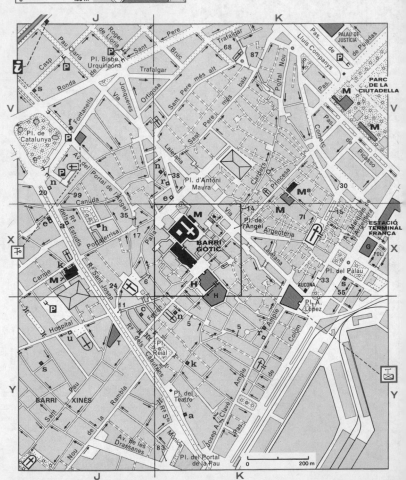

Restaurantes clásicos o modernos

XXXX ❀ **Ama Lur** entresuelo, Mallorca 275, ✉ 8, ☎ 215 20 24, « Agradable terraza-jardín » – 🍽.
E 𝑉𝐼𝑆𝐴. ✸ DU **h**
cerrado domingos y agosto – Com (reservación imprescindible) carta 2 575 a 3 175
Espec. Arroz con almejas, Lenguado al vinagre viejo y trufa, Becada "Ama Lur" (noviembre-febrero).

XXXX ❀❀ **Reno,** Tuset 27, ✉ 6, ☎ 200 91 29, « Elegante restaurante clásico » – 🍽 🅿. 𝔸𝔼 ⓞ E
𝑉𝐼𝑆𝐴. ✸ FU **r**
Com carta 2 250 a 3 000
Espec. Soufflé de trufas frescas, Lenguado soufflé a la mousse de salmón ahumado, Solomillo Matignon.

XXXX ❀ **Vía Veneto,** Ganduxer 10, ✉ 21, ☎ 250 31 00, « Estilo belle époque » – 🍽 🅿. 𝔸𝔼 ⓞ E
𝑉𝐼𝑆𝐴. ✸ BT **e**
Com carta 1 860 a 2 920
Espec. Sopa de bacalao ahumado, Ensalada tibia de pintada, Filet de porc a l'all dolç.

XXX ❀ **Finisterre,** av. de la Diagonal 469, ✉ 36, ☎ 230 91 14 – 🍽. 𝔸𝔼 ⓞ E 𝑉𝐼𝑆𝐴. ✸ EU **e**
Com carta 2 250 a 3 850
Espec. Soufflé de trufas frescas, Langostinos al champan, Filete de buey a la Stroganoff.

XXX **Germán,** Dr Rizal 8, ✉ 6, ☎ 217 71 85 – 🍽. 𝔸𝔼 ⓞ E 𝑉𝐼𝑆𝐴 FU **m**
Com carta 2 200 a 3 125.

XXX **Hostal del Sol** piso 1°, passeig de Gràcia 44, ✉ 7, ☎ 215 62 25, Cenas amenizadas al piano
– 🍽. 𝔸𝔼 ⓞ E 𝑉𝐼𝑆𝐴. ✸ GU **n**
Com carta 955 a 1 475.

XXX **Chalet Suisse,** av. de la Diagonal 493, ✉ 29, ☎ 259 19 23 – 🍽 EU **m**

XXX **Gueridón,** pasaje Permanuyer 2, ✉ 9, ☎ 318 09 94 – 🍽. 𝔸𝔼 ⓞ E 𝑉𝐼𝑆𝐴. ✸ HU **b**
cerrado domingos – Com carta 1 565 a 2 765.

XXX **Il Giardinetto,** La Granada 22, ✉ 6, ☎ 218 75 36, Cocina italiana – 🍽. 𝔸𝔼 ⓞ E 𝑉𝐼𝑆𝐴. ✸
Com carta 1 305 a 2 085. FU **b**

XXX **Txapela,** Teodora Lamadrid 34, ✉ 22, ☎ 212 69 16, Cocina vasca – 🍽 BS **a**

XXX **Koldobika,** Bruc 46, ✉ 10, ☎ 302 36 46 – 🍽. 𝔸𝔼 ⓞ E. ✸ JU **q**
cerrado domingos – Com carta 925 a 1 675.

XX ❀ **Ara-Cata,** Dr Ferràn 33, ✉ 34, ☎ 204 10 53 – 🍽. ⓞ BT **v**
cerrado agosto, sábados noche y festivos en verano, festivos noche y lunes en invierno – Com
carta 1 450 a 2 150
Espec. Merluza Ara-Cata, Gambas Ara-Cata, Pato a las fresas de Sant Pol.

XX ❀ **Quo Vadis,** Carme 7, ✉ 1, ☎ 317 74 47 – 🍽. 𝔸𝔼 ⓞ E. ✸ JX **k**
cerrado sábados mediodía, domingos y agosto – Com carta 1 175 a 2 250
Espec. Pot-pourri de setas, Morillas a la crema (marzo-abril), Pie de cerdo con nabos negros (octubre-enero).

XX **Chévere,** rambla del Prat 14, ✉ 12, ☎ 217 03 59 – 🍽. ⓞ E 𝑉𝐼𝑆𝐴. ✸ FU **q**
cerrado domingos y agosto – Com carta 1 475 a 1 840.

XX **Lalos,** Santaló 88, ✉ 21, ☎ 200 10 90 – 🍽 EU **h**

XX **Aitor,** Carbonnell 5, ✉ 3, ☎ 319 94 88, Cocina vasca – 🍽 LXY **m**
cerrado domingos y 15 agosto-15 septiembre – Com carta 1 050 a 2 750.

XX **La Odisea,** Copons 7, ✉ 2, ☎ 302 37 88 – 𝑉𝐼𝑆𝐴 KV **n**
cerrado domingos y agosto – Com carta 1 625 a 2 740.

XX **El Túnel de Muntaner,** Sant Mario 22, ✉ 22, ☎ 212 60 74 – 🍽 🅿. 𝔸𝔼 ⓞ E 𝑉𝐼𝑆𝐴. ✸ BT **k**
cerrado 25 julio-25 agosto, domingos y festivos – Com carta 1 650 a 1 900.

XX **Cathay,** Santaló 86, ✉ 21, ☎ 209 37 86, Rest. chino, « Decoración elegante » – 🍽. ✸ EU **f**
cerrado lunes y agosto – Com carta 940 a 1 570.

XX ❀ **Jaume de Provença,** Provença 88, ✉ 29, ☎ 230 00 29, Decoración moderna – 🍽. 𝔸𝔼 E
𝑉𝐼𝑆𝐴. ✸ EX **h**
cerrado domingos noche, lunes y agosto – Com carta 1 350 a 3 000
Espec. Muselina de salmonetes, Pies de cerdo salsa chorón, Graten de naranjas.

XX **Neichel,** av. de Pedralbes 16 bis, ✉ 34, ☎ 203 84 08 – 🍽. 𝔸𝔼 ⓞ E 𝑉𝐼𝑆𝐴 ABT **z**
cerrado domingos y agosto – Com carta 1 250 a 2 450.

XX **Las Indias,** passeig Manuel Girona 38 bis, ✉ 34, ☎ 204 69 63 – 🍽. 𝔸𝔼 ⓞ E 𝑉𝐼𝑆𝐴. ✸ BT **v**
cerrado domingos – Com carta 1 395 a 2 225.

XX **Hipopótamus,** pasaje Llovera 11, ✉ 6, ☎ 200 20 09 – 🍽 EU **k**

XX **O Botafumeiro,** Major de Gràcia 81, ✉ 12, ☎ 218 42 30, Pescados y mariscos – 🍽. 𝔸𝔼 ⓞ
E 𝑉𝐼𝑆𝐴 FU **v**
cerrado lunes del 2 al 30 agosto – Com carta 1 550 a 3 950.

XX **Pedralbes Paradis,** paseo Manuel Girona 7, ✉ 34, ☎ 203 76 37, Rest con buffet – 🍽. 𝔸𝔼 ⓞ E
𝑉𝐼𝑆𝐴. ✸ AT **t**

XX **Soley,** Bailén 29, ✉ 10, ☎ 245 21 75 – 🍽 🅿. ⓞ E 𝑉𝐼𝑆𝐴 KU **b**
cerrado sábados en verano – Com carta 1 000 a 2 000.

XX **Satélite,** av. de Sarriá 10, ✉ 29, ☎ 321 34 31 – 🍽. 𝔸𝔼 E 𝑉𝐼𝑆𝐴 EV **d**
cerrado domingos, festivos noche en verano y sábados – Com carta 1 150 a 2 440.

XX ۞ **Hostal Sant Jordi,** Travessera de Dalt 123, ✉ 24, ☎ 213 10 37 – ▤. ⑩. ⊱   CS **u**
cerrado domingos noche y agosto – Com carta 1 150 a 1 850
Espec. Chipirones encebollados, Filetes de lenguado Hostal, Fricando con setas del tiempo.

XX **Gorría,** Diputació 421, ✉ 13, ☎ 245 11 64, Cocina vasco-navarra – ▤. ﭏ ⑩ E 𝘝𝘐𝘚𝘈. ⊱
cerrado domingos y agosto – Com carta 1 555 a 2 480.   KU **a**

XX Farín, Valéncia 153, ✉ 11, ☎ 254 42 91 – ▤   FV **n**

XX Le Petit Soleil, pl. Villa de Madrid 4, ✉ 28, ☎ 302 61 64 – ▤   JX **h**

XX **Tramonti 1980,** av. de la Diagonal 501, ✉ 29, ☎ 250 15 35, Cocina italiana – ▤. ﭏ ⑩ E
𝘝𝘐𝘚𝘈. ⊱   EU **s**
Com carta 1 165 a 1 975.

XX **Au Périgord,** Roberto Bassas 34 C, ✉ 28, ☎ 339 30 19, Cocina francesa – ▤. ﭏ ⑩ E. ⊱
Com carta 875 a 1 200.   BT **x**

XX **Azulete,** Camp 63, ✉ 22, ☎ 211 37 96 – ▤. E 𝘝𝘐𝘚𝘈   BT **m**
cerrado domingos, festivos, 1 semana por Pascua, 1 semana por Navidad y agosto-5 septiembre
– Com carta 1 120 a 2 035.

XX **Amaya,** rambla Santa Mónica 20, ✉ 2, ☎ 302 10 37, Cocina vasca – ▤ ﭏ ⑩ E 𝘝𝘐𝘚𝘈. ⊱
Com carta 750 a 2 020.   KY **a**

XX La Soupe à l'Oignon, Padua 60, ✉ 6, ☎ 212 77 42, Cocina francesa – ▤   BT **a**

XX **El Pescador,** Mallorca 314, ✉ 37, ☎ 207 10 24, Pescados y mariscos – ▤. ﭏ ⑩ 𝘝𝘐𝘚𝘈. ⊱
cerrado domingos – Com carta 1 220 a 2 800.   HU **a**

XX **7 Puertas,** passeig d'Isabel II - 14, ✉ 3, ☎ 319 30 33, Cenas amenizadas al piano – ▤. ﭏ
⑩ E 𝘝𝘐𝘚𝘈. ⊱   KX **s**
Com carta 905 a 1 825.

X Tinell, Frenería 8, ✉ 2, ☎ 302 42 42 – ▤   MR **t**

X **Portofino 2,** Ganduxer 50, ✉ 21, ☎ 201 00 09, Cocina italiana – ▤. 𝘝𝘐𝘚𝘈. ⊱   BT **g**
Com carta 1 240 a 2 445.

X Poñón de Ifach, Travessera de Gràcia 35, ✉ 21, ☎ 209 65 75 – ▤   EU **c**

X Vila Plana, pl. Sant Gregorio Taumaturgo 4, ✉ 21, ☎ 201 13 00 – ▤   BT **d**

X **Cal Sardineta 2,** Casp 35, ✉ 10, ☎ 302 68 44 – ▤. ⑩ 𝘝𝘐𝘚𝘈. ⊱   JU **r**
cerrado domingos noche – Com carta 950 a 1 700.

X **Es Plá,** passeig de Sant Gervasi 86, ✉ 22, ☎ 212 65 54 – ▤. E 𝘝𝘐𝘚𝘈   BST **u**
cerrado lunes – Com carta 1 265 a 2 025.

X **Azpiolea,** Casanova 167, ✉ 36, ☎ 230 90 30, Cocina vasca – ▤. ⑩ E 𝘝𝘐𝘚𝘈. ⊱   EU **q**
cerrado domingos y festivos noche en agosto – Com carta 850 a 1 275.

X **Can Bara,** passeig Nacional 70, ✉ 3, ☎ 319 50 22 – ﭏ ⑩ E 𝘝𝘐𝘚𝘈. ⊱   LZ **r**
Com carta 775 a 1 650.

X La Porte Louise, Mariano Cubí 94, ✉ 21, ☎ 200 91 74, Cocina franco-belga – ▤   EU **p**

X Casa Isidro, Flores 12, ✉ 1, ☎ 241 11 39 – ▤   HY **e**

X La Balsa, Infanta Isabel 4, ✉ 23, ☎ 211 50 48   BS **k**

X **Abrevadero,** Vilá y Vilá 77, ✉ 4, ☎ 241 22 06 – ▤. ﭏ ⑩ E ⊱   HZ **s**
cerrado jueves – Com carta 1 700 a 1 800.

X **La Puñalada,** passeig de Grácia 104, ✉ 8, ☎ 218 83 44 – ▤. ⑩ E 𝘝𝘐𝘚𝘈   FU **e**
Com carta 1 265 a 2 045.

X **Viña Rosa,** av. de Sarriá 17, ✉ 29, ☎ 230 00 03 – ▤. ﭏ ⑩ E 𝘝𝘐𝘚𝘈   EV **y**
cerrado domingos y festivos noche – Com carta 1 315 a 2 355.

X Chicoa, Aribau 71, ✉ 36, ☎ 253 11 23 – ▤   FV **a**

X **El Trapio Jardín,** Esperanza 25, ✉ 17, ☎ 211 58 17, Rest. al aire libre – E 𝘝𝘐𝘚𝘈   BT **t**
cerrado domingos noche – Com carta 950 a 1 800.

X **La Venta,** pl. del Funicular, ✉ 22, ☎ 212 64 55, Antiguo café con gran terraza – ﭏ ⑩ E 𝘝𝘐𝘚𝘈
cerrado domingos – Com carta 1 200 a 1 800.   BS **d**

X Giorgi, Muntaner 231, ✉ 21, ☎ 209 91 86   EU **u**

X **Da Peppo,** av. de Sarriá 17, ✉ 29, ☎ 259 01 60 – ▤. 𝘝𝘐𝘚𝘈   EV **y**
cerrado martes – Com carta 705 a 1 340.

X Café de París, Maestro Nicolau 16, ✉ 21, ☎ 200 19 14, Cocina francesa – ▤   EU **b**

X Julivert Meu, Jorge Girona Salgado 12, ✉ 34, ☎ 204 11 96 – ▤   AT **d**

X **Can Solé,** Sant Carlos 4, ✉ 3, ☎ 319 50 12, Pescados y mariscos – ▤   LY **a**
cerrado sábados noche, domingos, del 1 al 15 febrero y del 1 al 15 septiembre – Com
carta 726 a 1 475.

X **La Nao,** Londres 35, ✉ 29, ☎ 230 91 86 – ▤. ﭏ ⑩ E 𝘝𝘐𝘚𝘈. ⊱   EV **r**
cerrado sábados y agosto – Com carta 1 235 a 2 205.

X **El Vol de Nit,** Anglí 4, ✉ 17, ☎ 203 91 81, Cocina vasca – E. ⊱   BT **c**
cerrado domingos y agosto – Com carta 1 110 a 1 755.

X **Casa Agustín,** Vergara 5, ✉ 2, ☎ 301 97 45 – ▤. E 𝘝𝘐𝘚𝘈   HV **g**
cerrado sábados – Com carta 725 a 1 450.

X **El Túnel,** Ample 33, ⊠ 2, ℱ 315 27 59 – ⬯⬰ KY r
cerrado domingos noche y lunes – Com carta 1 250 a 2 050.

X El Retiro, Paris 200, ⊠ 36, ℱ 217 68 40 – ▤ FU k

X **Bienservida,** Roselló 307, ⊠ 37, ℱ 257 85 87 – E 𝑽𝑰𝑺𝑨 GU a
cerrado martes – Com carta 615 a 815.

X Casa Leopoldo, Sant Rafael 24, ⊠ 1, ℱ 241 30 14, Pescados y mariscos JY s

X Le Pot au Feu, Francisco Giner 8, ⊠ 12, ℱ 218 74 64, Cocina francesa – E 𝑽𝑰𝑺𝑨. ⬯⬰ FU h
cerrado domingos y agosto.

X **Montse Guillén,** Mariano Cubi 195, ⊠ 21, ℱ 200 27 31 – ▤. E 𝑽𝑰𝑺𝑨 EU t
cerrado domingos y festivos – Com carta 1 575 a 2 475.

Restaurantes de ambiente típico

XX ❀ **Agut d'Avignon,** Trinidad 3, ⊠ 2, ℱ 302 60 34, « Decoración regional » – ▤. 𝔸𝔼 ⓞ E KY n
cerrado domingos, Semana Santa y agosto – Com carta 1 250 a 1 975
Espec. Sopa de melon (verano y otoño), Pollo con gambas, Filetes de lenguado a la sidra.

XX **Font del Gat,** passeig Santa Madrona, Montjuïc, ⊠ 4, ℱ 224 02 24, Decoración regional –
🅿. 𝔸𝔼 ⓞ. ⬯⬰ CT x
Com carta 875 a 2 000.

XX **La Dida,** Roger de Flor 230, ⊠ 25, ℱ 207 23 91, « Decoración regional » – ▤ 🅿. 𝔸𝔼 E 𝑽𝑰𝑺𝑨
⬯⬰ JU c
cerrado Semana Santa, domingos y festivos en verano y sábados – Com carta 1 400 a 2 575.

X L'Alberg, Ramón y Cajal 13, ⊠ 12, ℱ 214 10 25, Decoración rústica – ▤ FU d

X **La Cuineta,** Paradis 4, ⊠ 2, ℱ 315 01 11, « Instalado con buen gusto en una antigua
bódega del siglo XVII » – 𝔸𝔼 ⓞ E 𝑽𝑰𝑺𝑨. ⬯⬰ MR e
cerrado lunes – Com carta 1 150 a 2 325.

X **Los Caracoles,** Escudillers 14, ⊠ 2, ℱ 301 20 41 – ▤. 𝔸𝔼 ⓞ E 𝑽𝑰𝑺𝑨 KY k
Com carta 1 175 a 1 860.

X **Can Culleretes,** Quintana 5, ⊠ 2, ℱ 317 64 85 – ▤ JY c
cerrado domingos noche, lunes y del 1 al 28 julio – Com carta 800 a 1 225.

X **Pá i Trago,** Parlamento 41, ⊠ 15, ℱ 241 13 20 – ▤. 𝑽𝑰𝑺𝑨. ⬯⬰ GY a
cerrado lunes no festivos y agosto – Com carta 1 200 a 2 050.

X **A la Menta,** passeig Manuel Girona 50, ⊠ 34, ℱ 204 15 49, Taberna – ▤. 𝔸𝔼 ⓞ E 𝑽𝑰𝑺𝑨. ⬯⬰
cerrado domingos noche – Com carta 1 125 a 2 225. BT r

Cafeterías, Restaurantes rápidos

XX Navarra, passeig de Grácia 4, ⊠ 7, ℱ 318 16 43 – ▤ JV s

XX **Plazza,** pl. de Catalunya 15, ⊠ 2, ℱ 301 17 97 – ▤. 𝑽𝑰𝑺𝑨 JV f
Com carta 1 080 a 1 650.

XX **Sol 9,** passeig de Grácia 44, ⊠ 7, ℱ 215 30 65 – ▤. 𝔸𝔼 ⓞ E 𝑽𝑰𝑺𝑨. ⬯⬰ GU n
cerrado domingos y agosto – Com carta 930 a 1 550.

XX **Treno,** Diputació 257, ⊠ 7, ℱ 302 40 30 – ▤. 𝔸𝔼 ⓞ E 𝑽𝑰𝑺𝑨. ⬯⬰ GV t
Com carta 700 a 1 950.

X Don Chon, Pau Claris 122, ⊠ 9, ℱ 317 31 00 – ▤ GU e

X **Kok d'Or,** Balmes 149, ⊠ 6, ℱ 218 88 82 – ▤. ⬯⬰ FU g
Com carta 695 a 1 060.

X La Poma, Rambla de Canaletas 117, ⊠ 2, ℱ 301 94 00 – ▤ JX e

en Esplugues de Llobregat – AT – – ⊠ Esplugues de Llobregat – ☎ 93 :

XXX **La Masía,** av. Països Catalans 58 ℱ 371 37 42, « Terraza bajo los pinos » – ▤ 🅿. 𝔸𝔼 ⓞ E
𝑽𝑰𝑺𝑨. ⬯⬰ AT s
Com carta 1 025 a 1 700.

X ❀ **Casa Quirze,** Laureano Miró 202 ℱ 371 10 84 – ▤ 🅿. 𝑽𝑰𝑺𝑨. ⬯⬰ AT e
cerrado domingos, lunes y agosto – Com carta 1 200 a 2 450
Espec. Mousseline de rascasse, Estofado de oca, Liebre a la montañesa (14 octubre-10 marzo).

en el Tibidabo AS – ⊠ Barcelona 6 – ☎ 93 :

X **La Masía,** ℱ 247 63 50, < ciudad, mar y montaña – 𝔸𝔼 ⓞ E 𝑽𝑰𝑺𝑨 AS a
cerrado 24 enero-25 febrero – Com carta 1 050 a 1 600.

en la carretera de Sant Cugat por ⑦ : 11 km – ⊠ Barcelona 6 – ☎ 93 :

X **Can Cortés,** urbanización Ciudad Condal Tibidabo ℱ 674 17 04, <, « Antigua masía, decoración rústica », ⌁ de pago – 🅿. ⓞ E 𝑽𝑰𝑺𝑨
cerrado domingos noche – Com carta 850 a 1 465.

en el aeropuerto por ⑤ : 12 km – ⊠ Aeropuerto de Barcelona – ☎ 93 :

XX **Aeropuerto de Barcelona y Salón Sant Jorge,** ℱ 379 02 54 – ▤. 𝔸𝔼 ⓞ. ⬯⬰
Com carta 1 590 a 2 890.

France

Paris

Nice

Cannes

Monaco

PARIS
et sa banlieue

PARIS Ⓟ 75 Plans : **10, 11, 12 et 14 G. Paris** − 2 317 227 h. − Région d'Ile-de-France 9 878 500 h.

Aérogares urbaines (Terminal) : esplanade des Invalides (7ᵉ) ☏ 550.32.30 et Palais des Congrès Porte Maillot ☏ 758.20.05.

Aéroports : voir au Bourget, à Orly et à Roissy-en-France, rubrique Proche banlieue.

Trains Autos : Renseignements ☏ 261.50.50 − Gare de Lyon ☏ 345.92.22 − Gare de l'Est ☏ 208.49.90 — Gare d'Austerlitz ☏ 584.16.16 — Gare Montparnasse ☏ 538.52.29.

Distances : A chacune des localités du Guide est donnée la distance du centre de l'agglomération à Paris (Notre-Dame) calculée par la route la plus pratique.

Paris et ses environs ont toujours offert aux visiteurs une grande variété d'hôtels et de restaurants, depuis les plus célèbres de renommée mondiale, jusqu'aux plus modestes. Nous ne prétendons pas les signaler tous, mais nos sélections indiquent des établissements dans toutes les catégories. Toutes précisions sont données sur le confort, les prix, la qualité de la table, les spécialités, le genre ou l'agrément.

Nous espérons ainsi vous aider dans votre choix et nous vous souhaitons un agréable séjour dans la capitale française.

---

sommaire

■ RENSEIGNEMENTS PRATIQUES

BUREAUX DE CHANGE

De 6 h 30 à 23 h 30 **à l'aéroport d'Orly.**
De 6 h à 23 h 30 **à l'aéroport Charles de Gaulle.**

DÉPANNAGE AUTOMOBILE

Il existe, à Paris et dans la Région Parisienne, des ateliers et des services permanents de dépannage.

Les postes de Police vous indiqueront le dépanneur le plus proche de l'endroit où vous vous trouvez.

MICHELIN à Paris et en banlieue

Services généraux :
46 av. Breteuil ☎ (1) 539.25.00 — 75341 PARIS CEDEX 07 — Télex MICHLIN 270789 F
Ouverts du lundi au vendredi de 8 h 45 à 16 h 30 (16 h le vendredi).

Agences régionales :
Ouvertes du lundi au vendredi de 8 h à 12 h 15 et de 14 h à 18 h (17 h 45 le vendredi).
Arcueil : 24 bis r. Berthollet ☎ (1) 735.13.20 — BP 19 — 94110 ARCUEIL.
Aubervilliers : 34 r. des Gardinoux ☎ (1) 833.07.58 — BP 79 — 93302 AUBERVILLIERS CEDEX.
Montreuil : 3 r. François-Debergue ☎ (1) 287.35.80 — BP 206 — 93103 MONTREUIL SOUS BOIS CEDEX.
Nanterre : 13, 15, 17 r. des Fondrières ☎ (1) 721.67.21 — BP 505 — 92005 NANTERRE CEDEX.
Agences :
Buc : 417 av. R.-Garros — Z.I. Centre — ☎ (3) 956.10.66 — 78530 BUC.
Maisons-Alfort : r. Charles-Martigny — Z.I. des Petites Haies — ☎ (1) 899.55.60 — BP 50 — 94702 MAISONS ALFORT CEDEX.
Entrepôts :
Gennevilliers : 121 av. du Vieux Chemin de St-Denis ☎ (1) 790.65.32 — 92230 GENNEVILLIERS.

■ OFFICES DE TOURISME

Paris

Syndicat d'Initiative et Accueil de France :
(de Pâques au 31 oct. tous les jours de 9 à 22 h, hors sais., de 9 h à 20 h), 127 av. des Champs-Élysées (8e) ☎ 723.61.72 ; Télex 611984 — Informations et réservations d'hôtels (pas plus de 5 jours à l'avance pour la province) — Change : U.B.P., 125 av. des Champs-Élysées.

Hôtesses de Paris :
Gare de l'Est ☎ 607.17.73 ; Gare de Lyon ☎ 343.33.24 ; Gare du Nord ☎ 526.94.82. Aérogare des Invalides ☎ 705.82.81 ; Gare d'Austerlitz ☎ 584.91.70.

France et Province

Les offices ci-dessous sont fermés le dimanche, nous précisons seulement les autres fermetures. S = Samedi, SA = Samedi Après-midi, L = Lundi.

France				fermé
Aéro-Club de France	6 r. Galilée	16e	720.93.02	S
Air France	119 av. Champs-Élysées	8e	299.23.64	
Air France	2 r. Scribe	9e	299.23.57	
Air France	Esplanade des Invalides	7e	323.96.53	
Air France	2 pl. Porte-Maillot	17e	299.20.05	
Air France	30 r. Fg-Poissonnière	10e	824.52.02	SA
Air France	23 bd Vaugirard	15e	323.98.94	
Air France	62 r. Mr-le-Prince	6e	325.73.95	
Air France	4 bis pl. Mar. Juin	17e	227.65.45	
Air Inter	1 av. Mar.-Devaux 91550 Paray-Vieille-Poste		687.12.12	
Air Inter	12 r. Castiglione	1er	260.36.46	
Association Française des Automobilistes	9 r. A. de la Forge	17e	227.82.00	S
Association des Stations Françaises des Sports d'Hiver	61 bd Haussmann	8e	742.23.32	S
Automobile-Club de France	6 pl. Concorde	8e	265.34.70	S
Automobile-Club de l'Ile-de-F.	8 pl. Concorde	8e	266.43.00	S
Club Alpin Français	9 r. La Boétie	8e	742.38.46	SA et L
F. F. de Camping et Caravaning	78 r. Rivoli	4e	272.84.08	S

Inter-Service-Route   858.33.33

Cie Française du Thermalisme	32 av. Opéra	2°	742.67.91	SA*
Touring-Club de France	6. r. F.-Gillot	16°	502.14.00	
Tourisme S.N.C.F.	127 av. Champs-Élysées	8°	723.54.02	
Tourisme S.N.C.F.	16 bd Capucines	9°	742.00.26	
Tourisme Vert	35 r. Godot de Mauroy	9°	742.25.43	S
Union Nle des Associations de Tourisme et de Plein Air	8 r. C.-Franck	15°	783.21.73	S

* de mai à déc.

Province — Maison de :

Alpes-Dauphiné	2 pl. André-Malraux	1er	296.08.43 - 296.08.56	SA
Alsace	39 av. Champs-Élysées	8°	256.15.94 - 225.93.42	
Auvergne	194 bis r. Rivoli	1er	261.82.38	
Bretagne	17 r. Arrivée	15°	538.73.15	
Corse	82 bd Haussmann	8°	878.97.91	
Drôme	14 bd Haussmann	9°	246.66.67	
Gers et de l'Armagnac	16 bd Haussmann	9°	770.39.61	
Hautes-Alpes et de l'Ubaye	4 av. Opéra	1er	206.05.09 - 296.01.88	
Limousin	18 bd Haussmann	9°	770.32.63 - 246.60.76	S
Lot-et-Garonne	15-17 Passage Choiseul	2°	297.51.43	S
Principauté de Monaco	6 pl. Madeleine	8°	260.32.46	S
Nord et Pas-de-Calais	18 bd Haussmann	9°	770.59.62	S
Normandie	342-344 r. St-Honoré	1er	260.08.67	S*
Périgord	30 r. Louis-le-Grand	2°	742.09.15	S
Poitou-Charente	4 av. Opéra	1er	296.05.08	
Pyrénées	24 r. Quatre-Septembre	2°	742.21.34 - 266.41.88	S
Rouergue (Aveyron)	3 r. Chaussée-d'Antin	9°	246.94.03	SM
Savoie	16 bd Haussmann	9°	246.59.26 - 770.76.84	

* sauf matin en saison

Étranger

AFRIQUE	2 r. Viarmes	1er	233.44.01	S
AFRIQUE DU SUD	9 bd Madeleine	1er	261.82.30	S
ALLEMAGNE	4 pl. Opéra	2°	742.04.38	S
AUTRICHE	47 av. Opéra	2°	742.78.57	S
BELGIQUE	21 bd Capucines	2°	742.41.18	SA
BULGARIE	45 av. Opéra	2°	261.69.58	S
CANADA	37 av. Montaigne	8°	723.01.01	S
CHYPRE	50 av. Champs-Élysées	8°	225.25.97	S
COLOMBIE	25 r. Artois	8°	563.57.51	S
COREE	33 av. du Maine	15°	538.71.23	S
DANEMARK	142 av. Champs-Élysées	8°	562.17.02	S*
EGYPTE	90 av. Champs-Élysées	8°	562.94.42	S
ESPAGNE	43 ter av. P.-1er-de-Serbie	8°	720.90.54	SA
FINLANDE	13 r. Auber	9°	742.65.52 - 266.40.13	S
GRANDE-BRETAGNE	6 pl. Vendôme	1er	296.47.60	S
GRANDE-BRETAGNE Royal Automobile Club	8 pl. Vendôme	1er	260.51.19	SA
GRÈCE	3 av. Opéra	1er	260.65.34 - 260.65.75	S
HAITI	64 r. La Boétie	8°	563.66.97	S
HONGRIE	27 r. Quatre-Septembre	2°	742.50.25	S
INDE	8 bd Madeleine	9°	265.83.86	S
IRLANDE	9 bd Madeleine	1er	261.84.26	SA
ISRAEL	14 r. Paix	2°	261.01.97 - 261.03.67	S
ITALIE	CIT 3 bd Capucines	2°	266.00.90	SA
ITALIE	ENIT 23 r. Paix	2°	266.66.68	S
JAPON	4 r. Ste Anne	1er	296.07.94 - 296.20.29	S
JERSEY	19 bd Malesherbes	8°	742.93.68	S
KENYA	5 r. Volney	2°	260.66.00	S
LIBAN	124 fg St-Honoré	8°	359.10.36 - 562.34.73	S
LUXEMBOURG	21 bd des Capucines	2°	742.90.56	S
MAROC	161 r. St-Honoré	1er	260.63.50 - 260.47.24	
MEXIQUE	34 av. George-V	8°	720.69.15 - 720.69.19	
PAYS-BAS	31 et 33 av. Champs-Élysées	8°	225.41.25 - 225.96.25	S
POLOGNE	49 av. Opéra	2°	742.07.42	S
PORTUGAL	7 r. Scribe	9°	742.59.81	S
ROUMANIE	38 av. Opéra	2°	742.25.42 - 742.27.14	SA
SUÈDE	11 r. Payenne	3°	278.87.06	matin et S
SUISSE	11 bis rue Scribe	9°	742.45.45	SA
TCHÉCOSLOVAQUIE	32 av. Opéra	2°	742.38.45	S
TUNISIE	32 av. Opéra	2°	742.72.67	S
TURQUIE	102 av. Champs-Élysées	8°	562.78.68	S
U.R.S.S.	7 bd Capucines	2°	742.47.40	S
YOUGOSLAVIE	31 bd Italiens	2°	297.57.56 - 742.99.20	SA

* sauf matin en saison

ARRONDISSEMENTS QUARTIERS

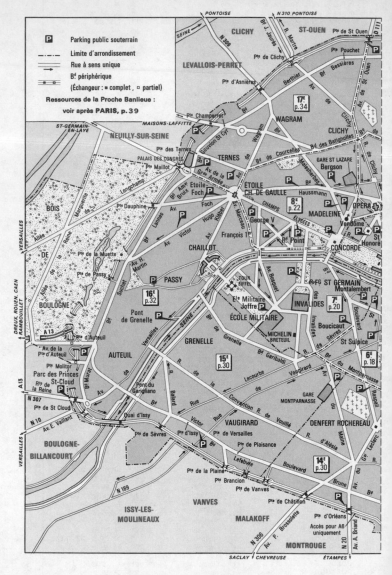

Pour la pratique journalière de Paris

Les Plans de Paris MICHELIN

précis - complets - détaillés

10 Plan, 12 Plan avec répertoire, 11 Paris Atlas, 14 plan de Paris

PRINCIPAUX PARCS DE STATIONNEMENT

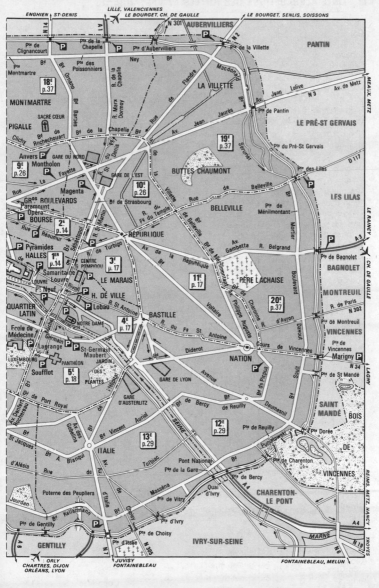

CARTES ET GUIDES MICHELIN
Bureau d'informations et de vente
46, avenue de Breteuil, Paris 7e - ☎ 539.25.00.
*Ouvert du lundi au vendredi de 9 h à 12 h et
de 13 h à 16 h 30.*

■ LISTE ALPHABÉTIQUE DES HOTELS ET RESTAURANTS

◼ RESTAURANTS de PARIS et de la BANLIEUE

Nous vous présentons ci-après une liste d'établissements sélectionnés pour la qualité de leur table ou pour leurs spécialités. Vous trouverez également des adresses pour souper après le spectacle ou pour déjeuner en plein air à Paris ou en banlieue.

Les bonnes tables... à étoiles

❀ ❀ ❀ 3 étoiles

		Arr.	Page
❀❀❀❀❀	Lasserre	8e	24
❀❀❀❀❀	Taillevent	8e	24
❀❀❀❀❀	Tour d'Argent	5e	19
❀❀❀❀	Archestrate	7e	21
❀❀❀❀	Grand Vefour	1er	15
❀❀❀❀	Vivarois	16e	33

❀ ❀ 2 étoiles

❀❀❀❀❀	Laurent	8e	24	
❀❀❀❀❀	Ledoyen	8e	24	
❀❀❀❀❀	Lucas-Carton	8e	24	
❀❀❀❀	Faugeron	16e	33	
❀❀❀❀	Marée (La)	8e	25	
❀❀❀❀	Pré Catelan	16e	34	
❀❀❀❀	Trois Marches	à Versailles	49	
❀❀❀	Bernardin (Le)	17e	35	
❀❀❀	Camélia (Le)	à Bougival	39	
❀❀❀	Chiberta	8e	25	
❀❀❀	Cochon d'Or	19e	37	

❀❀❀	Gérard Besson	1er	15	
❀❀❀	Gérard Pangaud	à Boulogne-Billancourt	40	
❀❀❀	Pressoir (Le)	12e	29	
❀❀❀	Rostang	17e	35	
❀❀❀	Tastevin (Le)	à Maisons-Laffitte	42	
❀❀❀	Vieille Fontaine	à Maisons-Laffite	42	
❀❀	Michel (Chez)	10e	28	
❀❀	Trou Gascon	12e	29	

❀ 1 étoile

❀❀❀❀❀	Bristol	8e	24	
❀❀❀❀❀	Régence Plaza	8e	24	
❀❀❀❀❀	Ritz Vendôme	1er	15	
❀❀❀❀	Célébrités	15e	31	
❀❀❀❀	Coq Hardi	à Bougival	39	
❀❀❀❀	Crillon	8e	25	
❀❀❀❀	Duc d'Enghien	à Enghien-les-Bains	41	
❀❀❀❀	El Chiquito	à Rueil-Malmaison	44	
❀❀❀❀	Fouquet's	8e	25	
❀❀❀❀	Grande Cascade	16e	34	
❀❀❀❀	Lamazère	8e	25	
❀❀❀❀	Maxim's	à Orly	43	
❀❀❀	Ambassade d'Auvergne	3e	17	
❀❀❀	Anges (Chez les)	7e	21	
❀❀❀	Aub. St-Quentinoise	à Livry-Gargan	42	
❀❀❀	Beauvilliers	18e	37	

❀❀❀	Bourgogne (La)	7e	21	
❀❀❀	Cazaudehore	à St-Germain-en-Laye	46	
❀❀❀	Champs d'Ors (Les)	7e	21	
❀❀❀	Comte de Gascogne (Au)	à Boulogne-Billancourt	40	
❀❀❀	Copenhague	8e	25	
❀❀❀	Étoile d'Or	17e	35	
❀❀❀	Jacqueline Fénix	à Neuilly	43	
❀❀❀	Jacques Cagna	6e	19	
❀❀❀	Jamin	16e	33	
❀❀❀	Louis XIV (Le)	10e	28	
❀❀❀	Marcande (Le)	8e	25	
❀❀❀	Marius et Janette	8e	25	
❀❀❀	Mercure Galant	1er	15	
❀❀❀	Morot-Gaudry	15e	31	

✿ 1 étoile

XXX	Nicolas 10ᵉ	28	
XXX	Récamier 7ᵉ	21	
XXX	Relais des Gardes . à Meudon	42	
XXX	Relais Louis XIII 6ᵉ	19	
XXX	Relais Pyrénées . . . 20ᵉ	37	
XXX	Timgad 17ᵉ	36	
XXX	Yan-Toit de Passy . . 16ᵉ	33	
XX	Albert (Chez) 14ᵉ	31	
XX	Ambroisie 5ᵉ	19	
XX	Aquitaine 15ᵉ	31	
XX	Augusta (Chez) . . . 17ᵉ	36	
XX	Barrière de Clichy (La) à Clichy	40	
XX	Belle Époque (La) à Chateaufort	40	
XX	Bistro 121 . . . . . 15ᵉ	31	
XX	Boule d'Or (La) . . . 7ᵉ	21	
XX	Bourrier . . . . . à Neuilly	43	
XX	Bretonnière à Boulogne-Billancourt	40	
XX	Cantine des Gourmets 7ᵉ	21	
XX	Châteaubriant (Au) . 10ᵉ	28	
XX	Clodenis 18ᵉ	38	
XX	Conticini 7ᵉ	21	
XX	Coq de la Maison Blanche . . . à St-Ouen	46	
XX	Coquille (La) 17ᵉ	36	
XX	Dariole (La) 8ᵉ	25	
XX	Dariole (La) . à Viry-Chatillon	49	
XX	Dodin Bouffant . . . 5ᵉ	19	
XX	Le Duc 14ᵉ	31	
XX	Ferme St-Simon . . . 7ᵉ	21	
XX	Flamberge (La) . . . 7ᵉ	21	
XX	Gambetta . . . à Houilles	41	

XX	Gasnier . . . . à Puteaux	44	
XX	Gildo 7ᵉ	22	
XX	Grandgousier (Le) . 18ᵉ	37	
XX	Guy Savoy 16ᵉ	34	
XX	Guyvonne (Chez) . . 17ᵉ	36	
XX	Julius . . . . à Gennevilliers	41	
XX	Michel Pasquet . . . 16ᵉ	33	
XX	Olympe 15ᵉ	31	
XX	Paul Chêne 16ᵉ	34	
XX	Pauline (Chez) . . . 1ᵉʳ	15	
XX	Petit Coin de la Bourse 2ᵉ	16	
XX	Petit Montmorency (Au) 8ᵉ	25	
XX	Petit-Pré 19ᵉ	38	
XX	Pierre 1ᵉʳ	16	
XX	Pierre Vedel 15ᵉ	32	
XX	P'tite Tonkinoise (La) . 10ᵉ	28	
XX	Quai des Ormes . . . 4ᵉ	17	
XX	Rêve d'Alsace à Morangis	42	
XX	Semailles (Les) . . . 18ᵉ	38	
XX	Sousceyrac (A) . . . 11ᵉ	17	
XX	Vert Bocage 17ᵉ	21	
X	Allard 6ᵉ	19	
X	Benoît 4ᵉ	17	
X	Bistro d'Hubert . . . 1ᵉʳ	16	
X	Mère Michel 17ᵉ	36	
X	Pantagruel 7ᵉ	22	
X	Petite Auberge (La) . 17ᵉ	36	
X	Petits Pères (Aux) . . 2ᵉ	16	
X	Pharamond 1ᵉʳ	16	
X	Pouilly-Reuilly au Pré St-Gervais	44	

Pour le souper après le spectacle

(Nous indiquons entre parenthèses l'heure limite d'arrivée)

XXXX	Café de la Paix (Relais des Capucines, snack) (1 h 15) 9ᵉ	28	
XXXX	Drouant-Grill (1 h) . . 2ᵉ	15	
XXX	Charlot Iᵉʳ « Merveille des Mers » (1 h) . . 18ᵉ	37	
XXX	✿ Louis XIV (1 h) . . 10ᵉ	28	
XXX	Relais Plaza (1 h 30) . 8ᵉ	25	
XX	Baumann (1 h) . . . 17ᵉ	36	
XX	Baumann-Baltard (2h) 1ᵉʳ	16	

XX	Coupe Chou (1 h) . . 5ᵉ	19	
XX	La Coupole (2 h) . . 14ᵉ	31	
XX	Dôme (Le) (1 h) . . 14ᵉ	31	
XX	Flo (Brasserie) (2 h) . 10ᵉ	28	
XX	Julien (2 h) 10ᵉ	28	
XX	Pied de Cochon (jour et nuit) 1ᵉʳ	16	
XX	Wepler (1 h) 18ᵉ	38	
X	Robert Vattier (5 h) . 1ᵉʳ	16	
X	Vaudeville (Le) (2 h) . 2ᵉ	16	

Le plat que vous recherchez

Une andouillette

Ambassade d'Auvergne . . .	3e	17
Casimir (Chez)	10e	28
Charbon de Bois	6e	19
Deux Taureaux	19e	38
Foux (La)	6e	19
Gasnier . . . . à Puteaux		44
Georges (Chez)	2e	16
Gourmet de l'Isle	4e	17
Grilladin (Au)	6e	19
Joséphine	6e	19
Pauline (Chez)	1er	15
Petit Coin de la Bourse (Le) .	2e	16
Petit Riche	9e	28
Pied de Cochon	1er	16
Robert Vattier	1er	16
Traversière (Le)	12e	30

Une bouillabaisse

Augusta (Chez)	17e	36
Charlot 1er		
« Merveilles des Mers » .	18e	37
El Chiquito . . à Rueil-Malmaison		44
Galan	4e	17
Grand Pavillon . . . . à Rungis		44
Jarasse . . . . à Neuilly-sur-Seine		43
Marius	16e	33
Marius et Janette	8e	25
Moulin d'Orgemont . . à Argenteuil		39
Prunier-Madeleine . . .	1er	15
Prunier-Traktir	16e	33
Senteurs de Provence (Les) .	15e	32
Truite Vagabonde	17e	36

Un cassoulet

Braisière (La)	17e	36
Chaumière Paysanne . . .	14e	32
Galan	4e	17
Gasnier . . . . à Puteaux		44
Giberne (La)	15e	32
Grand Veneur	17e	36
Julien	10e	28
Lamazère	8e	25
Mon Pays	14e	32
Morens	16e	33
Pyrénées-Cévennes . . .	11e	17
Quercy (Le)	9e	28
Quincy (Le)	12e	30
Relais du Périgord	13e	30
Sarladais	8e	25
Table de Jeannette (La) .	1er	16
Trois Marches . . à Versailles		49
Trou Gascon (Le)	12e	29
Truffière (La)	5e	19
Valéry (Le)	16e	34

Une choucroute

Baumann	17e	36
Baumann-Baltard	1er	16
Cochon Doré	2e	16
Flo (Brasserie)	10e	28
Petite Alsace	12e	30
Robert Vattier	1er	16
Taverne d'Alsace	9e	28

Un confit

Artois	8e	25
Auberge Landaise à Enghien-les-Bains		41
Braisière (La)	17e	36
Cazaudehore . . à St-Germain-en-Laye		46
Comte de Gascogne à Boulogne-Billancourt		40
Etchegorry	13e	30
Étienne de Bigorre . . .	6e	19
Gasnier . . . . à Puteaux		44
Giberne (La)	15e	32
Lamazère	8e	25
Maison des Foies Gras (La) .	1er	16
Mange Tout (Le)	5e	20
Mon Pays	14e	32
Pizou (Le)	6e	19
Pouilly-Reuilly . . au Pré-St-Gervais		44
Pyrénées-Cévennes . . .	11e	17
Quercy (Le)	9e	28
Relais des Pyrénées . . .	20e	37
Relais du Périgord	13e	30
Sarladais	8e	25
Taverne Basque	6e	19
Trou Gascon	12e	29
Valéry (Le)	16e	34

Des coquillages, crustacés, poissons

Arêtes (Les)	6e	19
Armes de Bretagne . . .	14e	31
Augusta (Chez)	17e	36
Bernardin (Le)	17e	35
Champs d'Ors (Les) . . .	7e	21
Charlot 1er		
« Merveille des Mers» »	18e	37
Drouant	2e	15
Duc (Le)	14e	31
El Chiquito . . à Rueil-Malmaison		44
Glénan (Les)	7e	22
Goumard	1er	15
Grand Pavillon . . . . à Rungis		44
Jarasse . . . . à Neuilly-sur-Seine		43
Louis XIV	10e	28
Marée (La)	8e	25
Marius (Chez)	7e	21
Marius	16e	33
Marius et Janette	8e	25
Moniage Guillaume . . .	14e	31
Pied de Cochon	1er	16
Prunier-Madeleine . . .	1er	15
Prunier-Traktir	16e	33
Truite Vagabonde	17e	36
Ty Coz	9e	28
Wepler	18e	38

Des escargots

Baumann	17e	36
Bourgogne (La)	7e	21
Camélia (Le) . . . . . à Bougival		39
Coquille (La)	17e	36
Fontaine aux Carmes . .	7e	22
Léon (Chez)	17e	36
Maître Paul	6e	20
Saintongeais (Le)	9e	28
Sancerre (Le)	19e	38
Truffière (La)	5e	19

Une grillade

Charbon de Bois (Au) . . .	6e	19
Cochon d'Or	19e	37
Dagorno	19e	37
Deux Taureaux	19e	38
Grilladin (Au)	6e	19
Hilton (Western)	15e	30
Pied de Cochon	1er	16
Robert Vattier	1er	16
Trois Limousins	8e	25
Trois Moutons	8e	25

Du boudin

Ambassade d'Auvergne . . .	3e	17
Artois	8e	25
Benoit	4e	17
Cochon d'Or	19e	37
Coquille (La)	17e	36
Giberne (La)	15e	32
Gourmet de l'Isle	4e	17
Quincy (Le)	12e	30
Terrasse (La)	à Créteil	41

Une paëlla

Etchegorry	13e	30
Étienne de Bigorre	6e	19
Pralognan (Le)	6e	20
Pyrénées-Cévennes	11e	17

Des tripes

La Foux	6e	19
Pharamond	1er	16
Pied de Cochon	1er	16
Relais du Périgord . . .	13e	30
Robert Vattier	1er	16

Des fromages choisis

Androuët	8e	25

Des soufflés

Le Soufflé	1er	16

Spécialités étrangères

Allemandes

Vieux Berlin (Au)	8e	25

Chinoises et Indochinoises

Délices de Szechuen (Aux) .	7e	21
Focly	à Neuilly-s-Seine	43
Grand Chinois (Le) . . .	16e	34
Moï (Le)	16e	34
Pagoda	9e	28
P'tite Tonkinoise (La) . . .	10e	28
Petite Tonkinoise .	à Enghien-les-Bains	41
Tan Dinh	7e	22
Tong-Yen	8e	25
Tsé-Yang	16e	33

Indiennes

Annapurna	8e	25
Indra	8e	25

Japonaises

Aï	1er	15
Nikko (Benkay)	15e	30
Méridien (Yamato) . . .	17e	34

Italiennes

Chateaubriant (Au) . . .	10e	28
Cour (La)	15e	32
Gildo (Chez)	7e	22
Main à la Pâte (La) . . .	1er	16
Pinocchio	14e	32
Pinocchio	10e	28
Stresa	8e	25

Orientales et Nord Africaines

Abel	10e	28
Al Mounia	16e	33
Caroubier (Le)	15e	32
Michèle (Chez)	13e	30
Timgad	17e	36
Wally	4e	17

Russes

Dominique	6e	19

Scandinaves

Copenhague	8e	25

Suisses : Mövenpick . . . . | 9e | 28

Plein air

Bois de Boulogne

XXXX ❀	Grande Cascade .	16e	34
XXXX ❀❀	Pré Catelan . . .	16e	34

Bois de Vincennes

XX	Chalet des Iles (Le)	. 12e	30

Champs-Elysées

XXXXX ❀❀	Laurent	8e	24
XXXXX ❀❀	Ledoyen	8e	24

Bougival	XXXX	❀ Coq Hardi	39
Chennevières	XXX	Écu de France	40
Maisons-Laffite	XXX	❀❀ Vieille Fontaine	42
»	XXX	❀❀ Tastevin	42
Meudon	XX	Ermitage Villebon	42
St-Germain-en-L.	XXX	❀ Cazaudehore	46
Vaucresson	XX	La Poularde	46
Le Vésinet	XX	Les Ibis	49

■ HOTELS, RESTAURANTS

par arrondissements

(Liste alphabétique des Hôtels et Restaurants, voir p. 6 à 9)

G 12 : Ces lettres et chiffres correspondent au carroyage du **Plan de Paris** Michelin n° **⑩**, **Paris Atlas** n° **⑪** et **Plan de Paris** n° **⑭**.

En consultant ces trois publications vous trouverez également les parkings les plus proches des établissements cités.

Opéra, Palais-Royal,
Halles, Bourse.
1er et 2e arrondissements.
1er : ✉ 75001
2e : ✉ 75002

🏨 **Ritz** 🥂, 15 pl. Vendôme (1er) ☎ 260.38.30, Télex 220262, « Jardin intérieur » – ⦀ ▤ 📺 ☎ 👌
℗ 🝙 🝓 ⓞ **E**   G 12
R Restaurant **Ritz-Vendôme voir ci-après** – ⊊ 36 – **163 ch** 700/950, 42 appart.

🏨 **Inter-Continental,** 3 r. Castiglione (1er) ☎ 260.37.80, Télex 220114 – ⦀ ▤ 📺 ☎ 👌 – 🝗
1000. 🝙 🝓 ⓞ **E**. 🍴 rest   G 12
rôtiss. Rivoli **R** 140/175 – **Café Tuileries R** carte 80 à 135 – ⊊ 37 – **500 ch** 556/754, 24 appart.

🏨 **Meurice,** 228 r. Rivoli (1er) ☎ 260.38.60, Télex 230673 – ⦀ ▤ 📺 ☎ 👌 – 🝖 25 à 40. 🝙 🝓
ⓞ **E**   G 12
Grill Copper Bar R carte 135 à 180 – ⊊ 50 – **159 ch** 676/1 040, 35 appart.

🏨 **Lotti,** 7 r. Castiglione (1er) ☎ 260.37.34, Télex 240066 – ⦀ ▤ rest ☎ 👌 – 🝖 25. 🝙 ⓞ **E**.
🍴 rest   G 12
R carte 120 à 180 - **Grill R** 150 – **126 ch** ⊊ 520/830, 12 appart.

🏨 **Westminster,** 13 r. Paix (2e) ☎ 261.57.46, Télex 680035 – ⦀ 📺 ☎ – 🝖 80. 🝙 🝓 ⓞ **E**   G 12
SC : Grill le **Bulldog R** carte 110 à 165 – **102 ch** ⊊ 600/710, 18 appart.

🏨 **Résidence St-James et Albany** Ⓜ, 202 r. Rivoli (1er) ☎ 260.31.60, Télex 213031 – ⦀
cuisinette 📺 ☎ – 🝖 50 à 150. 🝙 🝓 ⓞ **E**. 🍴   H 12
SC : rest. **Le Noailles** *(fermé dim.)* **R** carte 120 à 155 – **Bistro Lafayette R** carte environ 75 🍷 –
⊊ 30 – **142 ch** 450/550, 3 appart..

🏨 Louvre-Concorde, pl. A.-Malraux (1er) ☎ 261.56.01, Télex 220412 – ⦀ 📺 ☎ 👌   H 13
226 ch.

🏨 **Édouard VII,** 39 av. Opéra (2e) ☎ 261.56.90, Télex 680217 – ⦀ 📺 ☎ – 🝖 30. 🝙 🝓 ⓞ
SC : **R** voir rest **Delmonico** – **95 ch** ⊊ 390/490, 4 appart.   G 13

🏨 **Mayfair** Ⓜ sans rest, 3 r. Rouget-de-Lisle (1er) ☎ 260.38.14, Télex 240037 – ⦀ 📺 ☎   G 12
SC : ⊊ 22 – **52 ch** 358/501.

🏨 **France et Choiseul,** 239 r. St-Honoré (1er) ☎ 261.54.60, Télex 680959 – ⦀ ▤ rest 📺 ☎ –
🝖 30 à 200. 🝙 🝓 ⓞ. 🍴 rest   G 12
SC : **R** carte 75 à 120 🍷 – **135 ch** ⊊ 395/525, 7 appart.

🏨 **Cusset** Ⓜ, 95 r. Richelieu (2e) ☎ 297.48.90, Télex 670245 – ⦀ ▤ rest ☎. 🝓   F 13
les **Deux Ducs** *(fermé dim.)* **R** carte 65 à 95 🍷 – **115 ch** ⊊ 95/320.

🏨 **François** Ⓜ sans rest, 3 bd Montmartre (2e) ☎ 233.51.53, Télex 211097 – ⦀. 🝙. 🍴   F 14
SC : **64 ch** ⊊ 300/350, 11 appart. 465/510.

🏨 **Normandy,** 7 r. Échelle (1er) ☎ 260.30.21, Télex 670250 – ⦀ 📺 ☎ – 🝖 50. 🝙 🝓 ⓞ **E**.
🍴 rest   H 13
SC : **R** *(fermé sam. et dim.)* 80 – ⊊ 25 – **122 ch** 350/580, 8 appart.

🏨 **Métropole Opéra** Ⓜ sans rest, 2 r. Gramont (2e) ☎ 296.91.03, Télex 212276 – ⦀ 📺 ☎. 🝙
SC : ⊊ 18 – **51 ch** 110/310.   G 13

🏨 **Cambon** Ⓜ sans rest, 3 r. Cambon (1er) ☎ 260.38.09, Télex 240814 – ⦀ 📺 🛁wc ⬛wc ☎.
🝥 🝙 🝓 ⓞ   G 12
SC : ⊊ 24 – **44 ch** 350/460.

🏨 **Du Piémont** Ⓜ sans rest, 22 r. Richelieu (1er) ☎ 296.44.50 – ⦀ 📺 🛁wc ⬛wc ☎. 🝙 🝓 ⓞ
SC : **28 ch** ⊊ 218/275.   G 13

🏨 **Ascot Opéra** 〽 sans rest, 2 r. Monsigny (2ᵉ) ☎ 296.87.66, Télex 680461 — |\$| 🔟 ⇔wc ⋔wc
🕿, 🖚 ÆE ⒼⒷ ⓪ E
G 13
SC : ☲ 16 – **36 ch** 110/298.

🏨 **Richepanse** sans rest, 14 r. Richepanse (1ᵉʳ) ☎ 260.36.00 — |\$| 🔟 ⇔wc ⋔wc 🕿, 🖚 ÆE
🕉
G 12
SC : **43 ch** ☲ 262/294.

🏨 **Tuileries** sans rest, 10 r. St-Hyacinthe (1ᵉʳ) ☎ 261.04.17, Télex 240744 — |\$| 🔟 ⇔wc ☏, 🖚
ÆE
G 12
SC : **28 ch** ☲ 205/340.

🏨 **Favart** sans rest, 5 r. Marivaux (2ᵉ) ☎ 297.59.83 — |\$| ⇔wc ⋔wc 🕿, 🖚, 🕉
F 13
SC : **40 ch** ☲ 185/205.

🏨 **Montana H. Tuileries** 〽 sans rest, 12 r. St-Roch (1ᵉʳ) ☎ 260.35.10 — |\$| 🔟 ⇔wc ⋔wc 🕿,
🖚 ⒼⒷ 🕉
G 12
SC : ☲ 20 – **25 ch** 250/350.

🏨 **Molière** sans rest, 21 r. Molière (1ᵉʳ) ☎ 296.22.01 — |\$| ⇔wc ⋔wc 🕿, 🖚 ÆE ⓪, 🕉   G 13
SC : ☲ 16 – **30 ch** 178/280, 3 appart. 490.

🏨 **Gd H. de Champagne** sans rest, 17 r. J.-Lantier (1ᵉʳ) ☎ 261.50.05 — |\$| ⇔wc ⋔wc 🕿, 🖚
J 14
SC : **45 ch** ☲ 230/297.

🏨 **Ile de France** sans rest, 26 r. St-Augustin (2ᵉ) ☎ 742.40.61 — |\$| ⇔wc ⋔ 🕉   G 13
18 ch

🏨 **Ducs d'Anjou** sans rest, 1 r. Ste-Opportune (1ᵉʳ) ☎ 236.92.24 — |\$| ⇔wc ⋔wc 🕿, 🖚   H 14
SC : **38 ch** ☲ 100/185.

🏨 **Ducs de Bourgogne** sans rest, 19 r. Pont-Neuf (1ᵉʳ) ☎ 233.95.64 — |\$| ⇔wc ⋔wc 🕿, 🖚
🕉
H 14
SC : **49 ch** ☲ 194/220.

🏨 **St-Romain** sans rest, 7 r. St-Roch (1ᵉʳ) ☎ 260.31.70 — |\$| ⇔wc ⋔wc 🕿   G 13
SC : **33 ch** ☲ 155/220.

🏨 **Family** sans rest, 35 r. Cambon (1ᵉʳ) ☎ 261.54.84 — |\$| ⇔wc ⋔wc 🕿 ⅋, 🖚   G 12
SC : ☲ 13,50 – **25 ch** 123/198.

XXXXX ✿ **Ritz-Vendôme,** 15 pl. Vendôme (1ᵉʳ) ☎ 260.38.30 — ⓟ, ÆE ⒼⒷ ⓪ E, 🕉   G 12
R carte 190 à 290
Spéc. Poissons marinés à l'aneth, Omble chevalier, Aiguillettes de canard gras.

XXXX **Drouant,** pl. Gaillon (2ᵉ) ☎ 742.56.61 — ÆE ⒼⒷ ⓪ ▸   G 13
au rest. *(fermé sam.)* **R** carte 160 à 220, **au Grill** *(fermé 16 au 31 août et dim.)* **R** carte environ
150.

XXXX ✿✿✿ **Grand Vefour,** 17 r. Beaujolais (1ᵉʳ) ☎ 296.56.27, ancien café du Palais Royal fin 18ᵉ s.
— 🍽, 🕉
G 13
fermé août, sam. midi sauf du 1ᵉʳ sept. au 1ᵉʳ mai et dim. — **R** carte 185 à 220
Spéc. Filet de bar aux poireaux confits, Ris de veau "Yves Labrousse", Caneton nantais rôti.

XXXX **Prunier Madeleine,** 9 r. Duphot (1ᵉʳ) ☎ 260.36.04 — ÆE ⒼⒷ ⓪ E   G 12
fermé août — **R** carte 145 à 215.

XXX **Delmonico,** 39 av. Opéra (2ᵉ) ☎ 261.44.26 — 🍽, ÆE ⒼⒷ ⓪   G 13
fermé dim. — **R** carte 140 à 185.

XXX ✿✿ **Gérard Besson,** 5 r. Coq Héron (1ᵉʳ) ☎ 233.14.74 — ⒼⒷ ⓪   H 14
fermé 3 au 25 juil., 24 déc. au 2 janv., sam. et dim. — **R** 140 (déj.) et carte 125 à 180
Spéc. Terrines de viandes et de foie de canard, œufs brouillés "G. Garin", Biscuit glacé à la framboise.

XXX ✿ **Mercure Galant,** 15 r. Petits-Champs (1ᵉʳ) ☎ 297.53.85   G 13
fermé sam. midi, dim. et fêtes — **R** carte 135 à 170
Spéc. Feuilleté de langoustines, Foie de veau au vinaigre, Mille et une feuilles.

XXX **Aï,** 20 av. Opéra (1ᵉʳ) ☎ 296.01.81 — ÆE ⒼⒷ ⓪   G 13
fermé lundi — **R** 160/250.

XX **Goumard,** 17 r. Duphot (1ᵉʳ) ☎ 260.36.07 — ÆE ⒼⒷ ⓪   G 12
fermé dim. en août — **R** carte 110 à 165.

XX ✿ **Chez Pauline** (Génin), 5 r. Villedo (1ᵉʳ) ☎ 296.20.70   G 13
fermé sam. soir et dim. — **R** (🍽 1ᵉʳ étage) carte 110 à 185
Spéc. Foie gras frais, Ris de veau en croûte, Entrecôte à la moelle.

XX **La Table de Jeannette,** 14 r. Duphot (1er) ℡ 260.05.64 — 🆎 🆖 ⓞ ●   G 12
fermé 1er au 22 août, 24 déc. au 3 janv., sam. et dim. − SC : **R** carte 105 à 160.

XX **Baumann Baltard,** 9 r. Coquillière (1er) ℡ 236.22.00 — 🍽. 🆖   H 14
SC : **R** carte 105 à 140.

XX **La Main à la Pâte,** 35 r. St-Honoré (1er) ℡ 508.85.73 — 🆎 ⓞ ●   H 14
fermé sam. midi et dim. − SC : **R** carte 125 à 175 🍷.

XX **La Ferme Irlandaise,** 30 pl. Marché St.-Honoré (1er) ℡ 296.02.99 — 🆎 🆖 ⓞ   G 12
fermé août, 20 au 30 déc., dim. soir et lundi − **R** carte 85 à 125.

XX ❀ **Le Petit Coin de la Bourse** (Girard), 16 r. Feydeau (2e) ℡ 508.00.08   F 14
fermé sam., dim. et le soir sauf jeudi et vend. − SC : **R** carte 105 à 150
Spéc. Terrine de tourteau, Salade de St-Jacques (oct. à fin avril).

XX **La Corbeille,** 154 r. Montmartre (2e) ℡ 261.30.87 — 🆎 🆖 ⓞ   G 14
fermé sam. et dim. − **R** carte 115 à 150.

XX **Pied de Cochon** (ouvert jour et nuit), 6 r. Coquillière (1er) ℡ 236.11.75 — 🆎 🆖 ⓞ   H 14
SC : **R** 99.

XX **La Maison des Foies Gras,** 7 r. Gomboust (1er) ℡ 261.02.93 — 🆎 🆖 ⓞ   G 13
fermé sam. midi et dim. − **R** (nombre de couverts limité - prévenir) carte 115 à 165.

XX **Chez Gabriel,** 123 r. St-Honoré (1er) ℡ 233.02.99 — 🆎 🆖 ⓞ   H 14
fermé août, dim. soir et lundi − **R** carte 75 à 110.

XX ❀ **Pierre,** 10 r. Richelieu (1er) ℡ 296.09.17 — 🆎 🆖   H 13
fermé août, sam. et dim. − **R** carte 115 à 175
Spéc. Foie gras en terrine, Mousseline de rougets au fenouil, Rognon de veau à l'échalote.

XX **Le Soufflé,** 36 r. Mt-Thabor (1er) ℡ 260.27.19 — 🍽. 🆖 ⓞ E   G 12
fermé dim. et fériés − **R** carte 85 à 135.

XX **Pasadena,** 7 r. du 29-Juillet (1er) ℡ 260.68.96 — 🆎 🆖   G 12
fermé août, et fêtes − **R** carte 85 à 120 🍷.

XX **La Barrière Poquelin,** 17 r. Molière (1er) ℡ 296.22.19 — 🆎 🆖 ⓞ   G 13
fermé sam. midi et dim. − **R** carte 135 à 195.

XX **Caveau du Palais,** 19 pl. Dauphine (1er) ℡ 326.04.28 — 🆖   J 14
fermé Noël-Jour de l'An, sam. soir et dim. − **R** carte 95 à 145.

X ❀ **Pharamond,** 24 r. Grande-Truanderie (1er) ℡ 233.06.72 — 🆎 🆖 ⓞ   H 15
fermé juil., lundi midi et dim. − **R** carte 90 à 130
Spéc. Tripes à la mode de Caen, St-Jacques au cidre (oct. à mai), Canette au citron.

X **La Vigne aux Moineaux,** 15 r. N.-D.-Victoires (2e) ℡ 260.00.15 — 🍽. 🆎 🆖 ⓞ   G 14
fermé août, sam. et dim. − SC : **R** (déj. seul.) 35 bc/43 bc.

X **Chez Georges,** 1 r. Mail (2e) ℡ 260.07.11 — 🆎 🆖 ⓞ   G 14
fermé dim. et fêtes − **R** carte 80 à 120.

X ❀ **Bistro d'Hubert,** 36 pl. Marché St-Honoré (1er étage) ℡ 260.03.00 — 🆖   G 12
fermé dim. lundi et fériés − **R** 120, dîner à la carte
Spéc. Salade fine de foie gras, Turbot aux baies roses (oct. à mai), Feuillantine de poires (sept.-mars).

X **Vaudeville,** 29 r. Vivienne (2e) ℡ 233.39.31 — 🆖   FG 14
R carte 75 à 115 🍷.

X **La Bonne Fourchette,** 320 r. St-Honoré (1er) ℡ 260.45.27 — 🆎 🆖 ⓞ E   G 12
fermé 23 déc. au 6 janv., vac. scol. de fév. et sam. − SC : **R** 62.

X **Cochon Doré,** 16 r. Thorel (2e) ℡ 233.29.70 — 🍽   G 15
fermé merc. − SC : **R** 58 bc, carte le dim. 🍷.

X ❀ **Aux Petits Pères** (Chez Yvonne), 8 r. N.-D.-des-Victoires (2e) ℡ 260.91.73 — 🆎 🆖   G 14
fermé fin juil. à début sept., sam., dim. et fériés − **R** (prévenir) carte 80 à 120
Spéc. St-Jacques à la provençale (oct.-fin avril), Ris de veau toulousaine, Faisan (saison de chasse) ou pintade aux choux.

X **Louis XIV,** 1bis pl. Victoires (1er) ℡ 261.39.44   G 14
fermé août, sam. et dim. − **R** carte 85 à 130.

X **Robert Vattier,** 14 r. Coquillière (1er) ℡ 236.51.60 — 🆎 🆖 ⓞ E   H 14
fermé août et dim. − **R** carte 75 à 120.

X **La Vigne,** 30 r. Arbre-Sec (1er) ℡ 260.13.55   H 14
fermé août, dim. et lundi − **R** carte 70 à 100.

X **Paul,** 15 pl. Dauphine (1er) ℡ 354.21.48 — ✂   J 14
fermé août, lundi et mardi − **R** carte 70 à 100.

X **Gérard,** 4 r. Mail (2e) ℡ 296.24.36   G 14
fermé août, sam. midi, dim. et fêtes − **R** carte 70 à 105.

Pour traverser Paris et vous diriger en banlieue,
utilisez la carte Michelin **« Banlieue de Paris »** n° 101 à 1/50 000.

**Bastille, République,
Hôtel de Ville.**

3e, 4e et 11e arrondissements.
  3e : ⊠ *75003*
  4e : ⊠ *75004*
  11e : ⊠ *75011*

🏛 **Deux Iles** sans rest, 59 r. St.-Louis-en-l'Ile (4e) ☏ 326.13.35 — 🛗 ⌂wc 🎣wc ☎. 🚗. K 16
SC : ⌸ 20 — **17 ch** 250/300.

🏛 **Lutèce** Ⓜ sans rest, 65 r. St-Louis-en-l'Ile (4e) ☏ 326.23.52 — 🛗 ⌂wc 🎣wc ☜. 🚗. 🎎
SC : ⌸ 20 — **23 ch** 280/300. K 16

🏛 **Bretonnerie** sans rest, 22 r. Ste-Croix-de-la-Bretonnerie (4e) ☏ 887.77.63 — 🛗 ⌂wc 🎣wc
☎. 🚗. 🎎 J 16
SC : **32 ch** ⌸ 150/290.

🏛 **Nord et Est** sans rest, 49 r. Malte (11e) ☏ 700.71.70 — 🛗 ⌂wc 🎣wc ☎. 🎎 G 17
fermé août et 22 déc. au 2 janv. — SC : ⌸ 14 — **44 ch** 130/170.

🏛 **Place des Vosges** sans rest, 12 r. Birague (4e) ☏ 272.60.46 — 🛗 ⌂wc 🎣wc ☎. 🚗 GB
⓪ J 17
SC : ⌸ 16 — **16 ch** 140/200.

🏛 **Notre-Dame** sans rest, 51 r. Malte (11e) ☏ 700.78.76 — 🛗 ⌂wc 🎣wc 🚗. 🎎 G 17
fermé août — SC : ⌸ 14 — **58 ch** 45/170.

🏛 **Roubaix** sans rest, 6 r. Greneta (3e) ☏ 272.89.91 — 🛗 🎣wc 🚗. 🚗 G 15
SC : ⌸ 12 — **48 ch** 70/160.

🏛 **Sansonnet** sans rest, 48 r. Verrerie (4e) ☏ 887.96.14 — 🎣 ☎. 🚗. 🎎 J 15
SC : ⌸ 13 — **30 ch** 70/140.

XXX ✸ **Ambassade d'Auvergne,** 22 r. Grenier St-Lazare (3e) ☏ 272.31.22 — ▤. ▥ GB ⓪ E
fermé dim. — SC : **R** carte 100 à 145 H 15
Spéc. Andouillette aligot, Potée d'Auvergne, Cassoulet aux lentilles.

XX ✸ **Quai des Ormes** (Masraff), 72 quai Hôtel de Ville (4e) ☏ 274.72.22 — 🎎 J 15
fermé août, sam., dim. et fériés — **R** carte 115 à 150
Spéc. Poêlée d'artichauts et langoustines, St-Pierre grillé au basilic, Chaud froid de poires à la glace pistache.

XX **L'Acadien,** 35 bd Temple (3e) ☏ 272.27.94 — ▥ GB ⓪ E G 17
fermé août et dim. soir — **R** carte 105 à 185.

XX **Guirlande de Julie,** 25 pl. des Vosges (4e) ☏ 887.94.07 J 17
fermé 22 au 30 déc. et merc. — **R** carte environ 120.

XX ✸ **A Sousceyrac** (Asfaux), 35 r. Faidherbe (11e) ☏ 371.65.30 J 19
fermé 4 au 10 avril, août, sam. et dim. — **R** carte 110 à 145
Spéc. Foie gras frais, Cassoulet (merc. et vend.), Escalopes de rognons de veau aux asperges.

XX **Pyrénées Cévennes,** 106 r. Folie-Méricourt (11e) ☏ 357.33.78 G 17
fermé août, sam. dim. et fêtes — **R** carte 105 à 160.

XX **Chardenoux,** 1 r. J.-Vallès (11e) ☏ 371.49.52 K 20
fermé août, 23 déc. au 3 janv., sam. sauf le soir de sept. à Pâques, dim. et fêtes – SC : **R** carte
130 à 160.

XX **Taverne des Templiers,** 106 r. Vieille-du-Temple (3e) ☏ 278.74.67 — GB H 17
fermé août, sam. midi et dim. — SC : **R** carte 95 à 140.

XX **Repaire de Cartouche,** 8 bd Filles-du-Calvaire (11e) ☏ 700.25.86 — GB H 17
fermé 24 juil. au 22 août, sam. et dim. — **R** carte 85 à 125.

XX **Coconnas,** 2 bis pl. Vosges (4e) ☏ 278.58.16 — ⓪ J 17
fermé 19 déc. au 12 janv., lundi et mardi – SC : **R** 125 bc.

XX **Wally,** 16 r. Le Regrattier (4e) ☏ 325.01.39 K 15
fermé 23 déc. au 2 janv. et le midi ; sam. dim. et lundi — **R** 150.

XX **Au Gourmet de l'Isle,** 42 r. St-Louis-en-l'Ile (4e) ☏ 326.79.27 — ▤ K 16
fermé 25 juil. au 1er sept., lundi et jeudi — **R** 65.

XX **Victor,** 12 pl. Bastille (11e) ☏ 343.42.68 J 17
fermé août, dim. et fêtes — **R** carte 80 à 130 🍷.

XX **Galan,** 36 bd Henri-IV (4e) ☏ 272.17.09 — GB K 17
fermé août, sam. sauf le soir en hiver — **R** carte 90 à 135.

X ✸ **Benoît,** 20 r. St-Martin (4e) ☏ 272.25.76 J 15
fermé 5 au 12 avril, 24 juil. au 30 août, sam. et dim. — SC : **R** carte 125 à 190
Spéc. Bœuf et museau en salade, Boudin fait maison, Rognon de veau en cocotte.

X **Au Trou Normand,** 117 av. Parmentier (11e) ☏ 357.39.62 — GB G 18
fermé août, sam. soir, dim. et fêtes — **R** 47/57 🍷.

Quartier Latin, Luxembourg, Jardin des Plantes.

5ᵉ et 6ᵉ arrondissements.
5ᵉ : ⊠ 75005
6ᵉ : ⊠ 75006

🏨 **Victoria Palace** Ⓜ ⑤, 6 r. Blaise-Desgoffe (6ᵉ) 📞 544.38.16, Télex 270557 – 🔄 📺 ☎ 🚗.　L 11
　🅰🅴. 🛇
　SC : **R** carte environ 110 – **110 ch** ⊡ 370/490.

🏨 **Littré,** 9 r. Littré (6ᵉ) 📞 544.38.68, Télex 203852 – 🔄 📺 ☎ 🚗 – 🔬 25. 🅰🅴 🆖. 🛇　L 11
　SC : **R** carte environ 110 – **100 ch** ⊡ 370/415. 3 appart. 490.

🏨 **Lutétia Concorde,** 45 bd Raspail (6ᵉ) 📞 544.38.10, Télex 270424 – 🔄 📺 ☎ – 🔬 25 à 600.
　🅰🅴 🆖 ⓞ 🅴　K 12
　SC : **R** 48/74 🍴 – **285 ch** ⊡ 450/635, 11 appart.

🏨 **Abbaye St-Germain** Ⓜ ⑤ sans rest, 10 r. Cassette (6ᵉ) 📞 544.38.11, 🌳 – 🔄 ☎. 🛇　K 12
　SC : **45 ch** ⊡ 300/380.

🏨 **Odéon H.,** Ⓜ sans rest, 3 r. Odéon (6ᵉ) 📞 325.90.67, Télex 202943 – 🔄 ☎. 🅰🅴 ⓞ. 🛇　K 13
　fermé 29 juil. au 26 août – SC : **34 ch** ⊡ 280/310.

🏨 **Madison H.** sans rest, 143 bd St-Germain (6ᵉ) 📞 329.72.50 – 🔄 ☎. 🛇　J 13
　SC : **56 ch** ⊡ 176/280.

🏨 **Scandinavia** sans rest, 27 r. Tournon (6ᵉ) 📞 329.67.20 – ➡wc ☎. 🏧. 🛇　K 13
　fermé août – SC : ⊡ 17 – **22 ch** 220/240.

🏨 **Angleterre** sans rest, 44 r. Jacob (6ᵉ) 📞 260.34.72 – 🔄 📺 ➡wc ☎. 🏧. 🛇　J 13
　SC : ⊡ 18 – **31 ch** 220/350.

🏨 **Colbert** sans rest, 7 r. Hôtel-Colbert (5ᵉ) 📞 325.85.65, Télex 260690 – 🔄 ➡wc 🚿wc ☎. 🏧
　🅰🅴. 🛇　K 15
　SC : **40 ch** ⊡ 210/420.

🏨 **Ferrandi** sans rest, 92 r. Cherche-Midi (6ᵉ) 📞 222.97.40 – 🔄 ➡wc 🚿wc ☎. 🏧　L 11
　SC : ⊡ 18 – **41 ch** 240/260.

🏨 **Delavigne** sans rest, 1 r. C.-Delavigne (6ᵉ) 📞 329.31.50, Télex 201579 – 🔄 ➡wc 🚿wc ☎.
　🛇　K 13
　SC : ⊡ 15 – **34 ch** 155/200.

🏨 **Pas-de-Calais** sans rest, 59 r. Sts-Pères (6ᵉ) 📞 548.78.74 – 🔄 ➡wc 🚿wc ☎. 🏧　J 12
　SC : ⊡ 15 – **41 ch** 220/275.

🏨 **St-Germain-des-Prés** sans rest, 36 r. Bonaparte (6ᵉ) 📞 326.00.19 – 🔄 ➡wc 🚿wc ☎. 🏧　J 13
　SC : ⊡ 16 – **28 ch** 240/300.

🏨 **Gd H. des Principautés Unies** Ⓜ sans rest, 42 r. Vaugirard (6ᵉ) 📞 634.44.90 – 🔄 ➡wc
　🚿wc ☎. 🏧.　K 13
　fermé août – SC : **25 ch** ⊡ 90/242.

🏨 **d'Isly** sans rest, 29 r. Jacob (6ᵉ) 📞 326.32.39 – 🔄 ➡wc 🚿wc ☎. 🏧. 🛇　J 13
　SC : **35 ch** ⊡ 135/280.

🏨 **Marronniers** Ⓜ ⑤ sans rest, 21 r. Jacob (6ᵉ) 📞 325.30.60, 🌳 – 🔄 ➡wc 🚿wc ☎. 🏧. 🛇　J 13
　SC : ⊡ 18 – **37 ch** 160/245.

🏨 **Seine** sans rest, 52 r. Seine (6ᵉ) 📞 634.22.80 – 🔄 📺 ➡wc 🚿wc ☎. 🏧 🅰🅴 🆖 ⓞ. 🛇　J 13
　SC : **30 ch** ⊡ 140/270.

🏨 **Rennes Montparnasse** sans rest, 151 bis r. Rennes (6ᵉ) 📞 548.97.38 – 🔄 ➡wc 🚿wc ☎.
　🏧 🅰🅴 🆖 ⓞ 🅴　L 12
　fermé 1ᵉʳ au 29 août – SC : **38 ch** ⊡ 160/290.

🏨 **Welcome** Ⓜ sans rest, 66 r. Seine (6ᵉ) 📞 634.24.80 – 🔄 ➡wc 🚿wc ☎. 🏧. 🛇　J 13
　SC : ⊡ 17 – **30 ch** 165/215.

🏨 **Gd H. Suez** sans rest, 31 bd St-Michel (5ᵉ) 📞 634.08.02, Télex 202019 – 🔄 ➡wc 🚿wc ☎.
　🏧 🅰🅴 🆖 ⓞ 🅴. 🛇　K 14
　SC : **50 ch** ⊡ 153/213.

🏨 **Odéon** sans rest, 13 r. St-Sulpice (6ᵉ) 📞 325.70.11 – 🔄 📺 ➡wc 🚿wc ☎. 🏧 🅰🅴 ⓞ　K 13
　SC : **24 ch** ⊡ 120/275.

🏨 **Albe** sans rest, 1 r. Harpe (5ᵉ) 📞 634.09.70 – 🔄 ➡wc 🚿wc ☎. 🏧. 🛇　K 14
　SC : **41 ch** ⊡ 136/240.

🏨 **St-Sulpice** sans rest, 7 r. C.-Delavigne (6ᵉ) 📞 634.23.90 – 🔄 ➡wc 🚿wc ☎. 🏧　K 13
　SC : ⊡ 14 – **42 ch** 90/180.

XXXXX ✿✿✿ **Tour d'Argent** (Terrail), 15 quai Tournelle (5ᵉ) ☎ 354.23.31, « Petit musée de la table,
≤ Notre-Dame, dans les caves : spectacle historique sur le vin » – 🆎 ⑩ K 16
fermé lundi – **R** 180 (déj.) et carte 275 à 325
Spéc. Panaché de la marée, Caneton Tour d'Argent, Rosettes d'agneau à l'estragon.

XXX ✿ **Jacques Cagna,** 14 r. Gds-Augustins (6ᵉ) ☎ 326.49.39, « Maison du Vieux Paris » – 🖾
🆎 ☒ ⑩ J 14
fermé 31 juil. au 24 août, 24 déc. au 3 janv., sam. et dim. – **R** carte 180 à 240
Spéc. Cassolette d'huîtres et de homard, Filets de Sole au pamplemousse, Pigeon de Bresse en Bécasse.

XXX ✿ **Relais Louis XIII,** 8 r. Gds Augustins (6ᵉ) ☎ 326.75.96, « Caveau 16ᵉ siècle, beau mobilier » – 🆎 ☒ ⑩ 🇪 J 14
fermé août et dim. – **R** carte 150 à 190
Spéc. Sole braisée au foie gras, Ris de veau à l'oseille, Gourmandises.

XX **Aub. des Deux Signes,** 46 r. Galande (5ᵉ) ☎ 325.46.56, « Cadre médiéval » – 🆎 ☒ ⑩ 🇪
fermé dim. et fériés – **R** carte 130 à 200. K 14

XX ✿ **Dodin-Bouffant,** 25 r. F.-Sauton (5ᵉ) ☎ 325.25.14 – 🖾. ☒ ⑩ K 15
fermé août, vacances scolaires de Noel sam. et dim. – **R** carte 105 à 155
Spéc. Fricassée de tête de veau, Daube d'huîtres et pieds de porc, Cassoulet de tripes.

XX ✿ **Ambroisie** (Pacaud), 65 quai de la Tournelle (5ᵉ) ☎ 633.18.65 K 15
fermé 15 août au 15 sept., dim. soir et lundi – SC : **R** carte 150 à 185
Spéc. Salade de petits légumes à la coriandre, Raie aux choux, Mille-feuille aux fruits de saison.

XX **Le Pactole,** 44 bd St-Germain (5ᵉ) ☎ 633.31.31 – ☒ K 15
fermé sam. midi et dim. – SC : **R** carte 130 à 190.

XX **Coupe-Chou,** 11 r. Lanneau (5ᵉ) ☎ 633.68.69 K 14
fermé midi – **R** carte 100 à 150.

XX **Atelier Maître Albert,** 1 r. Maître-Albert (5ᵉ) ☎ 633.13.78 – 🖾 K 15
fermé dim. et fériés – **R** (dîner seul.) 120 bc.

XX **Taverne Basque,** 45 r. Cherche-Midi (6ᵉ) ☎ 222.51.07 – 🆎 ☒ K 12
fermé 1ᵉʳ au 16 août, dim. soir et lundi – **R** carte 80 à 115.

XX **La Foux,** 2 r. Clément (6ᵉ) ☎ 325.77.66 – 🖾. 🆎 ⑩ K 13
fermé dim. – SC : **R** carte 90 à 160.

XX **Les Arètes,** 165 bd Montparnasse (6ᵉ) ☎ 326.23.98 – 🆎 M 11
fermé sam. midi et lundi – **R** carte 125 à 190.

XX **Chez Tante Madée,** 11 r. Dupin (6ᵉ) ☎ 222.64.56 K 12
fermé juil., sam. midi et dim. – SC : **R** carte 130 à 175.

XX **Le Sybarite,** 6 r. Sabot (6ᵉ) ☎ 222.21.56 – 🖾. ☒ ⑩ K 12
fermé dim. – SC : **R** 105 bc.

XX **Au Grilladin,** 13 r. Mézières (6ᵉ) ☎ 548.30.38 K 12
fermé vacances de Pâques, août, vacances de Noel et dim. – **R** carte 85 à 120.

XX **Le Pizou,** 19 r. Regard (6ᵉ) ☎ 548.87.67 – ☒ ⑩ K 12
fermé août, vacances de fév., dim. et fériés – **R** carte 80 à 140 ♨.

XX **La Truffière,** 4 r. Blainville (5ᵉ) ☎ 633.29.82 – 🖾. 🆎 ☒ ⑩ 🇪 L 15
fermé 28 juin au 27 juil. et lundi – **R** carte 90 à 140.

XX **Joséphine** (Chez Dumonet), 117 r. Cherche-Midi (6ᵉ) ☎ 548.52.40 – ☒ L 11
fermé 3 juil. au 3 août, 25 au 31 déc., sam. et dim. – **R** carte 100 à 180.

XX **Dominique,** 19 r. Bréa (6ᵉ) ☎ 327.08.80 – 🆎 ☒ ⑩ 🇪 L 12
fermé juil. – **R** carte 75 à 130.

X ✿ **Allard** (Mme Allard), 41 r. St-André-des-Arts (6ᵉ) ☎ 326.48.23 – 🖾. ☒ ⑩ K 14
fermé août, dim. et fêtes – SC : **R** (nombre de couverts limité - prévenir) carte 120 à 180
Spéc. Poissons au beurre blanc, Canard aux olives, Gibiers (saison).

X **Balzar,** 49 r. Écoles (5ᵉ) ☎ 354.13.67 – ✎ K 14
fermé août et mardi – **R** carte 80 à 110.

X **Moissonnier,** 20 r. Fossés-St-Bernard (5ᵉ) ☎ 329.87.65 K 15
fermé août, dim. soir et lundi – **R** carte 90 à 125.

X **Étienne de Bigorre,** 14 r. Dauphine (6ᵉ) ☎ 326.49.81 – 🆎 ⑩ J 14
fermé août et dim. – **R** carte 80 à 130 ♨.

X **Au Charbon de Bois,** 16 r. Dragon (6ᵉ) ☎ 548.57.04. Ambiance début du siècle – 🖾. ☒
⑩ J 12
fermé août, dim. et fériés – **R** carte 85 à 120.

✗ **Chez Maître Paul,** 12 r. Monsieur-le-Prince (6ᵉ) ☏ 354.74.59 — 🆎 🇬🇧 ⓞ ●   K 13
fermé août, dim. et lundi – **R** carte 80 à 110.

✗ **Moulin à Vent,** 20 r. Fossés-St-Bernard (5ᵉ) ☏ 354.99.37 — 🆎 🇬🇧 ⓞ   K 15
fermé août et dim. – **R** carte 95 à 135.

✗ **Le Mange Tout,** 30 r. Lacépède (5ᵉ) ☏ 535.53.93 — ⓞ   L 15
fermé 15 août au 15 sept., dim. soir et lundi – SC : **R** carte 80 à 110.

✗ **Le Pralognan,** 3 r. Hautefeuille (6ᵉ) ☏ 354.35.46 — 🇬🇧 ⓞ   K 14
fermé 30 juil. au 2 sept., sam. midi et dim. – SC : **R** carte 90 à 140.

✗ Vellu, 12 rue Mirbel (5ᵉ) ☏ 331.64.89   M 15

✗ Chez Marcel, 7 r. Stanislas (6ᵉ) ☏ 548.29.94   L 12

**Faubourg-St-Germain,
Invalides,
École Militaire.**

7ᵉ arrondissement.
7ᵉ : ⊠ *75007*

🏨 **Pont Royal et rest. Les Antiquaires,** 7 r. Montalembert ☏ 544.38.27, Télex 270113 — 📶
cuisinette 📺 ☎ – 🕮 25 à 50. 🆎 🇬🇧 ⓞ 🇪   J 12
SC : **R** *(fermé dim.)* 120 – **74 ch** ⌺ 320/550, 6 appart.

🏨 **Sofitel Bourbon** Ⓜ, 32 r. St-Dominique ☏ 555.91.80, Télex 250019 — 📶 ▤ 📺 ☎ 🕭 ⇦
🕮 30 à 50. 🆎 🇬🇧   H 10
SC : rest. **Le Dauphin R** carte 140 à 190 – ⌺ 35 – **102 ch** 490/670.

🏨 **Cayré-Copatel** Ⓜ sans rest, 4 bd Raspail ☏ 544.38.88, Télex 270577 — 📶 📺 ☎. 🆎 🇬🇧 ⓞ.
✻   J 12
SC : **130 ch** ⌺ 431/471.

🏨 **Université** sans rest, 22 r. Université ☏ 261.09.39 — 📶 ☎. ✻   J 12
SC : ⌺ 22 – **27 ch** 250/450.

🏨 **de La Bourdonnais,** 111 av. La Bourdonnais ☏ 705.45.42, Télex 201416 — 📶 ☎   J 9
SC : **R** voir rest. **La Cantine des Gourmets** – **56 ch** ⌺ 220/270.

🏨 **Suède** Ⓜ sans rest, 31 r. Vaneau ☏ 705.00.08, Télex 200596 — 📶 ⌂wc 🛁wc ☎. 📶🅱 🆎. ✻
SC : **40 ch** ⌺ 268/350.   K 11

🏨 **De Varenne** Ⓜ ⌂ sans rest, 44 r. Bourgogne ☏ 551.45.55 — 📶 📺 ⌂wc 🛁wc ☎. 📶🅱 🆎
SC : ⌺ 18 – **24 ch** 195/295.   J 10

🏨 **Bourgogne et Montana,** 3 r. Bourgogne ☏ 551.20.22, Télex 270854 — 📶 ⌂wc 🛁wc ☎.
📶🅱 🆎 🇬🇧   H 11
R *(fermé août, sam. et dim.)* 70 🍴 – **30 ch** ⌺ 220/320, 5 appart. 450.

🏨 **Saxe Résidence** ⌂ sans rest, 9 villa Saxe ☏ 783.98.28, Télex 270139 — 📶 📺 ⌂wc 🛁wc
☎. 📶🅱 🆎. ✻   K 9
SC : **50 ch** ⌺ 270/350.

🏨 **Lenox** Ⓜ sans rest, 9 r. Université ☏ 296.10.95 — 📶 📺 ⌂wc 🛁wc ☎. 📶🅱   J 12
SC : ⌺ 18 – **32 ch** 198/310.

🏨 **St-Germain** sans rest, 88 r. Bac ☏ 548.62.92 — 📶 ⌂wc 🛁wc ☎. 📶🅱 🆎. ✻   J 11
SC : ⌺ 17 – **29 ch** 190/270.

🏨 **Derby H.** sans rest, 5 av. Duquesne ☏ 705.12.05 — 📶 ⌂wc 🛁wc ☎. 📶🅱 🆎 ⓞ 🇪   J 9
SC : ⌺ 15 – **36 ch** 200/230.

🏨 **Quai Voltaire** sans rest, 19 quai Voltaire ☏ 261.50.91, ≤ – 📶 ⌂wc 🛁wc ☎. 📶🅱   J 12
SC : ⌺ 18 – **34 ch** 100/300.

🏨 **Lindbergh** sans rest, 5 r. Chomel ☏ 548.35.53 — 📶 ⌂wc 🛁wc ☎. 📶🅱 🇬🇧 🇪. ✻   K 12
SC : ⌺ 15 – **26 ch** 180/220.

🏨 **Tourville** Ⓜ sans rest., 16 av. Tourville ☏ 705.52.15 — 📶 📺 ⌂wc 🛁wc ☎. ✻   J 9
SC : ⌺ 15 – **31 ch** 180/230.

🏠 **Solférino** sans rest, 91 r. Lille ☏ 705.85.54 — 📶 ⌂wc 🛁wc ☎. 📶🅱 ✻   H 11
fermé 20 déc. au 5 janv. – SC : **35 ch** ⌺ 120/250.

🏠 **Mars H.** sans rest, 117 av. La Bourdonnais ☏ 705.42.30 — 📶 ⌂wc 🛁wc ☎. 📶🅱 ✻   J 9
SC : ⌺ 14 – **24 ch** 85/190.

🏠 **Verneuil-St-Germain** sans rest, 8 r. Verneuil ☏ 260.24.16 — 📶 ⌂wc 🛁wc ☎. 📶🅱   J 12
SC : ⌺ 16 – **26 ch** 170/220.

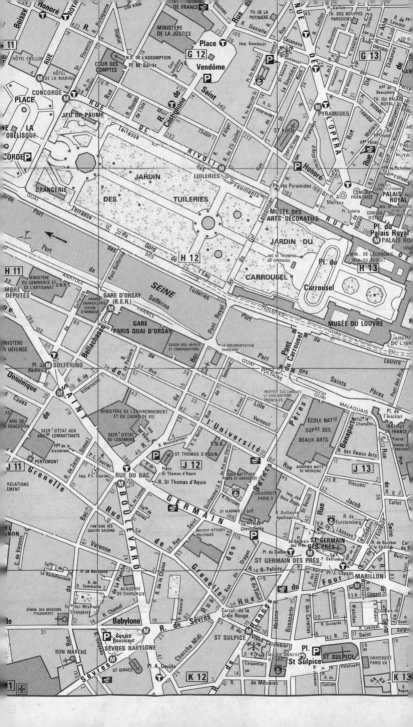

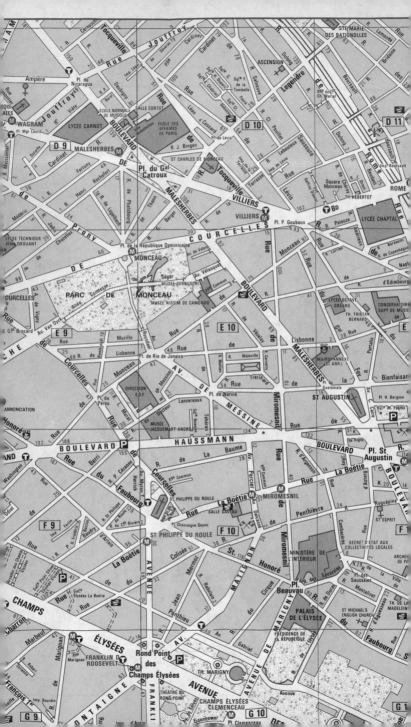

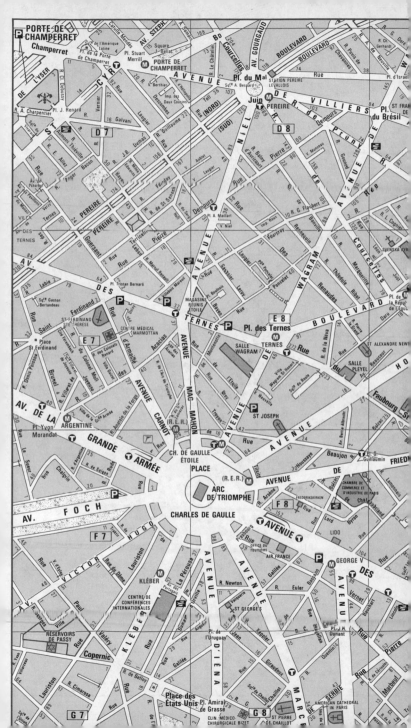

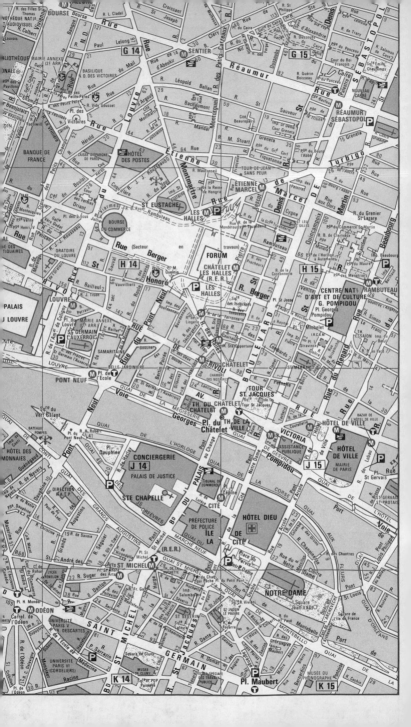

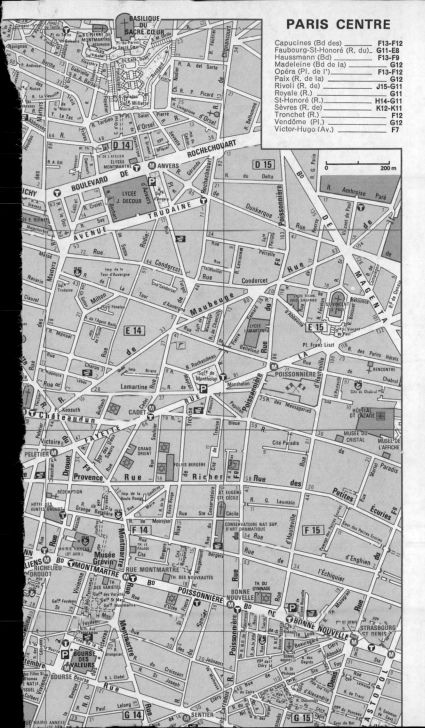

PARIS CENTRE

BASILIQUE DU SACRÉ CŒUR

0   200 m

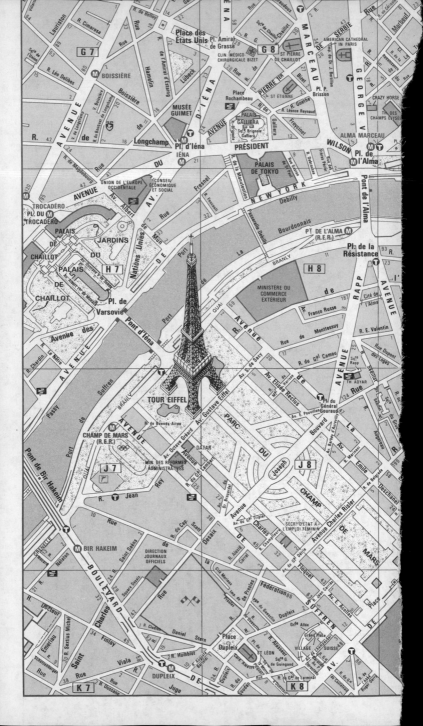

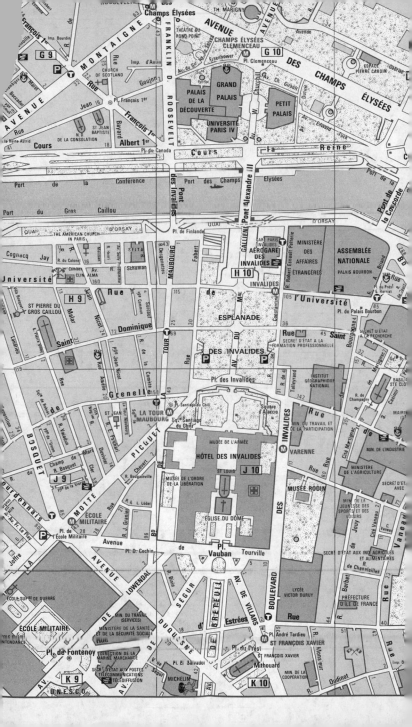

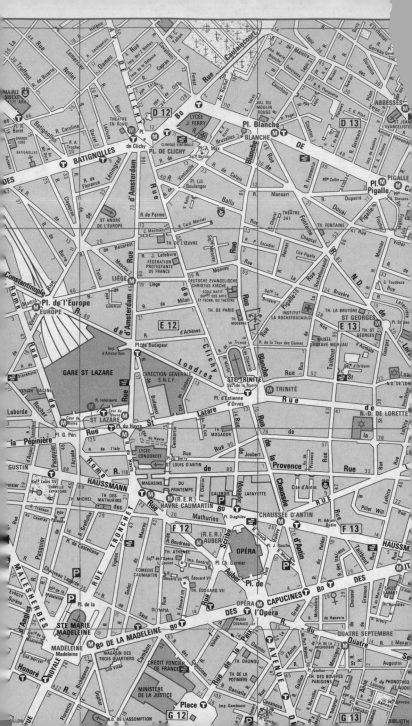

🏠 **Turenne** sans rest, 20 av. Tourville ☎ 705.99.92 – 🕃 🛏wc ⋔wc 🖭. 🚗 ÆE   J 9
SC : ⚌ 14 – **34 ch** 132/187.

🏠 **Kensington** sans rest, 79 av. La Bourdonnais ☎ 705.74.00 – 🕃 🛏wc ⋔wc ☎. 🚗 ÆE ⚏   J 9
SC : ⚌ 12 – **26 ch** 140/180.

🏠 **Résidence d'Orsay** sans rest, 93 r. Lille ☎ 705.05.27 – 🕃 🛏wc ⋔wc 🖭. 彩   H 11
fermé août – SC : ⚌ 16 – **32 ch** 110/210.

🏠 **Muguet** sans rest, 11 r. Chevert ☎ 705.05.93 – 🕃 🛏wc ⋔wc 🖭. 🚗   J 9
fermé 25 juil. au 30 août – SC : ⚌ 15 – **43 ch** 80/170.

XXXX 🏵🏵🏵 **Archestrate** (Senderens), 84 r. Varenne ☎ 551.47.33 – ÆE   J 10
fermé 1er au 24 août, 23 déc. au 2 janv. sam. et dim. – **R** carte 280 à 350
Spéc. Langoustines en papillote de poireaux, Foie gras au chou à la vapeur, Canard Apicius.

XXX 🏵 **Chez les Anges**, 54 bd Latour-Maubourg ☎ 705.89.86 – 🍽. ÆE ⚏ ⓞ 🗲   J 9
fermé dim. soir et lundi – **R** carte 120 à 180
Spéc. Oeufs en meurette, Suprême de barbue au beurre de poivrons rouges, Foie de veau.

XXX 🏵 **Chez Marius**, 5 r. Bourgogne ☎ 551.79.42 – ⚏ ⓞ. 彩   H 11
fermé fin juil. au 1er sept. et sam. – **R** carte 120 à 190.

XXX 🏵 **La Bourgogne** (Julien), 6 av. Bosquet ☎ 705.96.78 – ÆE ⚏ ⓞ   H 9
fermé août, sam. midi et dim. – **R** carte 125 à 180
Spéc. Foie gras de canard chaud aux raisins, Choux farci truffé, Ris de veau aux morilles.

XXX 🏵 **Récamier** (Cantegrit), 4 r. Récamier ☎ 548.86.58 – 🍽. ÆE ⚏ ⓞ E   K 12
fermé dim. – **R** carte 135 à 180
Spéc. Oeufs en meurette, Mousse de brochet, Sauté de bœuf bourguignon.

XXX 🏵 **Les Champs d'Ors** (Cloet), 22 r. Champ-de-Mars ☎ 551.52.69 – ⚏ ⓞ   J 9
fermé dim. et lundi – **R** carte 115 à 170
Spéc. Salade aux huîtres chaudes, Waterzooi de poissons (oct. à avril), Mille-feuille.

XXX **Chez Françoise**, Aérogare des Invalides ☎ 705.49.03 – ⚏   H 10
fermé 9 au 31 août et lundi – **R** carte 85 à 135.

XX 🏵 **Ferme St Simon** (Vandenhende), 6 r. St-Simon ☎ 548.35.74 – ⚏   J 11
fermé 1er au 15 août, sam. midi et dim. – **R** 105 (déj.) et carte 110 à 155
Spéc. Ballotine de lièvre à la Royale (15 oct.-15 déc.), Grillandine "Denise Fabre".

XX 🏵 **La Boule d'Or**, 13 bd Latour-Maubourg ☎ 705.50.18 – 🍽. ÆE ⚏   H 10
fermé août, sam. midi et dim. – **R** carte 120 à 160
Spéc. Foie gras de canard, Montgolfière de turbot aux petits légumes, Soufflé au citron.

XX 🏵 **Conticini**, 4 r. Pierre-Leroux ☎ 306.99.39 – ⚏ E   K 11
fermé août et dim. – **R** carte 125 à 155
Spéc. Salade de melon aux langoustines (juin à sept.), Coquilles St-Jacques aux oursins (oct. à mai), Panaché de ris et foie de veau au gingembre.

XX 🏵 **La Flamberge** (Albistur), 12 av. Rapp ☎ 705.91.37 – ÆE ⚏ ⓞ E   H 8
fermé 10 août au 10 sept. et dim. – SC : **R** carte 155 à 200
Spéc. Foie gras frais en terrine, Paupiettes de soles et langoustines à la crème de corail, Gibier (oct. à mars).

XX 🏵 **La Cantine des Gourmets**, 113 av. de La Bourdonnais ☎ 705.47.96 – ÆE ⚏ ⓞ   J 9
fermé lundi midi et dim. – SC : **R** carte 140 à 190
Spéc. Tarte fine au confit de poireaux, Ragoût de la mer, Gourmandise de pâtes fraîches.

XX **Le Galant Verre**, 12 r. Verneuil ☎ 260.84.56 – 🍽. ⚏ ⓞ   J 12
fermé août, sam. midi et dim. – **R** carte 110 à 160.

XX **Le Bistrot de Paris**, 33 r. Lille ☎ 261.16.83, évocation bistrot 1900 – ⚏   J 12
fermé sam., dim. et fêtes – **R** carte 135 à 170.

XX **Aux Délices de Szechuen**, 40 av. Duquesne ☎ 306.22.55 – ÆE ⚏   K 10
fermé lundi – **R** carte 60 à 100 🍷.

XX 🏵 **Vert Bocage**, 96 bd Latour-Maubourg ☎ 551.48.64 – 🍽. ÆE ⚏ ⓞ   J 9
fermé août, sam. soir et dim. – **R** carte 120 à 165
Spéc. Tarte à la tomate, Turbot au beurre blanc, Ris de veau normande.

XX **Le Petit Laurent**, 38 r. Varenne ☎ 548.79.64 – ÆE ⓞ   J 11
fermé fin juil. à début sept., dim. et lundi – **R** carte 95 à 130.

XX **La Calèche**, 8 r. Lille ☎ 260.24.76 – ÆE ⚏ ⓞ   J 12
fermé en août, sam. et dim. – SC : **R** carte 100 à 140.

9   167

XX **Le Bellecour,** 22 r. Surcouf ☎ 551.46.93 — AE GB ① E   H 9
fermé 15 août au 1er sept., sam. sauf le soir du 1er oct. au 1er juin et dim. — **R** carte 110 à 180.

XX **La Fontaine aux Carmes,** 124 r. Grenelle ☎ 551.77.23 — GB   J 11
fermé août, vend. soir et sam. — **R** carte 110 à 150.

XX **Le Champ de Mars,** 17 av. Motte-Picquet ☎ 705.57.99 — GB ①   J 9
fermé 14 juil. au 15 août et lundi — **R** carte 80 à 130.

XX **Les Glénan,** 54 r. de Bourgogne ☎ 551.61.09   J 10
fermé août, sam. midi, dim. et fêtes — **R** carte 115 à 160.

XX ✿ **Gildo** (Bellini), 153 r. Grenelle ☎ 551.54.12 — 🔲   J 9
fermé Pâques, Pentecôte, 14 juil. au 1er sept., vacances de Noël, dim. et lundi — **R** carte 85 à 120
Spéc. Felelto alla Carpaccio, Pâtes aux champignons sauvages, Saumon au basilic.

XX **Quai d'Orsay,** 49 quai d'Orsay ☎ 551.58.58 — 🔲 AE GB ① E   H 9
fermé août et dim. — **R** carte 125 à 170.

X ✿ **Pantagruel** (Israël), 20 r. Exposition ☎ 551.79.96 — AE GB ①   J 9
fermé sam. midi et dim. — **SC : R** carte 120 à 170
Spéc. Mousse de St-Jacques (15 oct. au 31 mars), Soufflé aux oursins (15 oct. au 31 mars), Foie chaud de canard.

X **Tan Dinh,** 60 r. Verneuil ☎ 544.04.84   J 12
fermé 1er au 29 août et dim. — **R** carte 65 à 90.

X **Délices St André,** 2 r. Sédillot ☎ 551.95.82 — AE ①   H 8
fermé 1er au 25 août, sam. et dim. — **R** carte 100 à 155.

X **La Chaumière,** 35 r. Beaune ☎ 261.26.09   J 12
fermé août, sam. soir et dim. — **SC : R** carte 75 à 125.

Champs-Élysées, St-Lazare, Madeleine.

8e arrondissement.
8e : ✉ *75008*

🏨🏨🏨🏨 **Plaza-Athénée** Ⓜ, 25 av. Montaigne ☎ 723.78.33, Télex 650092 — 🛗 🔲 📺 ☎ — 🏛 30. AE
① E. 🌸 rest   G 9
R voir rest. **Régence Plaza et Relais Plaza** — ☲ 40 — **216 ch** 780/1 720, 37 appart.

🏨🏨🏨🏨 **Bristol,** 112 fg St-Honoré ☎ 266.91.45, Télex 280961, 🔲 — 🛗 🔲 📺 ☎ 🅿 — 🏛 40 à 400. AE
①   F 10
SC : R voir rest **Bristol** — ☲ 40 — **211 ch** 660/1 300, 57 appart.

🏨🏨🏨🏨 **Crillon,** 10 pl. Concorde ☎ 296.10.81, Télex 290204 — 🛗 🔲 📺 ☎ 🔥 — 🏛 80. AE GB ①   G 11
R voir rest. ci-après — ☲ 45 — **169 ch** 750/1 075, 38 appart.

🏨🏨🏨🏨 **George V** Ⓜ, 31 av. George-V ☎ 723.54.00, Télex 650082 — 🛗 🔲 📺 ☎ 🔥 — 🏛 1 000. AE GB
① E. 🌸 rest   G 8
rest. **Les Princes R** carte 170 à 225 — ☲ 46 — **230 ch** 850/1 300, 59 appart.

🏨🏨🏨🏨 **Prince de Galles,** 33 av. George-V ☎ 723.55.11, Télex 280627 — 🛗 📺 ☎ 🔥 — 🏛 40 à 200.
AE GB ① E   G 8
R carte 150 à 190 — ☲ 46 — **119 ch** 811/1 068, 39 appart.

🏨🏨🏨 **Warwick** Ⓜ, 5 r. Berri ☎ 563.14.11, Télex 642295 — 🛗 🔲 📺 ☎ 🚗 — 🏛 120   F 9
SC : R carte 130 à 195 — ☲ 48 — **150 ch** 600/820, 5 appart.

🏨🏨🏨 **La Trémoille,** 14 r. La Trémoille ☎ 723.34.20, Télex 640344 — 🛗 📺 ☎. AE GB ① E   G 9
R carte 125 à 160 — ☲ 35 — **104 ch** 600/810, 13 appart.

🏨🏨🏨 **Lancaster,** 7 r. Berri ☎ 359.90.43, Télex 640991 — 🛗. AE E   F 9
R *(fermé sam. soir et dim. soir)* carte 130 à 190 — ☲ 40 — **57 ch** 500/880, 10 appart.

🏨🏨🏨 **San Regis** sans rest, 12 r. Jean-Goujon ☎ 359.41.90 — 🛗 ☎. 🌸   G 9
SC : ☲ 30 — **31 ch** 330/550, 12 appart.

🏨🏨🏨 **Royal Monceau,** 35 av. Hoche ☎ 561.98.00, Télex 650361, 🌴 — 🛗 📺 ☎ 🔥 — 🏛 600. AE ①
E. 🌸 rest   E 8
SC : Le Royal R carte 185 à 245 — ☲ 42 — **200 ch** 700/930, 28 appart.

🏨🏨🏨 **Frantel-Windsor** Ⓜ, 14 r. Beaujon ☎ 563.04.04, Télex 650902 — 🛗 🔲 rest 📺 ☎ — 🏛 120.
① E. 🌸 rest   F 8
SC : rest. Le Clovis *(fermé août, sam., dim. et fêtes)* **R** carte 170 à 220 — ☲ 30 — **135 ch** 545/677.

🏨🏨🏨 **Claridge Bellman** Ⓜ, 37 r. François 1er ☎ 723.90.03, Télex 641150, « Beau mobilier ancien »
— 🛗 🔲 rest 📺 ☎. AE ①. 🌸   G 9
SC : R *(fermé sam. soir et dim.)* carte 135 à 190 — ☲ 33 — **42 ch** 430/588.

🏨 **Napoléon,** 40 av. Friedland ☏ 227.74.20, Télex 640609 — |🛗| 📺 ☎ – 🛗 30 à100. 🅰🅴 ⓞ 🄴 F 8
SC : **R** voir rest. **Napoléon** – ⛄ 28 – **140 ch** 396/605, 32 appart.

🏨 **California,** 16 r. Berri ☏ 359.93.00, Télex 660634 — |🛗| 📺 ☎ – 🛗 70 à 150. 🅰🅴 🅶🅱 ⓞ 🄴.
✋ rest F 9
R *(fermé dim.)* carte 110 à 145 – **188 ch** ⛄ 485/630.

🏨 **Château Frontenac et rest. Pré Carré,** 54 r. P.-Charron ☏ 723.55.85, Télex 660994 — |🛗|
📺 ☎ – 🛗 25. 🅰🅴 🅶🅱 ⓞ. ✋ G 9
fermé août – SC : **R** *(fermé dim.)* 150/250 – ⛄ 28 – **101 ch** 430/600.

🏨 **Concorde-St-Lazare,** 108 r. St-Lazare ☏ 261.51.20, Télex 650442 — |🛗| 📺 ☎ – 🛗 100. 🅰🅴
🅶🅱 ⓞ 🄴 E 12
SC : **Café Terminus R** carte environ 105 ⅛ – **300 ch** ⛄ 480/650.

🏨 **Bedford,** 17 r. Arcade ☏ 266.22.32, Télex 290506 — |🛗| 📺 ☎ ⅙ – 🛗 80. 🄴. ✋ rest F 11
SC : **R** *(fermé sam. et dim.)* (déj. seul.) 92 bc – **140 ch** ⛄ 296/416, 10 appart.

🏨 **Castiglione,** 40 r. Fg-St-Honoré ☏ 265.07.50, Télex 240362 — |🛗| 📺 ☎ – 🛗 30 G 11
85 ch.

🏨 **Etap St-Honoré** M sans rest, 15 r. Boissy d'Anglas ☏ 266.93.62, Télex 240366 — |🛗| 📺 ☎ –
🛗 40. 🅰🅴 🅶🅱 ⓞ 🄴 G 11
SC : ⛄ 21 – **104 ch** 305/362, 8 appart. 600.

🏨 **Queen Elizabeth,** 41 av. Pierre-1er-de-Serbie ☏ 720.80.56, Télex 641179 — |🛗| 📺 ☎ – 🛗 25.
🅰🅴 🅶🅱 ⓞ 🄴 G 8
R *(fermé dim. et le soir en sem.)* 52 bc – ⛄ 30 – **60 ch** 400/500, 6 appart.

🏨 **Roblin et rest. Le Mazagran,** 6 r. Chauveau-Lagarde ☏ 265.57.00, Télex 640154 — |🛗| ☎.
🅰🅴 ⓞ F 11
R *(fermé sam. et dim.)* carte 115 à 155 - **Grill R** carte environ 105 – **70 ch** ⛄ 228/370.

🏨 **Résidence Champs-Elysées** M sans rest, 92 r. La Boëtie ☏ 359.96.15, Télex 650695 — |🛗|
📺 ☎ 🅰🅴 🅶🅱 🄴. ✋ F 9
SC : ⛄ 30 – **85 ch** 375/475.

🏨 **Vernet,** 25 r. Vernet ☏ 723.43.10, Télex 290347 — |🛗| 🅰🅴 🅶🅱 ⓞ 🄴 F 8
SC : **R** *(fermé août, sam. et dim.)* 150 – ⛄ 22 – **63 ch** 388/580.

🏨 **Celtic,** 6 r. Balzac ☏ 563.28.34, Télex 290298 — |🛗| 📺 ☎ – 🛗 60. 🅰🅴 🅶🅱 ⓞ. ✋ rest F 8
SC : **R** carte 95 à 135 – ⛄ 20 – **79 ch** 275/580.

🏨 **P.L.M. Royal-Madeleine** sans rest, 29 r. Arcade ☏ 266.13.81, Télex 641458 — |🛗| 📺 ☎. 🅰🅴
ⓞ. ✋ F 11
SC : ⛄ 31 – **70 ch** 460/600.

🏨 **Printemps et rest. Chez Martin,** 1 r. Isly ☏ 261.82.14, Télex 290744 — |🛗| 📺 ☎ – 🛗 30. 🄴 F 12
SC : **R** *(fermé dim.)* 70 bc/40 ⅛ – **66 ch** ⛄ 238/486.

🏨 **Elysées-Marignan** sans rest, 12 r. Marignan ☏ 359.58.61, Télex 660018 — |🛗| 📺 ☎. 🅰🅴 🅶🅱
ⓞ 🄴 G 9
SC : **71 ch** ⛄ 400/495.

🏨 **Royal H.,** 33 av. Friedland ☏ 359.08.14, Télex 280965 — |🛗| 📺 ☎. 🅰🅴 🅶🅱 ⓞ 🄴. ✋ F 8
SC : ⛄ 20 – **57 ch** 290/375.

🏨 **Powers** sans rest, 52 r. François-1er ☏ 723.91.05, Télex 642051 — |🛗| ☎. 🅰🅴 🅶🅱. ✋ G 9
SC : ⛄ 25 – **57 ch** 300/450, 3 appart. 500.

🏨 **Bradford** sans rest, 10 r. St-Philippe-du-Roule ☏ 359.24.20 — |🛗|. ✋ F 9
SC : **48 ch** ⛄ 230/290.

🏨 **Alison** M sans rest, 21 r. Surène ☏ 265.54.00, Télex 640435 — |🛗| 📺 ⌿wc ⌿wc ☎. 🅰🅴 🅶🅱
ⓞ 🄴. ✋ F 11
SC : ⛄ 17 – **35 ch** 190/285.

🏨 **L'Arcade** sans rest, 7 r. Arcade ☏ 265.43.85 — |🛗| 📺 ⌿wc ☎. 🆑 F 11
SC : **47 ch** ⛄ 210/270.

🏨 **Angleterre-Champs-Élysées** M sans rest, 91 r. La Boëtie ☏ 359.35.45, Télex 640317 — |🛗|
📺 ⌿wc ⌿wc ☎. 🆑 🅰🅴 ⓞ F 9
SC : ⛄ 17 – **40 ch** 185/285.

🏨 **Rochambeau-Copatel** sans rest, 4 r. La Boëtie ☏ 265.27.54, Télex 640030 — |🛗| 📺 ⌿wc
⌿wc ☎. 🆑 🅰🅴 ⓞ 🄴. ✋ F 11
SC : **49 ch** ⛄ 242/265.

🏨 **Résidence Saint-Philippe** sans rest, 123 r. Fg-St-Honoré ☏ 359.86.99 — |🛗| 📺 ⌿wc ⌿wc
🆑. ✋ F 9-10
SC : **38 ch** ⛄ 248/342.

🏨 **Concortel** sans rest, 19 r. Pasquier ☏ 265.45.44, Télex 660228 — |🛗| 📺 ⌿wc ⌿wc ☎. 🆑
🅰🅴 ⓞ F 11
SC : ⛄ 18 – **38 ch** 180/300, 8 appart. 300/400.

🏨 Royal Alma et rest. Le Bonaventure, 35 r. Jean-Goujon ☏ 225.83.30, Télex 641428 — |🛗| ⌿wc
⌿wc ☎ G 9
83 ch.

🏨 **Franklin Roosevelt** sans rest, 18 r. Clément-Marot 𝒯 723.61.66 − 📶 📺 ⇔wc 🛁wc ☎. 🚗 ⒶⒺ ⒼⒷ. 🦐
SC : **45 ch** ⇆ 280/300.
G 9

🏨 **Colisée** Ⓜ sans rest, 6 r. Colisée 𝒯 359.95.25, Télex 643101 − 📶 📺 ⇔wc ☎. 🚗 ⒶⒺ ⒼⒷ ① Ⓔ
SC : **45 ch** ⇆ 295/370.
F 9

🏨 **Rond-Point des Champs-Elysées** sans rest, 10 r. Ponthieu 𝒯 359.55.58 − 📶 📺 ⇔wc ☎. 🚗 ⒶⒺ ① Ⓔ. 🦐
SC : **46 ch** ⇆ 170/300.
F 10

🏨 **Brescia** sans rest, 16 r. Edimbourg 𝒯 522.14.31, Télex 660714 − 📺 ⇔wc 🛁wc ☎. 🚗 ⒶⒺ ⒼⒷ ① Ⓔ. 🦐
SC : ⇆ 15 − **38 ch** 145/200.
E 11

🏨 **Washington** sans rest, 43 r. Washington 𝒯 561.10.76 − 📶 📺 ⇔wc 🛁wc ☎. 🚗 ⒶⒺ.
SC : ⇆ 16 − **23 ch** 140/230.
F 9

🏨 **West End** sans rest, 7 r. Clément-Marot 𝒯 720.30.78 − 📶 ⇔wc ☎ ょ. 🚗 ⒶⒺ
SC : **60 ch** ⇆ 304/343.
G 9

🏨 **Queen Mary** sans rest, 9 r. Greffulhe 𝒯 266.40.50, Télex 640419 − 📶 ⇔wc 🛁wc ☎. 🚗. 🦐
SC : ⇆ 20 − **36 ch** 210/285.
F 12

🏨 **Atlantic** sans rest, 44 r. Londres 𝒯 387.45.40, Télex 650477 − 📶 ⇔wc 🛁wc ☎. 🚗. 🦐 E 12
SC : ⇆ 16 − **93 ch** 165/245.

🏨 **Lido** sans rest, 4 passage Madeleine 𝒯 266.27.37 − 📶 ⇔wc 🛁wc ☜. 🚗 ⒶⒺ. 🦐
SC : **29 ch** ⇆ 125/270.
F 11

🏨 **Opal** sans rest, 19 r. Tronchet 𝒯 265.77.97 − 📶 📺 ⇔wc 🛁wc ☎. 🚗 ⒶⒺ ⒼⒷ
SC : ⇆ 17 − **36 ch** 230/300.
F 12

🏨 **Élysées** sans rest, 100 r. La Boétie 𝒯 359.23.46 − 📶 📺 ⇔wc 🛁wc ☜. 🚗 ⒶⒺ ⒼⒷ ① Ⓔ. 🦐 F 9
SC : **30 ch** ⇆ 265/303.

🏨 **Lord Byron** sans rest, 5 r. Chateaubriand 𝒯 359.89.98, 🌹 − 📶 📺 ⇔wc ☎. 🚗. 🦐 F 9
SC : ⇆ 18 − **16 ch** 285, 10 appart. 375/490.

🏠 **Ministère** sans rest, 31 r. Surène 𝒯 266.21.43 − 📶 ⇔wc 🛁wc ☜. 🚗
SC : **32 ch** ⇆ 130/240.
F 11

🏠 **Lavoisier-Malesherbes** sans rest, 21 r. Lavoisier 𝒯 265.10.97 − 📶 ⇔wc 🛁wc ☜. 🚗
SC : **32 ch** ⇆ 140/210.
F 11

🏠 **Ouest H.** sans rest, 3 r. Rocher 𝒯 387.57.49 − 📶 ⇔wc 🛁wc ☎. 🚗. 🦐 EF 11
SC : ⇆ 15 − **58 ch** 125/250.

🍴🍴🍴🍴🍴 ❀❀❀ **Lasserre,** 17 av. Franklin-D.-Roosevelt 𝒯 359.53.43, Toit ouvrant − ▤. 🦐 G 10
fermé 1ᵉʳ au 30 août, dim. et lundi − **R** carte 210 à 300
Spéc. Turbotin braisé aux échalotes, Mignon de veau en papillote, Gourmandise Marigny.

🍴🍴🍴🍴🍴 ❀❀ **Laurent,** 41 av. Gabriel 𝒯 359.14.49 − ⒶⒺ ⒼⒷ ①. 🦐 G 11
fermé sam., dim. et fêtes − **R** carte 200 à 325
Spéc. Salade de homard, Canard nantais au cassis, Les deux soufflés.

🍴🍴🍴🍴🍴 ❀❀❀ **Ledoyen,** carré Champs-Élysées 𝒯 266.54.77 − ⓟ G 10
fermé 31 juil. au 1ᵉʳ sept. et dim. − **R** carte 190 à 250
Spéc. Fricassée de poissons, Canard sauvage aux poires (16 sept. au 28 fév.), Soufflé aux fruits frais.

🍴🍴🍴🍴🍴 ❀❀❀ **Taillevent,** 15 r. Lamennais 𝒯 561.12.90 − ▤. 🦐 F 9
fermé 24 juil. au 24 août, sam., dim. et fériés − **R** carte 175 à 235
Spéc. Cervelas de fruits de mer aux pistaches, Pintade en pot au feu, Farandole de desserts.

🍴🍴🍴🍴🍴 ❀ **Régence Plaza,** 25 av. Montaigne 𝒯 723.78.33 − ⒶⒺ ① Ⓔ. 🦐 G 9
fermé 17 déc. au 3 janv. − **R** carte 185 à 250
Spéc. Sole Reine Astrid, Suprême de volaille Montaigne, Mignon d'agneau.

🍴🍴🍴🍴🍴 ❀❀ **Lucas-Carton,** 9 pl. Madeleine 𝒯 265.22.90, « Authentique décor 1900 » − ⓟ. ⒶⒺ ⒼⒷ ① Ⓔ
G 11
R carte 155 à 250
Spéc. Sole Tante Marie, Canard à la Rouennaise, Surprise St-Moritz (dessert chaud).

🍴🍴🍴🍴🍴 ❀ **Bristol,** 112 r. fg St-Honoré 𝒯 266.91.45 − ⓟ. ⒶⒺ ①. 🦐 F 10
SC : **R** carte 220 à 275
Spéc. Salade de homard et aiguillettes de soles tièdes, Feuilleté de langoustines au St Emilion, Filet de canard sauvage en venaison (1ᵉʳ sept. au 1ᵉʳ mars).

XXXX ✿ **Lamazère,** 23 r. Ponthieu ☎ 359.66.66 — 🍽. AE GB ① E. ✻   F 9
fermé août et dim. – **R** 190/230
Spéc. Truffe Lamazère, Sole aux pâtes fraîches, Cassoulet aux trois confits.

XXXX ✿✿ **La Marée,** 1 r. Daru ☎ 763.52.42 — 🍽. AE ①   E 8
fermé 25 juil. au 1er sept., sam. et dim. – **R** carte 170 à 250
Spéc. Belons au Champagne, Petite marmite marseillaise, Pâtisseries.

XXXX ✿ **Crillon,** 10 pl. Concorde ☎ 296.10.81, « cadre 18e s. » — AE GB ①. ✻   G 11
R carte 175 à 250
Spéc. Marinière de St-Jacques (oct. à avril), Foie de veau aux truffes, Les trois gâteaux au Chocolat.

XXXX ✿ **Fouquet's,** 99 av. Champs-Élysées ☎ 723.70.60 — AE GB ①   F 8
R (1er étage) *(fermé août)* carte 135 à 195.
Spéc. Jambon chaud à l'os, Gratin de macaronis, Merlan Colbert.

XXX ✿✿ **Chiberta,** 3 r. Arsène-Houssaye ☎ 563.77.90 — 🍽. AE GB ①   F 8
fermé août, sam., dim. et fériés – **R** carte 165 à 220
Spéc. Coquilles St-Jacques aux endives et citron vert (oct. à avril), Fricassée de homard, Charlotte d'aubergines aux noisettes d'agneau.

XXX **Napoléon Baumann,** 38 av. Friedland ☎ 227.99.50 — AE GB ① E   F 8
R carte 130 à 165.

XXX ✿ **Le Marcande** (Ferrero), 52 r. Miromesnil ☎ 265.76.85 — AE GB ① E   F 10
fermé 13 août au 10 sept., 20 déc. au 5 janv., sam. et dim. – **R** carte 170 à 220
Spéc. Dégustation de champignons (oct. et nov.), St-Pierre au melon (en saison), St-Jacques aux asperges (en saison).

XXX **Au Vieux Berlin,** 32 av. George-V ☎ 720.88.96 — 🍽. AE GB ①   G 8
fermé sam. et dim – **R** carte 105 à 165.

XXX ✿ **Copenhague,** 142 Champs-Élysées ☎ 359.20.41 — 🍽. AE GB ① E. ✻   F 8
R *(fermé août, sam. midi en été, dim. et fêtes)* carte 110 à 165 - **Flora Danica R** carte 100 à 155
Spéc. Saumon grillé, Canard salé à la danoise, Mignon de renne au genièvre.

XXX ✿ **Marius et Janette,** 4 av. George-V ☎ 723.41.88 — GB   G 8
fermé dim. – **R** carte 155 à 235
Spéc. Bouillabaisse, Loup grillé, St-Jacques "Soubise" (d'oct au 15 avril).

XXX **Relais-Plaza,** 21 r. Montaigne ☎ 723.46.36 — 🍽. AE ① E   G 9
fermé août – **R** carte 150 à 210.

XXX **Indra,** 10 r. Cdt-Rivière ☎ 359.46.40 — AE GB ① E   F 9
fermé sam. midi et dim. – SC : **R** carte 75 à 125.

XXX **Chez Tante Louise,** 41 r. Boissy-d'Anglas ☎ 265.06.85 — 🍽. AE GB ①   G 11
fermé août et dim. – **R** carte 125 à 170.

XX ✿ **Le Petit Montmorency** (Bouché), 5 r. Rabelais ☎ 225.11.19 — 🍽. GB. ✻   F 10
fermé août, sam. et dim. – SC : **R** carte 150 à 190
Spéc. Foie gras de canard, Canard "Figani", Soufflé au chocolat.

XX ✿ **La Dariole** (Drouelle), 49 r. Colisée ☎ 225.66.76 — AE GB   F 10
fermé sam. sauf le soir du 25 sept. au 29 mai, dim. et fêtes – SC : **R** carte 140 à 210.
Spéc. Salade de caille et foie gras, Noix de St-Jacques (saison), Panaché de poissons au basilic.

XX **Ruc,** 2 r. Pépinière ☎ 522.66.70 — 🍽. AE GB ① E   F 11
fermé août – **R** (1er étage) carte 120 à 180.

XX **Le Relais,** 12 av. George-V ☎ 723.39.58   AE ①   G 8
fermé août et dim. – **R** carte 110 à 150.

XX **Les Trois Limousins,** 8 r. Berri ☎ 562.35.97 — 🍽. AE GB ①   F 9
SC : **R** 162 bc/185 bc.

XX **Les Trois Moutons,** 63 av. F.-D.-Roosevelt ☎ 225.26.95 — 🍽. AE GB ①   F 10
SC : **R** 162 bc/188 bc.

XX **Tong Yen,** 1 bis r. Jean-Mermoz ☎ 225.04.23 — 🍽. AE GB ① E   F 10
fermé en août – **R** carte 85 à 130

XX **Chez Max,** 19 r. Castellane ☎ 265.33.81 — GB   F 11
fermé sam., dim. et fêtes – **R** carte 115 à 160.

XX **Androuët,** 41 r. Amsterdam ☎ 874.26.93 — AE GB ①   E 12
fermé dim. et fêtes – **R** carte 90 à 140.

XX **Annapurna,** 32 r. Berri ☎ 563.91.62 — AE ①   F 9
fermé sam. midi et dim. – **R** carte 80 à 110.

XX **Stresa,** 7 r. Chambiges ☎ 723.91.62 — AE ①   G 9
fermé août, 18 déc. au 4 janv., sam. soir, dim. et fêtes – **R** carte 100 à 170.

XX **Le Sarladais,** 2 r. Vienne ☎ 522.23.62 — 🍽   E 11
fermé 14 juil. au 15 août, Noël au Jour de l'an, sam. midi, dim. et fériés – **R** carte 90 à 130.

XX **Artois,** 13 r. Artois ☎ 225.01.10   F 9
fermé 14 juil. au 7 sept., sam. et dim. – **R** (prévenir) carte 75 à 130.

XX **Chez Bosc,** 7 r. Richepanse ☎ 260.10.27 — GB   G 12
fermé août, sam. sauf le midi de sept. à avril, dim. et fériés – **R** carte 115 à 155.

XX **Le Manoir Normand,** 77 bd Courcelles ☎ 227.38.97 — AE GB ①   E 8
fermé août et sam. soir – **R** carte 90 à 145.

171

※ **André,** 12 r. Marbeuf ℡ 720.59.57 — G 9
fermé août et mardi – **R** carte 70 à 110.

※ **Le Capricorne,** 81 r. Rocher ℡ 522.64.99 — E 10-11
fermé 31 juil. au 7 sept., vacances de fév., sam. et dim. – **R** carte 55 à 80.

**Opéra, Gare du Nord,
Gare de L'Est,
Grands Boulevards.**

9ᵉ et 10ᵉ arrondissements.
9ᵉ : ⊠ 75009
10ᵉ : ⊠ 75010

Le Gd Hôtel, 2 r. Scribe (9ᵉ) ℡ 260.33.50, Télex 220875 – 📶 📺 ☎ ċ – 🏌 25 à 600. 🆎 🇬🇧 ⓘ Ε. ※ rest — F 12
SC : **Salons Ravel R** (déj. seul) 145 bc et voir **Café de la Paix** – **564 ch** � 690/860, 19 appart.

Scribe Ⓜ, 1 r. Scribe (9ᵉ) ℡ 742.03.40, Télex 214653 – 📶 ▤ 📺 ☎ ċ – 🏌 150. 🆎 🇬🇧 ⓘ Ε — F 12
SC : **R** carte 105 à 185 – ⊏ 50 – **206 ch** 650/940, 5 appart.

Ambassador-Concorde, 16 bd Haussmann (9ᵉ) ℡ 246.92.63, Télex 650912 – 📶 📺 ☎ ċ. 🆎 🇬🇧 ⓘ ※ — F 13
SC : **R** *(fermé juil. et 5 au 20 déc.)* 105/125 – **300 ch** ⊏ 560/665, 4 appart.

Commodore, 12 bd Haussmann (9ᵉ) ℡ 246.72.82, Télex 280601 – 📶 ▤ rest 📺 ☎ ċ. 🆎 🇬🇧 ⓘ Ε. ※ rest — F 13
R carte environ 105 – ⊏ 25 – **153 ch** 451/511, 11 appart.

St-Pétersbourg sans rest, 33 r. Caumartin (9ᵉ) ℡ 266.60.38, Télex 680001 – 📶 📺 ☎. 🆎 🇬🇧 ⓘ — F 12
SC : ⊏ 16 – **120 ch** 219/300.

Terminus Nord sans rest, 12 bd Denain (10ᵉ) ℡ 280.20.00, Télex 660615 – 📶 📺 ☎ ċ – 🏌 40. 🆎 🇬🇧 ⓘ Ε. ※ — E 15-16
SC : **230 ch** ⊏ 230/390.

Blanche Fontaine 🐾 sans rest, 34 r. Fontaine (9ᵉ) ℡ 526.72.32, Télex 660311 – 📶 ċ. 🚗 🆎. ※ — D 13
43 ch ⊏ 190/260, 6 appart. 260/340.

Carlton's H. sans rest, 55 bd Rochechouart (9ᵉ) ℡ 281.91.00, Télex 640649 – 📶 ☎. 🆎 🇬🇧 ⓘ Ε. ※ — D 14
SC : **100 ch** ⊏ 260/310, 6 appart. 408/456.

Franklin et du Brésil, 19 r. Buffault (9ᵉ) ℡ 280.27.27, Télex 640988 – 📶 📺 ☎. 🆎 🇬🇧 ⓘ Ε. ※ rest — E 14
Les Années Folles *(fermé août, sam. midi et dim.)* **R** 65 – **65 ch** ⊏ 335/395.

Astra sans rest, 29 r. Caumartin (9ᵉ) ℡ 266.15.15, Télex 210408 – 📶 ▤ rest 🚽wc ☎. 🛏️ 🆎 🇬🇧 ⓘ Ε — F 12
SC : **85 ch** ⊏ 290/400.

Paris Est Ⓜ sans rest, cour d'Honneur (10ᵉ) ℡ 241.00.33 – 📶 🚽wc 🚿wc ☎. 🇬🇧 — E 16
SC : ⊏ 15 – **31 ch** 130/330.

Gisendre Ⓜ sans rest, 6 r. Fromentin (9ᵉ) ℡ 280.36.86 – 📶 📺 🚽wc 🚿wc ☎. 🛏️ 🆎 🇬🇧 ⓘ Ε — D 13
SC : ⊏ 13 – **32 ch** 190/210.

Caumartin Ⓜ sans rest, 27 r. Caumartin (9ᵉ) ℡ 742.95.95, Télex 680702 – 📶 📺 🚽wc 🚿wc ☎. 🛏️ 🆎 🇬🇧 ⓘ Ε — F 12
SC : **40 ch** ⊏ 300/370.

Chamonix Ⓜ sans rest, 8 r. d'Hauteville (10ᵉ) ℡ 770.19.49, Télex 641177 – 📶 🚽wc 🚿wc ☎. 🛏️ 🆎 ⓘ Ε. ※ — F 15
SC : ⊏ 19,50 – **35 ch** 297/418.

Amiot sans rest, 76 bd Strasbourg (10ᵉ) ℡ 607.57.17 – 📶 📺 🚽wc 🚿wc ☎. 🛏️ 🆎 — E 16
SC : ⊏ 15 – **68 ch** 140/210.

London Palace sans rest, 32 bd Italiens (9ᵉ) ℡ 824.54.64, Télex 642360 – 📶 🚽wc 🚿wc ☎. 🛏️ 🇬🇧 Ε. ※ — F 13
SC : ⊏ 16 – **49 ch** 185/260.

Hélios sans rest, 75 r. Victoire (9ᵉ) ℡ 874.28.64, Télex 641255 – 📶 🚽wc 🚿wc ċ. 🛏️ 🆎 🇬🇧 ⓘ — F 13
SC : ⊏ 16 – **51 ch** 169/250.

🏨 **Mondial** 🦱 sans rest, 5 cité Bergère (9ᵉ) 𝒯 770.55.56, Télex 642308 — 🛗 🛏wc 🚿wc ☎.
🚗 AE ① E. 🛝
SC : ⌂ 15 — **60 ch** 158/250.
F 14

🏨 **Gare du Nord** sans rest, 33 r. St-Quentin (10ᵉ) 𝒯 878.02.92, Télex 642415 — 🛗 🛏wc 🚿wc
🚗. 🚗 GB E. 🛝
SC : ⌂ 16 — **49 ch** 140/260.
E 16

🏨 **Florida** sans rest, 7 r. Parme (9ᵉ) 𝒯 874.47.09, Télex 640410 — 🛗 TV 🛏wc 🚿wc ☎. 🚗 AE
GB ①
SC : **34 ch** ⌂ 105/280.
D 12

🏨 **Résidence Mauroy** Ⓜ sans rest, 11 bis r. Godot-de-Mauroy (9ᵉ) 𝒯 742.50.78 — 🛗 TV
🛏wc 🚿wc 🚗. 🚗 AE GB ① E
fermé août — SC : ⌂ 18 — **26 ch** 150/270.
F 12

🏨 **Montholon-Lafayette** sans rest, 4 r. Riboutté (9ᵉ) 𝒯 246.83.44 — 🛗 🛏wc 🚿wc 🚗. 🚗
SC : **38 ch** ⌂ 100/200.
E 14

🏨 **Florence** sans rest, 26 r. Mathurins (9ᵉ) 𝒯 742.63.47 — 🛗 🛏wc 🚿wc 🚗. 🚗 AE ①
SC : ⌂ 20 — **20 ch** 210/275.
F 12

🏨 **Morny** sans rest, 4 r. Liège (9ᵉ) 𝒯 285.47.92, Télex 660822 — 🛗 TV 🛏wc 🚿wc ☎. 🚗 AE
GB ① E
SC : **43 ch** ⌂ 275/300.
E 12

🏨 **Diamond** sans rest, 73 r. Dunkerque (9ᵉ) 𝒯 281.15.00 — 🛗 🛏wc 🚿wc 🚗. 🚗
SC : **52 ch** 🛒 112/194.
D 15

🏨 **Montréal** sans rest, 23 r. Godot-de-Mauroy (9ᵉ) 𝒯 265.99.54 — 🛗 🛏wc 🚿wc 🚗. 🚗 AE
① E
SC : ⌂ 15 — **14 ch** 130/230, 5 appart. 250.
F 12

🏨 **Pax H.** sans rest, 47 r. Trévise (9ᵉ) 𝒯 770.84.75, Télex 650197 — 🛗 🛏wc 🚿wc 🚗. 🚗 GB
SC : **50 ch** ⌂ 160/230.
E 14

🏨 **Peyris** sans rest, 10 r. Conservatoire (9ᵉ) 𝒯 770.50.83 — 🛗 🛏wc 🚿 🚗. GB
SC : **50 ch** ⌂ 180/230.
F 14

🏨 **Résidence Sémard** sans rest, 15 r. P.-Sémard (9ᵉ) 𝒯 878.26.72 — 🛗 🛏wc 🚿wc 🚗. 🚗
SC : **41 ch** ⌂ 134/195.
E 14-15

🏨 **Gd H. Haussmann** sans rest, 6 r. Helder (9ᵉ) 𝒯 824.76.10 — 🛗 🛏wc 🚿wc 🚗. 🚗 AE. 🛝
SC : **58 ch** ⌂ 235/290.
F 13

🏨 **Français** sans rest, 13 r. 8-Mai 1945 (10ᵉ) 𝒯 607.42.02 — 🛗 🛏wc 🚿wc 🚗. 🚗
SC : ⌂ 14 — **71 ch** 170/200.
E 16

🏨 **Gd H. Lafayette Buffault** sans rest, 6 r. Buffault (9ᵉ) 𝒯 770.70.96, Télex 642180 — 🛗
🛏wc 🚿wc 🚗. 🚗
SC : ⌂ 13 — **47 ch** 80/175.
E 14

🏨 **Victor Massé** sans rest, 32 bis r. Victor Massé (9ᵉ) 𝒯 874.37.53 — 🛗 🛏wc 🚿 🚗. 🚗 ①.
🛝
SC : ⌂ 14 — **42 ch** 105/185.
E 13

🏨 **Laffon** sans rest, 25 r. Buffault (9ᵉ) 𝒯 878.49.91 — 🛗 🛏wc 🚿wc 🚗. 🚗 GB E
fermé 25 juil. au 23 août — SC : **47 ch** ⌂ 86/215.
E 14

🏨 **Fénelon** sans rest, 23 r. Buffault (9ᵉ) 𝒯 878.32.18 — 🛗 🛏wc 🚿wc 🚗. 🚗 GB. 🛝
SC : ⌂ 14 — **36 ch** 106/198.
E 14

🏨 **Résidence Magenta** sans rest, 35 r. Y.-Toudic (10ᵉ) 𝒯 607.63.13 — 🛗 🚿wc 🚗. 🚗 AE
SC : **29 ch** ⌂ 155/185.
F 17

🏨 **Nord** sans rest, 47 r. A.-Thomas (10ᵉ) 𝒯 201.66.00 — 🛗 🚿wc 🚗. 🛝
SC : ⌂ 14,50 — **24 ch** 110/173.
F 16

🏨 **Londres et Anvers** sans rest, 133 bd Magenta (10ᵉ) 𝒯 285.28.26 — 🛗 🛏wc 🚿 🚗. 🚗
SC : ⌂ 15 — **43 ch** 90/198.
D 15

🏨 **Blanche H.** sans rest, 69 r. Blanche (9ᵉ) 𝒯 874.16.94 — 🛗 🛏wc 🚿 🚗. 🚗. 🛝
SC : ⌂ 13 — **54 ch** 50/160.
D 12

XXXX **Café de la Paix,** pl. Opéra (9ᵉ) ☎ 742.97.02 – 🖼. 🆎 🆖 ⓪   F 12
Rest. Opéra *(fermé août)* **R** carte environ 150 - **Relais Capucines R** snack carte environ 80 🍸.

XXX ❀ **Le Louis XIV,** 8 bd St-Denis (10ᵉ) ☎ 208.56.56 – 🆎 🆖 ⓪   G 16
fermé 1ᵉʳ juin au 31 août, lundi et mardi – **R** carte 105 à 165
Spéc. St-Jacques à la nage (oct. au 15 mars), Gigue de chevreuil Gd Veneur (oct. à fév.), Caneton au poivre vert
(sept. à mai).

XXX ❀ **Nicolas,** 12 r. Fidélité (10ᵉ) ☎ 246.84.74 – 🆎 🆖 ⓪   F 16
fermé août et sam. – **R** carte 100 à 150
Spéc. Foie gras frais, Coquilles St-Jacques (oct. à avril), Canard aux fruits de saison.

XX ❀ **Au Chateaubriant** (Forno), 23 r. Chabrol (10ᵉ) ☎ 824.58.94, Collection de tableaux – 🖼.   E 15
❀
fermé août, dim. et lundi – **R** carte 110 à 170
Spéc. Scampi fritti, Paglia e fieno alla contadina, Costoletta Villa d'Este.

XX ❀❀ **Chez Michel** (Tounissoux), 10 r. Belzunce (10ᵉ) ☎ 878.44.14 – 🖼. 🆎 ⓪   E 15
fermé août vend. et sam. – **R** (nombre de couverts limité - prévenir) carte 150 à 210
Spéc. Salade d'avocat aux noix, Salpicon de homard et de langouste, Sorbets.

XX **Atlantique,** 51 bd Magenta (10ᵉ) ☎ 208.27.20 – 🖼 🅿. 🆎 🆖 ⓪ 🅴   F 16
fermé 25 juil. au 3 sept., dim. et lundi – **R** carte 135 à 225.

XX **Mövenpick,** 12 bd Madeleine (9ᵉ) ☎ 742.47.93 – 🆎 🆖 ⓪   G 12
R carte environ 95 – 🍸 **Café des Artistes R** carte 130 à 185.

XX Aub. du Clou, 30 av. Trudaine (9ᵉ) ☎ 878.22.48   D 14

XX **Le Quercy,** 36 r. Condorcet (9ᵉ) ☎ 878.30.61 – 🆎 🆖 ⓪   E 15
fermé août et dim. – SC : **R** carte 95 à 150.

XX **Ty Coz,** 35 r. St-Georges (9ᵉ) ☎ 878.42.95, produits de la mer seulement   F 13
fermé 12 au 19 août, lundi de juil. à sept. et dim. – SC : **R** carte 140 à 200.

XX **Le Saintongeais,** 62 r. fg Montmartre (9ᵉ) ☎ 280.39.92   E 14
fermé 8 au 31 août, sam. midi et dim. – **R** carte 85 à 125.

XX **Julien,** 16 r. fg St-Denis (10ᵉ) ☎ 770.12.06, décor ''Belle Époque'' – 🆖   F 15
R carte 70 à 115.

XX **Petit Riche,** 25 r. Le Peletier (9ᵉ) ☎ 770.68.68, Cadre fin 19ᵉ s. – 🆖   F 13
fermé août et dim. – SC : **R** carte 70 à 115.

XX **Chez Casimir,** 6 r. Belzunce (10ᵉ) ☎ 878.32.53 – 🆎 🆖 ⓪   E 15
fermé sam. – SC : **R** carte 130 à 180.

XX **Abel,** 15 r. St-Vincent-de-Paul (10ᵉ) ☎ 878.41.88, plat principal : couscous – 🖼. 🆎 🅴   D-E 15
fermé 30 juil. au 31 août et dim. – **R** carte environ 90.

XX **Aux Deux Canards,** 8 r. Fg-Poissonnière (10ᵉ) ☎ 770.03.23 – 🆎 🆖 ⓪   F 15
fermé août et dim. – **R** carte 75 à 120.

XX **Pagoda,** 50 r. Provence (9ᵉ) ☎ 874.81.48 – 🆖. ❀   F 13
fermé dim. en août – **R** carte 55 à 85.

XX **Brasserie Flo,** 7 cour Petites-Écuries (10ᵉ) ☎ 770.13.59, cadre 1900 – 🆖   F 15
fermé août – **R** carte 60 à 110 🍸.

XX **Aub. Midi,** 12 r. Belzunce (10ᵉ) ☎ 878.40.03 – 🆖   E 15
fermé août et dim. – **R** carte 65 à 105.

XX ❀ **La P'tite Tonkinoise** (Costa), 56 fg Poissonnière (10ᵉ) ☎ 246.85.98   F 15
fermé 1ᵉʳ août au 15 sept., 15 au 28 fév. et lundi – **R** carte 75 à 130
Spéc. Banh Cuon, Crabe farci, My Sao (vend. et sam. seul.).

X **Les Frères Perraudin,** 18 r. d'Hauteville (10ᵉ) ☎ 770.41.05 – 🆎 🆖 ⓪   F 15
fermé 15 au 31 août, sam. midi et dim. – **R** carte 85 à 170.

X **Relais Beaujolais,** 3 r. Milton (9ᵉ) ☎ 878.77.91   E 14
fermé août, dim. et fêtes – **R** carte 75 à 110.

X **Taverne d'Alsace,** 42 r. Rochechouart (9ᵉ) ☎ 878.31.86 – 🆖   E 14
fermé août, dim. et lundi – **R** carte 60 à 85 🍸.

X Aub. Landaise, 23 r. Clauzel (9ᵉ) ☎ 878.74.40   E 13

X **Pinocchio,** 49 r. d'Enghien (10ᵉ) ☎ 770.01.98 – 🆎 🆖   F 15
fermé août, vacances de Noël, dim. et fêtes – **R** carte 65 à 105.

X **La Grille,** 80 fg Poissonnière (10ᵉ) ☎ 770.89.73 – ⓪   E 15
fermé août, vacances de fév., sam. et dim. – SC : **R** carte 85 à 135.

Pour vos promenades du dimanche
la nouvelle **carte** Michelin 🔲🔲🔲
'' Sports et loisirs Environs de Paris ''

Bastille, Gare de Lyon,
Place d'Italie,
Bois de Vincennes.

12e et 13e arrondissements.

12e : ⊠ 75012
13e : ⊠ 75013

🏨 **Modern H. Lyon** sans rest, 3 r. Parrot (12e) ☏ 343.41.52, Télex 230369 — 🛗 ☎. ᴁᴇ. 彩 L 18
SC : ⊡ 16,50 — **53 ch** 168/260.

🏨 **Paris-Lyon-Palace et Rest. Relais de la Méditerranée,** 11 r. Lyon (12e) ☏ 307.29.49,
Télex 213310 — 🛗 ☎ – 🏛 150. ᴁᴇ ᴳᴮ ⓞ ᴇ. 彩 rest L 18
SC : **R** carte 85 à 125 🍴 ⊡ 16 — **128 ch** 215/235.

🏨 **Équinoxe** Ⓜ sans rest, 40 r. Le Brun (13e) ☏ 337.56.56, Télex 201476 — 🛗 ᴛᴠ ☎ ℗. ᴁᴇ ᴳᴮ
ⓞ N 15
SC : **49 ch** ⊡ 290/370.

🏨 **Terminus-Lyon** sans rest, 19 bd Diderot (12e) ☏ 343.24.03, Télex 230702 — 🛗 ⌷wc ⊓wc
☎. ᴈᴈ8 ᴁᴇ ᴳᴮ ᴇ L 18
SC : ⊡ 16 — **61 ch** 206/249.

🏨 **Terrasses** sans rest, 74 r. Glacière (13e) ☏ 707.73.70 — 🛗 cuisinette ⌷wc ⊓wc ☎. ᴈᴈ8. 彩
SC : ⊡ 14,50 — **52 ch** 95/210. N 14

🏨 **Slavia** sans rest, 51 bd St-Marcel (13e) ☏ 337.81.25 — 🛗 ᴛᴠ ⌷wc ⊓wc ☎. ᴈᴈ8. 彩 M 16
SC : **36 ch** ⊡ 180/205, 6 appart. 240/310.

🏨 **Gd H. Gobelins** sans rest, 57 bd St-Marcel (13e) ☏ 331.79.89 — 🛗 ᴛᴠ ⌷wc ⊓wc ☎. ᴈᴈ8.
彩 M 16
SC : ⊡ 14 — **45 ch** 160/195.

🏨 **Viator** sans rest, 1 r. Parrot (12e) ☏ 343.11.00 — 🛗 ⌷wc ⊓wc ☎. ᴈᴈ8. 彩 L 18
SC : ⊡ 14 — **45 ch** 110/165.

🏨 **Marceau** sans rest, 13 r. Jules-César (12e) ☏ 343.11.65 — 🛗 ⌷wc ⊓wc ☎. 彩 K 17
fermé août – SC : ⊡ 15 — **53 ch** 70/160.

🏨 **Jules César** sans rest, 52 av. Ledru-Rollin (12e) ☏ 343.15.88, Télex 670945 — 🛗 ⌷wc ⊓wc
☎. 彩 K 18
SC : ⊡ 14 — **48 ch** 75/140.

🏨 **Rubens** sans rest, 35 r. Banquier (13e) ☏ 331.73.30 — 🛗 ⌷wc ⊓wc ☎. ᴈᴈ8 N 16
SC : ⊡ 13 — **50 ch** 95/160.

🏨 **Arts** sans rest, 8 r. Coypel (13e) ☏ 707.76.32 — 🛗 ⌷wc ⊓wc ☎ N 16
SC : ⊡ 14 — **42 ch** 60/150.

🏨 **Lux H.** sans rest, 8 av. Corbera (12e) ☏ 343.42.84 — 🛗 ⌷wc ⊓ ☎ L 19
SC : ⊡ 16 — **31 ch** 78/167.

🏨 **Terminus et Sports** sans rest, 96 cours Vincennes (12e) ☏ 343.97.93 — 🛗 ᴛᴠ ⌷wc ⊓wc
☎. ᴈᴈ8. 彩 L 23
SC : ⊡ 14 — **43 ch** 95/170.

🏨 **Palym H.** sans rest, 4 r. E.-Gilbert (12e) ☏ 343.24.48 — 🛗 ⌷wc ⊓wc ☎ L 18
SC : **51 ch** ⊡ 110/200.

🏨 **Trois Gares** sans rest, 1 r. Jules-César (12e) ☏ 343.01.70 — 🛗 ⊓wc ☎. 彩 K 17
SC : ⊡ 15 — **39 ch** 60/125.

XXX **Train Bleu,** Gare de Lyon (12e) ☏ 343.09.06, « Belles fresques évoquant le voyage de Paris à
la Méditerranée » — ᴁᴇ ᴳᴮ ⓞ L 18
R (1er étage) carte 110 à 160.

XXX ❀❀ **Le Pressoir** (Seguin), 257 av. Daumesnil (12e) ☏ 344.38.21 — ᴳᴮ M 22
fermé août, vacances scolaires de fév., dim. et lundi – SC : **R** carte 145 à 200
Spéc. Cassolette de pâtisson aux truffes (déc. à mars), Paupiette de choux au crabe, Rognon de veau à l'orange.

XX ❀❀ **Au Trou Gascon** (Dutournier), 40 r. Taine (12e) ☏ 344.34.26 — ▤. ᴳᴮ M 21
fermé sept., sam. et dim. – SC : **R** (nombre de couverts limité - prévenir) carte 135 à 200
Spéc. Ravioli de foie gras aux truffes, Saumon au lard fumé (début juin à fin août), Gigotin d'agneau de lait en
rognonnade (début janv. à fin avril).

XX **Sologne,** 164 av. Daumesnil (12ᵉ) ☎ 307.68.97 – GB M 21
fermé lundi soir et dim. – SC : **R** carte 95 à 135.

XX **Les Marronniers,** 53 bis bd Arago (13ᵉ) ☎ 707.58.57 – GB ⓞ E N 14
fermé août et dim. – SC : **R** carte 110 à 170.

XX **La Frégate,** 30 av. Ledru-Rollin (12ᵉ) ☎ 343.90.32 – GB. ⅍ L 18
fermé août, sam. et dim. – **R** carte 105 à 140.

XX **Le Traversière,** 40 r. Traversière (12ᵉ) ☎ 344.02.10 – AE GB ⓞ E N 18
fermé 12 juil. au 12 sept. et le soir des dim. et fêtes – **R** carte 80 à 140.

XX **Potinière du Lac,** 4 pl. E.-Renard (12ᵉ) ☎ 343.39.98 – ⓞ N 23
fermé 15 déc. au 15 janv., dim. soir et lundi – **R** carte 85 à 150.

X **Petite Alsace,** 4 r. Taine (12ᵉ) ☎ 343.21.80 – AE GB ⓞ M 20
fermé août, dim. soir et lundi – **R** carte 80 à 140.

X **Etchegorry,** 41 r. Croulebarbe (13ᵉ) ☎ 331.63.05 – AE GB ⓞ N 15
fermé dim. – SC : **R** 55 bc/90 bc.

X **Relais du Périgord,** 15 r. Tolbiac (13ᵉ) ☎ 583.07.48 – GB ⓞ P 18
fermé 15 août au 15 sept., sam. et dim. – **R** carte 100 à 180.

X **Les Algues,** 66 av. Gobelins (13ᵉ) ☎ 331.58.22 – GB N 15
fermé août dim. soir et lundi – **R** carte 100 à 135.

X **Quincy,** 28 av. Ledru-Rollin (12ᵉ) ☎ 628.46.76 – ⓞ L 17
fermé août au 15 sept., sam., dim. et lundi – **R** carte 80 à 140.

X **Le Rhône,** 40 bd Arago (13ᵉ) ☎ 707.33.57 – GB ⓞ E N 14
fermé août, sam. et dim. – **R** (nombre de couverts limité - prévenir) carte 50 à 85 ⚱.

X **Chez Michèle,** 39 r. Daviel (13ᵉ) ☎ 580.09.13 – GB P 14
fermé dim. – SC : **R** carte 95 à 125.

Au Bois de Vincennes :

XX **Chalet des Iles,** au lac Daumesnil Ile de Reuilly (12ᵉ) ☎ 307.77.07, ≼ – ⓟ. GB P 23
fermé mardi – **R** carte 110 à 170.

**Vaugirard,
Gare Montparnasse, Grenelle,
Denfert-Rochereau.**

14ᵉ et 15ᵉ arrondissements.
   14ᵉ : ✉ 75014
   15ᵉ : ✉ 75015

🏨 **Hilton** Ⓜ, 18 av. Suffren (15ᵉ) ☎ 273.92.00, Télex 200955 – 🛗 ▤ rest TV ☎ ⅃ ⇔ – 🏊
40 à 1200. AE GB ⓞ E J 7
SC : Rest : **Le Toit de Paris** ≼ *Paris, (fermé août et dim.)* **R** carte 175 à 250 ⅍ – **Western R** carte
environ 130 - **Coffee Shop R** carte environ 100 ⚱ – ⣌ 43 – **445 ch** 557/816, 32 appart.

🏨 **Sofitel Paris** Ⓜ, 8 r. L.-Armand (15ᵉ) ☎ 554.95.00, Télex 200432, piscine intérieure panoramique – 🛗 ▤ rest TV ☎ ⅃ ⓟ – 🏊 30 à 1 200. AE GB ⓞ E. ⅍ rest N 5
SC : rest. **Le Relais de Sèvres** *(fermé août)* **R** carte 150 à 210 - **La Poterie** (Brasserie) **R** carte
environ 80 ⚱ – ⣌ 33 – **635 ch** 450/640, 17 appart.

🏨 **Sheraton** Ⓜ, 19 r. Cdt-Mouchotte (14ᵉ) ☎ 320.15.51, Télex 200135 – 🛗 ▤ TV ☎ ⇔ ⓟ –
🏊 25 à 1 200. AE GB ⓞ E. ⅍ rest M 11
SC : **La Ruche R** carte environ 90 - **Montparnasse 25 R** carte 150 à 220 – ⣌ 45 – **917 ch**
490/605, 31 appart.

🏨 **Nikko** Ⓜ, 61 quai Grenelle (15ᵉ) ☎ 575.62.62, Télex 260012, ≼, ☒, – 🛗 ▤ TV ☎ ⓟ – 🏊
40 à 800. AE GB ⓞ E K 6
SC : **R** voir rest **Les Célébrités** - **Brasserie Pont Mirabeau R** carte environ 100 - **rest japonais
Benkay R** carte 100 à 200 – ⣌ 33 – **776 ch** 470/730, 6 appart.

🏨 **P.L.M. St-Jacques** Ⓜ, 17 bd St-Jacques (14ᵉ) ☎ 589.89.80, Télex 270740 – 🛗 ▤ TV ☎
⇔ – 🏊 40 à 1000. AE GB ⓞ E N 13-14
SC : **Café Français** (1ᵉʳ étage) *(fermé août)* **R** 110 bc/170 bc - **Le Patio** (3ᵉ étage) **R** carte 60 à 110
⚱ – ⣌ 30 – **797 ch** 490/590, 14 appart.

🏨 **L'Aiglon** sans rest, 232 bd Raspail (14ᵉ) ☎ 320.82.42 – 🛗 TV ☎ ⇔. AE GB. ⅍ M 12
SC : ⣌ 18 – **50 ch** 220/300, 8 appart. 360.

🏨 **Orléans Palace H.** sans rest, 185 bd Brune (14ᵉ) ☎ 539.68.50, Télex 260725 – 🛗 TV ☎ – 🏊
35. AE ⓞ R 11
SC : ⣌ 15 – **92 ch** 195/275.

🏢 **Carlton Palace H.** Ⓜ sans rest, 207 bd Raspail (14ᵉ) ℡ 320.62.94, Télex 200183 – 🎙 📺
🖭wc 🎴wc ☎. ✵   M 12
SC : 🖵 15 – **63 ch** 180/195.

🏢 **Résidence Champs de Mars** sans rest, 7 r. Gén. de Larminat (15ᵉ) ℡ 734.74.04 – 🎙
🖭wc 🎴wc ☎. ✵   K 8
fermé 10 juil. au 25 août – SC : 🖵 16 – **42 ch** 150/200.

🏢 **Midi** sans rest, 4 av. René-Coty (14ᵉ) ℡ 327.23.25 – 🎙 🖭wc 🎴wc 🕾. 🖾   N 13
SC : 🖵 8 – **50 ch** 92/162.

🏢 **France** sans rest, 46 r. Croix-Nivert (15ᵉ) ℡ 783.67.02   🎙 🖭wc 🎴wc 🕾. 🖾   L 8
SC : 🖵 16 – **30 ch** 180/230.

🏢 **Tourisme** sans rest, 66 av. La-Motte-Picquet (15ᵉ) ℡ 734.28.01 – 🎙 🖭wc 🎴wc 🕾. 🖾. ✵
SC : 🖵 12 – **60 ch** 95/165.   K 8

🏠 **Pacific H.** sans rest, 11 r. Fondary (15ᵉ) ℡ 575.20.49 – 🎙 🖭wc 🎴wc 🕾. 🖾. ✵   K 7
SC : **66 ch** 🖵 92/186.

🏠 **Pasteur** Ⓜ sans rest, 33 r. Dr. Roux (15ᵉ) ℡ 783.53.17 – 📺 🖭wc 🎴wc ☎   M 10
fermé août – SC : 🖵 15 – **19 ch** 140/180.

🏠 **Châtillon H.** 🐾 sans rest, 11 square Châtillon (14ᵉ) ℡ 542.31.17 – 🎙 🖭wc 🎴wc 🕾. 🖾.
✵   P 11
fermé août – SC : 🖵 13 – **32 ch** 120/155.

🏠 **Virgina** sans rest, 66 r. Père Corentin (14ᵉ) ℡ 540.70.90 – 🎙 🖭wc 🎴wc 🕾. ✵   R 12
SC : 🖵 12 – **54 ch** 70/130.

🏠 **Floréal** sans rest, 17 r. Poirier-de-Narçay (14ᵉ) ℡ 539.71.14 – 🎙 🖭wc 🎴wc 🕾. 🖾. ✵
fermé 7 au 26 août – SC : 🖵 14 – **42 ch** 55/150.   R 11-12

🏠 **Fondary** sans rest, 30 r. Fondary (15ᵉ) ℡ 575.14.75 – 🎙 🖭wc 🕾. ✵   L 8
SC : 🖵 14 – **24 ch** 70/130.

XXXX ✿ **Les Célébrités,** 61 quai Grenelle (15ᵉ) ℡ 575.62.62, ≼ – 🅿. 🆎 🆎 ⑩ 🖻   K 6
SC : **R** carte 160 à 240
Spéc. Paupiette de langoustines à la vapeur, Potée de bar et de ris de veau, Râble de garenne au thym et
champignons sauvages.

XXX **Armes de Bretagne,** 108 av. du Maine (14ᵉ) ℡ 320.29.50 – 🗎. 🆎 🆎 ⑩ 🖻   N 11
fermé 14 juil. au 15 août, dim. soir et lundi sauf fêtes – **R** carte 125 à 200.

XXX **Le Moniage Guillaume** avec ch, 88 r. Tombe-Issoire (14ᵉ) ℡ 327.09.88 – 🖭wc 🎴. 🖾 🆎
🆎 ⑩ 🖻   P 12
R *(fermé dim.)* carte 140 à 175 – 🖵 15 – **7 ch** 110/160.

XXX ✿ **Morot Gaudry,** 8 r. Cavalerie (15ᵉ) (8ᵉ étage) ℡ 567.06.85, ≼ – 🗎. 🆎   K 8
fermé sam. midi et dim. – SC : **R** 110 (déj.) et carte 115 à 160
Spéc. Foie de canard, Salmis de Grouse (oct.-janv.), Rognon de veau au jus d'échalotes.

XX ✿ **Olympe,** 8 r. N. Charlet (15ᵉ) ℡ 734.86.08 – 🆎 🆎 ⑩   L 10
fermé 1ᵉʳ au 22 août, 22 déc. au 2 janv., lundi et le midi sauf jeudi – SC : **R** 146/240
Spéc. St-Jacques en papillote d'oseille (oct. à mai), Canard sauvage rôti (saison de chasse).

XX ✿ **Le Duc** (Minchelli), 243 bd Raspail (14ᵉ) ℡ 322.59.59   M 12

XX ✿ **Aquitaine** (Mme Massia), 54 r. Dantzig (15ᵉ) ℡ 828.67.38 – 🆎 🆎 ⑩   N 8
fermé dim. et lundi – SC : **R** carte 150 à 200
Spéc. Salade de Gésiers confits, Panaché de poissons au beurre blanc, Rognon de veau sauté.

XX ✿ **Bistro 121,** 121 r. Convention (15ᵉ) ℡ 557.52.90 – 🆎 🆎 ⑩ 🖻   M 7
fermé 14 juil. au 18 août, dim. soir et lundi – **R** carte 125 à 190
Spéc. Marmite de poissons, Lièvre à la royale (oct. à déc.), Poule au pot.

XX ✿ **Chez Albert,** 122 av. Maine (14ᵉ) ℡ 320.21.69 – 🆎 🆎 ⑩ 🖻   N 11
fermé 9 au 24 août et sam. – SC . **R** (nombre de couverts limité - prévenir) carte 140 à 200.

XX **Le Pfister,** 1 r. Dr Jacquemaire-Clemenceau (15ᵉ) ℡ 828.51.38 – 🆎   L 8
fermé août, 23 déc. au 4 janv., sam. midi et dim. – **R** carte 105 à 150.

XX **La Coupole,** 102 bd Montparnasse (14ᵉ) ℡ 320.14.20 – 🆎   L 12
R carte 70 à 130.

XX **Le Dome,** 108 bd du Montparnasse (14ᵉ) ℡ 354.53.61 – 🆎 🆎 ⑩   LM 12
fermé lundi – **R** carte 105 à 160.

XX **Napoléon et Chaix,** 46 r. Balard (15ᵉ) ☏ 554.09.00 — 𝔸𝔼 𝗚𝗕   M 5
fermé dim. – **R** carte 130 à 200.

XX **La Chaumière des Gourmets,** 22 pl. Denfert-Rochereau (14ᵉ) ☏ 321.22.59 — 𝔸𝔼 𝗚𝗕 ⓘ   N 12
fermé août, sam. et dim. – **R** carte 130 à 180.

XX **Bocage Fleuri,** 19 r. Duranton (15ᵉ) ☏ 558.43.17 — 𝔸𝔼 𝗚𝗕 ⓘ   M 6
fermé août, dim. et fêtes – **R** carte 100 à 130.

XX ✿ **Pierre Vedel,** 50 r. Morillons (15ᵉ) ☏ 828.04.37 — ✂   N 8
fermé 10 juil. au 8 août, Noël au Jour de l'An, sam. et dim. – **R** carte 110 à 140
Spéc. Oeufs pochés au vin rouge, Bourride de lotte à l'aïoli, Charlotte au chocolat amer et praslin.

XX **Pinocchio,** 124 av. Maine (14ᵉ) ☏ 321.26.10 — 𝔸𝔼 𝗚𝗕 ⓘ   N 11
fermé août et dim. – **R** carte 90 à 130.

XX **Chaumière Paysanne,** 7 r. L.-Robert (14ᵉ) ☏ 320.76.55 — 𝗚𝗕   M 12
fermé août, 24 déc. au 4 janv., lundi midi et dim. – SC : **R** carte 120 à 175.

XX **Petite Bretonnière,** 2 r. Cadix (15ᵉ) ☏ 828.34.39 — ⓘ   N 7
fermé en juil., Noël-Jour de l'An, sam. midi et dim. – SC : **R** carte 100 à 140.

XX **La Chaumière,** 54 av. F.-Faure (15ᵉ) ☏ 554.13.91 — 𝗚𝗕   M 7
fermé août, lundi soir et mardi – **R** carte 95 à 130.

XX **La Giberne,** 42 bis av. Suffren (15ᵉ) ☏ 734.82.18 — 𝔸𝔼 𝗚𝗕 ⓘ   J 8
fermé 15 août au 15 sept., sam. et dim. – **R** carte 85 à 135.

XX **Le Caroubier,** 8 av. Maine (15ᵉ) ☏ 548.14.38   M 11
fermé 16 juil. au 30 sept. et dim. soir du 1ᵉʳ oct. au 30 mai – **R** carte environ 90 🍷.

X **La Bonne Table,** 42 r. Friant (14ᵉ) ☏ 539.74.91 — 𝗚𝗕   R 11
fermé août, 24 déc. au 4 janv., sam. et dim. – SC : **R** carte 100 à 170.

X **La Rabolière,** 13 r. Mademoiselle (15ᵉ) ☏ 250.35.29   L 7
fermé août, dim. soir et lundi – SC : **R** carte 70 à 120.

X **Bonne Auberge,** 33 r. Volontaires (15ᵉ) ☏ 734.65.49 — 𝔸𝔼 𝗚𝗕 ⓘ 𝖤   M 9
fermé sam. et dim. – SC : **R** carte 75 à 130.

X **Mon Pays,** 49 av. Jean-Moulin (14ᵉ) ☏ 539.71.54 — 𝔸𝔼 ⓘ   R 11
fermé 10 juil. au 10 août, dim. et fêtes – SC : **R** carte 70 à 110.

X **Senteurs de Provence,** 295 r. Lecourbe (15ᵉ) ☏ 557.11.98 — 𝗚𝗕. ✂   M 6
fermé août et lundi – **R** carte environ 130.

X **La Cour,** 12 r. Cepré (15ᵉ) ☏ 566.66.17 — 𝔸𝔼 𝗚𝗕 ⓘ. ✂   L 9
fermé dim. – **R** carte 80 à 100 🍷.

X **Gérard et Nicole,** 6 av. J.-Moulin (14ᵉ) ☏ 542.39.56 — 𝗚𝗕   P 12
fermé mi juil. à mi août, sam. et dim. – SC : **R** carte 125 à 170.

**Passy, Auteuil,
Bois de Boulogne,
Chaillot, Porte Maillot.**

16ᵉ arrondissement.

🏨 **La Pérouse** Ⓜ, 40 r. La Pérouse ✉ 75116 ☏ 500.83.47, Télex 613420 — 📶 🍽 📺 ☎. 𝔸𝔼 𝗚𝗕
ⓘ 𝖤   F 7
SC : **R** *(fermé sam. et dim.)* carte 170 à 200 – 🖵 32 – **11 ch** 560/675, 25 appart.

🏨 **Baltimore** Ⓜ, 88 bis av. Kléber, ✉ 75116, ☏ 553.83.33, Télex 611591 — 📶 📺 ☎ – 🏋 180.
𝔸𝔼 𝗚𝗕 ⓘ 𝖤   G 7
SC : **R** voir rest l'Estournel – **118 ch** 🖵 460/590.

🏨 **Résidence du Bois** 🌳 sans rest, 16 r. Chalgrin, ✉ 75116, ☏ 500.50.59, « Beaux aménage-
ments, jardin », 🚗 – 📺 ☎   F 7
SC : **17 ch** 🖵 460/710, 3 appart.

🏨 **Alexander** Ⓜ sans rest, 102 av. Victor-Hugo, ✉ 75116, ☏ 553.64.65, Télex 610373 — 📶 📺
☎. ✂   G 6
SC : **60 ch** 🖵 290/395.

🏨 **Victor Hugo** Ⓜ sans rest, 19 r. Copernic, ✉ 75116, ☏ 553.76.01, Télex 630939 — 📶 📺 ☎. 𝔸𝔼
𝗚𝗕 ⓘ 𝖤   G 7
SC : **76 ch** 🖵 245/365.

🏨 **Union H. Étoile** Ⓜ sans rest, 44 r. Hamelin, ✉ 75116, ☏ 553.14.95, Télex 611394 — 📶
cuisinette 📺 ☎. 𝔸𝔼   G 7
SC : 🖵 20 – **29 ch** 220/320, 13 appart. 400/500.

🏨 **Régina de Passy** sans rest, 6 r. Tour, ✉ 75016, ☏ 524.43.64, Télex 630004 — 📶 ☎. 𝔸𝔼 ⓘ.
✂   H6-J6
SC : 🖵 20 – **56 ch** 285.

🏨 **Résidence Foch** sans rest, 10 r. Marbeau, ⊠ 75116, ℘ 500.46.50, Télex 630886 – 🛗 📺 ☎.
🖭 ⬤ E. 🛇   F 6
SC : ⟷ 18 – **21 ch** 295/350, 4 appart. 425.

🏨 Majestic sans rest, 29 r. Dumont-d'Urville, ⊠ 75116, ℘ 500.83.70 – 🛗 ☎   F 7
28 ch.

🏨 **Massenet** sans rest, 5 bis r. Massenet, ⊠ 75016, ℘ 524.43.03, Télex 620682 – 🛗 📺 ☎. 🖭
GB ⬤. 🛇   J 6
SC : **41 ch** ⟷ 160/350.

🏨 **Fremiet** M ⌂ sans rest, 6 av. Fremiet, ⊠ 75016, ℘ 524.52.06, Télex 630329   🛗 📺 ☎ 🖭
GB ⬤ E   J 6
SC : **36 ch** ⟷ 240/350.

🏨 **Kléber** M sans rest, 7 r. Belloy, ⊠ 75116, ℘ 723.80.22, Télex 612830 – 🛗 📺 ☎. 🖭 ⬤   G 7
SC : **22 ch** ⟷ 290/350.

🏨 **Sévigné** sans rest 6 r. Belloy ⊠ 75116, ℘ 720.88.90, Télex 610219 – 🛗 📺 ☎. 🖭 ⬤ E   G 7
SC : ⟷ 20 – **30 ch** 270/340.

🏨 **Farnèse** sans rest, 32 r. Hamelin, ⊠ 75116, ℘ 720.56.66, Télex 611732 – 🛗 📺 ⌂wc ⌂wc
☎. 🖾. 🛇   G 7
SC : ⟷ 25 – **37 ch** 240/255.

🏨 **Rond-Point de Longchamp et rest Belles Feuilles,** 86 r. Longchamp, ⊠ 75116, ℘
505.13.63, Télex 620663   🛗 📺 ⌂wc ⌂wc ☎. 🖾 🖭 ⬤   G 6
R *(fermé 1 au 30 août, sam. et dim.)* carte environ 110 – ⟷ 22 – **59 ch** 240/330.

🏨 **Résidence Marceau** sans rest, 37 av. Marceau, ⊠ 75116, ℘ 720.43.37 – 🛗 ⌂wc ⌂wc 🖾.
🖾   G 8
fermé août – SC : **22 ch** ⟷ 175/220.

🏨 **Sylva** sans rest, 3 r. Pergolèse, ⊠ 75116, ℘ 500.38.12, Télex 612245 – 🛗 ⌂wc ☎. 🖾.
GB ⬤ E   E 6
SC : ⟷ 15 – **36 ch** 235/290.

XXXX ❀❀ **Faugeron,** 52 r. Longchamp, ⊠ 75116, ℘ 704.24.53 – 🍽. 🛇   G 7
fermé août, Noël à Jour de l'An, sam. sauf le soir d'oct. à avril, dim. et fêtes – **R** 140 (déj.) et
carte 150 à 210
Spéc. Oeufs à la coque à la purée de truffes, Caneton de Challans aux fèves (avril à août), Crottin de Chavignol
rôti.

XXXX ❀❀ **Vivarois** (Peyrot), 192 av. V.-Hugo, ⊠ 75116, ℘ 504.04.31 – 🍽 ⓟ. 🛇   G 5
fermé 1er août au 1er sept., sam., dim. et fêtes – **R** carte 170 à 250
Spéc. Huîtres chaudes au curry, Interlude à trois poissons, Poularde bressane au vinaigre.

XXX ❀ **Jamin** (Robuchon), 32 r. Longchamp, ⊠ 75116, ℘ 727.12.27 – 🍽. 🖭 GB ⬤   G 7
fermé juil., sam. et dim. – **R** 110/210.

XXX ❀ **Yan-Toit de Passy** (6e étage), 94 av. P.-Doumer ⊠ 75016, ℘ 524.55.37 – GB   H J 5
fermé 23 déc. au 18 janv., sam. midi, dim. et fériés – **R** 95 (déj.) et carte 135 à 200
Spéc. Soupe d'huîtres (15 sept.-15 avril), Ragoût de Soles et d'écrevisses, Delice de Yan.

XXX **Tsé-Yang,** 25 av. Pierre 1er de Serbie ⊠ 75016, ℘ 720.68.02 – 🍽. 🖭 GB ⬤ E   G 8
R carte 125 à 185.

XXX **Ile de France,** quai Debilly, ⊠ 75116, ℘ 723.60.21, < rest. flottant – ⓟ. 🖭 GB ⬤ E   H 8
fermé sam. midi et dim. – **R** carte 130 à 195.

XXX **Prunier Traktir,** 16 av. Victor-Hugo, ⊠ 75116, ℘ 500.89.12 – 🖭 GB ⬤   F 7
fermé dim. en juil.-août et lundi – **R** carte 170 à 210.

XXX **L'Estournel,** 1 r. L.-Delibes ⊠ 75116 ℘ 553.83.33 – 🍽 rest. 🖭 GB ⬤ E   G 7
fermé août sam. et dim. – **R** carte 140 à 190.

XXX **Morens,** 10 av. New-York, ⊠ 75116, ℘ 723.75.11 – 🖭 GB ⬤   H 8
fermé août, 24 déc. au 2 janv., vend. soir et sam. – **R** carte 110 à 180.

XXX **Ramponneau,** 21 av. Marceau ⊠ 75116 ℘ 720.59.51 – 🖭 GB   G 8
fermé août – **R** carte 125 à 160.

XX ❀ **Michel Pasquet,** 59 r. La-Fontaine, ⊠ 75016, ℘ 288.50.01 – GB ⬤   K 4
fermé août, sam. sauf le soir d'oct. à avril et dim. – SC : **R** carte 145 à 210.
Spéc. Salade de homard, Turbot rôti au beurre ciboulette, Pigeon sauté au Pomerol.

XX **Al Mounia,** 16 r. Magdebourg, ⊠ 75116, ℘ 727.57.28 – 🍽. 🖭. 🛇   G 7
fermé août et dim. – **R** carte environ 110.

XX **Marius,** 82 bd Murat, ⊠ 75016, ℘ 651.67.80 – 🖭 GB ⬤ E   M 2
fermé fin juin à début sept., dim. soir et lundi – **R** carte 115 à 185.

XX ✪ **Guy Savoy,** 28 r. Duret ⊠ 75116 ☎ 500.17.67 – ⊖B   F 6
fermé 1er au 15 janv., sam. et dim. – **R** carte 155 à 200
Spéc. Ragoût de légumes (mars à oct.) Eminçé de rognon de veau, Millefeuille "Minute".

XX ✪ **Paul Chêne,** 123 r. Lauriston, ⊠ 75116, ☎ 727.63.17 – ⊟ ◉ ℗   G 6
fermé en août, Noël au Jour de l'An, sam. et dim. – **R** carte 130 à 190
Spéc. Soupe d'écrevisses et de filets de sole, Rognon de veau aux trois moutardes, Beignets de pommes.

XX **Le Petit Bedon,** 38 r. Pergolèse ⊠ 75116 ☎ 500.23.66 – ⊟. ⊖B ◉   F 6
fermé août, sam., dim. et fériés – **R** carte 120 à 160.

XX **Jenny Jacquet,** 136 r. Pompe ⊠ 75116 ☎ 727.50.26 – ⊖B. ⋘   G 6
fermé août, sam. midi et dim. – **R** carte environ 125.

XX **Petit Victor Hugo,** 143 av. V.-Hugo ⊠ 75116, ☎ 553.02.68   G 5-6
fermé dim. – SC : **R** 60/100.

XX **Le Gd Chinois,** 6 av. New York, ⊠ 75116, ☎ 723.98.21 – ◭ ◉   H 8
fermé 9 au 23 août et lundi – **R** carte 60 à 100.

XX **Le Carrefour,** 131 bd Murat, ⊠ 75016, ☎ 288.82.15 – ⊖B   M 2-M 3
fermé 6 au 31 août, 23 déc. au 3 janv., dim. soir et sam. – **R** carte 85 à 135.

X **Au Clocher du Village,** 8 bis r. Verderet, ⊠ 75016, ☎ 288.35.87 – ⊖B   L 4
fermé août, sam., dim. et fêtes – **R** carte 75 à 125.

X **Le Valéry,** 55 r. Lauriston, ⊠ 75016, ☎ 553.55.48 – ⊖B   F 7
fermé sam. et dim. – SC : **R** carte 80 à 130.

X La Française, 120 r. La Pompe, ⊠ 75116, ☎ 553.47.18   G 6

X **Le Moï,** 7 r. G. Courbet ⊠ 75016 ☎ 704.95.10   G 6
fermé août et lundi – SC : **R** 80 bc/130 bc.

X **Saratoga,** 7 r. Lauriston, ⊠ 75116 ☎ 500.96.24 – ⊖B   F 7
fermé 1er au 31 août et dim. – SC : **R** carte 70 à 100.

Au Bois de Boulogne :

XXXX ✪✪ **Pré Catelan,** ⊠ 75016, ☎ 524.55.58 – ℗. ⊖B   H 2
fermé fév., dim. soir et lundi – **R** carte 175 à 240
Spéc. Soufflé au corail d'oursins (oct. à fin avril), Aile de faisan P. Lenotre (saison de chasse), Tourte feuilletée de volaille.

XXXX ✪ **Grande Cascade,** ⊠ 75016, ☎ 506.33.51, ⩤ – ℗. ◭ ◉ ⴹ
fermé 20 déc. au 21 janv. – **R** *(du 15 oct. au 15 mai déj. seul. et fermé lundi)* carte 155 à 230
Spéc. Huîtres chaudes au beurre de citron vert (sept. à mai), Filet de sandre au safran, Filet à la moelle et au vin.

Clichy, Ternes, Wagram.

17e arrondissement.
17e : ⊠ 75017

🏨 **Concorde Lafayette** Ⓜ, 3 pl. Pte des Ternes ☎ 758.12.84, Télex 650892, « Bar panoramique au 33e étage » – ⧖ ⊟ ⏍ ☎. ◭ ⊖B ◉ ⴹ   E 6
SC : **L'Arc-en-Ciel R** 120 ⌀ - Coffee Shop **Les Saisons R** carte environ 75 ⌀ - **L'Étoile d'Or** voir p. 35 – ⌷ 35 – **972 ch** 575/705, 28 appart.

🏨 **H. Méridien** Ⓜ, 81 bd Gouvion-St-Cyr (pte Maillot) ☎ 758.12.30, Télex 290952 – ⧖ ⊟ ⏍ ☎ – ⚗ 150 à 1 000. ◭ ⊖B ◉ ⴹ   E 6
SC : **Le Clos de Longchamp** *(fermé sam. et dim. du 14 juil. au 31 août)* **R** carte 130 à 200 ⋘ - **Café l'Arlequin R** carte environ 90 ⌀ ⋘ - **Le Yamato** (rest. Japonais) *(fermé en août, dim. et lundi)* **R** carte environ 80 ⌀ ⋘ - **La Maison Beaujolaise R** 90 bc/115 bc ⋘ – ⌷ 38 – **1 027 ch** 550/685, 14 appart.

🏨 **Splendid Etoile et rest. Pré Carré** Ⓜ, 1 bis av. Carnot ☎ 766.41.41, Télex 280773 – ⧖ ⏍ ☎. ◭ ⊖B ◉. ⋘ ch   F 7
R *(fermé en août, sam. soir et dim.)* 100/150 – ⌷ 25 – **58 ch** 250/450, 3 appart.

🏨 **Regent's Garden** ⧉ sans rest, 6 r. P.-Demours ☎ 574.07.30, Télex 640127, « Jardin fleuri » – ⧖ ⏍ ☎ ℗. ◭ ⊖B ◉ ⴹ   E 7
SC : ⌷ 18 – **41 ch** 275/360, 3 appart. 380.

🏨 **Mercure** Ⓜ sans rest, 27 av. Ternes ☎ 766.49.18, Télex 650679 – ⧖ ⊟ ⏍ ☎. ◭ ⊖B ◉ ⴹ   E 8
SC : ⌷ 25 – **56 ch** 380/395.

🏨 **Magellan** Ⓜ ⧉ sans rest, 17 r. J.B.-Dumas ☎ 572.44.51, Télex 660728 – ⧖ ☎. ◭ ⊖B ◉ ⴹ   D 7
SC : ⌷ 15 – **75 ch** 163/209.

🏨 **Balmoral** sans rest, 6 r. Gén.-Lanrezac ☎ 380.30.50, Télex 642435 – ⧖ ☎. ◭ ◉   E 7
SC : **57 ch** ⌷ 245/350.

🏨 **Cécilia** sans rest, 11 av. Mac-Mahon ☎ 380.32.10, Télex 280750 — 🛗 ➯wc ☎. 🚗🅿 🆎 ⓪ **E**. E 7
⠀⠀SC : ⇌ 18 – **45 ch** 301/331.

🏨 **Banville** sans rest, 166 bd Berthier ☎ 755.70.16, Télex 643025 — 🛗 ➯wc 🛁wc ☎. 🚗🅿 D 8
⠀⠀SC : **40 ch** ⇌ 245/260.

🏨 **Etoile** Ⓜ sans rest, 3 r. Etoile ☎ 380.36.94, Télex 642028 — 🛗 📺 ➯wc 🛁wc ☎. 🚗🅿 🆎 🇬🇧 E 8
⠀⠀⓪
⠀⠀SC : **25 ch** ⇌ 295/350.

🏨 **Stella** Ⓜ sans rest, 20 av. Carnot ☎ 380.84.50 — 🛗 📺 ➯wc 🛁wc ☎. 🚗🅿 🆎 🇬🇧 ⓪. 🌂 E 7
⠀⠀SC : ⇌ 14 – **36 ch** 170/250.

🏨 **Belfast** sans rest, 10 av. Carnot ☎ 380.12.10, Télex 642777 — 🛗 ➯wc 🛁wc ☎. 🚗🅿 🆎 🇬🇧
⠀⠀⓪. 🌂 E 7
⠀⠀SC : ⇌ 15 – **47 ch** 235/250.

🏨 **Royal Magda** sans rest, 7 r. Troyon ☎ 704.10.13, Télex 041066 — 🛗 📺 ➯wc 👔 🚗🅿 🔠
⠀⠀🇬🇧 ⓪ E 8
⠀⠀SC : **27 ch** ⇌ 270/284, 11 appart. 334/387.

🏨 **Empire H.** sans rest, 3 r. Montenotte ☎ 380.14.55, Télex 643232 — 🛗 📺 ➯wc 🛁wc ☎.
⠀⠀🚗🅿 🆎 🇬🇧 ⓪ **E**. 🌂 E 8
⠀⠀fermé 20 juil. au 20 août – SC : ⇌ 19 – **47 ch** 264/330.

🏨 **Tivoli Étoile** Ⓜ sans rest, 7 r. Brey ☎ 380.31.22, Télex 643107 — 🛗 📺 ➯wc ☎. 🚗🅿 🇬🇧
⠀⠀⓪ **E**. 🌂 E 8
⠀⠀SC : ⇌ 17 – **30 ch** 255/290.

🏨 **Mercédès** Ⓜ sans rest, 128 av. Wagram ☎ 227.77.82 — 🛗 ➯wc 🛁wc ☎. 🚗🅿 🆎 ⓪ D 8
⠀⠀SC : ⇌ 18 – **37 ch** 230/240.

🏨 **Régence-Étoile** sans rest, 24 av. Carnot ☎ 380.75.60 — 🛗 📺 ➯wc 🛁wc ☎. 🚗🅿 🇬🇧.
⠀⠀🌂 E 7
⠀⠀SC : ⇌ 16 – **38 ch** 175/250.

🏨 **Étoile Park H.** sans rest, 10 av. Mac-Mahon ☎ 755.69.63 — 🛗 ➯wc 🛁wc 🚗🅿 🆎 🇬🇧
⠀⠀⓪. 🌂 E 8
⠀⠀fermé 31 juil. au 23 août – SC : ⇌ 16 – **28 ch** 220/275.

🏨 **Astrid** sans rest, 27 av. Carnot ☎ 380.56.20, Télex 642065 — 🛗 ➯wc 🛁wc ☎. 🚗🅿. 🌂 E 7
⠀⠀SC : **40 ch** ⇌ 185/245.

🏨 **Astor** sans rest, 36 r. P.-Demours ☎ 227.44.93 — 🛗 ➯wc 🛁wc ☎. 🌂 D 8
⠀⠀SC : ⇌ 14 – **48 ch** 169/199.

🏨 **Prima H.**, 167 r. Rome ☎ 622.21.09 — 🛗 📺 ➯wc 🛁wc 🚗🅿 C-D 10
⠀⠀**R** snack (fermé dim. en août et sept.) carte environ 70 🥄 – ⇌ 13 – **30 ch** 150/200.

🏨 **Parc Monceau** sans rest, 38 r. Cardinet ☎ 763.88.60 — 🛗 🛁wc 🚗 D 9
⠀⠀**23 ch**.

🏨 **Palma** sans rest, 46 r. Brunel ☎ 574.29.93 — 🛗 📺 ➯wc 🛁wc 🚗. 🌂 E 7
⠀⠀SC : ⇌ 15 – **32 ch** 150/195.

🏨 **Néva** sans rest, 14 r. Brey ☎ 380.28.26 — 🛗 ➯wc 🛁wc 🚗. 🚗🅿 🇬🇧. 🌂 E 8
⠀⠀SC : ⇌ 16 – **35 ch** 170/195.

🏨 **Bel'Hôtel** sans rest, 20 r. Pouchet ☎ 627.34.77, 🌳 — 🛗 ➯wc 🛁 ☎. 🇬🇧 B 11
⠀⠀fermé août – SC : ⇌ 14 – **30 ch** 70/180.

🏨 **Niel** sans rest, 11 r. Saussier-Leroy ☎ 766.58.15 — 🛗 🛁wc 🚗. 🌂 E 8
⠀⠀fermé août, Noel et Jour de l'An – SC : **37 ch** ⇌ 92/169.

XXX ❀ **Étoile d'Or,** 3 pl. Porte des Ternes ☎ 758.12.84 — 🍽. 🆎 🇬🇧 ⓪ **E** E 6
⠀⠀SC : **R** carte 160 à 215
⠀⠀Spéc. Mesclun au jambon d'oie fumé, Panaché des mareyeurs, Filet d'agneau à la crème d'estragon.

XXX ❀❀ **Le Bernardin** (Le Coze), 18 r. Troyon ☎ 380.40.61 — 🇬🇧 E 8
⠀⠀fermé août, dim. et lundi – **R** carte 135 à 205
⠀⠀Spéc. Oursins chauds au beurre d'oursins (nov. à mai). St-Jacques à l'oseille et tomate (oct. à mai), Escalope de
⠀⠀saumon aux truffes (fév. à oct.).

XXX ❀❀ **Rostang**, 10 r. G.-Flaubert ☎ 763.40.77 — 🍽. 🇬🇧 D 8
⠀⠀fermé 1er au 24 août, 24 déc. au 5 janv. sam. midi, dim. et fériés – **R** 125 (déj.) et carte 180 à 215
⠀⠀Spéc. Fricassée de soles aux choux, Oeufs de caille en coque d'oursins (oct.-avril), Poulette de Bresse en pot au
⠀⠀feu.

XXX **Grand Veneur,** 6 r. Pierre-Demours ℡ 574.61.58 — ᴬᴱ ᴳᴮ ⓄⒺ   E 7
fermé août, sam. midi et dim. — **R** carte 125 à 165.

XXX ✿ **Timgad,** 21 r. Brunel ℡ 574.23.70, « Décor mauresque » — 🍴. ᴳᴮ Ⓞ   E 7
fermé août et dim. — **R** carte environ 120
Spéc. Tagine, Couscous, Méchoui.

XXX **Michel-Péreire,** 122 av. Villiers ℡ 380.19.66 — ᴳᴮ Ⓞ   D 8
fermé 17 juil. au 17 août et sam. — **R** carte 110 à 160.

XXX **La Devinière,** 97 av. Ternes ℡ 574.10.60 — ᴬᴱ ᴳᴮ Ⓞ   E 7
fermé 1ᵉʳ au 22 août, 25 déc. au 1ᵉʳ janv., sam. midi et dim. — **R** carte 120 à 170.

XX ✿ **La Coquille,** 6 r. Débarcadère ℡ 574.25.95 — 🍴. ᴳᴮ   E 7
fermé 30 juil. au 2 sept., dim., lundi et fériés — **R** carte 120 à 175
Spéc. St-Jacques au naturel (oct. à mai), Ris de veau sauté à la crème et morilles, Soufflé au praslin de noisettes.

XX **Baumann,** 64 av. Ternes ℡ 574.16.66 — 🍴. ᴬᴱ ᴳᴮ ⓄⒺ   E 7
SC : **R** carte 100 à 150 🍺.

XX **La Truite Vagabonde,** 17 r. Batignolles ℡ 387.77.80 — ᴬᴱ ᴳᴮ Ⓞ   D 11
fermé dim. — **R** carte 105 à 160.

XX **L'Écrevisse,** 212bis bd Péreire ℡ 572.17.60 — ᴬᴱ ᴳᴮ   E 7
fermé août, sam. midi et dim. — **R** carte 110 à 155.

XX **Paul et France,** 27 av. Niel ℡ 763.04.24 — ᴬᴱ ᴳᴮ Ⓞ   D 8
fermé 15 juil. au 15 août, sam. et dim. — **R** 100/170.

XX **La Braisière,** 54 r. Cardinet ℡ 763.40.37 — ᴬᴱ ᴳᴮ Ⓞ   D 9
fermé août, sam. et dim. — SC : **R** carte 130 à 175.

XX ✿ **Chez Guyvonne** (Cros), 14 r. Thann ℡ 227.25.43   D 9-10
fermé 9 au 31 juil., 24 déc. au 9 janv., sam., dim. et fêtes — **R** carte 120 à 175
Spéc. Pain d'écrevisses (sauf mai-juin), Soupe de St Jacques aux huîtres (oct. à avril), Rognon de veau au Cornas.

XX **Ma Cuisine,** 18 r. Bayen ℡ 572.02.19 — ᴬᴱ ᴳᴮ Ⓞ   E 7
fermé sam. midi et dim. — **R** carte 90 à 145.

XX ✿ **Chez Augusta** (Bareste), 98 r. Tocqueville ℡ 763.39.97 — ᴳᴮ Ⓞ   C 9
fermé août, dim. et fériés — **R** carte 125 à 165
Spéc. Salade Augusta, Fricassée des mareyeurs, Filets de rougets.

XX **Chez Georges,** 273 bd Pereire ℡ 574.31.00 — ᴳᴮ   E 6
fermé 29 juil. au 31 août et sam. — **R** carte 110 à 145.

XX **Le Petit Colombier,** 42 r. Acacias ℡ 380.28.54 — ᴳᴮ   E 7
fermé 1ᵉʳ au 16 août, 26 déc. au 2 janv., dim. midi, sam. et lundi fériés — **R** carte 105 à 150.

XX **Le Santenay,** 75 av. Niel ℡ 227.88.44 — ᴬᴱ ᴳᴮ   D 8
fermé dim. soir et lundi — **R** carte 100 à 155.

XX **Chez Léon,** 32 r. Legendre ℡ 227.06.82 — ᴳᴮ Ⓞ   D 10
fermé août, sam. soir et dim. — SC : **R** carte 95 à 155.

XX **Le Beudant,** 97 r. des Dames ℡ 387.11.20 — ᴬᴱ ᴳᴮ Ⓞ   D 11
fermé sam. midi et dim. — **R** carte 105 à 155.

XX **La Toque,** 16 r. Tocqueville ℡ 227.97.75 — ᴳᴮ   D 10
fermé 10 juil. au 2 août, Noël-Jour de l'an, sam. et dim. — SC : **R** 65/155.

X ✿ **La Petite Auberge** (Harbonnier), 38 r. Laugier ℡ 763.85.51 — Ⓞ   D 7-8
fermé 1ᵉʳ août au 1ᵉʳ sept., dim., lundi et fêtes — **R** (nombre de couverts limité - prévenir) carte 125 à 170
Spéc. Turbot Camille Renault, Carré d'agneau Emile Compard, Tarte aux pommes.

X **La Soupière,** 154 av. Wagram ℡ 227.00.73 — ᴳᴮ   D 9
fermé août, Noël au Jour de l'An, dim., lundi et fériés — **R** carte 105 à 150.

X **Brazais,** 42 bd Pereire ℡ 763.82.17 — ᴬᴱ ᴳᴮ Ⓞ   C 9
fermé mai, sam. d'avril à oct. et dim. — SC : **R** 92 bc/160 bc.

X ✿ **Mère Michel** (Gaillard), 5 r. Rennequin ℡ 763.59.80   E 8
fermé août, sam., dim. et fériés — SC : **R** (nombre de couverts limité - prévenir) carte 105 à 155
Spéc. Cressonnette de foies de volaille au Xérès, Poissons beurre blanc, Omelette soufflée.

Donnez-nous votre avis sur les tables que nous

recommandons,

sur leurs spécialités et leurs vins.

Montmartre, La Villette, Belleville.

18e, 19e et 20e arrondissements.
18e : ✉ 75018
19e : ✉ 75019
20e : ✉ 75020

Terrass'H. Ⓜ, 12 r. J.-de-Maistre (18e) ☎ 606.72.85, Télex 280830 – 🕴 📺 ☎ ﬨ – 🅰 30. 🆎 ᏀᏴ ⓘ 🄴 — C 13
SC : Coffee - Shop **L'Albaron** **R** carte environ 70 🍸 et voir rest. **Guerlande** – **95 ch** ⇆ 325/480, 13 appart. 470/540.

Résidence Montmartre sans rest, 10 r. Burq (18e) ☎ 606.45.28 – 🕴 ⛲wc ᵐwc ☎. 🖼 ᏀᏴ — D 13
ᏴᏟ : ⇆ 1ᵇ   **46 ch** 150/200.

H. Le Laumière sans rest, 4 r. Petit (19e) ☎ 206.10.77 – 🕴 ⛲wc ᵐwc ☎. ⅏ — D 19
SC : ⇆ 12 – **54 ch** 65/160.

Super H. Ⓜ, 208 r. Pyrénées (20e) ☎ 636.97.48 – 🕴 ▤ rest ⛲wc ᵐwc ☎. 🖼 ᏀᏴ — G 21
SC : **R** *(fermé dim.)* 55/110 – ⇆ 15 – **27 ch** 85/220.

Pyrénées Gambetta sans rest, 12 av. Père Lachaise (20e) ☎ 366.32.47 – 🕴 ⛲wc ᵐwc ☎ — H 21
SC : ⇆ 14 – **30 ch** 85/185.

Prima-Lepic sans rest, 29 r. Lepic (18e) ☎ 606.44.64 – 🕴 ⛲wc ᵐwc ☎. 🖼 🆎 — D 13
SC : **35 ch** ⇆ 128/188.

Luxia sans rest, 8 r. Seveste (18e) ☎ 606.84.24 – 🕴 ⛲ ᵐwc ☎. 🖼 🆎. ⅏ — D 14
SC : ⇆ 13 – **48 ch** 97/205.

Palma sans rest, 77 av. Gambetta (20e) ☎ 636.13.65 – 🕴 ⛲wc ᵐwc ☎. 🖼 ᏀᏴ. ⅏ — G 21
SC : ⇆ 13 – **34 ch** 65/152.

Puy de Dôme sans rest, 180 r. Ordener (18e) ☎ 627.78.55 – ⛲ ᵐ ☎. 🖼. ⅏ — B 13
fermé 13 juil. au 31 août – SC : **28 ch** ⇁ 70/130.

※※※ ✿ **Beauvilliers** (Carlier), 52 r. Lamarck (18e) ☎ 254.19.50, « Décor original, terrasse » – ᏀᏴ. ⅏ — C 14
fermé 30 août au 28 sept., lundi midi et dim. – **R** carte 165 à 210
Spéc. Flan de moules à la courgette, Tronçon de turbot en meurette, Col vert aux figues (15 oct. au 15 fév.).

※※※ ✿✿ **Cochon d'Or**, 192 av. Jean-Jaurès (19e) ☎ 607.23.13 – ▤. 🆎 ᏀᏴ ⓘ 🄴 — C 20
R carte 110 à 170
Spéc. Escargots de Bourgogne, Pied de porc sauce Choron, Grillades.

※※※ ✿ **Relais Pyrénées** (Marty), 1 r. Jourdain (20e) ☎ 636.65.81 – 🆎 ⓘ 🄴 — F 20
fermé août et sam. – **R** carte 140 à 190
Spéc. Foie gras frais de canard, Saumon frais au Champagne, Confit d'oie.

※※※ **Le Guerlande**, 12 r. Caulaincourt (18e) ☎ 606.59.05 – ▤. 🆎 ᏀᏴ ⓘ 🄴 — C 13
SC : **R** carte 115 à 160.

※※※ **Charlot 1er ''Merveilles des Mers''**, 128 bis bd Clichy (18e) ☎ 522.47.08 – 🆎 ᏀᏴ ⓘ 🄴 — D 12
fermé 14 juil. au 15 août – **R** carte 145 à 210.

※※※ **Auberge du XVIII e**, 6 r. Caulaincourt (18e) ☎ 387.64.78 – 🆎 ᏀᏴ ⓘ — D 12
fermé août, lundi midi et dim. – **R** carte 100 à 145.

※※※ **Dagorno**, 190 av. J.-Jaurès (19e) ☎ 607.02.29 – 🆎 ᏀᏴ ⓘ 🄴 — C 20
fermé sam. – **R** carte 115 à 160.

※※ **Sanglier Bleu**, 102 bd Clichy (18e) ☎ 606.07.61 – ▤. 🆎 ᏀᏴ ⓘ 🄴 — D 12
fermé juil. – **R** carte 105 à 165.

※※ ✿ **Grandgousier** (Vigato), 17 av. Rachel (18e) ☎ 387.66.12 – ᏀᏴ — D 12
fermé août, sam. et dim. – **R** carte 100 à 140
Spéc. Mousseline de foies blonds aux raisins, Poissons au miel et au vinaigre, Desserts au chocolat amer.

XX ⊛ **Les Semailles** (Jouteux), 3 r. Steinlen (18e) ☎ 606.37.05 — ⊖⊟   C 13
fermé dim. et lundi – SC : **R** carte 195 à 250
Spéc. Soupe de foie gras tiède aux pleurotes, Mignon de veau au chasselas, Selle d'agneau à l'aneth.

XX ⊛ **Petit Pré** (Verges), 1 r. Bellevue (19e) ☎ 208.92.62 — ⊖⊟   E 21
fermé 14 juil. au 15 août, sam., dim. et fériés – SC : **R** carte 130 à 170
Spéc. Terrine de filets de sole au basilic, Boutifare de lièvre (saison de chasse), Cassoulet de poisson.

XX ⊛ **Le Clodenis** (Gentes), 57 r. Caulaincourt (18e) ☎ 606.20.26   C 13
fermé 1er au 9 mai, 8 au 31 août, 26 déc. au 3 janv., dim. et lundi – **R** 100 (déj.) et carte 130 à 190
Spéc. Huîtres chaudes aux œufs de saumon (1er sept. au 28 fév.), Foie gras frais au naturel, Assiette de poissons.

XX **Deux Taureaux,** 206 av. J.-Jaurès (19e) ☎ 607.39.31 — ▧ ⊖⊟ ⓞ ▮   C 21
fermé sam. et dim. – **R** carte 110 à 140.

XX **Boeuf Couronné,** 188 av. Jean-Jaurès (19e) ☎ 607.89.52 — ▧ ⊖⊟ ⓞ ▮ ⊟   C 20
fermé dim. – **R** carte 105 à 140.

XX **La Chaumière,** 46 av. Secrétan (19e) ☎ 607.98.62 — ▧ ⊖⊟ ⓞ ▮   E 18
fermé août et dim. – SC : **R** carte 90 à 125.

XX **Wepler,** 14 pl. Clichy (18e) ☎ 522.53.24 — ⊖⊟ ⊟   D 12
R carte 85 à 130.

XX **La Manna,** 148 av. St-Ouen (18e) ☎ 627.42.35   B 12
fermé 10 août au 10 sept. mardi soir et merc. – **R** carte 75 à 125.

XX **Chez Frézet,** 181 r. Ordener (18e) ☎ 606.64.20   B 13
fermé août, vacances de fév., sam., dim. et fériés – **R** carte 95 à 130.

X **Marie-Louise,** 52 r. Championnet (18e) ☎ 606.86.55 — ⓞ ▮   B 15
fermé fin juil. à début sept., dim., lundi et fériés – **R** carte 75 à 115.

X **Le Pichet,** 174 r. Ordener (18e) ☎ 627.85.28 — ⊖⊟ ⓞ ▮   B 13
fermé août et dim. – **R** carte 85 à 130 ⅄.

X **Le Sancerre,** 13 av. Corentin Cariou (19e) ☎ 607.80.44 — ⊗   B 19 B 20
fermé août, sam., dim. et fêtes – **R** carte 90 à 115.

X **La Comète des Abattoirs,** 35 av. Corentin Cariou (19e) ☎ 607.74.26 — ▧ ⊖⊟ ⓞ ▮   B 19
fermé sam. soir et dim. – **R** carte 75 à 110.

en français

Visitez la capitale avec le
guide Vert Michelin

in English

Visit the capital with the
Michelin Green Guide

in Deutsch

Besuchen Sie die französische Hauptstadt mit dem
Grünen Michelin-Führer

Proche banlieue

26 km environ autour de Paris

Argenteuil ◁◉▷ **95100** Val-d'Oise 🔟🔟🔟 ⑭ – 103 141 h. alt. 42 – ✿ 3.

Paris 14 – Chantilly 36 – Pontoise 20 – St-Germain-en-Laye 15.

XXX **Moulin d'Orgemont**, r. Clos des Moines 🍴 410.21.47, « Moulin à vent sur la colline, manège de chevaux de bois » – 🅿
fermé août, 23 déc. au 5 janv. et dim. – **R** carte 105 à 155.

XX **Aub. Jacques Pichon**, 26 r. H.-Barbusse 🍴 961.07.86 – 🆎 ⒼⒷ
fermé 8 au 31 août, dim. soir et lundi soir – SC : **R** 100/160.

XX **Ferme d'Argenteuil**, 2 bis r. Verte 🍴 961.00.62 – 🆎 ⒼⒷ ⓪
fermé 1er au 15 août, dim. (sauf le midi en hiver) et lundi – SC : **R** 100.

X **La Colombe** avec ch, 20 bd Héloïse 🍴 961.01.38 – cuisinette 🔲 🛁wc ☎ 🅿 – 🄰 25 à 200.
🏠🏠 🆎 ⒼⒷ ⓪. ⚡ ch
R *(fermé dim.)* carte 80 à 120 – 🖵 15 – **14 ch** 55/185.

Aulnay-sous-Bois **93600** Seine-St-Denis 🔟🔟🔟 ⑰ G. Paris – 78 271 h. alt. 50 – ✿ 1.

Paris 19 – Lagny 21 – Meaux 30 – St-Denis 12 – Senlis 38.

🏘🏘 **Novotel** Ⓜ, rte Gonesse 🍴 866.22.97, Télex 230121, 🏊 – 📶 🔲 rest 📺 ☎ 🔥 🅿 – 🄰 300. 🆎
ⒼⒷ ⓪
R snack carte environ 75 – 🖵 25 – **139 ch** 230/260.

🏠 **Strasbourg** sans rest, 43 bd Strasbourg 🍴 866.60.38 – 🛁wc ☎. 🏠🏠 ⒼⒷ ⓪
fermé 30 juil. au 29 août et 24 déc. au 2 janv. – SC : 🖵 12 – **18 ch** 124/152.

Bagnolet **93170** Seine-St-Denis 🔟🔟🔟 ⑯ – 35 907 h. alt. 86 – ✿ 1.

Paris 6 – Lagny 27 – Meaux 40.

🏘🏘 **Novotel Paris Bagnolet** Ⓜ, av. République, échangeur porte de Bagnolet 🍴 360.02.10,
Télex 670216, 🏊 – 📶 🔲 📺 ☎ 🅿 – 🄰 25 à 800. 🆎 ⒼⒷ ⓪
L'Oeuf et la Poule **R** 120 bc - snack **R** carte environ 90 – 🖵 28 – **610 ch** 350/370.

Bougival **78380** Yvelines 🔟🔟🔟 ⑬ G. Environs de Paris – 8 744 h. alt. 40 – ✿ 3.

Paris 18 – Rueil-Malmaison 3,5 – St-Germain-en-Laye 7 – Versailles 7 – Le Vésinet 4.

🏘🏘 **Forest Hill** Ⓜ ⚡, 12 r. Y.-Tourgueneff 🍴 918.17.16, Télex 695580, 🏊 – 📶 🔲 rest 📺 ☎ 🚗
– 🄰 200. 🆎 ⒼⒷ ⓪ Ⓔ
SC : **R** 90/125 🍴 – 🖵 35 – **175 ch** 250/380.

XXXX ✿ **Coq Hardy**, 16 quai Rennequin-Sualem (N 13) 🍴 969.01.43, « Jardins fleuris en terrasses,
intérieur élégant » – 🅿 🆎 ⒼⒷ ⓪
fermé 17 janv. au 17 fév., mardi soir du 1er nov. au 15 mars et merc. – **R** (dim. prévenir) 170
(déj.) et carte 175 à 220
Spéc. Foie gras frais de canard, Aiguillettes de canard aux fruits, Millefeuilles au praliné.

XXX ✿✿ **Le Camelia** (Delaveyne), 7 quai G.-Clemenceau 🍴 969.03.02 – 🆎 ⒼⒷ
fermé dim. soir et lundi – **R** 140 (déj.) et carte 155 à 200
Spéc. Fricassée de champignons des bois (oct. à janv.), Tourtière de petite pêche à l'orange, Blanquette de veau.

XX **Cheval Noir**, 14 quai G.-Clemenceau 🍴 969.00.96 – ⒼⒷ
fermé fin juil. à début sept., merc. soir et jeudi – **R** carte 85 à 130.

Boulogne-Billancourt ◁◉▷ **92100** Hauts-de-Seine 🔟🔟🔟 ㉔ G. Paris – 103 948 h. alt. 35 – ✿ 1.

Voir Bois de Boulogne★★ : Jardin d'acclimatation★ – Jardin Albert Kahn★ – Musée Paul
Landowski★.

Paris (par Porte de St-Cloud) 10 – Versailles 11.

🏨 **Sélect H.** Ⓜ sans rest, 66 av. Gén.-Leclerc 🍴 604.70.47 – 📶 🛁wc 🛁wc ☎ 🅿
SC : 🖵 16 – **57 ch** 180/190.

🏠 **Excelsior** sans rest, 12 r. Ferme 🍴 621.08.08 – 📶 🛁wc ☎. 🏠🏠 🆎 ⚡
SC : 🖵 13 – **52 ch** 140/170.

XXX ✿✿ **Gérard Pangaud,** 1 rd point Rhin et Danube ☎ 605.34.42 – 🗏. 🖭 ⬤⬤ ⓘ
fermé sam. et dim. – **R** 135 (déj.) et carte 165 à 220
Spéc. Hure de langoustines et ris de veau, Pigeon au homard, Pommes soufflées.

XXX ✿ **Au Comte de Gascogne,** 89 av. J.-B.-Clément ☎ 603.47.27, « Jardin d'hiver » – 🗏. ⬤⬤
fermé août, sam., dim. et fériés – **R** carte 140 à 190
Spéc. Foie de canard, Panaché de poissons, Emincé de magret de canard au basilic.

XX ✿ **La Bretonnière,** 120 av. J.-B.-Clément ☎ 605.73.56 – 🖭 ⬤⬤ ⓘ
fermé sam. et dim. – **R** carte 125 à 170
Spéc. Ragoût de ris de veau, Assortiment de poissons, Escalope de foie gras au cassis.

XX **La Bergerie,** 87 av. J.-B.-Clément ☎ 605.39.07 – 🖭 ⬤⬤ ⓘ
fermé 13 au 20 août, lundi soir, dim. et fêtes – **R** carte 100 à 145.

XX **Laux... à la Bouche,** 117 av. J.-B.-Clément ☎ 825.43.88 – ⬤⬤
fermé août – **R** carte 85 à 115.

XX **La Petite Auberge Franc Comtoise,** 86 av. J.-B.-Clément ☎ 605.67.19 – 🖭 ⬤⬤ ⓘ
fermé 31 juil. au 29 août, dim. et fériés – **R** carte 120 à 170.

X **La Galère,** 112 r. Gén.-Gallieni ☎ 605.64.51 – ⬤⬤. 🍴
fermé août, sam. et dim. – **R** carte 75 à 105.

Le Bourget (Aéroport de Paris) 93350 Seine-St-Denis 🔟🔟 ⑰ G. Paris – 10 534 h. alt. 66 –
Renseignements : ☎ 862.12.12.

Voir Musée de l'Air (en cours d'installation).

Paris 15 – Aulnay-sous-Bois 6 – Chantilly 34 – Meaux 38 – St-Denis 6,5 – Senlis 36.

🏨 **Novotel** 🅼, à Blanc-Mesnil ZA pont Yblon ⊠ 93150 Le Blanc-Mesnil ☎ 867.48.88, Télex
230115, 🏊 – 劇 🗏 rest 📺 ☎ 🅿 – 🛦 250. 🖭 ⬤⬤ ⓘ
R carte environ 75 – 🖵 25 – **143 ch** 230/265.

Châteaufort 78 Yvelines 🔟🔟 ㉒ – 812 h. alt. 153 – ⊠ 78530 Buc – ✿ 3.

Paris 27 – Arpajon 28 – Rambouillet 25 – Versailles 10.

XX ✿ **La Belle Epoque** (Peignaud), 10 pl. Mairie ☎ 956.21.66, « Auberge rustique dominant le
vallon » – 🖭 ⬤⬤ ⓘ
fermé 13 août au 5 sept. et 23 déc. au 4 janv. – **R** carte 130 à 185
Spéc. St-Jacques aux cèpes en mousseline, Risettes et rognons de veau, Soufflé au noyau de Poissy.

Chennevières-sur-Marne 94430 Val-de-Marne 🔟🔟 ㉘ G. Paris – 17 571 h. alt. 100 – ✿ 1.

Voir Terrasse 🍴*.

🏌 d'Ormesson ☎ 576.20.71, SE : 3 km.

Paris 17 – Coulommiers 49 – Lagny 22.

🏠 **Jardins de France** sans rest, 27 r. Champigny ☎ 576.01.66, 🌳 – ⌂wc 🚿wc 🅿
fermé août – SC : 🖵 12 – **17 ch** 94/140.

XXX **Écu de France,** 31 r. Champigny ☎ 576.00.03, « Cadre rustique, terrasse fleurie en bordure
de rivière » – 🅿 🍴
fermé dim. soir et lundi – SC : **R** carte 95 à 150.

XXX **Aub. Vieux Clodoche,** 18 r. Champigny ☎ 576.09.39 – 🅿 🖭 ⓘ
R carte 120 à 160.

Chilly-Mazarin 91380 Essonne 🔟🔟 ㉟ – 17 413 h. alt. 77 – ✿ 6.

Paris 21 – Étampes 33 – Évry 16 – Versailles 27.

XXX **Pavillon Mazarin,** 31 rte Longjumeau ☎ 909.81.11, 🌳 – 🅿 🖭 ⬤⬤ ⓘ 🇪
fermé août et sam. – **R** (déj. seul.) carte 115 à 160.

Clichy 92110 Hauts-de-Seine 🔟🔟 ⑮ – 47 956 h. alt. 30 – ✿ 1.

Paris 6,5 – Argenteuil 7 – Pontoise 27 – St-Germain-en-Laye 17.

🏨 **Le Ruthène** sans rest, 35 r. Klock ☎ 737.02.51, Télex 613461 – 劇 ⌂wc 🚿wc 🅿. 🍴
SC : 🖵 20 – **20 ch** 200/220.

🏨 **Girbal** sans rest, 14 r. Dagobert ☎ 737.54.24 – 劇 ⌂wc 🚿wc 🅿 🚗 ⬤⬤
SC : 🖵 15 – **42 ch** 170/180.

XX ✿ **Barrière de Clichy,** 1 r. de Paris ☎ 737.05.18 – 🖭 ⬤⬤ ⓘ
fermé sam. midi et dim. – **R** carte 165 à 210.
Spéc. Feuilleté des 4 saisons, Aiguillettes de canard aux pêches, Panaché de l'océan.

XX **La Bonne Table,** 119 bd J.-Jaurès ☎ 737.38.79 – 🗏
fermé sept., dim. et lundi – SC : **R** 100 bc/150 bc.

XX **La Colombe d'Or,** 18 bd Gén. de Gaulle ☎ 731.73.61 – 🖭 ⬤⬤ ⓘ
fermé août, sam. midi et dim. – SC : **R** carte 105 à 145.

Cormeilles-en-Parisis 95240 Val-d'Oise 🗺 ④ – 14 309 h. alt. 115 – ❄ 3.

Paris 28,5 – Argenteuil 5 – Maisons-Laffitte 8 – Pontoise 14,5.

XX **Aub de l'Hexagone,** 32 r. Pommiers ⏰ 978.77.49 – **P**. ஊ 🅶🅱 ⓞ
fermé août dim. et fêtes – SC : **R** 80/100.

Courbevoie 92400 Hauts-de-Seine 🗺 ⑭ **G. Paris** – 54 578 h. alt. 34 – ❄ 1.

Voir La Défense★★ : Palais de la Défense★ (Centre National des Industries et des Techniques),
Tour Manhattan★★★ – Tour Fiat★★, Tour GAN★★ et Tour Roussel - Nobel★.

Paris (par Porte Champerret) 11 – Asnières 3 – Levallois-Perret 3,5 – St-Germain-en-Laye 14.

🏨 **Penta** Ⓜ, 18 r. Baudin 🕿 788.50.51, Télex 610470 – 🛗 🍽 root ☎ **P** – 🔬 25 à 300. ஊ 🅶🅱 ⓞ.
🍴 rest
SC : l'**Atelier R** carte 70 à 115 🔏 – **493 ch** ⊆ 330/360.

🏠 **Marina** sans rest, 18 av. Marceau 🕿 333.57.04 – 🛗 🛁wc 🖭. 🅾🅱. 🍴
SC : ⊆ 12 – **30 ch** 80/160.

🏠 **Central** sans rest, 99 r. Cap.-Guynemer 🕿 789.25.25 – 🛗 🚿wc 🛁wc 🖭. 🅾🅱
SC : ⊆ 10 – **55 ch** 60/120.

X **A la Potinière,** 65 bis av. Gambetta 🕿 333.07.99 – ஊ 🅶🅱 ⓞ
fermé août, sam. et dim. – **R** carte 90 à 135.

X **Clocher de Rodez,** 40 r. Bezons 🕿 333.52.19 – ⓞ
fermé août, dim. et lundi – **R** carte 75 à 130.

Créteil **P** 94000 Val-de-Marne 🗺 ㉗ **G. Paris** – 65 447 h. alt. 49 – ❄ 1.

Voir Hôtel de ville★ : parvis★.

🛈 Office de Tourisme, 1 r. F.-Mauriac (fermé sam. après-midi et dim.) 🕿 898.58.18.

Paris 12 – Bobigny 17 – Évry 20 – Lagny 26 – Melun 35.

🏨 **Novotel** Ⓜ 🐾, 🕿 207.91.02, Télex 670396, 🏊, – 🛗 🖭 📺 ☎ **P** – 🔬 25 à 200. ஊ 🅶🅱 ⓞ
R snack carte environ 75 – ⊆ 25 – **110 ch** 230/265.

XX **La Terrasse,** 39 av. Verdun 🕿 207.16.94 ஊ 🅶🅱
fermé 13 juil. au 28 août, sam. et dim. – **R** carte 120 à 165.

Enghien-les-Bains 95880 Val d'Oise 🗺 ⑤ **G. Environs de Paris** (plan) – 10 713 h. alt. 50 – Stat.
therm. – Casino – ❄ 3.

Voir Lac★.

🏌 de Domont 🕿 991.07.50, N : 8 km.

🛈 Office de Tourisme 2 bd Cotte (fermé merc. et dim.) 🕿 412.41.15.

Paris 18 – Argenteuil 16 – Chantilly 32 – Pontoise 20 – St-Denis 6 – St-Germain-en-Laye 23.

🏨 **Gd H. des Bains,** 85 r. Gén.-de-Gaulle 🕿 412.80.00, Télex 697842, ≤, « Beau jardin fleuri »
– 🛗 📺 ☎ **P** – 🔬 35. 🅶🅱 ⓞ. 🍴 rest
SC : **R** carte 90 à 110 – ⊆ 25 – **50 ch** 290/370, 3 appartements 540.

🏠 **Villa Marie Louise** 🐾 sans rest, 49 r. Malleville 🕿 964.82.21, 🌲 – 🛗 🚿wc 🛁wc 🖭
SC : ⊆ 13 – **22 ch** 83/160.

XXXX ❀ **Duc d'Enghien,** au Casino 🕿 412.90.00, ≤ lac – 🖭 **P**. 🅶🅱 ⓞ. 🍴
R carte 150 à 190
Spéc. Escalope de foie gras chaud de canard, St-Pierre en meurette, Mille-feuille tiède caramélisé.

XX La Cascade, 97 r. Gén.-de-Gaulle 🕿 989.97.33, ≤ lac.

XX **Aub. Landaise,** 32 bd d'Ormesson 🕿 412.78.36 – ஊ 🅶🅱
fermé août, vacances de fév. et merc. – SC : **R** carte 80 à 110.

XX **A la Carpe d'Or,** 91 r. Gén.-de-Gaulle 🕿 412.79.53, ≤ – ஊ 🅶🅱 ⓞ
R carte 90 à 140 🔏.

X **La Petite Tonkinoise,** 9 av. Gallieni à Épinay-sur-Seine 🕿 826.92.64
fermé août, dim. soir et lundi – SC : **R** carte 55 à 80.

Gennevilliers 92230 Hauts-de-Seine 🗺 ⑮ **G. Paris** – 50 326 h. alt. 29 – ❄ 1.

🛈 Office de Tourisme 177 av. Gabriel Péri (fermé août, sam. et dim.) 🕿 799.33.92.

Paris 11 – Pontoise 23 – St-Denis 4 – St-Germain-en-Laye 20.

XX ❀ **Julius,** 6 bd Ornuillaut 🕿 790.75.37 – 🖭
fermé août, sam. midi et dim. – SC : **R** carte 120 à 185
Spéc. Cassolette de coques à la ciboulette, Émincé de lotte à la fondue de poireaux, Pétales de pamplemousse au
caramel.

Houilles 78800 Yvelines 🗺 ⑬ – 30 636 h. alt. 31 – ❄ 3.

Paris 17 – Argenteuil 6 – Maisons-Laffitte 5 – St-Germain-en-Laye 8.

XX ❀ **Gambetta** (Poirier), 41 r. Gambetta 🕿 968.52.12 – 🅶🅱
fermé mi août à début sept., vacances de fév., dim. soir et lundi – SC : **R** carte 125 à 180
Spéc. Terrine de brochet, St-Pierre au Brouilly, Escalope de ris de veau aux écrevisses.

Livry-Gargan 93190 Seine-St-Denis 101 ⑱ – 32 944 h. alt. 63 – ✪ 1.

🛈 Syndicat d'Initiative pl. H. de Ville (fermé matin, dim. et lundi) �ℑ 330.61.60.

Paris 19 – Aubervilliers 13 – Aulnay-sous-Bois 5,5 – Chelles 8 – Meaux 28 – Senlis 42.

XXX ✲ **Aub. St-Quentinoise** (Mme Faure), 23 av. République ℑ 381.13.08 – ⤬ ⅏
fermé août, dim. soir et lundi – SC : **R** (dîner prévenir) 120 (déj.) et carte 140 à 200
Spéc. Marmite du pêcheur (oct. à avril), Rognons de veau, Cœur de filet.

Longjumeau 91160 Essonne 101 ㉟ – 18 183 h. alt. 72 – ✪ 6.

Paris 21 – Chartres 70 – Dreux 82 – Évry 16 – Melun 38 – ♦Orléans 96 – Versailles 21.

🏨 **Relais St-Georges** M ⅏, à Saulx-les-Chartreux SO : 3 km ⊠ 91160 Longjumeau ℑ
448.36.40, ≼, parc – ⌷ 🆃🆅 ⇔ 🅿 – 🅰 60 à 100. 🆀🅴 ⤬ ⓪ 🅴
fermé août – SC : **R** 80/140 – ⌷ 25 – **26 ch** 180/220 – P 280/350.

🏨 **Relais des Chartreux** M, à Saulxier SO : 2 km ⊠ 91160 Longjumeau ℑ 909.34.31, Télex
691245, ≼, 🏊, ⅏ – ⌷ 🆃🆅 ☎ 🅿 – 🅰 250. 🆀🅴 ⤬ ⓪ 🅴
SC : **R** 85 – ⌷ 22 – **100 ch** 220/250.

Maisons-Laffitte 78600 Yvelines 101 ⑬ G. Environs de Paris – 23 807 h. alt. 40 – ✪ 3.

Voir Escalier d'honneur★★ du château★.

Paris 21 – Argenteuil 8,5 – Mantes-la-Jolie 37 – Poissy 8 – Pontoise 18 – St-Germain 8.

XXX ✲✲ **Vieille Fontaine** (Clerc), 8 av. Gretry ℑ 962.01.78, « Jardin » – 🆀🅴 ⤬ ⓪
fermé dim. et lundi – **R** carte 185 à 230
Spéc. Aumônière de caviar, Cuisses de grenouilles, Rognon de veau au chiroubles.

XXX ✲✲ **Le Tastevin** (Blanchet), 7 av. Ste-Hélène ℑ 962.11.67, 🏵 – 🅿 🆀🅴 ⤬ ⓪
fermé 16 août au 8 sept., lundi soir et mardi – SC : **R** carte 125 à 170
Spéc. St-Jacques au coulis de truffes (15 oct. au 15 mars), Cassoulet, Sanciaux (nov. à avril).

XX **Le Laffitte**, 5 av. St-Germain ℑ 962.01.53 – 🆀🅴 ⓪
fermé août, mardi soir et merc. – SC : **R** carte 90 à 150.

Marne-la-Vallée 77 S.-et-M. 101 ⑱ G. Environs de Paris – ⊠ 77140 Lagny – ✪ 6.

Paris 26 – Meaux 28 – Melun 35.

S.E : 6 km par échangeur de Lagny A 4 :

🏨 **Novotel** M, ℑ 005.91.15, Télex 691990, 🏊, – ⌷ 🆃🆅 ⇔wc ☎ 🅑 🅿 – 🅰 150. 🆀🅴 ⤬ ⓪
R carte environ 75 – ⌷ 25 – **92 ch** 255/275.

Meudon 92190 Hauts-de-Seine 101 ㉔ G. Paris (plan) – 53 413 h. alt. 100 – ✪ 1.

Voir Terrasse★ : ⁂★ – Forêt de Meudon★.

Paris 12 – Boulogne-Billancourt 3 – Clamart 3,5 – Versailles 10.

🏨 **Forest Hill** M, à Meudon-la-Forêt S : 3 km ℑ 630.22.55, Télex 203150, 🏊, ⅏ – ⌷ 🆅 ⇔wc
☎ 🅿 – 🅰 60. 🍴 🆀🅴 ⤬ ⓪ 🅴
SC : **R** 82/115 ♨ – 🍽 20 – **97 ch** 215.

XXX ✲ **Relais des Gardes**, à Bellevue, 42 av. Gallieni ℑ 534.11.79 – 🆀🅴 ⤬ ⓪
fermé août, lundi soir et sam. – SC : **R** carte 145 à 195
Spéc. Cotriade des Glénan, Pot-au-feu de canard saintongeaise, Feuilleté tiède aux pommes.

XX **Ermitage de Villebon**, près étang de Villebon S : 3 km ℑ 632.10.74, 🏵 – 🅿 🆀🅴 ⤬
fermé août, vac. scol. de fév., dim. soir et lundi – SC : **R** 60/100.

X **Le Lapin Sauté** avec ch, 12 av. Le Corbeiller ℑ 626.68.68 – 🍴. ⓪
fermé août, dim. soir et lundi – SC : **R** carte 110 à 150 – ⌷ 18 – **8 ch** 120.

Montrouge 92120 Hauts-de-Seine 101 ㉖ – 40 403 h. alt. 74 – ✪ 1.

Paris (par Porte d'Orléans) 6 – Boulogne-Billancourt 6,5 – Longjumeau 14 – Versailles 16.

🏨 **Mercure** M, 13 r. F.-Ory ℑ 657.11.26, Télex 202528 – ⌷ 🖃 rest 🆅 ☎ ⅖ ⇦. 🆀🅴 ⤬ ⓪
R carte environ 120 – ⌷ 25 – **186 ch** 350/370.

Morangis 91420 Essonne 101 ㉟ – 8 565 h. alt. 76 – ✪ 6.

Paris 22 – Évry 16 – Longjumeau 4,5 – Versailles 23.

🏨 **Pierre Loti** M sans rest, 110 av. République ℑ 909.09.97 – ⇔wc 🍴wc 🚗 ⇦ 🅿. 🍴 ⅏
SC : ⌷ 13,50 – **30 ch** 102/141.

XX ✲ **Rêve d'Alsace**, 65 av. E.-Rostand ℑ 909.14.78 – 🆀🅴 ⓪
SC : **R** carte 105 à 165
Spéc. Tarte à la confiture d'oignons, Jambonneau de Barbarie, Mousse aux deux chocolats.

To cross Paris rapidly and find your way in the
suburbs use the new Michelin Map no. 101, **Outskirts of Paris** scale 1/50 000.

Neuilly-sur-Seine 92200 Hauts-de-Seine 👁️👁️👁️ ⑮ – 66 095 h. alt. 36 – 🌳 1.

Voir Bois de Boulogne★★ : Jardin d'acclimatation★, Bagatelle★, Musée National des Arts et Traditions Populaires★★ – Centre International de Paris - Palais des Congrès★★ : grand auditorium★★★, ≤★ de la tour Concorde-La Fayette, G. Paris.

Paris (par Porte Neuilly) 8 – Argenteuil 12 – Pontoise 37 – St-Germain 14 – Versailles 18.

🏨 **H.-Club Méditerranée** Ⓜ, 58 bd V.-Hugo 🕾 758.11.00, Télex 610971, Ambiance club, ☞ – 🛗 🔲 🔟 🕿 ᚴ ⇔ – ᚴ 30 à 120 – 335 ch.

🏨 **Parc Neuilly** Ⓜ sans rest, 4 bd Parc 🕾 747.87.32 – 🛗 🔟 ⇔wc ⋔wc ☎ ☰⬚
SC : ⇆ 12 – **71 ch** 81/198.

🏨 **Roule** sans rest, 37 bis av. du Roule 🕾 624.60.09 – 🛗 ⇔wc ⋔wc ☎. ☰⬚
SC : ⇆ 13.50 – **35 ch** 123/164

XXX **Manoir,** 4 r. Église 🕾 624.04.61 – 🔲. ☞☞
fermé août, sam. et dim. – SC : **R** carte 145 à 180.

XXX ⋈ **Jacqueline Fénix,** 42 av. Ch.-de-Gaulle 🕾 624.42.61 – 🔲
fermé août, Noël-Jour de l'An, sam. et dim. – SC : **R** carte 130 à 175
Spéc. Poissons, Foie de veau en cocotte, Chocolat au macaron et café.

XX **Jarasse,** 4 av. Madrid 🕾 624.07.56 – ☎ ☞☞ ☎
fermé 15 juil. au 31 août, dim. soir et lundi – **R** carte 145 à 185.

XX ⋈ **Bourrier,** 1 pl. Parmentier 🕾 624.11.19 – ☞☞
fermé 14 juil. au 15 août, sam., dim. et fêtes – SC : **R** 170/250
Spéc. Salade de canard, Andouillette de saumon (saison), Faisan Louis XIV (saison de chasse).

XX **Truffe Noire,** 2 pl. Parmentier 🕾 624.94.14 – ☎ ☞☞
fermé août, vend. soir et sam. – **R** carte 110 à 150.

XX **Focly,** 10 r. P.-Chatrousse 🕾 624.43.36 – ☎ ☞☞
fermé 6 au 20 août – **R** carte 50 à 75.

X **Chau'veau,** 59 r. Chauveau 🕾 624.46.22 – ⓦ
fermé août, sam. et dim. – **R** carte 60 à 110.

Nogent-sur-Marne 🛞 94130 Val-de-Marne 👁️👁️👁️ ㉗ G. Paris – 25 801 h. alt. 58 – 🌳 1.
🚹 Office de Tourisme 5 av. Joinville (fermé matin, dim. et lundi) 🕾 873.73.97.
Paris 14 – Créteil 6,5 – Montreuil 5 – Vincennes 4.

🏨 **Nogentel** Ⓜ, 8 r. Port 🕾 872.70.00, Télex 210116, ≤ – 🛗 🔟 🕿 – ᚴ 250. ☎ ☞☞ ⓦ ☎
rest. **Le Panoramic** (fermé août) **R** carte 125 à 175 - Grill **Le Canotier R** carte environ 70 – ⇆ 22
– **61 ch** 230/280.

Orly (Aéroport de Paris) 94396 Val-de-Marne 👁️👁️👁️ ㉘ G. Paris (plan) – 26 244 h. alt. 89 - Renseignements 🕾 884.52.52 – 🌳 1.

Voir Aérogares★ : terrasse supérieure d'Orly-Sud ≤★.

Paris 16 – Corbeil-Essonnes 17 – Longjumeau 9 – Villeneuve-St-Georges 12.

🏨 **Hilton Orly** Ⓜ, près aérogare 🕾 687.33.88, Télex 250621, ≤ – 🛗 🔲 🔟 🕿 ᚴ 🅿 – ᚴ 500. ☎
☞☞ ⓦ ☎
Le Café du Marché R carte 75 à 100 ⋞ - **La Louisiane** (fermé août et sam. du 15/11 au 15/3) **R**
carte 90 à 135 – ⇆ 27 – **388 ch** 332/491.

🏨 **Le Senia,** 6 r. Bas-Marin 🕾 687.31.30 – ⇔wc ⋔wc ☎ ⇔ 🅿. ☰⬚ ☎ ☞☞
SC : **R** 70 bc – ⇆ 15 – **44 ch** 150/195.

Aérogare d'Orly Sud :

XXX **Le Grillardin,** 🕾 687.24.25, ≤ – 🔲. ☎ ☞☞ ⓦ ☎
SC : **R** 71/151.

Aérogare d'Orly Ouest :

XXXX ⋈ **Maxim's,** 🕾 687.16.16, ≤ – ☎ ☞☞ ⓦ
R carte 155 à 220
Spéc. Fricassée de Poisson, Aiguillette de caneton aux mangues, Soupe de fruits frais.

XXX **Grill Maxim's,** 🕾 687.16.16 – ☎ ☞☞ ⓦ
SC : **R** carte 140 à 170.

X **La Galerie,** 🕾 687.16.16, ≤ – ☞☞
SC : **R** 69 ᚴ.

Orsay 91400 Essonne 👁️👁️👁️ ㉝ – 22 579 h. alt. 90 – 🌳 6.
🚹 Office de Tourisme (fermé matin sauf mardi et vend., sam. après-midi et dim.) et T.C.F. 14 av.
St-Laurent 🕾 928.59.72.
Paris 27 – Évry 24 – Rambouillet 30 – Versailles 21.

Échangeur Courtabœuf S : 2 km intersection A 10 et F 18 – ✉ 91400 Orsay :

🏨 **Mercure** Ⓜ, Zone Industrielle 🕾 907.63.96, Télex 691247, ⵣ – 🛗 🔲 rest 🔟 🕿 ᚴ 🅿 – ᚴ
25 à 200. ☎ ☞☞ ⓦ
R carte environ 80 – ⇆ 25 – **110 ch** 230/250.

Palaiseau 91120 Essonne 101 ㉞ − 28 924 h. alt. 80 − ❀ 6.

Paris 22 − Arpajon 18 − Chartres 69 − Évry 19 − Rambouillet 37.

🏨 **Novotel** M, Zone industrielle de Massy ⬦ 920.84.91, Télex 691595, ⊒ − 🛗 ▤ rest 📺 ☎ 🕭
🅿 − 🔼 25 à 250. 🝙 🇬🇧 ⑩
R snack carte environ 75 − ⌷ 25 − **151 ch** 230/265.

Le Pré St-Gervais 93310 Seine-St-Denis 101 ⑯ − 14 106 h. alt. 71 − ❀ 1.

Paris (par Porte de Pantin) 7 − Lagny 27 − Meaux 38 − Montreuil 4,5 − Senlis 44.

✗ ❀ **Au Pouilly Reuilly** (Thibault), 68 r. A.-Joineau ⬦ 845.14.59 − 🝙 ⑩
fermé août, dim. et fêtes − **R** carte 75 à 125
Spéc. Pâté de grenouilles, Foie de veau aux girolles, Rognon de veau dijonnaise.

Puteaux 92800 Hauts-de-Seine 101 ⑭ − 35 564 h. alt. 36 − ❀ 1.

Voir La Défense★★ : Palais de la Défense★ (Centre National des Industries et des Techniques),
Tour Manhattan★★★, Tour Fiat★★, Tour GAN★★ et Tour Roussel Nobel★, G. Paris.

Paris 10 − Neuilly-sur-Seine 3 − Pontoise 35 − St-Germain-en-Laye 11 − Versailles 14.

✗✗ ❀ **Gasnier**, 7 bd Richard-Wallace ⬦ 506.33.63 − 🇬🇧
fermé 30 juin au 22 août, sam., dim. et fériés − **R** (nombre de couverts limité - prévenir) carte
145 à 190
Spéc. Foie gras frais de canard, Cassoulet, Confit de canard aux cèpes.

✗✗ **Camille Renault**, 60 r. République ⬦ 776.01.30 − 🝙 🇬🇧 ⑩. ❀
fermé août, dim. et fêtes − **R** carte 95 à 150.

Roissy-en-France 95 Val-d'Oise 101 ⑧ G. Paris (plan) − 1 364 h. − ✉ **95500** Gonesse − ❀ 3.

Voir Aérogare★ − ✈ Charles de Gaulle ⬦ 862.12.12.

Paris 26 − Chantilly 28 − Meaux 36 − Senlis 28.

dans le domaine de l'aéroport :

🏰 **Sofitel** M, ⬦ 862.23.23, Télex 230166, ⊠, ❀ − 🛗 📺 ☎ 🕭 🅿 − 🔼 25 à 500. 🝙 🇬🇧 ⑩ E.
❀ rest
rest panoramique **Les Valois** *(fermé juil.-août)* **R** (dîner seul.) carte 120 à 180 - **Le Jardin**
(brasserie) (rez de chaussée) **R** carte environ 85 🍷 - **Pizzeria** (rez de chaussée) *(fermé sam.,
dim. et fêtes)* **R** carte environ 50 🍷 − ⌷ 30 − **344 ch** 350/520, 8 appart.

dans l'aérogare 1 :

✗✗✗✗ **Maxim's**, ⬦ 862.24.16 − ▤. 🇬🇧
SC : **R** (déj. seul.) 185 - au **Grill Maxim's R** 124.

à la Gare SNCF :

🏨 **Arcade,** ⬦ 862.49.49, Télex 212989 − 🚿wc 🅿 🕭 ❀ rest
SC : **R** 47/52 − ➡ 16 − **360 ch** 145/201.

Rueil-Malmaison 92500 Hauts-de-Seine 101 ⑬ G. Paris − 64 429 h. alt. 15 − ❀ 1.

Voir Château de Bois-Préau★ − Buffet d'orgues★ de l'église − Malmaison : musée★★ du
château − Paris 15 − Argenteuil 12 − St-Germain-en-Laye 7,5 − Versailles 11.

✗✗✗✗ ❀ **El Chiquito**, 126 av. Paul-Doumer ⬦ 751.00.53, « Jardin » − 🅿
fermé août, sam., dim. et fériés − **R** carte 150 à 200
Spéc. Blanquette de sole (sept. à juil.), Soupe de St Jacques aux légumes (oct. à mai), Paupiette de barbue à la
fleur de thym.

✗✗ **Relais de St-Cucufa**, 114 r. Gén.-Miribel ⬦ 749.79.05 − 🅿. 🝙 🇬🇧 ⑩
fermé 15 au 31 août et merc. soir − SC : **R** carte 100 à 190.

à Nanterre N : 2 km − ✉ **92 000** Nanterre :

✗✗✗ **Ile de France,** 83 av. Mar. Joffre ⬦ 724.10.44 − 🅿. 🝙 🇬🇧 ⑩
fermé août, dim. soir et lundi soir − **R** carte 125 à 160.

Rungis 94150 Val-de-Marne 101 ㉖ G. Paris (plan) − 2 996 h. alt. 80 - Marché d'intérêt National − ❀ 1.

Paris 13 − Antony 5,5 − Corbeil-Essonnes 26 − Longjumeau 10.

🏰 **Frantel Rungis Orly** M accès Paris : A6, bretelle d'Orly, de province : A 6 et sortie
Rungis-Orly, 20 av. Ch.-Lindbergh ✉ 94656 ⬦ 687.36.36, Télex 260738, ≼, ⊒ − 🛗 ▤ 📺 ☎ 🕭
⟺ 🅿 − 🔼 50 à 300. 🝙 🇬🇧 ⑩ E. ❀ rest
SC : rest. **La Rungisserie R** carte 120 à 175 − ⌷ 25 − **206 ch** 319/424.

🏨 **Holiday Inn** M, accès de Paris : A 6 bretelle d'Orly, de province A 6 sortie Rungis-Orly ⬦
687.26.66, Télex 204679, ⊒ − 🛗 ▤ 📺 ☎ 🅿 − 🔼 50 à 250. 🝙 🇬🇧 ⑩ E
SC : **R** carte 110 à 150 🍷 − ⌷ 26 − **171 ch** 285/375.

✗✗✗ **Le Charolais,** 13 r. N-Dame à Rungis Ville ⬦ 686.16.42 − 🝙 ⑩
fermé août − **R** carte 120 à 170.

✗✗ **Le Gd Pavillon** (jour et nuit), 6 quai Lorient ⬦ 687.58.58 − 🝙 🇬🇧 ⑩
fermé dim., lundi et le soir sauf sam. − **R** carte 130 à 200.

Saclay 91400 Essonne 101 ㉓ – 2 037 h. alt. 157 – 🟢 6.

🏌 de St-Aubin ☎ 941.25.19, SO : 2,5 km.

Paris 21 – Arpajon 22 – Chartres 68 – Rambouillet 30 – Versailles 11.

🏨 **Novotel** Ⓜ, près rd-point Christ-de-Saclay ☎ 941.81.40, Télex 691856, 🏊, 🍽 – 🛗 ▤ rest
📺 ☎ 🅰 Ⓟ – 🏛 300. 🆎 ⒼⒷ ⓪
R snack carte environ 75 – 🖙 25 – **136 ch** 255/280.

☞ *Michelin n'accroche pas de panonceau aux hôtels et restaurants qu'il signale.*

ST-GERMAIN
EN-LAYE

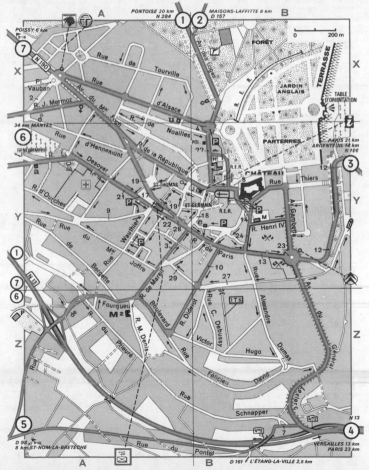

St-Germain-en-laye ⬢ **78100** Yvelines 🔟🔟🔟 ⑫ G. Environs de Paris – 40 471 h. alt. 78 – ✿ 3.

Voir Terrasse★★ BX – Jardin anglais★ BX – Château★ BY : musée des Antiquités nationales de la France★★ – Musée du Prieuré★ AZ **M2.**

📍 📍 ✈ 451.05.90 par ⑦ : 3 km ; 📍 📍 de Fourqueux ✈ 451.41.47 par ⑤ : 4 km.

🅱 Office de Tourisme 1 bis r. République (fermé dim.) ✈ 451.05.12.

Paris 21 ③ – Beauvais 73 ① – Chartres 81 ④ – Dreux 70 ④ – Mantes-la-Jolie 34 ⑥.

Plan page précédente

🏨 **Le Cèdre** 🏡, 7 r. Alsace ✈ 451.84.35, 🍴 – ⇌wc ☏. 🍴. 🎇   AX u
fermé fév. – SC : **R** 62/72 – **30 ch** 🛏 95/190 – P 182/264.

🏨🏨🏨 **Le 7 Rue des Coches,** 7 r. Coches ✈ 973.66.40 – 🍽. 🆎 🆑 ⓞ   BY e
fermé août, dim. soir et lundi – **R** carte 120 à 160.

🍴 **Petite Auberge,** 119 bis r. L.-Desoyer ✈ 451.03.99   AY a
fermé 1er au 28 juil., vacances de fév., mardi soir et merc. – **R** (nombre de couverts limité - prévenir) carte 70 à 105.

au NO par ① : 2,5 km sur N 284 et rte des Mares – ✉ **78100** St-Germain-en-Laye :

🏨🏨🏨 **La Forestière** Ⓜ 🏡, 1 av. Prés.-Kennedy ✈ 973.36.60, Télex 696055, 🍴 – 🛗 📺 ☏ Ⓟ – 🏛 40
SC : **R** voir rest Cazaudehore – 🛏 25 – **24 ch** 290/340, 6 appart. 410/440.

🏨🏨🏨 ✿ **Cazaudehore,** 1 av. Prés.-Kennedy ✈ 451.93.80, « Intérieur rustique, jardin fleuri en forêt » – Ⓟ
fermé lundi sauf fériés – **R** carte 115 à 160
Spéc. Foie gras de canard, Escalope de saumon frais, Confit d'oie ou de canard.

St-Ouen **93400** Seine-St-Denis 🔟🔟🔟 ⑮ G. Paris – 43 695 h. alt. 36 – ✿ 1.

🅱 Office de Tourisme pl. République (fermé août, sam. et dim.) ✈ 254.77.36.

Paris (par Porte de St-Ouen) 7 – Chantilly 34 – Meaux 45 – Pontoise 29 – St-Denis 3,5.

🏨 **Alhambra** sans rest, 23 r. E.-Renan ✈ 254.06.22 – ⇌wc 🚿wc ☏. 🍴. 🎇
fermé août – SC : ☎ 11 – **30 ch** 60/100.

🏨🏨 ✿ **Coq de la Maison Blanche,** 37 bd Jean-Jaurès ✈ 254.01.23 – 🍽. 🆑 ⓞ
fermé dim. soir et merc. soir – **R** carte 100 à 150
Spéc. Jambon persillé, Coq au vin.

Vaucresson **92420** Hauts-de-Seine 🔟🔟🔟 ㉓ – 9 349 h. alt. 142 – ✿ 1.

Voir Etang de St-Cucufa★ NE : 2,5 km, G. Paris.

Paris 19 – Mantes-la-Jolie 43 – St-Cloud 4 – St-Germain-en-Laye 11 – Versailles 5.

voir plan de Versailles

🏨🏨 **La Poularde,** 36 bd Jardy (près autoroute) D 182 ✈ 741.13.47 – Ⓟ 🆑   U a
fermé août, vac. de fév., mardi soir et merc. – SC : **R** carte 90 à 150.

Vélizy-Villacoublay **78140** Yvelines 🔟🔟🔟 ㉓ – 23 856 h. alt. 174 – ✿ 3.

Paris 18 – Antony 11 – Chartres 79 – Meudon 7,5 – Versailles 6,5.

🏨🏨🏨 **Ramada** Ⓜ, av. Europe, centre commercial Vélizy II ✈ 946.96.98, Télex 696537, 🔲 – 🛗 🍽 📺 ☏ Ⓟ – 🏛 300. 🆎 🆑 ⓞ Ⓔ
SC : **R** 82/130 – 🛏 35 – **183 ch** 345/395.

Versailles Ⓟ **78000** Yvelines 🔟🔟🔟 ㉒ G. Environs de Paris – 97 133 h. alt. 132 – ✿ 3.

Voir Château★★★ Y – Jardins★★★ (Grandes Eaux★★★ et fêtes de nuit★★★ en été) V – Grand Canal★★ U – Trianon★★ V – Musée Lambinet★ Y **M.**

📍📍📍 du Racing Club de France ✈ 950.59.41 par ③ : 2,5 km.

🅱 Office de Tourisme 7 r. Réservoirs (fermé jeudi) ✈ 950.36.22 - T.C.F. 2 r. Mar.-Foch ✈ 951.66.22.

Paris 23 ⑨ – Beauvais 87 ⑦ – Dreux 62 ⑥ – Évreux 86 ⑦ – Melun 61 ③ – ◆Orléans 120 ③.

Plans pages suivantes

🏨🏨🏨🏨 **Trianon Palace** 🏡, 1 bd Reine ✈ 950.34.12, Télex 698863, parc – 🛗 📺 ♿ Ⓟ – 🏛 300. 🆎 🆑 ⓞ. 🎇 rest   X r
R 96/130 – 🛏 28 – **120 ch** 250/480, 8 appartements – P 365/442.

🏨🏨 **Mercure** Ⓜ sans rest, r. Marly-le-Roi, face centre commercial Parly 2 ✉ 78150 Le Chesnay ✈ 955.11.41, Télex 695205 – 🛗 📺 ⇌wc ☏ Ⓟ. 🍴 🆎 🆑 ⓞ   U e
SC : 🛏 25 – **78 ch** 250/265.

🏨🏨 **Bellevue** Ⓜ sans rest, 12 av. Sceaux ✈ 950.13.41 – 🛗 📺 ⇌wc ☏ ♿. 🍴 🆎 🆑 ⓞ Ⓔ
SC : 🛏 18 – **24 ch** 120/200.   Z a

🏨🏨 **Le Versailles** sans rest, r. Ste-Anne (Petite Place) ✈ 950.64.65 – 🛗 📺 ⇌wc ☏ ♿ 🚗 🍴 🆎   Y m
SC : **48 ch** 🛏 180/250.

🏨🏨 **Richaud** sans rest, 16 r. Richaud ✈ 950.10.42 – 🛗 📺 ⇌wc 🚿wc ☏ Ⓟ. 🍴 🆎 🆑 ⓞ   Y z
SC : 🛏 15 – **39 ch** 120/180.

VERSAILLES

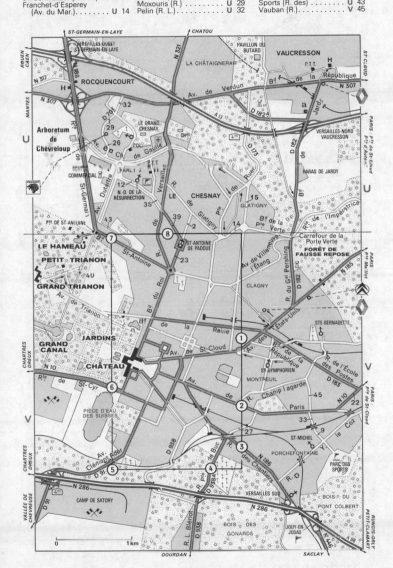

Les **guides Rouges,** les **guides Verts** et les **cartes Michelin**
sont complémentaires.
Utilisez les ensemble.

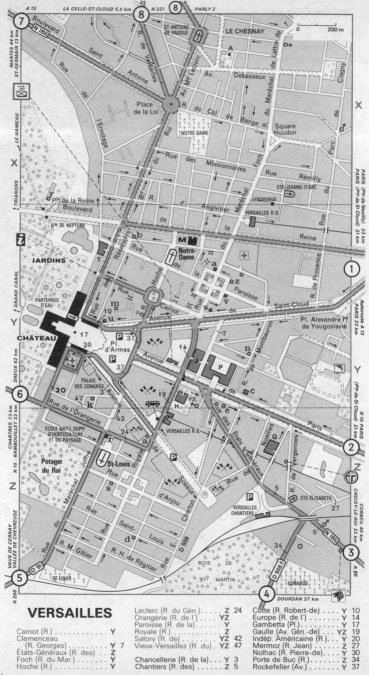

VERSAILLES

🏨 **Printania** sans rest, 7 bis r. Montbauron ☏ 950.44.10 — 🛁wc 🛏 📶 🕭 ᠖. 🚗 GB. 🛒   Y **n**
fermé 30 juil. au 30 août – SC : ⌑ 17 – **30 ch** 60/180.

🏨 **St-Louis** 🕭 sans rest, 28 r. St-Louis ☏ 950.23.55 — 🛁wc 📶wc 🕭 ᠖. 🚗   Z **d**
SC : ⌑ 14 – **27 ch** 100/160.

🏨 **Angleterre** sans rest, 2 bis r. Fontenay ☏ 951.43.50 — 🛁wc 📶wc 🕭. 🚗 ᴁ GB. 🛒
SC : ⌑ 14 – **22 ch** 100/170.   Y **k**

🏨 **Cheval Rouge,** 18 r. A.-Chenier ☏ 950.03.03 — 🛁wc 📶 🕭 ᠖ 🅿. 🚗 . 🛒   Y **z**
fermé 18 déc. au 11 janv. – SC : **R** *(fermé 6 au 23 août, vend. soir et sam.)* 65/80 🍷 – ⌑ 16,50 –
41 ch 70/235

🏨 **Paris** sans rest, 14 av. Paris ☏ 950.56.00 — 🛁wc 📶wc 🕭. 🚗 . 🛒   Y7 **e**
fermé août – SC : ⌑ 18 – **30 ch** 60/160.

🏨 **Résidence du Berry** sans rest, 14 r. Anjou ☏ 950.01.80 — 📶   Z **s**
fermé 24 déc. au 2 janv. – SC : 🍸 11,50 – **39 ch** 75/110.

XXXX ❀❀ **Trois Marches** (Vié), 3 r. Colbert ☏ 950.13.21, «Élégant hôtel particulier du 18ᵉ s. » –
🍴 ᴁ GB ⓪ 🄴   Y **u**
fermé dim. et lundi – **R** carte 180 à 235
Spéc. Flan chaud de foie gras aux huîtres et écrevisses, Ecrevisses pattes rouges (1er juil.-1er avril), Canard de
Challans au vinaigre de cidre et miel.

XXX **Boule d'Or ''Aub. Comtoise'',** 25 r. Mar.-Foch ☏ 950.22.97. «Intérieur rustique » – ᴁ
GB ⓪   Y **a**
fermé dim. soir (sauf juil.-août) et lundi – SC : **R** carte 115 à 170.

XX **Potager du Roi,** 1 r. Mar.-Joffre ☏ 950.35.34   Z **r**
fermé dim. et lundi – **R** 150 bc/75 (sauf fêtes).

XX **Rescatore,** 27 av. St-Cloud ☏ 950.23.60 – ᴁ GB   Y **s**
fermé sam. midi et dim. – **R** 79 bc.

XX **Au Chien qui Fume,** r. A.-Chenier ☏ 950.00.40 – GB   Y **v**
fermé août, vacances de fév., dim. soir et lundi – SC : **R** carte 100 à 160.

Le Vésinet 78110 Yvelines 🔟🔟🔟 ⑬ – 18 206 h. alt. 44 – ❀ 3.
🛈 Office de Tourisme 60 bd Carnot (fermé sam. après-midi, dim. et lundi matin) ☏ 976.00.27.
Paris 18 – Maisons-Laffitte 9 – Pontoise 21 – St-Germain-en-Laye 3 – Versailles 15.

XX **Les Ibis** 🕭 avec ch, île du Grand Lac ☏ 952.17.41, ≤, «Terrasses fleuries dans le parc » –
🛁wc 🕭 🅿 – 🔬 25 à 60. ᴁ GB ⓪ 🄴
R *(fermé 5 juil. au 3 sept.)* carte 100 à 140 – ⌑ 16 – **20 ch** 180/200.

XX **Rossello,** 8 bis av. H.-Vernet ☏ 976.37.50 – GB
fermé août, mardi soir et merc. – **R** carte 100 à 140.

Vincennes 94300 Val-de-Marne 🔟🔟🔟 ⑦ – 44 467 h. alt. 60 – ❀ 1.
Voir Château★★ – Bois de Vincennes★★ : Zoo★★, Parc floral de Paris★★, Musée des Arts
africains et océaniens★, G. Paris.
🛈 Office de Tourisme avec T.C.F. (☏ 328.07.03) 11 av. Nogent (fermé sam. et dim.) ☏ 808.13.00.
Paris 6 – Lagny 22 – Meaux 41 – Melun 48 – Montreuil 1,5 – Senlis 48.

🏨 **Donjon Vincennes** sans rest, 22 r. Donjon ☏ 328.19.17 – 🛗 🛁wc 📶 🕭
SC : ⌑ 14 – **28 ch** 60/150.

Viry-Châtillon 91170 Essonne 🔟🔟🔟 ㊱ – 32 490 h. alt. 36 – ❀ 6.
Paris 26 – Corbeil-Essonnes 11 – Évry 8,5 – Longjumeau 8,5 – Versailles 29.

XX **La Patinière,** 31 rte Nationale ☏ 905.06.16 – GB
fermé sam. midi – **R** carte 110 à 160.

XX ❀ **La Dariole,** 21 r. Pasteur ☏ 944.22.40 – 🍴 ᴁ GB
fermé août, sam., dim. et fêtes – SC : **R** carte 115 à 185
Spéc. Poêlée de foie gras, Feuilleté de St Jacques (15 oct.-15 avril), Coupe ''Jacqueline'' (oct.-avril).

NICE

NICE Ⓟ 06000 Alpes-Mar. 🎄84 ⑨⑩. 195 ㉖㉗ G. Côte d'Azur – 346 620 h. alt. au château 92 – Casino-Club GYZT, Casino Ruhl FZ – 🎄 93.

Voir Site** – Promenade des Anglais** EFZ – Vieux Nice* : Château ⩽** JZ, Intérieur* de l'église St-Martin-St-Augustin HY **D**, – Escalier monumental* du Palais Lascaris HZ **K**, Intérieur* de la cathédrale Ste-Réparate HZ **L**, – Église St-Jacques* HZ **N**, Décors* de la chapelle Saint-Giaume HZ **R** – Mosaïque* de Chagall dans la Faculté de droit DZ **U** – A Cimiez : Monastère* (Primitifs niçois** dans l'église) HV **Q**, ruines romaines* HV – Musées : Marc Chagall** GX, Matisse* HV **M2**, des Beaux-Arts** DZ **M**, Masséna* FZ **M1** – Carnaval*** (avant Mardi Gras) – Mont Alban ⩽** 5 km CT – Mont Boron ⩽* 3 km CT – Église St-Pons* : 3 km BS **Z**.

Env. Plateau St-Michel ⩽** 9,5 km par ①.

🅱 de Biot ☎ 65.08.48 par ④ : 22 km.

✈ de Nice-Côte d'Azur ☎ 83.91.03 AU 7 km.

🚗 ☎ 88.89.91.

🚢 pour la Corse : Société Nationale Maritime Corse-Méditerranée, 3 av. Gustave-V ☎ 89.89.89 FZ**D**.

🅱 Office de Tourisme 32 r. Hôtel desPostes ☎ 62.06.06, avenue Thiers (fermé dim. hors sais.) avec Accueil de France ☎ 87.07.07, Telex 46.00.42, 5 av. Gustave-V (fermé sam. et dim. hors sais.) ☎ 87.60.60 et Nice-Parking (près Aéroport) (fermé dim.) ☎ 83.32.64 - A.C. 9 r. Massenet ☎ 87.18.17 - T.C.F. 6 r. Paradis ☎ 87.79.95.

Paris 934 ⑤ – Cannes 34 ⑤ – Genova 192 ⑨ – ♦Lyon 471 ⑤ – ♦Marseille 188 ⑤ – Turino 219 ⑨.

Plans pages suivantes

🏨🏨 **Négresco**, 37 prom. des Anglais ☎ 88.39.51, Télex 460040, ⩽, « Chambres et salons d'époque 16e et 18e s., Empire, Napoléon III » – 🛗 🗐 ☎ 🕭 – 🏖 50 à 400. 🖭 🗔 🗑 **E**   FZ **k**
  La Rotonde R carte 90 à 145 et voir Nice p. 6 rest. **Chantecler** – 🖙 35 – **150 ch** 420/700, 16 appartements.

🏨🏨 **Sofitel Splendid** Ⓜ, 50 bd Victor-Hugo ☎ 88.69.54, Télex 460938, « 🏊 au 8e étage, ⩽ sur la ville » – 🛗 🗐 🖵 ☎ 🚗 – 🏖 30 à 100. 🖭 🗔 🗑 **E** 🛠 rest   FYZ **g**
  SC : **R** carte 80 à 120 – **130 ch** 🖙 300/500, 11 appartements 550/600 – P 400/460.

🏨🏨 **Hyatt Régency** Ⓜ, 223 prom. des Anglais ☎ 83.91.51, Télex 461635, ⩽ sur la baie, 🏊, 🎾 – 🛗 🗐 🖵 🖵 ☎ 🚗 📞 – 🏖 50 à 400. 🖭 🗔 🗑 **E**   AU **k**
  SC : **Rendez Vous R** 80/95 🍷, dîner à la carte - **Coffee Shop** (avril-oct.) **R** carte environ 95 🍷 – 🖙 43 – **325 ch** 395/620, 10 appartements.

🏨🏨 **Frantel** Ⓜ sans rest, 28 av. Notre-Dame ☎ 80.30.24, Télex 470662, « 🏊 au 8e, jardin suspendu au 2e étage, ⩽ » – 🛗 🗐 🖵 ☎ 🕭 – 🏖 25 à 120. 🖭 🗔 🗑 **E**   FXY **s**
  SC : 🖙 23 – **200 ch** 275/440.

🏨🏨 **Méridien** Ⓜ, 1 prom. des Anglais ☎ 82.25.25, Télex 470361, « 🏊 sur le toit, ⩽ la baie » – 🛗 🗐 🗐 – 🏖 30 à 400. 🖭 🗔 🗑 **E** 🛠 rest   FZ **d**
  SC : **R** carte 120 à 180 – 🖙 32 – **292 ch** 395/700, 24 appartements.

🏨🏨 **Plaza**, 12 av. Verdun ☎ 87.80.41, Télex 460979, ⩽, « Terrasse aménagée sur le toit » – 🛗 🗐 🖵 🖵 – 🏖 30 à 500. 🖭 🗔 🗑 **E**   GZ **f**
  SC : **R** carte 90 à 115 – **186 ch** 🖙 365/490.

🏨🏨 **Westminster Concorde**, 27 prom. des Anglais ☎ 88.29.44, Télex 460872, ⩽ – 🛗 🖵 ☎ 🕭 – 🏖 40 à 350. 🖭 🗑 **E**   FZ **m**
  SC : **R** rest. **Il Pozzo** (1er avril-2 nov.) carte environ 80 , rest. **Le Farniente** (fermé nov.) 110 – 🖙 25 – **110 ch** 300/480.

🏨🏨 **Aston-Concorde** Ⓜ, 12 av. F.-Faure ☎ 80.62.52, Télex 470290, « Terrasse sur le toit » – 🛗 🖵 – 🏖 50 à 180. 🖭 🗔 🗑 **E**   HZ **u**
  SC : **R** 100 – 🖙 25 – **157 ch** 275/375 – P 445/490.

🏨🏨 **Continental-Masséna** Ⓜ sans rest, 58 r. Gioffredo ☎ 85.49.25, Télex 470192 – 🛗 🗐 🖵 ☎ 🕭 – 🏖 60. 🖭 🗔 🗑 **E**   GZ **k**
  SC : 🖙 20 – **115 ch** 135/355.

🏨🏨 **Ambassador** Ⓜ sans rest, 8 av. Suède ☎ 87.90.19, Télex 460025, ⩽ – 🛗 ☎ 🕭, 🖭 🗔 🗑 **E**.
       FZ **x**
  fermé 15 nov. au 15 déc. – SC : **45 ch** 🖙 200/320.

🏨🏨 **Napoléon** sans rest, 6 r. Grimaldi ☎ 87.70.07, Télex 460949 – 🛗 🗐 🖵 🕭, 🖭 🗔 🗑 **E**   FZ **r**
  SC : 🖙 16 – **80 ch** 190/260.

🏨🏨 **La Pérouse** 🦢, 11 quai Rauba-Capeù ⊠ 06300 ☎ 62.34.63, Télex 461411, « ⩽ Nice et la promenade des Anglais », 🏊, 🎾 – 🛗 🗐 ch 🖵 ☎. 🖭 🗔 🗑. 🛠 rest   HZ **k**
  SC : **R** (snack en été) – **65 ch** 🖙 200/400.

🏨🏨 **La Malmaison,** 48 bd V.-Hugo ☎ 87.62.56, Télex 470410 – 🛗 🖵 ☎ – 🏖 40. 🖭 🗔 🗑 **E**. 🛠 rest   FYZ **e**
  SC : **R** (fermé mardi) 70/100 – **50 ch** 🖙 220/340 – P 310/360.

🏨🏨 **Atlantic,** 12 bd Victor-Hugo ☎ 88.40.15, Télex 460840 – 🛗 ☎ 📞 – 🏖 30 à 80. 🖭 🗔 🗑 **E**
  SC : **R** 60/70 – **130 ch** 🖙 220/340 – P 285/355.   FY **d**

🏨🏨 **Windsor** sans rest, 11 r. Dalpozzo ☎ 87.50.41, Télex 970072, 🏊, 🎾 – 🛗 🖵. 🖭 🗑 **E**   FZ **f**
  SC : **59 ch** 🖙 180/300.

🏨🏨 **Park et rest. Le Passage,** 6 av. Gustave-V ☎ 87.80.25, ⩽ – 🛗 🗐 rest ☎ 🕭 – 🏖 80. 🖭 🗑 🗑 **E**   FZ **x**
  SC : **R** 90/150 – 🖙 20 – **150 ch** 270/360 – P 280/380.

🏨 **Gd Hôtel de Florence** Ⓜ sans rest, 3 r. P.-Deroulède ⓟ 88.46.87, Télex 470652 — 🛗 🍴 📺.
🅰🅴 ⚙🅱 ⓞ. 🚳 GY **r**
SC : **53 ch** ⇌ 180/280.

🏨 **Victoria** sans rest, 33 bd V.-Hugo ⓟ 88.39.60, Télex 461337, 🌳 — 🛗 📺 ☎. 🅰🅴 ⚙🅱 ⓞ 🅴 FYZ **z**
SC : **40 ch** ⇌ 200/320.

🏨 **Locarno** sans rest, 4 av. Baumettes ⓟ 96.28.00, Télex 970015 — 🛗 🍴 📺 🚗 — 🛗 50. 🅰🅴 ⚙🅱
ⓞ 🅴 DEZ **t**
fermé 15 nov. au 15 déc. – SC : ⇌ 12 – **48 ch** 165/220.

🏨 **Gounod** Ⓜ sans rest, 3 r. Gounod ⓟ 88.26.20, Télex 461705 — 🛗 🍴 📺 🚿wc 🛁wc ☎ 🚗
🚗🚗 🅰🅴 ⚙🅱 ⓞ FYZ **g**
SC : **41 ch** ⇌ 200/280, 4 appartements 350.

🏨 **New York** sans rest, 44 av. Mar.-Foch ⓟ 92.04.19, Télex 470215 — 🛗 🚿wc 🛁wc ☎ Ⓟ 🚗🚗
🅰🅴 ⚙🅱 ⓞ 🅴 GY **g**
SC : **52 ch** ⇌ 205/280.

🏨 **Georges** Ⓜ 🚳 sans rest, 3 r. H.-Cordier ⓟ 86.23.41 — 🛗 🚿wc 🛁wc 🍴. 🚗🚗 🅰🅴 DZ **e**
SC : ⇌ 13 – **18 ch** 150/230.

🏨 **Suisse** sans rest, 15 quai Rauba-Capeu ✉ 06300 ⓟ 62.33.00, < — 🛗 🚿wc 🛁wc HZ **r**
SC : ⇌ 14 – **37 ch** 84/216.

🏨 **Avenida** sans rest, 41 av. J.-Médecin ⓟ 88.55.03 — 🛗 cuisinette 🍴 📺 🚿wc 🛁wc 🍴. 🚗🚗
🅰🅴. 🚳 FY **m**
SC : ⇌ 12 – **35 ch** 130/180.

🏨 **Carlton** sans rest, 26 bd V.-Hugo ⓟ 88.87.83 — 🛗 🚿wc 🛁wc 🍴. 🚗🚗 🅰🅴 ⚙🅱 ⓞ 🅴 FY **f**
SC : **29 ch** ⇌ 110/230.

🏨 **Chatham** Ⓜ sans rest, 9 r. A.-Karr ⓟ 87.80.61 — 🛗 🚿wc 🛁wc 🍴. 🚗🚗 🅰🅴 ⚙🅱 ⓞ 🅴 FY **x**
SC : **50 ch** ⇌ 130/230.

🏨 **Midi** Ⓜ sans rest, 16 r. Alsace-Lorraine ⓟ 88.49.17, Télex 970565 — 🛗 🍴 📺 🚿wc 🛁wc ☎.
🚗🚗. 🚳 FX **n**
1er fév.-31 oct. – SC : **40 ch** ⇌ 215/250.

🏨 **Brice**, 44 r. Mar.-Joffre ⓟ 88.14.44, Télex 470658 — 🛗 📺 🚿wc 🛁wc ☎ 🕭 – 🛗 30. 🚗🚗 🅰🅴
⚙🅱 ⓞ 🅴. 🚳 rest FZ **b**
SC : **R** 80 – **65 ch** ⇌ 190/290 – P 290/350.

🏨 **Albert 1er** sans rest, 4 av. Phocéens ✉ 06300 ⓟ 85.74.01, Télex 970575, < — 🛗 🚿wc 🛁wc
🍴. 🚗🚗 🅰🅴 ⚙🅱 ⓞ GZ **n**
SC : **69 ch** ⇌ 175/285, 5 appartements 450.

🏨 **Petit Palais** 🚳, 10 av. E.-Bieckert (par bd Cimiez) ⓟ 80.19.11, <, 🌳 — 🛗 📺 🚿wc 🛁wc ☎.
🚗🚗 HX **s**
SC : **R** 60/80 – ⇌ 15 – **22 ch** 180/220 – P 205/230.

🏨 **Busby**, 38 r. Mar.-Joffre ⓟ 88.19.41, Télex 461053 — 🛗 🚿wc 🛁wc 🍴 🕭. 🚗🚗 🅰🅴 ⓞ FZ **u**
fermé 15 nov. au 15 déc. et sans rest du 1er juin au 15 nov. – SC : **R** 60 – ⇌ 12 – **80 ch** 158/256
– P 260/290.

🏨 **Alfa** Ⓜ sans rest, 30 r. Masséna ⓟ 87.88.63 — 🛗 🍴 🚿wc 🛁wc ☎. 🅰🅴 ⚙🅱 🅴 FZ **a**
SC : ⇌ 11 – **38 ch** 115/180.

🏨 **Trianon** sans rest, 15 av. Auber ⓟ 88.30.69 — 🛗 🚿wc 🛁wc 🍴. 🚗🚗 🅰🅴 ⚙🅱 🅴 FY **u**
SC : **32 ch** ⇌ 120/174.

🏨 **Harvey** sans rest, 18 av. de Suède ⓟ 53.16.43 — 🛗 🍴 🚿wc 🛁wc 🍴. 🚗🚗 🅰🅴. 🚳 FZ **h**
1er fév.-1er nov. – SC : ⇌ 12 – **51 ch** 140/185.

🏨 **Univers** sans rest, 9 av. J.-Médecin ⓟ 87.88.81 — 🛗 🚿wc 🛁wc 🍴. 🚗🚗 ⚙🅱. 🚳 GYZ **x**
SC : **80 ch** ⇌ 80/190.

🏠 **Durante** 🚳 sans rest, 16 av. Durante ⓟ 88.84.40, 🌳 — cuisinette 🚿wc 🛁wc 🍴 Ⓟ 🚗🚗.
🚳 – fermé 25 oct. au 24 nov. – SC : ⇌ 12 – **30 ch** 95/165 FY **b**

🏠 **Midland** sans rest, 41 r. Lamartine ⓟ 62.14.43 — 🛗 🛁wc 🍴. 🚗🚗 FX **h**
SC : **50 ch** ⇌ 72/170.

🏠 **Flandres** sans rest, 6 r. Belgique ⓟ 88.78.94 — 🛗 🚿wc 🛁wc 🍴. 🚳 FX **u**
SC : **39 ch** ⇌ 150.

🏠 **Nouvel H.** sans rest, 19 bd V.-Hugo ⓟ 87.73.60 — 🛗 🚿wc 🛁 🍴 — **54 ch** FY **v**

🏠 **Cigognes** sans rest, 16 r. Maccarani ⓟ 88.65.02 — 🛗 🚿wc 🛁wc 🍴 🕭 — **32 ch** FY **s**

🏠 **Marbella Week-End,** 120 bd Carnot ✉ 06300 ⓟ 89.39.35, < baie de Nice, 🌳 — 🛁wc 🍴.
⚙🅱 – SC : **R** 38/65 – ⇌ 15 – **15 ch** 80/200 CT **b**

🏠 **Star H.** Ⓜ sans rest, 14 r. Biscarra ⓟ 85.19.03 — 🚿wc 🛁wc ☎ GY **k**
SC : ⇌ 10 – **19 ch** 90/155.

🏠 **St-Pierre** sans rest, 2 av. Fleurs ⓟ 96.93.10 — 🛗 🚿wc 🛁wc 🍴. 🚗🚗 🅰🅵 ⚙🅱 EZ **f**
fermé 15 nov. au 15 déc. – SC : ⇌ 10 – **35 ch** 72/182.

🏠 **Crillon** sans rest, 44 r. Pastorelli ⓟ 85.43.59 — 🛗 🚿wc 🛁wc 🍴. 🚗🚗. 🚳 GY **u**
SC : **42 ch** ⇌ 75/180.

🏠 **Plaisance H.** sans rest, 20 r. Paris ⓟ 85.11.90 — 🛗 🚿wc 🛁wc. 🚗🚗 GX **t**
fermé 15 nov. au 15 déc. – SC : ⇌ 12 – **30 ch** 65/140.

🏠 **L'Oasis** 🚳, 23 r Gounod ⓟ 88.12.29, 🌳 — 🛁 🍴 Ⓟ 🚗🚗. 🚳 rest FY **a**
fermé 20 oct. au 10 déc. – SC : **R** 40/45 – ⇌ 12 – 31 ch 60/120 – P 110/140.

RÉPERTOIRE DES RUES DU PLAN DE NICE

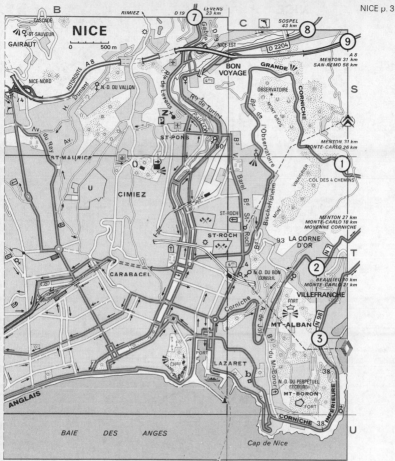

NICE

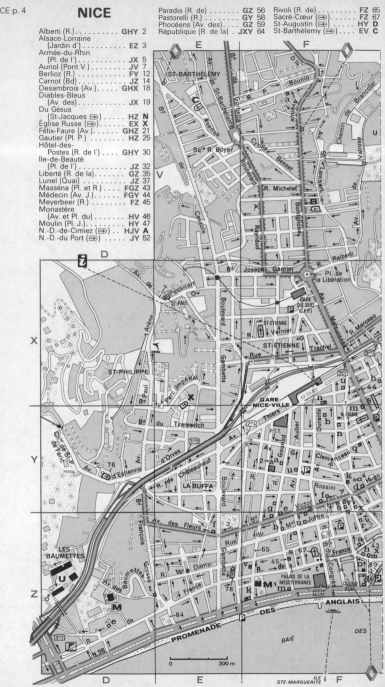

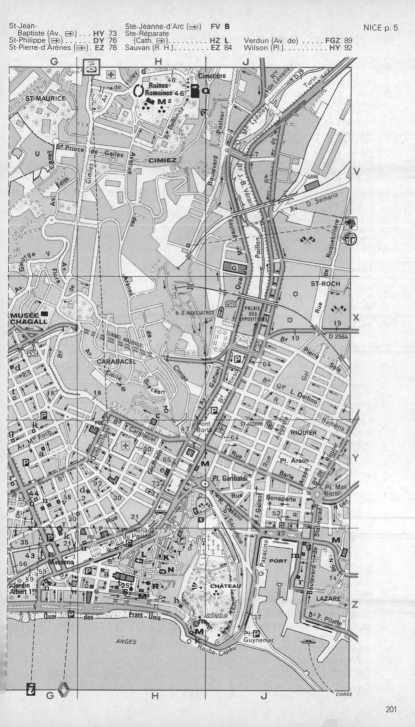

XXXX ✿✿ **Chantecler,** 37 prom. des Anglais ℡ 88.39.51 – ▤. 🆊 🆋 ➊ 🅴   FZ **k**
fermé nov. – **R** 150/220 et carte
Spéc. Courgettes aux truffes, Saumon frais au gros sel, Gratiné de lapereau aux champignons. **Vins** Bellet blanc.

XXX ✿ **La Poularde chez Lucullus** (Normand), 9 r. Deloye ℡ 85.22.90 – ▤. 🆊 🆋 ➊   GY **n**
fermé 11 juil. au 16 août et fériés – **R** 100/130
Spéc. Langouste grillée (15 mars-15 nov.), Rougets à la sauvage, Capilotade de volaille. **Vins** Gassin, Bellet.

XXX ✿ **Ane Rouge** (Vidalot), 7 quai Deux-Emmanuel ✉ 06300 ℡ 89.49.63 – 🆊 ➊   JZ **m**
fermé 14 juil. au 1ᵉʳ sept., dim. et fériés – **R** carte 145 à 230
Spéc. Belons au champagne (10 sept.-30 avril), Filets de sole Mentonnaise, Langouste ¨Ane Rouge¨.. **Vins** Bellet.

XXX **Madrigal,** 7 av. G.-Clemenceau ℡ 88.79.23, 🍴   FY **q**

XXX **Los Caracolès,** 5 r. St-François-de-Paule ✉ 06300 ℡ 80.98.23 – ▤. 🆊 🆋   HZ **e**
fermé mi-juil. à fin août et merc. – **SC** : **R** carte 120 à 165.

XXX **Garac,** 2 bd Carnot ✉ 06300 ℡ 89.57.36 – 🆊 🆋 ➊ 🅴   JZ **g**
fermé 1ᵉʳ au 22 fév. et lundi – **R** carte 125 à 165.

XXX **Petit Brouant,** 4 bis r. Deloye ℡ 85.25.84, 🍴 – 🆊 ➊   GY **n**
fermé juin et lundi – **R** 75/100.

XX **Don Camillo,** 5 r. Ponchettes ✉ 06300 ℡ 85.67.95, cuisine italienne – ▤. ➊ 🅴   HZ **h**
fermé juil. et lundi – **R** carte 95 à 145.

XX **Gourmet Lorrain** 🏡 avec ch, 7 av. Santa-Fior ✉ 06100 ℡ 84.90.78 – ▤ 🆊 ➊ 📺 🛏 🌳. 🍴🏧 🆊   FV **a**
R *(fermé oct. et dim. soir)* 50/150 – 🍽 12 – 13 ch 110/160 – P 130/160.

XX **Bon Coin Breton,** 5 r. Blacas ℡ 85.17.01 – ▤   GY **v**
fermé dim. soir et lundi – **SC** : **R** 45/110.

XX **Chez Rolando,** 3 r. Desboutins ℡ 85.76.79, cuisine italienne – ▤. 🆊   GZ **n**
fermé juil., dim., fêtes et le soir en août – **R** carte 90 à 115.

XX **Chez les Pêcheurs,** 18 quai des Docks ✉ 06300 ℡ 89.59.61, produits de la mer   JZ **r**
fermé nov. au 15 déc. et merc. – **R** carte 100 à 145.

XX **Aux Gourmets,** 12 r. Dante ℡ 96.83.53 – ▤. ➊   EZ **w**
fermé 14 juin, 15.nov. au 8 déc., dim. soir et lundi – **SC** : **R** 42/135.

XX **St-Moritz,** 5 r. Congrès ℡ 88.54.90 – ▤. 🆊   FZ **t**
fermé 1ᵉʳ au 10 août, 7 janv. au 7 fév. et jeudi – **SC** : **R** 90/160.

XX **Michel,** 1 r. Meyerbeer ℡ 88.77.42, produits de la mer – ▤   FZ **s**
fermé 1ᵉʳ juil. au 8 août et lundi – **SC** : **R** carte 95 à 150.

XX **Le Rive Droite,** 22 av. St-Jean Baptiste ℡ 62.16.72. 🆊   HY **e**
fermé lundi midi et dim. – **R** 60.

XX **La Cassole,** 22 av. St-Jean-Baptiste ℡ 85.01.14, spécialités du sud-ouest – 🆊 🆋 ➊   HY **e**
fermé 25 juil. au 25 août et lundi – **R** 55/120.

XX **La Madrague,** 13 bis cours Saleya ℡ 85.61.91, produits de la mer – 🆋   HZ **t**
fermé mardi – **SC** : **R** carte 90 à 140.

XX **Bông-Laï,** 14 r. Alsace-Lorraine ℡ 88.75.36, cuisine vietnamienne – ▤. ➊ 🅴   FX **n**
fermé 3 au 23 juin, 15 au 29 déc., lundi et mardi – **SC** : **R** carte 100 à 160.

X **La Nissarda,** 17 r. Gubernatis ℡ 85.26.29 – 🆊   HY **d**
fermé juil., mardi soir et merc. – **SC** : **R** 38/65.

X **Mireille,** 19 bd Raimbaldi ℡ 85.27.23   GX **d**
fermé 7 juin au 12 juil., lundi et merc sauf fêtes – **SC** : **R** plat unique : paella carte env. 70.

X **Rivoli,** 9 r. Rivoli ℡ 88.12.62 – ▤. 🆋 – *fermé juin et mardi* – **SC** : **R** 55   FZ **v**

X **Le St-Laurent,** 12 r. Paganini ℡ 87.18.94 – 🆊   FY **n**
fermé 15 nov. au 1ᵉʳ déc. et merc. – **SC** : **R** 32/60.

X **Florian,** 22 r. A.-Karr ℡ 88.47.83 – 🆊 🆋 ➊ 🅴   FY **k**
fermé déc. et merc. – **SC** : **R** 50/70 🍷.

X **La Casbah,** 3 r. Doct.-Balestre ℡ 85.58.81, couscous   GY **a**
fermé 15 juil. au 15 août et lundi – **R** carte environ 70.

X **La Merenda,** 4 r. Terrasse ✉ 06300, cuisine niçoise – ▤   HZ **a**
SC : **R** carte env. 70.

à l'Aéroport 7 km – ✉ 06200 Nice :

XXX ✿ **Ciel d'Azur,** 2ᵉ étage ℡ 83.18.57, Télex 970011, ≤ – ▤ 🅿. 🆋 ➊   AU **x**
R 95/160.
Spéc. Terrine de pigeonneau au foie d'oie, Filet de loup Mistral, Rognon de veau. **Vins** Bellet.

XX **Grill Soleil d'Or,** 1ᵉʳ étage aérogare ℡ 83.19.76, ≤ – ▤ 🅿. 🆋 ➊   AU **x**
SC : **R** carte environ 75 🍷.

au Cap 3000 par ④ : 8 km – ✉ 06700 St-Laurent-du-Var :

🏨 **Novotel** Ⓜ, ℡ 31.61.15, Télex 470643, 🏊, – 🔌▤ 📺 ☎ & 🅿 – 🔬 300. 🆊 🆋 ➊
R snack carte environ 75 – 🍽 25 – **103 ch** 245/305.

à St-Pancrace N : 8 km par D 914 AS – alt. 302 – ✉ 06100 Nice :

XXX ✿ **Rôtisserie de St-Pancrace** (Teillas), ℡ 84.43.69, ≤ – 🅿
fermé 5 janv. au 5 fév. et lundi hors sais. – **R** carte 120 à 165
Spéc. Frivolités, Selle de lapereau farcie, Gâteau de brochet aux écrevisses (sauf avril et mai). **Vins** Bellet, Bandol.

XX **Cicion,** ℡ 84.49.29, ≤ Nice et littoral – 🅿
fermé 15 oct. au 15 nov. et merc. – **R** *(juil. et août : dîner seul)* (sur réservation) 64/80.

CANNES

CANNES 06400 Alpes-Mar. 🎱 ⑨. 195 ㉟㊳ G. Côte d'Azur – 71 080 h. – Casinos : Les Fleurs BZ, Palm Beach X, Municipal BZ – 🌸 93.

Voir Boulevard de la Croisette✶✶ BCZ – Pointe de la Croisette✶ X – ≼✶ de la tour du Mont-Chevalier AZ **A** – Musée de la Castre✶ AZ **M** – Observatoire de Super-Cannes ✳✶✶✶ E : 4 km, VX **B** – Chemin des Collines✶ NE : 4 km V – La Croix des Gardes V E ≼✶ O : 5 km puis 15 mn.

🟥 Country-Club de Cannes-Mougins ☏ 75.79.13 par ⑤ : 9 km ; 🟥🟥 Golf Club de Cannes-Mandelieu ☏ 47.55.39 par ② : 6,5 km ; 🟥 de Biot 65.08.48 par ⑤ : 14 km ; 🟥 de Valbonne ☏ 42.00.08 par ⑤ : 15 km.

🅱 Office de Tourisme et Accueil de France (Informations, change et réservations d'hôtels, pas plus de 5 jours à l'avance). Gare S.N.C.F. ☏ 99.19.77, Télex 470795 et Palais des Festivals et des Congrès, La Croisette (fermé dim. hors saison) ☏ 39.24.53, Télex 470749 - A.C. 21 quai St-Pierre ☏ 39.38.94.

Paris 909 ⑤ – Aix-en-Provence 151 ⑥ – ✦Grenoble 314 ④ – ✦Marseille 163 ⑤ – ✦Nice 34 ⑤ – ✦Toulon 128 ⑤.

Plans pages suivantes

🏯🏯🏯 **Carlton**, 58 bd Croisette ☏ 68.91.68, Télex 470720, ≼, 🏍 – ‖ 🔲 📺 🕭 ⇔ 🅿 – 🏛 80. **E**. 🍴 rest — CZ **e**
R carte 205 à 265, **Grill** carte environ 175 – ⊑ 25 – **288 ch** 400/1 000, 30 appartements – P 610/1 150.

🏯🏯🏯 **Majestic** Ⓜ, bd Croisette ☏ 68.91.00, Télex 470787, ≼, ⌇, ⚞ – ‖ 🔲 📺 🕭 ⇔ – 🏛 30 à 120. 🖭 🆖 ⓞ **E**. 🍴 rest — BZ **n**
fermé 1er déc. – **R** carte 150 à 210 et Grill – ⊑ 25 – **248 ch** 640/950, 12 appartements.

🏯🏯 **Montfleury Inter-Continental** Ⓜ ⏩, 25 av. Beauséjour ☏ 68.91.50, Télex 470039, ≼, « Jardin », ⌇ – ‖ 🔲 📺 🕭 ⇔ 🅿 – 🏛 350. 🖭 🆖 ⓞ **E** — DY **r**
fermé 31 janv. au 12 mars – **R** 138 – ⊑ 35 – **230 ch** 500/740, 5 appartements.

🏯🏯 🌸 **Gray d'Albion** Ⓜ, 38 r. Serbes ☏ 48.54.54, Télex 470744, ⌇ – ‖ 🔲 📺 🕭 – 🏛 30 à 200. 🖭 🆖 ⓞ **E** — BZ **d**
fermé fév. – SC : **Royal Gray** *fermé dim. soir hors sais.. et lundi* **R** carte 140 à 190 **Coffee Shop R** carte environ 90 🍸 – ⊑ 35 – **172 ch** 585/810, 14 appartements.
Spéc. Galette de ris de veau, Fricassée de homard, Noisettes de veau aux truffes.

🏯🏯 **Martinez-Concorde**, bd Croisette ☏ 68.91.91, Télex 470708, ≼, 🏍 – ‖ 🔲 ch 🕭 🕭 🅿 – 🏛 40 à 500. 🖭 ⓞ **E**. 🍴 rest — CDZ **n**
fermé oct. à déc. – SC : **R** 140/200 – ⊑ 35 – **400 ch** 290/730, 14 appartements.

🏯🏯 **Sofitel Méditerranée** Ⓜ, 2 bd J.-Hibert ☏ 99.22.75, Télex 470728, ≼, « Piscine et terrasses sur le toit, ≼ baie de Cannes » – ‖ 🔲 📺 🕭 ⇔ 🅿 – 🏛 160. 🖭 🆖 ⓞ **E**. 🍴 rest — AZ **u**
fermé 15 nov. au 15 déc. – SC : **R** carte 90 à 125 – **152 ch** ⊑ 306/555, 5 appartements – P 340/415.

🏯🏯 **Gd Hôtel** ⏩, 45 bd Croisette ☏ 38.15.45, Télex 470727, ≼, 🏍 – ‖ 🔲 📺 🕭 🅿. 🖭 — CZ **q**
R voir rest. Lamour - SC : **75 ch** ⊑ 470/800 – P 505/1 000.

🏯🏯 **Frantel Beach** Ⓜ sans rest, 13 r. Canada ☏ 38.22.32, Télex 470034, ⌇ – ‖ 🔲 📺 🕭 🕭 🕭 – 🏛 30 à 60. 🖭 🆖 ⓞ **E** — CZ **v**
fermé 10 nov. au 14 déc. – SC : ⊑ 26 – **80 ch** 475/615, 7 appartements.

🏯🏯 **Victoria** Ⓜ sans rest, 122 r. d'Antibes ☏ 99.36.36, Télex 470817, ⌇ – ‖ 🔲 📺 ⇔. 🖭 🆖 ⓞ — CZ **x**
SC : **25 ch** ⊑ 265/490.

🏯🏯 **Gonnet et de la Reine**, 42 bd Croisette ☏ 38.40.01, ≼ – ‖. 🖭 🆖. 🍴 — CZ **h**
21 janv.-15 oct. – SC : **R** (résid. seul.) – **58 ch** ⊑ 240/460, 5 appartements.

🏯🏯 **Splendid** sans rest, 4 r. F.-Faure ☏ 99.53.11, Télex 470990, ≼ – ‖ cuisinette 📺 🕭. 🖭 ⓞ **E** — BZ **a**
SC : **63 ch** ⊑ 185/375.

🏯🏯 **Fouquet's** Ⓜ sans rest, 2 Rd-Pt Duboys-d'Angers ☏ 38.75.81 – 🔲 📺 ⇔. 🖭 ⓞ **E** — DZ **y**
fermé 20 oct. au 20 déc. – SC : **10 ch** ⊑ 500.

🏯🏯 **Solhotel** Ⓜ, 61 av. Dr Picaud par ③ ⊠ 06150 Cannes La Bocca ☏ 47.63.00, Télex 970956, ⌇, ⚞ – ‖ 🔲 📺 🕭 ⇔ – 🏛 100. 🆖 ⓞ
fermé 1er nov. au 15 déc. – SC : **R** 80 – **101 ch** ⊑ 300/440 – P 400/495.

🏯🏯 **Beau Séjour** Ⓜ, 100 r. G.-Clemenceau ☏ 39.63.00, Télex 470975, ⌇, ⚞ – ‖ 🔲 rest 📺 ⇔. 🖭 ⓞ. 🍴 rest — AZ **d**
fermé 11 nov. au 20 déc. – SC : **R** 90 – **46 ch** ⊑ 360/400 – P 520/720.

🏯🏯 **Century** Ⓜ sans rest, 133 r. d'Antibes ☏ 99.37.64, Télex 470090 – ‖ 🔲 📺 🕭 ⇔ — CZ **r**
35 ch.

🏯🏯 **Abrial** Ⓜ sans rest, 24 bd Lorraine ☏ 30.70.02, Télex 470761 🔲 🕭 🕭 ⇔. 🖭 🆖 — CY **s**
15 janv.-31 oct. – SC : **48 ch** ⊑ 250/330.

🏯🏯 **Embassy** sans rest., 6 r. Bône ☏ 38.79.02, Télex 470081 – ‖ 🔲 📺 🕭 ⇔. 🖭 🆖 ⓞ — CZ **j**
SC : **60 ch** ⊑ 300/320.

🏯🏯 **Paris** sans rest, 34 bd d'Alsace ☏ 38.30.89, Télex 470995, ⌇, ⚞ – ‖ 🔲 – 🏛 40 — CY **a**
fermé nov. au 20 janv. – SC : ⊑ 20 – **48 ch** 208/308.

🏯🏯 **Canberra** sans rest, 120 r. d'Antibes ☏ 38.20.70, Télex 470817 – ‖ 🔲 📺 🅿. 🖭 🆖 ⓞ **E** — CZ **u**
SC : **37 ch** ⊑ 230/425.

🏨 **Licorn'H.** Ⓜ, 23 av. Fr.-Tonner par ③ ⊠ 06150 Cannes-La-Bocca ☎ 47.18.46, Télex 470818
– 📶 🍴 rest 📺 🛏wc 🛁wc ☎ 🅿 🛢 🔱 Ⓔ
SC : **R** 70 – **45 ch** ⬛ 150/320 – P 220/280.

🏨 **Acapulco** Ⓜ, 16 bd Alsace ☎ 99.16.16, Télex 470929, 🔱 – 📶 🍴 📺 🛏wc 🛁wc ☎ 🚗 🛢
🅰🅴 🅶🅱 Ⓝ Ⓔ 🎜 rest   BY **t**
SC : **R** *(fermé 15 nov. au 20 déc.)* 50/75 – **59 ch** ⬛ 250/370 – P 335/500.

🏨 **Univers** Ⓜ, 2 r. Mar.-Foch ☎ 39.59.19, Télex 470972 – 📶 🍴 ch 📺 🛏wc 🛁wc ☎ 🛢 🅰🅴
🅶🅱 Ⓝ   BZ **r**
SC : **R** *(au 6e étage)* 60/65 – ⬛ 10 – **68 ch** 260/360 – P 255/310.

🏨 **Clarice**, 48 bd Alexandre-III ☎ 43.07.55, 🌿 – 📶 🛏wc 🛁wc 🐾 Ⓟ   DZ **a**
25 ch.

🏨 **Ruc H.** sans rest, 15 bd Strasbourg ☎ 38.64.32 – 📶 🚪 📺 🛏wc ☎ 🛢 Ⓔ   CY **v**
fermé 15 oct. à fin déc. – SC : **30 ch** ⬛ 240/315.

CANNES - LE CANNET - VALLAURIS

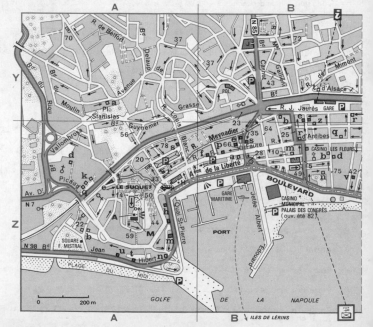

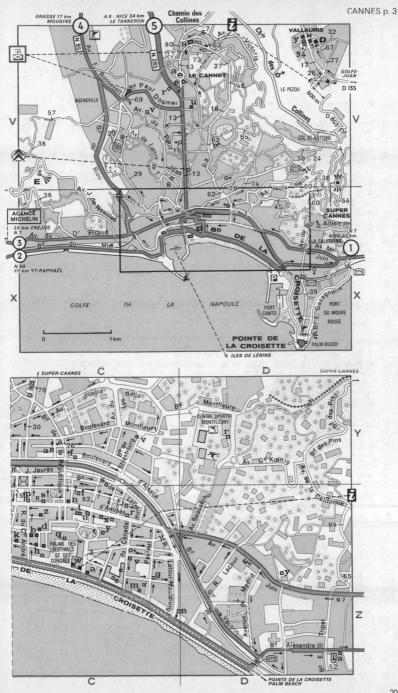

🏨 **La Madone** ⑤ sans rest, 5 av. Justinia ℡ 43.57.87, « Coquette installation », 🖙 – cuisinette
📺 🅿🗕wc 🍴 🕾 🖭 🅰🗉 🖭 . 🗱 rest   DZ **y**
SC : **25 ch** ⊇ 200/390.

🏨 **Provence,** 9 r. Molière ℡ 38.44.35 – 🛗 🖃 ch 📺 🖃wc 🍴wc 🕾. 🕾🗉 🅰🗉 🖭 🖭 **E**   CZ **t**
SC : **R** *(fermé 14 nov. au 20 déc. et lundi)* 65/80 – ⊇ 18 – **30 ch** 130/260.

🏨 **Les Orangers,** 1 r. des Orangers ℡ 39.99.92, Télex 470873, ≤, ⊿, 🕾 – 🛗 🖃wc 🍴wc 🕾.
🕾🗉 🅰🗉 🖭 **E.** 🗱 rest   AZ **k**
fermé 1ᵉʳ nov. au 20 déc. – SC : **R** 80 – **40 ch** ⊇ 202/322 – P 276.

🏨 **Belle Plage** sans rest, 6 r. J.-Dollfus ℡ 39.08.12 – 🛗 📺 🖃wc 🍴wc 🕾. 🕾🗉 AZ **b**
15 janv.-1ᵉʳ nov. – SC : ⊇ 25 – **42 ch** 185/350.

🏨 **Host. de L'Olivier** sans rest, 90 r. G.-Clemenceau ℡ 39.53.28, ⊿, 🕾 – 🖃wc 🍴wc 🕾 🅿.
🕾🗉 🅰🗉 🖭   AZ **k**
SC : **25 ch** ⊇ 160/300.

🏨 **Dauphins Verts** sans rest, 9 r. J.-Dollfus ℡ 39.45.83, 🖙 – 🛗 🖃 📺 🖃wc 🍴wc 🕾. 🕾🗉 🅰🗉
fermé 30 nov. au 5 janv. – SC : **17 ch** ⊇ 126/220.   AZ **b**

🏨 **Ligure** Ⓜ sans rest, 5 pl. Gare ℡ 39.03.11 – 🛗 🖃wc 🍴wc 🕾. 🕾🗉 🅰🗉 🖭 🖭 BY **b**
SC : ⊇ 10 – **36 ch** 240/320.

🏨 **Mondial** sans rest, 1 r. Teisseire ℡ 39.28.70 – 🛗 🖃wc 🍴wc 🕾. 🕾🗉   CZ **p**
fermé 15 nov. au 15 déc. – SC : **65 ch** ⊇ 109/247.

🏨 **Château de la Tour** ⑤, av. Font-de-Veyre par ③ ⊠ 06150 Cannes-la-Bocca ℡ 47.34.64,
Télex 470906, 🖙 – 🛗 🖃wc 🍴wc 🕾 🅿. 🅰🗉 🖭 . 🗱 rest
SC : **R** 70 – 42 ch ⊇ 180/300 – P 260/280.

🏨 **Select** sans rest, 16 r. H.-Vagliano ℡ 99.51.00 – 🛗 🖃wc 🍴wc 🕾   BY **r**
fermé 15 nov. au 15 déc. – SC : ⊇ 12 – **30 ch** 182/192.

🏨 **Régina** sans rest, 31 r. Pasteur ℡ 94.05.43 – 🛗 🖃wc 🍴wc 🕾 🅿. 🕾🗉 CZ **g**
15 janv.-15 oct. – SC : **23 ch** ⊇ 175/330.

🏨 **Vendôme** sans rest, 37 bd Alsace ℡ 38.34.33, 🖙 – 🖃wc 🍴wc 🕾 🅿. 🖭 CY **f**
fermé nov. – SC : ⊇ 16 – **18 ch** 130/350.

🏨 **France** sans rest, 85 r. Antibes ℡ 39.23.34 – 🛗 🖃 📺 🖃wc 🍴wc 🕾. 🕾🗉 🅰🗉 CZ **s**
SC : ⊇ 15 – **34 ch** 175/225.

🏨 **Corona** sans rest, 55 r. d'Antibes ℡ 39.69.85 – 🛗 🖃wc 🍴wc 🕾. 🕾🗉 🅰🗉 🖭 **E** BZ **q**
SC : – **20 ch** ⊇ 120/220.

🏨 **Molière** sans rest, 5 r. Molière ℡ 38.16.16, 🖙 – 🛗 🖃wc 🍴wc 🕾. **E**   CZ **t**
fermé 1ᵉʳ au 20 déc. – SC : ⊇ 12 – **33 ch** 160/230.

🏚 **El Puerto** ⑤, 45 av. Petit-Juas ℡ 68.39.75, 🖙 – 🖃wc 🍴wc 🕾 🅿. 🕾🗉 🅰🗉. 🗱 V **s**
fermé 1ᵉʳ oct. au 15 déc. – SC : **R** *(fermé lundi)* 65 – ⊇ 15 – 22 ch 140/220 – P 150/200.

🏚 **Cheval Blanc** sans rest, 3 r. de-Maupassant ℡ 38.88.60 – 📺 🖃wc 🍴wc 🕾. 🕾🗉 AY **a**
SC : ⊇ 13,50 – **16 ch** 175/185.

🏚 **Athénée** sans rest, 6 rue Lecerf ℡ 38.69.54 – 🖃wc 🍴wc 🕾. 🅰🗉 🖭 **E.** 🗱 CZ **f**
15 janv.-15 oct. – SC : ⊇ 13 – **17 ch** 140/300.

🏚 **Wagram,** 140 r. d'Antibes ℡ 38.55.53, 🖙 – 🛗 🖃 ch 🖃wc 🍴wc 🕾. 🗱 CZ **x**
fermé nov. – SC : **R** 77 – ⊇ 17 – **23 ch** 132/253 – P 237/298.

🏚 **Roches Fleuries** sans rest, 92 r. G.-Clemenceau ℡ 39.28.78, 🖙 – 🛗 🖃wc 🍴wc 🕾 🅿. 🗱
fermé 15 nov. au 20 déc. – SC : **24 ch** ⊇ 65/172.   AZ **q**

🏚 **Campanile,** Aérodrome de Cannes-Mandelieu par ③ : 6 km ⊠ 06150 Cannes-la-Bocca ℡
48.69.41 – 📺 🖃wc 🅿. 🖭
SC : **R** 46 bc/70 bc – ☕ 18 – **49 ch** 160.

🏚 **Modern** sans rest, 11 r. Serbes ℡ 39.09.87 – 🛗 📺 🍴wc 🕾. 🕾🗉   BZ **b**
fermé 2 nov. au 20 déc. – SC : **19 ch** ⊇ 130/275.

🏚 **Poste** sans rest, 31 r. Bivouac-Napoléon ℡ 39.22.58 – 🛗 🖃wc 🍴wc 🕾. 🕾🗉. 🗱 BZ **m**
SC : ⊇ 12 – **22 ch** 70/180.

🏚 **Touring** sans rest, 11 r. Hoche ℡ 38.34.40 – 🛗 📺 🖃wc 🍴wc 🕾. 🕾🗉 🖭 BYZ **z**
SC : ⊇ 12 – **30 ch** 80/180.

XXX **Félix,** 64 bd Croisette ℡ 94.00.61, ≤ – 🖃 🅰🗉   CZ **m**
fermé mi-déc. à mi-déc. et merc. sauf fêtes – **R** carte 110 à 160.

XXX **Le Festival,** 52 bd Croisette ℡ 38.04.81, ≤ – 🖃 🅰🗉 🖭   CZ **a**
fermé fin oct. au 10 déc. – **R** carte 110 à 170.

XXX **Poêle d'Or,** 23 r. États-Unis ℡ 39.77.65 – 🖃 🅰🗉 🖭   BZ **v**
fermé 26 juil. au 12 août., 31 janv. au 17 fév., mardi soir et merc. d'oct. à Pâques – **R** carte 140 à
210.

XXX **Gaston et Gastounette,** 7 quai St-Pierre ℡ 39.47.92, ≤ – 🅰🗉 🖭 🖭 **E** AZ **h**
fermé 3 au 20 déc., 3 au 16 janv. et lundi du 15 oct. au 1ᵉʳ avril – **R** 120.

XXX ✿ **Reine Pédauque** (Dorange), 6 r. Mar.-Joffre ℡ 39.40.91 – 🖃. 🖭 BZ **s**
fermé 28 juin au 19 juil., 13 au 21 déc. et lundi – **R** (nombre de couverts limité - prévenir)
110/200
Spéc. Mousseline de rascasse, Nage de poissons au beurre blanc, Filet d'agneau en croûte. **Vins** Château-Minuty,
Château-Simone.

XXX **Lamour,** 45 bd Croisette ℡ 99.49.60 – **P.** AE GB   CZ **q**
R 90.

XXX **Le Piccolo,** 14 r. Bateguier ℡ 39.75.96 – 🗐. AE GB ◐   CZ **h**
fermé nov. et merc. – **R** 65/95.

XX **Rescator,** 7 r. Mar.-Joffre ℡ 39.44.57 – 🗐. GB   BZ **e**
fermé 15 oct. au 15 nov. et lundi sauf juil., août – **R** (du 15 mai au 15 sept. dîner seul.) 88/250.

XX **Blue Bar,** Palais des Festivals ℡ 39.03.04, ≤ – 🗐   CZ **w**
fermé juin – **R** carte 95 à 135.

XX **Voile au Vent,** 17 quai St-Pierre ℡ 39.27.84 – AE GB ◐   AZ **m**
fermé 20 oct. au 20 déc. et joudi sauf juil.-août – **R** carte 100 à 140.

XX **J. J. Garé,** 18 r. Frères-Pradignac ℡ 39.18.66 🗐. AE OD ◐   CZ **b**
fermé mars et dim. – SC : **R** 70.

XX **Caveau Provençal,** 45 r. Félix-Faure ℡ 39.06.33 – 🗐. AE GB ◐ E   BZ **f**
fermé 15 au 30 mars – **R** 60/120.

XX **Monsieur Madeleine,** 12 bd Jean Hibert ℡ 39.72.22, ≤   AZ **t**
fermé janv. et jeudi sauf juil.-août – SC : **R** 80/110.

XX ✿ **Le Croquant** (Peytour), 18 bd J.-Hibert ℡ 39.39.79 – 🗐 AE ◐ E   AZ **u**
fermé 10 fév. au 10 mars., 15 nov. au 15 déc. et lundi – **R** (en hiver ouvert dim. et dîner en sem.)
carte 95 à 170.
Spéc. Délice périgourdin, Confit de canard, Millassou aux pruneaux.

XX **Mère Besson,** 13 r. Frères-Pradignac ℡ 39.59.24, Cuisine provençale – AE   CZ **d**
fermé juin et dim. – SC : **R** carte 100 à 130.

XX **Poivre Vert,** 11 r. L.-Blanc ℡ 39.07.67 – 🗐. AE ◐   AZ **s**
fermé 15 juil. au 14 août et merc. – SC : **R** 45/150.

XX **Gilbert de Cassis,** 17 r. G.-Monod ℡ 39.24.95 – 🗐. AE GB ◐ E   CZ **h**
fermé 28 juin au 12 juil. et lundi – SC : **R** 75.

XX **Taverna Romana,** pl. Suquet ℡ 39.96.05, spécialités italiennes – 🗐   AZ **e**
R 90.

XX **La Cigale,** 1 r. Florian ℡ 39.65.79 – 🗐   CZ **z**
fermé 10 nov. au 17 déc., jeudi midi en sais. et merc. – SC : **R** 65/93.

XX **La Croisette,** 15 r. Cdt-André ℡ 39.86.06 – AE GB ◐   CZ **b**
fermé 15 nov. au 15 déc. et mardi – SC : **R** 48/60.

XX **La Coquille,** 65 r. Félix-Faure ℡ 39.26.33 – 🗐. AE GB ◐ E   BZ **p**
fermé 20 nov. au 10 déc. – **R** 45/68.

XX **Au Mal Assis,** 15 quai St-Pierre ℡ 39.13.38, ≤ – GB   AZ **h**
fermé mi-oct. au 20 déc. – SC : **R** 53.

X **L'Esquinade,** 3 r. G.-Monod ℡ 39.36.25 – AE GB ◐   CZ **k**
fermé 1er au 10 juin, nov. et lundi – SC : **R** 48/60 ♨.

X **L'Olivier,** 9 r. Rouguière ℡ 39.91.63 – AE GB ◐   BZ **e**
fermé 15 nov. au 15 déc. et sam. – SC : **R** 45/65.

X **Le Monaco,** 15 r. 24-août ℡ 38.37.76   BY **e**
fermé nov. et dim. – SC : **R** 42/55.

X **Côte d'Azur,** 3 r. J.-Daumas ℡ 38.60.02   CZ **n**
fermé 1er au 20 juil., 1er au 20 nov. et dim. – SC : **R** *(fermé le soir d'oct. à avril)* 48 bc.

X **Aux Bons Enfants** (Chez Romain), 80 r. Meynadier – ✿   AZ **r**
fermé avril, mai, merc. soir hors sais. et dim. – SC : **R** 45 ♨.

X **Au Bec Fin,** 12 r. 24-Août ℡ 38.35.86 – AE GB   BY **e**
fermé 24 déc. au 24 janv. et dim. – SC : **R** 45/60 ♨.

Route de Pégomas par ③ : 8 km – ✉ 06150 Cannes-la-Bocca :

XXX L'Oriental, 286 av. M.-Jourdan ℡ 47.43.99, « Décor Mauresque », cuisine du Maghreb – **P**
fermé janv., dim. soir et lundi hors sais. – SC : **R** 140.

MONACO

MONACO (Principauté de) 84 ⑩, 195 ㉗㉘ G. Côte d'Azur – 24 600 h. alt. 65 – Casino – ✿ 93.
Paris 958 ⑤ – Menton 9 ② – ♦Nice (par la Moyenne Corniche) 18 ④ – San Remo 44 ①.

Monaco Capitale de la Principauté – ⊠ Monaco.

Voir Jardin exotique★★ DZ : ≤★ – Grotte de l'Observatoire★ DZ**E** – Jardins St-Martin★ EFZ
– Ensemble de primitifs niçois★★ dans la cathédrale EZ **B** – Christ gisant★ dans la chapelle
de la Miséricorde EZ**D** – Place du Palais★ EZ**35** – Palais du Prince★ EZ – Musées : océano-
graphique★★ FZ**M2** (aquarium★★, ≤★★ de la terrasse), d'anthropologie préhistorique★ DZ**M1**,
– napoléonien et des archives monégasques★ EZ**M4**.

Circuit automobile urbain - A.C. 23 bd Albert-1er ☏ 30.32.20, Télex 469003.

à Monaco Ville sur le Rocher :

✕ **Castelroc**, pl. Palais ☏ 30.36.68, ≤   EZ **p**
fermé 1er déc. au 31 janv. et sam. – SC : **R** (déj. seul.) 45/68.

à la Condamine – ⊠ La Condamine :

🏨 **Terminus** Ⓜ, 9 av. Prince Pierre ☏ 30.20.70 – ❙❘ ⊟ wc 🚿wc ☎ – ⛟ 35. ☞🄱. ⚲   DZ **a**
SC : **R** *(fermé 15 oct. au 15 nov., vend. soir et sam.)* 55/70 ⅋ – ☷ 18 – **54 ch** 125/183.

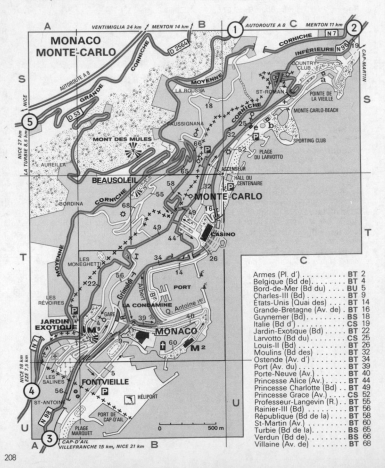

Monte-Carlo Centre mondain de la Principauté - Grand casino FX, Casino du Sporting Club CS, Casino Loews FX − ⊠ Monte-Carlo.

Voir Terrasse★★ du Grand casino FX − Musée de poupées et automates★ FV **M5.**

ᵣₛ de Monte-Carlo Golf Club ⏰ 41.09.11 par : ④ 11 km.

🛈 Direction Tourisme et Congrès, 2 a bd Moulins (fermé dim. après-midi) ⏰ 30.87.01, Télex 469760.

⛨ ❀ **Paris,** pl. Casino ⏰ 50.80.80, Télex 469925, ⟨, « Salle à manger Empire », ⟱, ⟰ − ❘▮❘ ▤
▣ ☎ ఉ ❶ − ⚚ 50. ⅄ ⅁⅊ ⑩ ⅀. ℀ rest   FX **y**
R *(fermé merc.)* carte 160 à 240 − ⟱ 35 − **250 ch** 500/950, 22 appartements
Spéc. Terrine de volaille aux écrevisses et corail d'oursins, Langouste à la ficelle, Carré d'agneau. **Vins** Bellet, Coteaux d'Aix.

⛨ **Hermitage,** square Beaumarchais ⏰ 50.67.31, Télex 479432, « Salle à manger de style baroque », ⟱ − ❘▮❘ ▤ ▣ ☎ ❶ − ⚚ 80. ⅄ ⅁⅊ ⑩ ⅀. ℀ rest   FX **r**
R carte 140 à 200 − ⟱ 32 − **200 ch** 450/750, 11 appartements.

⛨ **Loews** Ⓜ, av. Spélugues ⏰ 50.65.00, ⟨, casino et cabaret sur place, ⟱ − ❘▮❘ ▤
▣ ☎ ❶ − ⚚ 50 à 1 200   FX **e**
Le Foie Gras (dîner seul.) **L'Argentin** (dîner seul.) **Café Jardin** snack − 550 ch. 72 appartements.

⛨ **Mirabeau** Ⓜ, 1 av. Princesse-Grace ⏰ 30.90.01, Télex 479413, ⟨, ⟱ − ❘▮❘ ▤ ▣ ☎ ఉ ❶ −
⚚ 150. ⅄ ⅁⅊ ⑩ ⅀. ℀ rest   FV **n**
R 120/135 − ⟱ 32 − **86 ch** 380/630, 14 appartements − P 600/700.

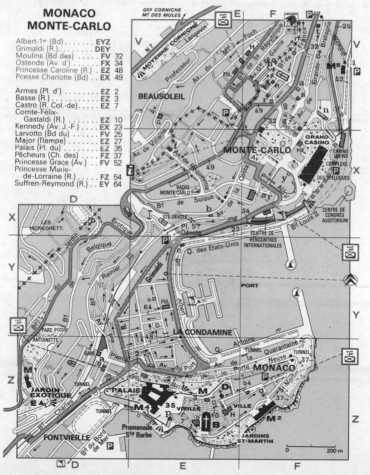

Beach Plaza Ⓜ 🦢, av. Princesse-Grace, à la Plage du Larvotto ℡ 30.98.80, Télex 479617, ≤ mer et Principauté, « Bel ensemble balnéaire », 🏊, 🏌 – 🛗 🖥 📺 ☎ 🅖 🚗 – 🔬 30 à 300
306 ch
CS **b**

Balmoral 🦢, 12 av. Costa ℡ 50.62.37, Télex 479436, ≤ – 🛗 🖥 📺 ☎. ⒶⒺ ⒼⒷ ⓘ **E**. 🎿
SC : **R** *(fermé dim. soir et lundi)* snack 70 – 🍽 22 – **65 ch** 160/310.
EX **b**

Louvre sans rest, 16 bd Moulins ℡ 50.65.25, Télex 479645 – 🛗 📺 🚽wc ☎ 🅖. 🚗 ⓘ
E. 🎿
FV **a**
SC : **32 ch** 🍽 270/360.

Alexandra sans rest, 35 bd Princesse-Charlotte ℡ 50.63.13 – 🛗 🚽wc 🛁wc 🅖. ⒶⒺ ⓘ
SC : 🍽 21 – **55 ch** 130/257.
FV **r**

XXX **Grill de l'Hôtel de Paris,** pl. Casino ℡ 50.80.80, « Grill-rôtisserie sur le toit avec ≤ sur la
Principauté et la côte » – 🖥 🅿. ⒶⒺ ⒼⒷ ⓘ **E**. 🎿
FX **y**
fermé 4 janv. au 8 fév. et lundi – **R** carte 190 à 250.

XXX **P'tit Bec,** 11 av. Grde Bretagne ℡ 50.97.48 – 🖥. ⒶⒺ ⓘ
FV **s**
fermé 2 janv. au 2 fév. et dim. – **R** 100.

XX **Rampoldi,** 3 av. Spélugues ℡ 50.70.65 – 🖥. ⒶⒺ ⒼⒷ ⓘ
FV **z**
fermé 15 nov. au 15 déc. – **R** carte 110 à 150.

XX ❀ **Bec Rouge,** 12 av. St-Charles ℡ 30.74.91 – ⒶⒺ ⓘ
FV **e**
fermé 20 nov. au 20 déc. et lundi de janv. à avril – **R** carte 125 à 175
Spéc. Foie gras frais, Gratin de langouste, Médaillon de foie de canard aux raisins. **Vins** Cassis, Bandol.

XX **Chez Gianni,** 39 av. Princesse Grace ℡ 30.46.33, cuisine italienne – 🖥. ⒶⒺ ⒼⒷ ⓘ
CS **e**
fermé 1er au 15 oct. et mardi – SC : **R** carte 110 à 145

XX **Costa Rica,** 40 bd Moulins ℡ 50.63.00 – 🖥
FV **t**

XX **du Port,** quai Albert 1er ℡ 50.77.21, ≤, cuisine italienne – 🖥. ⒶⒺ ⒼⒷ **E**
EY **e**
fermé déc. et lundi sauf du 20 juil. au 20 août – SC : **R** 85/150.

X **La Calanque,** 33 av. St-Charles ℡ 50.63.19, produits de la mer – ⒶⒺ
FV **r**
fermé 20 juin au 20 juil. et dim. – SC : **R** carte 130 à 190.

X **Polpetta,** 6 av. Roqueville ℡ 50.67.84, cuisine italienne
EX **f**
fermé 10 janv. au 10 fév. et mardi – SC : **R** 60.

à Monte-Carlo Beach (06 Alpes-Mar.) par ① : 2,5 km – ✉ **06190** Roquebrune-Cap-Martin :

Monte-Carlo Beach H. Ⓜ 🦢, ℡ 78.21.40, ≤ sur mer et Monaco, « Remarquable ensemble
balnéaire, 🏊, 🏌 », 🎿 – 🛗 🖥 ch 📺 ☎ 🅿 – 🔬 30. ⒶⒺ ⒼⒷ ⓘ **E**. 🎿 rest
CS **a**
Hôtel : avril-oct. Rest. : juin-sept. – **R** carte 150 à 200 – 🍽 35 – **46 ch** 550/750.

Great-Britain

London

Manchester

London

LONDON (Greater) 404 @ to 44 – pop. 7,452,346 – 🌣 01.

Heathrow, ☏ 759 4321, Telex 934892 p. 8 AY.

Gatwick, ☏ 0293 (Crawley) 28822 and ☏ 01 (London) 668 4211, p. 9 : by A 23 EZ and M 23.

Stansted, at Bishop's Stortford, ☏ 0279 (Bishop's Stortford) 502380, Telex 81102, NE: 34 m. off M 11 and A 120.

BA Air Terminal : Buckingham Palace Rd, Victoria, SW1, ☏ 834 2323, p. 30 AX.

British Caledonian Airways, Victoria Air Terminal : Victoria Station, SW1, ☏ 833 9411, p. 30 BX.

Kensington Olympia ☏ 603 4555 – King's Cross ☏ 837 4200 ext 4700 – Paddington ☏ 723 7000 ext 3148.

🛈 London Tourist Board, Head Office : 26 Grosvenor Gardens, SW1W 0DU, ☏ 730 3450.

Victoria Station (adjacent to Platform 15), Buckingham Palace Rd, SW1.

British Tourist Authority, 64 St. James's St., SW1, ☏ 499 9325.

Telephone Information Service ☏ 730 0791 or Teletourist ☏ 246 8041 (English), 246 8043 (French), 246 8045 (German).

The maps in this section of the Guide are based upon the Ordnance Survey of Great Britain with the permission of the Controller of Her Majesty's Stationery Office. Crown Copyright reserved.

> Remember the speed limits that apply in the United Kingdom, unless otherwise signposted.
>
>   — 60 mph on single carriageway roads
>   — 70 mph on dual carriageway roads and Motorways

SIGHTS
CURIOSITÉS
LE CURIOSITÀ
SEHENSWÜRDIGKEITEN

■ **HISTORIC BUILDINGS AND MONUMENTS**

Palace of Westminster*** : House of Lords**, Westminster Hall** (hammerbeam roof***), Robing Room*, Central Lobby*, House of Commons*, Big Ben*, Victoria Tower*, p. 19 NX — Tower of London*** (Crown Jewels***, White Tower or Keep***, Beauchamp Tower*, St. John's Chapel**) p. 20 QU.

Banqueting House** p. 19 NV — Buckingham Palace** (Changing of the Guard**, Royal Mews**) p. 30 BV — Kensington Palace** p. 18 JV — Lincoln's Inn** p. 31 FV — London Bridge** p. 20 QV — Royal Hospital Chelsea** p. 29 FU — St. James's Palace** p. 27 EP — South Bank Arts Centre** (Royal Festival Hall*, National Theatre*, County Hall*) p. 19 NV — The Temple** (Middle Temple Hall*) p. 15 NU — Tower Bridge** p. 20 QV.

Albert Memorial* p. 28 CQ — Apsley House* p. 26 BP — Bloomsbury* p. 15 NT — Burlington House* p. 27 EM — Charterhouse* p. 16 PT — Commonwealth Institute* p. 17 HX — Design Centre* p. 27 FM — HMS Discovery* p. 20 QV A — George Inn*, Southwark p. 20 QV — Gray's Inn* p. 15 NT — Guildhall* (Lord Mayor's Show**) p. 16 PT — Dr Johnson's House* p 16 PTU A — Lancaster House* p. 27 EP — Leighton House* p. 17 GX — Mansion House* (plate and insignia**) p. 16 QU P — The Monument* (❋*) p. 16 QU G — New Zealand House (Royal Opera Arcade*) p. 27 FGN — Old Admiralty* p. 19 MV — Royal Exchange* p. 16 QU V — Royal Opera House* (Covent Garden) p. 31 EV — Somerset House* p. 31 EV — Staple Inn* p. 15 NT Y — Stock Exchange* p. 16 QTU — Westminster Bridge* p. 19 NX.

■ **CHURCHES**

The City Churches

St. Paul's Cathedral*** (Dome ⩽***) p. 16 PU.

St. Bartholomew the Great** (vessel*) p. 16 PT K — St. Dunstan-in-the-East** p. 16 QU F — St. Mary-at-Hill** (plan*, woodwork**) p. 16 QU B — Temple Church** p. 15 NU.

All Hallows-by-the-Tower (font cover**, brasses*) p. 16 QU Y — Christ Church* p. 16 PT E — St. Andrew Undershaft (monuments*) p. 16 QU A — St. Bride* (steeple**) p. 16 PU J — St. Clement Eastcheap (panelled interior**) p. 16 QU E — St. Edmund the King and Martyr (tower and spire*) p. 16 QU D — St. Giles Cripplegate* p. 16 PT N — St. Helen Bishopsgate* (monuments**) p. 16 QTU R — St. James Garlickhythe (tower and spire*, sword rests*) p. 16 PU R — St. Katherine Cree (sword rest*) p. 16 QU J — St. Magnus the Martyr (sword rest*) p. 16 QU K — St. Margaret Lothbury* (tower and spire*, woodwork*, screen*, font*) p. 16 QT S — St. Margaret Pattens (woodwork*) p. 16 QU N — St. Martin Ludgate (tower and spire*, door cases*) p. 16 PU B — St. Mary Abchurch* (dome*, reredos*) p. 16 QU X — St. Mary-le-Bow (tower and steeple*) p. 16 PU G — St. Michael Paternoster Royal (tower and spire*) p. 16 PU D — St. Nicholas Cole Abbey (tower and spire*) p. 16 PU F — St. Olave* p. 16 QU S — St. Peter upon Cornhill (screen*) p. 16 QU L — St. Stephen Walbrook* (tower and steeple*, dome*) p. 16 QU Z — St. Vedast (tower and spire*, ceiling*) p. 16 PTU E.

Other Churches

Westminster Abbey*** (Chapel of Edward the Confessor**, Henry VII Chapel***, Chapter House**) p. 19 MX.

Southwark Cathedral** p. 20 QV.

Queen's Chapel* p. 27 EP — St. Clement Danes* p. 31 FV — St. James's* p. 27 EM — St. Margaret's* p. 19 NX A — St. Martin-in-the-Fields* p. 31 DX — St. Paul's* (Covent Garden) p. 31 DV — Westminster Roman Catholic Cathedral* p. 19 MX B.

■ PARKS

Regent's Park*** p. 14 KS (terraces**), Zoo***.
Hyde Park** p. 18 JU — St. James's Park** p. 19 MV.
Kensington Gardens* p. 18 JV (Orangery* A).

■ STREETS AND SQUARES

The City*** p. 16 PU.

Bedford Square** p. 15 MT — Belgrave Square** p. 30 AV — Burlington Arcade** p. 27 DM —
The Mall** p. 27 FP — Piccadilly** p. 27 EM — The Thames** pp. 18-20 — Trafalgar Square**
p. 31 DX — Whitehall** (Horse Guards*) p. 19 MV.

Barbican* p. 16 PT — Bond Street* pp. 26-27 CK-DM — Canonbury Square* p. 16 PR — Carlton
House Terrace* p. 27 GN — Charing Cross* p. 31 DX — Cheyne Walk* p. 18 JZ — Fitzroy Square*
p. 15 LT — Jermyn Street* p. 27 EN — Montpelier Square* p. 29 EQ — Piccadilly Arcade* p. 27
DEN — Portman Square* p. 26 AJ — Portobello Road* p. 13 GU — Queen Anno's Gate* p. 19 MX —
Regent Street* p. 27 EM — St. James's Square* p. 27 FN — St. James's Street* p. 27 EN — Shepherd
Market* p. 26 CN — Strand* p. 31 DX — Trinity Church Square* p. 20 PX — Victoria Embankment*
p. 31 EX — Waterloo Place* p. 27 FN.

■ MUSEUMS

British Museum*** p. 15 MT — National Gallery*** p. 27 GM — Science Museum*** p. 28
CR — Tate Gallery*** p. 19 MY — Victoria and Albert Museum*** p. 29 DR.

Courtauld Institute Galleries** p. 15 MT M — Museum of London** p. 16 PT M — National Portrait
Gallery** p. 27 GM — Natural History Museum** p. 28 CS — Queen's Gallery** p. 30 BV — Wallace
Collection** p. 26 AH.

Clock Museum* (Guildhall) p. 16 PT — Geological Museum* p. 28 CR — Imperial College of
Science and Technology* p. 28 CR — Imperial War Museum* p. 20 PX — Madame Tussaud's* p. 14
KT M — Museum of Mankind* p. 27 DM — National Army Museum* p. 29 FU — Percival David
Foundation of Chinese Art* p. 15 MS M — Sir John Soane's Museum* p. 15 NT M — Wellington
Museum* p. 26 BP.

■ OUTER LONDON

Hampton Court p. 8 BZ (The Palace***, gardens***) — **Kew** p. 9 CY Royal Botanic Gardens*** : Palm House**, Temperate House*, Kew Palace or Dutch House**, Orangery*,
Pagoda*, Japanese Gateway* — Windsor (Castle***) by A 4, M 4 AX.

Blackheath p. 11 GY terraces and houses*, Eltham Palace* **A** — **Brentford** p. 8 BY Syon
Park**, gardens* — **Chiswick** p. 9 CX Chiswick Mall**, Chiswick House* **D**, Hogarth's
House* **E** — **Greenwich** pp. 10 and 11 : Cutty Sark** FX **F**, National Maritime Museum**
(Queen's House**) FX **M**, Royal Naval College** (Painted Hall*, the Chapel*) FX **G**,Old Royal
Observatory* (Meridian Building : collection**) GX **K**, Ranger's House* FY **N** — **Hampstead**
Kenwood House** (Adam Library**, paintings**) p. 5 EV **P**, Fenton House* p. 13 GR — **Hendon**
p. 5 CU Royal Air Force Museum** **M** — **Hounslow** p. 8 BX Osterley Park** — **Lewisham**
p. 10 FY Horniman Museum* **M** — **Richmond** pp. 8 and 9 : Richmond Park**, ※*** CY,
Richmond Bridge** BY **R**, Richmond Green** BY **S** (Maids of Honour Row**, Trumpeter's
House*), Asgill House* BY **B**, Ham House** BY **V**.

Dulwich p. 10 FY Dulwich College Picture Gallery* **X** — **Shoreditch** p. 6 FV Geffrye Museum*
M — **Tower Hamlets** p. 6 FX St. Katharine Dock* **Y** — **Twickenham** p. 8 BY Marble Hill House* **Z**,
Strawberry Hill* **A**.

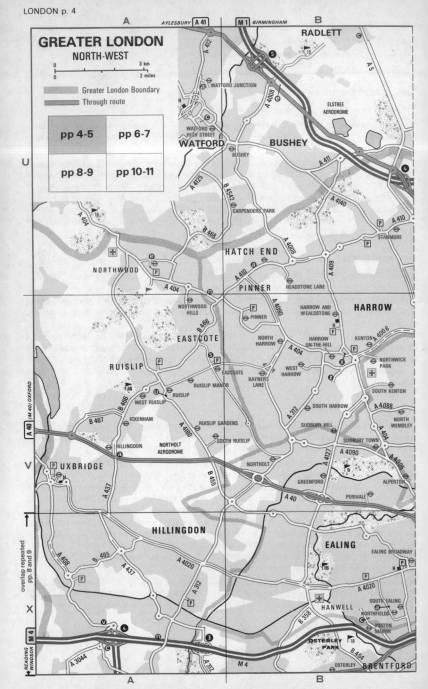

GREATER LONDON
NORTH-WEST

Greater London Boundary
Through route

pp 4-5	pp 6-7
pp 8-9	pp 10-11

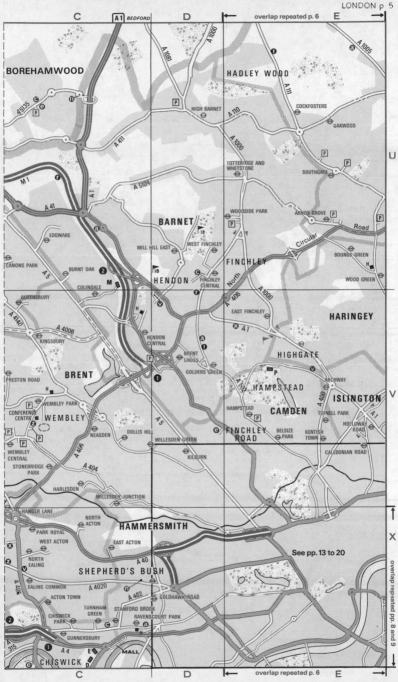

overlap repeated p. 6

C D E

A1 BEDFORD

A 1000

A 1081

A 1005

BOREHAMWOOD

HADLEY WOOD

A 111

A5135

HIGH BARNET

A 110

COCKFOSTERS

OAKWOOD

A 411

A 1000

U

A 5109

TOTTERIDGE AND WHETSTONE

SOUTHGATE

M 1

A 1

BARNET

WOODSIDE PARK

ARNOS GROVE

A 41

EDGWARE

MILL HILL EAST

WEST FINCHLEY

Circular

Road

CANONS PARK

BURNT OAK

2

18

FINCHLEY

BOUNDS GREEN

A 5

COLINDALE

M

18

HENDON

FINCHLEY CENTRAL

North

WOOD GREEN

QUEENSBURY

A 4006

H

A 406

A 1000

HARINGEY

A 4140

KINGSBURY

HENDON CENTRAL

EAST FINCHLEY

A 1

HIGHGATE

PRESTON ROAD

BRENT

BRENT CROSS

GOLDERS GREEN

HAMPSTEAD

ARCHWAY

A 400

H

1

A 502

ISLINGTON

V

WEMBLEY PARK

CONFERENCE CENTRE

WEMBLEY

HAMPSTEAD

CAMDEN

TUFNELL PARK

A 1

NEASDEN

DOLLIS HILL

A 5

FINCHLEY ROAD

BELSIZE PARK

KENTISH TOWN

HOLLOWAY ROAD

WEMBLEY CENTRAL

STONEBRIDGE PARK

A 406

WILLESDEN GREEN

KILBURN

CALEDONIAN ROAD

A 404

HARLESDEN

WILLESDEN JUNCTION

HANGER LANE

PARK ROYAL

NORTH ACTON

HAMMERSMITH

X

WEST ACTON

EAST ACTON

A 40

See pp. 13 to 20

NORTH EALING

SHEPHERD'S BUSH

A 406

EALING COMMON

A 4020

ACTON TOWN

A 402

GOLDHAWK ROAD

CHISWICK PARK

TURNHAM GREEN

STAMFORD BROOK

RAVENSCOURT PARK

GUNNERSBURY

A 315

A 4

E

MALL

CHISWICK

A 4

D

overlap repeated p. 6

overlap repeated pp. 8 and 9

C D E

217

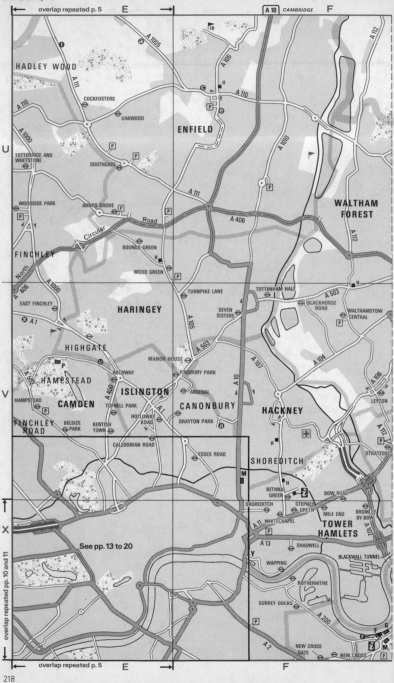

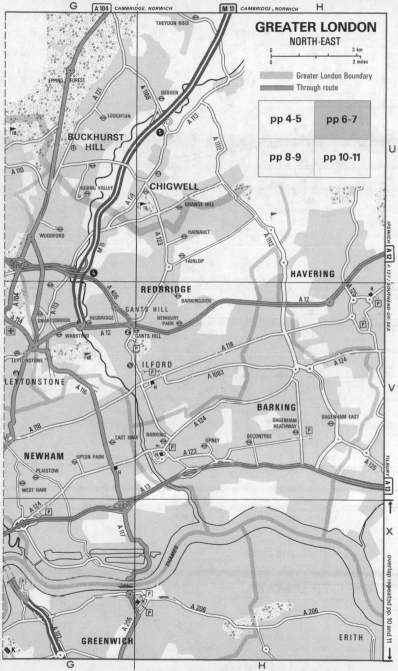

219

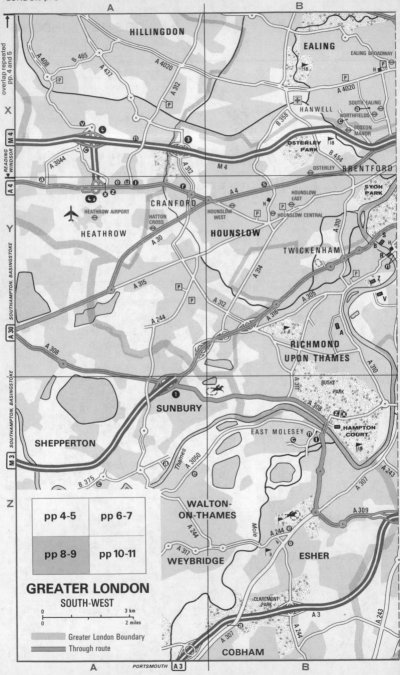

A

B

HILLINGDON

EALING

EALING BROADWAY

A 408
B 465
A 437
A 4020
A 312

HANWELL

SOUTH EALING
NORTHFIELDS
BOSTON MANOR

X

overlap repeated pp. 4 and 5

M 4

READING WINDSOR

A 4

A 3044

OSTERLEY PARK

B 358

A 4020

BRENTFORD

SYON PARK

OSTERLEY

M 4

A 4

CRANFORD

HOUNSLOW EAST

HOUNSLOW WEST

HOUNSLOW CENTRAL

HEATHROW AIRPORT

HATTON CROSS

A 30

HEATHROW

HOUNSLOW

A 314

TWICKENHAM

A 310

Y

SOUTHAMPTON, BASINGSTOKE

A 315

A 312

A 305

A 316

A 310

A 30

A 308

RICHMOND UPON THAMES

BUSHY PARK

SUNBURY

A 311

A 308

HAMPTON COURT

SOUTHAMPTON, BASINGSTOKE

A 244

EAST MOLESEY

A 310

SHEPPERTON

Thames

A 3050

M 3

B 375

A 307

A 243

Z

pp 4-5	pp 6-7
pp 8-9	pp 10-11

WALTON-ON-THAMES

A 244

Mole

A 309

ESHER

A 311

WEYBRIDGE

A 244

GREATER LONDON
SOUTH-WEST

CLAREMONT PARK

A 3

A 243

0 ___ 3 km
0 ___ 2 miles

Greater London Boundary
Through route

COBHAM

A

PORTSMOUTH A 3

B

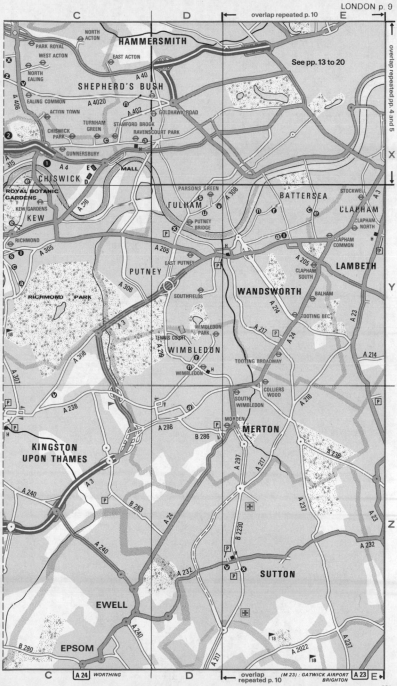

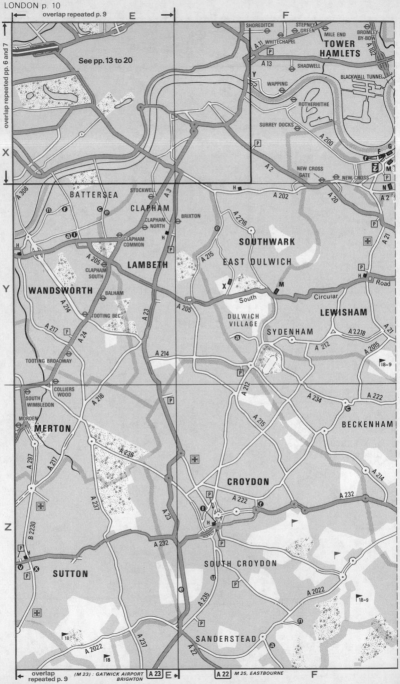

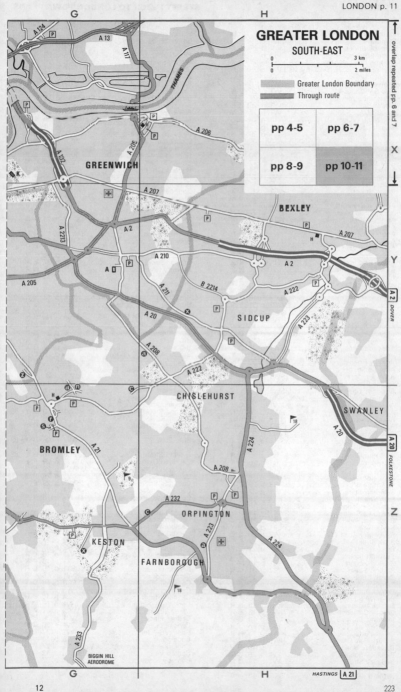

GREATER LONDON
SOUTH-EAST

0 — 3 km
0 — 2 miles

▓▓▓ Greater London Boundary
▬▬▬ Through route

| pp 4-5 | pp 6-7 |
| pp 8-9 | pp 10-11 |

overlap repeated pp. 6 and 7

GREENWICH

BEXLEY

SIDCUP

CHISLEHURST

SWANLEY

BROMLEY

ORPINGTON

KESTON

FARNBOROUGH

BIGGIN HILL
AERODROME

A 124
A 13
A 117
THAMES
A 206
A 102
A 205
A 2213
A 2
A 207
A 207
A 210
A 211
B 2214
A 222
A 20
A 208
A 222
A 223
A 224
A 20
A 208
A 232
A 224
A 223
A 233

X
Y
Z

A 2 DOVER
A 20 FOLKESTONE

HASTINGS A 21

12

223

Continued p. 21

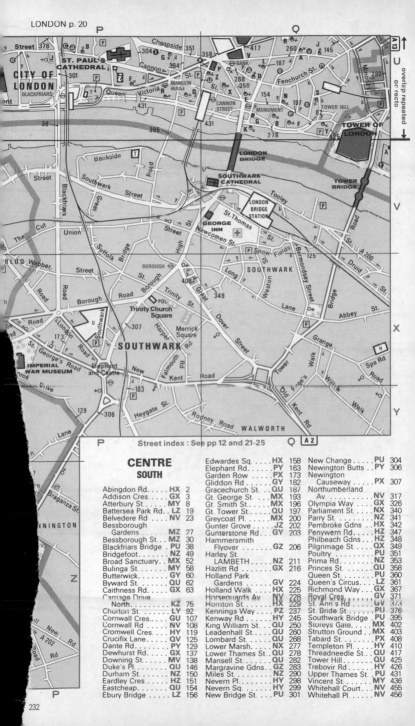

Street index : See pp 12 and 21-25

232

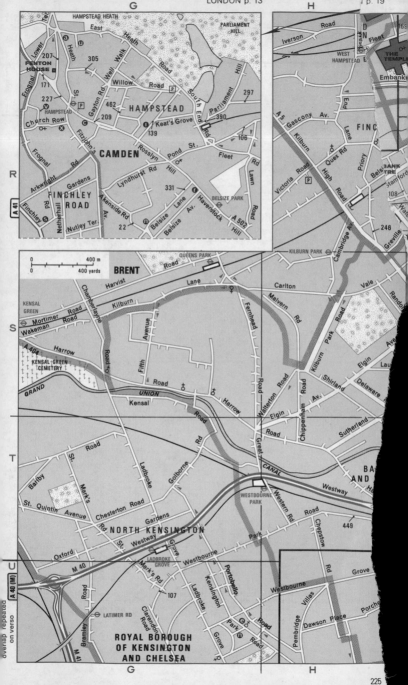

STRAND AND COVENT GARDEN

SOHO

MAYFAIR

Brook Street

Bruton St.

Berkeley St.

Curzon Street

Piccadilly

GREEN PARK

Constitution Hill

BUCKINGHAM PALACE GARDENS

ail p 30

Regent Street

Wardour Street

Shaftesbury Av.

Endell St.

Long Acre

Bow St.

Aldwych

Victoria

A Detail pp 26-27

Piccadilly Circus

LEICESTER SQ

D Detail p 31

Strand

Regent St.

Trafalgar Square

CHARING CROSS STATION

SOUTH ARTS CEN

ST. JAMES'S

St. James's St.

The Mall

Pall Mall

OLD ADMIRALTY

HORSE GUARDS

Whitehall

317

456   455

228

BANQUETING HOUSE

23

138

WATERLOO STATION

ST. JAMES'S PARK

Birdcage Walk

WESTMINSTER

340

193

COUNTY HALL

277

WA

Queen Anne's Gate

Road

Petty France

Buckingham Gate

ST. JAMES'S PARK

Tothill St.

402

52

WESTMINSTER ABBEY

A

WESTMINSTER BRIDGE

PALACE OF WESTMINSTER

York Rd

Baylis Rd

LAMBETH NOR

B

POL

Victoria

H

NEW SCOTLAND YARD

196

Great Peter Street

Millbank

Palace Rd

LAMBETH

403   200

Marsham

Westminster

VICTORIA STATION

Belgrave

Francis

Rochester

Vincent Sq.

Row

Horseferry

Page St. Rd

Lambeth Bridge

LAMBETH PALACE

Lambeth

Walk

Lollard

St.

Saint

Way

Wilton Rd.

Tachbrook

St.

Regency

Islip

St.

436

88

Embankment

Lambeth

Black Prince Road

LAMBETH

VICTORIA

VAUXHALL

Vincent

Bridge

TATE GALLERY

Vauxhall Walk

St.

Tyers

St.

Newburn St.

Lane

156

P

Sutherland

St.

Gloucester

Denbigh St.

Claverton St.

St.

Vauxhall

Millbank

Rd.

John

St.

30

27

8

THAMES

Albert

Kennington

49

Lane

gham

Palace

Road

Warwick

St. George's

Drive

PIMLICO

St.George's Square

Rd

VAUXHALL

150

Kennington Street

Clayton St.

Lupus

Street

a

Vauxhall Bridge

P

Kennington

Oval

Chelsea

Grosvenor

341

THE OVAL

211   OVAL

Kenningt

Queenstown

Road

Elms

Lane

290

SOUTH LAMBETH

Fentiman Road

353

East

Road

Nine

Wandsworth

Road

Lambeth

Dorset

South

Rd.

Clapham

Road

Brixton

19

COVENT GARDEN MARKET

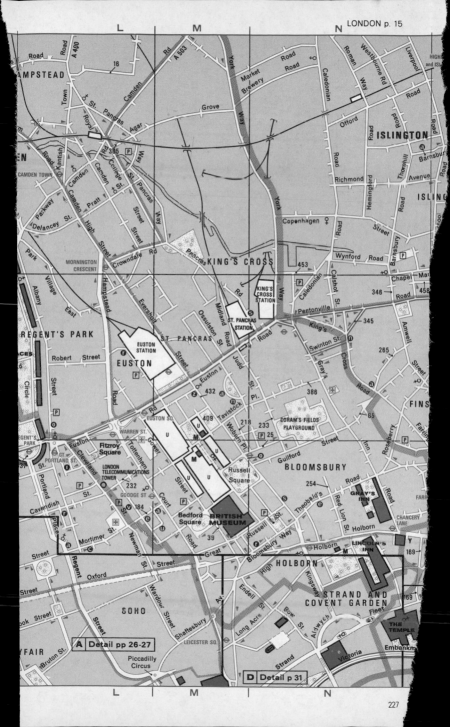

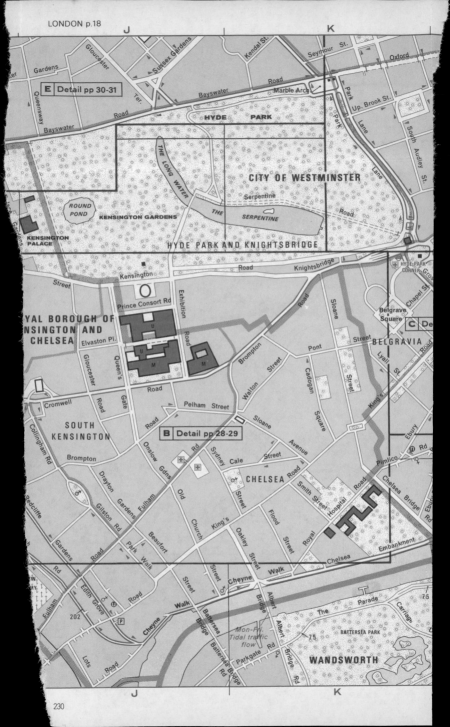

CENTRE
NORTH

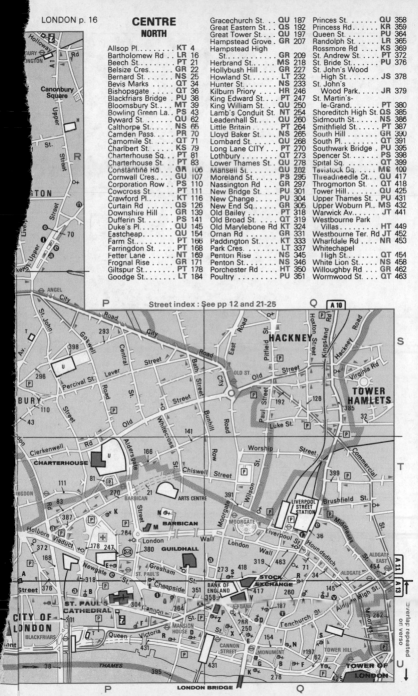

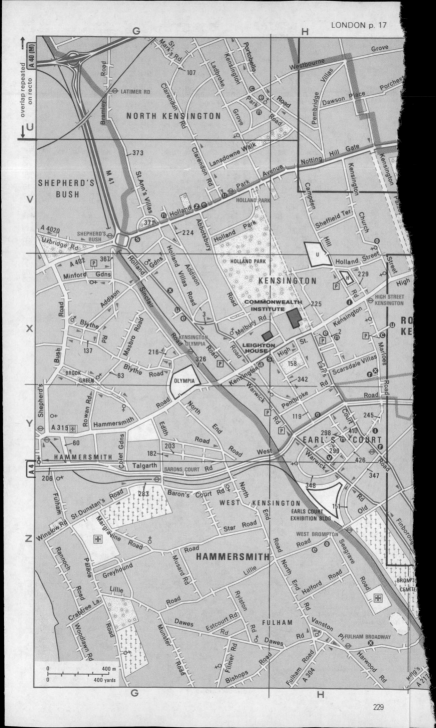

Continued on next page

13

STREET INDEX TO LONDON

Continued on next page

Street index: See pp 12 and 21-25

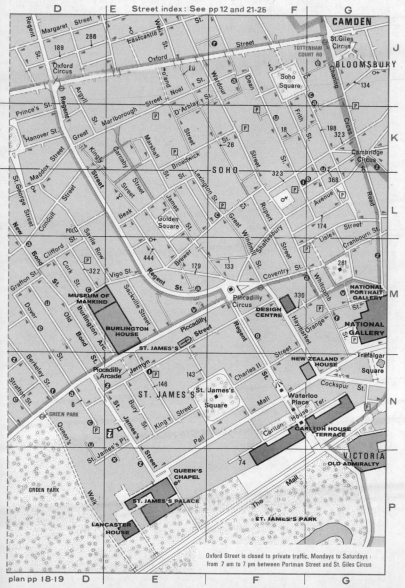

Oxford Street is closed to private traffic, Mondays to Saturdays : from 7 am to 7 pm between Portman Street and St. Giles Circus

plan pp 18·19

239

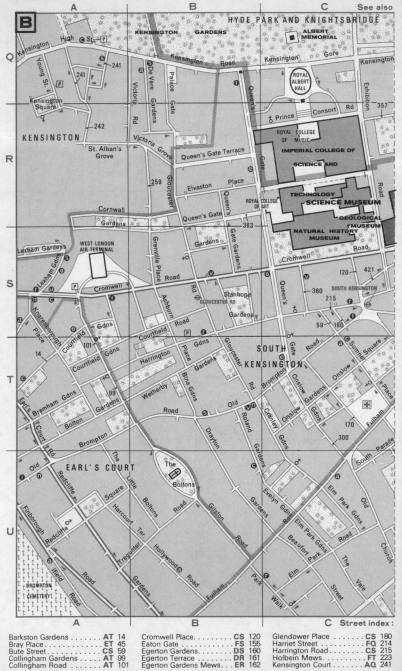

B

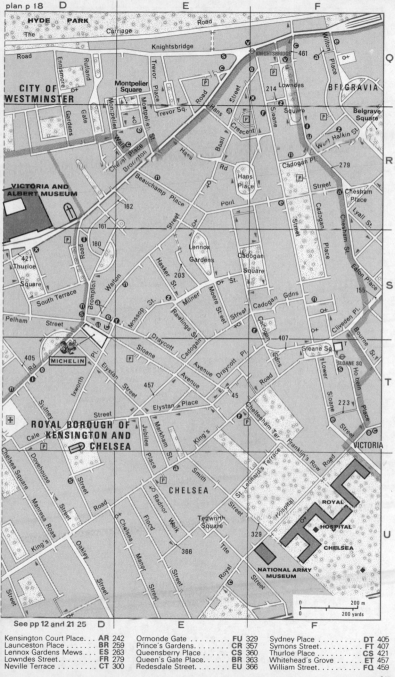

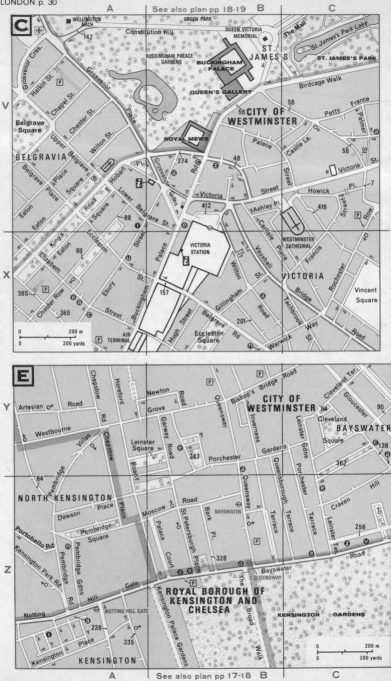

C

WELLINGTON ARCH

Constitution Hill

GREEN PARK

QUEEN VICTORIA MEMORIAL

The Mall

St. James's Park Lake

ST. JAMES'S

ST. JAMES'S PARK

142

Grosvenor Cres.

BUCKINGHAM PALACE GARDENS

BUCKINGHAM PALACE

Halkin St.

Chapel St.

Grosvenor Place

QUEEN'S GALLERY

Birdcage Walk

V

Chester St.

Wilton St.

56 **CITY OF WESTMINSTER**

56

Petty France

Palmer St.

Belgrave Square

Upper Belgrave

ROYAL MEWS

Palace

Castle La.

56

BELGRAVIA

Belgrave Place

Wilton Pl.

Grosvenor Gdns.

274

48

Street

Victoria

H Victoria St.

7

Belgrave Place

Square

Hobart Pl.

Lower Belgrave St.

Victoria

Street

Howick Pl.

416

Eaton

King's Road

Eaton Square

88

412

Ashley Pl.

Street

P Row

X

Elizabeth

Eccleston

St.

Carlisle Place

WESTMINSTER CATHEDRAL

Francis

389

Chester Row

88

Eaton St.

Ebury

VICTORIA STATION

Wilton St.

Vauxhall

Place

Rochester

Vincent Square

389

Street

Buckingham

157

Hugh Street

Belgrave Rd

Gillingham St.

201

Bridge Road

Tachbrook St.

Way

0   200 m
0   200 yards

AIR TERMINAL

Eccleston Square

Warwick St.

E

Chepstow Road

Newton Road

Bishop's Bridge Road

CITY OF WESTMINSTER

Cleveland Ter.

Artesian Road

Hereford Road

Grove

Garway Road

Queensway

Inverness

94

Gloucester

90

Y

Westbourne

Chepstow Rd

Leinster Square

Porchester

Leinster Gdns

Cleveland Square

BAYSWATER

136

Villas

243

Queensborough Terrace

Porchester Terrace

362

84

Chepstow Road

Moscow Rd

Bark Pl.

BAYSWATER

Queensway

Leinster Ter.

Craven Hill

256

NORTH KENSINGTON

Pembridge Place

Dawson Place

St.Petersburgh Place

Palace Court

328

Leinster

Road

Portobello Rd

Pembridge Square

Bayswater

Queensway

Z

Kensington Park Rd

Pembridge Gdns

Pembridge Villas

ROYAL BOROUGH OF KENSINGTON AND CHELSEA

The Broad Walk

KENSINGTON GARDENS

Notting

Pembridge Rd

Gate Hill

NOTTING HILL GATE

Kensington Palace Gardens

238

335

0   200 m
0   200 yards

KENSINGTON

Kensington Place

A   B   C

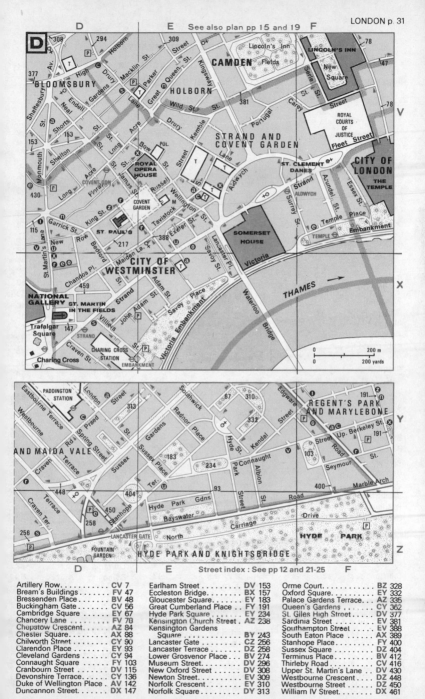

ALPHABETICAL LIST OF HOTELS AND RESTAURANTS
LISTE ALPHABÉTIQUE DES HOTELS ET RESTAURANTS
ELENCO ALFABETICO DEGLI ALBERGHI E RISTORANTI
ALPHABETISCHES HOTEL- UND RESTAURANTVERZEICHNIS

STARRED ESTABLISHMENTS IN LONDON
LES ÉTABLISSEMENTS A ÉTOILES DE LONDRES
GLI ESERCIZI CON STELLE A LONDRA
DIE STERN-RESTAURANTS LONDONS

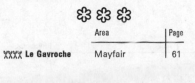

	Area	Page
XXXX Le Gavroche	Mayfair	61

	Area	Page
XXX La Tante Claire	Chelsea	53

	Area	Page		Area	Page
🏠 Connaught	Mayfair	60	XXX Chez Nico	Battersea	58
🏠 Capital	Chelsea	52	XXX Le Poulbot	City	49
XXXX Boulestin	Strand & Covent Garden	64	XX Carrier's	Islington	52
XXXX Chelsea Room	Chelsea	53	XX Interlude de Tabaillau	Strand & Covent Garden	65
XXXX Inigo Jones	Strand & Covent Garden	64	XX Lichfield's	Richmond	58
XXXX Waltons	Chelsea	53	XX Ma Cuisine	Chelsea	53
			XX Tiger Lee	Earl's Court	54

FURTHER ESTABLISHMENTS WHICH MERIT YOUR ATTENTION
AUTRES TABLES QUI MÉRITENT VOTRE ATTENTION
ALTRE TAVOLE PARTICOLARMENTE INTERESSANTI
WEITERE EMPFEHLENSWERTE HÄUSER

M

XX Bagatelle	Chelsea	53	XX Langan's Brasserie	Mayfair	61
XX Chez Moi	North Kensington	55			
XX Eatons	Victoria	66	XX Parke's	Chelsea	53
XX Frederick's	Islington	52	X Bubb's	City	49
XX Gavvers	Chelsea	53	X Poons of Covent Garden	Strand & Covent Garden	65
XX Grange	Strand & Covent Garden				

247

RESTAURANTS CLASSIFIED ACCORDING TO TYPE
RESTAURANTS CLASSÉS SUIVANT LEUR GENRE
RISTORANTI CLASSIFICATI SECONDO IL LORO GENERE
RESTAURANTS NACH ART UND EINRICHTUNG GEORDNET

Borough	Area	Restaurant		Page

BISTRO

Borough	Area		Restaurant	Page
Hammersmith	Fulham	✗	Carlo's Place	50
—	—	✗	Trencherman Bistro	50
Islington	Islington	✗	M'sieur Frog	52
Kingston-upon-Thames	Kingston	✗	Stonewalls	57
Wandsworth	Battersea	✗	Jacks Place	58
—	Clapham	✗	Pollyanna's	59
—	Putney	✗	Cassis	59
Westminster (City of)	Regent's Park & Marylebone	✗	Langan's Bistro	63
—	Victoria	✗	Bumbles	66
—	—	✗	Pimlico	66

DANCING

Borough	Area		Restaurant	Page
Hammersmith	Fulham	✗✗	Barbarella	50
Redbridge	Ilford	✗✗	Marios	57
Westminster (City of)	Bayswater & Maida Vale	✗✗	Concordia Notte	59
—	—	✗✗	Lotus House	59
—	Mayfair	✗✗✗	Tiberio	61
—	Strand & Covent Garden	✗✗✗	Bussola (La)	65

SEAFOOD

Borough	Area		Restaurant	Page
Camden	Bloomsbury	✗	Trattoria dei Pescatori	47
City of London	City of London	✗✗	Bill Bentley's	49
Croydon	Croydon	✗✗	Hook, Line and Sinker	49
Kensington & Chelsea (Royal Borough of)	Chelsea	✗✗	Poissonnerie de l'Avenue	53
—	—	✗✗	Suquet (Le)	53
—	—	✗✗	Wheeler's George and Dragon	53
—	Earl's Court	✗✗	Croisette (La)	54
—	Kensington	✗✗	Quai St. Pierre (Le)	55
Westminster (City of)	Belgravia	✗✗	Wheeler's Carafe	60
—	Mayfair	✗✗✗✗	Scott's	61
—	—	✗✗	Golden Carp	61
—	Regent's Park & Marylebone	✗✗	Bill Bentley's	63
—	Strand & Covent Garden	✗✗	Sheekey's	65

AUSTRIAN

Borough	Area		Restaurant	Page
Westminster (City of)	Regent's Park & Marylebone	✗✗	Kerzenstüberl	63

Borough	Area	Restaurant	Page

CHINESE

Borough	Area	Restaurant	Page
Barnet	Mill Hill	XX Good Earth	46
City of London	City of London	X Mandarin	49
Ealing	Ealing	XX Maxim	49
—	Hanwell	X Happiness Garden	49
Kensington & Chelsea (Royal Borough of)	Chelsea	XX Good Earth	54
—	Earl's Court	XX ⊛ Tiger Lee	54
—	—	X Crystal Palace	54
—	Kensington	XX Mama San	55
—	—	XX Sailing Junk	55
Richmond-upon-Thames	Richmond	XX Evergreen	58
—	—	XX Kew Rendezvous	58
—	—	X Richmond Rendezvous	58
Westminster (City of)	Bayswater & Maida Vale	XX Lotus House	59
—	Hyde Park & Knightsbridge	XX Mr. Chow	60
—	Mayfair	XX Mr Kai	61
—	Regent's Park & Marylebone	XX Lords Rendezvous	63
—	Soho	X Soho Rendezvous	64
—	Strand & Covent Garden	X Poons of Covent Garden	65
—	Victoria	XX Ken Lo's Memories of China	66

ENGLISH

Borough	Area	Restaurant	Page
Camden	Hampstead	X Turpin's	48
Kensington & Chelsea (Royal Borough of)	Chelsea	XX English House	53
Westminster (City of)	Belgravia	X Upper Crust in Belgravia	60
—	Strand & Covent Garden	XXX Simpson's-in-the-Strand	65
—	Victoria	XXX Lockets	66
—	—	X Tate Gallery Rest.	66

FRENCH

Borough	Area	Restaurant	Page
Barnet	Finchley	X Aubergade (L')	46
Bromley	Beckenham	XX Bon Bec (Le)	46
—	Orpington	XXX Oven d'Or	47
Camden	Bloomsbury	XXX Etoile (L')	47
—	—	XX Les Halles	47
—	—	X Mon Plaisir	47
—	Hampstead	XXX Keats	48
—	—	X Cellier du Midi (Le)	48
City of London	City of London	XXX ⊛ Poulbot (Le) (basement)	49
—	—	X Bourse Plate (La)	49
—	—	X Bubb's	49
—	—	X Gamin (Le)	49
Harrow	Central Harrow	XX Old Etonian	50
Islington	Islington	X Four Seasons	52
Kensington & Chelsea (Royal Borough of)	Chelsea	XXX Français (Le)	53
—	—	XXX ⊛⊛ Tante Claire (La)	53
—	—	XX Bagatelle	53
—	—	XX Brasserie St. Quentin	53

249

Borough	Area		Restaurant	Page

FRENCH *(continued)*

Borough	Area		Restaurant	Page
Kensington & Chelsea (Royal Borough of)	Chelsea	XX	Gavvers	53
—	—	XX ⊗	Ma Cuisine	53
—	—	X	Brasserie (La)	54
	Kensington			
—	—	XX	Détour (Le)	55
—	—	XX	Pomme d'Amour (La)	55
—	—	XX	Quai St. Pierre (Le)	55
—	—	XX	Toque Blanche (La)	55
—	—	X	Ark (The)	55
—	—	X	Jardinière (La)	55
—	North Kensington	XX	Chez Moi	55
Merton	Merton	X	Les Amoureux	57
Richmond-upon-Thames	Hampton Court	XX	Bastians	57
Wandsworth	Battersea	XXX ⊗	Chez Nico	58
—	—	XX	Grenouille (La)	58
—	Mayfair	XXXX ⊗⊗⊗	Gavroche (Le)	61
Westminster (City of)	Regents Park & Marylebone	X	Aventure (L')	63
—	—	X	Bois St. Jean (Au)	63
—	Soho	XX	Jardin des Gourmets (Au)	64
—	Strand & Covent Garden	XXXX ⊗	Boulestin	64
—	—	XX	Chez Solange	65
—	—	XX ⊗	Interlude de Tabaillau	65
—	Victoria	XX	Mijanou	66
—	—	XX	Restaurant (The)	66
—	—	X	Poule au Pot (La)	66

GREEK

Borough	Area		Restaurant	Page
Camden	Bloomsbury	XXX	White Tower	47
Westminster (City of)	Bayswater & Maida Vale	X	Kalamaras Taverna	60

HUNGARIAN

Borough	Area		Restaurant	Page
Westminster (City of)	Soho	XX	Gay Hussar	64

INDIAN & PAKISTANI

Borough	Area		Restaurant	Page
Camden	Holborn	X	Last Days of the Raj	48
Hammersmith	Hammersmith	XX	Aziz	50
—	—	X	Rajdoot	50
—	Shepherd's Bush	XX	Shireen	50
Kensington & Chelsea (Royal Borough of)	Chelsea	XX	Tandoori	53
—	Earl's Court	X	Naraine	54
—	North Kensington	X	Rama Sita	55
—	South Kensington	X	Star of India	56
Westminster (City of)	Belgravia	XX	Salloos	60
—	Hyde Park & Knightsbridge	XXX	Shezan	60
—	Mayfair	XXX	Tandoori	61
—	—	XX	Gaylord	61
—	Regent's Park & Marylebone	XX	Gaylord	63
—	—	XX	Viceroy of India	63
—	Victoria	XX	Kundan	66

Borough	Area	Restaurant	Page

ITALIAN

Borough	Area	Restaurant	Page
Barnet	Finchley	XX Luigi's " Belmont "	46
—	—	X Palme (Le)	46
Bexley	Sidcup	X Botte (La)	46
Bromley	Bromley	XX Chariot Wheel	47
—	—	X Capisano	47
—	Chislehurst	XX Franco	47
—	Farnborough	XX Ombrello (L')	47
—	Keston	XX Giannino's	47
Camden	Finchley Road	XX Trattoria del Buonamico	48
—	Hampstead	X Villa Bianca	48
City of London	City of London	XXX City Tiberio	49
—	—	XX Villa Augusta	49
Croydon	Sanderstead	X Elio	49
—	South Croydon	X Trattoria Bella Venezia	49
Ealing	Ealing	XX Gino's	49
Hammersmith	Fulham	XX Barbarella	50
—	—	XX Clessidra (La)	50
Haringey	Highgate	XX San Carlo	50
Harrow	Hatch End	XX Canaletto 2	51
Hillingdon	Eastcote	X Sambuca	51
—	Northwood	XX Martini	51
Islington	Islington	XX Ristorante Portofino	52
Kensington & Chelsea (Royal Borough of)	Chelsea	XX Beccofino	53
—	—	XX Don Luigi	54
—	—	XX Eleven Park Walk	53
—	—	XX Meridiana	53
—	—	XX Sale e Pepe	54
—	—	XX San Frediano	54
—	—	XX San Ruffillo	54
—	Earl's Court	XX Pontevecchio	54
—	Kensington	XX Franco Ovest	55
—	—	XX Gallo d'Oro	55
—	—	XX Gatamelata	55
—	—	XX Topo d'Oro	55
—	—	XX Trattoo	55
—	—	X Barbino (Il)	55
—	—	X Paesana (La)	55
—	South Kensington	XX Pulcinella	56
Merton	Wimbledon	XX San Lorenzo Fuoriporta	57
Richmond-upon-Thames	Richmond	XX Franco's	58
—	—	XX Gino's	58
Southwark	Dulwich Village	XX Luigi's	58
Sutton	Sutton	X Trattoria Toscana	58
Waltham Forest	Leytonstone	X Trattoria Parmigiana	58

251

Borough	Area	Restaurant		Page

ITALIAN (continued)

Borough	Area	Restaurant		Page
Westminster (City of)	Bayswater & Maida Vale	XX	Canaletto	60
—	—	XX	Concordia Notte	59
—	—	XX	Lupa (La)	60
—	—	XX	San Marino	59
—	—	XX	Trat-West	59
—	—	X	Concordia	60
—	Hyde Park & Knightsbridge	XX	Montpeliano	60
—	Mayfair	XXX	Cecconi's	61
—	—	XXX	Tiberio	61
—	—	X	Trattoria Fiori	61
—	Regent's Park & Marylebone	XX	Loggia (La)	63
—	—	XX	Tonino	63
—	—	X	Barbino (II)	63
—	—	X	Biagi's	63
—	—	X	Vecchio Parioli	63
—	St. James's	XX	Frank's	63
—	Soho	XXX	Leonis Quo Vadis	64
Westminster (City of)	Soho	XX	Romeo e Giulietta	64
—	—	XX	Rugantino	64
—	—	XX	Terrazza (La)	64
—	—	XX	Venezia	64
—	—	X	Trattoria Imperia	64
—	Strand & Covent Garden	XXX	Bussola (La)	65
—	—	XX	Luigi's	65
—	—	XX	San Martino	65
—	—	X	Colosseo	65
—	—	X	Laguna 50	65
—	Victoria	XX	Gran Paradiso	66
—	—	X	Mimmo d'Ischia	66

JAPANESE

Borough	Area	Restaurant		Page
City of London	City of London	X	Ginnan	49
Kensington & Chelsea (Royal Borough of)	Kensington	XX	Hiroko	55
Westminster (City of)	Mayfair	X	Ikeda	61
—	—	X	Saga	61
—	Regent's Park & Marylebone	XX	Asuka	63
—	—	XX	Masako	63
—	—	X	Mikado	63
—	St. James's	XXX	Suntory	63
—	Soho	XX	Fuji	64
—	Strand & Covent Garden	XX	Azami	65

MALAYSIAN

Borough	Area	Restaurant		Page
Westminster (City of)	Regent's Park & Marylebone	X	Singapore	63

SWISS

Borough	Area	Restaurant		Page
Westminster (City of)	Soho	XX	Chesa (Swiss Centre)	64

RESTAURANTS OPEN ON SUNDAY (L : lunch - D : dinner) AND RESTAU-RANTS TAKING LAST ORDERS AFTER 11.30 p.m.

RESTAURANTS OUVERTS LE DIMANCHE (L : déjeuner - D : diner) ET RES-TAURANTS PRENANT LES DERNIÈRES COMMANDES APRÈS 23 h 30

RISTORANTI APERTI LA DOMENICA (L : colazione - D : pranzo) E RISTO-RANTI CHE ACCETTANO ORDINAZIONI DOPO LE 23. 30

RESTAURANTS, DIE SONNTAGS GEÖFFNET SIND (L : Mittagessen - D : Abendessen), BZW. BESTELLUNGEN AUCH NACH 23.30 UHR ANNEHMEN

Borough	Area	Restaurant	Sunday	11.30 p. m.	Page
Barnet					
	Finchley	XX Fogareiro		x	46
—	—	XX Luigi's « Belmont »	L D		46
—	—	X Otello	L D		46
—	Mill Hill	XX Good Earth	L D		46
Bexley	Sidcup	X La Botte (12.00)		x	46
Bromley	Beckenham	XX Bon Bec (Le)	L		46
Camden	Finchley Road	XX Capability Brown		x	48
—	—	XX Trattoria del Buonamico (11.45)	L D	x	48
—	Hampstead	XXX Keats		x	48
—	—	X Cellier du Midi (Le)		x	48
—	—	X Chateaubriand (12.00)		x	48
—	—	X Turpin's	L		48
—	—	X Villa Bianca		x	48
—	Holborn	XXX Opera (L') (12.00)		x	48
—	—	X Last Days of the Raj	D	x	48
—	Swiss Cottage	XX Peter's	L	x	48
Croydon	South Croydon	X Trattoria Bella Venezia		x	49
Ealing	Ealing	XX Maxim (12.00)	D	x	49
—	Hanwell	X Happiness Garden (12.00)		x	49
Greenwich	Greenwich	X Meantime	L		50
Hammersmith	Fulham	XX Barbarella (1.00)		x	50
—	—	XX Clessidra (La) (12.00)		x	50
—	—	X Carlo's Place		x	50
—	Hammersmith	XX Aziz		x	50
—	—	X Rajdoot (11.45)	L D	x	50
—	Shepherd's Bush	XX Shireen		x	50
Haringey	Highgate	XX San Carlo	L D	x	50
Harrow	Pinner	X Giralda (La)	L D		51
Hillingdon	Eastcote	X Sambuca		x	51

253

Borough	Area	Restaurant	Sunday	11.30 p. m.	Page
Islington	Islington	XX ✿ Carrier's		x	52
—	—	XX Frederick's		x	52
—	—	XX Julius's (11.45)		x	52
—	—	X M'sieur Frog		x	52
Kensington & Chelsea (Royal Borough of)	Chelsea	🏛🏛🏛 Carlton Tower (Rib Room)	L D		52
—	—	🏛🏛 ✿ Capital	L D		52
—	—	XXXX ✿ Chelsea Room	L D		53
—	—	XXXX ✿ Waltons	L D	x	53
—	—	XX Beccofino		x	53
—	—	XX Bewick's		x	53
—	—	XX Brasserie St. Quentin (1.00)	L D	x	53
—	—	XX Daphne's (12.00)		x	53
—	—	XX Don Luigi	L D	x	54
—	—	XX Eleven Park Walk (12.00)		x	53
—	—	XX Good Earth (12.00)	L D	x	54
—	—	XX Meridiana (12.00)	L D	x	53
—	—	XX Poissonnerie de l'Avenue		x	53
—	—	XX Sale e Pepe		x	54
—	—	XX San Frediano		x	54
—	—	XX Tandoori (12.00)	L D	x	53
—	—	X Brasserie (La) (12.00)	L D	x	54
—	Earl's Court	XX Pontevecchio	L D	x	54
—	—	XX ✿ Tiger Lee	D	x	54
—	—	X Crystal Palace (11.45)	L D	x	54
—	—	X Naraine (11.45)	L D	x	54
—	Kensington	🏛🏛 Royal Garden (Royal Roof 12.30)		x	55
—	—	XX Détour (Le)	L D		55
—	—	XX Franco Ovest		x	55
—	—	XX Gatamelata		x	55
—	—	XX Mama San	L D		55
—	—	XX Quai St. Pierre (Le)	L D	x	55
—	—	XX Sailing Junk		x	55
—	—	XX Topo d'Oro	L D	x	55
—	—	XX Trattoo (11.45)	L D	x	55
—	—	X Ark (The)	D	x	55
—	—	X Barbino (Il) (12.00)		x	55
—	—	X Jardinière (La)	L D		55
—	—	X Paesana (La) (12.00)		x	55
—	North Kensington	XXX Leith's (11.45)	D	x	55
—	—	XX Chez Moi		x	55
—	South Kensington	XX Pulcinella (11.45)		x	56
—	—	X Chanterelle	L D		56
—	—	X Star of India (11.50)	L D	x	56
Kingston-upon-Thames	Kingston	X Stonewalls	L D		57
Merton	Wimbledon	XX San Lorenzo Fuoriporta	L D		57

Borough	Area		Restaurant	Sunday	11.30 p. m.	Page
Richmond-upon-Thames	Richmond	XX	Evergreen		x	58
—	—	XX	Franco's (12.00)	L D	x	58
—	—	XX	Gino's	L D	x	58
—	—	XX	Kew Rendezvous	L D		58
—	—	X	Richmond Rendezvous	L D		58
Waltham Forest	Leytonstone	X	Trattoria Parmigiana (12.00)		x	58
Wandsworth	Battersea	XX	Grenouille (La) (12.00)		x	58
—	—	X	Routier (Le)		x	58
—	Clapham	X	Pollyanna's	L D	x	59
Westminster (City of)	Bayswater & Maida Vale	XX	Concordia Notte (1.00)		x	59
		XX	Lotus House (1.00)	L D	x	59
—	—	XX	Lupa (La)		x	60
—	—	XX	San Marino		x	59
—	—	XX	Trat-West	L D	x	59
—	—	X	Concordia (11.45)		x	60
—	—	X	Kalamaras Taverna (12.00)		x	60
	Belgravia	XX	Salloos		x	60
—	—	XX	Wheeler's Carafe	L D		60
—	—	X	Upper Crust in Belgravia	L D		60
—	Hyde Park & Knightsbridge	XXX	Shezan		x	60
		XX	Mr. Chow (11.45)	L D	x	60
—	—	XX	Montpeliano (12.00)		x	60
—	—	XX	Newports		x	60
—	Mayfair	命命命	Dorchester (Grill)	L D		60
—	—	命命命	Inn on the Park (Four Seasons 12.00)	L D	x	
			(Lanes 12.00)	L	x	60
—	—	XXXX	✿✿✿ Gavroche (Le) (11.45)		x	61
—	—	XXXX	Scott's	D		61
—	—	XXX	Snooty Fox (12.00)		x	61
—	—	XXX	Tandoori (12.00)		x	61
—	—	XXX	Tiberio (1.00)		x	61
—	—	XX	Gaylord	L D	x	61
—	—	XX	Golden Carp		x	61
—	—	XX	Langan's Brasserie		x	61
—	—	XX	Mr Kai		x	61
—	Regent's Park & Marylebone	XX	Gaylord	L D	x	63
—		XX	Loggia (La)		x	63
—	—	XX	Lords Rendezvous		x	63
—	—	XX	Viceroy of India	L D	x	63
—	—	X	Aventure (L')	L		63
—	—	X	Barbino (Il) (12.00)		x	63
—	—	X	Biagi's	L D		63

255

Borough	Area	Restaurant		Sunday	11.30 p.m.	Page
Westminster (City of)	St. James's	XXX	Hunting Lodge	L D	x	63
—	—	XX	Caprice (Le) (11.45)		x	63
—	Soho	XXXX	Café Royal Grill	L D	x	64
—	—	XXXX	Relais du Café Royal (Le)	L D	x	64
—	—	XXX	Leonis Quo Vadis (11.45)	D		64
—	—	XX	Chesa (Swiss Centre) (12.00)	L D	x	64
—	—	XX	Fuji	D		64
—	—	XX	Gay Hussar		x	64
—	—	XX	Rugantino		x	64
—	—	XX	Terrazza (La)	L D	x	64
—	—	X	Soho Rendezvous (11.45)	L D	x	64
—	Strand & Covent Garden	⛨⛨⛨	Savoy (River Room)	L D	x	64
—	—	XXXX	❀ Inigo Jones (11.45)		x	64
—	—	XXX	Bussola (La) (12.00)		x	65
—	—	XX	Chez Solange (12.15)		x	65
—	—	XX	Grange		x	65
—	—	XX	❀ Interlude de Tabaillau		x	65
—	—	XX	Luigi's		x	65
—	—	XX	San Martino		x	65
—	—	XX	Sheekey's		x	65
—	—	X	Cellier de Medici		x	65
—	—	X	Colosseo		x	65
—	—	X	Laguna 50		x	65
—	—	X	Poons of Covent Garden (11.45)		x	65
—	Victoria	XX	Ken Lo's Memories of China		x	66
—	—	XX	Kundan (12.00)		x	66
—	—	XX	Restaurant (The)	L D	x	66
—	—	X	Fontana (La)		x	66
—	—	X	Pimlico	L D	x	66

When visiting London use the Green Guide " **London** "
- Detailed descriptions of places of interest
- Useful local information
- A section on the historic square-mile of the City of London with a detailed fold out plan
- The lesser known London boroughs — their people, places and sights
- Plans of selected areas and important buildings.

ALPHABETICAL LIST OF AREAS INCLUDED
LISTE ALPHABÉTIQUE DES QUARTIERS CITÉS
ELENCO ALFABETICO DEI QUARTIERI CITATI
LISTE DER ERWÄHNTEN BEZIRKE

BOROUGHS and AREAS

Greater London is divided, for administrative purposes, into 32 boroughs plus the City ; these sub-divide naturally into minor areas, usually grouped around former villages or quarters, which often maintain a distinctive character.

◎ of Greater London : 01 except special cases.

BARNET pp. 4 and 5.

Finchley – ✉ N3/N12/NW11.
🛇 Nether Court, Frith Lane ℡ 346 2436.

XX **Luigi's Belmont,** 2-4 Belmont Par., Finchley Rd, NW11 6XP, at Temple Fortune ℡ 455 0210, Italian rest. – 🖾 🖾 ⓞ 𝘝𝘐𝘚𝘈   DV **a**
closed Monday, Christmas Day and Bank Holidays – **M** a la carte 5.40/8.10 **st.** 🔥 2.00.

XX **Fogareiro,** 16-18 Hendon Lane, N 3, ℡ 346 0315 – 🖾 🖾 ⓞ 𝘝𝘐𝘚𝘈   DU **c**
closed Saturday lunch, Sunday and Bank Holidays – **M** a la carte 8.90/15.70 **t.** 🔥 2.25.

X Le Palme, 46 Market Pl., NW11, ℡ 458 7305, Italian rest.   EV **x**
X **Otello,** 241 Regents Park Rd, N3 3LA, ℡ 346 5232 – 🖾 ⓞ   DUV **r**
M a la carte 5.35/15.65 **t.** 🔥 1.90.

X **L'Aubergade,** 816 Finchley Rd, NW11 6XL, at Temple Fortune ℡ 455 8853, French rest. – 🖾 𝘝𝘐𝘚𝘈   DV **i**
closed Saturday lunch, Sunday and 2 weeks at Christmas – **M** a la carte 7.60/9.70 **t.** 🔥 2.00.

Hendon – ✉ NW4/NW7.
🛇 off Sanders Lane ℡ 346 7810.

🏨 **Hendon Hall,** Ashley Lane, NW4 1HF, ℡ 203 3341, Telex 8956088, 🚿 – 🛗 📺 🅿. 🏝. 🖾 🖾 ⓞ 𝘝𝘐𝘚𝘈   DV **v**
M 5.95 **st.** 🔥 2.35 – **50 rm** ⬜ 30.00/36.00 **st.** – P 42.00/46.00 **st.**

🏨 **TraveLodge** (T.H.F.) without rest., NW7 3HB, at Scratchwood Service Area on M 1 ℡ 906 0611 – 📺 ⎚wc 🚿 ♿ 🅿. 🏝. 🖾 🖾 ⓞ 𝘝𝘐𝘚𝘈   CU **r**
100 rm 23.00/32.00 **st.**

Mill Hill – ✉ NW7.
XX **Good Earth,** 143-145 The Broadway, NW 7, ℡ 959 7011, Chinese rest. – 🖾 🖾 ⓞ 𝘝𝘐𝘚𝘈   CU **a**
M a la carte 4.25/6.20 **t.** 🔥 2.00.

Le Grand Londres (GREATER LONDON) est composé de la City et de 32 arrondissements administratifs (Borough) eux-mêmes divisés en quartiers ou villages ayant conservé leur caractère propre (Area).

BEXLEY pp. 10 and 11.

Sidcup – ✉ Kent.
X La Botte, 9 Marechal Neil Par., Main Rd, DA14 6QF, ℡ 300 5233, Italian rest.   HY **x**

BRENT pp. 4 and 5.

Wembley – ✉ Middx.
🛇 Horsenden Hill, Whitton Av. ℡ 902 4555.

🏨 **Crest** (Crest), Empire Way, HA9 8DS, ℡ 902 8839, Telex 24837 – 🛗 📺 ♿ 🅿. 🏝. 🖾 🖾 ⓞ 𝘝𝘐𝘚𝘈   CV **z**
M 6.30 **s.** 🔥 2.60 – ⬜ 3.60 – **320 rm** 20.50/47.20 **st.**

BROMLEY pp. 10 and 11.

Beckenham – ✉ Kent.
🛇, 🛇 Beckenham Place Park ℡ 650 2292.

XX **Le Bon Bec,** 189a High St., BR3 1AH, ℡ 658 3614, French rest. – 🖾 🖾 ⓞ 𝘝𝘐𝘚𝘈   FZ **c**
closed Saturday lunch and Sunday dinner – **M** a la carte 7.55/10.65 **t.** 🔥 2.10.

Bromley – ⊠ Kent.

🇫 Magpie Hall Lane ☏ 462 7014.

↑ **Grianan,** 23 Orchard Rd, BR1 2PR, ☏ 460 1795 – **℗**   GYZ **n**
10 rm ⊊ 9.20/18.40 st.

↑ **Bromley Continental,** 56 Plaistow Lane, BR1 3JE, ☏ 464 2415, 🚗 – **℗**   GZ **a**
18 rm ⊊ 9.75/25.00 t.

XX **Chariot Wheel,** 21-22 Westmoreland Pl., Bromley South Shopping Centre, BR2 0TE, ☏
460 8477, Italian rest. – 🔄 ⒶⒺ *VISA*   GZ **r**
closed Sunday, Monday and Bank Holidays – **M** a la carte 8.50/14.00 t. 🍷 2.50.

X **Capisano,** 9 Simpson Rd, BR2 9AP, ☏ 464 8036, Italian rest. – 🔄 ⒶⒺ *VISA*   GZ **s**
closed Sunday, Monday, 15 August-7 September and Bank Holidays – **M** a la carte 6.95/11.65 t.
🍷 2.20.

Chislehurst – ⊠ Kent.

XX **Foxes,** 43 High St., BR7 5AF, ☏ 467 2094 – 🔄 ⒶⒺ ⑩ *VISA*   IIY **a**
closed Sunday, Monday and last 2 weeks July – **M** a la carte 6.85/10.10 t. 🍷 3.00.

XX **Franco,** 53 Chislehurst Rd, BR7 5NP, ☏ 467 1341, Italian rest. – 🔄 ⒶⒺ ⑩ *VISA*   GZ **c**
closed Sunday – **M** a la carte 7.85/10.35 t. 🍷 1.95.

Farnborough – ⊠ Kent – ☎ 0689 Farnborough.

🇫 High Elms, High Elms Rd ☏ 58175, off A 21 via Shire Lane.

XX **L'Ombrello,** 360 Crofton Rd, Locksbottom, ☏ 52286, Italian rest. – 🔄 ⑩ *VISA*   HZ **c**
closed Sunday – **M** a la carte 7.05/12.30 t. 🍷 1.75.

Keston – ⊠ Kent – ☎ 0689 Farnborough.

XX Giannino's, 6 Commonside, BR4 2TS, ☏ 56410, Italian rest.   GZ **x**

Orpington – ⊠ Kent – ☎ 0689 Orpington.

🇫 Cray Valley, St. Paul's Cray ☏ 37909.

XXX **Oven d'Or,** 4a Crescent Way, BR5 2GT, ☏ 52170, French rest. – 🔄 ⒶⒺ ⑩ *VISA*   HZ **a**
closed Saturday lunch, Sunday, Monday, 2 to 23 August, 1 to 12 January and Bank Holidays –
M a la carte 8.30/14.45 st.

CAMDEN Except where otherwise stated see pp. 13-16.

Bloomsbury – ⊠ NW1/W1/WC1.

🏨 **Russell** (T.H.F.), Russell Sq., WC1B 5BE, ☏ 837 6470, Telex 24615 – 🛗 📺 ☎. 🅰. 🔄 ⒶⒺ ⑩
VISA   NT **o**
M (carvery rest.) 6.95 st. 🍷 2.10 – ⊊ 4.50 – **318 rm** 37.50/46.00 st.

🏨 **Cora,** Upper Woburn Pl., WC1H 0HT, ☏ 387 5111, Telex 261591 – 🛗 📺 🛏wc ☎. 🅰. 🔄 ⒶⒺ
⑩ *VISA*   MS **z**
M 6.00 t. 🍷 2.55 – **133 rm** ⊊ 18.00/40.00 t.

🏨 **Bonnington,** 92 Southampton Row, WC1B 4BH, ☏ 242 2828, Telex 261591 – 🛗 📺 🛏wc
☎. 🅰. 🔄 ⒶⒺ ⑩ *VISA*   NT **s**
M (grill rest. only) a la carte 5.75/7.70 t. 🍷 2.55 – **250 rm** ⊊ 20.00/42.50 t.

🏨 **Kingsley** (T.H.F.), Bloomsbury Way, WC1A 2SD, ☏ 242 5881, Telex 21157 – 🛗 📺 🛏wc ☎.
🅰. 🔄 ⒶⒺ ⑩ *VISA*   NT **r**
M (carvery rest.) 6.95 st. 🍷 2.50 – ⊊ 2.75 – **169 rm** 17.00/35.00 st.

↑ **Harlingford,** 61-63 Cartwright Gdns, WC1H 9EL, ☏ 387 1551   MS **n**
40 rm ⊊ 12.00/20.00 st.

↑ **Crescent,** 49-50 Cartwright Gdns, WC1H 9EL, ☏ 387 1515   MS **a**
28 rm ⊊ 9.00/16.00 st.

XXX **White Tower,** 1 Percy St., W1P 0ET, ☏ 636 8141, Greek rest. – 🔄 ⒶⒺ ⑩ *VISA*   MT **u**
closed Sunday, Sunday, 3 weeks August, 1 week at Christmas and Bank Holidays – **M** a la
carte 10.00/16.00 t. 🍷 2.50.

XXX **L'Etoile,** 30 Charlotte St., W1P 1HJ, ☏ 636 7189, French rest. – ⒶⒺ ⑩   LT **e**
closed Saturday, Sunday, first 3 weeks August and Bank Holidays – **M** a la carte approx. 14.40 t.

XX **Lacy's,** 26-28 Whitfield St., W1P 5RD, ☏ 636 2411 – 🔄 ⒶⒺ ⑩ *VISA*   MT **a**
closed Saturday lunch, Sunday and 3 weeks in summer – **M** a la carte 12.15/18.75.

XX **Les Halles,** 57 Theobald's Rd, WC1 8SP, ☏ 405 3609, French rest. – 🔄 ⒶⒺ ⑩ *VISA*   NS **e**
closed Saturday, Sunday, 25-26 December and Bank Holidays – **M** a la carte 10.50/12.50 t.
🍷 2.20.

X **Trattoria dei Pescatori,** 55-57 Charlotte St., W1P 1LA, ☏ 580 3289, Italian rest., Seafood –
🔄 ⒶⒺ ⑩ *VISA*   LT **v**
closed Saturday lunch, Sunday and Bank Holidays – **M** a la carte 6.55/10.50 t. 🍷 2.25.

X **Mon Plaisir,** 21 Monmouth St., WC2H 9DD, ☏ 836 7243, French rest.   p. 31 DV **a**
closed Saturday and Sunday – **M** a la carte 5.80/8.60 t. 🍷 2.50.

P.T.O. →

Euston – ✉ NW1.

🏨 **Kennedy** (Gd. Met.), 43 Cardington St., NW1 2LP, ☎ 387 4400, Telex 28250 – ⌷ �📺 🛏wc
☎. 🔒 🖭 🟰 **VISA**   LS   r
M 4.95/5.50 st. – ⌷ 1.85 – **324 rm** 20.00/34.00 s.

Finchley Road – ✉ NW1/NW3.

🏨 **Charles Bernard,** 5 Frognal, NW3 6AL, ☎ 794 0101, Telex 23560 – ⌷ 📺 🛏wc 🅿 🔒 🖭
🟰 **VISA**   GR   s
M a la carte 3.15/7.60 st. ⌷ 2.00 – **57 rm** ⌷ 24.00/30.00 s.

⌂ **Dawson House,** 72 Canfield Gdns, NW6 3ED, ☎ 624 0079, 🚗   HR   a
15 rm ⌷ 7.50/15.00 st.

✗✗ **Capability Brown,** 351 West End Lane, NW6, ☎ 794 3234 – 🔒 🖭 🟰 **VISA**
closed Sunday, Easter, 2 weeks in summer, Christmas and Bank Holidays – **M** (dinner only) a
la carte 9.15/13.85 t. ⌷ 2.10.   pp. 4 and 5   DV   e

✗✗ **Trattoria del Buonamico,** 122a Finchley Rd, NW3 5HT, ☎ 794 5784, Italian rest. – 🔒 🖭
🟰 **VISA**   JR   o
closed Christmas – **M** a la carte 5.25/9.25 t. ⌷ 2.05.

Hampstead – ✉ NW3.

🏨 **Clive** (Ladbroke), Primrose Hill Rd, NW3 3NA, ☎ 586 2233 – ⌷ 📺 🅿. 🔒. 🔒 🖭 🟰 **VISA**
M 6.00/8.00 st. ⌷ 3.00 – ⌷ 3.75 – **83 rm** 37.00/42.00 st.   KR   a

🏨 **Swiss Cottage,** 4 Adamson Rd, NW3 3HP, ☎ 722 2281, Telex 27950, « Antique furniture
collection » – ⌷ 📺 🛏wc ⧖wc 🍴. 🔒 🖭 🟰 **VISA**   JR   n
M 4.50/6.50 s. ⌷ 2.00 – **65 rm** ⌷ 19.00/46.00 st. – P 28.00/50.00 st.

🏨 **Post House** (T.H.F.), 215 Haverstock Hill, NW3 4RB, ☎ 794 8121, Telex 262494 – ⌷ 📺
🛏wc 🚗 🅿. 🔒 🖭 🟰 **VISA**   GR   r
M 5.50/10.00 st. ⌷ 2.10 – ⌷ 4.35 – **140 rm** 29.00/38.50 st.

⌂ **Sandringham** 🐾, 3 Holford Rd, NW3 1AD, ☎ 435 1569, ≼, 🚗 – 🅿   GR   u
13 rm ⌷ 8.50/20.00.

⌂ **Frognal Lodge,** 14 Frognal Gdns (off Church Row), NW3 6UX, ☎ 435 8238 – ⌷ 🛏wc 🚗.
🔒 🖭 🟰 **VISA**   GR   v
17 rm ⌷ 15.00/32.00 st.

✗✗✗ **Keats,** 3-4 Downshire Hill, NW3 1NR, ☎ 435 1499, French rest. – 🔒 🖭 🟰 **VISA**   GR   i
closed Sunday, 3 weeks August and Bank Holidays – **M** (dinner only) a la carte 14.30/20.80 t.
⌷ 5.00.

✗ Villa Bianca, 1 Perrin's Court, NW3 1QR, ☎ 435 3131, Italian rest.   GR   c

✗ **Turpin's,** 118 Heath St., NW3 1DR, ☎ 435 3791, English rest. – 🔒 🖭 🟰 **VISA**   GR   a
closed Sunday dinner and Monday – **M** a la carte 6.75/10.20 t. ⌷ 2.10.

✗ **Le Cellier du Midi,** 28 Church Row, NW3 6UP, ☎ 435 9998, French rest. – 🔒 🖭 🟰 **VISA**
closed Sunday and Bank Holidays – **M** (dinner only) a la carte 7.55/10.45 t. ⌷ 2.00.   GR   x

✗ **Chateaubriand,** 48 Belsize Lane, NW3 5AR, ☎ 435 4882 – 🔒 🖭 🟰 **VISA**
closed Sunday, 24 to 26 December and New Year – **M** (dinner only) a la carte 7.20/12.00 t.
⌷ 2.70.

Holborn – ✉ WC2.

🏨 **Drury Lane** (Gd. Met.), 10 Drury Lane, High Holborn, WC2B 5RE, ☎ 836 6666, Telex 8811395
– ⌷ 📺 ☎. 🔒. 🔒 🖭 🟰 **VISA**   p. 31   DV   c
M 10.25/11.25 st. ⌷ 2.50 – ⌷ 4.60 – **128 rm** 38.00/44.00 s.

✗✗✗ **L'Opera,** 32 Great Queen St., WC2B 5AA, ☎ 405 9020 – 🔒 🖭 🟰 **VISA**   p. 31   EV   n
closed Saturday lunch and Sunday – **M** a la carte approx. 8.50 t. ⌷ 1.90.

✗ **Last Days of the Raj,** 22 Drury Lane, WC2, ☎ 836 1628, Indian rest. – 🔒 🖭 🟰 **VISA**
closed Sunday lunch – **M** a la carte 6.20/7.05 t.   p. 31   DV   s

King's Cross – ✉ N1.

🏨 Great Northern (B.T.H.), N1 9AN, ☎ 837 5454, Telex 299041 – ⌷ 📺 🛏wc 🚗. 🔒. 🔒 🖭 🟰
VISA   MNS   s
M (grill rest. only) – **66 rm** ⌷ 23.00/42.50 st.

Regent's Park – ✉ NW1.

🏨 **White House** (Rank), Albany St., NW1 3UP, ☎ 387 1200, Telex 24111 – ⌷ 📺 ☎ 🔒. 🔒.
🖭 🟰 **VISA**   LS   o
M *(closed Saturday lunch and Sunday)* 9.00 t. – ⌷ 4.25 – **587 rm** 36.50/49.50 st.

Swiss Cottage – ✉ NW3.

🏨 **Holiday Inn,** 128 King Henry's Rd, NW3 3ST, ☎ 722 7711, Telex 267396, 🏊 – ⌷ 📺 ☎ 🔒 🅿.
🔒. 🔒 🖭 🟰 **VISA**   JR   a
M (buffet lunch) a la carte 13.00/16.00 t. ⌷ 3.60 – ⌷ 4.75 – **291 rm** 41.50/52.50 s.

✗✗ **Peter's,** 65 Fairfax Rd, NW6 4EE, ☎ 624 5804 – 🖭 🟰 **VISA**   JR   i
closed Saturday lunch, Sunday dinner and Bank Holidays – **M** a la carte 6.65/8.90 t. ⌷ 1.85.

CITY OF LONDON Except where otherwise stated see p. 16.

🖪 St. Paul's Churchyard, EC4, 🕾 606 3030 ext 2456/7.

🏨 **Great Eastern (B.T.H.),** Liverpool St., EC2M 7QN, 🕾 283 4363, Telex 886812 – 🛊 📺 🅿. 🛦. 🖾
 🖾 ⓞ 𝘝𝘐𝘚𝘈
  QT **r**
 closed 4 days at Christmas – **M** (coffee shop only except lunch Monday to Friday) a la carte
 4.40/15.00 **st.** – **145 rm**

XXX ✿ **Le Poulbot** (basement), 45 Cheapside, EC2V 6AR, 🕾 236 4379, French rest. – 🖾 🖾 ⓞ
 𝘝𝘐𝘚𝘈
  PU **i**
 closed Saturday, Sunday and Bank Holidays – **M** (lunch only) 13.50 **st.**
 Spec. Boudin blanc sauce Périgueux, Filets de sole Leonora, Grenadins de veau vallée d'Auge.

XXX **City Tiberio,** 8-11 Lime St., EC3M 7AA, 🕾 623 3616, Italian rest. – 🖾 🖾 ⓞ 𝘝𝘐𝘚𝘈 QU **i**
 closed Saturday and Sunday – **M** (lunch only) a la carte 7.70/13.60 **t.**

XX **Bill Bentley's,** Swedeland Court, 202-204 Bishopsgate, EC2M 4NR, 🕾 283 1763, Seafood –
 🖾 🖾 𝘝𝘐𝘚𝘈
  QT **e**
 closed Saturday, Sunday and Bank Holidays – **M** (lunch only) a la carte 7.95/11.55 **t.** ⏶ 2.65.

XX **Villa Augusta,** Bucklersbury House, Queen Victoria St., EC4, 🕾 248 0005, Italian rest. – 🖾
 🖾 ⓞ 𝘝𝘐𝘚𝘈
  PQU **x**
 closed Saturday and Sunday – **M** (lunch only) a la carte 8.35/13.60 **t.**

X **Le Gamin,** 32 Old Bailey, EC4M 7HS, 🕾 236 7931, French rest. – 🖾 🖾 ⓞ 𝘝𝘐𝘚𝘈 PU **a**
 closed Saturday, Sunday and Bank Holidays – **M** (lunch only) 12.75 **st.**

X La Bourse Plate, 78 Leadenhall St., EC3, 🕾 623 5159, French rest. QU **v**

X **Bubb's,** 329 Central Market, Farringdon St., EC1A 9NB, 🕾 236 2435, French rest. PT **a**
 closed Saturday, Sunday, August and Bank Holidays – **M** (lunch only) a la carte 7.05/10.05 **t.**
 ⏶ 2.10.

X **Ginnan,** 5 Cathedral Pl., St. Paul's, EC4M 7EA, 🕾 236 4120, Japanese rest. – 🖾 🖾 ⓞ 𝘝𝘐𝘚𝘈
 closed Saturday and Sunday – **M** a la carte 4.60/9.20. PT **e**

X **Mandarin,** 7 Basinghall St., EC2 7XX, 🕾 600 0921, Chinese rest. – 🖾 🖾 ⓞ 𝘝𝘐𝘚𝘈 QT **u**
 closed Saturday, Sunday, 25-26 December and 1 January – **M** a la carte 4.90/6.40 **t.**

CROYDON pp. 10 and 11.

🖪₈ Woodcote Park 🕾 660 0176, 2 m. from Purley.

Croydon – ✉ Surrey.

🖪₈,🖪₈ Featherbed Lane 🕾 657 0281, E : 3 m. – 🖪₈ Coulsdon 🕾 660 0468, S : 5 m.

🖪 Katherine St. 🕾 688 3627 ext 45/46.

🏨 **Aerodrome** (Anchor), Purley Way, CR9 4LT, 🕾 688 5185, Telex 893814, 🚗 – 📺 🛏wc ☜
 🅿. 🛦. 🖾 🖾 ⓞ 𝘝𝘐𝘚𝘈
  EZ **e**
 M 5.00 **st.** ⏶ 2.00 – **80 rm** ⋤ 28.50/35.00 **st.**

↑ **Briarley,** 8-10 Outram Rd, CR0 6XE, 🕾 654 1000, 🚗 – 📺 🛏wc ☜ 🅿. 🖾 🖾 𝘝𝘐𝘚𝘈
 19 rm ⋤ 18.00/28.00 **st.** FZ **r**

XX Hook, Line and Sinker, 3 George St., CR10 1LA, 🕾 688 8604, Seafood FZ **i**

Sanderstead – ✉ Surrey.

🏨 **Selsdon Park,** Addington Rd, CR2 8YA, 🕾 657 8811, Telex 945003, ≼, 🏊 heated, 🖪₈, 🚗,
 park, ≶ – 🛊 📺 ⟜ 🅿. 🛦. 🖾 🖾 ⓞ 𝘝𝘐𝘚𝘈
  FZ **n**
 M 8.75/9.75 **st.** – **160 rm** ⋤ 45.00/75.00 **st.**

X **Elio,** 17 Limpsfield Rd, CR2 9LA, 🕾 657 2953, Italian rest. – 🖾 ⓞ 𝘝𝘐𝘚𝘈 FZ **a**
 closed Sunday, 2 weeks August and Bank Holidays – **M** a la carte 6.40/9.70 **t.** ⏶ 2.20.

South Croydon – ✉ Surrey.

X Trattoria Bella Venezia, 248 Brighton Rd, CR2 6AH, 🕾 686 2680, Italian rest. FZ **u**

EALING pp. 4 and 5.

Ealing – ✉ W5.

🖪₈ Church Rd, Hanwell 🕾 567 4230.

🏨 **Carnarvon,** Ealing Common, W5 3HN, 🕾 992 5399, Telex 935114 – 🛊 📺 🛏wc ☜ 🅿. 🛦.
 🖾 🖾 ⓞ 𝘝𝘐𝘚𝘈
  CX **v**
 M a la carte 3.80/8.90 **st.** ⏶ 2.70 – **150 rm** ⋤ 32.50/42.50 **st.**

🏨 **Kenton House,** 5 Hillcrest Rd, Hanger Hill, W5 2JL, 🕾 997 8436, Telex 8812544 – 📺 🛏wc
 🛀wc ☜ 🅿. 🖾 🖾 ⓞ 𝘝𝘐𝘚𝘈
  CX **x**
 M (bar lunch) a la carte 5.60/8.20 **st.** – **51 rm** ⋤ 29.75/36.00 **st.**

XX **Gino's,** 4 The Mall, W5 2PJ, 🕾 567 3681, Italian rest. – 🖾 🖾 ⓞ 𝘝𝘐𝘚𝘈 CX **z**
 closed Sunday and Bank Holidays – **M** a la carte 5.15/13.05 **t.**

XX **Maxim,** 153-155 Northfield Av., W13 9QU, 🕾 567 1719, Chinese rest. – 🖾 🖾 ⓞ BX **a**
 closed Sunday lunch and 25-26 December – **M** a la carte 5.80/8.50 **t.** ⏶ 2.00.

Hanwell – ✉ W7.

X **Happiness Garden,** 22 Boston Par., Boston Rd, W7 2DG, 🕾 567 9314, Chinese rest. – 🖾 🖾
 ⓞ 𝘝𝘐𝘚𝘈
  BX **c**
 closed Sunday – **M** a la carte 5.50/13.00 **t.** ⏶ 1.80.

ENFIELD pp. 6 and 7.

Enfield – ⊠ Middx.

🛅 Enfield Municipal GC., Whitewebbs Park ℐ 363 4458, N : 1 m.

🏛 **Royal Chace,** 162 The Ridgeway, EN2 3AR, ℐ 366 6500, Telex 266628, ≤, ⊐ heated, 🖛 –
📺 ஃ 🅿. ஃ. ⊠ 쯔 ⓪ ⅥⓈⒶ   EU **a**
M a la carte 10.60/16.55 **t.** ▯ 3.00 – ⊊ 3.00 – **92 rm** 24.00/34.50 **t.**

🏠 **Holtwhites,** 92 Chase Side, EN2 0QN, ℐ 363 0124, Telex 299670 – 📺 ⇔wc 🕾 🅿. ⊠ 쯔
⓪ ⅥⓈⒶ   FU **c**
M *(closed Friday, Saturday and Sunday)* (bar lunch) 6.00 **t.** ▯ 2.50 – **28 rm** ⊊ 18.75/32.50 **t.**

XXX **Norfolk,** 80 London Rd, EN2 6AP, ℐ 363 0979 – ⊠ 쯔 ⓪ ⅥⓈⒶ   FU **e**
closed Saturday lunch, Monday dinner, Sunday and Bank Holidays – **M** a la carte 8.00/12.25 **t.**
▯ 2.80.

Hadley Wood – ⊠ Herts.

🏛 **West Lodge Park** ⑤, off Cockfosters Rd, ⊠ Barnet, EN4 0PY, ℐ 440 8311, ≤, 🖛, park –
▮ 📺 🅿. ஃ. ⊠ 쯔 ⓪ ⅥⓈⒶ   EU **i**
M a la carte 5.95/10.75 **st.** – **53 rm** ⊊ 30.00/45.00 **st.**

MICHELIN Branch, Eley's Estate, Angel Rd, N18 3DQ, ℐ 803 7341/2/3/4

GREENWICH pp. 10 and 11.

Greenwich – ⊠ SE10.

🛈 Cutty Sark Gardens, near Greenwich Pier, SE10, ℐ 858 6376 (summer only).

X Le Papillon, 57 Greenwich Church St., SE10 9BL, ℐ 858 2668   FX **r**
X **Meantime,** 47-49 Greenwich Church St., SE10 9BL, ℐ 858 8705 – ⊠ 쯔 ⓪ ⅥⓈⒶ   FX **r**
closed Saturday lunch and Sunday dinner – **M** a la carte 8.05/10.60 **t.** ▯ 2.30.

HAMMERSMITH Except where otherwise stated see pp. 17-20.

Fulham – ⊠ SW6.

XX **Barbarella,** 428 Fulham Rd, SW6 1DU, ℐ 385 9434, Italian rest., Dancing – ⊠ 쯔 ⓪ ⅥⓈⒶ
closed Sunday and Bank Holidays – **M** (dinner only) a la carte 6.95/8.75 ▯ 1.75.   HZ **x**
XX La Clessidra, 175 New King's Rd, SW6, ℐ 731 6404, Italian rest.   pp. 8 and 9   DY **v**
X **Trencherman Bistro,** 271 New King's Rd, SW6 4RD, ℐ 736 4988, Bistro – ⊠ 쯔 ⓪ ⅥⓈⒶ
closed Saturday lunch, Sunday and August – **M** a la carte 6.70/10.80 **t.** ▯ 1.95.
                                                                    pp. 8 and 9   DY **u**
X **Carlo's Place,** 855 Fulham Rd, SW6 5HJ, ℐ 736 4507, Bistro – 쯔 ⓪ ⅥⓈⒶ
closed Saturday lunch, Sunday, 24 to 30 December – **M** a la carte 9.50/11.00 **st.** ▯ 2.25.
                                                                    pp. 8 and 9   DY **s**

Hammersmith – ⊠ W6/W12/W14.

XX Aziz, 116 King St., W6, ℐ 748 1826, Indian rest.   pp. 8 and 9   CX **a**
X **Rajdoot,** 291 King St., W6 9HY, ℐ 748 7345, Indian rest. – ⊠ 쯔 ⓪ ⅥⓈⒶ pp. 8 and 9   CX **c**
M a la carte 5.35 **t.** ▯ 2.50.

Shepherd's Bush – ⊠ W 12.

XX Shireen, 270 Uxbridge Rd, W12 8NR, ℐ 749 5927, Indian rest.   CX **n**

West Kensington – ⊠ SW6/W14.

🏨 **West Centre** (Crest), Lillie Rd, SW6 1UQ, ℐ 385 1255, Telex 917728 – ▮ 📺 ⇔wc 🕾 🅿.
ஃ. ⊠ 쯔 ⓪ ⅥⓈⒶ   HZ **e**
M 3.50 **s.** ▯ 2.50 – ⊊ 3.60 – **497 rm** 19.00/37.50 **st.**
🏠 **Lily,** 23-33 Lillie Rd, SW6 1UG, ℐ 381 1881, Telex 918922 – ▮ 📺 ⇔wc 🕾 🅿. ⊠ 쯔 ⓪ ⅥⓈⒶ
M (dinner only) 7.50 **s.** ▯ 1.75 – **99 rm** ⊊ 15.00/23.00 **s.**   HZ **o**

HARINGEY pp. 6 and 7.

Highgate – ⊠ N6.

XX **San Carlo,** 2 High St., N6 5JL, ℐ 340 5823, Italian rest. – ⊠ 쯔 ⓪ ⅥⓈⒶ   EV **v**
closed Monday and Bank Holidays – **M** a la carte 6.35/11.15 **t.**

HARROW pp. 4 and 5.

Central Harrow – ⊠ Middx.

🏠 **Cumberland,** 1 St. John's Rd, HA1 2EF, ℐ 863 4111 – 📺 ⇔wc 🎜wc 🕾 🅿. ⊠ 쯔   BV **x**
M 5.00/5.95 **t.** ▯ 1.90 – **66 rm** ⊊ 20.70/34.05 **t.**
XX **Old Etonian,** 38 High St., Harrow Hill, HA1 3LL, ℐ 422 8482, French rest. – ⊠ 쯔 ⓪ ⅥⓈⒶ
closed Saturday lunch, Sunday and Bank Holidays – **M** a la carte 6.75/9.05 **t.** ▯ 2.20.   BV **z**

Hatch End – ⊠ Middx.

XX **Canaletto 2,** 302 Uxbridge Rd, HA5 4HR, ☎ 428 4232, Italian rest. – 🔄 AE ⓪ VISA   BU **a**
   closed Saturday lunch, Sunday and Bank Holidays – **M** a la carte 7.95/11.55 t. ⓖ 2.85.

Pinner – ⊠ Middx.

X **La Giralda,** 66-68 Pinner Green, HA5 2AB, ☎ 868 3429 – 🔄 AE ⓪ VISA   AUV **n**
   closed Christmas Day – **M** 6.60/10.10 t. ⓖ 1.60.

HAVERING pp. 6 and 7.

Hornchurch – by A 12 – HU – on A 127 – ✪ 040 23 Ingrebourne.

🏨 **Ladbroke Mercury,** Southend Arterial Rd (A 127), RM11 3UJ, ☎ 46789, Telex 897315 – TV
   ⇔wc ☎ ⓖ ⓟ. 🅰. 🔄 AE ⓪ VISA
   M 6.00/8.00 st. ⓖ 3.00 – � 3.75 – **140 rm** 28.75/36.80 t.

HILLINGDON pp. 4 and 8.

Eastcote – ⊠ Middx.

X **Sambuca,** 113 Field End Rd, HA5 1QG, ☎ 866 7500, Italian rest. – 🔄 AE ⓪ VISA   AV **s**
   closed Sunday – **M** (dinner only) 4.90/6.75 t. ⓖ 1.70.

Heathrow Airport – ⊠ Middx.
🛈 Heathrow Central Station, London Airport ☎ 730 0791.

🏨🏨 **Sheraton Skyline,** Bath Rd, Harlington, Hayes, UB3 5BP, ☎ 759 2535, Telex 934254, « Exotic
   indoor garden with 🔲 » – 🛗 TV ☎ ⓖ ⓟ. 🅰. 🔄 AE ⓪ VISA   AY **u**
   M 7.00 st. – ⇌ 4.45 – **353 rm** 42.00/59.00 s. – P 46.00/67.50 st.

🏨 **Excelsior** (T.H.F.), Bath Rd, West Drayton, UB7 0DU, ☎ 759 6611, Telex 24525, 🔲 heated –
   🛗 TV ☎ ⓖ ⓟ. 🅰. 🔄 AE ⓪ VISA   AY **x**
   M 7.50 st. ⓖ 2.35 – ⇌ 4.50 – **662 rm** 40.50/50.50 st.

🏨 **Heathrow Penta,** Bath Rd, Hounslow, TW6 2AQ, ☎ 897 6363, Telex 934660, <, 🔲 – 🛗 TV
   ⓖ ⓟ. 🅰. 🔄 AE ⓪ VISA   AY **z**
   M 7.85/8.50 st. – ⇌ 4.10 – **670 rm** 46.00/55.20 st.

🏨 **Holiday Inn,** Stockley Rd, West Drayton, UB7 9NA, ☎ 089 54 (West Drayton) 45555, Telex
   934518, 🔲, 🔄, 💥 – 🛗 TV ☎ ⓖ ⓟ. 🅰. 🔄 AE ⓪ VISA   AX **v**
   M 6.95 st. – **401 rm** ⇌ 43.75/62.15 t.

🏨 **Sheraton Heathrow,** Colnbrook by-pass, West Drayton, UB7 0HJ, ☎ 759 2424, Telex
   934331, 🔲 – 🛗 TV ☎ ⓖ ⓟ. 🅰. 🔄 AE ⓪ VISA   AXY **a**
   M 4.70/6.80 st. – ⇌ 3.30 – **440 rm** 32.50/45.00 s. – P 37.40/45.50 s.

🏨 **Skyway** (T.H.F.), 140 Bath Rd, Hayes, UB3 5AW, ☎ 759 6311, Telex 23935, 🔲 heated – 🛗 TV
   ☎ ⓖ ⓟ. 🅰. 🔄 AE ⓪ VISA   AY **e**
   M 6.50 st. ⓖ 2.10 – ⇌ 4.50 – **440 rm** 32.50/42.00 st.

🏨 **Post House** (T.H.F.), Sipson Rd, West Drayton, UB7 0JU, ☎ 759 2323, Telex 934280 – 🛗 TV
   ⓖ ⓟ. 🔄 AE ⓪ VISA   AX **c**
   M a la carte 9.80/14.50 st. ⓖ 2.10 – ⇌ 4.35 – **594 rm** 32.50/40.50 st.

🏨 **Ariel** (T.H.F.), Harlington Corner, Bath Rd, Hayes, UB3 5AJ, ☎ 759 2552, Telex 21777 – 🛗 TV
   ⇔wc ☎ ⓖ ⓟ. 🅰. 🔄 AE ⓪ VISA   AY **l**
   M 9.50/12.00 st. ⓖ 2.25 – ⇌ 4.50 – **178 rm** 33.00/44.00 st.

🏨 **Arlington** (Norfolk Cap.), Shepiston Lane, Hayes, UB3 1LP, ☎ 573 6162, Group Telex 23241 –
   TV ⇔wc 🔥wc ☎ ⓟ. 🅰. 🔄 AE ⓪ VISA   AX **n**
   78 rm.

Hillingdon – ⊠ Middx. – ✪ Uxbridge.
🛈 Civic Centre, Uxbridge ☎ 50600.

🏨 **Master Brewer Motel,** Western Av., Hillingdon Circus, UB10 9BR, ☎ 51199 – TV ⇔wc ☎
   ⓟ. 🅰. 🔄 AE ⓪ VISA   AV **a**
   M 4.50 t. ⓖ 2.00 – ⇌ 2.50 – **64 rm** 28.00/33.00 st.

Northwood – ⊠ Middx. – ✪ Northwood.

XX **Martini,** 27 Green Lane, ☎ 27052, Italian rest. – 🔄 AE ⓪ VISA   AU **e**
   closed Sunday – **M** a la carte 6.25/10.45 t. ⓖ 3.10.

Ruislip – ⊠ Middx. – ✪ Ruislip.
🏌 Ickenham Rd ☎ 32004.

🏠 **Barn,** West End Rd, HA4 6JD, ☎ 36057, Telex 892514, 🌿 – TV ⇔wc ⓟ   AV **u**
   closed 1 week at Christmas and New Year – **M** *(closed Saturday)* (bar lunch) 6.00 ⓖ 2.50 –
   57 rm ⇌ 20.90/35.50 st.

Benachrichtigen Sie sofort das Hotel,
wenn Sie ein bestelltes Zimmer nicht belegen können.

HOUNSLOW pp. 8 and 9.

Ⓡ₈ Wyke Green, Syon Lane, Isleworth, ℡ 560 8777, ½ m. from Gillettes Corner (A 4).

Cranford – ✉ Middx.

🏨 **Berkeley Arms (Embassy)**, Bath Rd, TW5 9QE, ℡ 897 2121, Telex 935728, 🚗 – 🕮 📺 ⌁wc
@ Ⓟ. 🎿. 🝙 ⒜ ⓪ 𝘝𝘐𝘚𝘈   AY r
M 5.65/7.15 **st.** ⌑ 2.20 – **42 rm**.

Hounslow – ✉ Middx.

🏨 **Master Robert Motel**, 366 Great West Rd, TW5 0BD, ℡ 570 6261, 🚗 – 📺 ⌁wc 🝙wc @
Ⓟ. 🎿. 🝙 ⒜ ⓪ 𝘝𝘐𝘚𝘈   BY s
M (closed Saturday lunch, Sunday and Bank Holidays) 5.50 **t.** ⌑ 2.00 – ☲ 2.50 – **63 rm**
28.00/33.00 **st.**

ISLINGTON pp. 13-16.

Canonbury – ✉ N 1.

✗ **Anna's Place**, 90 Mildmay Park, N1, ℡ 249 9379   pp. 6 and 7 FV a
closed Sunday, Monday, 3 weeks at Easter, August and 3 weeks at Christmas – **M** (booking essential) (dinner only) a la carte 9.15/11.65 **t.**

Finsbury – ✉ WC1/EC1.

🏨 **Royal Scot (Thistle)**, 100 King's Cross Rd, WC1X 9DT, ℡ 278 2434, Telex 27657 – 🕮 📺 ⌁wc
@ Ⓟ. 🎿.   NS n
☲ 3.95 – **349 rm** 29.00/39.00 **t.**

🏨 **London Ryan**, Gwynne Pl., King Cross Rd, WC1X 9QN, ℡ 278 2480, Telex 27728 – 🕮 📺
⌁wc @ Ⓟ. 🝙 ⒜ ⓪ 𝘝𝘐𝘚𝘈   NS a
M (buffet lunch) 3.75/6.00 **st.** ⌑ 2.00 – ☲ 2.00 – **213 rm** 26.00/36.00 **st.**

Islington – ✉ N1.

✗✗ ❀ **Carrier's**, 2 Camden Passage, N1 8ED, ℡ 226 5353 – ⒜ ⓪   PR e
closed Sunday, Easter Saturday and Bank Holidays – **M** 14.25/16.50
Spec. Brandade of smoked trout, Calf's liver with avocado, Soufflés glacés.

✗✗ **Frederick's**, Camden Passage, N1 8EG, ℡ 359 2888, « Conservatory and walled garden » –
🝙 ⒜ 𝘝𝘐𝘚𝘈   PR a
closed Sunday, Christmas Day and New Years Day – **M** a la carte 8.55/13.80 **t.** ⌑ 2.30.

✗✗ **Ristorante Portofino**, 39 Camden Passage, N1 8EA, ℡ 226 0884, Italian rest. – 🝙 ⒜ ⓪
𝘝𝘐𝘚𝘈   PR o
closed Sunday, Easter, Christmas and Bank Holidays – **M** a la carte 6.10/10.80 **t.**

✗✗ **Julius's**, 39 Upper St., N1 0PN, ℡ 226 4380 – 🝙 ⒜ ⓪ 𝘝𝘐𝘚𝘈   PR i
closed Saturday lunch, Sunday, August and Bank Holidays – **M** a la carte 7.85/9.65 **t.** ⌑ 1.75.

✗ **Four Seasons**, 69 Barnsbury St., N1 1EJ, ℡ 607 0857, French rest. – 🝙 𝘝𝘐𝘚𝘈   NR a
closed lunch Saturday and Bank Holidays and Sunday – **M** a la carte 12.80/14.55 **t.** ⌑ 2.40.

✗ **M'sieur Frog**, 31a Essex Rd, N1 2SE, ℡ 226 3495, Bistro   PR n
closed Sunday, Easter Monday, 3 weeks August and 1 week at Christmas – **M** (dinner only) a la carte 8.60/10.50 **t.** ⌑ 1.95.

Groß-London (GREATER LONDON) besteht aus der City und 32 Verwaltungsbezirken (Borough) : diese sind wiederum in kleinere Bezirke (Area) unterteilt, deren Mittelpunkt ehemalige Dörfer oder Stadtviertel sind, die oft ihren eigenen Charakter bewahrt haben.

KENSINGTON and CHELSEA (Royal Borough of).

Chelsea – ✉ SW1/SW3/SW10 – Except where otherwise stated see pp. 28 and 29.

🏨🏨 **Carlton Tower**, 2 Cadogan Pl., SW1X 9PY, ℡ 235 5411, ≼, 🚗, ✗ – 🕮 📺 ☎ & Ⓟ. 🎿. 🝙
⒜ ⓪ 𝘝𝘐𝘚𝘈   FR n
M (see **Chelsea Room** below) – **Rib Room** a la carte 13.70/18.70 **st.** ⌑ 3.40 – ☲ 5.80 – **236 rm**
50.00/90.00 **st.**

🏨🏨 **Sheraton Park Tower**, 101 Knightsbridge, SW1X 7RN, ℡ 235 8050, Telex 917222 – 🕮 📺
☎ & Ⓟ. 🎿. 🝙 ⒜ ⓪ 𝘝𝘐𝘚𝘈   FQ v
M 13.00/17.00 **st.** – ☲ 6.50 – **295 rm** 72.00/80.00 **s.**

🏨🏨 ❀ **Capital**, 22-24 Basil St., SW3 1AT, ℡ 589 5171, Telex 919042 – 🕮 📺 ☎. 🝙 ⒜ ⓪ 𝘝𝘐𝘚𝘈
M a la carte 12.00/17.50 – ☲ 4.00 – **60 rm** 45.00/65.00   ER a
Spec. Coeur d'artichaut farci à la Nissarda, Carré d'agneau persillé aux herbes de Provence, Sorbet à la fine Champagne.

🏨🏨 **Holiday Inn**, 17-25 Sloane St., SW1X 9NU, ℡ 235 4377, Telex 919111, 🏊 – 🕮 📺 ☎. 🎿. 🝙
⒜ ⓪ 𝘝𝘐𝘚𝘈   FR r
M 8.50/10.50 **st.** – ☲ 4.25 – **217 rm** 59.00/79.00 **st.**

🏨 **London Belgravia,** 20 Chesham Pl., SW1X 8HQ, ℡ 235 6040, Telex 919020 – 🕸 📺 ☎. 🔄 🅰🅴
⓿ 𝑽𝑰𝑺𝑨   FR a
M a la carte 6.80/8.30 **st.** 🍷 2.50 – 🖵 4.50 – **110 rm** 50.60/69.00 **st.**

🏨 **Basil Street,** 8 Basil St., SW3 1AH, ℡ 581 3311, Telex 28379 – 🕸. 🦺. 🔄 🅰🅴 ⓿ 𝑽𝑰𝑺𝑨   FQ o
M a la carte 7.50/10.75 **st.** 🍷 2.80 – 🖵 4.00 – **103 rm** 28.00/58.00 **st.**

🏨 **Cadogan** (Thistle), 75 Sloane St., SW1X 9SG, ℡ 235 7141, Telex 267893 – 🕸 📺 ☎. 🔄 🅰🅴 ⓿
𝑽𝑰𝑺𝑨   FR e
🖵 4.25 – **69 rm** 45.00/52.00 **t.**

🏨 **Wilbraham,** 1-5 Wilbraham Pl., Sloane St., SW1X 9AE, ℡ 730 8296 – 🕸 🛁wc ☎   FS n
M (closed, Saturday lunch, Sunday and Bank Holidays) 11 00 **t.** 🍷 2.00 – 🖵 2.10 – **50 rm**
17.00/30.00.

🏠 **Fenja** without rest., 69 Cadogan Gdns, SW3 2RB, ℡ 589 1183 – 🕸 🛁wc ☎. 🔄 🅰🅴 ⓿ 𝑽𝑰𝑺𝑨
16 rm 🖵 19.00/45.00 **st.**   FS r

🏠 **Park House** without rest., 47 Egerton Gdns, SW3 2DD, ℡ 589 0715 – 🕸 📺 🛁wc ☎. 🅰🅴
16 rm 10.00/36.00 **st.**   DS i

🏠 **Willett** without rest., 32 Sloane Gdns, Sloane St., SW1W 8DJ, ℡ 730 0634 – 📺 🛁wc
17 rm 🖵 19.00/20.50 **st.**   FT s

XXXX ❀ **Chelsea Room** (at Carlton Tower H.), 2 Cadogan Pl., SW1X 9PY, ℡ 235 5411 – 🄿. 🔄 🅰🅴
⓿ 𝑽𝑰𝑺𝑨   FR n
M a la carte 16.45/22.60 **st.** 🍷 3.70
Spec. Salade de saison aux crustacés, Fricassée de turbot et homard aux concombres, Filet d'agneau au basilic et
tomate.

XXXX ❀ **Waltons,** 121 Walton St., SW3 2HP, ℡ 584 0204 – 🔄 🅰🅴 ⓿ 𝑽𝑰𝑺𝑨   DS a
closed Christmas and Bank Holidays – **M** 15.50/21.00 🍷 2.50
Spec. Tournedos Waltons style, Paupiette of sole, Calves liver and avocado.

XXX ❀❀ **La Tante Claire,** 68 Royal Hospital Rd, SW3 2HP, ℡ 352 6045, French rest. – 🅰🅴   EU ∩
closed Saturday, Sunday, 2 weeks at Easter, 3 weeks August, 2 weeks at Christmas and New
Year and Bank Holidays – **M** a la carte 14.80/22.10 **st.**
Spec. Terrine de poireaux, vinaigrette truffée (spring/summer), Andouillette de la mer au vinaigre de cassis, Pied
de cochon farci aux morilles et ris de veau.

XXX **Le Français,** 257-259 Fulham Rd, SW3 6HY, ℡ 352 4748, French rest. – 🅰🅴 𝑽𝑰𝑺𝑨   CU a
closed Sunday – **M** 7.50/10.00 **s.**

XX **Gavvers,** 61-63 Lower Sloane St., SW1W 8DH, ℡ 730 5983, French rest. – 🔄 🅰🅴 ⓿ 𝑽𝑰𝑺𝑨
closed Sunday, 30 August-10 September, 24 December-8 January and Bank Holidays –   FT e
M (dinner only) 12.75 **st.**

XX **Bewick's,** 87-89 Walton St., SW3 2HP, ℡ 584 6711 – 🔄 🅰🅴 𝑽𝑰𝑺𝑨   ES n
closed Saturday lunch, Sunday, Easter, 30 August and Christmas – **M** a la carte 12 15/17.00 **t.**
🍷 2.75.

XX **Daphne's,** 112 Draycott Av., SW3 3AE, ℡ 589 4257 – 🔄 🅰🅴 ⓿ 𝑽𝑰𝑺𝑨   DS e
closed Sunday and Bank Holidays – **M** (dinner only) a la carte 8.70/12.50 **t.** 🍷 3.00.

XX ❀ **Ma Cuisine,** 113 Walton St., SW3 2JY, ℡ 584 7585, French rest. – 🅰🅴   DS a
closed Saturday, Sunday, 1 week at Easter, 1 week at Christmas, 15 July-15 August and Bank
Holidays – **M** a la carte 11.40/13.55 **t.** 🍷 4.25
Spec. Terrine de volaille aux algues, Noisette d'agneau pastourelle, Mousse brûlée.

XX **English House,** 3 Milner St., SW3 2QA, ℡ 584 3002, English rest. – 🔄 🅰🅴 ⓿ 𝑽𝑰𝑺𝑨   ES z
closed Sunday and Bank Holidays – **M** a la carte 11.50/17.25 **st.** 🍷 2.50.

XX **Bagatelle,** 5 Langton St., SW10 0JL, ℡ 351 4185, French rest. – 🔄 🅰🅴 ⓿ 𝑽𝑰𝑺𝑨
closed Sunday and Bank Holidays – **M** a la carte 9.25/13.00 **t.** 🍷 2.40.   pp. 17-20   JZ u

XX **Parke's,** 4-5 Beauchamp Pl., SW3 1NG, ℡ 589 1390 – 🔄 🅰🅴 ⓿ 𝑽𝑰𝑺𝑨   ER n
closed Saturday lunch, Sunday, Easter and Christmas – **M** 9.00/20.00 **t.** 🍷 1.60.

XX **Poissonnerie de l'Avenue,** 82 Sloane Av., SW3 3DZ, ℡ 589 2457, Seafood – 🔄 🅰🅴 ⓿ 𝑽𝑰𝑺𝑨
closed Sunday and Bank Holidays – **M** a la carte 7.40/13.20 **t.** 🍷 2.50.   DS u

XX **Wheeler's George and Dragon,** 256 Brompton Rd, SW3 2AS, ℡ 584 2626, Seafood – 🔄
🅰🅴 𝑽𝑰𝑺𝑨   DS n
closed Sunday, 25-26 December and Bank Holidays – **M** a la carte 10.30/17.30 **t.** 🍷 2.00.

XX Le Suquet, 104 Draycott Av., SW3 3AE, ℡ 581 1785, French rest., Seafood   DS c

XX **Tandoori,** 153 Fulham Rd, SW3 6SN, ℡ 589 7749, Indian and Pakistani rest. – 🔄 🅰🅴 ⓿ 𝑽𝑰𝑺𝑨
closed 25 to 26 December – **M** (dinner only and Sunday lunch) a la carte 7.60/9.90 **t.** 🍷 2.20.
    DT o

XX **Beccofino,** 100 Draycott Av., SW3 3BT, ℡ 584 3600, Italian rest. – 🔄 🅰🅴 𝑽𝑰𝑺𝑨   ES r
closed Sunday – **M** a la carte 8.00/10.20 **t.** 🍷 2.20.

XX **Eleven Park Walk,** 11 Park Walk, SW10, ℡ 352 3449, Italian rest. – 🅰🅴   CU r
closed Sunday and Bank Holidays – **M** a la carte 7.50/11 00 **t.** 🍷 2.00.

XX **Meridiana,** 169 Fulham Rd, SW3 6SP, ℡ 589 8815, Italian rest. – 🔄 🅰🅴 ⓿ 𝑽𝑰𝑺𝑨   DT i
closed Easter, 25-26 December and Bank Holidays – **M** a la carte 10.50/16.20 **t.** 🍷 2.00.

XX **Brasserie St. Quentin,** 243 Brompton Rd, SW3 2EP, ℡ 589 8005, French rest. – 🔄 🅰🅴 ⓿
𝑽𝑰𝑺𝑨   DR a
M a la carte 8.60/14.80 **t.** 🍷 2.95.

P.T.O. →

XX **San Ruffillo,** 8 Harriet St., SW1, ☏ 235 3969, Italian rest. – 🖹 ΛΕ ⓞ *VISA*   FQ **z**
   closed Sunday and Bank Holidays – **M** a la carte 6.85/8.65 **t.** ⓘ 1.90.

XX **Good Earth,** 91 King's Rd, SW3, ☏ 352 9231, Chinese rest. – 🖹 ΛΕ ⓞ *VISA*   EU **a**
   M a la carte 7.45/8.70 **t.** ⓘ 1.95.

XX **Sale e Pepe,** 13-15 Pavilion Rd, SW1, ☏ 235 0098, Italian rest.   FQ **x**

XX **Don Luigi,** 33c King's Rd, SW3 4LX, ☏ 730 3023, Italian rest. – 🖹 ΛΕ ⓞ *VISA*
   M a la carte 5.95/10.05 **t.**   ET **r**

XX **San Frediano,** 62-64 Fulham Rd, SW3 6HH, ☏ 584 8375, Italian rest. – 🖹 ΛΕ ⓞ *VISA*   DT **n**
   closed Sunday and Bank Holidays – **M** a la carte 6.90/8.90 **st.** ⓘ 2.00.

X **Dan's,** 119 Sydney St., SW3 6NR, ☏ 352 2718 – ΛΕ *VISA*   DU **s**
   closed Saturday lunch and Sunday – **M** a la carte 10.85/16.85 **t.** ⓘ 2.25.

X **La Brasserie,** 272 Brompton Rd, SW3 2AW, ☏ 584 1668, French rest. – ΛΕ ⓞ *VISA*   DS **s**
   M a la carte 5.40/10.35 **t.** ⓘ 2.15.

Earl's Court – ✉ SW5/SW10 – Except where otherwise stated see pp. 28 and 29.

🏨 **Barkston** (T.H.F.), Barkston Gdns, SW5 0ER, ☏ 373 7851 – 🛗 📺 ➟wc 🚿wc ☎. 🅰. 🖹 ΛΕ
   ⓞ *VISA*   AT **c**
   M 4.00 **st.** ⓘ 2.50 – ☷ 3.95 – **72 rm** 28.50/35.00 **st.**

🏨 **Hogarth,** 27-35 Hogarth Rd, SW5 0QQ, ☏ 370 6831 – 🛗 📺 ➟wc 🚿wc ☎ 🅿. 🖹 ΛΕ ⓞ
   closed 4 days at Christmas – **M** (grill rest. only) a la carte approx. 6.40 **st.** ⓘ 1.50 – ☷ 2.50 –
   82 rm 20.00/26.00 **st.**   AS **a**

🏨 **Town House,** 44-48 West Cromwell Rd, SW5 9QL, ☏ 373 4546 – 📺 🚿wc ☎. 🖹 ΛΕ ⓞ *VISA*
   M 6.90 **st.** – ☷ 2.30 – **46 rm** 16.90/29.90 **st.** – P 33.05 **st.**   pp. 17-20 HY **o**

🏨 **Kensington Court** (Ladbroke) without rest., 33-35 Nevern Pl., SW5 9NP, ☏ 370 5151, Telex
   8814451 – 🛗 📺 ➟wc ☎. 🖹 ΛΕ ⓞ *VISA*   pp. 17-20 HY **n**
   ☷ 3.75 – **35 rm** 28.00/36.00 **st.**

🏨 Manor Court, 33-35 Courtfield Gdns, SW5, ☏ 373 8585, Telex 885230 – 🛗 📺 ➟wc ☎
   88 rm.   AS **e**

🏠 **Terstan,** 29-31 Nevern Sq., SW5 9PE, ☏ 373 5368 – 🛗 ➟wc ☎. 🖹 *VISA*   pp. 17-20 HY **v**
   56 rm ☷ 10.50/21.00 **st.**

XX ⊛ **Tiger Lee,** 251 Old Brompton Rd, SW5 9HP, ☏ 370 2323, Chinese rest. – ΛΕ ⓞ *VISA*   AU **n**
   M (dinner only) a la carte 11.00/25.50 **t.**
   Spec. Lobster Emperor, Chicken in spicy nut sauce, Sharks fin treasure.

XX La Croisette, 168 Ifield Rd, SW10 9AF, ☏ 373 3694, French rest., Seafood   AU **a**

XX **Pontevecchio,** 254-258 Old Brompton Rd, SW5 9HP, ☏ 373 9082, Italian rest. – 🖹 ΛΕ ⓞ
   VISA   AU **i**
   closed Bank Holidays – **M** a la carte 6.20/8.50 **t.** ⓘ 1.80.

XX **Brinkley's,** 47 Hollywood Rd, SW10 9HY, ☏ 351 1683 – 🖹 ΛΕ ⓞ *VISA*   BU **n**
   closed Sunday and Bank Holidays – **M** (dinner only) a la carte 10.00/12.70 **t.**

X **Crystal Palace,** 10 Hogarth Pl., Hogarth Rd, SW5, ☏ 373 0754, Chinese rest. – 🖹 ΛΕ ⓞ
   VISA   pp. 17-20 HY **r**
   M a la carte 8.00/10.50 **t.**

X **Naraine,** 10 Kenway Rd, SW5 0RR, ☏ 370 3853, Indian rest. – 🖹 ⓞ *VISA*   pp. 17-20 HY **i**
   M a la carte 5.90/7.00 **t.** ⓘ 1.95.

Kensington – ✉ SW7/W8/W11/W14 – Except where otherwise stated see pp. 17-20.

🏨🏨 **Royal Garden** (Rank), Kensington High St., W8 4PT, ☏ 937 8000, Telex 263151, ≼ – 🛗 📺 ☎
   🅿. 🅰. 🖹 ΛΕ ⓞ *VISA*   pp. 28 and 29 AQ **c**
   M 9.50/13.50 **st.** ⓘ 3.25 – **Royal Roof** *(closed Sunday and Bank Holidays)* (Dancing) (dinner
   only) a la carte 19.75/24.75 **st.** – ☷ 4.75 – **434 rm** 42.50/71.00 **st.**

🏨🏨 Kensington Palace (Thistle), De Vere Gdns, W8 5AF, ☏ 937 8121, Telex 262422 – 🛗 📺 ☎.
   🅰. 🖹 ΛΕ ⓞ *VISA*   pp. 28 and 29 BQ **a**
   ☷ 4.25 – **315 rm** 38.50/49.00 **t.**

🏨🏨 **Tara,** Scarsdale Pl., W8 5SR, ☏ 937 7211, Telex 918834 – 🛗 📺 ☎ ♿ 🅿. 🅰. 🖹 ΛΕ ⓞ *VISA*
   M 4.95 **st.** – ☷ 3.80 – **843 rm** 35.00/45.00 **t.**   HX **u**

🏨🏨 Hilton International, 179-199 Holland Park Av., W11 4UL, ☏ 603 3355, Telex 919763 – 🛗 📺 ☎
   ♿ 🅿. 🅰   GV **s**
   611 rm.

🏨🏨 **Kensington Close** (T.H.F.), Wrights Lane, W8 5SP, ☏ 937 8170, Telex 23914, 🌂 – 🛗 📺.
   🅰. 🖹 ΛΕ ⓞ *VISA*   HX **c**
   M 4.80/9.60 **st.** ⓘ 2.45 – ☷ 4.35 – **530 rm** 31.00/38.50 **st.**

🏨🏨 **De Vere** (De Vere), 60 Hyde Park Gate, W8 5AS, ☏ 584 0051, Telex 8953644 – 🛗 📺 ♿. 🅰.
   🖹 ΛΕ ⓞ *VISA*   pp. 28 and 29 BQ **s**
   M approx. 8.25 **st.** ⓘ 2.60 – ☷ 2.50 – **83 rm** 24.00/48.00 **st.**

🏠 **One-Two-Eight,** 128 Holland Rd, W14 8BD, ☏ 602 3395, 🌳 – 🛗 🚿wc ☎   GX **x**
   closed 24 December-2 January – **30 rm** ☷ 14.00/24.00 **st.**

XX **La Pomme d'Amour,** 128 Holland Park Av., W11 4UE, ☎ 229 8532, French rest. – ⏻ 🅰🅴 ⓞ 🆅🆂🅰
GV **e**
closed Saturday lunch, Sunday and Bank Holidays – **M** a la carte 7.05/10.95 **t.** ⚱ 2.00.

XX **La Toque Blanche,** 21 Abingdon Rd, W8 6AH, ☎ 937 5832, French rest. – 🅰🅴 ⓞ
HX **n**
closed Saturday, Sunday, Easter, August, Christmas and Bank Holidays – **M** a la carte
7.95/11.45 **t.**

XX Gallo d'Oro, 353 Kensington High St., W8 6NW, ☎ 603 6951, Italian rest.
GX **a**

XX **Mama San,** 11 Russell Gdns, W14, ☎ 602 0312, Chinese rest. – ⏻ 🅰🅴 ⓞ 🆅🆂🅰
GX **e**
closed Saturday lunch – **M** a la carte 11.00/15.30 **t.** ⚱ 2.40.

XX **Trattoo,** 2 Abingdon Rd, W8 6AF, ☎ 937 4448, Italian rest. – ⏻ 🅰🅴 ⓞ 🆅🆂🅰
HX **e**
M a la carte 6.45/12.85 **t.**

XX **Topo d'oro,** 39 Uxbridge St., W8, ☎ 727 5813, Italian rest. – ⏻ 🅰🅴 ⓞ 🆅🆂🅰
pp. 30 and 31 AZ **a**
M a la carte 5.35/10.05 **st.** ⚱ 1.95.

XX **Le Quai St. Pierre,** 7 Stratford Rd, W8, ☎ 937 6388, French rest., Seafood
HX **r**
closed Tuesday lunch, Monday and 21 December-4 January – **M** a la carte 10.80/10.50 **t.**

XX **Le Détour,** 5 Campden Hill Rd, W0 7AD, ☎ 937 9602, French rest. – ⏻ 🅰🅴 ⓞ 🆅🆂🅰
HX **i**
closed Bank Holidays – **M** a la carte 10.95/14.55 **t.**

XX Hiroko (at Hilton International H.), 179-199 Holland Park Av., W11, ☎ 603 5003, Japanese rest.
– ⓟ
GV **s**

XX **Gatamelata,** 343 Kensington High St., W8 6NW, ☎ 603 3613, Italian rest. – ⏻ 🅰🅴 ⓞ 🆅🆂🅰
closed Saturday lunch, Sunday and Bank Holidays – **M** a la carte 6.85/8.65 **t.** ⚱ 2.00.
GHX **s**

XX **Franco Ovest,** 3 Russell Gdns, W14 8EZ, ☎ 602 1242, Italian rest. – ⏻ 🅰🅴 ⓞ 🆅🆂🅰
GX **u**
closed Sunday – **M** a la carte 9.00/15.00 **t.** ⚱ 2.00.

XX Sailing Junk, 59 Marloes Rd, W8 6LE, ☎ 937 5833, Chinese rest.
HX **x**

X **La Paesana,** 30 Uxbridge St., W8 7TA, ☎ 229 4332, Italian rest. – 🅰🅴 ⓞ 🆅🆂🅰
closed Sunday, Good Friday, Easter Monday and 25-26 December – **M** a la carte 6.30/7.40 **t.**
⚱ 1.80.
pp. 30 and 31 AZ **i**

X **Il Barbino,** 32 Kensington Church St., W8, ☎ 937 8752, Italian rest. – ⏻ 🅰🅴 ⓞ 🆅🆂🅰
HV **o**
closed Saturday lunch, Sunday, 25-26 December, 1 January and Bank Holidays – **M** a la carte
6.70/8.70 **t.** ⚱ 1.80.

X **The Ark,** Kensington Court, 35 Kensington High St., W8 5BA, ☎ 937 4294, French rest. – ⏻
🅰🅴 ⓞ 🆅🆂🅰
pp. 28 and 29 AQ **s**
closed lunch Sunday and Bank Holidays, 4 days at Easter and 4 days at Christmas – **M** a la
carte 7.05/10.35 **t.** ⚱ 1.60.

X **La Jardinière,** 148 Holland Park Av., W11, ☎ 221 6090, French rest. – 🅰🅴
GV **z**
closed Monday – **M** (dinner only and Sunday lunch) a la carte 5.10/6.90 **t.** ⚱ 1.85

North Kensington – ✉ W2/W10/W11 – Except where otherwise stated see pp. 13-16.

🏠 **Portobello,** 22 Stanley Gdns, W11 2NG, ☎ 727 2777 – 📶 📺 ⌢wc ▥wc ☎. ⏻ 🅰🅴 ⓞ 🆅🆂🅰
closed 5 days at Christmas – **M** a la carte 5.90/8.25 **s.** – ☲ 3.00 – **25 rm** 25.50/46.00 **s.**
GU **n**

🏠 **Pembridge Court,** 34 Pembridge Gdns, W2 4DX, ☎ 229 9977, Telex 298363 – 📺 ⌢wc
▥wc ☜. ⏻ 🅰🅴 ⓞ 🆅🆂🅰
pp. 30 and 31 AZ **n**
M *(closed Sunday dinner and Bank Holidays)* (bar lunch) a la carte 6.40/10.45 **t.** ⚱ 2.10 – **35 rm**
☲ 21.50/30.50 **s.**

XXX Leith's, 92 Kensington Park Rd, W11 2PN, ☎ 229 4481 – ⏻ 🅰🅴 ⓞ 🆅🆂🅰
GU **e**
closed August, Christmas and Bank Holidays – **M** (dinner only) 18.90 **st.**

XX Chez Moi, 3 Addison Av., Holland Park, W11 4QS, ☎ 603 8267, French rest. – 🅰🅴 🆅🆂🅰
closed Sunday, last 2 weeks August, 2 weeks at Christmas and Bank Holidays – **M** (dinner
only) a la carte 8.90/13.50 **t.** ⚱ 2.40.
pp. 17-20 GV **n**

X Rama Sita, 6 Clarendon Rd, Holland Park, W11 5QS, ☎ 727 9359, Indian rest. – ⏻ 🅰🅴 ⓞ
🆅🆂🅰
pp. 17-20 GV **u**
closed Sunday, 15 to 31 August and 25-26 December – **M** a la carte 5.70/10.65 **t.** ⚱ 2.40.

In London, at any time of the year,
it is wise to book a room in advance.

A Londres, en toutes saisons,
il est prudent de réserver sa chambre à l'avance.

A Londra, in qualsiasi periodo dell'anno,
è consigliabile prenotare la camera in anticipo.

Wir empfehlen, in London zu jeder Jahreszeit
Ihr Hotelzimmer im voraus zu bestellen.

South Kensington – ⊠ SW5/SW7/W8 – pp. 28 and 29.

🏨 **Gloucester** (Rank), 4-18 Harrington Gdns, SW7 4LH, ☎ 373 6030, Telex 917505 – 🛗 TV ☎ ⚹
ⓟ. 🏛. 🔼 AE ⓞ VISA
BS **r**
M 4.50/6.00 t. ⒜ 2.50 – **550 rm**.

🏨 **John Howard** without rest., 4 Queen's Gate, SW7 5EH, ☎ 581 3011, Telex 8813397 – 🛗 🔼
☎. 🔼 AE ⓞ VISA
BQ **i**
⌕ 4.95 – **32 rm** 34.35/54.90 s.

🏨 **Elizabetta,** 162 Cromwell Rd, SW5 0TT, ☎ 370 4282, Telex 918978 – 🛗 TV ☎ ⓟ. 🔼 AE ⓞ
VISA
AS **r**
M 4.50 t. ⒜ 1.85 – ⌕ 2.50 – **84 rm** 25.30/32.20 st. – P 35.80 st.

🏨 London International (Gd. Met.), 147c Cromwell Rd, SW5 0TH, ☎ 370 4200, Telex 27260 – 🛗
TV. 🏛. 🔼 AE ⓞ VISA
AS **n**
415 rm.

🏨 **Blakes,** 33-35 Roland Gdns, SW7 3PF, ☎ 370 6701, Telex 8813500, « Tasteful decor » – 🛗 TV
⌷wc ☎. 🔼 AE ⓞ VISA
BU **c**
M (bar lunch) a la carte 11.40/16.95 t. ⒜ 3.00 – ⌕ 5.75 – **45 rm** 50.00/187.00 st.

🏨 **Eden Plaza,** 68-69 Queen's Gate, SW7 5JT, ☎ 370 6111, Telex 916228 – 🛗 TV ⌷wc ⌷wc
☜. 🔼 AE ⓞ VISA
CS **o**
M a la carte 5.20/7.70 t. ⒜ 1.95 – **61 rm** ⌕ 22.00/33.00 st.

🏨 Adelphi, without rest., 127-129 Cromwell Rd, SW7 4DT, ☎ 373 7177, Telex 8813164 – 🛗 TV
⌷wc ☜
AS **i**
57 rm.

🏨 Vanderbilt, 76-86 Cromwell Rd, SW7 5BT, ☎ 584 0491, Telex 919867 – 🛗 TV ⌷wc ☜   BS **v**
113 rm.

🏨 **Majestic,** 158-160 Cromwell Rd, SW5, ☎ 373 3083, Telex 8811844 – 🛗 TV ⌷wc ☜. 🔼 AE
ⓞ VISA
AS **u**
M 4.00 st. ⒜ 1.80 – ⌕ 1.75 – **92 rm** 24.65/31.65 st. – P 34.45/46.45 st.

🏨 Embassy House (Embassy), 31-33 Queen's Gate, ☎ 584 7222, Telex 8813387 – 🛗 TV ⌷wc
⌷wc ☜. 🔼 AE ⓞ VISA
BR **e**
M (bar lunch) a la carte 4.25/8.15 st. ⒜ 2.00 – **70 rm**.

🏨 **Rembrandt,** 11 Thurloe Pl., SW7 2RS, ☎ 589 8100, Telex 917575 – 🛗 TV ⌷wc ☜. 🏛. 🔼
AE ⓞ VISA
DS **x**
M 7.50 st. ⒜ 2.50 – ⌕ 2.25 – **198 rm** 16.50/33.50 s.

🏨 **Regency,** 100-105 Queen's Gate, SW7 5AG, ☎ 370 4595, Telex 267594 – 🛗 TV ⌷wc ⌷wc
☜. 🏛. 🔼 AE ⓞ VISA
CT **e**
M 6.00 st. ⒜ 3.00 – ⌕ 2.00 – **200 rm** 33.00/44.00 st.

🏨 Norfolk (Norfolk Cap.), 2-10 Harrington Rd, SW7 3ER, ☎ 589 8191, Group Telex 23241 – 🛗 TV
⌷wc ⌷wc ☜. 🔼 AE ⓞ VISA
CS **r**
94 rm.

🏨 **Cranley Gardens,** 8 Cranley Gdns, SW7 3DB, ☎ 373 3232, Group Telex 267465 – 🛗 TV
⌷wc ⌷wc ☜. 🔼 AE ⓞ VISA
BT **n**
M (grill rest. only) a la carte 2.75/6.75 st. – ⌕ 2.00 – **85 rm** 18.50/23.50 st.

🏨 **Number Sixteen** without rest., 15-17 Sumner Pl., SW7 3EG, ☎ 589 5232, ⚘ – ⌷wc ⌷wc
☎. 🔼 AE ⓞ
CT **c**
24 rm ⌕ 20.00/48.00 s.

🏨 **Alexander** without rest., 9 Sumner Pl., SW7 3EE, ☎ 581 1591, Telex 917133, ⚘ – 🛗 TV
⌷wc ⌷wc ☜. 🔼 AE ⓞ VISA
CT **a**
36 rm ⌕ 25.00/38.00 st.

🏨 Queensberry Court, without rest., 7-11 Queensberry Pl., SW7 2DW, ☎ 589 3693 – 🛗 ⌷wc
⌷wc ☜
CS **v**
42 rm.

🏨 **Apollo,** 18-22 Lexham Gdns, W8 5JE, ☎ 373 3236, Telex 264189 – 🛗 ⌷wc ☜. 🔼 AE ⓞ VISA
M (dinner only) 4.00 st. ⒜ 2.00 – ⌕ 1.20 – **57 rm** 10.50/22.00 st.
AS **o**

🏨 **Atlas** without rest., 24-30 Lexham Gdns, W8 5JE, ☎ 373 7873, Telex 264189 – 🛗 ⌷wc ☜.
🔼 AE ⓞ VISA
AS **s**
⌕ 1.20 – **70 rm** 10.50/22.00 st.

🏠 Concord, 155-157 Cromwell Rd, SW5 0TQ, ☎ 370 4151 – ⌷wc ⌷wc ☜. AE
AS **c**
40 rm ⌕ 10.00/22.45 st.

🗙🗙 **Pulcinella,** 30 Old Brompton Rd, SW7 3DA, ☎ 589 0529, Italian rest. – 🔼 AE ⓞ VISA   CS **i**
closed Sunday and Bank Holidays – **M** a la carte 6.50/9.25 t.

🗙 **Chanterelle,** 119 Old Brompton Rd, SW7 3RN, ☎ 373 5522 – 🔼 AE ⓞ VISA
BT **v**
closed 25 to 27 December – **M** a la carte 7.90/9.90 t. ⒜ 2.20.

🗙 **Star of India,** 154 Old Brompton Rd, SW5 0BE, ☎ 373 2901, Indian rest. – 🔼 AE ⓞ VISA
BT **s**
closed Bank Holidays – **M** a la carte 5.00/8.05 t.

Pour parcourir l'Europe,

utilisez les cartes Michelin **Grandes Routes** à 1/1 000 000.

KINGSTON-UPON-THAMES pp. 8 and 9 – ⊠ Surrey.
᠗₈ Hampton Wick ⏃ 977 6645, W : 2 ½ m.

Kingston – ⊠ Surrey.

✗ **Stonewalls,** 14 Kingston Hill, KT2 7NH, ⏃ 549 5984, Bistro – ▣ ① *VISA* CZ **v**
  closed lunch Saturday and Bank Holidays – **M** a la carte 6.85/8.50 **st.** ᐗ 1.70.

LEWISHAM pp. 10 and 11.

Bromley – ⊠ SE3.

🏨 **Bromley Court** ⚘, Bromley Hill, BR1 4JD, ⏃ 464 5011, Telex 090310, ⭤ – ⧈ ▣ ❷ ⚐. ▣
  Æ ① *VISA* GY **z**
  M 6.00/7.50 **st.** ᐗ 2.40 – **130 rm** ⇆ 25.00/45.00 **st.**

LONDON HEATHROW AIRPORT – see Hillingdon, London p. 51.

MERTON pp. 8 and 9.

Merton – ⊠ SW19.

✗ Les Amoureux, 156 Merton Hall Rd, SW19 3PZ, ⏃ 543 0567, French rest. DZ **a**

Wimbledon – ⊠ SW19.

↑ **Worcester House,** 38 Alwyne Rd, SW19 7AE, ⏃ 946 1300 – ▣ ⋒wc DY **r**
  8 rm ⇆ 16.00/28.00 **st.**

✗✗ **San Lorenzo Fuoriporta,** Worple Rd Mews, SW19 4DB, ⏃ 946 8463, Italian rest. – ▣ Æ
  ① *VISA* DY **n**
  closed Bank Holidays – **M** a la carte 8.70/12.70 **t.**

MICHELIN Branch, Deer Park Rd, Merton, SW19 3UD, ⏃ 540 9034/7

REDBRIDGE pp. 6 and 7.

Gants Hill – ⊠ Essex.

↑ **Blenheim House,** 2 Blenheim Av., IG2 6JG, ⏃ 554 4138 GV **z**
  8 rm ⇆ 13.00 **s.**

Ilford – ⊠ Essex.
᠗₈ Wanstead Park Rd ⏃ 554 5174.

✗✗ Mario's, 251 Cranbrook Rd, IG1 4TG, ⏃ 554 2921, Dancing GV **s**

RICHMOND-UPON-THAMES pp. 8 and 9.

Hampton Court – ⊠ Middx.
᠗₅ Twickenham ⏃ 941 2206, NW : 2 m.

🏛 Henekey's (T.H.F.), Hampton Court Rd, East Molesey, KT8 9BZ, ⏃ 977 8121 – ▣ ⌷wc 🅿
  ❷. ▣ Æ ① *VISA* BZ **x**
  29 rm ⇆ 19.00/32.00 **st.**

✗✗ **Bastians,** Hampton Court Rd, East Molesey, KT3 9BX, ⏃ 977 6074, French rest. – ▣ Æ ①
  VISA BZ **z**
  closed Saturday lunch, Sunday and Bank Holidays – **M** a la carte 7.00/11.95 **t**

Kew – ⊠ Surrey.

✗ **Jasper's Bun in the Oven,** 11 Kew Green, TW9 3AA, ⏃ 940 3987 – ▣ Æ ① *VISA* CX **e**
  closed Sunday and Bank Holidays – **M** a la carte 5.80/10.50 **t.** ᐗ 2.20.

Richmond – ⊠ Surrey.
᠗₈, ᠗₈ Richmond Park ⏃ 876 3205.
🅱 Central Library, Little Green ⏃ 940 9125.

🏨 **Petersham,** Richmond Hill, Nightingale Lane, TW10 6RP, ⏃ 940 7471, Telex 928556 – ⧈ ▣
  ⌷wc ☎ 🅿. ⚐ CY **c**
  M a la carte 9.00/12.00 **t.** ᐗ 2.00 – **58 rm** ⇆ 32.50/42.00 **t.**

🏨 **Richmond Gate,** Richmond Hill, TW10 6RP, ⏃ 940 0061, Telex 928556, ⭤ – ▣ ⌷wc ☎
  🅿. ⚐ CY **a**
  M a la carte 7.50/8.80 **t.** ᐗ 2.00 – **52 rm** ⇆ 32.50/42.00 **t.**

P.T.O. →

XX ❀ **Lichfield's,** 13 Lichfield Terr., Sheen Rd, ☎ 940 5236 – 🖪 🖭 𝘝𝘐𝘚𝘈   CY **i**
closed Sunday, Monday, last 2 weeks August and 1 week at Christmas –
M (dinner only) a la carte 12.80/16.50 t. ₰ 2.25
Spec. Royale of artichokes and mushrooms (seasonal), Roast duck with limes, Charlotte Malakoff au chocolat.

XX **Gino's,** 15-17 Hill Rise, ☎ 940 3002, Italian rest. – 🖪 🖭 ➀ 𝘝𝘐𝘚𝘈   BY **n**
closed Monday and Bank Holidays – **M** a la carte 6.00/14.10 t. ₰ 2.50.

XX **Evergreen,** 102-104 Kew Rd, TW9 1RZ, ☎ 940 9044, Chinese rest.   CY **e**

XX **Kew Rendezvous,** 110 Kew Rd, TW9 2PQ, ☎ 948 4343, Chinese rest. – 🖪 🖭 ➀ 𝘝𝘐𝘚𝘈
closed Bank Holidays – **M** approx. 7.00 t.   CY **e**

XX **Franco's,** 5 Petersham Rd, TW9 1EN, ☎ 940 9051, Italian rest. – 🖪 🖭 ➀ 𝘝𝘐𝘚𝘈   BY **n**
M a la carte 8.25/10.00 t. ₰ 2.15.

X **Richmond Rendezvous,** 1 Wakefield Rd, TW9 1RX, ☎ 940 6869, Chinese rest. – 🖪 🖭 ➀
𝘝𝘐𝘚𝘈   CY **s**
M approx. 6.00 t.

SOUTHWARK pp. 10 and 11.

Dulwich Village – ✉ SE21.

XX **Luigi's,** 129 Gipsy Hill, SE19 1QS, ☎ 670 1843, Italian rest. – 🖪 🖭 ➀ 𝘝𝘐𝘚𝘈   FY **a**
closed Saturday lunch, Sunday, 3 weeks August and Bank Holidays – **M** a la carte 9.75/10.80 t.
₰ 1.95.

East Dulwich – ✉ SE22.

X **Pyramid,** 78 East Dulwich Grove, SE22, ☎ 693 0372   FY **e**
closed Sunday, Monday and Bank Holidays – **M** (dinner only) a la carte approx. 10.85 t. ₰ 1.90.

SUTTON pp. 8 and 9.
🏁 Oak Sports Centre, Woodmansterne Rd, Carshalton ☎ 642 9608.

Sutton – ✉ Surrey.

↑ **The Dene,** 39 Cheam Rd, SM1 2AT, ☎ 642 3170, 🍴 – 📺 ⌂wc ℗   EZ **v**
17 rm ⊏ 9.00/24.00 **s.**

X Trattoria Toscana, 6-7 Station Par., Brighton Rd, SM2 5AD, ☎ 642 3341, Italian rest.   EZ **x**

Carte
Hotels and restaurants
offering set meals generally also serve
« a la carte ».

TOWER HAMLETS Except where otherwise stated see pp. 6 and 7.

Tower Hamlets – ✉ E1.
🅱 88 Roman Rd, E2 OPG, ☎ 980 3749 and 4831 ext. 211.

🏨 Tower (Thistle), St. Katharine's Way, E1 9LD, ☎ 481 2575, Telex 885934, ≼ Tower Bridge and
River Thames – 🛗 📺 ☎ ௹ ℗. 🔼. 🖪 🖭 ➀ 𝘝𝘐𝘚𝘈   pp. 17-20 QV **r**
⊏ 4.00 – **826 rm** 35.00/42.00 t.

WALTHAM FOREST pp. 6 and 7.
🏁 at Chingford, 158 Station Rd ☎ Silverstone 529 2107.

Leystonstone – ✉ E11.

X **Trattoria Parmigiana,** 715 High Rd, E11 4RD, ☎ 539 1700, Italian rest. – 🖪 🖭 ➀ 𝘝𝘐𝘚𝘈
closed Sunday and Bank Holidays – **M** a la carte 6.60/10.10 t. ₰ 2.20.   GV **a**

WANDSWORTH pp. 8 and 9.

Battersea – ✉ SW8/SW11.

XXX ❀ **Chez Nico,** 129 Queenstown Rd, SW8, ☎ 720 6960, French rest. – 🖪 𝘝𝘐𝘚𝘈   EY **c**
closed Sunday, Monday, 7 days at Easter, August and 10 days at Christmas – **M** (dinner only)
(booking essential) a la carte approx. 17.50 **st.**
Spec. La soupe de poissons avec sa rouille, Suprême de canard aux fruits, Les sorbets.

XX **Alonso's,** 32 Queenstown Rd, SW8 3RX, ☎ 720 5986 – 🖭 ➀   EY **e**
closed Saturday lunch, Sunday and Bank Holidays – **M** 7.20/11.00 t.

XX **La Grenouille,** 515 Battersea Park Rd, SW11, ☎ 228 5385, French rest. – 🖪 🖭 ➀ 𝘝𝘐𝘚𝘈
closed Sunday, last week August, first week September and 1 week at Christmas – **M** (dinner
only) a la carte 9.10/13.80 t.   EY **r**

X **Le Routier,** 245 Lavender Hill, SW11 1JW, ☎ 228 9824 – 🖪 🖭 𝘝𝘐𝘚𝘈   EY **i**
closed Sunday – **M** (dinner only) a la carte 7.00/9.25 t. ₰ 2.00.

X **Jacks Place,** 12 York Rd, SW11 3PX, ☎ 228 8519, Bistro – 🖪   EY **n**
closed Saturday lunch, Sunday, Monday, August and Bank Holidays – **M** a la carte 6.15/10.55 st.
₰ 1.95.

Clapham – ⊠ SW11.

✗ **Pollyanna's,** 2 Battersea Rise, SW11, ℡ 228 0316, Bistro – 🔆 🆎 ⓞ 𝐕𝐈𝐒𝐀 EY **a**
closed 24 to 26 December and 1 January – **M** (dinner only and Sunday lunch) a la carte 6.90/9.45 **t.** ⁑ 2.05.

Putney – ⊠ SW15.

✗ Cassis, 30 Putney High St., SW15 1SQ, ℡ 788 8668, French bistro. DY **x**

WESTMINSTER (City of).

Bayswater and Maida Vale – ⊠ W2/W9 – Except where otherwise stated see pp. 30 and 31.

🏨🏨 **Royal Lancaster** (Rank), Lancaster Terr., W2 2TY, ℡ 262 6737, Telex 24822, ≤ – 🛗 📺 ☎ ⅍ ₱. ⌂. 🔆 🆎 ⓞ 𝐕𝐈𝐒𝐀 DZ **e**
M 10.00/12.50 **st.** – ⊆ 4.75 – **433 rm** 39.50/10.50 **st.**

🏨 **Great Western Royal** (D.T.H.), Praed St., W2 1HE, ℡ 723 8064, Telex 263972 – 🛗 📺 ⅍. ⌂. 🔆 🆎 ⓞ 𝐕𝐈𝐒𝐀 DY **c**
closed Christmas – **M** 7.50 **st.** ⁑ 3.00 – ⊆ 2.00 – **169 rm** 25.00/39.00 **st.**

🏨🏨 **Metropole,** Edgware Rd, W2 1JU, ℡ 402 4141, Telex 23711, ≤ – 🛗 📺 ₱. ⌂. 🔆 🆎 ⓞ 𝐕𝐈𝐒𝐀 pp. 13-16 JT **c**
M 7.50 ⁑ 1.50 – ⊆ 2.50 – **586 rm** 43.00/51.00 **s.**

🏨 **Post House** (T.H.F.), 104 Bayswater Rd, W2 3HL, ℡ 262 4461, Telex 22667, ≤ – 🛗 📺 ⇌wc ⌕ ₱. 🔆 🆎 ⓞ 𝐕𝐈𝐒𝐀 CZ **o**
M 4.95/7.50 **st.** ⁑ 2.20 – ⊆ 4.35 – **175 rm** 31.00/40.50 **st.**

🏨 **London Embassy** (Embassy), 150 Bayswater Rd, W2 4RT, ℡ 229 1212, Telex 27727 – 🛗 📺 ⇌wc ☎ ⅍ ₱. ⌂. 🔆 🆎 ⓞ 𝐕𝐈𝐒𝐀 BZ **o**
M (carvery lunch) 4.50/6.30 **st.** ⁑ 2.15 – ⊆ 2.75 – **193 rm** 37.00/48.00 **st.**

🏨 **White's** (T.H.F.), Bayswater Rd, 90-92 Lancaster Gate, W2 3NR, ℡ 262 2711, Group Telex 23922 – 🛗 📺 ⇌wc ☎ ₱. 🔆 🆎 ⓞ 𝐕𝐈𝐒𝐀 CZ **v**
M 5.50 **st.** ⁑ 2.50 – ⊆ 4.25 – **61 rm** 31.00/43.50 **st.**

🏨 **Park Court** (T.H.F.), 75 Lancaster Gate, W2 3NN, ℡ 402 4272, Group Telex 23922, 🚗 – 🛗 📺 ⇌wc ☎. ⌂. 🔆 🆎 ⓞ 𝐕𝐈𝐒𝐀 CZ **z**
M 3.75 **st.** ⁑ 2.50 – ⊆ 4.25 – **434 rm** 27.00/37.50 **st.**

🏨 **Clarendon Court,** Edgware Rd, W9 1AG, ℡ 286 8080, Telex 27374 – 🛗 📺 ⇌wc 🚻wc ⌕. ⌂. 🔆 🆎 ⓞ 𝐕𝐈𝐒𝐀 pp. 13-16 JS **a**
M 7.00 **st.** ⁑ 1.05 – ⊆ 1.75 – **155 rm** 27.50/38.50 **s.**

🏨 **Coburg** (Best Western), 129 Bayswater Rd, W2 4RJ, ℡ 229 3654, Telex 268235 – 🛗 📺 ⇌wc ⌕. ⌂. 🔆 🆎 ⓞ 𝐕𝐈𝐒𝐀 BZ **a**
M a la carte 4.75/8.00 **st.** – **120 rm** ⊆ 18.50/44.00 **st.** – P 21.00 **st.**

🏨 **Grosvenor Court** (Gd. Met.), 144 Praed St., W2 1HU, ℡ 262 3464, Group Telex 25971 – 🛗 📺 ⇌wc ☎. 🔆 🆎 ⓞ 𝐕𝐈𝐒𝐀 DY **a**
M 3.60/4.65 **st.** ⁑ 2.15 – ⊆ 1.85 – **93 rm** 20.15/29.35 **st.**

🏨 **Mornington Lancaster** without rest., 12 Lancaster Gate, W2 3LG, ℡ 262 7361, Telex 24281 – 🛗 📺 ⇌wc ⌕. 🔆 🆎 ⓞ 𝐕𝐈𝐒𝐀 DZ **s**
⊆ 1.75 – **65 rm** 27.00/40.00 **st.**

🏨 **Colonnade,** 2 Warrington Cres., W9 1ER, ℡ 286 1052, Telex 298930 – 🛗 📺 ⇌wc 🚻wc ⌕ ₱. 🆎 JT **e**
M (dinner only) 6.00 ⁑ 1.50 – **54 rm** ⊆ 16.00/45.00.

🏨 **Westland,** 154 Bayswater Rd, W2 4HP, ℡ 229 9191 – 🛗 📺 ⇌wc ⌕ ₱. 🔆 🆎 ⓞ 𝐕𝐈𝐒𝐀 BZ **a**
M (dinner only) a la carte 3.85/5.00 ⁑ 1.60 – **49 rm** ⊆ 27.50/34.50.

🏠 **Garden Court,** 30-31 Kensington Gardens Sq., W2 4BG, ℡ 229 2553 – ⇌wc 🚻wc BY **e**
37 rm ⊆ 9.00/18.00 **s.**

🏠 **Dylan,** 14 Devonshire Terr., W2 3DW, ℡ 723 3280 – ⇌wc 🚻wc. 🆎 ⓞ 𝐕𝐈𝐒𝐀 CY **c**
18 rm ⊆ 10.00/22.00 **t.**

🏠 **Allandale,** 3 Devonshire Terr., Lancaster Gate, W2 3DN, ℡ 723 8311 – ⇌wc 🚻wc. 🔆 𝐕𝐈𝐒𝐀 CY **a**
18 rm ⊆ 9.00/18.00 **s.**

🏠 **Caring,** 24 Craven Hill Gdns, Leinster Terr., W2 3EA, ℡ 262 8708 – 📺 ⇌wc 🚻 CZ **e**
26 rm ⊆ 11.50/18.50 **s.**

✗✗ **San Marino,** 26 Sussex Pl., W2 2TH, ℡ 723 8395, Italian rest. – 🔆 🆎 ⓞ 𝐕𝐈𝐒𝐀 EY **u**
closed Sunday and Bank Holidays – **M** a la carte 7.80/14.10 **t.** ⁑ 1.90.

✗✗ **Trat-West,** 143 Edgware Rd, W2 2HR, ℡ 723 8203, Italian rest. – 🔆 🆎 ⓞ 𝐕𝐈𝐒𝐀 pp. 13-10 KI **i**
M a la carte 7.35/11.80 **t.**

✗✗ **Lotus House,** 61-69 Edgware Rd, W2 2HZ, ℡ 262 4341, Chinese rest., Dancing – 🔆 🆎 ⓞ 𝐕𝐈𝐒𝐀 FY **o**
closed Christmas – **M** a la carte 8.00/10.00 **t.** ⁑ 2.70.

✗✗ **Concordia Notte,** 29-31 Craven Rd, W2 3BX, ℡ 402 4985, Italian rest., Dancing – 🔆 🆎 ⓞ 𝐕𝐈𝐒𝐀 DY **r**
closed Sunday and August – **M** a la carte 12.00/16.50 **t.** ⁑ 2.50.

P.T.O. →

XX **La Lupa,** 23 Connaught St., W2 2AY, ☎ 723 0540, Italian rest. – ☒ AE ⓪ VISA   EY **v**
    closed Sunday – **M** a la carte 5.10/9.80 **t.** ⓵ 1.90.

XX **Canaletto,** 451 Edgware Rd, W2 1TH, ☎ 262 7027, Italian rest. – ☒ AE ⓪ VISA ⓵ 2.85.
    closed Saturday lunch, Sunday and Bank Holidays – **M** a la carte 7.95/11.55 **t.** ⓵ 2.85.
                                pp. 13-16   JT **v**

X **Kalamaras Taverna,** 76-78 Inverness Mews, W2 3JQ, ☎ 727 9122, Greek rest. – AE ⓪
    closed Sunday and Bank Holidays – **M** (dinner only) a la carte 6.15/8.35 **t.** ⓵ 2.00.   BY **a**

X **Concordia,** 29-31 Craven Rd, W2 3BX, ☎ 402 4985, Italian rest. – ☒ AE ⓪ VISA   DY **r**
    closed Sunday – **M** a la carte 5.75/7.90 **t.**

Belgravia – ✉ SW1 – Except where otherwise stated see pp. 28 and 29.

🏨 Berkeley, Wilton Pl., SW1X 7RL, ☎ 235 6000, Telex 919252, ☒ – 📶 TV ᴋ ⟲ . 🏛 . ☒   FQ **e**
    M Restaurant *(closed Saturday)* – **Le Perroquet** *(closed Sunday)* – **152 rm**.

🏨 Lowndes (Thistle), 21 Lowndes St., SW1X 9ES, ☎ 235 6020, Telex 919065 – 📶 TV ☎ . ☒ AE
    ⓪ VISA   FR **i**
    � 4.25 – **80 rm** 54.00/67.00 **t.**

XX **Salloos,** 62-64 Kinnerton St., SW1 8ER, ☎ 235 4444, Indian and Pakistani rest. – ☒ AE ⓪
    VISA   FQ **a**
    closed Sunday and Bank Holidays – **M** a la carte 7.80/10.25 **t.** ⓵ 2.25.

XX **Motcombs,** 26 Motcomb St., SW1X 8JU, ☎ 235 6382 – ☒ AE ⓪ VISA   FR **z**
    closed Saturday, Sunday and Bank Holidays – **M** a la carte 8.30/13.45 **t.** ⓵ 2.50.

XX **Wheeler's Carafe,** 15-16 Lowndes St., SW1X 9EY, ☎ 235 2525, Seafood – ☒ AE ⓪ VISA
    closed Monday and Bank Holidays – **M** a la carte 10.00/17.00 **t.** ⓵ 2.00.   FR **u**

X **Upper Crust in Belgravia,** 9 William St., SW1X 9HL, ☎ 235 8444, English rest. – ☒ AE ⓪
    VISA   FQ **c**
    closed 25 and 26 December – **M** a la carte 5.90/7.75 **t.** ⓵ 2.10.

Hyde Park and Knightsbridge – ✉ SW1/SW7 – pp. 28 and 29.

🏨 **Hyde Park** (T.H.F.), 66 Knightsbridge, SW1Y 7LA, ☎ 235 2000, Telex 262057, ≤ – 📶 TV . 🏛 .
    ☒ AE ⓪ VISA   EQ **v**
    M a la carte 12.55/21.05 **st.** ⓵ 3.70 – � 5.60 – **201 rm** 74.00/85.00 **st.**

XXX **Shezan,** 16-22 Cheval Pl., Montpelier St., SW7 1ES, ☎ 589 7918, Indian and Pakistani rest. –
    ☒ AE ⓪ VISA   ER **c**
    closed Sunday, 25-26 December and Bank Holidays – **M** a la carte 8.40/17.15 **t.** ⓵ 2.70.

XX **Mr Chow,** 151 Knightsbridge, SW1X 7PA, ☎ 589 7347, Chinese rest. – ☒ AE ⓪ VISA   EQ **s**
    closed Bank Holidays – **M** a la carte 10.55/14.35 **st.** ⓵ 2.50.

XX Newports, Knightsbridge Green, 22 Brompton R, SW1, ☎ 589 8772   EQ **c**

XX Montpeliano, 13 Montpelier St., SW7 1HQ, ☎ 589 0032, Italian rest.   ER **e**

Mayfair – ✉ W1 – pp. 26 and 27.

🏨 Claridge's, Brook St., W1A 2JQ, ☎ 629 8860, Telex 21872 – 📶 TV ᴋ. ☒   BL **c**
    M a la carte 11.60/16.10 **t.** ⓵ 2.50 – **Causerie** *(closed Saturday)* – **205 rm**.

🏨 Inn on the Park, Hamilton Pl., Park Lane, W1A 1AZ, ☎ 499 0888, Telex 22771 – 📶 TV ☎ ᴋ
    🄿. 🏛 . ☒ AE ⓪ VISA   BP **a**
    M Four Seasons a la carte 16.60/20.10 **st.** ⓵ 3.50 – **Lanes** *(closed Sunday dinner)* 12.85 (wine
    included) a la carte approx. 10.75 **st.** ⓵ 3.50 – ⊏⊐ 4.30 – **228 rm** 72.00/83.00 **s.**

🏨 Dorchester, Park Lane, W1A 2HJ, ☎ 629 8888, Telex 887704 – 📶 TV ᴋ 🄿. 🏛 . ☒ AE ⓪ VISA
    M The Terrace *(closed Sunday)* (dinner only) 18.15/22.50 **st.** ⓵ 2.20 – **Grill** a la carte
    10.00/15.70 **st.** ⓵ 2.20 – ⊏⊐ a la carte 6.00 – **285 rm** 65.00/95.00 **st.**   BN **z**

🏨 Grosvenor House (T.H.F.), Park Lane, W1A 3AA, ☎ 499 6363, Telex 24871, ☒ – 📶 TV ☎ ᴋ
    🄿. 🏛 . ☒ AE ⓪ VISA   AM **a**
    M a la carte 12.45/19.65 **st.** ⓵ 3.50 – ⊏⊐ 5.25 – **478 rm** 71.50/82.50 **st.**

🏨 ❀ Connaught, 16 Carlos Pl., W1Y 6AL, ☎ 499 7070 – 📶 TV ☎ . ☒   BM **e**
    M (booking essential) – **90 rm**
    Spec. Pâté de turbot froid au homard sauce pudeur, Rendez-vous du pêcheur, sauce légère au parfum d'Armorique,
    Salmis de canard strasbourgeoise en surprise.

🏨 **Inter-Continental,** 1 Hamilton Pl., Hyde Park Corner, W1V 0QY, ☏ 409 3131, Telex 25853 –
🛗 📺 ☎ & 🅿. 🔺. 🔼 🖭 ⑩ 𝘝𝘐𝘚𝘈   BP **o**
M (French rest.) a la carte 10.50/20.00 **t.** – � 5.60 – **497 rm** 69.00/87.00.

🏨 Hilton International, 22 Park Lane, W1A 2HH, ☏ 493 8000, Telex 24873, ≤ London – 🛗 📺 ☎
& 🅿. 🔺   BP **e**
509 rm.

🏨 **Athenaeum** (Rank), 116 Piccadilly, W1V 0BJ, ☏ 499 3464, Telex 261589 – 🛗 📺 ☎. 🔺. 🔼
🖭 ⑩ 𝘝𝘐𝘚𝘈   CP **s**
M 9.50/12.50 **st.** ▮ 3.85 – ⊑ 5.00 – **112 rm** 71.00/89.00 **st.**

🏨 **Brown's** (T.H.F.), 29-34 Albemarle St., W1A 4SW, ☏ 493 6020, Telex 28686 – 🛗 📺 ☎. 🔺.
🔼 🖭 𝘝𝘐𝘚𝘈   DM **e**
M approx. 9.95 **st.** ▮ 3.40 – ⊑ 5.50 – **129 rm** 65.00/82.50 **st.**

🏨 **Westbury** (T.H.F.), New Bond St., W1Y 0PD, ☏ 629 7755, Telex 24378 – 🛗 📺 ☎ & 🅿. 🔺.
🔼 🖭 𝘝𝘐𝘚𝘈   DM **a**
M approx. 9.25 **t.** ▮ 3.50 – ⊑ 5.00 – **254 rm** 57.00/74.00 **st.**

🏨 **Britannia** (Gd. Met.), 42 Grosvenor Sq., W1A 3AN, ☏ 629 9400, Telex 23041 – 🛗 📺 ☎ 🅿. 🔺.
🔼 🖭 ⑩ 𝘝𝘌𝘈   BM **i**
435 rm.

🏨 **May Fair** (Gd. Met.), Stratton St., W1A 2AN, ☏ 629 7777, Telex 262526 – 🛗 📺 ☎. 🔺. 🔼 🖭
⑩ 𝘝𝘐𝘚𝘈   DN **z**
M a la carte 15.20/18.10 **st.** ▮ 2.85 – ⊑ 5.45 – **390 rm** 42.55/64.40 **st.**

🏨 **Bristol,** 3 Berkeley St., W1X 6NE, ☏ 493 8282, Telex 24561 – 🛗 📺 ☎ & 🅿. 🔺. 🔼 🖭 ⑩
𝘝𝘐𝘚𝘈   DN **r**
M 8.50/9.50 **st.** ▮ 2.50 – ⊑ 5.00 – **190 rm** 63.00/66.00 **s.**

🏨 **Chesterfield** (Gd. Met.), 35 Charles St., W1X 8LX, ☏ 491 2622, Telex 269394 – 🛗 📺 ☎. 🔼
🖭 ⑩ 𝘝𝘐𝘚𝘈   CN **c**
M 8.00 **st.** ▮ 2.50 – ⊑ 4.95 – **87 rm** 37.00/60.00 **s.**

🏨 **Europa** (Gd. Met.), Grosvenor Sq., W1A 4AW, ☏ 493 1232, Telex 268101 – 🛗 📺 ☎ 🅿. 🔺.
🔼 🖭 ⑩ 𝘝𝘐𝘚𝘈   BL **n**
M 7.75 **st.** ▮ 2.50 – ⊑ 4.95 – **275 rm** 37.00/60.0 **s.**

🏨 **Piccadilly** (Gd. Met.), 21 Piccadilly, W1V 0BH, ☏ 734 8000, Telex 25795 – 🛗 📺 ⌁wc 📼.
🔺. 🔼 🖭 ⑩ 𝘝𝘐𝘚𝘈   EM **v**
M (carvery rest.) 7.25 **st.** – ⊑ 4.60 – **290 rm** 32.00/52.00.

🏨 Washington (Gd. Met.), 5-7 Curzon St., W1Y 8DT, ☏ 499 7030, Telex 24540 – 🛗 📺 ⌁wc 📼.
🔺. 🔼 🖭 ⑩ 𝘝𝘐𝘚𝘈   CN **n**
M a la carte 5.40/9.05 **st.** ▮ 2.50 – **159 rm**.

XXXXX **Mirabelle** (De Vere), 56 Curzon St., W1Y 8DL, ☏ 499 4636, 🌭 – 🔼 🖭 ⑩ 𝘝𝘐𝘚𝘈   CN **a**
closed Sunday and Bank Holidays – **M** a la carte approx. 16.50 **t.** ▮ 5.00.

XXXX ✸✸✸ **Le Gavroche,** 43 Upper Brook St., W1, ☏ 408 0881, French rest. – 🔼 🖭 ⑩ 𝘝𝘐𝘚𝘈
closed Saturday, Sunday, 30 August-10 September, 24 December-8 January and Bank Holidays
– **M** (booking essential) 16.50/a la carte approx. 26.10 **st.**   AM **c**
Spec. Soufflé suissesse, Caneton Gavroche, Sablé aux fraises.

XXXX **Scott's,** 20 Mount St., W1Y 5RB, ☏ 629 5248, Seafood – 🔼 🖭 ⑩ 𝘝𝘐𝘚𝘈   BM **r**
closed Sunday lunch and Bank Holidays – **M** a la carte 15.85/22.70 **t.** ▮ 2.80.

XXX Cecconi's, 5a Burlington Gdns, W1Y 5DT, ☏ 434 1500, Italian rest.   DM **c**

XXX **Tiberio,** 22 Queen St., W1X 7PJ, ☏ 629 3561, Italian rest., Dancing – 🔼 🖭 ⑩ 𝘝𝘐𝘚𝘈   CN **z**
closed Saturday lunch and Sunday – **M** a la carte 9.15/17.50 **t.**

XXX **Snooty Fox,** 51-52 Hertford St., Shepherd Market, W1Y 7HJ, ☏ 629 1786 – 🔼 🖭 ⑩ 𝘝𝘐𝘚𝘈
closed Saturday lunch, Sunday and Bank Holidays – **M** 9.00/9.75 **t.** ▮ 2.50.   BN **c**

XXX **Tandoori,** 37a Curzon St., W1Y 7AF, ☏ 629 0600, Indian and Pakistani rest. – 🔼 🖭 ⑩ 𝘝𝘐𝘚𝘈
closed Sunday and 25-26 December – **M** a la carte 8.30/10.30 **t.**   BN **i**

XX **Langan's Brasserie,** Stratton St., W1X 5FD, ☏ 493 6437 – 🔼 🖭 ⑩ 𝘝𝘐𝘚𝘈   DN **e**
closed Saturday lunch, Sunday and Bank Holidays – **M** (booking essential) a la carte
8.40/12.00 **t.** ▮ 2.95.

XX **Greenhouse,** 27a Hay's Mews, W1X 7RJ, ☏ 499 3331 – 🔼 🖭 ⑩ 𝘝𝘐𝘚𝘈   BN **a**
closed Saturday lunch, Sunday and 1 week at Christmas and New Year – **M** a la carte
9.80/11.95 **t.** ▮ 3.45.

XX Mr. Kai, 65 South Audley St., W1, ☏ 493 8988, Chinese rest.   BM **v**

XX **Marquis,** 121a Mount St., W1Y 5HB, ☏ 499 1256 – 🔼 🖭 ⑩ 𝘝𝘐𝘚𝘈   BM **u**
closed Sunday – **M** a la carte 7.05/10.75 **t.** ▮ 2.75.

XX **Golden Carp,** 8a Mount St., W1Y 5AD, ☏ 499 3385, Seafood – 🔼 🖭 ⑩ 𝘝𝘐𝘚𝘈   BM **x**
closed Saturday lunch, Sunday, 3 weeks August and Bank Holidays – **M** a la carte 6.10/10.70 **t.**
▮ 2.50.

XX **Gaylord,** 16 Albemarle St., W1 3HA, ☏ 629 9802, Indian rest. – 🔼 🖭 ⑩ 𝘝𝘐𝘚𝘈   DM **u**
M a la carte approx. 6.45 **t.** ▮ 3.10.

X Ikeda, 30 Brook St., W1Y 1AG, ☏ 629 2730, Japanese rest.   CKL **a**

X **Trattoria Fiori,** 87-88 Mount St., W1Y 5HG, ☏ 499 1447, Italian rest. – 🔼 🖭 ⑩ 𝘝𝘐𝘚𝘈   BM **o**
closed Sunday and Bank Holidays – **M** a la carte 7.95/13.45 ▮ 2.05.

X Saga, 43 South Molton St., W1, ☏ 408 2236, Japanese rest.   BK **s**

Regent's Park and Marylebone – ⊠ NW1/NW6/NW8/W1 – Except where otherwise stated see pp. 26 and 27.

Churchill, 30 Portman Sq., W1A 4ZX, ☏ 486 5800, Telex 264831 – 🛗 📺 ☎ 🕭 🅿. 🚗. 🖾 🖭 ⓞ 𝖵𝖨𝖲𝖠
AJ x
M a la carte 9.55/18.55 **st.** ⓝ 2.35 – 🖙 5.30 – **489 rm** 54.00/60.00.

Portman, 22 Portman Sq., W1H 9FL, ☏ 486 5844, Telex 261526 – 🛗 📺 ☎ 🕭 🅿. 🚗
AJ o
275 rm.

Selfridge (Thistle), 400 Orchard St., W1H 0JS, ☏ 408 2080, Telex 22361 – 🛗 📺 ☎ 🕭 🅿. 🚗.
🖾 🖭 ⓞ 𝖵𝖨𝖲𝖠
AK e
🖙 4.70 – **298 rm** 55.00/68.00 **t.**

Montcalm, Great Cumberland Pl., W1A 2LF, ☏ 402 4288, Telex 28710 – 🛗 📺 ☎. 🚗. 🖾 🖭
ⓞ 𝖵𝖨𝖲𝖠
pp. 30 and 31   FY x
M (closed lunch Saturday and Sunday) a la carte 9.65/15.05 **st.** ⓝ 2.75 – 🖙 5.20 – **116 rm** 46.00/54.00.

Ladbroke Westmoreland (Ladbroke), 18 Lodge Rd, NW8 7JT, ☏ 722 7722, Telex 23101 –
🛗 📺 ☎ 🚐 🅿. 🚗. 🖾 🖭 ⓞ 𝖵𝖨𝖲𝖠
pp. 13-16   JS v
M 6.00/8.00 **t.** ⓝ 3.00 – 🖙 3.75 – **345 rm** 35.00/46.00 **t.**

Holiday Inn, 134 George St., W1H 6DN, ☏ 723 1277, Telex 27983, 🖾 – 🛗 📺 ☎ 🕭 🅿. 🚗.
🖾 🖭 ⓞ 𝖵𝖨𝖲𝖠
pp. 30 and 31   FY i
M a la carte 6.40/14.80 **st.** ⓝ 3.60 – 🖙 4.30 – **243 rm** 51.50/60.00 **s.**

St. George's (T.H.F.), Langham Pl., W1N 8QS, ☏ 580 0111, Telex 27274, ≤ – 🛗 📺 ☎. 🖾 🖭
ⓞ 𝖵𝖨𝖲𝖠
pp. 13-16   LT a
M approx. 9.25 **st.** ⓝ 2.10 – 🖙 4.50 – **85 rm** 49.50/60.50 **st.**

Cumberland (T.H.F.), Marble Arch, W1A 4RF, ☏ 262 1234, Telex 22215 – 🛗 📺 ☎ 🕭 🅿. 🚗.
🖾 🖭 ⓞ 𝖵𝖨𝖲𝖠
AK n
M 7.45 **t.** ⓝ 3.00 – 🖙 4.50 – **894 rm** 43.00/58.50 **st.**

Durrants, 26-32 George St., W1H 6BJ, ☏ 935 8131, Telex 894919 – 🛗 📺 ⇌wc ☎. 🚗. 🖾
🖭 ⓞ
AH e
M (closed 25 and 26 December) a la carte 8.30/16.50 **t.** ⓝ 2.50 – **102 rm** 🖙 25.00/45.00 **st.**

New Berners (Gd. Met.), Berner St., W1A 3BE, ☏ 636 1629, Telex 25759 – 🛗 📺 ⇌wc ☎ 🕭.
🚗. 🖾 🖭 ⓞ 𝖵𝖨𝖲𝖠
FJ r
M (carvery rest.) 6.95 **st.** ⓝ 2.20 – **238 rm**.

Regent Centre (Crest), Carburton St., W1P 8EE, ☏ 388 2300, Telex 22453 – 🛗 📺 ⇌wc ☎
🅿. 🚗. 🖾 🖭 ⓞ 𝖵𝖨𝖲𝖠
pp. 13-16   LT i
M 6.10 **s.** ⓝ 3.25 – **335 rm** 32.00/44.00 **st.**

Londoner (Gd. Met.), 57-59 Welbeck St., W1M 8HS, ☏ 935 4442, Group Telex 894630 – 🛗
📺 ⇌wc ☎. 🖾 🖭 ⓞ 𝖵𝖨𝖲𝖠
BJ v
M 5.25 **st.** ⓝ 2.75 – **142 rm**.

Stratford Court (Gd. Met.), 350 Oxford St., W1N 0BY, ☏ 629 7474, Telex 22270 – 🛗 📺 ⇌wc
☎
BK n
M (grill rest. only) – **137 rm**.

Clifton Ford (Gd. Met.), 47 Welbeck St., W1M 8DN, ☏ 486 6600, Group Telex 22569 – 🛗 📺
⇌wc ☎. 🚗. 🖾 🖭 ⓞ 𝖵𝖨𝖲𝖠
BH a
M 7.95 **st.** ⓝ 2.50 – **229 rm**.

Harewood, Harewood Row, NW1 6SE, ☏ 262 2707, Telex 267465 – 🛗 📺 ⇌wc ☎. 🖾 🖭
ⓞ 𝖵𝖨𝖲𝖠
pp. 13-16   KT x
M (grill rest. only) a la carte 2.90/5.45 **st.** – 🖙 2.50 – **93 rm** 24.50/34.00 **st.**

Bryanston Court, 56-60 Great Cumberland Pl., W1H 7FD, ☏ 262 3141, Telex 21120 – 🛗 📺
⇌wc 🕼wc ☎. 🖾 🖭 ⓞ 𝖵𝖨𝖲𝖠
pp. 30 and 31   FY z
M (closed Saturday and Sunday) 4.95/6.95 **t.** ⓝ 1.80 – 🖙 1.80 – **55 rm** 26.50/36.00 **st.**

Concorde without rest., 50 Great Cumberland Pl., W1H 7FD, ☏ 402 6169, Group Telex 21120
– 🛗 📺 ⇌wc 🕼wc ☎. 🖾 🖭 ⓞ 𝖵𝖨𝖲𝖠
pp. 30 and 31   FY n
🖙 1.80 – **28 rm** 25.00/32.00 **st.**

Hallam without rest., 12 Hallam St., W1N 5LJ, ☏ 580 1166 – 🛗 ⇌wc 🕼wc ☎. 🖾 🖭 𝖵𝖨𝖲𝖠
23 rm 🖙 17.50/27.50 **st.**
pp. 13-16   LT r

Portman Court, 30 Seymour St., W1H 5WD, ☏ 402 5401 – ⇌wc ☎. 🖾 🖭 ⓞ 𝖵𝖨𝖲𝖠   AK x
🖙 1.00 – **30 rm** 14.00/25.00 **st.**

XXX **Odins,** 27 Devonshire St., W1N 1RJ, ☏ 935 7296   pp. 13-16   KT   **n**
closed Saturday lunch, Sunday and Bank Holidays – **M** a la carte 10.75/16.75 **t.**

XX **La Loggia,** 68 Edgware Rd, W2 2EG, ☏ 723 0554, Italian rest. – 🖸 🆎 **VISA**
closed Sunday and Bank Holidays – **M** a la carte 7.60/10.40.   pp. 30 and 31   FY   **a**

XX **Asuka,** Berkeley Arcade, 209A Baker St., NW1 6AB, ☏ 486 5026, Japanese rest. – 🖸 🆎 ⓪
VISA   pp. 13-16   KT   **u**
closed Saturday lunch and Sunday – **M** a la carte 11.20/14.90 🍷 3.80.

XX Tonino, Berkeley Court, 12 Glentworth St., NW1 5PG, ☏ 935 4220, Italian rest.
     pp. 13-16   KT   **c**

XX Bill Bentley's, 239 Baker St., NW1 6XE, ☏ 935 3130, Seafood   pp. 13-16 KST   **a**

XX **Viceroy of India,** 3-5 Glentworth St., NW1, ☏ 486 3401, Indian rest. – 🖸 🆎 ⓪ **VISA**
M a la carte 6.05/8.50 **t.**   pp. 13-16   KT   **o**

XX **Kerzenstüberl,** 9 St. Christopher's Pl., W1M 6DU, ☏ 486 3196, Austrian rest. – 🖸 🆎
VISA   BJ   **a**
closed Saturday lunch, Sunday, 10 August-10 September and Bank Holidays – **M** a la carte
7.95/11.10 **et.** 🍷 0.20.

XX **Gaylord,** 79-81 Mortimer St., W1N 7TB, ☏ 636 0808, Indian and Pakistani rest. – 🖸 🆎 ⓪
VISA   pp. 13-16   LT   **c**
M a la carte approx. 5.10 **t.** 🍷 3.10.

XX Masako, 6-8 St. Christopher's Pl., W1M 5HB, ☏ 935 1579, Japanese rest.   BJ   **e**

XX Lords Rendezvous, 24 Finchley Rd, NW8 6ES, ☏ 586 4280, Chinese rest.   pp. 13-16   JR   **r**

X **Au Bois St-Jean,** 122 St. John's Wood High St., NW8 7SG, ☏ 722 0400, French rest. – 🖸
🆎 ⓪ **VISA**   pp. 13-16   JS   **e**
closed Sunday and Bank Holidays – **M** (dinner only) a la carte 7.05/11.00 **t.** 🍷 2.00.

X **Mikado,** 110 George St., W1H 6DJ, ☏ 935 8320, Japanese rest. – 🆎 ⓪ **VISA**   AH   **s**
closed Saturday lunch, Sunday, 1 week September, 1 week December and Bank Holidays –
M a la carte 11.10/22.50 🍷 4.00.

X **Langan's Bistro,** 26 Devonshire St., W1, ☏ 935 4531   pp. 13-16   KT   **r**
closed Saturday lunch, Sunday and Bank Holidays – **M** a la carte 6.50/10.25 **t.**

X **Biagi's,** 39 Upper Berkeley St., W1H 7PG, ☏ 723 0394, Italian rest. – 🖸 🆎 ⓪ **VISA**
closed Bank Holidays – **M** a la carte 6.35/9.80 **t.**   pp. 30 and 31   FY   **c**

X L'Aventure, 3 Blenheim Terr., NW8, ☏ 624 6232, French rest. – 🆎   pp. 13-16   JR   **s**
closed Saturday lunch and Sunday dinner.

X **Il Barbino,** 64 Seymour St., W1H 5AF, ☏ 402 6866, Italian rest. – 🖸 🆎 ⓪ **VISA**
closed Saturday lunch, Sunday and Bank Holidays – **M** a la carte 7.50/10.00 **t.** 🍷 1.80.
     pp. 30 and 31   FY   **r**

X **Vecchio Parioli,** 129 Crawford St., W1H 1AA, ☏ 935 3791, Italian rest. – 🖸 🆎
closed Saturday lunch, Sunday, Good Friday and 25-26 December – **M** a la carte 5.80/10.50 **st.**
🍷 1.90.   pp. 13-16   KT   **s**

X Singapore, 62 Marylebone Lane, W1M 5FF, ☏ 486 2004, Malaysian rest.   BJ   **c**

St. James's – ✉ W1/SW1/WC2 – pp. 26 and 27.

🏯🏯🏯 **Ritz,** Piccadilly, W1V 9DG, ☏ 493 8181, Telex 267200 – 🛗 📺 ☎. 🖸 🆎 ⓪ **VISA**   DN   **a**
M a la carte 16.25/23.00 **st.** 🍷 3.00 – ⊒ 5.00 – **141 rm** 46.00/80.00.

🏯🏯 **Dukes** 🍸, 35 St. James's Pl., SW1A 1NY, ☏ 491 4840, Telex 28283 – 🛗 📺 ☎. 🖸 🆎 ⓪ **VISA**
M a la carte 12.50/20.00 **st.** 🍷 3.50 – ⊒ 5.25 – **54 rm** 49.00/78.00 st.   EP   **x**

🏯🏯 **Stafford** 🍸, 16-18 St. James's Pl., SW1A 1NJ, ☏ 493 0111, Telex 28602 – 🛗 📺 ☎. 🏠. 🆎
⓪   DN   **u**
M 7.60/8.60 **st.** 🍷 3.70 – ⊒ 5.50 – **60 rm** 61.00/86.00 **st.**

🏯🏯 **Cavendish** (T.H.F.), Jermyn St., SW1Y 6JF, ☏ 930 2111, Telex 263187 – 🛗 📺 ☎ 🚻 🅿. 🏠.
🖸 🆎 ⓪ **VISA**   EN   **i**
M 7.75 **st.** 🍷 3.45 – ⊒ a la carte 4.50 – **255 rm** 58.50/77.00 **st.**

🏯🏯 Royal Trafalgar (Thistle), Whitcomb St., WC2H 7HG, ☏ 930 4477, Telex 298564 – 🛗 📺 🚿wc
☎. 🖸 🆎 ⓪ **VISA**   GM   **r**
⊒ 3.95 – **108 rm** 36.00/49.00 **t.**

🏯🏯 Royal Angus (Thistle), 39 Coventry St., W1V 8EL, ☏ 930 4033, Group Telex 24616 – 🛗 📺
🚿wc ☎. 🖸 🆎 ⓪ **VISA**   FGM   **a**
⊒ 3.95 – **92 rm** 31.50/39.50 **t.**

🏯 Pastoria, St. Martin's St., WC2H 7HL, ☏ 930 8641, Telex 8813164 – 🛗 📺 🚿wc ☎   GM   **v**
54 rm.

XXX Suntory, 72-73 St. James's St., SW1, ☏ 409 0201, Japanese rest.   🖸 🆎 ⓪ **VISA**   EP   **z**
closed Sunday – **M** a la carte 9.30/24.00 🍷 3.50.

XXX **Hunting Lodge** (T.H.F.), 16 Regent St., SW1Y 4PH, ☏ 930 4222 – 🖸 🆎 ⓪ **VISA**   FM   **o**
M a la carte 9.60/16.60 **t.**

XX **Le Caprice,** Arlington House, Arlington St., SW1, ☏ 629 2239 – 🆎 **VISA**   DN   **c**
closed Saturday lunch, Sunday, 25-26 December and Bank Holidays – **M** a la carte 9.15/13.40 **t.**
🍷 2.00.

XX **Frank's,** 63 Jermyn St., SW1Y 6LX, ☏ 493 3645, Italian rest. – 🖸 🆎 ⓪ **VISA**   EN   **z**
closed Sunday, 3 weeks August and Bank Holidays – **M** a la carte 6.75/9.15 **t.** 🍷 2.05.

Soho – ⊠ W1/WC2 – pp. 26 and 27.

XXXX **Le Relais du Café Royal** (T.H.F.), 68 Regent St., W1R 6EL, ☏ 439 6082, Telex 261679 – 🔄 ⚠️ ⓘ 💳
EM **a**
closed Saturday lunch – **M** a la carte 11.70/15.00 **t.** ◊ 4.30.

XXXX **Café Royal Grill** (T.H.F.), 68 Regent St., W1R 6EL, ☏ 439 6320, Telex 261679 – 🔄 ⚠️ ⓘ 💳
EM **a**
closed Saturday lunch – **M** a la carte 12.65/15.85 **t.** ◊ 4.30.

XXX **Leonis Quo Vadis**, 26-29 Dean St., W1V 6LL, ☏ 437 9585, Italian rest. – 🔄 ⚠️ ⓘ 💳
closed Sunday lunch, Good Friday, Easter Sunday and Christmas Day – **M** a la carte 8.30/11.55 **t.**
◊ 1.90.
FK **u**

XX **La Terrazza**, 19 Romilly St., W1T 5TG, ☏ 734 2504, Italian rest. – 🔄 ⚠️ ⓘ 💳
FL **i**
M a la carte 7.30/12.40 **t.**

XX **Au Jardin des Gourmets**, 5 Greek St., Soho Sq., W1V 5LA, ☏ 437 1816, French rest. – 🔄 ⚠️ ⓘ 💳
GJ **a**
closed Saturday lunch and Sunday – **M** a la carte 7.95/10.75 **t.** ◊ 2.00.

XX **Venezia**, 21 Great Chapel St., W1V 5HA, ☏ 437 6506, Italian rest. – 🔄 ⚠️ ⓘ 💳
FJ **a**
closed Saturday lunch, Sunday and Bank Holidays – **M** a la carte 7.00/11.75 **t.** ◊ 2.15.

XX **Romeo e Giulietta**, 11 Sutton Row, W1V 5FE, ☏ 734 4914, Italian rest. – 🔄 ⚠️ ⓘ 💳
GJ **e**
closed Saturday lunch, Sunday and Bank Holidays – **M** a la carte 6.45/10.45 **t.** ◊ 1.80.

XX **Chesa (Swiss Centre)**, 10 Wardour St., W1V 3HG, ☏ 734 1291, Swiss rest. – 🔄 ⚠️ ⓘ 💳
GM **n**
M a la carte 7.40/12.80 **st.** ◊ 2.85.

XX **Rugantino**, 26 Romilly St., W1V 5TQ, ☏ 437 5302, Italian rest. – 🔄 ⚠️ ⓘ 💳
GK **u**
closed Saturday lunch, Sunday and Bank Holidays – **M** a la carte 7.25/9.25 **t.** ◊ 2.00.

XX **Gay Hussar**, 2 Greek St., W1V 6NB, ☏ 437 0973, Hungarian rest.
GJ **c**
closed Sunday and Bank Holidays – **M** a la carte 8.50/11.00 **t.** ◊ 2.70.

XX **Fuji**, 36-40 Brewer St., W1R 3HP, ☏ 734 0957, Japanese rest. – 🔄 ⚠️ ⓘ 💳
FL **c**
closed Saturday, Sunday and Bank Holidays for lunch – **M** a la carte 4.90/12.00 **st.**

X **Soho Rendezvous**, 21 Romilly St., W1V 5TG, ☏ 437 1486, Chinese rest. – 🔄 ⚠️ ⓘ 💳
GL **o**
closed Bank Holidays – **M** a la carte 8.00/12.90 **t.**

X **Trattoria Imperia**, 19 Charing Cross Rd, WC2H 0ES, ☏ 930 8364, Italian rest. – 🔄 ⚠️ ⓘ
💳
GM **z**
closed Sunday – **M** a la carte 5.35/9.45 **st.** ◊ 1.95.

Strand and Covent Garden – ⊠ WC2 – p. 31.

🏨 **Savoy**, Strand, WC2R 0EU, ☏ 836 4343, Telex 24234 – 📶 📺 ⇦. 🏊. 🔄 ⚠️ 💳
EX **a**
M Grill Room *(closed Saturday and Sunday)* a la carte 13.30/21.75 **t.** ◊ 2.50 – **River Room** a la carte 12.30/23.80 **t.** ◊ 2.50 – 🍽 4.15 – **200 rm** 60.00/85.00 **st.**

🏨 **Waldorf** (T.H.F.), Aldwych, WC2B 4DD, ☏ 836 2400, Telex 24574 – 📶 📺 ☎. 🏊. 🔄 ⚠️ ⓘ
💳
EV **x**
M 8.25/8.50 **st.** ◊ 2.10 – 🍽 4.50 – **310 rm** 49.50/60.50 **st.**

🏨 **Howard**, 12 Temple Pl., WC2R 2PR, ☏ 836 3555, Telex 268047 – 📶 📺 ⚙ ⇦. 🏊. 🔄 ⚠️ ⓘ
💳
FV **e**
M a la carte 10.50/14.70 **st.** ◊ 2.70 – **137 rm**

🏨 **Strand Palace** (T.H.F.), Strand, WC2R 0JJ, ☏ 836 8080, Telex 24208 – 📶 📺 ☎. 🏊. 🔄 ⚠️ ⓘ
💳
EV **u**
M (carvery rest.) 6.95 **t.** ◊ 2.50 – **761 rm**

🏨 **Charing Cross** (B.T.H.), Strand, WC2N 5HX, ☏ 839 7282, Telex 261101 – 📶 📺 ⇔wc ☎ ♿.
🏊. 🔄 ⚠️ ⓘ 💳
DX **s**
closed 1 week at Christmas – **M** (carvery rest.) 6.50 **st.** – 🍽 4.00 – **206 rm** 25.00/35.00 **st.**

XXXX ❀ **Boulestin**, 25 Southampton St., WC2, ☏ 836 7061, French rest. – 🔄 ⚠️ ⓘ 💳
EV **r**
closed Saturday lunch, Sunday, last 3 weeks August and Bank Holidays – **M** a la carte 12.00/16.25 **t.** ◊ 4.00
Spec. Corbeille croquante d'oeufs de caille au roquefort, Pléiade de homard aux pistils de safran, Aiguillettes de canard sauvage et sa cuisse en roinselle.

XXXX ❀ **Inigo Jones**, 14 Garrick St., WC2E 9BJ, ☏ 836 6456 – 🔄 ⚠️ ⓘ 💳
DV **n**
closed Saturday lunch, Sunday and Bank Holidays – **M** a la carte 13.60/19.70 **st.** ◊ 2.90
Spec. Pâté du pêcheur, Carré d'agneau en croûte sauce à la menthe, Lou Magret aux deux purées.

XXX **Ivy,** 1-5 West St., WC2H 9NE, ☏ 836 4751 – ᴬ ᴬᴱ Ⓞ 𝗩𝗜𝗦𝗔   DV **e**
closed Saturday lunch, Sunday and Bank Holidays – **M** a la carte 11.20/17.20 **t.** ⸸ 2.20.

XXX **Simpson's in-the-Strand,** 100 Strand, WC2R 0EW, ☏ 836 9112, English rest. – ᴬ 𝗩𝗜𝗦𝗔
closed Sunday, Good Friday, Christmas Day and Bank Holidays – **M** a la carte 8.85/13.85 **st.**
⸸ 2.50.   EV **o**

XXX **La Bussola,** 42-49 St. Martin's Lane, WC2N 4EJ, ☏ 240 1148, Italian rest., Dancing – ᴬ ᴬᴱ
Ⓞ 𝗩𝗜𝗦𝗔   DX **r**
closed Sunday and Bank Holidays – **M** a la carte 7.90/12.30 **t.** ⸸ 2.75.

XX **Thomas de Quincey's,** 36 Tavistock St., WC2E 7PB, ☏ 240 3972 – ᴬ ᴬᴱ Ⓞ 𝗩𝗜𝗦𝗔   EV **c**
closed Saturday lunch, Sunday, last 3 weeks August and Bank Holidays – **M** a la carte
13.00/14.50 **t.** ⸸ 2.70.

XX ✿ **Interlude de Tabaillau,** 7-8 Bow St., WC2, ☏ 379 6473, French rest. – ᴬ ᴬᴱ Ⓞ 𝗩𝗜𝗦𝗔
closed Saturday lunch, Sunday and Bank Holidays – **M** 17.50/19.00 **st.** (wine included) DEV **x**
Spec. Feuilleté d'agneau sauce moëlle, Filet de barbue Karpinski, Suprême de caneton Juliette.

XX **San Martino,** 46 St. Martin's Lane, WC2N 4EJ, ☏ 240 2336, Italian rest. – ᴬ ᴬᴱ Ⓞ 𝗩𝗜𝗦𝗔
closed Saturday lunch, Sunday, Good Friday and Christmas Day – **M** a la carte 6.75/9.65 **t.**
⸸ 2.05.   DX **x**

XX **Luigi's,** 15 Tavistock St., WC2E 7PA, ☏ 240 1795, Italian rest. – ᴬ 𝗩𝗜𝗦𝗔   EV **a**
closed Sunday and Bank Holidays – **M** a la carte 10.70/13.30 **t.** ⸸ 2.50.

XX **Grange,** 39 King St., WC2E 8JS, ☏ 240 2939 – ᴬᴱ   DV **z**
closed Saturday lunch, Sunday, 7 August 8 September and Bank Holidays – **M** 8.75/11.25 **t.**
⸸ 2.50.

XX **Chez Solange,** 35 Cranbourn St., WC2H 7AD, ☏ 836 5886, French rest. – ᴬ ᴬᴱ Ⓞ 𝗩𝗜𝗦𝗔
closed Sunday and Bank Holidays – **M** a la carte 6.70/11.80 **t.** ⸸ 2.60.   DV **i**

XX **Sheekey's,** 28-32 St. Martin's Court, WC2N 4AL, ☏ 240 2565, Seafood – ᴬ ᴬᴱ Ⓞ 𝗩𝗜𝗦𝗔
closed Sunday and Bank Holidays – **M** a la carte 9.40/12.75 **t.**   DV **v**

XX Azami, 13-15 West St., WC2H 9BL, ☏ 240 0634, Japanese rest.   pp. 26 and 27   GK **z**

X **Poons of Covent Garden,** 41 King St., WC2E 8JS, ☏ 240 1743, Chinese rest. – ᴬᴱ Ⓞ
closed Sunday and 24 to 26 December – **M** a la carte approx. 9.35 **t.**   DV **r**

X **Laguna 50,** 50 St. Martin's Lane, WC2N 4EA, ☏ 836 0960, Italian rest. – ᴬ ᴬᴱ Ⓞ 𝗩𝗜𝗦𝗔
closed Sunday and Bank Holidays – **M** a la carte 5.80/8.50 **t.** ⸸ 1.95.   DV **u**

X **Colosseo,** 12 May's Court, St. Martin's Lane, WC2N 4BS, ☏ 836 6140, Italian rest. – ᴬ ᴬᴱ
Ⓞ 𝗩𝗜𝗦𝗔   DX **e**
closed Saturday lunch and Sunday – **M** a la carte 5.85/9.05 **t.** ⸸ 1.95.

X **Cellier de Medici,** 5-8 May's Court, St. Martin's Lane, WC2N 4BS, ☏ 836 9180 – ᴬ ᴬᴱ Ⓞ
𝗩𝗜𝗦𝗔   DX **o**
closed Saturday lunch, Sunday and Bank Holidays – **M** a la carte 8.20/9.95 **t.** ⸸ 2.20.

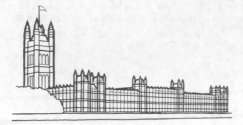

Victoria – ✉ SW1 – Except otherwise stated see p. 30.
🛈 West Passageway, Victoria Station ☏ 730 0791.

🏨 **Goring,** 15 Beeston Pl., Grosvenor Gdns, SW1W 0JW, ☏ 834 8211, Telex 919166 – 🛗 📺 ☎.
🗜. ᴬ ᴬᴱ Ⓞ 𝗩𝗜𝗦𝗔   BV **a**
M 9.00/11.00 **t.** ⸸ 3.50 – ⇌ 4.50 – **100 rm** 45.00/58.00 **st.** – P 49.00 **st.**

🏨 **Royal Horseguards (Thistle),** 2 Whitehall Court, SW1A 2EJ, ☏ 839 3400, Telex 917096 – 🛗 📺
☎. 🗜. ᴬ ᴬᴱ Ⓞ 𝗩𝗜𝗦𝗔   pp. 17-20 NV **u**
⇌ 3.95 – **280 rm** 38.00/43.50 **t.**

🏨 **Royal Westminster (Thistle),** Buckingham Palace Rd, SW1W 0QT, ☏ 834 1021, Telex 916821
– 🛗 📺. 🗜. ᴬ ᴬᴱ Ⓞ 𝗩𝗜𝗦𝗔   BV **z**
⇌ 3.95 – **135 rm** 39.50/49.80 **t.**

🏨 **St. Ermin's (Gd. Met.),** Caxton St., SW1H 0QW, ☏ 222 7888, Telex 917731 – 🛗 📺 ☎ 🅿. 🗜.
ᴬ ᴬᴱ Ⓞ 𝗩𝗜𝗦𝗔   CV **a**
M a la carte 9.30/14.40 **st.** ⸸ 2.50 – **229 rm.**

P.T.O. →

🏨 **Grosvenor** (B.T.H.), 101 Buckingham Palace Rd, SW1W 0SJ, ☏ 834 9494, Telex 916006 – 📶
📺 🛏wc 📻wc 📞. 🅰. ⚡ 🆎 ⓪ VISA BV e
M a la carte 3.75/7.60 **st.** 🍷 3.35 – ☑ 3.00 – **356 rm** 28.00/35.00 **st.**

🏨 **Ebury Court,** 24-32 Ebury St., SW1W 0LU, ☏ 730 8147 – 📶 🛏wc 📻. ⚡ VISA AV i
M a la carte 5.20/9.15 **t.** 🍷 2.10 – **37 rm** ☑ 23.50/43.00 **t.**

🏨 **Hamilton House,** 60-66 Warwick Way, SW1V 1SA, ☏ 821 7113 – 📺 🛏wc 📻. ⚡ 🆎 ⓪
VISA BX n
M (grill rest. only) a la carte approx. 2.85 **t.** 🍷 1.75 – **41 rm** ☑ 14.00/27.00 **t.**

🏠 **Elizabeth,** 37 Eccleston Sq., SW1V 1PB, ☏ 828 6812 – 📻 pp. 17-20 LY c
24 rm ☑ 14.00/36.00 **st.**

XXX **Lockets,** Marsham Court, Marsham St., SW1P 4JY, ☏ 834 9552, English rest. – ⚡ 🆎 ⓪
VISA pp. 17-20 MY z
closed Saturday, Sunday and Bank Holidays – **M** a la carte 8.30/10.80 **t.** 🍷 2.00.

XX **Kundan,** 3 Horseferry Rd, SW1P 2AN, ☏ 834 3434, Indian and Pakistani rest. – ⚡ 🆎 ⓪ VISA
closed Sunday and Bank Holidays – **M** a la carte 6.80/8.50 🍷 2.80. pp. 17-20 NXY a

XX **Ken Lo's Memories of China,** 67-69 Ebury St., SW1W 0NZ, ☏ 730 7734, Chinese rest. –
⚡ 🆎 ⓪ VISA AX u
closed Sunday and Bank Holidays – **M** a la carte 11.10/18.10 **st.**

XX **Pomegranates,** 94 Grosvenor Rd, SW1V 3LG, ☏ 828 6560 – ⚡ 🆎 ⓪ VISA
closed Saturday lunch, Sunday and Bank Holidays – **M** a la carte 9.30/13.00 **t.** 🍷 2.55.
pp. 17-20 LMZ a

XX **Eatons,** 49 Elizabeth St., SW1W 9PP, ☏ 730 0074 – ⚡ 🆎 ⓪ VISA AX a
closed Saturday, Sunday and Bank Holidays – **M** a la carte 6.80/10.40 **s.** 🍷 2.25.

XX **The Restaurant,** Dolphin Square, Chichester St., SW1, ☏ 828 3207, French rest., « Art
deco » – ⚡ 🆎 ⓪ VISA LZ e
M a la carte 5.85/13.35 **t.** 🍷 2.50.

XX **Mijanou,** 143 Ebury St., SW1W 9QN, ☏ 730 4099, French rest. – ⚡ 🆎 ⓪ AX c
closed Saturday, Sunday, 1 week at Easter, 3 weeks August and 2 weeks at Christmas – **M** a la
carte 10.85/17.15 **t.** 🍷 2.00.

XX **Gran Paradiso,** 52 Wilton Rd, SW1V 1DE, ☏ 828 5818, Italian rest. – ⚡ 🆎 ⓪ VISA BX a
closed Saturday lunch, Sunday and Bank Holidays – **M** a la carte 7.00/9.20 **t.** 🍷 1.65.

X **La Fontana,** 101 Pimlico Rd, SW1W 8PH, ☏ 730 6630 – 🆎 ⓪ pp. 28 and 29 FT o
closed Saturday lunch and Sunday – **M** a la carte 7.30/9.30 **t.** 🍷 2.50.

X **La Poule au Pot,** 231 Ebury St., SW1W 8UT, ☏ 730 7763, French rest. pp. 17-20 KY n

X **Mimmo d'Ischia,** 61 Elizabeth St., SW1W 9PP, ☏ 730 5406, Italian rest. – ⚡ 🆎 ⓪ VISA
closed Sunday and Bank Holidays – **M** a la carte 9.30 **t.** 🍷 1.75.
AX o

X **Pimlico,** 89 Pimlico Rd, SW1W 9PH, ☏ 730 5323, Italian Bistro – 🆎 ⓪
closed Tuesday lunch and Monday – **M** a la carte 6.50/8.10 **t.** 🍷 2.40. pp. 28 and 29 FT c

X **Bumbles,** 16 Buckingham Palace Rd, SW1W 0QP, ☏ 828 2903, Bistro – ⚡ 🆎 ⓪ VISA
closed Saturday lunch, Sunday and Bank Holidays – **M** a la carte 6.40/7.85 **t.** BV c

X **Tate Gallery Rest.,** Tate Gallery, Millbank, SW1P 4RG, ☏ 834 6754, English rest., « Rex
Whistler murals » pp. 17-20 NY c
closed Sunday, Good Friday, 1 May, 24 to 26 December, New Year and Bank Holidays – **M**
(lunch only) a la carte 6.35/11.80 **t.** 🍷 2.60.

MANCHESTER

MANCHESTER Greater Manchester **402 403 404** N 23 – pop. 543,650 – ECD : Wednesday – ✪ 061.

See : Town Hall★ 19C DZ – City Art Gallery★ DZ **M** – Whitworth Art Gallery★ – Cathedral 15C (chancel★) DZ **B** – John Ryland's Library (manuscripts★) CZ **A**.

Envir. : Heaton Hall★ (18C) *AC*, N : 5 m.

🛦 Heaton Park, ☎ 773 1085, N : by A 576 – 🛦 Booth Rd, Audenshaw, ☎ 370 1641, E : by A 635 – 🛦 Brookdale, Woodhouses ☎ 681 4534, N : 5 m.

✈ ☎ (061) 437 5233, S : 10 m. by A 5103 and M 56 – **Terminal :** Victoria Station.

🖪 Magnum House, Portland St. Piccadilly ☎ 247 3094 and 3712/3 – Town Hall Extension, Lloyd St. ☎ 236 1606/1697.

♦London 202 – ♦Birmingham 86 – ♦Glasgow 213 – ♦Leeds 42 – ♦Liverpool 36 – ♦Nottingham 69.

MANCHESTER
CENTRE

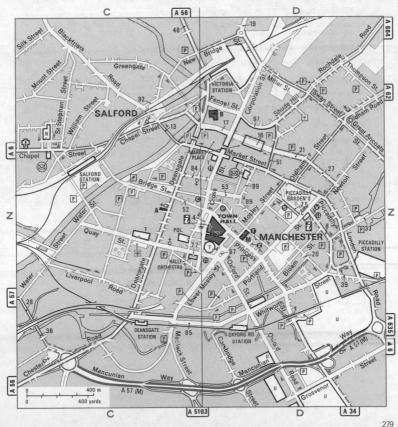

🏨 Piccadilly (Embassy), Piccadilly Plaza, M60 1QR, ☏ 236 8414, Telex 668765, ≼ – 🛗 📺 ☎ 🕭 ⓟ. 🖎 🖎 Æ ⓞ 𝘝𝘐𝘚𝘈
DZ s
M 9.95 st. ⌗ 2.50 – **246 rm**.

🏨 Midland (B.T.H.), Peter St., M60 2DS, ☏ 236 3333, Telex 667797 – 🛗 📺. 🖎. 🖎 Æ ⓞ 𝘝𝘐𝘚𝘈
M 7.25/8.25 st. ⌗ 3.50 (see also **French Restaurant**) – � 2.50 – **302 rm** 39.60/54.00 st.   CDZ n

🏨 Portland (Thistle), Piccadilly Gdns., M1 6DP, ☏ 228 3400, Telex 669157 – 🛗 📺 ☎ 🕭. 🖎. 🖎 Æ ⓞ 𝘝𝘐𝘚𝘈
DZ v
⊃ 3.95 – **221 rm** 33.50/40.00 t.

🏨 Grand (T.H.F.), Aytoun St., M1 3DR, ☏ 236 9559, Telex 667580 – 🛗 📺. 🖎. 🖎 Æ ⓞ 𝘝𝘐𝘚𝘈
M 6.25 st. ⌗ 2.90 – ⊃ 3.75 – **146 rm** 34.00/44.00 st.   DZ u

XXXX French Restaurant (B.T.H.), (at Midland H.) Peter St., M60 2DS, ☏ 236 3333, Telex 667797
– 🖎 Æ ⓞ 𝘝𝘐𝘚𝘈   CDZ n
closed Sunday and Bank Holidays – **M** (dinner only) a la carte 11.50/18.50 **st.**

XXX La Terrazza, 14 Nicholas St., M1 4FE, ☏ 236 4033, Italian rest. – 🖎 Æ ⓞ 𝘝𝘐𝘚𝘈   DZ r
closed Saturday lunch and Sunday – **M** a la carte approx. 15.50 **st.**

XX Via Veneto, 35 George St., M1 4HQ, ☏ 236 4887, Italian rest. – 🖎 ⓞ 𝘝𝘐𝘚𝘈   DZ z
closed Saturday lunch and Sunday – **M** a la carte 8.00/10.00 **t.** ⌗ 2.00.

XX Isola Bella, 6a Booth St., M2 4AW, ☏ 236 6417, Italian rest. – ⓞ 𝘝𝘐𝘚𝘈   DZ e
closed Sunday, 25-26 December and Bank Holidays – **M** a la carte 7.30/12.60 **st.** ⌗ 2.00.

XX Rajdoot, St. James' House, South King St., ☏ 834 2176, Indian rest. – 🖎 Æ ⓞ 𝘝𝘐𝘚𝘈   CZ c
closed lunch Sunday and Bank Holidays and 25-26 December – **M** a la carte 6.70/8.20 **t.** ⌗ 2.00.

XX Casa España, 100 Wilmslow Rd, M14 5AJ, S : 2 m. on A 34 ☏ 224 6826, Spanish rest..

X Danish Food Centre (Copenhagen Room), Cross St., M2 7BY, ☏ 832 9924, Smorrebrod –
🖎 Æ ⓞ 𝘝𝘐𝘚𝘈   DZ n
closed Sunday and Bank Holidays – **M** a la carte 4.60/11.55 **st.** ⌗ 2.80.

at Whalley Range S : 2 ½ m. – ✉ ✆ 061 Manchester :

🏛 Simpson's, 122 Withington Rd, M16 8FB, ☏ 226 2235, ☔ – ⏥wc ☎ ⓟ. 🖎 ⓞ 𝘝𝘐𝘚𝘈
closed 24 December-2 January – **M** 3.00/5.50 ⌗ 3.50 – **38 rm** ⊃ 12.00/24.00.

at Fallowfield S : 3 m. on B 5093 – ✉ ✆ 061 Manchester :

🏨 Willow Bank, 340-342 Wilmslow Rd, M14 6AF, ☏ 224 0461, Telex 666387 – 📺 ⏥wc ☎ ⓟ.
🖎 Æ ⓞ 𝘝𝘐𝘚𝘈
M *(closed Sunday lunch)* 4.00/6.00 **t.** ⌗ 1.75 – ⊃ 3.00 – **122 rm** 15.00/27.00 t. – P 25.00/35.00 st.

at West Didsbury S : 5 ½ m. by B 5093 – ✉ ✆ 061 Manchester :

XX George's Armenian Rest., 125 Palatine Rd, M20 9YA, ☏ 434 1122, Armenian rest. – ⓟ. Æ
closed Sunday and 25-26 December – **M** a la carte 5.95/9.50 **t.**

at Northenden S : 6 ½ m. by A 5103 and M 56 – ✉ ✆ 061 Manchester :

🏨 Post House (T.H.F.), Palatine Rd, M22 4FH, ☏ 998 7090, Telex 669248 – 🛗 📺 ⏥wc ☎ 🕭
ⓟ. 🖎. 🖎 Æ ⓞ 𝘝𝘐𝘚𝘈
M 4.95/6.95 **st.** ⌗ 2.90 – ⊃ 3.75 – **201 rm** 29.00/36.50 st.

at Manchester Airport S : 9 m. by A 5103 and M 56 – ✉ ✆ 061 Manchester :

🏨 Excelsior (T.H.F.), M22 5NS, ☏ 437 5811, Telex 668721, ⊒ heated – 🛗 📺 ☎ 🕭 ⓟ. 🖎. 🖎 Æ
ⓞ 𝘝𝘐𝘚𝘈
M a la carte 9.80/13.40 **st.** ⌗ 2.10 – ⊃ 3.75 – **304 rm** 36.00/44.00 st.

at Heald Green S : 10 m. by A 5103 and M 56 – ✉ ✆ 061 Manchester :

XX La Bonne Auberge, 224 Finney Lane, SK8 3QA, ☏ 437 5701, French rest. – ⓟ. 🖎 Æ ⓞ
closed Monday dinner, Sunday and Bank Holidays – **M** a la carte 7.30/9.60 **st.** ⌗ 2.50.

at Pendleton W : 4 m. by A 6 and A 576 – ✉ ✆ 061 Manchester :

⏡ Beaucliffe, 254 Eccles Old Rd, M6 8ES, ☏ 789 5092 – ⏢wc ⓟ. 🖎 𝘝𝘐𝘚𝘈
21 rm ⊃ 12.50/20.50.

Italia

Roma

Milano

Venezia

ROMA

ROMA 00100 ▣ 🄳🄸🄸 ㉙ – 2 916 414 ab. alt. 20 – ✿ 06.

Curiosità
La maggior parte delle più note curiosità di Roma è ubicata sulle piante da p. 4 a 11. Per una visita turistica più dettagliata consultate la guida Verde Michelin Italia.

Curiosités
Les plans des p. 4 à 11 situent la plupart des grandes curiosités de Rome. Pour une visite touristique plus détaillée, consultez le guide Vert Italie et plus particulièrement le guide Vert Rome.

Sehenswürdigkeiten
Auf den Städtplänen S. 4 bis 11 sind die hauptsächlichsten Sehenswürdigkeiten verzeichnet. Eine ausführliche Beschreibung aller Sehenswürdigkeiten finden Sie im Grünen Reiseführer Italien.

Sights
Rome's most famous sights are indicated on the town plans pp. 4 to 11. For a more complete visit see the Green Guide to Italy.

🕤 (chiuso lunedi) ad Acquasanta ✉ 00178 Roma 🕿 783407, SE : 12 km MS;

🕤 e 🕤 (chiuso lunedi) ad Olgiata ✉ 00123 Roma 🕿 3788040, per ⑩ : 19 km.

✈ di Ciampino SE : 15 km NS 🕿 600251.

✈ Leonardo da Vinci di Fiumicino per ⑧ : 26 km 🕿 4687 – Alitalia, via Giolitti 36 ✉ 00185 🕿 481650; via Bissolati 13 ✉ 00187 🕿 4688 e piazzale Pastore o dell'Arte (EUR) ✉ 00144 🕿 5454.

🚃 Tèrmini 🕿 464923 – Tiburtina 🕿 4956626.

🛈 via Parigi 5 ✉ 00185 🕿 463748 – sulle autostrade : A1 Roma Nord 🕿 6919958 e A2 Roma Sud 🕿 9420058.

A.C.I. via Cristoforo Colombo 261 ✉ 00147 🕿 5106 e via Marsala 8 ✉ 00185 🕿 4998, Telex 610686.

Distanze : nel testo delle altre città elencate nella Guida è indicata la distanza chilometrica da Roma.

Zona nord Monte Mario, Stadio Olimpico, via Flaminia-Parioli, Villa Borghese, via Salaria, via Nomentana (pianta : Roma p. 6 e 7, salvo indicazioni speciali)

Cavalieri Hilton ⑤, via Cadlolo 101 ⊠ 00136 ℡ 3151, Telex 610296, ≤ città, « Terrazze e parco », ⌿ (coperta d'inverno), ※ – 🗐 🖸 ☎ ⑆ ⇔ 🅿 - 🔊. 🄰🄴 ① 🅴 𝘝𝘐𝘚𝘈. ※ rist   AT **n**
Pas carta 34000/45000 al Rist. **La Pergola** carta 36000/52000 – ☑ 10500 – **398 cam** 135000/176000.

Lord Byron e Rist. le Jardin ⑤, via De Notaris 5 ⊠ 00197 ℡ 3609541, Telex 611217, ⇌ –
🗐 🖸 ☎ ⑆ 🅿. 🄰🄴 ① 𝘝𝘐𝘚𝘈. ※ rist   ET **a**
Pas (prenotare e *chiuso domenica*) carta 25000/37000 – ☑ 7500 – **55 cam** 95000/120000.

Borromini senza rist, via Lisbona 7 ⊠ 00198 ℡ 841321, Telex 680485 – 🗐 🖸 ☎ - 🔊. 🄰🄴 ①
🅴 𝘝𝘐𝘚𝘈. ※   GT **e**
☑ 6000 – **75 cam** 61000/88000.

Albani senza rist, via Adda 41 ⊠ 00198 ℡ 84991, Telex 612414 – 🗐 🖸 ☎ ⑆ ⇔ - 🔊. 🄰🄴 ①
𝘝𝘐𝘚𝘈   GT **g**
☑ 3500 – **157 cam** 60000/95000.

Parco dei Principi, via Frescobaldi 5 ⊠ 00198 ℡ 841071, Telex 610517, « Piccolo parco con
⌿ » – 🗐 🖸 ☎ ⇔ - 🔊. 🄰🄴 ①. ※   FT **h**
Pas 18000/28000 – ☑ 9000 – **179 cam** 90000/130000 – P 93000.

Claridge e Rist. lo Chef, viale Liegi 62 ⊠ 00198 ℡ 868556 e rist ℡ 8449482, Telex 610340 –
🗐 ☎ ⑆ - 🔊. 🄰🄴 ① 𝘝𝘐𝘚𝘈   GT **u**
Pas carta 15000/23000 – ☑ 5000 – **88 cam** 55000/75000.

Panama senza rist, via Salaria 336 ⊠ 00199 ℡ 862558, ⇌ – 🛗 🗐 ⌷wc 🖩wc ☎. ※   HT **e**
43 cam ☑ 37000/64000, 🗐 4500.

Fenix, viale Gorizia 5 ⊠ 00198 ℡ 850741, ⇌ – 🛗 🗐 ⌷wc 🖩wc ☎ ⑆ ⇔. 𝘝𝘐𝘚𝘈. ※   JT **g**
Pas 13000/16000 – **69 cam** ☑ 33000/65000, 🗐 3000.

Degli Aranci, via Oriani 11 ⊠ 00197 ℡ 870202, « Terrazza-aranceto » – 🛗 ⌷wc 🖩wc ☎.
※   ET **r**
Pas 15000 – **42 cam** ☑ 36000/56000.

Villa del Parco senza rist, via Nomentana 110 ⊠ 00161 ℡ 864115, ⇌ – 🗐 ⌷wc 🖩wc ☎.
🄰🄴 𝘝𝘐𝘚𝘈. ※   JT **n**
23 cam ☑ 33000/55000, 🗐 5000.

Villa Florence senza rist, via Nomentana 28 ⊠ 00161 ℡ 864461 – 🛗 ⌷wc 🖩wc ☎ ⑆ 🅿.
🄰🄴. ※   HT **r**
☑ 4000 – **25 cam** 33000/50000.

Colony Flaminio senza rist, via Monterosi 18 ⊠ 00191 ℡ 3276843 – 🛗 🗐 ⌷wc 🖩wc ☎ ⑆.
🄰🄴 ①   Roma p.5 MQ **m**
☑ 3500 – **72 cam** 35000/50000.

Rivoli senza rist, via Torquato Taramelli 7 ⊠ 00197 ℡ 878161, Telex 614615 – 🛗 ⌷wc 🖩wc ☎.
🄰🄴 ① 🅴 𝘝𝘐𝘚𝘈. ※   ET **b**
47 cam ☑ 32000/50000.

Lloyd senza rist, via Alessandria 110 ⊠ 00198 ℡ 862977, Telex 612598 – 🛗 🗐 ⌷wc 🖩wc
☎. 🄰🄴 ① 🅴   HT **f**
☑ 3500 – **48 cam** 25000/40000, 🗐 3500.

Clodio senza rist, via di Santa Lucia 10 ⊠ 00195 ℡ 317541 – 🛗 ⌷wc 🖩wc ☎. ※   ABT **e**
☑ 5000 – **117 cam** 35000/55000.

Astor senza rist, via Tevere 5/d ⊠ 00198 ℡ 851224, ⇌ – 🛗 🗐 ⌷wc ☎. 🄰🄴 ① 🅴 𝘝𝘐𝘚𝘈
※   GT **a**
27 cam ☑ 36000/46000, 🗐 3500.

Delle Muse, via Salvini 18 ⊠ 00197 ℡ 870095, Telex 612537, « Rist. estivo in giardino » – 🛗
🗐 rist ⌷wc 🖩wc ☎. 🄰🄴 ① 🅴 𝘝𝘐𝘚𝘈   GT **n**
Pas 12000 – **62 cam** ☑ 30000/47000 – P 41000/52000.

La Vigna dei Cardinali, piazzale Ponte Milvio 34 ⊠ 00191 ℡ 3965846, « Servizio estivo in
giardino » – 🅿. 🄰🄴 ① 𝘝𝘐𝘚𝘈   Roma p. 5 MQ **x**
chiuso sabato – Pas carta 16000/26000.

Il Caminetto, via dei Parioli 89 ⊠ 00197 ℡ 803946 – 🗐   ET **q**
chiuso giovedì e dal 14 al 18 agosto – Pas carta 13000/20000.

Al Ceppo, via Panama 2 ⊠ 00198 ℡ 84409696, Rist. caratteristico – 🗐. ① 𝘝𝘐𝘚𝘈   GT **u**
chiuso lunedì e dal 7 al 31 agosto – Pas carta 13000/20000.

Celestina-Fazi, viale dei Parioli 184 ⊠ 00197 ℡ 878242 – 🗐   ET **k**
chiuso domenica ed agosto – Pas carta 14000/20000.

La Pariolina, via dei Parioli 93/d e f ⊠ 00197 ℡ 879734 – **Pas** carta 12000/18000.   ET **q**
chiuso lunedì e dal 10 al 25 agosto – **Pas** carta 12000/18000.

Trattoria Capri, viale Tirreno 252 ⊠ 00141 ℡ 8182268   MQ **e**

La Scala, viale dei Parioli 79/d ⊠ 00197 ℡ 803978, Rist.-pizzeria   ET **q**
chiuso mercoledì e dal 10 al 30 agosto – Pas carta 12000/20000.

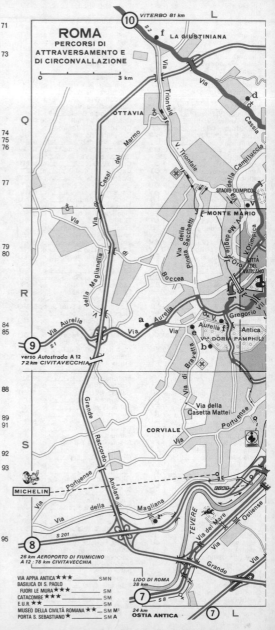

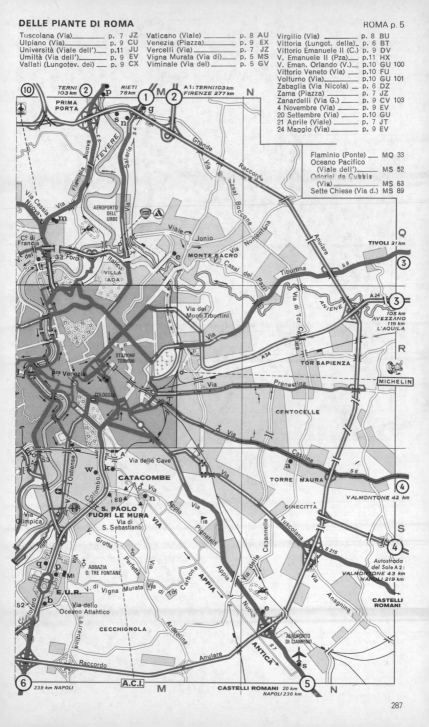

A

MUSEO BORGHESE ★★★	FT M²
VILLA GIULIA ★★★	DT M³
S. SABINA ★★	DEZ C
TERME DI CARACALLA ★★	FGZ
VILLA BORGHESE ★★	EFT
AVENTINO ★	EZ
GALLERIA NAZ. D'ARTE MODERNA ★	ET M⁴
PIRAMIDE DI CAIO CESTIO ★	EZ B
PORTA S. PAOLO ★	EZ K
S. AGNESE E S. COSTANZA ★	JT F
S. CROCE IN GERUSALEMME ★	JY G
S. LORENZO FUORI LE MURA ★	JV D
S. SABA ★	EZ E

VITERBO 81 km — TERNI 103 km

STADIO OLIMPICO

Vedere indice toponomastico, Roma p. 3, 4 e 5.

72 km CIVITAVECCHIA

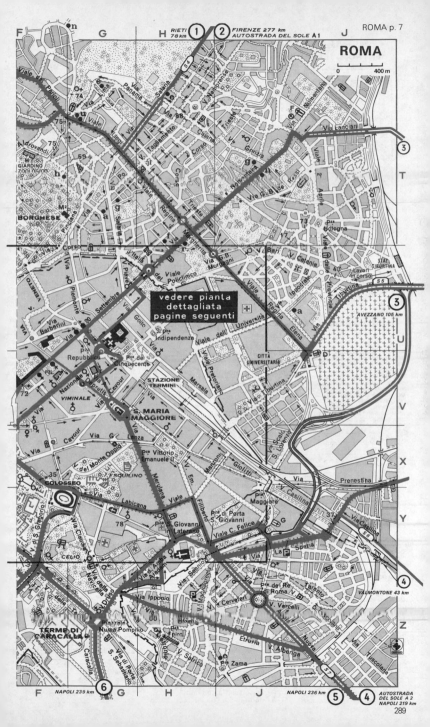

ROMA

ROMA
CENTRO OVEST

0   400 m

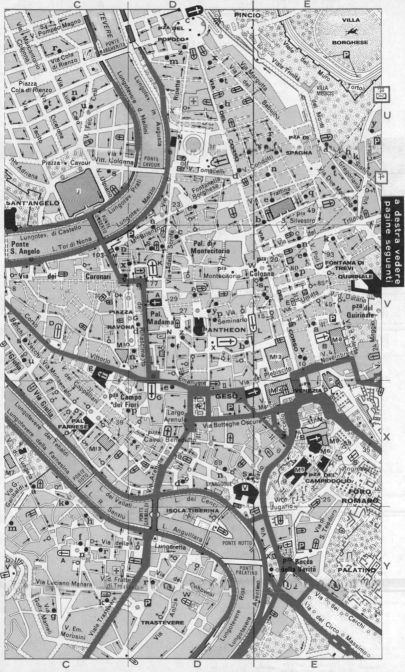

a destra vedere pagine seguenti

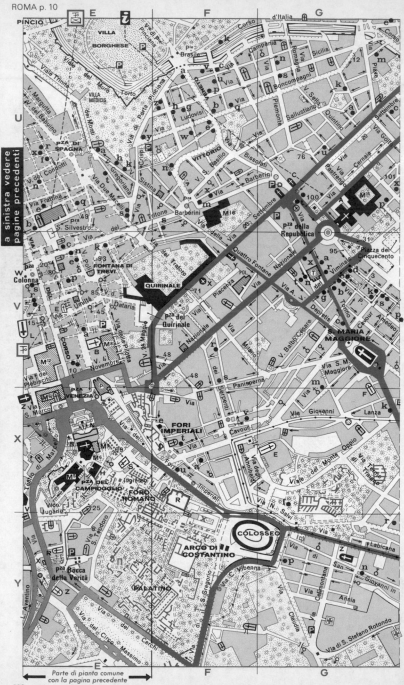

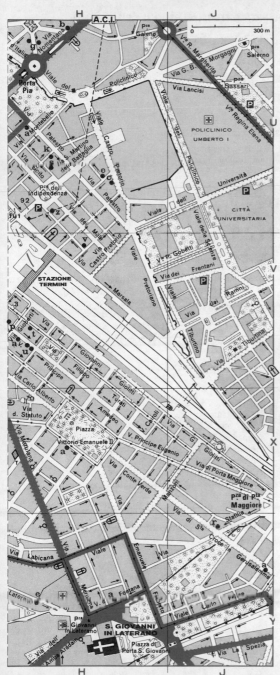

ROMA
CENTRO EST

ELENCO ALFABETICO DEGLI ALBERGHI E RISTORANTI

For Gourmets

We distinguish for your use
certain hotels and restaurants
by awarding them ❀ or ❀❀.

X **Delle Vittorie,** via Monte Santo 62/64 ⊠ 00195 ℱ 386847 – ⋘   BT **a**
   chiuso domenica e dal 22 dicembre al 10 gennaio – Pas carta 13000/18000.

X **Da Benito,** via Flaminia Nuova 230/232 ⊠ 00191 ℱ 3272752, Trattoria-pizzeria – ⚏ ⓿
   chiuso lunedì – Pas carta 14000/24000.   Roma p. 5 MQ **m**

X **Nino alla Camilluccia,** via della Camilluccia 64 ⊠ 00135 ℱ 340829, Trattoria di campagna;
   servizio estivo all'aperto con ⩸ – ❸   Roma p. 4 LQ **v**
   chiuso venerdì ed agosto – Pas carta 16000/24000.

   Zona centro ovest San Pietro (Città del Vaticano), Gianicolo, corso Vittorio Emanuele, piazza
   Venezia, Pantheon e Quirinale, Pincio e Villa Medici, piazza di Spagna, Palatino e Fori (pianta :
   Roma p. 8 e 9, salvo indicazioni speciali)

🏨 **Hassler-Villa Medici,** piazza Trinità dei Monti 6 ⊠ 00187 ℱ 6792651, Telex 610208, ⩸ città
   dal rist. roof-garden – ⬛ ☎. ⋘   EU **a**
   Pas carta 30000/45000 – ⌑ 8500 – **100 cam** 130000/180000.

🏨 **Eden,** via Ludovisi 49 ⊠ 00187 ℱ 4743551, Telex 610567, « Rist. roof-garden con ⩸ città » –
   ⬛ ☎. ⋘   EU **y**
   Pas carta 30000/40000 – ⌑ 6000 – **116 cam** 100000/150000.

🏨 **Plaza** senza rist, via del Corso 126 ⊠ 00186 ℱ 672101 – ⬛ ⤶ - 🚗. ⚏. ⋘   DU **d**
   ⌑ 5000 – **207 cam** 53000/80000, ⬛ 3000.

🏨 **Gd G. de La Ville,** via Sistina 69 ⊠ 00187 ℱ 6733, Telex 611676 – ⬛ ☎ ⤶ ⇋ - 🚗. ⚏ ⓿
   E 𝕍𝕀𝕊𝔸   EU **h**
   Pas carta 19000/28000 – 189 cam ⌑ 79000/120000.

🏨 **Leonardo da Vinci,** via dei Gracchi 324 ⊠ 00192 ℱ 382091, Telex 611182 – ⬛ 📺 ☎ ⇋ -
   🚗. ⚏. ⋘   CU **r**
   Pas *(chiuso domenica)* 21000 – ⌑ 6000 – **250 cam** 71000/105000 – P 116000.

🏨 **Cicerone** senza rist, via Cicerone 55 ⊠ 00193 ℱ 3576, Telex 680514 – ⬛ 📺 ☎ ⤶ ⇋ - 🚗.
   ⚏ ⓿ **E** 𝕍𝕀𝕊𝔸. ⋘   CU **t**
   237 cam ⌑ 75000/100000.

🏨 **Visconti Palace** senza rist, via Cesi 37 ⊠ 00193 ℱ 3684, Telex 680407 – ⬛ 📺 ☎ ⤶ ⇋
   ⚏ ⓿ **E** 𝕍𝕀𝕊𝔸   CU **u**
   247 cam ⌑ 70000/100000.

🏨 **D'Inghilterra** senza rist, via Bocca di Leone 14 ⊠ 00187 ℱ 672161, Telex 614552 – ⬛ 📺 ☎
   ⚏ ⓿ **E** 𝕍𝕀𝕊𝔸   EU **n**
   ⌑ 7000 – **102 cam** 85000/110000.

🏨 **Marini Strand Hotel,** via del Tritone 17 ⊠ 00187 ℱ 672061, Telex 612295 – ⬛ ☎. ⚏ ⓿ **E**
   𝕍𝕀𝕊𝔸. ⋘ rist   EV **c**
   Pas 14000 – **115 cam** ⌑ 61000/94000.

🏨 **Delle Nazioni** senza rist, via Poli 7 ⊠ 00187 ℱ 6792441, Telex 614193 – ⬛ ☎. ⚏ ⓿ **E** 𝕍𝕀𝕊𝔸
   75 cam ⌑ 60000/85000, ⬛ 5000.   EV **e**

🏨 **Colonna Palace** senza rist, piazza Montecitorio 12 ⊠ 00186 ℱ 6781341, Telex 721467 – ⬛
   ☎. ⚏ ⓿ **E** 𝕍𝕀𝕊𝔸   EV **s**
   ⌑ 5000 – **100 cam** 60000/90000.

🏨 **Accademia** senza rist, piazza Accademia di San Luca 75 ⊠ 00187 ℱ 6786705 – 🛗 ⬛ 🚻wc
   🛁wc ☜. ⚏ ⓿ **E** 𝕍𝕀𝕊𝔸   EV **k**
   41 cam ⌑ 48000/70000.

🏨 **Della Torre Argentina** senza rist, corso Vittorio Emanuele 102 ⊠ 00186 ℱ 6548251 – 🛗
   🚻wc 🛁wc ☜. ⚏ ⓿ 𝕍𝕀𝕊𝔸. ⋘   DX **e**
   ⌑ 3000 – **32 cam** 33000/52000.

🏨 **Atlante,** via Vitelleschi 34 ⊠ 00193 ℱ 6564196, Telex 680258, « Rist. roof-garden con ⩸
   Basilica di San Pietro » – 🛗 ⬛ cam 🚻wc 🛁wc ☜. ⚏ ⓿ **E** 𝕍𝕀𝕊𝔸. ⋘ rist   BU **r**
   Pas 14000/17000 – **76 cam** ⌑ 65000/90000 – P 72000/85000.

🏨 **Diplomatic,** via Vittoria Colonna 28 ⊠ 00193 ℱ 6542084, Telex 610506 – 🛗 ⬛ 🚻wc 🛁wc
   ☜. ⚏ ⓿ **E** 𝕍𝕀𝕊𝔸   CU **s**
   Pas carta 12000/18000 (15%) – **35 cam** ⌑ 45000/68000.

🏨 **Bologna** senza rist, via Santa Chiara 4/a ⊠ 00186 ℱ 6568951 – 🛗 🚻wc 🛁wc ☜ ⤶   DV **z**
   118 cam ⌑ 38000/58000.

🏨 **Arcangelo** senza rist, via Boezio 15 ⊠ 00192 ℱ 311098 – 🛗 🚻wc 🛁wc ☜   BU **e**
   30 cam ⌑ 35000/60000.

🏨 **Carriage** senza rist, via delle Carrozze 36 ⊠ 00187 ℱ 6795166 – 🛗 ⬛ 🚻wc ☜. ⋘   EU **x**
   ⌑ 2500 – **24 cam** 37000/55000, ⬛ 2500.

🏨 **Della Conciliazione** senza rist, borgo Pio 165 ⊠ 00193 ℱ 6567910 – 🛗 🚻wc 🛁wc ☜ ⤶
   ⚏ ⓿   BU **k**
   ⌑ 3500 – **80 cam** 26000/42000.

🏨 **Gregoriana** senza rist, via Gregoriana 18 ⊠ 00187 ℱ 6794269 – 🛗 ⬛ 🚻wc 🛁wc ☜ ⤶   EU **t**
   19 cam ⌑ 45000/70000.

🏨 **Adriano,** via di Pallacorda 2 ⊠ 00186 ℱ 6542451 – 🛗 🚻wc 🛁wc ☜. ⚏ ⓿ **E** 𝕍𝕀𝕊𝔸. ⋘
   Pas (solo per clienti alloggiati) 8000/12000 – ⌑ 4000 – **82 cam** 21000/43000 – P 34000/47000.
         DV **c**

Tritone senza rist, via del Tritone 210 ⊠ 00187 ☎ 6782624, Telex 614254 – |‡| ▤ ⊟wc ⋒wc ☏. AE ⓓ E VISA — EV **n**
43 cam ☕ 43000/65000.

Madrid senza rist, via Mario de' Fiori 95 ⊠ 00187 ☎ 6791249 – |‡| ▤ TV ⊟wc ⋒wc ☏. AE ⓓ VISA. ✗ — EU **q**
24 cam ☕ 60000.

Atlante Garden senza rist, via Crescenzio 78/a ⊠ 00193 ☎ 350338 – |‡| ▤ ⊟wc ⋒wc ☏. AE ⓓ E VISA — BU **f**
42 cam ☕ 65000/90000.

Internazionale senza rist, via Sistina 79 ⊠ 00187 ☎ 6793047, Telex 614333 – |‡| ▤ ⊟wc ⋒wc ☏. AE ⓓ E VISA — EU **k**
38 cam ☕ 55000/85000.

Gerber senza rist, via degli Scipioni 241 ⊠ 00192 ☎ 3595148 – |‡| ⊟wc ⋒wc ☏ ♿. AE ⓓ VISA. ✗ — BU **s**
28 cam ☕ 20000/44000.

Cesàri senza rist, via di Pietra 89/a ⊠ 00186 ☎ 6792386 – |‡| ⊟wc ☏. AE VISA — EV **r**
50 cam ☕ 34000/46000.

Senato senza rist, piazza della Rotonda 73 ⊠ 00186 ☎ 6793231, ≤ Pantheon – |‡| ⊟wc ⋒wc ☏. AE ⓓ VISA. ✗ — DV **y**
☕ 3000 – **50 cam** 20000/40000.

San Silvestro senza rist, via del Gambero 3 ⊠ 00187 ☎ 6794169 – |‡| ▤ ⋒wc ☏. AE ⓓ E VISA. ✗ — EU **b**
☕ 3500 – **21 cam** 28000/33000.

Sant'Anna senza rist, borgo Pio 134 ⊠ 00193 ☎ 6541602 – ⊟wc ⋒wc ☏ — BU **h**
18 cam ☕ 30000/48000.

Mozart senza rist, via dei Greci 23/b ⊠ 00187 ☎ 6787422 – |‡| ▤ ⊟wc ⋒wc ☎ ♿. AE ⓓ E VISA. ✗ — DU **h**
☕ 3500 – **31 cam** 28000/45000.

Tre Alpi, senza rist, via del Mancino 12 ⊠ 00187 ☎ 6783500 – |‡| ▤ ⋒wc ☏ — EV **v**
20 cam.

Portoghesi senza rist, via dei Portoghesi 1 ⊠ 00186 ☎ 6564231 – |‡| ▤ ⊟wc ⋒wc ☏. ✗ — DV **s**
29 cam ☕ 28000/47000.

Condotti senza rist, via Mario de' Fiori 37 ⊠ 00187 ☎ 6794661 – |‡| ⊟wc ⋒ ☏ — EU **r**
☕ 2500 – **21 cam** 18000/35000.

Margutta senza rist, via Laurina 34 ⊠ 00187 ☎ 6798440 – |‡| ⊟wc ⋒wc ☏ ♿. AE ⓓ E — DU **t**
21 cam ☕ 23000/30000.

Prati senza rist, via Crescenzio 87 ⊠ 00193 ☎ 655357 – ⊟wc ⋒wc — BU **d**
☕ 2500 – **25 cam** 12000/29000.

XXXXX **Hostaria dell'Orso,** via Monte Brianzo 93 ⊠ 00186 ☎ 6564250, Rist. elegante - night club; prenotare, « Edificio quattrocentesco e decorazioni in stile » – ▤. AE ⓓ E VISA. ✗ — CV **n**
chiuso a mezzogiorno e domenica – Pas carta 33000/42000.

XXXX ✿ **El Toulà,** via della Lupa 29 ⊠ 00186 ☎ 6786471, Rist. elegante-specialità venete; prenotare – ▤. AE ⓓ E VISA. ✗ — DU **e**
chiuso sabato a mezzogiorno, domenica ed agosto – Pas carta 30000/40000 (13%)
Spec. Risotto allo champagne, Fiorentina di manzo in ardesia, Sorbetto ai frutti di stagione. **Vini** Pinot Bianco, Venegazzù.

XXX ✿ **Passetto,** via Zanardelli 14 ⊠ 00186 ☎ 6543696 – ▤. AE ⓓ VISA. ✗ — CV **v**
chiuso domenica – Pas carta 24000/32000
Spec. Fettuccine alla crema con funghi, Lombatina di vitello al cartoccio, Scaloppine Passetto. **Vini** Frascati, Chianti.

XXX ✿ **Ranieri,** via Mario de' Fiori 26 ⊠ 00187 ☎ 6791592, Rist. intimo a coperti limitati; prenotare – ▤. AE ⓓ — EU **f**
chiuso domenica – Pas carta 23000/34000
Spec. Crêpes alla Ranieri, Mignonnettes Regina Vittoria, Costoletta Imperiale. **Vini** Frascati, Sangiovese.

XXX **4 Colonne,** via della Posta 4 ⊠ 00186 ☎ 6547152, prenotare – ▤. ✗ — DV **n**
chiuso domenica e dal 5 al 30 agosto – Pas carta 20000/30000.

XX **Mastrostefano,** piazza Navona 94 ⊠ 00186 ☎ 6541669, Rist. american bar, « Servizio estivo all'aperto con ≤ fontana del Bernini » – ▤. AE — DY **d**
chiuso lunedì, dal 20 al 30 agosto e dal 7 al 20 gennaio – Pas carta 18000/26000.

XX **Taverna Giulia,** vicolo dell'Oro 23 ⊠ 00186 ☎ 6569768, Rist. con specialità liguri; prenotare – ▤ — BV **a**
chiuso domenica e dal 10 al 30 agosto – Pas carta 17000/23000 (15%).

XX **Dal Bolognese,** piazza del Popolo 1 ⊠ 00187 ☎ 3611426, Rist. con specialità bolognesi, « Raccolta di quadri » – ▤. ⓓ — DU **z**
chiuso domenica sera, lunedì, dal 9 al 25 agosto e dal 24 dicembre al 2 gennaio – Pas carta 18000/28000.

XX ⚙ **Piperno,** Monte de' Cenci 9 ✉ 00186 ☎ 6540629, Rist. con specialità romane – 🍴. 🍴
chiuso domenica sera, lunedì, agosto e dal 23 dicembre al 2 gennaio – Pas carta 19000/30000
Spec. Carciofi alla giudia, Filetti di baccalà con fritto vegetariano, Coda alla vaccinara. Vini Frascati.　　DX **d**

XX ⚙ **L'Eau Vive,** via Monterone 85 ✉ 00186 ☎ 6541095, Rist. con cucina francese e specialità
internazionali, « Edificio cinquecentesco » – 🍴. 🆎. 🍴　　DV **f**
chiuso domenica ed agosto – Pas turistico 25000/25000
Spec. Soupe à l'oignon gratinée et escargots de Bourgogne, Crêpe à la parisienne, Filet congolais. Vini Francesi.

XX **Au Lapin Blond,** via Visconti 39 ✉ 00193 ☎ 314014, Rist. con specialità francesi – 🍴
chiuso domenica e dal 24 dicembre al 2 gennaio – Pas carta 18000/26000.　　CU **n**

XX **La Maiella,** piazza Sant'Apollinare 45/46 ✉ 00186 ☎ 6564174, Rist. con specialità abruzzesi
ed internazionali – 🍴. 🆎 ⓞ 🖃 𝘝𝘐𝘚𝘈　　CDV **x**
chiuso domenica ed agosto – Pas carta 18000/28000.

XX **Alfredo alla Scrofa,** via della Scrofa 104 ✉ 00186 ☎ 6540163 – 🍴. 🆎 ⓞ 🖃 𝘝𝘐𝘚𝘈　　DV **r**
chiuso martedì – Pas carta 16000/24000 (12%).

XX **Osteria St. Ana,** via della Penna 68 ✉ 00186 ☎ 3610291, Taverna caratteristica – 🍴. 🆎 ⓞ
𝘝𝘐𝘚𝘈. 🍴　　DU **m**
chiuso domenica, dal 15 al 30 agosto e dal 23 dicembre al 6 gennaio – Pas carta 17000/24000.

XX **Da Pancrazio,** piazza del Biscione 92 ✉ 00186 ☎ 6561246, « Taverna ispirata allo stile
dell'antica Roma » – 🆎 ⓞ 🖃 𝘝𝘐𝘚𝘈　　CDX **p**
chiuso mercoledì e dal 5 al 25 agosto – Pas carta 14000/24000.

XX **Pierdonati,** via della Conciliazione 39 ✉ 00193 ☎ 6543557, Rist. con taverna　　BV **m**
chiuso martedì e dal 15 al 31 agosto – Pas carta 14000/23000 (15%).

XX **Da Mario,** via della Vite 55 ✉ 00187 ☎ 6783818, Rist. con specialità toscane – 🍴　　EU **e**
chiuso domenica e dal 5 al 30 agosto – Pas carta 14000/20000.

X **Abruzzi,** via del Vaccaro 1 ✉ 00187 ☎ 6793897 – 🍴. 🍴　　EV **a**
chiuso sabato ed agosto – Pas carta 12000/18000.

X **Il Buco,** via Sant'Ignazio 8 ✉ 00186 ☎ 6793298, Rist. con specialità toscane – 🍴. 🆎 ⓞ
chiuso lunedì e dal 30 luglio al 25 agosto – Pas carta 14000/24000.　　DV **b**

X **Al Moro,** vicolo delle Bollette 13 ✉ 00187 ☎ 6783495, Trattoria romana; prenotare – 🍴. 🍴
chiuso domenica ed agosto – Pas carta 16000/28000.　　EV **p**

X **Il Drappo,** vicolo del Malpasso 9 ✉ 00186 ☎ 657365, Rist. a coperti limitati; specialità sarde
– 🍴. 🆎　　CV **u**
chiuso domenica ed agosto – Pas carta 15000/20000 (15%).

X **La Cantinella,** via Crispi 19 ✉ 00187 ☎ 6795069, Trattoria d'habitués con specialità sarde –
🍴　　EU **s**
chiuso mercoledì ed agosto – Pas carta 10000/17000 (10%).

X **Polese,** piazza Sforza Cesarini 40 ✉ 00186 ☎ 6561709, Trattoria d'habitués – 🍴　　CV **s**
chiuso martedì, dall'11 al 25 agosto e dal 22 dicembre al 5 gennaio – Pas carta 12000/17000.

X ⚙ **Carmelo alla Rosetta,** via della Rosetta 9 ✉ 00187 ☎ 6561002, Trattoria con specialità
siciliane e di mare – 🍴　　DV **e**
chiuso domenica, lunedì a mezzogiorno ed agosto – Pas carta 22000/33000
Spec. Zuppa alla Nostrromo, Pappardelle ai frutti di mare, Pesce spada alla messinese. Vini Regaleali bianco e
rosato.

X **La Buca di Ripetta,** via di Ripetta 36 ✉ 00187 ☎ 3619004, Trattoria d'habitués con specialità
romane e toscane – 🍴　　DU **x**
chiuso domenica sera, lunedì ed agosto – Pas carta 12000/19000.

X **Campana,** vicolo della Campana 18 ✉ 00186 ☎ 6567820, Trattoria d'habitués – 🍴. 🆎. 🍴
chiuso lunedì ed agosto – Pas carta 15000/22000.　　DUV **a**

X **Crispi,** via Crispi 29 ✉ 00187 ☎ 6792481, Rist. con specialità romane　　EU **s**
chiuso domenica – Pas carta 12000/19000 (12%).

X **Toto alle Carrozze,** via delle Carrozze 10 ✉ 00187 ☎ 6785558 – 🍴. 🍴　　DU **r**
chiuso domenica ed agosto – Pas carta 12000/19000.

X **Barroccio,** via dei Pastini 13 ✉ 00186 ☎ 6793797, Rist. con specialità toscane – 🍴. 🆎 ⓞ 🖃
𝘝𝘐𝘚𝘈. 🍴　　DV **y**
chiuso lunedì ed agosto – Pas carta 15000/25000.

X **Da Giggetto,** via del Portico d'Ottavia 21/a ✉ 00186 ☎ 6561105, Trattoria tipica con specialità
romane – 🍴　　DX **n**
chiuso lunedì e dal 10 al 30 agosto – Pas carta 12000/19000.

X **La Sacrestia,** via del Seminario 89 ✉ 00186 ☎ 6797581, Rist.-pizzeria-soupers, « Caratteris-
tiche decorazioni » – 🍴　　DV **p**
chiuso mercoledì, dal 14 al 16 agosto e 24-25 dicembre – Pas carta 14000/21000 (15%).

X **Topo Gigio al Tre Api,** vicolo del Piombo 6 ✉ 00187 ☎ 6783991, Rist. d'habitués – 🍴　　EV **v**

X **Il Falchetto,** via Montecatini 12/14 ✉ 00186 ☎ 6791160, Trattoria rustica – 🆎　　EV **f**
chiuso venerdì e dal 5 al 20 agosto – Pas carta 12000/19000.

X **Taverna Negma,** borgo Vittorio 92 ✉ 00193 ☎ 6565143, Tipico locale con specialità arabe
– 🍴　　BU **q**
chiuso martedì ed agosto – Pas carta 12000/19000 (12%).

X **Zi' Gaetana,** via Cola di Rienzo 263 ✉ 00192 ☎ 3595342, Taverna tipica-pizzeria – ⓞ. 🍴
chiuso lunedì e dal 1° al 12 agosto – Pas carta 13000/20000.　　BU **g**

Zona centro est via Vittorio Veneto, via Nazionale, Viminale, Santa Maria Maggiore, Colosseo, Porta Pia, via Nomentana, Stazione Termini, Porta San Giovanni (pianta : Roma p. 10 e 11, salvo indicazioni speciali)

🏨🏨 **Le Grand Hotel,** via Vittorio Emanuele Orlando 3 ⊠ 00185 ℑ 4709, Telex 610210 – 🗐 📺 ☎
&. - 🛦. 🛦 ① Ε 🚾. 🛠 rist GU **t**
Pas al Rist. **Le Rallye** carta 40000/66000 – 🖙 11000 – **175 cam** 174000/243000.

🏨🏨 **Excelsior,** via Vittorio Veneto 125 ⊠ 00187 ℑ 4708, Telex 610232 – 🗐 📺 ☎ &. - 🛦. 🛦 ①
Ε 🚾. 🛠 rist FU **b**
Pas carta 40000/62000 – 🖙 11000 – **368 cam** 162000/226000.

🏨🏨 **Jolly,** corso d'Italia 1 ⊠ 00198 ℑ 8495, Telex 612293 – 🗐 📺 ☎ 🚗 - 🛦. 🛦 ① Ε 🚾.
🛠 rist FU **k**
Pas 21000 – 🖙 6000 – **200 cam** 85000/120000 – P 127000.

🏨🏨 **Regina Carlton,** via Vittorio Veneto 72 ⊠ 00187 ℑ 4758841, Telex 611684 – 🗐. 🛦 ① Ε
🚾. 🛠 FU **e**
Pas carta 25000/38000 – 🖙 6500 – **134 cam** 72000/108000 – P 115000.

🏨🏨 **Ambasciatori Palace,** via Vittorio Veneto 70 ⊠ 00187 ℑ 473831, Telex 610241 – 🗐 📺 &.
🛦 Ε 🚾. 🛠 FU **e**
Pas carta 20000/30000 – 🖙 7000 – **147 cam** 91000/143000.

🏨🏨 **Bernini Bristol,** piazza Barberini 23 ⊠ 00187 ℑ 463051, Telex 610554 – 🗐 📺 ☎ - 🛦. 🛦 ①
Ε. 🛠 rist FU **m**
Pas *(chiuso domenica sera e lunedì)* carta 22000/32000 – 🖙 7000 – **125 cam** 97000/133000.

🏨🏨 **Majestic,** via Vittorio Veneto 50 ⊠ 00187 ℑ 486841, Telex 680463 – 🗐 📺. 🛦 ① Ε 🚾.
🛠 rist TU **n**
Pas carta 16000/29000 – 🖙 4500 – **100 cam** 55000/97000.

🏨🏨 **Mediterraneo,** via Cavour 15 ⊠ 00184 ℑ 464051 – 🗐 📺 ☎ - 🛦. 🛦 ① Ε 🚾. 🛠 rist
Pas 21000 – **272 cam** 🖙 79000/113000. GV **k**

🏨🏨 **Londra Cargill,** piazza Sallustio 18 ⊠ 00187 ℑ 473871, Telex 680412 – 🗐 📺 ☎ 🚗 - 🛦.
🛦. 🛠 GU **k**
Pas carta 18000/25000 – **105 cam** 🖙 76000/115000.

🏨🏨 **Massimo D'Azeglio,** via Cavour 18 ⊠ 00184 ℑ 460646, Telex 610556 – 🗐 ☎ - 🛦. 🛦 ① Ε
🚾. 🛠 rist GV **s**
Pas *(chiuso domenica)* 18000 – **210 cam** 🖙 68000/97000.

🏨🏨 **Metropole e Rist. Apicio,** via Principe Amedeo 3 ⊠ 00185 ℑ 4751441 e rist ℑ 461446, Telex
611061 – 🗐 ☎ 🚗 GV **e**
285 cam.

🏨🏨 **Quirinale,** via Nazionale 7 ⊠ 00184 ℑ 479901, Telex 610332 – 🗐 &. 🛦 ① Ε 🚾. 🛠 rist
Pas carta 18000/30000 – 🖙 6500 – **200 cam** 65000/98000. GV **x**

🏨🏨 **Etap Boston,** via Lombardia 47 ⊠ 00187 ℑ 473951, Telex 680460 – 🗐 ☎ &. 🛦 ① Ε.
🛠 rist FU **z**
Pas carta 17000/28000 – **121 cam** 🖙 70000/105000.

🏨🏨 **Napoleon,** piazza Vittorio Emanuele 105 ⊠ 00185 ℑ 737646, Telex 611069 – 🗐 - 🛦. 🛦 ①
Ε 🚾. 🛠 HX **a**
Pas (solo per clienti alloggiati; *chiuso a mezzogiorno e mercoledì*) 13000 – 🖙 4000 – **80 cam**
33000/64000.

🏨🏨 **Commodore** senza rist, via Torino 1 ⊠ 00184 ℑ 485656, Telex 612170 – 🗐. 🛦 ① Ε 🚾. 🛠
🖙 4000 – **65 cam** 42000/66000. GV **c**

🏨🏨 **Imperiale,** via Vittorio Veneto 24 ⊠ 00187 ℑ 4756351 – 🗐 &. 🛦 ①. 🛠 FU **n**
Pas 16500 – **84 cam** 🖙 46000/80000 – P 73000.

🏨🏨 **Victoria,** via Campania 41 ⊠ 00187 ℑ 473931, Telex 610212 – 🗐 ☎ &. 🛦 Ε. 🛠 rist FU **c**
Pas carta 18000/28000 – 🖙 5000 – **110 cam** 60000/100000. 🗐 2000.

🏨🏨 **San Giorgio** senza rist, via Amendola 61 ⊠ 00185 ℑ 4751341 – 🗐. 🛦 ① Ε 🚾 GV **s**
186 cam 🖙 60000/92000.

🏨🏨 **Forum,** via Tor de' Conti 25 ⊠ 00184 ℑ 6792446, Telex 680252, « Rist. roof-garden con ≼
Fori Imperiali » – 🗐 🚗. 🛦 ① Ε 🚾. 🛠 FX **t**
Pas (solo per clienti alloggiati) carta 24000/32000 – 🖙 8000 – **81 cam** 85000/115000 – P
100000/128000.

🏨🏨 **Mondial** senza rist, via Torino 127 ⊠ 00184 ℑ 471801, Telex 612219 – 🗐 📺 ☎ &. 🛦 Ε 🛠
🖙 5500 – **77 cam** 53000/81000. GV **a**

🏨🏨 **Atlantico** senza rist, via Cavour 23 ⊠ 00184 ℑ 485951 – 🗐 ☎. 🛦 ① Ε 🚾 GV **k**
83 cam 🖙 60000/92000.

🏨🏨 **Universo,** via Principe Amedeo 5 ⊠ 00185 ℑ 4750542, Telex 610342 – 🗐 &. - 🛦. 🛦. 🛠
Pas 15000 – **206 cam** 🖙 58000/85000 – P 84000. GV **e**

🏨🏨 **Britannia** senza rist, via Napoli 64 ⊠ 00184 ℑ 463153, Telex 611292 – 🛊 🗐 🛏wc 🍴 ☎ ℗.
🛦 ① Ε 🚾 GV **t**
32 cam 🖙 56000/82000.

🏨 **Diana,** via Principe Amedeo 4 ⊠ 00185 ℱ 4751541, Telex 611198 – |₿| 🗏 rist 🛏wc 🏿wc 🕾.
　　🖭. 🚿 rist　　　　　　　　　　　　　　　　　　　　　　　　　　　　　　　　GV **e**
Pas (solo per clienti alloggiati) 13500 – 🗷 3500 – **187 cam** 30000/48000 – P 53000/59000.

🏨 **Nord-Nuova Roma** senza rist, via Amendola 3 ⊠ 00185 ℱ 465441 – |₿| 🗏 🛏wc 🏿wc 🕾.
　　🖭 ⓞ **E** 𝒱𝐼𝑆𝐴. 🚿　　　　　　　　　　　　　　　　　　　　　　　　　　　　　GV **d**
156 cam 🗷 42000/70000.

🏨 **La Residenza** senza rist, via Emilia 22 ⊠ 00187 ℱ 6799592 – |₿| 🗏 🛏wc 🕾 ⓟ　　FU **w**
　　🗷 5500 – **27 cam** 44000/66000, 🗏 3500.

🏨 **Sitea** senza rist, via Vittorio Emanuele Orlando 90 ⊠ 00185 ℱ 4743647, Telex 614163 – |₿| 🗏
　　🛏wc 🏿wc 🕾. 🖭　　　　　　　　　　　　　　　　　　　　　　　　　　　　　　GU **t**
37 cam 🗷 56000/82000.

🏨 **Milani** senza rist, via Magenta 12 ⊠ 00185 ℱ 4952641, Telex 614356 – |₿| 🛏wc 🏿wc 🕾. 🚿
　　🗷 4000 – **78 cam** 33000/45000.　　　　　　　　　　　　　　　　　　　　　　HU **z**

🏨 **Globus** senza rist, viale Ippocrate 119 ⊠ 00161 ℱ 4953994 – |₿| 🗏 🛏wc 🏿wc 🕾 - 🔥. 🖭
　　ⓞ 𝒱𝐼𝑆𝐴　　　　　　　　　　　　　　　　　　　　　　　Roma p. 7　　JU **a**
96 cam 🗷 45000/73000.

🏨 **Alpi** senza rist, via Castelfidardo 84/a ⊠ 00185 ℱ 464618, Telex 611677 – |₿| 🗏 🛏wc 🕾. 🖭
　　ⓞ **E** 𝒱𝐼𝑆𝐴. 🚿　　　　　　　　　　　　　　　　　　　　　　　　　　　　　　HU **s**
46 cam 🗷 35000/55000.

🏨 **Galles** senza rist, viale Castro Pretorio 66 ⊠ 00185 ℱ 4954741, Telex 680556 – |₿| 🗏 🛏wc
　　🏿wc 🕾 ₺. 🖭 ⓞ **E** 𝒱𝐼𝑆𝐴. 🚿　　　　　　　　　　　　　　　　　　　　　　HU **c**
45 cam 🗷 38000/59000, 🗏 5000.

🏨 **Siviglia** senza rist, via Gaeta 12 ⊠ 00185 ℱ 4750004, Telex 612225 – |₿| 🛏wc 🏿wc 🕾. 🖭 ⓞ
　　E 𝒱𝐼𝑆𝐴　　　　　　　　　　　　　　　　　　　　　　　　　　　　　　　　HU **k**
41 cam 🗷 35000/50000.

🏨 **Colosseum** senza rist, via Sforza 10 ⊠ 00184 ℱ 4751228 – |₿| 🏿wc 🕾. 🖭 ⓞ 𝒱𝐼𝑆𝐴　　GVX **m**
50 cam 🗷 32000/54000.

🏨 **Fiamma** senza rist, via Gaeta 61 ⊠ 00185 ℱ 4758436 – |₿| 🗏 🛏wc 🏿wc 🕾. 🖭. 🚿　　GU **p**
　　🗷 3000 – **67 cam** 42000/62000, 🗏 4000.

🏨 **Fiume** senza rist, via Brescia 5 ⊠ 00198 ℱ 864010 – |₿| 🛏wc 🏿wc 🕾. 🖭 ⓞ　　　　GU **e**
55 cam 🗷 33000/52000.

🏨 **Rex** senza rist, via Torino 149 ⊠ 00184 ℱ 462743 – |₿| 🛏wc 🏿wc 🕾. 🖭　　　　　GV **b**
　　🗷 4000 – **54 cam** 26000/43000.

🏨 **Terminal** senza rist, via Principe Amedeo 103 ⊠ 00185 ℱ 734041 – |₿| 🛏wc 🏿wc 🕾. 🖭. 🚿
　　🗷 4000 – **35 cam** 32000/52000.　　　　　　　　　　　　　　　　　　　　　HV **u**

🏨 **Lux Messe** senza rist, via Volturno 32 ⊠ 00185 ℱ 4741741, Telex 612376 – |₿| 🛏wc 🏿wc
　　🕾. 🚿　　　　　　　　　　　　　　　　　　　　　　　　　　　　　　　　　GU **x**
99 cam 🗷 36000/56000, 🗏 3500.

🏨 **Ariston** senza rist, via Turati 16 ⊠ 00185 ℱ 7310341, Telex 614479 – |₿| 🛏wc 🏿wc 🕾. 🚿
　　🗷 3500 – **110 cam** 23000/37000.　　　　　　　　　　　　　　　　　　　　　HV **t**

🏨 **Bled,** via di Santa Croce in Gerusalemme 40 ⊠ 00185 ℱ 777102 – |₿| 🗏 🛏wc 🏿wc 🕾 ⓟ.
　　🚿 rist　　　　　　　　　　　　　　　　　　　　　　　　　　　　　　　　　JY **r**
Pas *(chiuso domenica e dal 15 al 30 agosto)* carta 17000/24000 – **45 cam** 🗷 39000/58000 – P
62000.

🏨 **Medici** senza rist, via Flavia 96 ⊠ 00187 ℱ 4751319 – |₿| 🛏wc 🏿wc 🕾. 🖭 ⓞ **E** 𝒱𝐼𝑆𝐴. 🚿
57 cam 🗷 32000/55000.　　　　　　　　　　　　　　　　　　　　　　　　　GU **a**

🏨 **Edera** senza rist, via Poliziano 75 ⊠ 00184 ℱ 738355, Telex 721472, 🛱 – |₿| 🛏wc 🏿wc 🕾
　　ⓟ. 🚿　　　　　　　　　　　　　　　　　　　　　　　　　　　　　　　　　GY **r**
38 cam 🗷 23000/49000.

🏨 **Igea** senza rist, via Principe Amedeo 97 ⊠ 00185 ℱ 7311212 – |₿| 🏿wc 🕾. 🚿　　　HV **u**
　　🗷 2000 – **42 cam** 20000/30000.

🏨 **Canada** senza rist, via Vicenza 58 ⊠ 00185 ℱ 4950749, Telex 613037 – |₿| 🗏 🛏wc 🏿wc 🕾.
　　🖭 ⓞ **E** 𝒱𝐼𝑆𝐴. 🚿　　　　　　　　　　　　　　　　　　　　　　　　　　　HU **e**
48 cam 🗷 24000/40000, 🗏 3500.

🏨 **Centro** senza rist, via Firenze 12 ⊠ 00184 ℱ 464142, Telex 612125 – |₿| 🛏wc 🏿wc 🕾. 🖭
　　ⓞ. 🚿　　　　　　　　　　　　　　　　　　　　　　　　　　　　　　　　　GV **n**
36 cam 🗷 38000/60000.

🏨 **Alba** senza rist, via Leonina 12 ⊠ 00184 ℱ 484471 – |₿| 🛏wc 🏿wc 🕾 ₺. - 🔥. 🖭 ⓞ　　FX **v**
25 cam 🗷 23000/30000.

🏨 **Flavio** senza rist, via Frangipane 34 ⊠ 00184 ℱ 6797203 – |₿| 🏿wc ₺. 🚿　　　　FX **a**
　　🗷 2000 – **23 cam** 19000/20000.

🏨 **Galileo** senza rist, via Palestro 33 ⊠ 00185 ℱ 464910 – |₿| 🛏wc 🏿wc 🕾. 🖭. 🚿　　　HU **a**
　　🗷 4000 – **30 cam** 32000/48000.

XXXX ❀ **Sans Souci,** via Sicilia 20/24 ⌧ 00187 ☎ 493504, Taverna elegante-soupers; prenotare –
    🍽. 🖭 ⓪ 𝘝𝘐𝘚𝘈. 🍴   FU **p**
chiuso a mezzogiorno, lunedì e dal 10 agosto al 2 settembre – Pas carta 26000/45000
Spec. Variété de soufflé (per 2 persone), Les délices de sole "Sans Souci", Escalope de veau "St Bruno". **Vini**
Torre di Giano, Rubesco.

XXX **Harry's Bar,** via Vittorio Veneto 150 ⌧ 00187 ☎ 4745832, Rist. a coperti limitati; prenotare
    – 🍽. 🖭 ⓪. 🍴   FU **a**
chiuso domenica – Pas carta 25000/40000.

XXX **Domus Aurea,** nel parco del viale del Monte Oppio ⌧ 00184 ☎ 7315325, Rist. elegante;
diners dansants, ⪕ Colosseo – 🍽 🅿. 🖭. 🍴   GX **f**
chiuso martedì – Pas carta 25000/35000 (15%).

XXX **La Graticola del Jackie O',** via Boncompagni 11 ⌧ 00187 ☎ 461401 – 🍽. 🖭 ⓪ 🇪   FU **q**
chiuso a mezzogiorno ed agosto – Pas carta 27000/37000.

XX **Cesarina,** via Piemonte 109 ⌧ 00187 ☎ 460828, Rist. con specialità bolognesi – 🍽   GU **n**
chiuso domenica e dal 1° al 15 agosto – Pas carta 15000/22000 (15%).

XX **Coriolano,** via Ancona 14 🖼 00198 ☎ 001122, Rist. a coperti limitati; prenotare – 🍽   HU **g**
chiuso domenica e dal 1° al 24 agosto – Pas carta 21000/31000 (15%).

XX ❀ **Girarrosto Toscano,** via Campania 29 ⌧ 00187 ☎ 493759, Taverna moderna – 🍽. 🖭 ⓪
chiuso mercoledì – Pas carta 18000/27000 (15%)   FU **v**
Spec. Antipasto misto della Casa, Costoletta d'abbacchio a scottadito, Bistecca alla fiorentina. **Vini** Frascati,
Chianti.

XX **Loreto,** via Valenziani 19 ⌧ 00187 ☎ 4745286, Rist. con specialità di mare – 🍽. 🍴   GU **m**
chiuso domenica e dal 10 al 25 agosto – Pas carta 21000/35000.

XX **Giovanni,** via Marche 64 ⌧ 00187 ☎ 493576, Rist. d'habitués – 🍽   FU **u**
chiuso sabato ed agosto – Pas carta 17000/28000 (15%).

XX ❀ **Al Chianti,** via Ancona 17 ⌧ 00198 ☎ 861083, Trattoria toscana con tavernetta – 🍽
chiuso domenica ed agosto – Pas carta 17000/25000   HU **g**
Spec. Cacciagione (ottobre-marzo), Carni alla griglia, Stracotto alla toscana con fagioli. **Vini** Pinot Grigio, Case-
nuove.

XX **Piccolo Mondo,** via Aurora 39/d ⌧ 00187 ☎ 4754595, Tipica tavernetta – 🍽. 🖭 ⓪ 𝘝𝘐𝘚𝘈. 🍴
chiuso domenica ed agosto – Pas carta 15000/24000 (13%).   FU **h**

XX **Angelino ai Fori,** largo Corrado Ricci 40 ⌧ 00184 ☎ 6786198 – 🍽. 🖭 ⓪ 𝘝𝘐𝘚𝘈   FX **u**
chiuso martedì – Pas carta 14000/22000.

XX **Al Gladiatore,** piazza del Colosseo 5/a ⌧ 00184 ☎ 736276, Rist. rustico caratteristico con ⪕
    – 🍽. 🖭 ⓪ 🇪 𝘝𝘐𝘚𝘈.   GY **p**
chiuso martedì e dal 20 gennaio al 10 febbraio – Pas carta 12000/18000.

XX **Taverna Flavia-da Mimmo,** via Flavia 9 ⌧ 00187 ☎ 4745214, Tipica tavernetta – 🍽
chiuso domenica – Pas carta 20000/30000.   GU **u**

XX **Scoglio di Frisio,** via Merulana 256 ⌧ 00185 ☎ 734619, Rist. tipico napoletano con specialità
di mare – 🍽. 🖭 ⓪ 🇪 𝘝𝘐𝘚𝘈. 🍴   GX **k**
chiuso a mezzogiorno e lunedì – Pas carta 14000/24000.

XX **Il Tinello,** via di Porta Pinciana 16/b ⌧ 00187 ☎ 486847, Taverna caratteristica – 🍽. 🖭 ⓪
🇪 𝘝𝘐𝘚𝘈. 🍴   FU **z**
chiuso domenica e dal 15 al 30 agosto – Pas carta 18000/26000.

XX **Mario's Hostaria,** piazza del Grillo 9 ⌧ 00184 ☎ 6793725 – 🖭 ⓪ 🇪 𝘝𝘐𝘚𝘈   FX **e**
chiuso domenica e dal 10 al 31 agosto – Pas carta 15000/22000.

XX **Mino,** via Magenta 48 ⌧ 00185 ☎ 4959202 – 🍽   HV **v**
chiuso sabato – Pas carta 15000/22000.

XX **Peppone,** via Emilia 60 ⌧ 00187 ☎ 483976 – 🍽. 🖭 ⓪ 𝘝𝘐𝘚𝘈. 🍴   FU **g**
chiuso domenica ed agosto – Pas carta 19000/28000.

XX **Charly's Saucière,** via di San Giovanni in Laterano 270 ⌧ 00184 ☎ 736666, Rist. con
specialità francesi – 🍽. 🖭 ⓪ 🇪 𝘝𝘐𝘚𝘈   UY **e**
chiuso domenica ed agosto – Pas carta 18000/24000.

XX **La Matriciana,** via Viminale 44 ⌧ 00184 ☎ 461775, Rist. d'habitués – 🍽. 🖭 ⓪ 🇪 𝘝𝘐𝘚𝘈. 🍴
chiuso sabato – Pas carta 16000/23000.   GV **g**

X **Tullio,** via di San Nicola da Tolentino 26 ⌧ 00187 ☎ 4758564, Trattoria toscana – 🍽. 🍴
chiuso domenica ed agosto – Pas carta 14000/22000.   FU **x**

X **Mariano,** via Piemonte 79 ⌧ 00187 ☎ 4745256, Trattoria d'habitués – 🍽. 🖭 ⓪ 🇪 𝘝𝘐𝘚𝘈. 🍴
chiuso domenica ed agosto – Pas carta 12000/19000.   GU **s**

X **Cannavota,** piazza San Giovanni in Laterano 20 ⌧ 00184 ☎ 775007, Trattoria romana 🍴
chiuso mercoledì ed agosto – Pas carta 11000/17000.   HY **a**

X **Del Giglio,** via Torino 137 ⌧ 00184 ☎ 461606, Rist. d'habitués – 🖭 ⓪ 🇪 𝘝𝘐𝘚𝘈. 🍴   GV **r**
chiuso domenica ed agosto – Pas carta 12000/20000.

X **Severini a Santa Croce,** via di Santa Croce in Gerusalemme 1 ⌧ 00185 ☎ 7591512,
Trattoria e pizzeria – 🖭   JY **a**
chiuso giovedì e dal 15 al 30 luglio – Pas carta 11000/18000.

X **Costa Balena,** via Messina 5 ⌧ 00198 ☎ 857686, Trattoria con specialità di mare – 🍽. 🖭
⓪   HU **b**
chiuso domenica ed agosto – Pas carta 14000/22000.

X **Tavernelle,** via Panisperna 48 ⊠ 00184 ℱ 4740724, Trattoria d'habitués – 🖭. ✾   FV **s**
  chiuso lunedì – Pas carta 15000/20000 (14%).

X **Crisciotti-al Boschetto,** via del Boschetto 30 ⊠ 00184 ℱ 4744770, Trattoria rustica
  chiuso sabato ed agosto – Pas carta 12000/18000 (10%).   FV **r**

X **Elettra,** via Principe Amedeo 72 ⊠ 00185 ℱ 4745397, Trattoria d'habitués – ✾   GHV **p**
  chiuso venerdì sera, sabato ed agosto – Pas carta 13000/21000.

X **Colline Emiliane,** via degli Avignonesi 22 ⊠ 00187 ℱ 4757538 – ▤   FU **s**
  chiuso venerdì ed agosto – Pas carta 13000/19000.

X **Peppino,** via Principe Amedeo 70/a ⊠ 00185 ℱ 4745387, Trattoria di stazione   GHV **p**
  chiuso domenica ed agosto – Pas carta 10000/15000.

X **Hostaria da Vincenzo,** via Castelfidardo 6 ⊠ 00185 ℱ 484596 – ▤. 🖭 ⓞ   GU **c**
  chiuso mercoledì ed agosto – Pas carta 10000/18000.

X **Da Domenico,** via di San Giovanni in Laterano 134 ⊠ 00184 ℱ 734774, Trattoria d'habitués
  – ▤. 🖭 ⓞ.   DY **n**
  chiuso lunedì e dal 15 agosto al 15 settembre – Pas carta 11000/18000.

X **Guarnieri,** via Principe Amedeo 75/b ⊠ 00185 ℱ 7311285, Trattoria-pizzeria   HV **a**
  chiuso venerdì – Pas carta 11000/17000 (12%).

Zona sud Aventino, Porta San Paolo, Terme di Caracalla, via Appia Nuova (pianta : Roma p. 6
e 7)

🏨 **Villa San Pio** senza rist, via di Sant'Anselmo 19 ⊠ 00153 ℱ 5781325, ⇌ – |‡| ⌷wc ▥wc
  ⊛ ⑃. ✾   DEZ **e**
  59 cam ⊑ 25000/36000.

🏨 Santa Prisca, largo Manlio Gelsomini 25 ⊠ 00153 ℱ 571917 – |‡| ▥wc ⊛ ⓟ   DZ **h**
  45 cam.

🏠 **Domus Maximi** ⟋ senza rist, via Santa Prisca 11/b ⊠ 00153 ℱ 576135 – ⌷wc ▥wc ☎.
  ✾   EZ **b**
  21 cam ⊑ 28000/41000.

🏠 **Aventino** ⟋ senza rist, via di San Domenico 10 ⊠ 00153 ℱ 572831, ⇌ – ⌷wc ⊛ ⑃
  19 cam ⊑ 25000/36000.   EZ **r**

🏠 **Sant'Anselmo** senza rist, piazza Sant'Anselmo 2 ⊠ 00153 ℱ 573547 – ⌷wc ⊛   DEZ **e**
  26 cam ⊑ 25000/36000.

XX ❀ **Severino,** piazza Zama 5/c ⊠ 00183 ℱ 7550872 – ▤. 🖭 ⓞ 𝐕𝐈𝐒𝐀   JZ **e**
  chiuso domenica sera, lunedì ed agosto – Pas carta 17000/25000
  Spec. Bucatini all'amatriciana, Taglierini rosa (al salmone), Abbacchio e Saltimbocca alla romana. Vini dei Colli
  Albani.

XX **Apuleius,** via Tempio di Diana 15 ⊠ 00153 ℱ 572160, « Taverna ispirata allo stile dell'antica
  Roma » – 🖭 ⓞ. ✾   EZ **a**
  chiuso domenica – Pas carta 14000/25000 (15%).

Zona Trastevere (quartiere tipico) (pianta : Roma p. 9)

XX **Galeassi,** piazza di Santa Maria in Trastevere 3 ⊠ 00153 ℱ 5803775, Rist. con specialità
  romane – ▤. ✾   CY **f**
  chiuso lunedì e dal 24 dicembre al 24 gennaio – Pas carta 18000/26000.

XX **Sabatini a Santa Maria in Trastevere,** piazza di Santa Maria in Trastevere 13 ⊠ 00153
  ℱ 582026, Rist. con specialità romane e di mare   CY **n**
  chiuso mercoledì e dal 13 agosto al 4 settembre – Pas carta 15000/27000 (15%).

XX **Corsetti-il Galeone,** piazza San Cosimato 27 ⊠ 00153 ℱ 5816311, Rist. tipico con specialità
  di mare e pizzeria – ▤. 🖭 ⓞ 𝐄 𝐕𝐈𝐒𝐀. ✾   CY **g**
  chiuso mercoledì e dal 1° al 28 luglio – Pas carta 13000/23000.

XX **Carlo in Trastevere all'Alberata,** via Cardinal Merry del Val 16 ⊠ 00153 ℱ 5816674, Rist.
  tipico con specialità romane e di mare – ▤. 🖭 ⓞ 𝐕𝐈𝐒𝐀   CY **k**
  chiuso lunedì – Pas carta 17000/25000.

XX **Checco er Carettiere,** via Benedetta 10 ⊠ 00153 ℱ 5817018, Rist. tipico con specialità
  romane e di mare – ▤. ✾   CX **k**
  chiuso lunedì e dal 10 agosto al 10 settembre – Pas carta 16000/25000.

XX **Taverna Trilussa,** via del Politeama 23 ⊠ 00153 ℱ 588918, Rist. tipico con specialità
  romane – ▤. 🖭 𝐕𝐈𝐒𝐀. ✾   CY **h**
  chiuso domenica sera, lunedì e dal 1° al 20 agosto – Pas carta 15000/22000.

XX **Antica Pesa,** via Garibaldi 18 ⊠ 00153 ℱ 5809326, Servizio estivo in cortile – ▤. 🖭   CY **m**
  chiuso giovedì – Pas carta 15000/24000.

XX **Pastarellaro,** via di San Crisogono 33 ⊠ 00153 ℱ 5810871, Rist. tipico con specialità
  romane – ▤. 🖭   DY **r**
  chiuso martedì – Pas carta 15000/25000.

X **Romolo,** via di Porta Settimiana 8 ⊠ 00153 ℱ 588284, Trattoria tipica, « Servizio estivo in un
  fresco cortiletto » – 🖭   CX **a**
  chiuso lunedì e dal 13 agosto al 2 settembre – Pas carta 17000/24000.

X **Da Gino,** via della Lungaretta 85 ⊠ 00153 ℱ 5803403, Trattoria con specialità romane e di
  mare – ▤. 🖭 ⓞ 𝐕𝐈𝐒𝐀   CY **r**
  chiuso domenica ed agosto – Pas carta 20000/25000.

Dintorni di Roma

sulla strada statale 1 - via Aurelia (pianta : Roma p. 4) :

🏨 **Villa Pamphili,** via della Nocetta 105 ⊠ 00164 ℡ 5862, Telex 611675, ⤢ (coperta d'inverno),
🐾, ⚒ – ▤ 🐎 ⚿ ⓟ - ⚐. 🆎 ① ☰ *VISA*. ⚘ rist
LR **b**
Pas 20000 – **257 cam** ⊑ 60000/85000.

🏨 **Holiday Inn-St Peter's,** via Aurelia Antica 415 ⊠ 00165 ℡ 5872, Telex 680195, ⤢, 🐾, ⚒
– ▤ 📺 🐎 ⚿ ⓟ - ⚐. 🆎 ① ☰ *VISA*
LR **e**
Pas 16000/21000 – ⊑ 6500 – **337 cam** 61000/90000.

🏨 **Motelagip,** ⊠ 00163 ℡ 626843, Telex 613699, <, ⤢, 🐎 – 📶 ▤ 🚿wc ☎ ⓟ - ⚐. 🆎 ① *VISA*.
⚘ rist
LR **a**
Pas 11000 - senza ⊑ – **222 cam** 30000/50000.

✕ **La Maielletta,** via Aurelia Antica 270 ⊠ 00165 ℡ 6377464, Rist. tipico con specialità abruzzesi; servizio estivo all'aperto – ⓟ 🈺
LR **f**
chiuso lunedì – Pas carta 13000/23000.

sulla strada statale 2 - via Cassia (pianta : Roma p. 4) :

✕✕ **Severini alla Cassia,** via Oriolo Romano 59 ⊠ 00189 ℡ 3282643, Rist. con servizio estivo
all'aperto – ▤. 🆎
LQ **p**
chiuso lunedì ed agosto – Pas carta 17000/23000.

✕ **La Giustiniana,** via Cassia 1298 ⊠ 00123 ℡ 3765203, Rist. rustico con servizio estivo
all'aperto – ⓟ. 🆎
LQ **f**
chiuso martedì e dal 4 al 18 agosto – Pas carta 13000/23000.

sulla strada statale 3 - via Flaminia Nuova (pianta : Roma p. 5) :

✕ **La Cuccagna,** via Flaminia ⊠ 00188 ℡ 6912827, Rist. di campagna con servizio estivo
all'aperto – ⓟ. 🆎
MQ **p**
chiuso lunedì – Pas carta 15000/22000.

✕ **La Fattoria,** via Flaminia 1432 ⊠ 00188 ℡ 6910033, Rist. di campagna con servizio estivo
all'aperto – ▤ ⓟ. 🆎 ① *VISA*
MQ **p**
chiuso martedì e dal 10 al 25 agosto – Pas carta 20000/29000.

sulla strada statale 4 - via Salaria (pianta : Roma p. 5) :

🏨 **Motel la Giocca,** via Salaria 1223 ⊠ 00138 ℡ 6910411, ⤢ – 📶 ▤ 🚿wc 🚗 🚕 ⓟ - ⚐ ⚘
Pas *(chiuso domenica e dall'8 al 28 agosto)* carta 16000/24000 (12%) – ⊑ 5500 – **47 cam**
37000/51000. ⊑ 5000 – P 50000/60000.
MQ **n**

🏨 **Eurogarden Motel** senza rist, raccordo anulare Salaria-Flaminia ⊠ 00138 ℡ 6420059, ⤢,
🐎 – 🚿wc 🚿wc 🚗 ⚿ ⓟ. 🆎 ① *VISA*
MQ **s**
⊑ 4000 – **40 cam** 35000/42000.

🏠 **Motel Salaria** senza rist, via Salaria 1256 ⊠ 00138 ℡ 6919656 – 🚿wc 🚿wc 🚗 ⚿ ⓟ
MQ **g**
⊑ 3500 – **29 cam** 16000/29000.

sulla strada statale 6 - via Casilina (pianta : Roma p. 5) :

✕ **El Patio,** via Casilina 1108 ⊠ 00169 ℡ 260201, Rist. tipico con specialità spagnole, 🐎 – ▤
ⓟ
NS **a**
chiuso sabato – Pas carta 12000/19000.

sulla strada statale 7 - via Appia Nuova (pianta : Roma p. 5) :

✕✕ **Rinaldo all'Acquedotto,** via Appia Nuova 1267 ⊠ 00178 ℡ 7993910, 🐎 – ⓟ. 🆎. ⚘
NS **e**
chiuso martedì e dal 5 al 25 agosto – Pas carta 15000/21000.

✕ **Da Giacobbe,** via Appia Nuova 1681 ⊠ 00043 Ciampino ℡ 600131, Trattoria di campagna
con servizio estivo all'aperto – ⓟ. ⚘
NS **s**
chiuso lunedì ed agosto – Pas carta 10000/16000.

sulla via Appia Antica (pianta : Roma p. 5) :

✕✕ **Cecilia Metella,** via Appia Antica 125 ⊠ 00179 ℡ 5126710, Rist. con servizio estivo all'aperto,
« Giardino ombreggiato » – ⓟ. 🆎
MS **n**
chiuso lunedì – Pas carta 16000/24000.

✕✕ **Quo Vadis,** via Appia Antica 38 ⊠ 00179 ℡ 5136795, Rist. con servizio estivo all'aperto –
ⓟ. ⚘
MS **k**
chiuso martedì ed agosto – Pas carta 17000/25000.

sulla via Cristoforo Colombo (pianta : Roma p. 5) :

🏨 **Caravel** senza rist, via Colombo 124/c ⊠ 00147 ℡ 5115046 – 📶 🚿wc 🚿wc 🚗. ⚘ MS **w**
100 cam ⊑ 42000/59000.

all'E.U.R. Città Giardino (pianta : Roma p. 5) :

🏨 **Shangri Là-Corsetti,** viale Algeria 141 ✉ 00144 ☏ 5916441, ⌿, ☞ – 🗏 📺 🅿 - 🛦. 🆎 ⓪
E 𝘝𝘐𝘚𝘈. ⅋⅋   MS **b**
Pas carta 13000/23000 – ⬡ 6000 – **52 cam** 44000/70000.

🏨 **Dei Congressi** senza rist, viale Shakespeare 29 ✉ 00144 ☏ 5926021, Telex 614140 – 🗏 -
🛦. 🆎 ⓪ E 𝘝𝘐𝘚𝘈. ⅋⅋   MS **p**
chiuso dal 5 al 25 agosto – **96 cam** ⬡ 50000/75000.

✗✗ **Vecchia America-Corsetti,** piazza Marconi 32 ✉ 00144 ☏ 5926601, Rist. tipico e birreria
– 🗏. 🆎 ⓪ E 𝘝𝘐𝘚𝘈   MS **q**
chiuso martedì – Pas carta 16000/23000.

sull'autostrada per Fiumicino in prossimità raccordo anulare (pianta : Roma p. 4) :

🏨 **Holiday Inn-Parco dei Medici,** viale Castello della Magliana 65 ✉ 00148 ☏ 5475, Telex
613302, ⌿, ☞, ⅋⅋ – 🗏 📺 ☎ 🅿 - 🛦. 🆎 ⓪ E 𝘝𝘐𝘚𝘈. ⅋⅋ rist   LS **r**
Pas 18000 – ⬡ 5500 – **324 cam** 59000/87000.

MILANO

MILANO 20100 P 988 ③, 26 ⑲ – 1 655 599 ab. alt. 122 – a.s. 12-27 aprile e settembre-ottobre – ☎ 02.

Vedere : Duomo★★★, ascesa al Duomo e visita dei terrazzi★★★ – Palazzo e pinacoteca di Brera★★★ – Castello Sforzesco★★ (civiche collezioni d'arte★★) – Museo Poldi-Pezzoli★★ (Salone Dorato : ritratto di donna★★★, tappeto persiano★, Cristo morto★★ di G. Bellini) CU **M1** – Via e piazza Mercanti★ – Teatro alla Scala★ – Santa Maria delle Grazie (cupola★, Cena di Leonardo da Vinci★★★) – Basilica di Sant'Ambrogio★ (atrio★★) – Galleria Vittorio Emanuele★ CV – Biblioteca Ambrosiana★ (pinacoteca★ due ritratti★★★ di Leonardo da Vinci, i cartoni★★★ della Scuola di Atene di Raffaello, Presepio★★ del Barocci, il Topo con la rosa★ di Breughel dei Velluti) BV **A** – Museo della Scienza e della Tecnica Leonardo da Vinci★ AV **M1** – Chiesa di Sant'Eustorgio★ (cappella Portinari★★) BY **B** – Chiesa di San Satiro★ CV **C** – Ospedale Maggiore★ DX **U** – Chiesa di San Maurizio (affreschi del Luini★) BV **E** – Parco Sempione★.

Dintorni : Abbazia di Chiaravalle★ SE : 7 km HN – N : Laghi : Lago di Como★★★, Lago Maggiore★★★ Lago di Lugano★★.

18 e 9 (chiuso lunedì) al Parco di Monza ✉ 20052 Monza ☎ (039) 703082, per ② : 20 km;

18 Barlassina (chiuso lunedì) a Birago di Camnago ✉ 20030 ☎ (0362) 560621, per ① : 26 km;

9 Le Rovedine a Noverasco di Opera ✉ 20090 Opera ☎ (02) 5442730, S : 8 km per via Ripamonti (GN Milano p. 5).

Autodromo al Parco di Monza per ② : 20 km, ☎ (039) 22366, vedere la pianta sotto Monza.

✈ Forlanini di Linate E : 8 km HMN ☎ 6281; della Malpensa per ⑫ : 45 km ☎ (0331) 868028 – Alitalia, viale Luigi Sturzo 37 ✉ 20154 ☎ 6281 e via Albricci 5 ✉ 20122 ☎ 6281.

🚗 Porta Garibaldi ☎ 228274.

ℹ via Marconi 1 ✉ 20123 ☎ 808813 – Stazione Centrale ✉ 20124 ☎ 206030.

A.C.I. corso Venezia 43 ✉ 20121 ☎ 7745.

Roma 572 ⑦ – Genève 323 ⑫ – Genova 142 ⑨ – Torino 140 ⑫.

Piante : Milano p. 4 a 11.

Alberghi e Ristoranti

(Elenco alfabetico : Milano p. 2 e 3)

Zona urbana nord Piazza della Repubblica, Stazione Centrale, viale Zara, Stazione Porta Garibaldi, Porta Volta, corso Sempione (pianta : Milano p. 6 e 7, salvo indicazioni speciali)

Excelsior Gallia, piazza Duca d'Aosta 9 ✉ 20124 ☎ 6277, Telex 311160 – ▤ TV ☎ - 🏃. E. ✗ rist DR **a**
Pas 28000 – ☕ 8500 – **248 cam** 121000/162000.

Principe e Savoia, piazza della Repubblica 17 ✉ 20124 ☎ 6230, Telex 310052 – ▤ TV ☎ ♿ Ⓟ - 🏃. AE ⓞ E VISA. ✗ rist DS **x**
Pas 46000/69000 – ☕ 11000 – **354 cam** 174000/243000.

Palace, piazza della Repubblica 20 ✉ 20124 ☎ 6336, Telex 311026 – ▤ TV ☎ Ⓟ - 🏃. AE ⓞ E VISA. ✗ rist DS **t**
Pas *(chiuso sabato)* carta 41000/74000 – ☕ 10000 – **203 cam** 128000/186000.

Milano Hilton, via Galvani 12 ✉ 20124 ☎ 6983, Telex 330433 – ▤ TV ☎ ♿ - 🏃. AE ⓞ E VISA. ✗ rist DR **t**
Pas carta 30000/45000 – ☕ 11000 – **339 cam** 90000/170000.

Michelangelo, via Scarlatti 33 ✉ 20124 ☎ 2055, Telex 340330 – ▤ TV ☎ 🚗 - 🏃. AE ⓞ E VISA. ✗ rist DR **c**
Pas 28000/30000 – **285 cam** ☕ 120000/160000.

Executive senza rist, viale Luigi Sturzo 45 ✉ 20154 ☎ 6294, Telex 310191 – ▤ TV ☎ ♿ - 🏃. AE ⓞ E VISA CRS **v**
420 cam ☕ 105000/135000.

Anderson senza rist, piazza Luigi Savoia 20 ✉ 20124 ☎ 2043741, Telex 321018 – ▤ TV ☎ 🚗. AE E VISA DR **v**
chiuso agosto – ☕ 6000 – **102 cam** 70000/87000

Jolly Touring, via Tarchetti 2 ✉ 20121 ☎ 665653, Telex 320118 – ▤ ☎ - 🏃. AE ⓞ E VISA. ✗ rist DT **v**
Pas 25000 – ☕ 8000 – **277 cam** 80000/103000 – P 130000.

Auriga senza rist, via Pirelli 7 ✉ 20124 ☎ 632851 – ▤. AE E VISA. ✗ DR **f**
chiuso agosto – ☕ 5000 – **65 cam** 59000/79000.

Windsor senza rist, via Galilei 2 ✉ 20124 ☎ 6346, Telex 330562 – ▤ TV ☎ - 🏃. AE ⓞ E VISA DS **j**
☕ 6000 – **114 cam** 70000/88000

Atlantic senza rist, via Napo Torriani 24 ✉ 20124 ☎ 2043941, Telex 321451 – ▤ ♿ 🚗. AE E VISA. ✗ DS **q**
☕ 6500 – **62 cam** 85000/133000.

Royal, via Cardano 1 ✉ 20124 ☎ 6709151, Telex 333167 – ▤ ♿ - 🏃. AE ⓞ E. ✗ rist
chiuso agosto – Pas *(chiuso sabato e domenica)* carta 21000/29000 – ☕ 6000 – **110 cam** 58000/79000 – P 85000. DR **b**

ELENCO ALFABETICO DEGLI ALBERGHI E RISTORANTI

Segnalateci il vostro parere sui ristoranti che
raccomandiamo, indicateci le loro specialità
ed i vini di produzione locale da essi serviti.

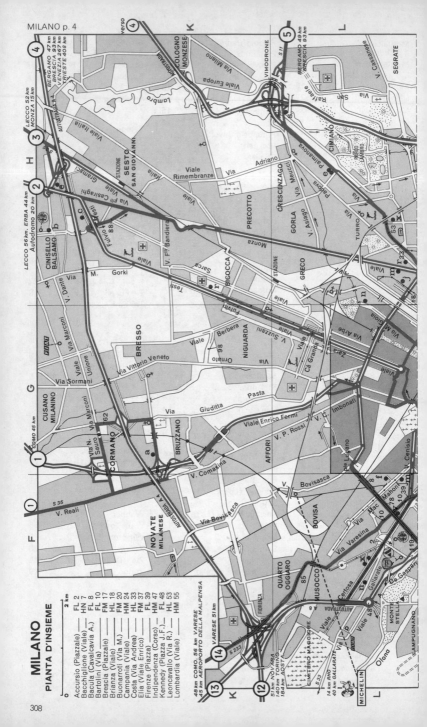

MILANO
PIANTA D'INSIEME

0   2 km

308

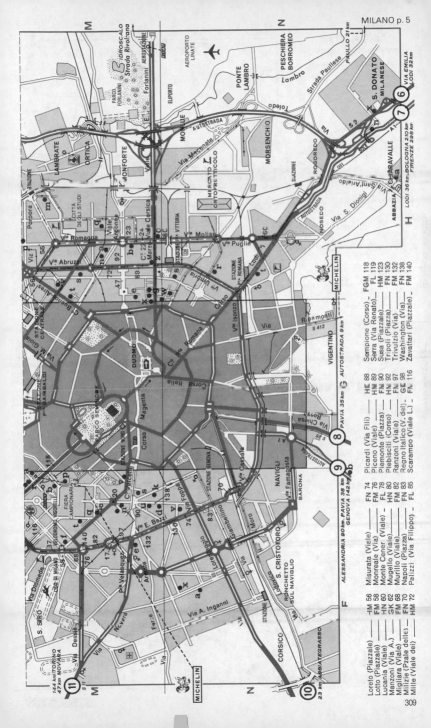

309

MILANO
ZONA URBANA NORD

0 — 500 m

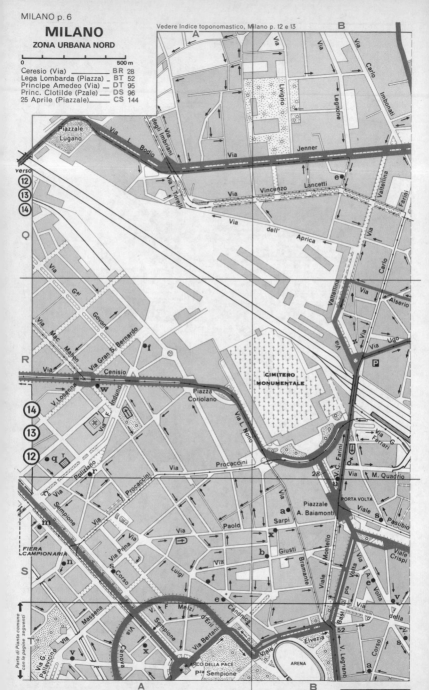

sotto, vedere

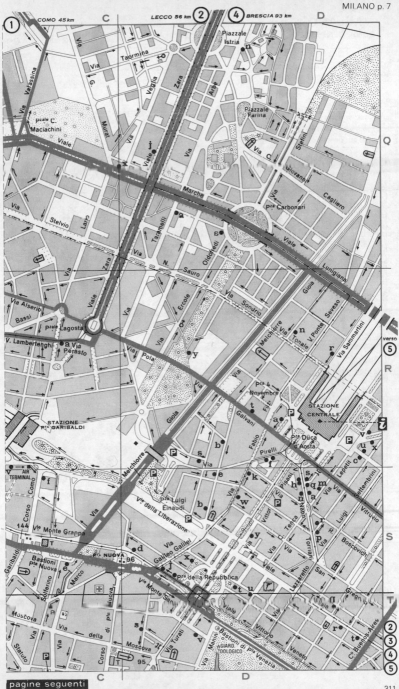

MILANO
ZONA CENTRALE

0 ——————— 500 m

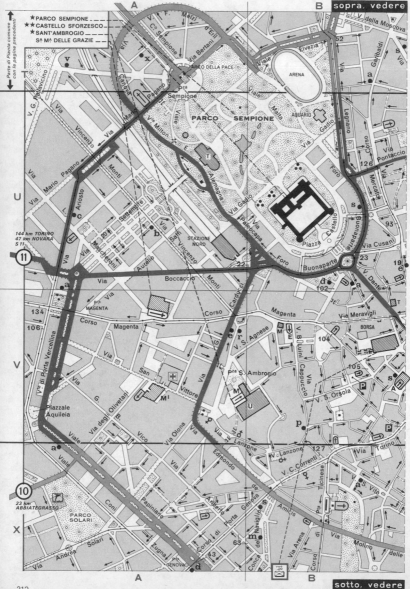

sopra, vedere

sotto, vedere

Vedere indice toponomastico,
Milano p. 12 e 13.

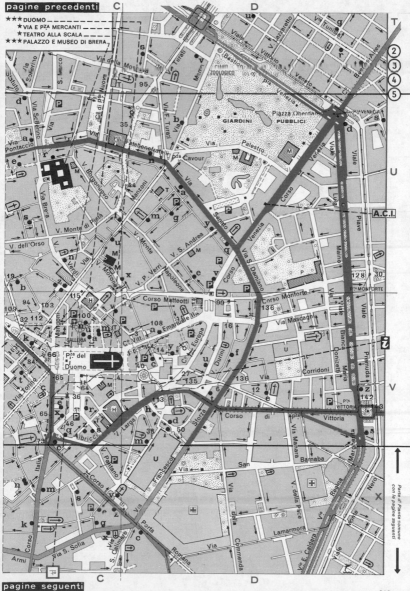

pagine precedenti

★★★ DUOMO
★ VIA E P^ZA MERCANTI
★ TEATRO ALLA SCALA
★★★ PALAZZO E MUSEO DI BRERA

pagine seguenti

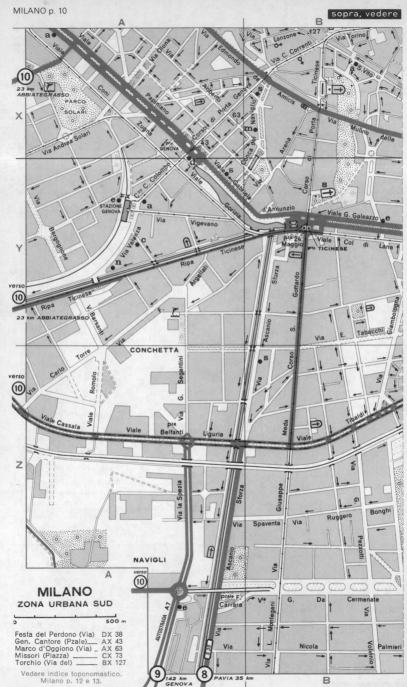

MILANO
ZONA URBANA SUD

0 — 500 m

Vedere indice toponomastico.
Milano p. 12 e 13.

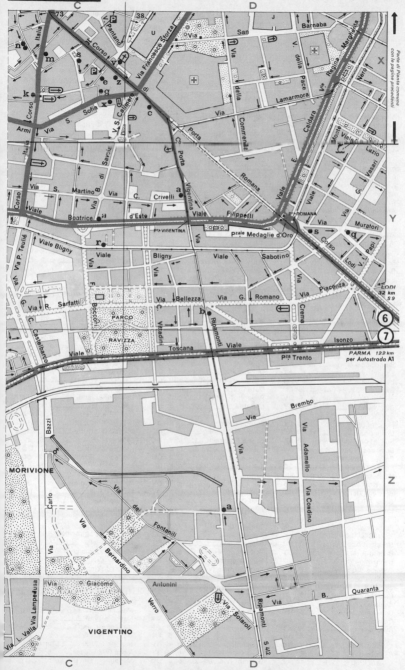

Splendido senza rist, viale Andrea Doria 4 ⊠ 20124 ℱ 2050, Telex 321413 – 🖿 📺 ☎ - 🏖.
🖭 ⓘ ☰ 𝘝𝘐𝘚𝘈. DR x
⊊ 6000 – **129 cam** 84000/114000.

Bristol senza rist, via Scarlatti 32 ⊠ 20124 ℱ 203751 – 🖿 📺 . 🏖. 🖭 ☰. ⅏ DR u
chiuso dal 7 al 26 agosto – ⊊ 10000 – **71 cam** 80000/110000.

Berna senza rist, via Napo Torriani 18 ⊠ 20124 ℱ 2046441, Telex 334695 – 🖿 ⅃. - 🏖. 🖭 ⓘ
☰ 𝘝𝘐𝘚𝘈. ⅏ DS a
⊊ 6500 – **83 cam** 63000/87000.

Europeo senza rist, via Canonica 38 ⊠ 20154 ℱ 344041, ⵤ, 🍴 – 🖿 📺 ⟵ - 🏖. 🖭 ☰ 𝘝𝘐𝘚𝘈
⅏ AS f
⊊ 7000 – **45 cam** 43000/63000.

Lancaster senza rist, via Abbondio Sangiorgio 16 ⊠ 20145 ℱ 344705 – |�| 🖿 📺 ⇔wc 🛁wc
⅏. 🖭 ☰ 𝘝𝘐𝘚𝘈. ⅏ AT v
chiuso dal 15 luglio al 28 agosto – ⊊ 6500 – **29 cam** 45000/65000.

Mediolanum senza rist, via Mauro Macchi 1 ⊠ 20124 ℱ 225834, Telex 310448 – |�| 🖿 ⇔wc
🛁wc ⅏ - 🏖. 🖭 ☰. ⅏ DS r
⊊ 5500 – **52 cam** 45000/65000.

Club Hotel senza rist, via Copernico 18 ⊠ 20125 ℱ 606128 – |�| 🖿 📺 ⇔wc 🛁wc ⅏ DR n
chiuso agosto – ⊊ 3500 – **31 cam** 38000/55000.

Augustus ⅏ senza rist, via Napo Torriani 29 ⊠ 20124 ℱ 6575741, Telex 333112 – |�| 🖿
⇔wc 🛁wc ⅏. 🖭 ⓘ ☰ 𝘝𝘐𝘚𝘈 DS h
chiuso dal 22 al 28 dicembre – **56 cam** ⊊ 47000/71000.

San Carlo senza rist, via Napo Torriani 28 ⊠ 20124 ℱ 203022, Telex 314324 – |�| 🖿 ⇔wc
🛁wc ⅏ ⅃. 🖭 ⓘ ☰ 𝘝𝘐𝘚𝘈 DS s
⊊ 4000 – **62 cam** 39000/58000.

Flora senza rist, via Napo Torriani 23 ⊠ 20124 ℱ 639522 – |�| 🖿 ⇔wc 🛁wc ⅏ ⅃. 🖭 ⓘ
𝘝𝘐𝘚𝘈. ⅏ DS h
⊊ 4500 – **45 cam** 38000/55000.

New York senza rist, via Pirelli 5 ⊠ 20124 ℱ 650551 – |�| ⇔wc ⅏ - 🏖. 🖭 ⓘ ☰ 𝘝𝘐𝘚𝘈
⊊ 4000 – **71 cam** 30000/45000. DR f

St. George senza rist, viale Tunisia 9 ⊠ 20124 ℱ 206375 – |�| 🖿 ⇔wc 🛁wc ⅏ DT r
⊊ 3500 – **54 cam** 40000/56000.

Sempione, via Finocchiaro Aprile 11 ⊠ 20124 ℱ 665285 – |�| 🖿 rist 🛁wc ⅏ DST u
Pas carta 14000/25000 – ⊊ 5000 – **38 cam** 32000/55000 – P 55000.

Domus senza rist, piazza Gerusalemme 6 ⊠ 20154 ℱ 3490251, Telex 335051 – |�| 🖿 ⇔wc
🛁wc ⅏ - 🏖. 🖭 ⓘ ☰ 𝘝𝘐𝘚𝘈. ⅏ AR r
chiuso dall'8 al 27 agosto – ⊊ 4000 – **84 cam** 43000/60000.

San Guido senza rist, via Carlo Farini 1/a ⊠ 20159 ℱ 662261 – |�| 🖿 ⇔wc 🛁wc ⅏ ⅃. 🖭 ☰
𝘝𝘐𝘚𝘈 BRS u
⊊ 3000 – **31 cam** 34000/49000, 🖿 2000.

Canova senza rist, via Napo Torriani 15 ⊠ 20124 ℱ 669541 – |�| 🖿 ⇔wc 🛁wc ⅏ ⅃. 🖭 ⓘ
☰ 𝘝𝘐𝘚𝘈 DS n
⊊ 4000 – **59 cam** 42000/60000.

Colombia senza rist, via Lepetit 15 ⊠ 20124 ℱ 225208 – |�| ⇔wc 🛁wc ⅏ DS m
⊊ 3000 – **42 cam** 24000/49000.

Gala senza rist, viale Zara 89 ⊠ 20159 ℱ 6890867 – |�| ⇔wc 🛁wc ⅏ ⅃. ☰ DQ j
chiuso dal 2 al 29 agosto – ⊊ 5000 – **22 cam** 22000/50000.

XXX ❀ **Romani,** via Trebazio 3 ⊠ 20145 ℱ 340738 – 🖿. 🖭 AS m
chiuso domenica ed agosto – Pas carta 23000/37000
Spec. Insalatina alla tropicale, Risotto alle fragole e champagne, Scampi all'armoricana con riso pilaw. Vini Gavi,
Dolcetto.

XXX **Grattacielo,** via Vittor Pisani 6 ⊠ 20124 ℱ 632330, Servizio estivo in giardino, « Raccolta di
quadri d'autore » – 🖭 ⓘ 𝘝𝘐𝘚𝘈 DS y
chiuso venerdì sera, sabato, dall'8 al 25 agosto e dal 26 dicembre al 6 gennaio – Pas
carta 18000/25000 (11%).

XXX **Cavallini,** via Mauro Macchi 2 ⊠ 20124 ℱ 200297, Servizio estivo all'aperto – 🖭 ⓘ 𝘝𝘐𝘚𝘈. ⅏
chiuso sabato, domenica, dal 1° al 25 agosto e dal 23 dicembre al 6 gennaio – Pas
carta 16000/25000 (12%). DS p

XX ❀ **A Riccione,** via Taramelli 70 ⊠ 20124 ℱ 6086807, Specialità di mare; prenotare – 🖿 ⓟ.
🖭 ⓘ ☰ 𝘝𝘐𝘚𝘈 DQ a
chiuso lunedì – Pas carta 35000/45000
Spec. e. Vini suggeriti della Casa.

XX **Da Lino Buriassi,** via Lecco (⊠ 20124 via Felice Casati 12) ℱ 273383, prenotare – 🖿. 🖭
chiuso sabato a mezzogiorno, domenica ed agosto – Pas carta 18000/26000. DT g

XX **Tre Pini,** via Tullo Morgagni 19 ⊠ 20125 ℱ 6898464, « Giardino-pergolato » – ⓟ. 🖭 𝘝𝘐𝘚𝘈
chiuso sabato ed agosto – Pas carta 16000/26000. DQ n

XX **Serafino,** via Bramante 35 ⊠ 20154 ℱ 3185363, Specialità piemontesi – ⓟ. 🖭 ⓘ ☰ 𝘝𝘐𝘚𝘈
chiuso lunedì, martedì a mezzogiorno ed agosto – Pas 20000 bc. BS a

XX **Wan Tong,** via Paolo Sarpi (✉ 20154 via Niccolini 20) ☏ 3453633, Rist. cinese a coperti
limitati; prenotare – 🍽. 🆎 ⓪ 𝗩𝗜𝗦𝗔. ✻ BS x
chiuso domenica, lunedì a mezzogiorno, agosto e dal 24 dicembre al 6 gennaio – Pas
carta 18000/27000 (10%).

XX **Pesce d'Oro,** via Cornalia 17 ✉ 20124 ☏ 6702532 – 🍽. 🆎 𝗩𝗜𝗦𝗔 DR s
chiuso sabato a mezzogiorno, domenica ed agosto – Pas carta 13000/25000 (12%).

XX **Al Griso,** via Fabio Filzi 12 ✉ 20124 ☏ 664963, Rist.rustico con servizio estivo all'aperto
chiuso domenica ed agosto – Pas carta 18000/25000 (12%). DS k

XX **Olivo 2,** viale Monte Santo 2 ✉ 20124 ☏ 653846 – 🍽. 🆎 ⓪ 𝗩𝗜𝗦𝗔 DS j
chiuso sabato e domenica – Pas carta 18000/27000.

XX **Endo,** via Fabio Filzi 8 ✉ 20124 ☏ 6595017, Rist. giapponese; prenotare – 🍽. 🆎 ⓪ 𝗩𝗜𝗦𝗔. ✻
chiuso domenica – Pas carta 20000/40000. DS w

XX ✿ **Alfredo-Gran San Bernardo,** via Borgese 14 ✉ 20154 ☏ 389000, Coperti limitati; prenotare – 🍽 AR f
chiuso domenica, agosto e dal 21 dicembre al 19 gennaio – Pas carta 21000/28000
Spec. Risotto alla milanese ed al salto, Costoletta alla milanese, Foiolo (trippa), Vini Pinot Grigio, Barbera.

XX **La Barcarola,** via Volta 9 ✉ 20121 ☏ 667265, Specialità di mare – 🍽. 🆎 𝗩𝗜𝗦𝗔. ✻ BS e
chiuso domenica sera, lunedì e dal 26 luglio al 26 agosto – Pas carta 15000/22000.

XX **5 Terre,** via Appiani 9 ✉ 20121 ☏ 653034, Specialità di mare – 🍽. 🆎 ⓪ 𝗩𝗜𝗦𝗔 DT s
chiuso domenica – Pas carta 16000/27000.

XX Da Berti, via Algarotti 20 ✉ 20124 ☏ 6081696, Servizio estivo in giardino – ⓟ DR y

XX **Osteria del Vecchio Canneto,** bastioni Porta Nuova (✉ 20121 via Solferino 56) ☏ 6598498,
Specialità di mare, «Originali decorazioni » – 🍽 CS e
chiuso a mezzogiorno, domenica ed agosto – Pas (menu tipico) 25000 bc.

XX **Taverna del Gran Sasso,** piazzale Principessa Clotilde 10 ✉ 20121 ☏ 6597578, Caratteristico rist. abruzzese; prenotare – 🍽 DS d
chiuso domenica, lunedì, mercoledì a mezzogiorno e luglio – Pas (menu tipico) 22000 bc.

XX **Altopascio,** via Gustavo Fara 17 ✉ 20124 ☏ 6702458, Rist.toscano – 🍽. 🆎 DS e
chiuso sabato ed agosto – Pas carta 15000/25000 (11%).

XX **Ca' d'Oro,** via Perasto 2 ✉ 20159 ☏ 683095, Rist. veneziano-specialità di mare – 🍽. 🆎 ⓪
chiuso domenica sera, lunedì a mezzogiorno ed agosto – Pas carta 18000/26000. CR a

XX **Ponticello 2,** via Statuto 16 ✉ 20121 ☏ 662219, Rist. moderno con servizio estivo in giardino
– 𝗩𝗜𝗦𝗔 BT s
chiuso sabato e dall'8 al 20 agosto – Pas carta 14000/23000.

XX **Cassinna de' Pomm,** via Melchiorre Gioia 194 ✉ 20125 ☏ 6081448, Trattoria vecchia
Milano con giardino – ⓟ. 🆎. ✻ Milano p. 4 HL n
chiuso domenica ed agosto – Pas carta 22000/30000.

XX All'Isola, corso Como 10 ✉ 20154 ☏ 0571024, solo su prenotazione – 🍽 CS f

XX **Le Colline Pisane,** largo La Foppa 5 ✉ 20121 ☏ 639136, Rist.toscano – 🍽. 🆎 𝗩𝗜𝗦𝗔 BT v
chiuso domenica ed agosto – Pas carta 14000/22000.

XX **Solferino,** via Castelfidardo 2 ✉ 20121 ☏ 639886, prenotare, Trattoria vecchia Milano
chiuso sabato a mezzogiorno, domenica, dal 9 al 16 agosto e dal 25 dicembre al 2 gennaio –
Pas carta 15000/25000. CT a

XX **Montecristo,** corso Sempione angolo via Prina 17 ✉ 20154 ☏ 312760, Specialità di mare –
🍽. ✻ AS s
chiuso martedì, sabato a mezzogiorno ed agosto – Pas carta 20000/30000.

XX **Da Fumino,** via Bernina 43 ✉ 20158 ☏ 606872, Trattoria toscana – 🍽. ⓪ BQ e
chiuso sabato, domenica sera ed agosto – Pas carta 17000/24000.

XX **Le Pietre Cavate,** via Castelvetro (✉ 20154 via Piero della Francesca 38) ☏ 344704 – 🍽.
🆎 AR q
chiuso mercoledì ed agosto – Pas carta 15000/25000.

X **Antica Trattoria della Pesa,** viale Pasubio 10 ✉ 20154 ☏ 665741, Tipica trattoria vecchia
Milano con cucina lombarda – 🍽 BS s
chiuso domenica ed agosto – Pas carta 15000/22000.

X **Casa Fontana,** piazza Carbonari 5 ✉ 20124 ☏ 6892684, Coperti limitati; prenotare – 🍽. ✻
chiuso lunedì, sabato a mezzogiorno ed agosto – Pas carta 15000/22000 (15%). DQ s

X **La Veneta,** via Giusti 14 ✉ 20154 ☏ 342881, Trattoria con specialità venete BS b
chiuso lunedì ed agosto – Pas carta 12000/17000 (12%).

X **Al Vecchio Passeggero,** via Gherardini 1 ✉ 20145 ☏ 312461 – 🍽 AT x
chiuso sabato a mezzogiorno, domenica, dall'8 al 29 agosto e dal 26 dicembre al 6 gennaio –
Pas carta 15000/27000.

X **Pupurry,** via Canonica 27 ✉ 20154 ☏ 301029, Rist. d'artisti-soupers – 🆎 𝗩𝗜𝗦𝗔 AS e
chiuso lunedì e dal 5 al 25 agosto – Pas (menu suggerito dal proprietario) 20000/23000.

X **Birreria Porta Renza,** viale Tunisia (✉ 20124 corso Buenos Aires 9) ☏ 276473, Rist. –
tavola calda – soupers; servizio estivo all'aperto – 🍽. 🆎 ⓪ 𝗩𝗜𝗦𝗔 DT t
chiuso giovedì – Pas carta 13000/20000 (12%).

X **Dalla Zia,** via Gustavo Fara 5 ✉ 20124 ☏ 666281, Trattoria toscana a coperti limitati – 𝗩𝗜𝗦𝗔.
✻ DS b
chiuso sabato ed agosto – Pas carta 15000/23000 (10%).

✗ **La Secchia Rapita,** viale Marche 56 ⊠ 20159 ℡ 603008, Trattoria tipica con specialità modenesi – ▤ CDQ **x**
chiuso lunedì – Pas (menù tipico) 15000 bc.

✗ **Taverna della Trisa,** via Francesco Ferruccio 1 ⊠ 20145 ℡ 341304, Specialità trentine; servizio estivo all'aperto AS **n**
chiuso domenica, lunedì ed agosto – Pas carta 15000/20000.

✗ **Da Gori,** via Sammartini 21 ⊠ 20125 ℡ 6081607, Trattoria toscana – ▤. 𝘝𝘐𝘚𝘈. ✁ DR **r**
chiuso sabato, domenica sera, dal 7 al 24 agosto e dal 24 al 31 dicembre – Pas carta 14000/25000 (10%).

✗ **Il Palio,** piazza Diocleziano (⊠ 20154 via Cenisio 37) ℡ 3453687, Trattoria toscana – ▤. ✁ AR **w**
chiuso sabato ed agosto – Pas carta 15000/22000.

✗ **Al Matarel,** via Laura Solera Montegazza (⊠ 20121 corso Garibaldi 75) ℡ 654204, Tipica trattoria con solo specialità milanesi BT **a**
chiuso martedì, luglio e dal 23 dicembre al 10 gennaio – Pas carta 18000/30000.

Zona centrale Duomo, Scala, Parco Sempione, Castello Sforzesco, Giardini Pubblici corso Venezia, via Manzoni, Stazione Nord, corso Magenta, Porta Vittoria (pianta : Milano p. 8 e 9)

🏨 **Gd H. Duomo,** via San Raffaele 1 ⊠ 20121 ℡ 8833, Telex 312086 – ▤ ♿ - ᴁ. E 𝘝𝘐𝘚𝘈.
Pas carta 20000/28000 – ⚏ 7500 – **158 cam** 75000/115000 – P 98000/120000. CV **m**

🏨 **Jolly President,** largo Augusto 10 ⊠ 20122 ℡ 7746, Telex 312054 – ▤ 📺 ☎ - ᴁ. ᴁᴇ ⓸ E 𝘝𝘐𝘚𝘈. ✁ rist DV **t**
Pas 25000 – ⚏ 8000 – **201 cam** 105000/127000 – P 155000.

🏨 **Plaza** senza rist, piazza Diaz 3 ⊠ 20123 ℡ 8058452, Telex 321162 – ▤ 📺 ☎ - ᴁ. ᴁᴇ. ✁ CV **r**
⚏ 11000 – **115 cam** 110000/150000.

🏨 **Cavour,** via Fatebenefratelli 21 ⊠ 20121 ℡ 650983, Telex 320498 – ▤ 📺 ☎ ♿. ᴁᴇ E 𝘝𝘐𝘚𝘈. ✁ rist DU **n**
Pas *(chiuso sabato e domenica)* 21000 – ⚏ 7000 – **113 cam** 67000/85000.

🏨 **Select** senza rist, via Baracchini 12 ⊠ 20123 ℡ 8843, Telex 312256 – ▤ 📺 ☎ ♿ - ᴁ. ᴁᴇ ⓸ E 𝘝𝘐𝘚𝘈 CV **s**
⚏ 6000 – **140 cam** 85000/115000.

🏨 **Carlton Hotel Senato,** via Senato 5 ⊠ 20121 ℡ 781780, Telex 331306 – ▤ 📺 ♿ ⟸. ᴁᴇ E 𝘝𝘐𝘚𝘈. ✁ rist DU **q**
chiuso agosto – Pas *(chiuso sabato e domenica)* 17000 – ⚏ 6000 – **73 cam** 70000/87000 – P 84000/110000.

🏨 **Grand Hotel et de Milan** senza rist, via Manzoni 29 ⊠ 20121 ℡ 870757, Telex 334505 – ☎ ♿ - ᴁ. ᴁᴇ ⓸ E 𝘝𝘐𝘚𝘈 CDU **f**
⚏ 6000 – **90 cam** 94000/134000.

🏨 **Dei Cavalieri** senza rist, piazza Missori 1 ⊠ 20123 ℡ 8857, Telex 312040 – ▤ ☎ - ᴁ. ᴁᴇ ⓸ E 𝘝𝘐𝘚𝘈 CVX **c**
175 cam ⚏ 70000/98000.

🏨 **De la Ville** senza rist, via Hoepli 6 ⊠ 20121 ℡ 867651, Telex 312642 – ▤ - ᴁ. ᴁᴇ E 𝘝𝘐𝘚𝘈 CV **v**
chiuso agosto – ⚏ 5000 – **105 cam** 75000/90000.

🏨 **Manin,** via Manin 7 ⊠ 20121 ℡ 667251, Telex 320385, ☞ – ▤ ☎ ♿ - ᴁ. ᴁᴇ E 𝘝𝘐𝘚𝘈. ✁ rist DU **b**
chiuso dal 6 al 22 agosto – Pas *(chiuso sabato e domenica)* 15000/25000 – ⚏ 6500 – **106 cam** 69000/86000 – P 82000/108000.

🏨 **Francia Europa** senza rist, corso Vittorio Emanuele 9 ⊠ 20122 ℡ 708301, Telex 320083 – ▤. ᴁᴇ 𝘝𝘐𝘚𝘈 DV **a**
chiuso agosto – ⚏ 6000 – **124 cam** 67000/88000.

🏨 **Gran Duca di York** senza rist, via Moneta 1/a ⊠ 20123 ℡ 874863 – ▤ 📺 ♿ - ᴁ. ✁ BV **s**
chiuso dal 2 al 30 agosto – ⚏ 3500 – **33 cam** 38000/56000.

🏨 **Ariosto** senza rist, via Ariosto 22 ⊠ 20145 ℡ 496038 – ▤ ♿. ᴁᴇ ⓸ 𝘝𝘐𝘚𝘈. ✁ AU **c**
chiuso agosto – ⚏ 4000 – **53 cam** 38000/56000.

🏨 **Marino alla Scala** senza rist, piazza della Scala 5 ⊠ 20121 ℡ 867831, Telex 312680 – ▤ ☎ - ᴁ. ᴁᴇ E 𝘝𝘐𝘚𝘈. ✁ CU **z**
chiuso dal 1° al 23 agosto – ⚏ 6000 – **78 cam** 80000/104000.

🏨 **Ambasciatori** senza rist, galleria del Corso 3 ⊠ 20122 ℡ 790241, Telex 315489 – ▐ ▤ ☐wc ▥wc ☎ ♿. ᴁᴇ ⓸ E 𝘝𝘐𝘚𝘈 DV **y**
89 cam ⚏ 38000/75000, ▤ 3000.

🏨 **Manzoni** senza rist, via Santo Spirito 20 ⊠ 20121 ℡ 705700 – ▐ ☐wc ▥wc ☎ ⟸. DU **g**
⚏ 3500 – **54 cam** 40000/60000.

🏨 **Casa Svizzera** senza rist, via San Raffaele 3 ⊠ 20121 ℡ 802246, Telex 316064 – ▐ ▤ 📺 ☐wc ▥wc ☜. ᴁᴇ ⓸ E 𝘝𝘐𝘚𝘈 CV **m**
45 cam ⚏ 52000/72000.

🏨 **Lord Internazionale** senza rist, via Spadari 11 ⊠ 20123 ℡ 803028 – ▐ ▤ ☐wc ▥wc. ᴁᴇ CV **t**
⚏ 3500 – **46 cam** 42000/61000.

🏨 **Centro** senza rist, via Broletto 46 ⊠ 20121 ℡ 875578 – ▐ ▤ ☐wc ▥wc ☜. ᴁᴇ ⓸ E 𝘝𝘐𝘚𝘈 BU **e**
⚏ 4000 – **54 cam** 39000/58000.

🏨 **Star** senza rist, via dei Bossi 5 ⊠ 20121 ℡ 871703 – ▐ ▤ ▥wc ☜ CU **b**
⚏ 4000 – **28 cam** 34000/50000, ▤ 4000.

XXXXX ❀ **Savini,** galleria Vittorio Emanuele 11 ⊠ 20121 ℡ 8058343, Gran tradizione; prenotare –
■. 🄰🄴 ⓪ 🄴 𝖵𝖨𝖲𝖠.   CV n
chiuso domenica, agosto e da Natale al 6 gennaio – Pas carta 31000/47000 (15%)
Spec. Risotto alla milanese ed al salto, Costoletta alla milanese, Branzino con frutti di mare al cartoccio.. **Vini**
Sauvignon, Dolcetto.

XXXX **St. Andrews,** via Sant'Andrea 23 ⊠ 20121 ℡ 793132, Confort accurato – soupers; prenotare
– ■. 🄰🄴 ⓪ 🄴 𝖵𝖨𝖲𝖠. ❄   DU y
chiuso domenica ed agosto – Pas carta 27000/38000 (15%).

XXXX **Biffi Scala,** piazza della Scala ⊠ 20121 ℡ 876332, Tea-room e soupers – ■. 🄰🄴 ⓪ 🄴 𝖵𝖨𝖲𝖠
chiuso domenica ed agosto – Pas carta 21000/34000 (13%).   CU z

XXXX **El Toulà,** piazza Paolo Ferrari 6 ⊠ 20121 ℡ 870302, Confort accurato – ■   CU z
chiuso domenica ed agosto – Pas carta 32000/45000 (13%).

XXXX **Suntory,** via Verdi 6 ⊠ 20121 ℡ 862210, Rist. giapponese – ■. 🄰🄴 ⓪ 𝖵𝖨𝖲𝖠. ❄   CU n
chiuso domenica e dal 9 al 18 agosto – Pas carta 25000/50000.

XXX **Prospero,** via Chiossetto 20 ⊠ 20122 ℡ 701345 – ■   DV e
chiuso sabato, domenica, agosto e dal 26 dicembre al 3 gennaio – Pas carta 16000/28000.

XXX **Luciano,** via Ugo Foscolo 1 ⊠ 20121 ℡ 866818 – ■. 🄰🄴 ⓪ 🄴 𝖵𝖨𝖲𝖠. ❄   CV a
chiuso sabato ed agosto – Pas carta 30000/40000 (12%).

XXX **Alfio,** via Senato 31 ⊠ 20121 ℡ 780731, Giardino d'inverno – ■. 🄰🄴 ⓪ 🄴 𝖵𝖨𝖲𝖠   DU a
chiuso sabato, domenica a mezzogiorno, dal 1° al 22 agosto e dal 26 dicembre al 3 gennaio –
Pas carta 21000/35000.

XXX **Rigoletto,** via Vincenzo Monti 33 ⊠ 20123 ℡ 860447 – ■. 🄰🄴 ⓪ 𝖵𝖨𝖲𝖠   AU b
chiuso domenica ed agosto – Pas carta 20000/33000.

XXX **Barbarossa,** via Cerva 10 ⊠ 20122 ℡ 781418, Ambiente vecchia Milano – ■. 🄰🄴 ⓪ 🄴 𝖵𝖨𝖲𝖠
chiuso domenica e dal 10 al 20 agosto – Pas carta 20000/33000.   DV f

XXX **Santa Monica,** piazzale Baracca 6 ⊠ 20123 ℡ 468850, « Raccolta di quadri » – ■. 🄰🄴 ⓪ 🄴
𝖵𝖨𝖲𝖠. ❄   AU a
chiuso domenica – Pas carta 20000/35000 (12%).

XXX **L'Innominato,** via Fiori Oscuri 3 ⊠ 20121 ℡ 8690552 – ■. 🄰🄴 ⓪ 🄴 𝖵𝖨𝖲𝖠. ❄   CU r
chiuso sabato a mezzogiorno, domenica, agosto e Capodanno – Pas carta 25000/35000.

XXX **4 Mori,** via San Giovanni sul Muro 2 ⊠ 20121 ℡ 870617, « Servizio estivo in giardino » – ■.
🄴 𝖵𝖨𝖲𝖠   BU d
chiuso sabato a mezzogiorno, domenica ed agosto – Pas carta 21000/36000.

XXX **Crispi,** corso Venezia 3 ⊠ 20121 ℡ 782010, Servizio estivo in giardino – ■. 🄰🄴 ⓪ 🄴 𝖵𝖨𝖲𝖠. ❄
chiuso lunedì e dal 6 al 30 agosto – Pas carta 19000/31000 (12%).   DU v

XXX **Boeucc,** piazza Belgioioso 2 ⊠ 20121 ℡ 790224, Servizio estivo all'aperto – ■. 🄰🄴 𝖵𝖨𝖲𝖠. ❄
chiuso venerdì sera, sabato ed agosto – Pas carta 19000/27000.   CDU x

XXX **Biffi Galleria,** galleria Vittorio Emanuele ⊠ 20121 ℡ 8052425, Rist. e self-service – ■. 🄰🄴
⓪ 🄴 𝖵𝖨𝖲𝖠. ❄   CV u
chiuso domenica e dal 24 dicembre al 1° gennaio – Pas carta 25000/40000.

XX **Don Lisander,** via Manzoni 12/a ℡ 790130, « Servizio estivo in cortile » – ■
chiuso sabato sera, domenica, dal 9 al 21 agosto e dal 21 dicembre al 3 gennaio – Pas
carta 24000/36000.   CU u

XX **Da Bice,** via Borgospesso 12 ⊠ 20121 ℡ 702572   DU m
chiuso lunedì, luglio ed agosto – Pas carta 20000/28000.

XX **Bagutta,** via Bagutta 14 ⊠ 20121 ℡ 702767, Rist. d'artisti; servizio estivo in giardino,
« Caratteristici dipinti e caricature » – 🄰🄴 ⓪ 🄴 𝖵𝖨𝖲𝖠. ❄   DU e
chiuso domenica, dal 7 al 31 agosto e dal 23 dicembre al 4 gennaio – Pas carta 20000/30000
(12%).

XX **Da Marino-al Conte Ugolino,** piazza Beccaria 6 ⊠ 20122 ℡ 876134 – ■. 🄰🄴 ⓪ 𝖵𝖨𝖲𝖠
chiuso domenica ed agosto – Pas carta 19000/30000.   DV c

XX **Tencitt,** via Laghetto 2 ⊠ 20122 ℡ 7490673, Rist. e piano-bar – ■. 🄰🄴   DV r
chiuso sabato a mezzogiorno, domenica ed agosto – Pas carta 19000/26000.

XX **Rigolo,** largo Treves (⊠ 20121 via Solferino 11) ℡ 8059768, Rist. d'habitués – ■. 🄰🄴 𝖵𝖨𝖲𝖠. ❄
chiuso lunedì, martedì a mezzogiorno ed agosto – Pas carta 18000/25000.   CU d

XX **Il Peschereccio,** Foro Bonaparte 52 (⊠ 20121 via Quintino Sella) ℡ 861418 – ■   BU s
chiuso lunedì sera, mercoledì ed agosto – Pas carta 20000/40000.

XX **Da Bruno,** via Maurizio Gonzaga 6 ⊠ 20123 ℡ 804364 – ■. 🄰🄴 𝖵𝖨𝖲𝖠   CV x
chiuso sabato e dal 1° al 20 agosto – Pas carta 14000/23000.

XX **La Pantera,** via Festa del Perdono 12 ⊠ 20122 ℡ 8057374, Rist. toscano – ■. 🄰🄴 ⓪ 𝖵𝖨𝖲𝖠
chiuso martedì ed agosto – Pas carta 17000/30000.   DV m

XX **La Muraglia,** piazza Oberdan 2 ⊠ 20129 ℡ 279528, Rist. cinese; servizio estivo in giardino
– ■. 🄰🄴 𝖵𝖨𝖲𝖠   DU d
chiuso lunedì e dal 10 al 25 agosto – Pas carta 11000/17000 (12%).

XX **Al Mercante,** piazza Mercanti 17 ⊠ 20123 ℡ 8052198, « Servizio estivo in una antica
loggia » – ❄   CV k
chiuso domenica e dal 15 al 30 agosto – Pas carta 14000/22000.

XX **Boccondivino,** via Carducci 17 ⊠ 20123 ℡ 866040, Specialità salumi, formaggi e vini tipici;
prenotare – ■. ❄   AV e
chiuso a mezzogiorno, domenica ed agosto – Pas carta 15000/22000.

XX **Franco il Contadino,** via Fiori Chiari 20 ⊠ 20121 ℱ 808153, Tipico rist. toscano e ritrovo d'artisti – ▤   CU **e**
chiuso martedì e luglio – Pas carta 16000/25000 (12%).

XX **Piccolo Padre,** viale Bianca Maria 2 ⊠ 20129 ℱ 798481, Caratteristico rist. umbro – ▤. 🅰🅴   DV **z**
chiuso a mezzogiorno, martedì ed agosto – Pas (menu tipico) 22000 bc.

XX **La Tampa,** via Laghetto 3 ⊠ 20122 ℱ 780940, Tipica trattoria toscana – ▤. 🅰🅴 ⓓ   DV **d**
chiuso sabato, Ferragosto e dal 25 dicembre al 12 gennaio – Pas carta 20000/35000 (12%).

XX **Albric,** via Albricci 3 ⊠ 20122 ℱ 806356, « Raccolta di quadri » – ▤. 🅰🅴 ⓓ Ɛ 𝖵𝖨𝖲𝖠. ⌘   CV **q**
chiuso domenica e dal 25 luglio al 25 agosto – Pas carta 17000/25000.

X **Ciovassino,** via Ciovassino 5 ⊠ 20121 ℱ 8053868, Coperti limitati; prenotare – ▤   CU **s**
chiuso sabato a mezzogiorno, domenica ed agosto – Pas carta 17000/25000.

X **I Matteoni,** viale Regina Margherita (⊠ 20129 piazzale 5 Giornate 6) ℱ 588293, Rist. d'habitués – ▤. 🅰🅴 𝖵𝖨𝖲𝖠   DV **s**
chiuso domenica ed agosto – Pas carta 16000/25000.

X **Dollaro,** via Paolo da Cannobio 11 ⊠ 20122 ℱ 804138, Rist., quick-lunches e pizzeria – ▤. 𝖵𝖨𝖲𝖠   CV **z**
chiuso domenica e dal 1° al 25 agosto – Pas carta 15000/24000.

X **Peppino,** via Durini 7 ⊠ 20122 ℱ 781729 – ▤. 🅰🅴 ⓓ 𝖵𝖨𝖲𝖠   DV **u**
chiuso venerdì sera, sabato, luglio e dal 2 dicembre al 4 gennaio – Pas carta 18000/25000.

X **'nderre a la lanze,** piazza Santo Stefano 10 ⊠ 20122 ℱ 873449, Rist. pugliese con specialità di mare – ▤. 🅰🅴 𝖵𝖨𝖲𝖠   DV **h**
chiuso lunedì e dal 1° al 25 agosto – Pas carta 14000/22000 (12%).

X **Allo Scudo,** via Mazzini 7 ⊠ 20123 ℱ 8052761, Rist. d'habitués – ▤. ⌘   CV **e**
chiuso domenica ed agosto – Pas carta 12000/22000 (10%).

X **Brasera Meneghina,** via Circo 10 ⊠ 20123 ℱ 808108, Trattoria vecchia Milano; servizio estivo all'aperto   BV **p**
chiuso venerdì, sabato a mezzogiorno, agosto e dal 25 dicembre al 4 gennaio – Pas carta 15000/24000 (12%).

X **Ai Tre Fratelli,** via Terraggio 11/13 ⊠ 20123 ℱ 873281, prenotare, Servizio estivo in giardino – ▤. 🅰🅴 𝖵𝖨𝖲𝖠. ⌘   AV **r**
chiuso domenica, dal 1° al 25 agosto e dal 24 dicembre al 6 gennaio – Pas carta 12000/21000.

X **Al Chico,** via Sirtori 24 ⊠ 20129 ℱ 2716883, Rist. toscano; servizio estivo all'aperto   DU **s**
chiuso sabato a mezzogiorno, domenica, dal 1° al 27 agosto e dal 25 al 31 dicembre – Pas carta 15000/25000.

X **Pizzeria le Briciole,** via Camperio 17 ⊠ 20123 ℱ 877185, Trattoria a coperti limitati; prenotare – ▤. ⌘   BU **a**
chiuso sabato a mezzogiorno, lunedì ed agosto – Pas carta 15000/20000.

X **Spaghetteria Emilio,** via Solferino 3 ⊠ 20122 ℱ 872735, prenotare, Trattoria caratteristica con specialità spaghetti; soupers – ▤   CU **a**
chiuso a mezzogiorno, domenica e dal 7 al 23 agosto – Pas carta 16000/22000.

Zona urbana sud Porta Ticinese, Porta Romana, Stazione Genova, Navigli, Parco Ravizza, Vigentino (pianta : Milano p. 10 e 11)

🏨 **Lloyd,** senza rist, corso di Porta Romana 48 ⊠ 20122 ℱ 867971, Telex 335028, « Raccolta di quadri d'autore » – ▤ 📺 - 🛗   CX **z**
52 cam.

🏨 **Ascot** senza rist, via Lentasio 3 ⊠ 20122 ℱ 862946, Telex 311303 – ▤ 🚗. 🅰🅴 Ɛ 𝖵𝖨𝖲𝖠   CX **e**
⬜ 7000 – **56 cam** 60000/90000.

🏨 **Crivi's** senza rist, corso Porta Vigentina 46 ⊠ 20122 ℱ 5463341, Telex 313255 – ▤ 📺 ⅍ 🚗 - 🛗. 🅰🅴   DY **a**
⬜ 5500 – **62 cam** 75000/95000.

🏨 **D'Este** senza rist, viale Bligny 23 ⊠ 20136 ℱ 5461041 – ▤ 📺 ☎ - 🛗. 🅰🅴 ⓓ Ɛ 𝖵𝖨𝖲𝖠. ⌘   CY **r**
⬜ 6000 – **54 cam** 40000/57000.

🏨 **Sant'Ambroeus** senza rist, viale Papiniano 14 ⊠ 20123 ℱ 4697451, Telex 313373 – ▤ ☎ ⅍ - 🛗. 𝖵𝖨𝖲𝖠   AX **a**
chiuso agosto – ⬜ 4500 – **52 cam** 45000/65000.

🏨 **Ambrosiano** senza rist, via Santa Sofia 9 ⊠ 20122 ℱ 580445 – ▤ ☎ ⓟ. 🅰🅴 Ɛ 𝖵𝖨𝖲𝖠. ⌘   CX **x**
chiuso luglio o agosto – ⬜ 4000 – **68 cam** 36000/60000.

🏨 **Mediterraneo** senza rist, via Muratori 14 ⊠ 20135 ℱ 5488151, Telex 335812 – |🛗| ▤ 📺 ⌷wc ⋔wc ☎ - 🛗. 🅰🅴 ⓓ Ɛ 𝖵𝖨𝖲𝖠   DY **q**
⬜ 4000 – **93 cam** 40000/57000, ▤ 2000.

🏨 **Imperial** senza rist, corso di Porta Romana 68 ⊠ 20122 ℱ 5468241 – ▤ ⌷wc ⋔wc ☎ ⓟ. 🅰🅴 Ɛ 𝖵𝖨𝖲𝖠. ⌘   DX **c**
⬜ 5000 – **36 cam** 40000/58000.

🏨 **Amedei** senza rist, via Amedei 2 ⊠ 20123 ℱ 8057065 – |🛗| ⌷wc ⊛. 🅰🅴 ⓓ 𝖵𝖨𝖲𝖠   CX **n**
chiuso agosto – ⬜ 7000 – **71 cam** 65000/90000.

🏨 **Adriatico** senza rist, via Conca del Naviglio 20 ⊠ 20123 ℱ 8324141 – |🛗| ▤ 📺 ⌷wc ⋔wc ⊛. 🅰🅴 ⓓ Ɛ 𝖵𝖨𝖲𝖠   BX **m**
⬜ 4000 – **105 cam** 41000/60000.

🏨 **Canada** senza rist, via Lentasio 15 (✉ 20122 via Santa Sofia 18) ☎ 8052527, Telex 313286 –
|𝄞| 🖙wc ⏚wc ⚑. ⁅⁆ 🝔 𝓥𝓢𝓐   CX **g**
chiuso agosto – ⟗ 4500 – **30 cam** 42000/60000.

🏨 **Motel dei Fiori** senza rist, raccordo autostrada A7 ✉ 20142 ☎ 8436441 – |𝄞| 🖳 🖙wc ⏚wc
🕭 ⬧ 𝐏. ⁅⁆ ⓞ ⁅   AZ **e**
55 cam ⟗ 28000/43000, 🖳 3000.

🏨 **Zurigo**, corso Italia 11/a ✉ 20122 ☎ 808909 – |𝄞| 🖙wc ⏚wc ⚑. ⁅⁆   CX **m**
⟗ 3500 – **36 cam** 36000/53000.

🏠 **Garden** senza rist, via Rutilia 6 ✉ 20141 ☎ 560838 – ⏚wc ⚑ 🖦 𝐏   DZ **a**
chiuso agosto – ⟗ 3000 – **23 cam** 25000/30000.

XXX **La Nôs**, via Amedei 2 ✉ 20123 ☎ 8058759, Ritrovo elegante stile vecchia Milano, « Decorazioni ottocentesche » – 🖳. ⁅⁆ ⓞ ⁅ 𝓥𝓢𝓐. ⚘   CX **n**
chiuso domenica, lunedì a mezzogiorno ed agosto – Pas carta 20000/36000 (13%).

XXX **Vecchia Milano**, viale Gian Galeazzo 25 (✉ 20136 via Aurispa 7) ☎ 8397365, Specialità
arabe ed internazionali – 🖳. ⁅⁆ ⓞ ⁅ 𝓥𝓢𝓐   BY **a**
chiuso lunedì, dal 5 al 25 agosto e Capodanno – Pas carta 20000/30000 (12%).

XXX **Malatesta,** via Bianca di Savoia 19 ✉ 20122 ☎ 5461079 – 🖳. ⁅⁆ ⓞ 𝓥𝓢𝓐. ⚘   CY **a**
chiuso sabato sera, domenica ed agosto – Pas carta 26000/38000.

XXX ⚙ **Scaletta Wine Bar,** piazzale stazione Porta Genova ✉ 20144 ☎ 8350290, Coperti limitati;
prenotare – 🖳. ⚘   AY **a**
chiuso domenica, lunedì, dal 10 al 20 aprile, agosto e dal 24 dicembre al 4 gennaio – Pas
carta 35000/43000
Spec. Risotto con ortiche e fragole, Dova (filetto crudo con spinaci crudi). Insalata di soncino e scampetti. Vini
Verduzzo, Le Rive Rosse.

XXX ⚙ **San Vito da Nino,** via San Vito 5 ✉ 20123 ☎ 8377029, Rist. a coperti limitati; prenotare
– 🖳. 𝓥𝓢𝓐. ⚘   BX **a**
chiuso lunedì e da agosto al 2 settembre – Pas carta 26000/36000 (13%)
Spec. Gingillo tartufato, Pollo allo champagne, Costa di manzo alla bourguignonne.

XX **Giordano,** via Torti (✉ 20123 corso Genova 3) ☎ 8350824, Rist. rustico moderno con specialità
bolognesi – 🖳   BX **s**
chiuso domenica e dal 2 al 23 agosto – Pas carta 15000/21000 (12%).

XX **Osteria del Binari,** via Tortona 1 ✉ 20144 ☎ 8399428, prenotare, Atmosfera vecchia Milano;
servizio estivo in giardino   AY **e**
chiuso a mezzogiorno.

XX **Al Porto,** piazzale Generale Cantore ✉ 20123 ☎ 8321481, prenotare, Trattoria con specialità
di mare – 🖳   AXY **d**
chiuso domenica, lunedì a mezzogiorno ed agosto – Pas carta 23000/30000

XX **Toscanino,** piazza Erculea 9 ✉ 20122 ☎ 873589 – ⓞ   CX **s**
chiuso domenica ed agosto – Pas carta 15000/25000.

XX **Il Montalcino-la Cucina di Edgardo,** via Valenza 17 ✉ 20144 ☎ 8353783, prenotare – 🖳.
⁅⁆ ⓞ 𝓥𝓢𝓐   AY **n**
chiuso domenica e in luglio-agosto anche sabato – Pas (menu suggerito dal proprietario)
26000 (10%).

X **Osteria Via Pré,** via Casale 4 ✉ 20144 ☎ 8373869, Trattoria tipica con specialità liguri – 🖳
chiuso lunedì, martedì, agosto e dal 24 dicembre al 1° gennaio – Pas carta 16000/23000.
                                                                                                   AY **c**

X **Ai Sabbioni,** viale d'Annunzio 7/9 ✉ 20123 ☎ 8390052, Coperti limitati; prenotare – 🖳
chiuso domenica, lunedì a mezzogiorno ed agosto – Pas carta 20000/30000.   AY **s**

X **La Cantinetta,** via Ripamonti 19 ✉ 20136 ☎ 580817 – 🖳   DY **b**
chiuso sabato a mezzogiorno, domenica ed agosto – Pas carta 12000/20000.

X **Al Buon Convento,** corso Italia 26 ✉ 20122 ☎ 8050623, Trattoria tipica a coperti limitati –
🖳   CX **k**
chiuso domenica ed agosto – Pas carta 18000/25000.

X **Il Torchietto,** via Ascanio Sforza 47 ✉ 20136 ☎ 8372910, Rist. rustico – 🖳   BZ **s**
chiuso lunedì, dal 27 luglio al 31 agosto e dal 26 dicembre al 5 gennaio – Pas carta 18000/24000.

X Osteria la Pergola, vicolo Santa Caterina 5 ✉ 20122 ☎ 800213, Trattoria a coperti limitati;
prenotare.   CX **v**

Zone periferiche

Rioni : Bruzzano, Niguarda, Bicocca, viale Fulvio Testi – N : verso ① ② ③ e ④ : Monza, Lecco,
Erba, Venezia (pianta : Milano p. 4)

🏨 **Leonardo da Vinci** ⚐, via Senigallia 6 ✉ 20161 ☎ 6407, Telex 331552, ⟒, ☀, ⚘ – 🖳 📺
🕿 🖦 ⟲ 𝐏 - ⚠. ⁅⁆ ⓞ ⁅ 𝓥𝓢𝓐. ⚘ rist   GK **a**
Pas carta – **282 cam** ⟗ 90000/123000.

🏨 **Tourist Motel e Rist. la Cuccagnina,** viale Fulvio Testi 300 ✉ 20126 ☎ 6437777 – |𝄞| 🖳
📺 ⏚wc 🕿 ⟲ 𝐏. ⁅⁆ ⓞ ⁅ 𝓥𝓢𝓐   HK **r**
Pas carta 13000/19000 – ⟗ 5000 – **60 cam** 37000/64000.

Rioni : corso Buenos Aires, Loreto, Lambrate – NE : verso ⑤ : Bergamo, Brescia (pianta : Milano p.4 e 5)

🏨 **Napoleon,** senza rist, via Ozanam 12 ⊠ 20129 ℱ 208280 – 🛗 🗐 ⇔wc 🛎wc ☎   HM **v**
43 cam.

🏨 **Adam** senza rist, via Palmanova 153 ⊠ 20132 ℱ 2592551 – 🛗 🗐 ⇔wc 🛎wc ☎. ⚘   HL **e**
⟺ 5500 – **48 cam** 38000/54000.

🏨 **Lombardia e Rist. la Festa,** viale Lombardia 74 ⊠ 20131 ℱ 2824938 – 🛗 🗐 ⇔wc 🛎wc
☎ ⟺ - 🔬. 🖭 ⓞ 🗉 𝓥𝓘𝓢𝓐   HLM **p**
Pas *(chiuso domenica ed agosto)* carta 15000/25000 – ⟺ 4000 – **69 cam** 40000/55000 – P 66000/73000.

🏨 **Gamma** senza rist, via Valvassori Peroni 85 ⊠ 20133 ℱ 2141116 – 🛗 🗐 ⇔wc 🛎wc ☎
chiuso agosto – ⟺ 3000 – **55 cam** 40000/60000.   HM **m**

✕✕ **Don Chisciotte,** via Palmanova 153 ⊠ 20132 ℱ 2564098, Rist. rustico moderno – 🗐. 🖭 ⓞ
𝓥𝓘𝓢𝓐   HL **e**
chiuso sabato, domenica e dal 9 al 31 agosto – Pas carta 14000/22000 (12%).

✕✕ **Montecatini Alto,** viale Monza 7 ⊠ 20125 ℱ 2846773 – 🗐   HL **m**
chiuso domenica ed agosto – Pas carta 15000/24000 (12%).

✕✕ **Mancini,** via Omboni 4 ⊠ 20129 ℱ 276472, Rist. d'habitués – 🗐. 🖭 ⓞ 𝓥𝓘𝓢𝓐   HM **t**
chiuso venerdì sera, sabato ed agosto – Pas carta 13000/25000 (12%).

✕✕ **Da Renzo,** via Teodosio 104 ⊠ 20131 ℱ 2846261, Rist. rustico con servizio estivo all'aperto
– ⚘   HL **x**
chiuso lunedì sera, martedì ed agosto – Pas carta 15000/22000.

✕✕ **Antica Hostaria la Gobba,** via Padova 395 ⊠ 20132 ℱ 2560081, Rist. rustico con servizio estivo all'aperto – ⓟ. 🖭 ⓞ. ⚘   HL **s**
chiuso domenica – Pas carta 18000/29000.

✕ **L'Aratro-da Sabatino,** via Pietro Marocco 12 ⊠ 20127 ℱ 2850126, Trattoria tipica con specialità alla brace – 🗐. ⓞ 𝓥𝓘𝓢𝓐   HL **j**
chiuso domenica e dal 1° al 24 agosto – Pas carta 12000/20000.

✕ **La Paranza,** via Padova 3 ⊠ 20127 ℱ 2843224, Rist. a coperti limitati; specialità di mare –
🗐. 🖭 ⓞ 𝓥𝓘𝓢𝓐   HL **r**
chiuso lunedì ed agosto – Pas carta 16000/22000.

Rioni : Città Studi, Monforte, corso 22 Marzo, viale Corsica – E : verso : aeroporto di Linate, Idroscalo, strada Rivoltana (pianta : Milano p. 5)

🏨 **Zefiro** senza rist, via Gallina 12 ⊠ 20129 ℱ 7384253 – 🛗 🗐 ⇔wc 🛎wc ☎ - 🔬. ⚘   HM **a**
chiuso dal 30 luglio al 29 agosto – ⟺ 4000 – **55 cam** 42000/58000.

🏨 **Vittoria** senza rist, via Pietro Calvi 32 ⊠ 20129 ℱ 793695 – 🛗 🗐 ⇔wc 🛎wc ☎. ⚘   HM **g**
chiuso agosto – **18 cam** ⟺ 37000/57000, 🗐 2000.

🏠 **Città Studi** senza rist, via Saldini 24 ⊠ 20133 ℱ 744602 – 🛗 ⇔wc 🛎wc ☎
⟺ 3000 – **45 cam** 23000/34000.   HM **q**

✕✕✕✕ ✿ **Giannino,** via Amatore Sciesa 8 ⊠ 20135 ℱ 5452948, Gran tradizione, « Originali decorazioni; giardino d'inverno » – 🗐 ⓟ. 🖭 ⓞ 🗉 𝓥𝓘𝓢𝓐   HN **w**
chiuso sabato, domenica, agosto e dal 24 al 30 dicembre – Pas carta 30000/45000
Spec. Risotto con frutti di mare, Branzino al piatto, Olivette di vitello tartufate.

✕✕✕ ✿✿ **Gualtiero Marchesi,** via Bonvesin de la Riva 9 ⊠ 20129 ℱ 741246, Confort accurato; prenotare – 🗐. 🖭. ⚘   HM **g**
chiuso domenica, lunedì a mezzogiorno ed agosto – Pas carta 42000/55000
Spec. Secondo stagione.

✕✕✕ **Alle Asse,** via Marcona 6 ⊠ 20129 ℱ 795359, Servizio estivo in giardino – 🗐. 🖭 𝓥𝓘𝓢𝓐 HM **x**
chiuso domenica, lunedì a mezzogiorno, dal 7 al 30 agosto e dal 2 al 12 gennaio – Pas carta 19000/35000.

✕✕ **La Pesa-da Rino,** via Morosini 12 ⊠ 20135 ℱ 592058, Rist. d'habitués – 🗐. 🖭 ⓞ 🗉 𝓥𝓘𝓢𝓐
chiuso mercoledì e dal 1° al 28 agosto – Pas carta 20000/27000.   HN **w**

✕✕ ✿ **La Bella Pisana,** via Pasquale Sottocorno 17 ⊠ 20129 ℱ 708376, Servizio estivo in giardino
– 🗐. 🖭 𝓥𝓘𝓢𝓐   HM **e**
chiuso domenica, lunedì a mezzogiorno, dal 5 al 31 agosto e dal 1° all 8 gennaio – Pas carta 20000/28000
Spec. Taglierini alla Bella Pisana, Tortelli di magro piacentini, Branzino alle erbe. **Vini** Gavi, Chianti.

✕✕ **Palazzo del Ghiaccio,** via Piranesi 14 ⊠ 20137 ℱ 7398 – 🗐   HM **c**
chiuso lunedì ed agosto – Pas carta 13000/19000 (12%).

✕ **Il Palio di Siena,** via Turroni 4 ⊠ 20129 ℱ 7387928, Trattoria toscana; servizio estivo all'aperto   HM **b**
chiuso domenica sera, lunedì e dal 9 al 30 agosto – Pas carta 14000/21000.

✕ **Lo Stuzzichino,** via Cadore 15 ⊠ 20135 ℱ 5484825, Servizio estivo all'aperto – 🗐. ⚘
chiuso lunedì ed agosto – Pas carta 20000/27000.   HN **s**

✕ **Da Claudio,** piazza Emilia 4 ⊠ 20129 ℱ 742438, Trattoria moderna; raccolta di quadri – 🖭
🗉 𝓥𝓘𝓢𝓐   HM **z**
chiuso domenica – Pas carta 13000/21000.

✗ **Sagittario,** via Eustachi 6 ⊠ 20129 ℱ 220045 – 🖭 🕸   HM s
chiuso domenica ed agosto – Pas carta 19000/30000.

✗ **Al Grissino,** via Tiepolo 54 ⊠ 20129 ℱ 730392 – 🗏. 🖭. 🕸   HM n
chiuso domenica sera, mercoledì ed agosto – Pas carta 18000/29000.

Rioni :corso Lodi, inizio Autostrada del Sole – SE : verso ⑥ : Lodi, Parma, via Emilia (pianta :
Milano p. 5, salvo indicazioni speciali)

🏨 **Mec** senza rist, via Tito Livio 4 ⊠ 20137 ℱ 544040 – 🛗 🗏 🛏wc 🎢wc 📼. 🖭 **E** 𝘝𝘐𝘚𝘈 🕸
� 3500 – **40 cam** 39000/56000, 🗏 2500.   HN r

✗✗ **Lo Scrigno,** corso Lodi 70 ⊠ 20139 ℱ 563081, Servizio estivo in giardino – 🗏 **E**   HN t
chiuso domenica e dall'8 al 24 agosto – Pas carta 12000/23000.

✗ **Da Costantino,** corso Lodi 3 ⊠ 20135 ℱ 541492, Servizio estivo in giardino – 🗏. 🖭 ⓪ **E**
𝘝𝘐𝘚𝘈   Milano p 11 DY s
chiuso lunedì ed agosto – Pas carta 14000/19000.

Rioni : Fiera Campionaria, San Siro, Porta Magenta – O : verso ⑩ e ⑪ : Novara, Torino (pianta :
Milano p. 5)

🏨 **Gd H. Fieramilano,** viale Boezio 20 ⊠ 20145 ℱ 3105, Telex 331426 – 🗏 📺 ☎ ⅄ - 🏛. 🖭
⓪ **E** 𝘝𝘐𝘚𝘈. 🕸 rist   FM p
Pas 25000 – **238 cam** ⊐ 105000/135000.

🏨 **Rubens** senza rist, via Rubens 21 ⊠ 20148 ℱ 405051, Telex 333503 – 🗏 ☎ ⓟ - 🏛. **E** 𝘝𝘐𝘚𝘈
🕸   FM e
chiuso dal 1° al 23 agosto – ⊐ 5000 – **76 cam** 46000/68000.

🏨 **Montebianco** senza rist, via Monte Rosa 90 ⊠ 20149 ℱ 4697941 – 🗏 ⓟ. 🖭 **E** 𝘝𝘐𝘚𝘈   FM f
chiuso agosto – ⊐ 4000 – **44 cam** 40000/60000.

🏨 **Fiera** senza rist, via Spinola 9 ⊠ 20149 ℱ 432374, «Piccolo giardino » – 🛗 🛏wc 🎢wc ☎
🚗 - 🏛. 🕸   FM q
chiuso agosto – ⊐ 4000 – **29 cam** 40000/58000.

🏨 **Capitol** senza rist, via Cimarosa 6 ⊠ 20144 ℱ 496024 – 🛗 🗏 🛏wc 🎢wc 📼 - 🏛. 🖭 **E** 𝘝𝘐𝘚𝘈
99 cam ⊐ 48000/73000.   FM s

🏨 **Wagner** senza rist, via Buonarroti 13 ⊠ 20149 ℱ 4696051 – 🛗 🗏 🛏wc 🎢wc 📼   FM n
chiuso agosto – **49 cam** ⊐ 44000/66000, 🗏 4000.

🏨 **Piemonte** senza rist, via Ruggero Settimo 1 ⊠ 20146 ℱ 4989939 – 🛗 🛏wc 🎢wc 📼 ⓟ
⊐ 3000 – **19 cam** 27000/37000.   FM u

✗✗✗ ❀ **La Corba,** via dei Gigli 14 ⊠ 20147 ℱ 4158977, Ambiente rustico, «Servizio estivo in
giardino »   FN a
chiuso domenica sera, lunedì e dal 10 al 25 agosto – Pas carta 20000/30000
Spec. Capriccio di paste, Spiedini alla Corba, Cosciotto di bue al Barolo (ottobre-aprile). **Vini** Chianti.

✗✗ **El Gamba de Legn,** via Elba 30 ⊠ 20144 ℱ 463091, Rist. con specialità milanesi; prenotare
– 🗏. 🖭 ⓪   FM k
chiuso domenica e dal 20 luglio al 31 agosto – Pas carta 18000/29000 (13%).

✗✗ **Su Nuraghe,** via Roncaglia 3 ⊠ 20146 ℱ 431475, Tipico rist. sardo – 🗏. 🖭 ⓪ **E** 𝘝𝘐𝘚𝘈. 🕸
chiuso agosto – Pas carta 15000/20000.   FN v

✗✗ Raffaello, via Raffaello Sanzio 8 ⊠ 20149 ℱ 495227, Servizio estivo in giardino.   FM n

✗✗ **Da Gino e Franco,** largo Domodossola 2 ⊠ 20145 ℱ 312003 – 🗏. 🕸   FM b
chiuso lunedì e dal 25 luglio al 25 agosto – Pas carta 15000/26000 (12%).

✗✗ ❀ **Da Aimo,** via Montecuccoli 6 ⊠ 20147 ℱ 416886, Servizio estivo in giardino – 🕸   FN x
chiuso domenica ed agosto – Pas carta 28000/48000
Spec. Gnocchi di rucola con ragù di insalate fresche, Capretto di Normandia alle olive (autunno-inverno) Stinco di
vitello delizia di Nadia. **Vini** Rosso delle colline lucchesi.

✗✗ **Furio-Montebianco,** via Monte Bianco 2 ⊠ 20149 ℱ 495677, Rist. toscano – 🗏   FM t
chiuso martedì ed agosto – Pas carta 17000/28000 (12%).

✗ **Pace,** via Washington 74 ⊠ 20146 ℱ 468567, Rist. d'habitués 🕸   FM d
chiuso mercoledì ed agosto – Pas carta 13000/20000.

✗ **Il Garfagnino,** via Cherubini 8 ⊠ 20145 ℱ 495191, Trattoria toscana – 🗏. 🖭 𝘝𝘐𝘚𝘈. 🕸
chiuso lunedì e luglio – Pas carta 13000/20000.   FM v

Rioni : Sempione-Bullona, viale Certosa – NO : verso ⑫ ⑬ e ⑭ : Varese, Como, Torino, Aeroporto della Malpensa (pianta : Milano p. 4 e 5)

🏨 **Raffaello** senza rist, viale Certosa 108 ⊠ 20156 ℱ 3270146, Telex 315499 – 🗏 - 🏛. 🖭 **E**
𝘝𝘐𝘚𝘈. 🕸   FL x
⊐ 4000 – **109 cam** 38000/55000.

🏨 **Berlino** senza rist, via Plana 33 ⊠ 20155 ℱ 387732 – 🛗 🗏 🛏wc 🎢wc ☎ - 🏛. **E** 𝘝𝘐𝘚𝘈   FL v
⊐ 3500 – **47 cam** 36000/53000.

🏨 **Mac Mahon** senza rist, via Mac Mahon 45/a ⊠ 20155 ℱ 341281 – 🛗 🛏wc 🎢wc 📼. 🕸
chiuso agosto – ⊐ 4000 – **27 cam** 28000/43000.   FL m

🏨 **Corallo** senza rist, via Cesena 20 ⊠ 20155 ℱ 314074 – 🛗 🛏wc 🎢wc 📼
⊐ 3500 – **35 cam** 27000/41000.   FL f

▥ **Piccolo Hotel** senza rist, via Piero della Francesca 60 ⊠ 20154 ℡ 340756 – 🛗 🛁wc ☜
chiuso dal 5 al 23 agosto – 🍽 3000 – **34 cam** 28000/40000.   FM   **r**

▥ **Parma** senza rist, via Piero della Francesca 48 ⊠ 20154 ℡ 315448 – 🛗 🛁wc 🛁wc ☜. ⌇
26 cam 🍽 21000/41000.   FGM   **a**

▥ **Casella** senza rist, via Casella 61 ⊠ 20156 ℡ 395938 – 🛗 🛁wc 🛁wc ☜   FL   **x**
chiuso agosto e dal 25 al 31 dicembre – 🍽 3000 – **29 cam** 29000/42000.

XX **La Pobbia,** via Gallarate 92 ⊠ 20151 ℡ 305641, Rist. rustico moderno, « Servizio estivo
all'aperto » – 🅿. 🖭   FL   **n**
chiuso domenica ed agosto – Pas carta 15000/30000 (12%).

X **Al Vöttantott,** corso Sempione 88 ⊠ 20154 ℡ 3182114, Trattoria d'habitués – 🍽. 🖭
chiuso domenica ed agosto – Pas carta 14000/23000.   FM   **r**

Dintorni di Milano

a Chiaravalle Milanese SE : 7 km (pianta : Milano p. 5 HN) :

XX ✿ **Antica Trattoria San Bernardo,** via San Bernardo 36 ⊠ 20139 Milano ℡ 5690831,
Trattoria della campagna lombarda, « Servizio estivo all'aperto » – 🅿. ⌇   HN   **a**
chiuso lunedì ed agosto – Pas carta 21000/31000
Spec. Terrina di legumi, Delizia San Bernardo, Brasato di stinco con polenta (settembre-aprile). Vini Sauvignon,
Nebbiolo.

sull'autostrada A 7 per ⑨ : 7 km (pianta : Milano p.5 FGN) :

🏨 **Motel f.i.n.i.** senza rist, via del Mare 93 ⊠ 20142 Milano ℡ 8464041 – 🍽 📺 ⛴ 🚗 🅿 - 🏛
🖭 ⓞ ☰ 𝘝𝘐𝘚𝘈. ⌇   FGN   **b**
🍽 4500 – **78 cam** 39000/55000.

sulla strada Nuova Vigevanese-quartiere Zingone per ⑩ : 11 km per via Lorenteggio :

🏨 **Motel Eur** senza rist, ⊠ 20090 Zingone di Trezzano ℡ 4451951 – 🍽 🅿 - 🏛. 🖭 ⓞ ☰
41 cam 🍽 36000/53000, 🍽 3000.

🏨 **Tiffany,** ⊠ 20090 Zingone di Trezzano ℡ 4452859, Servizio rist. estivo all'aperto – 🛗 🍽 cam
🛁wc 🛁wc ☜ 🅿. 𝘝𝘐𝘚𝘈
chiuso dal 13 al 23 agosto – Pas *(chiuso domenica e dal 28 luglio al 29 agosto)* carta 19000/28000
– 🍽 3000 – **36 cam** 28000/43000, 🍽 2500 – P 66000.

all'idroscalo (lato Est) E : 12 km (pianta : Milano p.5 HM) :

XX **La Viscontina,** località Plasticopoli ⊠ 20068 Peschiera Borromeo ℡ 5470391, Servizio
estivo in giardino – ⌇
chiuso mercoledì – Pas carta 16000/22000.

verso San Bovio E : 12 km per strada Rivoltana (pianta Milano p. 5 HM) :

X **Trattoria dei Cacciatori,** Cascina Longhignana ⊠ 20068 Peschiera Borromeo ℡ 7531154,
Vecchio cascinale con servizio estivo in giardino – 🅿
chiuso domenica sera, lunedì ed agosto – Pas carta 15000/23000.

sulla tangenziale ovest-Assago per ⑩ : 14 km :

🏨 **Motelagip,** ⊠ 20094 Assago ℡ 8463441, 🛁 – 🍽 ☎ 🅿 - 🏛. 🖭 ⓞ 𝘝𝘐𝘚𝘈. ⌇ rist
Pas 11000 - senza 🍽 – **222 cam** 39000/59000.

VENEZIA 30100 🄿 🄑🄑🄑 ⑤ – 352 453 ab. – a.s. aprile-ottobre e Natale – ☎ 041.

Vedere :

Piazza San Marco★★★ CY : Basilica★★★ (mosaici★★★, Pala d'Oro★★★, Tesoro★★★), Campanile★ (panorama★★), Torre dell'Orologio★, Procuratie★, museo Correr★★, Palazzo Ducale★★★ (Sala del Consiglio Maggiore★★★, Sala dello Scrutinio★★★), Piazzetta★★★ (Libreria Vecchia★) – Ponte dei Sospiri★ CY.

Canal Grande★★★ : Palazzo Venier (galleria d'arte moderna★) BZ, Palazzo Rezzonico★ (museo del Settecento veneziano AY, Ponte di Rialto★ CX, Cà d'Oro★★ (Galleria Franchetti, in corso di restauro) BX, Palazzo Pesaro★ (museo d'arte moderna) BX – Galleria dell'Accademia★★★ ABZ.

Scuola di San Rocco★★★ (dipinti del Tintoretto★★★) AX – Scuola di San Giorgio degli Schiavoni★ (dipinti del Carpaccio★★) DX – Scuola dei Carmini★ (dipinti del Tiepolo★) AY – Chiesa di Santa Maria della Salute★ BZ – Chiesa di San Giorgio Maggiore★ CZ – Chiesa di San Zanipolo★, statua equestre di Bartolomeo Colleoni★★ CX – Chiesa di Santa Maria Gloriosa dei Frari★ AX – Chiesa di San Zaccaria★ CY – Chiesa di Santa Maria dei Miracoli★ CX – Chiesa di San Sebastiano (soffitto del Veronese★) AY.

Dintorni : Lido★★★ SE : 15 mn di vaporetto – Murano★ (museo d'Arte Vetraria★) NE : 15mn di vaporetto – Burano★ NE : 30 mn di vaporetto – Torcello★★ (cattedrale di Santa Maria Assunta★, chiesa di Santa Fosca★) NE : 45 mn di vaporetto – Riviera del Brenta★★, O : andata in battello e ritorno in autopullman (una giornata).

☞ (chiuso lunedì) al Lido Alberoni ⊠ 30011 ☏ 731015, 15 mn di vaporetto e 9 km.

✈ Marco Polo di Tessera, NE : 13 km ☏ 957333 (pianta : Dintorni p. 3) – Alitalia, campo San Moisè 1483 ⊠ 30124 ☏ 700355.

🚂 a Mestre ☏ 929472.

🚋 per il Lido – San Nicolò da piazzale Roma (Tronchetto) giornalieri (35 mn).

🚢 per Punta Sabbioni da riva degli Schiavoni giornalieri (45 mn); per l'isola di Pellestrina-Santa Maria del Mare dal Lido Alberoni giornalieri (10 mn); per le isole di Murano (10 mn), Burano (45 mn) e Torcello (50 mn) giornalieri, dalle fondamente Nuove – Informazioni : ACTV - Azienda Consorzio Trasporti Veneziano, San Marco corte dell'Albero 3880 ⊠ 30124 ☏ 89620.

🛈 San Marco Ascensione 71/c ⊠ 30124 ☏ 26356 – piazzale Roma 540/d ⊠ 30125 ☏ 27402 – Stazione Santa Lucia ⊠ 30121 ☏ /15016.

A.C.I. fondamenta Santa Chiara 518/a ⊠ 30125 ☏ 700300.

Roma 528 ① – Bologna 152 ① – Milano 267 ① – Trieste 158 ①.

Salvo indicazioni speciali, vedere ubicazioni sulla pianta p. 6

🏨 **Gritti Palace,** campo Santa Maria del Giglio 2467 ⊠ 30124 ☏ 26044, Telex 410125, ≤ Canal Grande – 🗏 📺 🕿 ᴕ - 🟧 🕮 🖪 𝓥𝓘𝓢𝓐, 🦐 rist   BY **a**
Pas carta 49000/90000 – 🍷 17000 – **92 cam** 208000/266000.

🏨 **Danieli,** riva degli Schiavoni 4196 ⊠ 30122 ☏ 26480, Telex 410077, ≤ canale di San Marco, « Hall in cortiletto stile veneziano » – 🗏 📺 🕿 ᴕ - 🟧 🕮 🕦 🖪 𝓥𝓘𝓢𝓐, 🦐 rist   CY **a**
Pas carta 56000/82000 – 🍷 11000 – **246 cam** 168000/232000.

🏨 **Cipriani** ⑊, isola della Giudecca 10 ⊠ 30123 ☏ 707744, Telex 410162, ≤, 🏊 riscaldata – 🗏 ᴕ - 🟧.   Venezia p. 5 CZ **h**
18 febbraio-30 novembre – Pas carta 45000/60000 – **94 cam** 🍷 185000/260000

🏨 **Monaco e Grand Canal,** calle Vallaresso 1325 ⊠ 30124 ☏ 700211, Telex 410450, ≤ Canal Grande – 🗏 🕿, 🕮, 🦐 rist   CY **e**
Pas al Rist **Grand Canal** (chiuso martedì) carta 30000/45000 – **80 cam** 🍷 92000/146000.

🏨 **Europa e Regina,** calle larga 22 Marzo 2159 ⊠ 30124 ☏ 700477, Telex 410123, ≤ Canal Grande – 🗏 📺 🕿 ᴕ - 🟧 🕮 🖪 𝓥𝓘𝓢𝓐, 🦐 rist   CY **d**
Pas carta 39000/64000 – 🍷 10000 – **200 cam** 98000/158000.

🏨 **Metropole,** riva degli Schiavoni 4149 ⊠ 30122 ☏ 705044, Telex 410340, ≤ canale di San Marco – 🗏 📺 - 🟧, 🕮 🕦 𝓥𝓘𝓢𝓐, 🦐 rist   Venezia p. 5 DY **t**
Pas al **Grill Zodiaco** (chiuso martedì) carta 24000/35000 – 🍷 7000 – **64 cam** 78000/116000

🏨 **Bauer Grünwald e Grand Hotel,** campo San Moisè 1459 ⊠ 30124 ☏ 707022, Telex 410075, ≤ Canal Grande – 🗏 ᴕ - 🟧 🕮 🖪 𝓥𝓘𝓢𝓐, 🦐 rist   CY **h**
Pas carta 38000/50000 – **210 cam** 🍷 103000/172000 – P 107000/155000, b.s. 82000/110000.

🏨 **Gd H. Luna,** calle larga dell'Ascensione 1243 ⊠ 30124 ☏ 89840, Telex 410236 – 🗏 🕿 - 🟧. 🕮, 🦐 rist   CY **p**
Pas 25000 – **127 cam** 🍷 90000/150000.

🏨 **Etap-Park Hotel,** giardini Papadopoli ⊠ 30125 ☏ 85394, Telex 410310 – 🗏 - 🟧. 🕮 🕦 🖪 𝓥𝓘𝓢𝓐, 🦐 rist   Venezia p. 4 AX **k**
Pas carta 25000/35000 – **100 cam** 🍷 85000/140000 – P 115000/130000, b.s. 85000/100000.

🏨 **Londra Palace e Rist. Do Leoni,** riva degli Schiavoni 4171 ⊠ 30122 ☏ 700533, Telex 431315, ≤ canale di San Marco, « Servizio rist. estivo sulla riva » – 🗏 📺 🕿 ᴕ. 🕮 🕦 🖪 𝓥𝓘𝓢𝓐
Pas carta 25000/38000 – **70 cam** 🍷 87000/150000.   CY **t**

🏨 **Saturnia e International,** calle larga 22 Marzo 2398 ⊠ 30124 ☏ 708377, Telex 410355, « Palazzo patrizio del 14° secolo; servizio rist. estivo all'aperto » – 🗏 - 🟧. 🕮 🕦 🖪 𝓥𝓘𝓢𝓐, 🦐 rist   BY **n**
Pas (chiuso mercoledì) 22000/32000 vedere anche rist La Caravella – 🍷 8000 – **96 cam** 84000/134000.

🏨🏨 **La Fenice et des Artistes** senza rist, campiello de la Fenice 1936 ⌧ 30124 ☎ 32333, Telex 411150 – 🗏 🕭. ⚇ — BY **v**
☋ 4500 – **68 cam** 45000/81000, ▦ 4000.

🏨🏨 **Cavalletto e Doge Orseolo,** calle del Cavalletto 1107 ⌧ 30124 ☎ 700955, Telex 410684, ≼ – ⚇ — CY **f**
Pas 27000 – 81 cam ☋ 64000/95000.

🏨🏨 **Gabrielli Sandwirth,** riva degli Schiavoni 4110 ⌧ 30122 ☎ 31580, Telex 410228, ≼ canale di San Marco, « Cortiletto e piccolo giardino » – ▦. 🆎 ⚇ 🝔 𝗩𝗜𝗦𝗔. ⚇ rist   Venezia p. 5 DY **b**
15 marzo-15 novembre – Pas 35000 – **110 cam** ☋ 94000/158000 – P 144000.

🏨 **Concordia** senza rist, calle larga San Marco 367 ⌧ 30124 ☎ 706866, Telex 411069 – 🛗 ⌂wc ☏. 🆎 𝗩𝗜𝗦𝗔 — CY **k**
☋ 6000 – **60 cam** 54000/78000.

🏨 **Flora** ⚘ senza rist, calla larga 22 Marzo 2283/a ⌧ 30124 ☎ 705844, « Piccolo giardino fiorito » – 🛗 ▦ ⌂wc 🛁wc ☏ ሐ. 🆎 ⚇ 🝔 𝗩𝗜𝗦𝗔 — BY **c**
15 febbraio-10 novembre – ☋ 5500 – **47 cam** 47000/72000, ▦ 5000.

🏨 **Bonvecchiati,** calle Goldoni 4488 ⌧ 30124 ☎ 85017, Telex 410560, « Raccolta di quadri d'arte contemporanea » – 🛗 ▦ ⌂wc 🛁wc ☏. 🆎 🝔. ⚇ rist — CY **w**
Pas 20500 – ☋ 5500 – **90 cam** 49000/79000, ▦ 5000 – P 69000/98000, b.s. 52000/70000.

🏨 **Giorgione,** Santi Apostoli 4587 ⌧ 30121 ☎ 25810 – 🛗 ▦ ⌂wc 🛁wc ☏. 𝗩𝗜𝗦𝗔. ⚇ — CX **u**
chiuso dall'11 novembre al 21 dicembre – Pas 15000 – ☋ 5000 – **56 cam** 53000/75000, ▦ 5000 – P 65000/70000, b.s. 50000/56000.

🏨 **Ala** senza rist, campo Santa Maria del Giglio 2494 ⌧ 30124 ☎ 708333, Telex 410275 – 🛗 ▦ ⌂wc 🛁wc ☏. 🆎 ⚇ 🝔 𝗩𝗜𝗦𝗔 — BY **e**
87 cam ☋ 45000/85000, ▦ 3000.

🏨 **Casanova** senza rist, San Marco-Frezzeria 1284 ⌧ 30124 ☎ 706855 – 🛗 ⌂wc 🛁wc ☏ ሐ. 🆎 — CY **u**
45 cam ☋ 55000/81000.

🏨 **Montecarlo** senza rist, calle dei Specchieri 463 ⌧ 30124 ☎ 28026, Telex 411098 – 🛗 ⌂wc 🛁wc ☏. 🆎 🝔. ⚇ — CY **q**
☋ 5000 – **48 cam** 56000/80000.

🏨 **San Marco,** piazza San Marco 877 ⌧ 30124 ☎ 22447 – 🛗 ⌂wc 🛁wc ☏. ⚇ — CY **r**
Pas *(chiuso martedì)* carta 19000/39000 (12%) – 60 cam ☋ 61000/87000 – P 61000/83000, b.s. 51000/70000.

🏨 **Bisanzio** ⚘ senza rist, calle della Pietà 3651 ⌧ 30122 ☎ 703100 – 🛗 ▦ ⌂wc 🛁wc ☏. 🆎 ⚇ 🝔 𝗩𝗜𝗦𝗔 — DY **d**
chiuso gennaio – ☋ 5000 – **45 cam** 42000/65000, ▦ 3000.   Venezia p. 5

🏨 **Savoia e Jolanda,** riva degli Schiavoni 4187 ⌧ 30122 ☎ 706644, Telex 410620, ≼ canale di San Marco – 🛗 ⌂wc 🛁wc ☏. 🆎. ⚇ rist — CY **x**
Pas *(chiuso martedì)* 22000 – ☋ 6000 – **71 cam** 56000/81000 – P 58000/95000, b.s. 51000/74000.

🏨 **Patria Tre Rose** senza rist, calle dei Fabbri 905 ⌧ 30124 ☎ 22490 – 🛗 ⌂wc 🛁wc ☏. ⚇ — CY **g**
15 marzo-10 novembre – **31 cam** ☋ 55000/79000.

🏨 **Do Pozzi** ⚘, calle larga 22 Marzo 2373 ⌧ 30124 ☎ 707855 – 🛗 ▦ ⌂wc 🛁wc ☏. 🆎 🝔 𝗩𝗜𝗦𝗔 — BY **h**
Pas vedere rist Da Raffaele – **35 cam** ☋ 48000/80000, ▦ 3500.

🏨 **Boston** senza rist, calle dei Fabbri 848 ⌧ 30124 ☎ 87665 – 🛗 ⌂wc 🛁wc ☏. ⚇ — CY **r**
15 marzo-15 novembre – **42 cam** ☋ 45000/70000.

🏠 **Torino** senza rist, calle delle Ostreghe 2356 ⌧ 30124 ☎ 705222 – ▦ 🛁wc ☏. 🆎 ⚇ 𝗩𝗜𝗦𝗔 — BY **z**
20 cam ☋ 42000/77000, ▦ 5000.

🏠 **Nuovo Teson,** calle de la Pescaria 3980 ⌧ 30122 ☎ 705555 – 🛁wc ☏. ⚇ 🝔 𝗩𝗜𝗦𝗔 — DY **s**
Pas *(chiuso lunedì)* carta 14000/22000 – **27 cam** ☋ 30000/53000 – P 51000/53000, b.s. 41000/46000.

🏠 **Scandinavia** senza rist, Santa Maria Formosa 5240 ⌧ 30122 ☎ 23507 – ⌂wc 🛁wc ☏. 𝗩𝗜𝗦𝗔 — CX **s**
chiuso dal 1° al 20 marzo – ☋ 5000 – **29 cam** 21000/47000.

🏠 **Carpaccio** ⚘ senza rist, calle Corner 2765 ⌧ 30125 ☎ 35946, ≼ – ⌂wc 🛁wc ☏ ሐ. 𝗩𝗜𝗦𝗔 — BX **c**
18 marzo-10 novembre – **17 cam** ☋ 52000/77000.   Venezia p. 4

🏠 **Serenissima** senza rist, calle Goldoni 4486 ⌧ 30124 ☎ 700011 – ⌂wc 🛁wc ☏. 🆎 ⚇ — CY **w**
10 marzo-5 novembre – **34 cam** ☋ 30000/50000.

🏠 **Basilea** senza rist, rio Marin 817 ⌧ 30125 ☎ 21853 – ▦ ⌂wc 🛁wc. 🆎   Venezia p. 4 AX **d**
☋ 3500 – **30 cam** 24000/41000, ▦ 3500.

🏠 **Castello** senza rist, Castello-calle Figher 4365 ⌧ 30122 ☎ 30217 – ⌂wc 🛁wc ☏ — CY **b**
chiuso dal 1° al 19 dicembre e dall'11 gennaio al 19 febbraio – **26 cam** ☋ 32000/52000.

🏠 **La Residenza** senza rist, campo Bandiera e Moro 3608 ⌧ 30122 ☎ 85315, « Edificio del 14° secolo » – ▦ ⌂wc 🛁wc ☏. 🆎 𝗩𝗜𝗦𝗔 — DY **n**
chiuso dal 6 al 30 novembre e dal 6 gennaio al 10 febbraio – **14 cam** ☋ 26000/45000, ▦ 2000.

🏠 **Bel Sito** senza rist, campo Santa Maria del Giglio 2517 ⌧ 30124 ☎ 23365 – ⌂wc 🛁wc ☏ — BY **f**
☋ 5000 – **36 cam** 29000/68000.

🏠 **Brooklyn** senza rist, calle dei Fabbri 4712 ⌧ 30124 ☎ 23227 – 🛁wc. ⚇ — CY **y**
☋ 4500 – **12 cam** 19000/44000.

DINTORNI DI VENEZIA CON RISORSE ALBERGHIERE

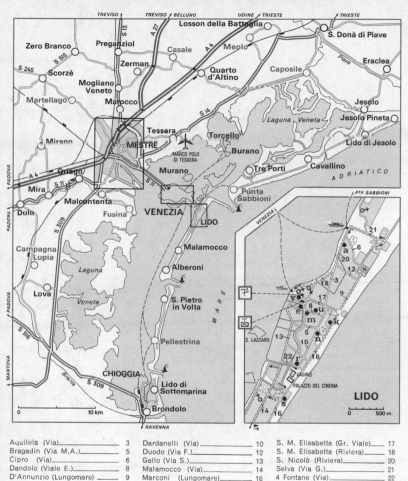

🏠 **Caprera,** lista di Spagna 219 ⊠ 30121 ☏ 715271 – 🛏wc 🛁wc ♿   Venezia p. 4 AX **b**
chiuso novembre e dicembre – Pas *(chiuso mercoledì)* carta 12000/19000 – ☲ 3500 – **22 cam**
15000/44000.

🏠 **Paganelli,** riva degli Schiavoni 4687 ⊠ 30122 ☏ 24324 – 🍽 rist 🛏wc 🛁wc. ⚓   CY **t**
Pas *(chiuso mercoledì e dal 15 novembre al 15 marzo)* carta 16000/27000 (12%) – ☲ 4000 –
23 cam 27000/45000 – P 46000/52000, b.s. 40000/44000.

🏠 **San Fantin** senza rist, campiello de la Fenice 1930/a ⊠ 30124 ☏ 31401 – 🛁wc. ⚓   RY **r**
aprile-5 novembre e 20 dicembre 15 gennaio – **14 cam** ☲ 7000/47000.

🏠 **Astoria** senza rist, calle Fiubera 951 ⊠ 30124 ☏ 25381 – 🛏wc 🛁wc. ⚏ ⓪ E 📼. ⚓   CY **v**
aprile 5 novembre – ☲ 4500 – **30 cam** 19000/44000.

🏠 **Trovatore** senza rist, calle delle Rasse 4535 ⊠ 30122 ☏ 24611 – 🛗 🛏wc 🛁wc. ⚓   CY **c**
15 marzo-novembre e 24 dicembre 6 gennaio – **34 cam** ☲ 32000/56000.

🏠 **La Calcina** senza rist, zattere ai Gesuati 780 ⊠ 30123 ☏ 27045, < canale ed isola della
Guidecca – 🛏wc 🛁wc   Venezia p. 4 BZ **s**
35 cam ☲ 22000/50000.

16

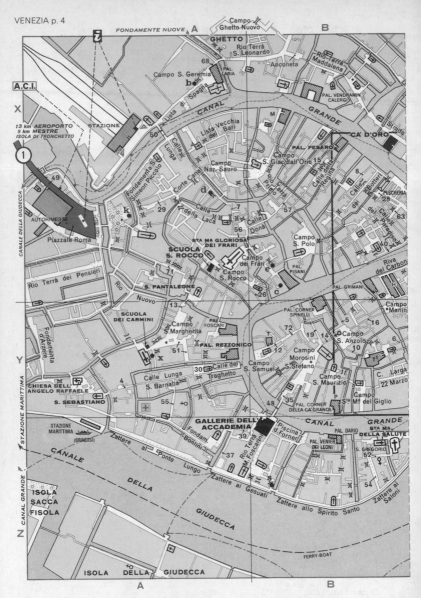

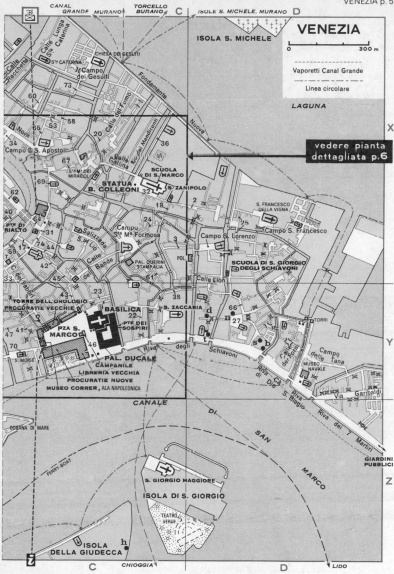

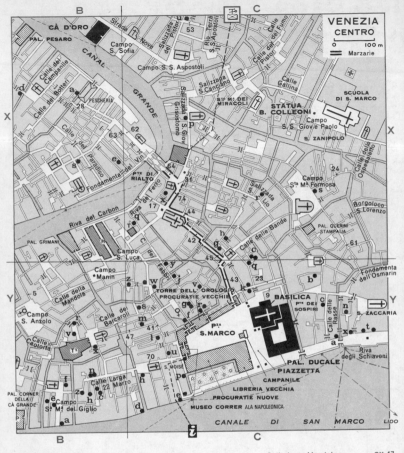

VENEZIA CENTRO
0   100 m
═══ Marzarie

Calle larga S. Marco	CY 23	Piazza S. Marco	CY	Calle larga Mazzini	CX 17
Calle larga 22 Marzo	BY	Ponte di Rialto	CX	Calle lunga S. M. Formosa	CX 24
Campo S. Bartolomeo	CX 31	Ruga degli Orefici	CX 62	Campo delle Beccarie	BX 28
Frezzeria	CY 41	Salizzada S. Moisè	CY 70	Piscina di Frezzeria	CY 47
Marzaria del Capitello	CX 42	Via 2 Aprile	CX 74	Rio Terrà dei Franceschi	CX 53
Marzaria dell'Orologio	CY 43			Ruga Giuffa S. M. Formosa	CX 61
Marzaria S. Salvador	CX 44	Calle degli Avvocati	BY 5	Ruga Vecchia S. Giovanni	BX 63
Marzaria S. Zulian	CX 45	Calle di Canonica	CY 9	Salizzada Pio X	CX 64

XXXX ❀ **Antico Martini,** campo San Fantin 1983 ⊠ 30124 ℡ 24121, Gran classe – 🍴 ᴀᴇ ⓞ 🄴 ᴠɪsᴀ, ⁒
BY x
18 marzo-novembre; chiuso martedì e mercoledì a mezzogiorno – Pas carta 32000/47000 (15%)
Spec. Cannelloni Dogaressa, Filetti di San Pietro alla Betty, Filetto di bue dello chef. **Vini** Malvasia, Cabernet.

XXX ❀❀ **Harry's Bar,** calle Vallaresso 1323 ⊠ 30124 ℡ 36797, Ristorante-american bar ''alla moda'' – 🍴 ᴀᴇ ⓞ 🄴 ᴠɪsᴀ
CY e
chiuso lunedì e dall'11 gennaio al 9 febbraio – Pas carta 36000/55000 (20%)
Spec. Risotto con seppioline (15 luglio-15 ottobre), Taglierini verdi gratinati, Scampi Carlina. **Vini** Pinot, Cabernet.

XXX ❀ **La Caravella,** calle larga 22 Marzo 2397 ⊠ 30124 ℡ 708901, Rist. caratteristico a coperti limitati; prenotare – 🍴 ᴀᴇ ⓞ 🄴 ᴠɪsᴀ, ⁒
BY n
chiuso mercoledì – Pas carta 28000/42000
Spec. Bigoli in salsa, Scampi allo Champagne, Filetto di bue Caravella. **Vini** del Montello.

XXX **Taverna La Fenice,** San Marco 1938 ⊠ 30124 ℡ 23856, Rist.elegante; servizio estivo all'aperto – 🍴 ᴀᴇ 🄴 ᴠɪsᴀ
BY v
chiuso domenica, lunedì a mezzogiorno e gennaio – Pas carta 24000/39000 (15%).

XXX **Al Campiello,** calle dei Fuseri 4346 ⊠ 30124 ℱ 706396, Rist.-american-bar-soupers a coperti
limitati; prenotare – 🗏 🗚 ⓞ 𝓥𝓘𝓢𝓐   CY **z**
chiuso a mezzogiorno, lunedì ed agosto – Pas carta 20000/30000.

XX **Al Graspo de Ua,** calle dei Bombaseri 5094 ⊠ 30124 ℱ 23647, Taverna caratteristica – 🗏
🗚 ⓞ 🗲 𝓥𝓘𝓢𝓐   CX **x**
chiuso lunedì, martedì e dal 14 novembre al 25 dicembre – Pas carta 22000/39000 (12%).

XX **Do Forni,** calle de Specchieri 457/468 ⊠ 30124 ℱ 32148, Rist. rustico moderno – 🗏 🗚 ⓞ
🗲 𝓥𝓘𝓢𝓐   CX **c**
chiuso giovedì e dal 22 novembre al 5 dicembre – Pas carta 25000/35000.

XX **Al Giglio,** campo Santa Maria del Giglio 2477 ⊠ 30124 ℱ 89456 – 🗏 🗚 ⓞ 🗲 𝓥𝓘𝓢𝓐 ⌘
chiuso mercoledì e gennaio – Pas carta 18000/30000 (15%).   BY **e**

XX **La Colomba,** piscina di Frezzeria 1665 ⊠ 30124 ℱ 23817, Trattoria caratteristica, « Raccolta
di quadri d'arte contemporanea » – 🗚 ⓞ 🗲 𝓥𝓘𝓢𝓐   CY **m**
chiuso martedì e novembre – Pas carta 26000/40000 (12%).

XX **Antico Panada** con cam. calle larga San Marco 646/656 ⊡ 00124 ℱ 703000 – 🛏 🛏 rist
🗕wc ⋔wc 🕾, 🗚 ⓞ 𝓥𝓘𝓢𝓐   CY **k**
Pas *(chiuso lunedì)* carta 20000/33000 (12%) – ⌘ 6000 – **5 cam** 54000/78000 – P 60000/75000,
b.s. 49000/55000.

XX **Da Ivo,** calle dei Fuseri 1809 ⊠ 30124 ℱ 705889, Coperti limitati; prenotare – 🗚 🗲 𝓥𝓘𝓢𝓐 ⌘
chiuso domenica e gennaio – Pas carta 20000/29000 (13%).   CY **s**

XX **Antico Pignolo,** calle dei Specchieri 451 ⊠ 30124 ℱ 28123, Rist. rustico moderno; servizio
estivo all'aperto – 🗏 🗚 ⓞ 🗲 𝓥𝓘𝓢𝓐   CX **c**
chiuso martedì e dal 10 al 21 gennaio – Pas carta 21000/29000.

XX ✿ **Noemi** con cam, calle dei Fabbri 909 ⊠ 30124 ℱ 38144 – 🗏 rist 🕾   CY **g**
Pas *(chiuso domenica sera, lunedì e da dicembre a febbraio)* carta 23000/39000 (12%) – **15 cam**
⌘ 23000/41000
Spec. Cannelloni alla Nonno Piero, Seppie in tecia con polenta, Filetti di sogliola Casanova. **Vini** Pinot Bianco,
Cabernet

XX **Al Conte Pescaor,** piscina San Zulian 544 ⊠ 30124 ℱ 21483, Rist.rustico – 🗏   CX **h**

XX **Da Raffaele,** calle larga 22 Marzo 2347 ⊠ 30124 ℱ 32317, Servizio estivo all'aperto – 🗏. 🗚
🗲 𝓥𝓘𝓢𝓐   BY **c**
chiuso giovedì e dal 2 gennaio al 28 febbraio – Pas carta 17000/30000 (12%).

XX **Città di Milano** con cam, campiello San Zulian 590 ⊠ 30124 ℱ 27002 – ⋔wc. 🗚 ⓞ 🗲 𝓥𝓘𝓢𝓐
⌘   CX **g**
Pas *(chiuso lunedì)* carta 18000/29000 (12%) – ⌘ 3500 – **26 cam** 19000/44000.

XX **Malamocco,** campiello del Vin 4650 ⊠ 30122 ℱ 27438   CY **n**
chiuso martedì e dal 7 gennaio al 14 febbraio – Pas carta 15000/25000 (12%).

XX **Shuang Hsi,** campo Santa Margherita 2894 ⊠ 30123 ℱ 38366, Rist.cinese – ⌘
chiuso lunedì e luglio – Pas carta 12000/22000 (10%).   Venezia p. 4 AY **x**

X **Madonna,** calle della Madonna 594 ⊠ 30125 ℱ 23824, Trattoria veneziana – 🗏   BX **e**
chiuso mercoledì, dal 5 al 20 agosto e dal 20 dicembre al 10 febbraio – **Pas** carta 14000/24000
(11%).

X **Da Bruno,** Castello-calle del Paradiso 5731 ⊠ 30122 ℱ 21480, Trattoria d'habitués – 🗏
chiuso martedì e dal 15 al 30 luglio – Pas carta 11000/18000 (10%).   CX **r**

X **Antica Carbonera,** calle Bembo 4648 ⊠ 30124 ℱ 25479, Trattoria veneziana – 🗏   CX **q**
chiuso lunedì sera, martedì e novembre – Pas carta 14000/23000 (12%).

X **Antica Trattoria Poste Vecie,** Pescheria 1608 ⊠ 30125 ℱ 23822, Tipica trattoria veneziana
chiuso martedì e dal 20 novembre al 20 dicembre – Pas carta 16000/27000 (12%).   BX **a**

X **Città di Vittorio,** San Marco-Frezzeria 1591 ⊠ 30124 ℱ 30537, Trattoria d'habitués   CY **l**
chiuso lunedì, novembre e dicembre – Pas carta 12000/22000 (12%).

X Ignazio, calle Saoneri 2749 ⊠ 30125 ℱ 34852, Trattoria veneziana.   Venezia p. 4 BX **e**

X **Al Pozzo,** calle dei Fabbri 1016 ⊠ 30124 ℱ 23649 – 🗏. 🗚 🗲 𝓥𝓘𝓢𝓐   CY **j**
chiuso lunedì, dall'11 novembre al 14 dicembre e dal 10 gennaio al 15 febbraio – Pas
carta 13000/20000 (12%).

X **Fiaschetteria Toscana,** San Giovanni Crisostomo 5719 ⊠ 30121 ℱ 85281, Rist. snack-bar
chiuso martedì, dal 29 giugno al 20 luglio e dal 26 dicembre al 7 gennaio – Pas carta 13000/23000
(12%).   CX **p**

X **Alla Letizia,** ruga Rialto 692 ⊠ 30125 ℱ 29526, Trattoria veneziana – 🗏   BX **s**
chiuso lunedì e luglio – Pas carta 13000/24000 (13%).

X **Nono Risorto,** sottoportego Siora Bettina 2337 ⊠ 30125 ℱ 27630, Trattoria con pergolato
chiuso martedì e dal 15 novembre al 15 febbraio – Pas carta 13000/18000 (12%).   BX **d**

al Lido 15 mn di vaporetto da San Marco CY – ⊠ **30126** (pianta : Dintorni p. 3) :

🏨🏨🏨🏨 **Excelsior,** lungomare Marconi 41 ℱ 760201, Telex 410023, ≼, ⊥ riscaldata, 🏖, ⌘, 🗐 – 🗏
📺 🕾 ➋, 🗚 ⓞ 🗲 𝓥𝓘𝓢𝓐 ⌘ rist   **s**
aprile-ottobre – Pas carta 46000/62000 – ⌘ 11000 – **236 cam** 191000/266000.

🏨🏨🏨 **Des Bains,** lungomare Marconi 17 ℱ 765921, Telex 410142, ≼, « Parco fiorito con ⌘ e ⊥
riscaldata », 🏖, 🗐 – 🗏 🕾 ♿ ➋ – 🔬 🗚 ⓞ 🗲 𝓥𝓘𝓢𝓐 ⌘ rist   **k**
aprile-ottobre – Pas carta 40000/55000 – ⌘ 10000 – **255 cam** 109000/174000.

🏛 **Quattro Fontane** ⚓, via 4 Fontane 16 ☎ 760227, ⚔, ✵ – ⊕   r
23 aprile-settembre – Pas 28000/34000 – ⌧ 7500 – **70 cam** 54000/88000 – P 83000/98000.

🏛 **Villa Mabàpa**, riviera San Nicolò 16 ☎ 760590, « Rist. estivo in giardino », ⚔ – 🛗 🖹 🚻wc
🚻wc ☎ ઙ. 🖭 ⓪ 𝚅𝙸𝚂𝙰. ✵ rist   a
Pas *(chiuso martedì)* carta 16000/25000 – ⌧ 5000 – **64 cam** 49000/80000, 🛏 3000 – P
50000/60000.

🏛 **Villa Otello** senza rist, via Lepanto 12 ☎ 760048 – 🛗 🚻wc 🚻wc ☎ ⊕. 🄴 𝚅𝙸𝚂𝙰   m
10 aprile-7 ottobre – **34 cam** ⌧ 48000/82000.

🏛 **Helvetia** senza rist, Gran Viale S. M. Elisabetta 4 ☎ 760105, ⚔ – 🛗 🚻wc 🚻wc ☎ ⊕. ✵ v
aprile-ottobre – ⌧ 5000 – **54 cam** 50000/80000.

🏛 **Adria, Urania, Villa Nora-Biasutti**, viale Dandolo 29 ☎ 760120, Telex 410666, ⚔ – 🛗
🚻wc 🚻wc ☎ ઙ. ⊕. 🖭 ⓪ 🄴 𝚅𝙸𝚂𝙰. ✵ rist   u
aprile-15 ottobre – Pas 10000/20000 – **73 cam** ⌧ 55000/90000.

🏛 **Rigel**, viale Dandolo 13 ☎ 760158 – 🛗 🚻wc 🚻wc ☎   e
stagionale – 44 cam.

🏛 **Byron Central Hotel**, via Bragadin 30 ☎ 760052, ⚔ – 🛗 🚻wc 🚻wc ☎   n
stagionale – 36 cam.

🏛 **Vianello**, località Alberoni ✉ 30011 ☎ 731072, ⚔ – 🚻wc 🚻wc. 𝚅𝙸𝚂𝙰. ✵ rist
aprile-settembre – Pas *(chiuso sino al 30 maggio e dal 10 al 30 settembre)* 13000/15000 – ⌧
3500 – **20 cam** 26000/42000 – P 34000/40000.

✕✕ **Al Porticciolo-da Danilo**, verso Malamocco ☎ 768384, « Servizio estivo in giardino » – 🖹 ⊕
stagionale.

✕ **Da Ciccio**, verso Malamocco ☎ 765489, Servizio estivo all'aperto
chiuso martedì e dal 15 al 30 novembre – Pas carta 15000/25000 (12%).

a Murano 10 mn di vaporetto dalle fondamenta Nuove CX – ✉ **30121** (pianta : Dintorni
p. 3) :

✕ **Ai Frati**, ☎ 736694, Trattoria marinara – ✵
chiuso giovedì e febbraio – Pas carta 18000/25000 (12%).

a Burano 45 mn di vaporetto dalle fondamenta Nuove CX – ✉ **30012** (pianta : Dintorni p. 3) :

✕ ✿ **Tre Stelle-da Romano**, ☎ 730030, Trattoria tipica della laguna, « Raccolta di quadri »
chiuso martedì, dal 23 novembre al 2 gennaio e dal 1° al 15 marzo – Pas carta 18000/25000
(12%).
Spec. Gran risotto alla Romano (di pesce), Anguilla in umido (su ordinazione), Pesce fritto o alla griglia. **Vini** Pinot
Grigio, Tocai.

✕ **Ai Pescatori**, ☎ 730650, Trattoria marinara – ⓪. ✵
chiuso lunedì, dal 28 luglio al 7 agosto e dal 25 dicembre al 4 febbraio – Pas carta 17000/25000
(10%).

✕ **Al Gatto Nero**, ☎ 730120, Trattoria tipica – 🖭
chiuso lunedì, dal 25 al 31 ottobre e dal 1° al 19 gennaio – Pas carta 15000/25000.

a Torcello 50 mn di vaporetto dalle fondamenta Nuove CX – ✉ **30012** Burano (pianta :
Dintorni p. 3) :

✕✕ ✿ **Locanda Cipriani** ⚓ con cam, ☎ 730150, Rist. caratteristico, « In un angolo fiorito » –
🖹 cam 🚻wc. 🖭. ✵ cam
20 marzo-1° novembre – Pas *(chiuso martedì)* carta 40000/52000 (15%) – 6 cam (solo pens) –
P 150000/190000
Spec. Tagliolini gratinati, Risotto di pesce, Zuppa di pesce. **Vini** Scave, Cabernet.

a Pellestrina - San Pietro in Volta 1 h e 10 mn di vaporetto ed autobus da riva degli
Schiavoni CY – ✉ **30010** (pianta : Dintorni p. 3) :

✕ **Da Nane**, ☎ 967100, Trattoria marinara con ⪭ – ✵
chiuso lunedì, gennaio e febbraio – Pas carta 17000/25000.

Portugal

Lisboa

LISBOA

LISBOA 1100 ℗ **37** ⑫ e ⑰ – 859 200 h. alt. 111.

Ver : Vista sob a cidade : ★★ da Ponte 25 de Abril (p. 2) BV , ★★ do Cristo-Rei por ②.

CENTRO

Ver : Rossio★ (Praça) p. 5 GY – Avenida da Liberdade★ p. 4 FX – Parque Eduardo VII★ (Estufa fria) p.4 EX – Igreja Sâo Roque★ (p.4) FY **M1** – Terreiro do Paço (Praça) p. 5 GZ.

CIDADE MEDIEVAL

Ver : Castelo de São Jorge★★ (p. 5) GY – Sé★ (p. 5) GZ – Miradauro de Santa Luzia★ (p. 7) JY – Alfama★★ (p. 7) JYZ.

CIDADE MANUELINA

Ver : Mosteiro dos Jerónimos★★ (igreja, claustro) p. 2 AV – Torre de Belém★★ (p. 2) AV – Padrão dos Descobrimentos★ (p. 2) AV F.

MUSEUS

Ver : Nacional de Arte Antiga★★ (poliptico de Nuno Gonçalves★★★) p. 2 BV **M6** – Calouste Gulbenkian★★★ (colecoês de arte) p. 3 CU **M7** – do Azulejo★ e Igreja de Madre de Deus★★ (p. 3) DU **N** – Nacional dos Coches★★ (p.2) AV **M12** – de Marinha★★ (p. 2) AV **M4**

⟦⟧, ⟦⟧ Club de golf do Estoril 25 km por ③ ☏ 268 01 76 Estoril – ⟦⟧ Lisbon Sports Club 20 km por ⑤ ☏ 96 00 77 – ⟦⟧ Club de Campo de Lisboa 15 km por ② ☏ 24 57 17 Aroeira – Fonte da Telha.

↗ de Lisboa, 8 km do Centro (CDU) – T.A.P., Praça Marquês de Pombal 3, ⊠ 1200, ☏ 53 88 52 e 57 50 20, Av. Guerra Junqueiro 15-C, ⊠ 1000 ☏ 89 60 73 e no aeroporto ☏ 89 91 21.

🚗 ☏ 86 46 75

⚓ para a Madeira : C.T.M., Rua de São Julião 63 ☏ 36 96 21, Telex 12440, Av. 24 de Julho 132 ☏ 60 71 81 e Roche Conde de Óbidos ☏ 60 22 21 – E.N.M., Rua de São Julião 5, ⊠ 1100, ☏ 87 01 21 e Rocha Conde de Óbidos, ⊠ 1300, ☏ 66 25 47, Telex 13669.

🛈 Palácio Foz, Praça dos Restauradores ☏ 36 36 24, jardim do Regedor ☏ 36 35 21 e no aeroporto ☏ 89 42 48 – **A.C.P.** Rua Rosa Araújo 24, ⊠ 1200, ☏ 56 39 31, Telex 12581 e Av. Barbosa do Bocage 23, ⊠ 1000, ☏ 77 54 00, Telex 14270.

◆ Madrid 646 ① – ◆ Bilbao 897 ① – Paris 1814 ① – ◆ Porto 315 ① – ◆ Sevilla 411 ②.

LISBOA

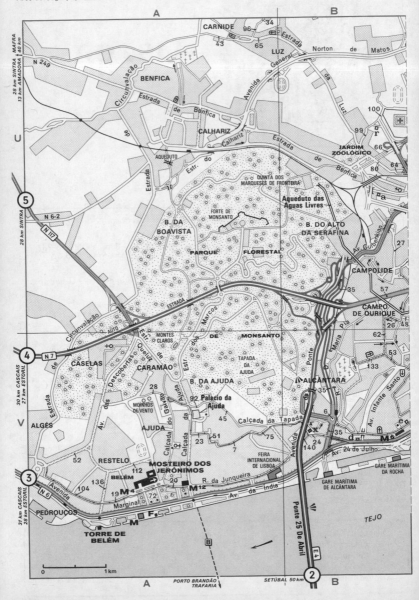

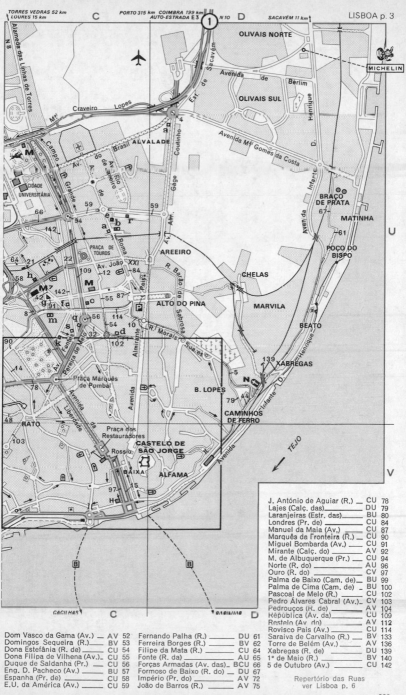

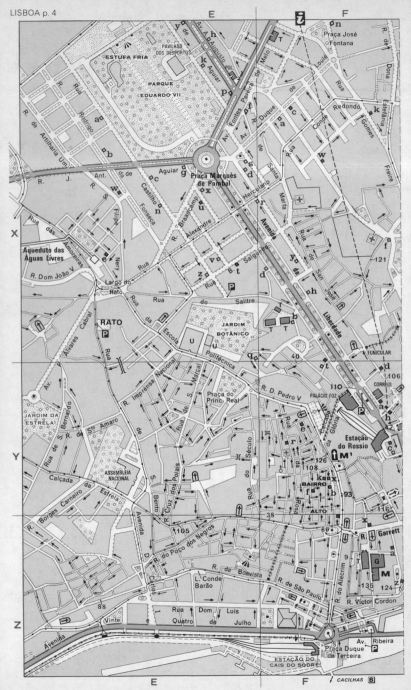

LISBOA

REPERTÓRIO DAS

ALFAMA

0   50 m

🏨🏨🏨 **Ritz Inter-Continental,** Rua Rodrigo da Fonseca 88, ⊠ 1000, ℡ 68 41 31, Telex 12589, ≤ –
■ ⇔ ❷ – 🏖. 🎩 ⓪ *VISA*. ⅍ rest EX **b**
Ref 950 – **306 qto** 🗲 5 300/6 300.

🏨🏨🏨 **Sheraton** Ⓜ, Rua Latino Coelho 1, ⊠ 1000, ℡ 57 57 57, Telex 12774, ≤, ⊿ climatizada – ■
⇔ – 🏖. 🎩 Ⅱ E *VISA*. ⅍ rest CU **s**
Ref lista 550 a 980 – **387 qto** 🗲 4 400/5 500.

🏨🏨🏨 **Altis** Ⓜ, Rua Castilho 11, ⊠ 1200, ℡ 56 00 71, Telex 13314 – ■ ⇔ – 🏖. 🎩 ⓪ E *VISA*. ⅍
Ref 850 – **225 qto** 🗲 4 100/5 100. EX **z**

🏨🏨🏨 **Tivoli e Tivoli Jardim,** Av. da Liberdade 185, ⊠ 1200, ℡ 53 01 81, Telex 12588 – ■ ❷ –
🏖. 🎩 ⓪ E *VISA*. ⅍ FX **d**
Ref 700 – **469 qto** 🗲 3 000/3 500.

🏨🏨🏨 **Lutécia,** Av. Frei Miguel Contreiras 52, ⊠ 1700, ℡ 80 31 21, Telex 12457, ≤ – ■ – 🏖. E
VISA. ⅍ CU **b**
Ref 900 – **151 qto** 🗲 2 800/3 500 – P 3 700/5 300.

🏨🏨 **Alfa Lisboa Husa,** Av. Columbano Bordalo Pinherio ℡ 73 21 21, Telex 18477, ≤ – ■ ❷. 🎩
⓪ E *VISA*. ⅍ rest BU **a**
Ref lista 650 a 1 700 – **270 qto** 🗲 4 200/6 000.

🏨🏨 **Diplomático,** Rua Castilho 74, ⊠ 1200, ℡ 56 20 41, Telex 13712 – ■ ❷ – 🏖. 🎩 ⓪ E *VISA*.
⅍ rest EX **c**
Ref 800 – **90 qto** 🗲 3 000 – P 4 200/6 700.

🏨🏨 **Flórida** sem rest, Rua Duque de Palmela 32, ⊠ 1200, ℡ 57 61 45, Telex 12256 – ■ – 🏖. 🎩
⓪ E *VISA*. ⅍ EX **x**
120 qto 🗲 2 300/2 800.

🏨🏨 **Mundial,** Rua D. Duarte 4, ⊠ 1100, ℡ 86 31 01, Telex 12308, ≤ – ■ ❷ – 🏖. 🎩 ⓪ E *VISA*.
⅍ rest GY **c**
146 qto.

🏨🏨 **Fénix e Rest. El Bodegón,** Praça Marquês de Pombal 8, ⊠ 1200, ℡ 53 51 21, Telex 12170
– ■. 🎩 ⓪ E *VISA*. ⅍ EX **g**
Ref 650 – **125 qto** 🗲 1 900/2 600 – P 3 100/3 200.

🏨🏨 **Lisboa Penta,** Av. dos Combatentes, ⊠ 1600, ℡ 74 01 41, Telex 18437, ⊿, ⇌ – ■ ⇔
❷ – 🏖. 🎩 ⓪ E *VISA*. ⅍ rest BU **r**
Ref 825 – **592 qto** 🗲 2 840/3 835 – P 4 295/6 875.

🏨🏨 **Roma,** Av. de Roma 33, ⊠ 1700, ℡ 76 77 61, Telex 16586, ≤, 🗔 – ■ – 🏖. ⅍ CU **a**
Ref 500 – **263 qto** 🗲 1 790/2 200 – P 2 100/2 790.

🏨🏨 **Dom Carlos** sem rest, Av. Duque de Loulé 121, ⊠ 1000, ℡ 53 90 71, Telex 16468 – ■. 🎩
VISA EX **s**
73 qto 🗲 1 650/2 200.

🏨🏨 **Lisboa Plaza,** Travessa do Salitre 7, ⊠ 1200, ℡ 36 39 22, Telex 16402 – ■ ❷. 🎩 ⓪ E *VISA*
⅍ FX **b**
Ref 800/1 000 – **93 qto** 🗲 2 700/3 300 – P 3 150/4 200.

🏨🏨 **Embaixador,** Av. Duque de Loulé 73, ⊠ 1000, ℡ 53 01 71, Telex 13773, ≤ – ■ 🎩 ⓪ E *VISA*.
⅍ rest FX **a**
Ref 690 – **96 qto** 🗲 2 200/2 900 – P 3 580/5 660.

🏨🏨 **Miraparque,** Av. Sidónio Pais 12, ⊠ 1000, ℡ 57 80 70, Telex 16745 – 🛗 🍴 ■ rest 🛁wc
🍴wc 🕾. ⅍ rest EX **k**
Ref 480 – **100 qto** 🗲 1 550/1 955 – P 2 510/3 875.

🏨🏨 Rex, Rua Castilho 169, ⊠ 1000, ℡ 68 21 61, ≤ – 🛗 🍴 ■ 🛁wc 🕾 EX **a**
70 qto.

🏨🏨 **Britânia** sem rest, Rua Rodrigues Sampiao 17, ⊠ 1100, ℡ 57 50 16, Telex 13733 – 🛗 🍴 ■
🛁wc 🕾. 🎩 ⓪ E *VISA*. ⅍ FX **y**
30 qto 🗲 1 840/2 300.

🏨🏨 **Principe Real** sem rest, Rua da Alegria 53, ⊠ 1200, ℡ 36 01 16, « Bela decoração » – 🛗 🍴
🛁wc 🕾. 🎩 ⓪ E EX **q**
24 qto 🗲 3 500.

🏨🏨 **Eduardo VII,** Av. Fontes Pereira de Melo 5, ⊠ 1000, ℡ 53 01 41, Telex 18340, ≤ – 🛗 🍴
■ rest 🛁wc 🍴wc 🕾. 🎩 ⓪ E *VISA*. ⅍ EX **p**
Ref 680 – **104 qto** 🗲 1 600/2 100 – P 2 210/2 760.

🏨🏨 **York House,** Rua das Janelas Verdes 32, ⊠ 1200, ℡ 66 24 35, « Instalado num convento do
século XVI decorado num estilo português » – 🍴 🛁wc 🍴wc 🕾. 🎩 ⓪ E *VISA*. ⅍ rest
Ref 420 – **63 qto** 🗲 1 600/2 800 – P 2 200/4 000. BV **e**

🏨🏨 **Vip** sem rest, Rua Fernão Lopes 25, ⊠ 1000, ℡ 57 03 59 – 🛗 🍴 🛁wc 🕾. 🎩 ⓪ E *VISA*. ⅍
54 qto 🗲 1 450/1 850. FX **n**

🏨🏨 Do Reno sem rest, Av. Duque d'Avila 195, ⊠ 1000, ℡ 54 81 81 – 🛗 🍴 🛁wc 🍴wc 🕾 ❷
54 qto. CU **m**

🏨🏨 **Príncipe,** Av. Duque d'Avila 201, ⊠ 1000, ℡ 53 61 51 – 🛗 🍴 ■ rest 🛁wc 🍴wc 🕾 ❷. 🎩
⓪ E *VISA*. ⅍ rest CU **m**
Ref 500 – **60 qto** 🗲 1 450/2 200 – P 2 100/2 450.

🏨 **Excelsior,** Rua Rodrigues Sampaio 172, ☒ 1100, ☏ 53 71 51, Telex 14223 – |≴| 🏛 ▤ rest
⇱wc 🛏wc 🕿. ⓪ 𝘝𝘐𝘚𝘈. ✄   EX **d**
Ref 550 – **80 qto** ⊑ 1 900/2 100 – P 2 150/3 000.

🏨 Presidente sem rest, Rua Alexandre Herculano 13, ☒ 1100, ☏ 53 95 01 – |≴| 🏛 ▤ ⇱wc 🕿
59 qto.   FX **r**

🏨 **Capitol,** Rua Eça de Queiroz 24, ☒ 1000, ☏ 53 68 11, Telex 13701 – |≴| 🏛 ▤ rest ⇱wc 🕿.
🜂 ⓪ 𝘝𝘐𝘚𝘈. ✄   EX **f**
Ref 600/750 – **58 qto** ⊑ 1 500/1 900 – P 1 450/2 000.

🏨 **Jorge V** sem rest, Rua Mouzinho da Silveira 3, ☒ 1200, ☏ 56 25 25 – |≴| 🏛 ⇱wc 🕿. 🜂 ⓪
E 𝘝𝘐𝘚𝘈   EX **v**
49 qto ⊑ 1 850/2 300.

🏨 **Flamingo,** Rua Castilho 41, ☒ 1200, ☏ 53 21 91, Telex 14736 – |≴| 🏛 ⇱wc 🛏wc 🕿. 🜂 ⓪ E
𝘝𝘐𝘚𝘈. ✄   EX **n**
Ref 690/1 050 – **39 qto** ⊑ 1 725/2 300 – P 3 105/5 060.

🏨 **Infante Santo** sem rest, Rua Tenente Valadim 14, ☒ 1300, ☏ 60 01 44, ← – |≴| 🏛 ▤ – ⇱wc
🕿. 🜂 ⓪ E 𝘝𝘐𝘚𝘈. ✄   BV **d**
27 qto ⊑ 1 550.

🏨 **Albergaria Términus** sem rest, Av. Almirante Gago Coutinho 153, ☒ 1700, ☏ 89 11 06, ⅀,
🞕 – 🏛 ⇱wc 🛏wc 🕿 ℗. ⓪ E 𝘝𝘐𝘚𝘈. ✄   DU **a**
23 qto ⊑ 1 050/1 500.

🏠 Nazareth 4° andar, sem rest, Av. António Augusto de Aguiar 25, ☒ 1000, ☏ 57 20 16 – |≴| 🏛
⇱wc 🕿   EX **y**
32 qto.

🏠 **São Pedro** sem rest, Rua Pascoal de Melo 130, ☒ 1000, ☏ 57 87 65 – |≴| 🏛 ⇱wc 🛏wc 🕿
𝘝𝘐𝘚𝘈. ✄   CU **d**
50 qto ⊑ 1 290.

🏠 Insulana 2° andar, sem rest, Rua da Assunção 52, ☒ 1100, ☏ 32 76 25 – |≴| 🏛 ⇱wc 🛏wc 🕿
32 qto   GY **e**

🏠 **Imperador** sem rest, Av. 5 de Outubro 55, ☒ 1000, ☏ 57 48 84 – |≴| 🏛 ⇱wc 🛏wc 🕿. ✄
43 qto ⊑ 1 790.   CU **f**

🏠 **Roma** 1° andar, sem rest, Travessa da Glória 22-A, ☒ 1200, ☏ 36 05 57 – 🏛 ⇱wc 🛏wc 🕿.
🜂. ✄   FY **t**
24 qto ⊑ 1150/1720.

🏠 **Americano** sem rest, Rua 1° de Dezembro 73, ☒ 1200, ☏ 32 09 75 – |≴| 🏛 ⇱wc 🛏wc 🕿
49 qto ⊑ 460/1 400.   FY **c**

🏠 **Lis** sem rest, Av de Liberdade 180, ☒ 1200, ☏ 56 34 34 – |≴| 🏛 ⇱wc 🛏 🕿. ✄   FX **h**
62 qto ⊑ 1 580/1 680.

🏠 **Albergaria Pax** sem rest, Rua José Estévão 20, ☒ 1100, ☏ 56 18 61 – |≴| 🏛 ⇱wc 🕿. 🜂 ⓪
𝘝𝘐𝘚𝘈. ✄   GX **q**
30 qto ⊑ 1 300/2 000.

🏠 Horizonte sem rest, Av. António Augusto de Aguiar 42, ☒ 1000, ☏ 53 94 26 – |≴| 🏛 ⇱ 🛏wc
🕿   EX **h**
52 qto.

🏠 Lisbonense 3° andar, sem rest, Rua Pinheiro Chagas 1, ☒ 1000, ☏ 54 46 28 – |≴| 🏛 ⇱wc 🛏
🕿   CU **q**
30 qto.

XXXX Aviz, Rua Serpa Pinto 12-B, ☒ 1200, ☏ 32 83 91 – ▤   FZ **x**

XXXX ✿ **Tágide,** Largo da Biblioteca Pública 18, ☒ 1200, ☏ 32 07 20, ← – ▤. 🜂 ⓪ E 𝘝𝘐𝘚𝘈. ✄
fechado Sábado meio dia e Domingo – Ref lista 1 040 a 2 120   FZ **z**
Espec. Pate de salmão a Tagide, Crepes de bacalhão a Tagide, Pecinhos de porco com molho de coentros.

XXXX **Clara,** Campo dos Martires da Patria 49 ☏ 55 73 41 – ▤. 🜂 ⓪ E 𝘝𝘐𝘚𝘈   FX **f**
Ref lista 1 030 a 1 630.

XXXX **Tavares,** Rua da Misericárdia 37, ☒ 1200, ☏ 32 11 12, Estilo fim do século XIX – ▤. 🜂 E
𝘝𝘐𝘚𝘈. ✄   FZ **t**
fechado Sábado – Ref lista 1 820 a 2 350.

XXX **Gambrinus,** Rua das Portas de Santo Antão 25, ☒ 1 100, ☏ 32 14 66 – ▤. 🜂 ⓪ E 𝘝𝘐𝘚𝘈. ✄
Ref lista 1 540 a 2 370.   GY **n**

XXX **Escorial,** Rua das Portas de Santo Antão 47, ☒ 1100, ☏ 36 44 29, Decoração moderna – ▤.
🜂 ⓪ E 𝘝𝘐𝘚𝘈   GY **n**
Ref lista 1 340 a 1 930.

XXX **Pabe,** Rua Duque de Palmela 27-A, ☒ 1200, ☏ 53 56 75, Pub inglês – ▤. 🜂 ⓪ E 𝘝𝘐𝘚𝘈. ✄
Ref lista 1 130 a 1 590.   EX **u**

XXX **Casa da Comida,** Travessa das Amoreiras 1, ☒ 1200, ☏ 65 93 86 – 🜂 ⓪ E 𝘝𝘐𝘚𝘈   EX **e**
fechado Domingo –

XXX **Chester,** Rua Rodrigo de Fonseca 87-D, ☒ 1000, ☏ 68 78 11, Carnes – ▤. 🜂 ⓪ E 𝘝𝘐𝘚𝘈. ✄
fechado Domingo – Ref lista 795 a 1 765.   EX **w**

XX ✿ **Michel,** Largo de Santa Cruz do Castelo 5, ⊠ 1100, ☎ 86 43 38, Rest. francês – 🄰🄴 ⓪ 🄴 *VISA*   GY **b**
   fechado Domingo e feriados – Ref lista 1 040 a 1 800
   Espec. Marmite aux trois délices de l'Atlantique, Bar à la vapeur d'algues Conde de Agueda, Carré d'agneau aux champignons sylvestres.

XX **Sancho,** Travessa da Glória 14, ⊠ 1200, ☎ 36 97 80 – 🍽. *VISA*. ✄   FX **t**
   fechado Domingo e feriados – Ref lista 420 a 755.

XX **O Policia,** Rua Marquês Sá da Bandeira 112, ⊠ 1000, ☎ 76 35 05 – 🍽. ✄   CU **g**
   fechado Sábado noite e Domingo – Ref lista 600 a 1 690.

XX **Solmar,** Rua das Portas de Santo Antáo 108-A, ⊠ 1100, ☎ 36 00 10, Mariscos – 🄰🄴 ⓪ 🄴 *VISA*. ✄   FY **d**
   Ref lista 840 a 1 250.

X **António,** Rua Tomàs Ribeiro 63, ⊠ 1000, ☎ 53 87 80 – 🍽. 🄰🄴 ⓪ 🄴 *VISA*. ✄   CU **k**
   Ref lista 740 a 1 060.

X **Macau,** Rua Barata Salgueiro 37-A, ⊠ 1200, ☎ 55 88 88, Rest. chinês – 🍽. 🄰🄴 ⓪ 🄴 *VISA*. ✄   EX **t**
   fechado Domingo, 2a feira meio dia e feriados.

X **Dragão de Ouro,** 1° andar, Av. Frei Miguel Contreiras 54-B, ⊠ 1700, ☎ 89 45 03, Rest. chinês – 🍽   CU **b**

X **Ibéria,** Rua Ivens 28, ⊠ 1200, ☎ 32 82 18 – 🍽   FZ **a**

X **Celta,** Rua Gomes Freire 148-C e D, ⊠ 1100, ☎ 57 30 69 – 🍽. 🄰🄴 ⓪ *VISA*   FX **k**

X **Quim Vuá** (Mandarim), Rua Luciano Cordeiro 34-A, ⊠ 1100, ☎ 57 68 91, Rest. chinês – 🍽. ✄   FX **w**
   Ref lista 300 a 600.

X **Arraial,** Rua Conde Sabugosa 13-A, ⊠ 1700, ☎ 89 73 43, Decoração rústica – 🍽. ✄   CU **e**

X **Adegada do Teixeira,** Rua do Teixeira 39, ⊠ 1200, ☎ 32 83 20 – 🍽   FY **e**

X **Galão,** com snack-bar, Rua 1° de Maio 2, ⊠ 1300, ☎ 64 06 13 – 🍽   BV **x**

X **Mordomo,** com snack-bar, Rua Dr Gama Barros 27-A, ⊠ 1700, ☎ 80 04 76 – 🍽   CU **r**

X **Arameiro,** Travessa de Santo Antão 21, ⊠ 1100, ☎ 36 71 85 – 🍽. ✄   FY **a**
   Ref lista 480 a 890.

X **Leâo de Ouro,** Rua 1° de Dezembro 89-107, ⊠ 1200, ☎ 32 61 95 – 🍽   FY **c**

X **A Lota,** 1° andar, Rua Jardim do Regedor 15, ⊠ 1100, ☎ 32 33 55 – 🍽   FY **h**

X **Paris,** Rua dos Sapateiros 126, ⊠ 1100, ☎ 36 97 97 – 🍽. 🄰🄴 ⓪ 🄴 *VISA*. ✄   GZ **a**
   Ref lista 520 a 970.

X **Cortador "Oh Lacerda",** Av. de Berna 36-A ☎ 77 40 57, Decoração rústica   CU **h**

   Restaurantes tipicos.

XX **O Faia,** Rua da Barroca 56, ⊠ 1200, ☎ 32 67 42, Fados – 🍽. 🄰🄴 ⓪ 🄴 *VISA*. ✄   FY **f**
   Ref lista 1 100 a 1 550.

XX **A Severa,** Rua das Gáveas 51, ⊠ 1200, ☎ 36 40 06, Fados – 🍽. 🄰🄴 ⓪. ✄   FY **b**
   fechado 5a feira – Ref lista 1 300 a 1 750.

XX **Lisboa à Noite,** Rua das Gáveas 69, ⊠ 1200, ☎ 36 85 57, Fados – 🍽   FY **x**
   Ref (só jantar).

X **Adega Machado,** Rua do Norte 91, ⊠ 1200, ☎ 36 00 95, Fados – 🍽. 🄰🄴 ⓪ 🄴 *VISA*   FY **k**
   fechado 2a feira.

X **O Farcado,** Rua da Rosa 221, ⊠ 1200, ☎ 36 85 79, Fados – 🍽   FY **r**
   Ref (só jantar).

X **Parreirinha de Alfama,** Beco do Espirito Santo 1, ⊠ 1100, ☎ 86 82 09, Fados   JZ **b**
   Ref (só jantar).

   Snack-Bares.

X **Galeto,** Av. da República 14, ⊠ 1000, ☎ 54 44 44 – 🍽. ✄   CU **c**
   fechado 1 Maio – Ref lista 460 a 920.

X **Noite e Dia,** Av. Duque de Loulé 51-A e B, ⊠ 1000, ☎ 57 35 14 – 🍽   FX **c**

Suisse
Schweiz

Genève

Zürich

GENÈVE

GENÈVE Suisse ⁷⁴ ⑥. ²³ ⑪ G. Suisse – 169 960 h. alt. 375 – Casino – ⊙ Genève et les environs : de France 19-41-22 ; de Suisse 022.

Voir Bords du Lac ≤*** – Parcs** : Mon Repos FX , la Perle du Lac BU B et Villa Barton BU D – Jardin botanique* : jardin alpin** BU E – Cathédrale* : ✴* ** FY – Monument de la Réformation* FYZ – Palais des Nations* BU F – Parc de la Grange* GY – Parc des Eaux-Vives* CV – Vaisseau* de l'église du Christ-Roi BV N – Musées : Art et Histoire*** FZ M1, Ariana** BU M2, Histoire naturelle** GZ M3, Petit Palais* FZ M4, – Collections Baur* (dans Hôtel particulier) FZ M5 , Instruments de musique* FZ M6.

Excurs. en bateau sur le lac. Rens. Cie Gén. de Nav., Jardin Anglais ↱ 21.25.21 – Mouettes genevoises, 8 quai du Mt-Blanc ↱ 32.29.44 – Swiss Boat, 4 quai du Mont-Blanc ↱ 32.47.47.

ᵷ à Cologny ↱ 35.75.40 - CU.

✈ de Genève-Cointrin : Air France ↱ 31.33.30 AU.

🛈 Office de Tourisme, 1 Tour de l'Ile (fermé dim. sauf sais.) ↱ 28.72.33, Télex 22795 et gare Cornavin (juin-sept.) ↱ 32.53.40 - A.C. Suisse, 10 bd Théâtre ↱ 28.07.66 - T.C. Suisse, 9 r. P.-Fatio ↱ 36.60.00.

Paris 548 ⑦ – Bern 166 ② – Bourg-en-Bresse 120 ⑦ – Lausanne 63 ② – ♦Lyon 190 ⑥ – Torino 253 ⑥.

Plans : Genève p. 2 à 5.

Les prix sont donnés en francs suisses

1ᵉʳ - *Rive droite (Gare Cornavin - Les Quais - B.I.T.)* – ⊠ 1201.

🏨🏨 **Richemond,** jardin Brunswick, ⊠ 1211, ↱ 31.14.00, Télex 22598, ≤ – ╡ ▤ rest ⊤ⱽ ☎ – 🏛 40. 🖭 ⑩ E 🆅🆂🅰 ⛗ rest FY **u**
SC : **rest Le Jardin R** carte 50 à 65 ⅃ et voir rest Le Gentilhomme – **110 ch** ⊇ 104/275, 21 appartements.

🏨🏨 **Rhône** Ⓜ, quai Turrettini, ⊠ 1211, ↱ 31.98.31, Télex 22213, ≤ – ╡ ⊤ⱽ ☎ ♿ ⊙ – 🏛 25 à 150. 🖭 E 🆅🆂🅰 EY **r**
SC : **R** voir Rôtisserie Le Neptune – **290 ch** ⊇ 115/310, 21 appartements 290/550.

🏨🏨 **Noga Hilton** Ⓜ, 19 quai Mt-Blanc ⊠ 1211, ↱ 31.98.11, Télex 289704, ≤ lac et Mt-Blanc, ⛴ ╡ cuisinette ▤ ch ⊤ⱽ ☎ – 🏛 1300. 🖭 ⑩ E 🆅🆂🅰 ⛗ rest FY **y**
SC : rest. **Le Cygne R** 40/100 - **La Grignotière R** carte environ 40 ⅃ - **Le Bistroquai R** carte environ 20 ⅃ – ⊇ 15 – **260 ch** 148/295.

🏨🏨 **Président** Ⓜ, 47 quai Wilson, ⊠ 1211, ↱ 31.10.00, Télex 22780, ≤ lac – ╡ ▤ ⊤ⱽ ☎ ♿ ⇌ ℗ – 🏛 25 à 80. 🖭 ⑩ E 🆅🆂🅰 ⛗ rest FX **d**
SC : **R** carte 60 à 100 – ⊇ 12 – **205 ch** 155/275, 25 appartements.

🏨🏨 **Les Bergues,** 33 quai Bergues, ⊠ 1201, ↱ 31.50.50, Télex 23383, ≤ – ╡ ▤ ⊤ⱽ ☎ – 🏛 100 à 300. 🖭 ⑩ E 🆅🆂🅰 FY **a**
SC : **R** voir rest. Amphitryon – ⊇ 12 – **117 ch** 150/270, 8 appartements.

🏨🏨 **Beau Rivage,** 13 quai Mont-Blanc, ⊠ 1201, ↱ 31.02.21, Télex 23362, ≤ lac – ╡ ▤ ⊤ⱽ ☎ ℗ – 🏛 30 à 200. 🖭 ⑩ E 🆅🆂🅰 ⛗ rest FY **n**
SC : **R** voir rest. Le Chat Botté – **120 ch** ⊇ 160/290, 6 appartements.

🏨🏨 **Paix,** 11 quai Mont-Blanc, ⊠ 1211, ↱ 32.61.50, Télex 22552, ≤ – ╡ ▤ rest ⊤ⱽ ☎ – 🏛 50. 🖭 ⑩ E 🆅🆂🅰 FY **s**
SC : **R** carte 60 à 85 ⅃ – **94 ch** ⊇ 100/260, 11 appartements – P 195.

🏨🏨 **Ramada** Ⓜ, 19 r. Zurich, ⊠ 1201, ↱ 31.02.41, Télex 289109, dégustation de fromages – ╡ ▤ ⊤ⱽ ☎ ℗ – 🏛 150. 🖭 ⑩ E 🆅🆂🅰 FX **x**
SC : **La Clef d'Or** *(fermé dim.)* **Rive Droite R** carte 60 à 90 ⅃ – ⊇ 12 – **206 ch** 130/200, 7 appartements.

🏨 **Méditerranée** Ⓜ, 14 r. Lausanne, ⊠ 1201, ↱ 31.62.50, Télex 23630 – ╡ ▤ ⊤ⱽ ☎ – 🏛 420. 🖭 ⑩ 🆅🆂🅰 EY **n**
SC : **R** carte 55 à 70 ⅃ – **168 ch** ⊇ 120/170.

🏨 **P.L.M. Rotary** Ⓜ, 18 r. Cendrier, ⊠ 1206, ↱ 31.52.00, Télex 289999 – ╡ cuisinette ⊤ⱽ ☎. 🖭 ⑩ E 🆅🆂🅰 FY **p**
SC : **R** carte 45 à 65 ⅃ – **95 ch** ⊇ 130/190, 12 appartements 170/350.

🏨 **Bristol** Ⓜ, 10 r. Mont-Blanc, ⊠ 1201, ↱ 32.44.00, Télex 23739 – ╡ ▤ ⊤ⱽ ♿ – 🏛 40 à 120. 🖭 ⑩ E 🆅🆂🅰 FY **w**
SC : **R** *(fermé sam. soir et dim.)* carte 50 à 80 – **69 ch** ⊇ 100/210, 6 appartements 210/400 – P 170/210.

🏨 **Angleterre,** 17 quai Mt-Blanc, ⊠ 1201, ↱ 32.81.80, Télex 22668, ≤ – ╡ ▤ rest ⊤ⱽ ☎. 🖭 ⑩ E 🆅🆂🅰 ⛗ rest FY **t**
SC : **R** carte 35 à 50 – **65 ch** ⊇ 115/240, 3 appartements 450 – P 165/210.

🏨 **Ambassador,** 21 quai Bergues, ⊠ 1201, ↱ 31.72.00, Télex 23231 – ╡ ⊤ⱽ ℗ – 🏛 40. 🖭 ⑩ E 🆅🆂🅰 EY **p**
SC : **R** 27/36 ⅃ – **92 ch** ⊇ 70/160.

🏨 **Cornavin** sans rest, 33 bd James-Fazy, ⊠ 1211, ↱ 32.21.00, Télex 22853 – ╡ ⊤ⱽ ☎ ℗. 🖭 ⑩ E 🆅🆂🅰 EY **t**
SC : **125 ch** ⊇ 75/150.

🏨🏨 **Amat-Carlton** Ⓜ, 22 r. Amat., ⊠ 1202, ☏ 31.68.50, Télex 27595 — 🛗 cuisinette 🍽 rest 📺 ☎
⟵, 🅰🅴 ⓞ 🄴 𝑉𝐼𝑆𝐴. 🍴 rest   FX **a**
SC : **R** *(fermé dim. midi et sam.)* 16/52 ♨ — **119 ch** ⌷ 98/175.

🏨🏨 **Berne** Ⓜ, 26 r. Berne, ⊠ 1201, ☏ 31.60.00, Télex 22764 — 🛗 📺 — 🏛 30 à 100. 🅰🅴 ⓞ 🄴 𝑉𝐼𝑆𝐴.
🍴 rest   FY **x**
SC : **R** 18/22 — **80 ch** ⌷ 95/135 — P 108/135.

🏨 **Midi** Ⓜ, pl. Chevelu, ⊠ 1201, ☏ 31.78.00, Télex 23482 — 🛗 📺 ⌷wc 🚾wc ☎. ⟵ 🅰🅴 ⓞ 🄴
𝑉𝐼𝑆𝐴. 🍴 rest   FY **r**
SC : **R** carte 40 à 50 ♨ — **84 ch** ⌷ 90/120.

🏨 **Alba** sans rest, 19 r. Mt-Blanc, ⊠ 1201, ☏ 32.56.00, Télex 23930 — 🛗 📺 ⌷wc ☎. ⟵ 🅰🅴
ⓞ 🄴 𝑉𝐼𝑆𝐴   EY **a**
SC : **60 ch** ⌷ 90/150.

🏨 **Suisse** Ⓜ sans rest, 10 pl. Cornavin, ⊠ 1201, ☏ 32.66.30, Télex 23868 — 🛗 📺 ⌷wc 🚾wc
☎ ⟵ 🅰🅴 ⓞ 🄴 𝑉𝐼𝑆𝐴   EY **y**
SC : **60 ch** ⌷ 70/120.

🏨 **Balzac** sans rest, pl. Navigation, ⊠ 1201, ☏ 31.01.60, Télex 289430 — 🛗 📺 ⌷wc 🚾wc ☎
🅟. ⟵ 🅰🅴 ⓞ 🄴 𝑉𝐼𝑆𝐴   FX **n**
SC : **40 ch** ⌷ 35/98, 4 appartements 120.

🏨 **California** sans rest, 1 r. Gevray, ⊠ 1201, ☏ 31.55.50, Télex 23560 — 🛗 cuisinette ⌷wc ☎.
⟵ 🅰🅴 ⓞ 🄴 𝑉𝐼𝑆𝐴. 🍴   FY **m**
SC : **51 ch** ⌷ 80/150, 9 appartements 185/265.

🏨 **International et Terminus,** 20 r. Alpes, ⊠ 1201, ☏ 32.80.95, Télex 27808 — 🛗 ⌷wc 🚾wc
☎. ⟵ 🅰🅴 ⓞ 🄴 𝑉𝐼𝑆𝐴. 🍴 rest   EY **n**
SC : **R** carte 55 à 90 ♨ — **51 ch** ⌷ 35/100 — P 65/105.

🏨 **Astoria** sans rest, 6 pl. Cornavin, ⊠ 1211, ☏ 32.10.25, Télex 22307 — 🛗 📺 ⌷wc 🚾wc ☎.
⟵ 🅰🅴 ⓞ 🄴 𝑉𝐼𝑆𝐴   EY **y**
SC : **62 ch** ⌷ 60/95.

🏨 **Moderne** sans rest, 1 r. Berne, ⊠ 1211, ☏ 32.81.00, Télex 289738 — 🛗 📺 ⌷wc 🚾wc ☎.
⟵ 🅰🅴 ⓞ 🄴 𝑉𝐼𝑆𝐴   EY **v**
SC : **55 ch** ⌷ 35/100.

🏨 **Bernina** sans rest, 22 pl. Cornavin, ⊠ 1211, ☏ 31.49.50, Télex 28795 — 🛗 📺 ⌷wc 🚾wc ☎.
⟵ 🅰🅴 🄴 𝑉𝐼𝑆𝐴   EY **e**
SC : **77 ch** ⌷ 38/86.

🏨 **Lido** sans rest, 8 r. Chantepoulet, ⊠ 1201, ☏ 31.55.30 — 🛗 ⌷wc 🚾wc ☎. ⟵ 🅰🅴 ⓞ 🄴 𝑉𝐼𝑆𝐴
SC : **31 ch** ⌷ 45/85.   EY **v**

XXXX ✤ **Le Chat Botté,** 13 quai Mont-Blanc, ⊠ 1201, ☏ 31.02.21 — ☰ 🅟. 🅰🅴 ⓞ 🄴 𝑉𝐼𝑆𝐴. 🍴
fermé dim. midi et sam. — SC : **R** 65/85   FY **n**
Spéc. Les trois feuilletés Chat-Botté, Saumon Janine, Aiguillettes de lapin au basilic. **Vins** Gamay, Pinot gris.

XXXX ✤ **Le Gentilhomme,** jardin Brunswick, ⊠ 1211, ☏ 31.14.00 — ☰. 🅰🅴 ⓞ 🄴 𝑉𝐼𝑆𝐴. 🍴   FY **u**
SC : **R** carte 65 à 90
Spéc. Coquille St-Jacques au basilic (oct.-avril), Navarin de homard à la crème d'estragon, Mignon de veau au
citron vert. **Vins** Pinot noir, Yvorne.

XXXX **Amphitryon,** 33 quai Bergues, ⊠ 1201, ☏ 31.50.50 — 🅰🅴 ⓞ 🄴 𝑉𝐼𝑆𝐴. 🍴   FY **a**
fermé sam. — SC : **R** carte 70 à 85.

XXX ✤ **Perle du Lac,** 128 r. Lausanne ⊠ 1202, ☏ 31.35.04, ⟵ — 🅟. 🅰🅴 ⓞ 🄴 𝑉𝐼𝑆𝐴   BU **f**
fermé 22 déc. au 31 janv. et lundi — SC : **R** 65/87
Spéc. Paupiettes de soles au coulis d'écrevisses, Mignons de veau au citron vert, Gibier en saison.

XXX **Rôtisserie Le Neptune,** quai Turrettini ⊠ 1211 ☏ 31.98.31 — ☰ 🅟. 🅰🅴 ⓞ 🄴 𝑉𝐼𝑆𝐴. 🍴
fermé sam., dim. et fériés — SC : **R** carte 60 à 85   EY **r**

XXX **Fin Bec,** 55 r. Berne, ⊠ 1201, ☏ 32.29.19 — 🅰🅴 ⓞ 🄴 𝑉𝐼𝑆𝐴   FX **k**
fermé 1er au 20 août, 25 déc. au 5 janv., sam. midi et dim. — SC : **R** carte 50 à 80 ♨.

XXX **Aub. Mère Royaume,** 9 r. Corps Saints, ⊠ 1201, ☏ 32.70.08, « Style vieux genevois » —
🅰🅴 ⓞ 🄴 𝑉𝐼𝑆𝐴   EY **k**
fermé sam. midi et dim. — SC : **R** carte 55 à 80 ♨.

XX **Buffet Cornavin,** 3 pl. Cornavin, ⊠ 1201, ☏ 32.43.06 — 🅰🅴 ⓞ 🄴 𝑉𝐼𝑆𝐴   EY
SC : **Rest français R** carte 40 à 60 ♨ - **Buffet (1er classe) R** carte environ 35.

XX **Mövenpick-Cendrier** (Beef Club), 17 r. Cendrier, ⊠ 1201, ☏ 32.50.30, Télex 23676 — ☰. 🅰🅴
ⓞ 🄴 𝑉𝐼𝑆𝐴   FY **f**
SC : **R** carte 50 à 75 ♨.

XX **Locanda Ticinese,** 13 r. Rousseau, ⊠ 1201, ☏ 32.31.70, Cuisine tessinoise et italienne —
🅰🅴 ⓞ 𝑉𝐼𝑆𝐴   EY **b**
fermé 1er au 22 août et dim. — SC : **R** carte environ 50 ♨.

X **Boeuf Rouge,** 17 r. A.-Vincent ⊠ 1201, ☏ 32.75.37, cuisine lyonnaise   FY **z**
fermé 12 au 31 juil., 23 déc. au 3 janv., sam., dim. et fériés — SC : **R** carte 35 à 55 ♨.

X **A la Diligence,** 2 r. Pécolat, ⊠ 1201, ☏ 32.44.95 — 🅰🅴 𝑉𝐼𝑆𝐴   FY **j**
fermé dim. — SC : **R** carte 35 à 55 ♨.

RÉPERTOIRE DES RUES DU

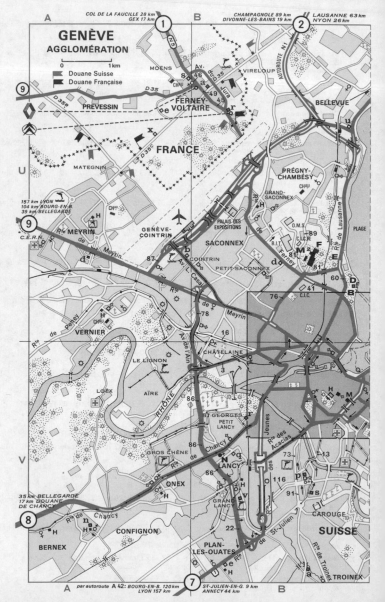

PLAN DE GENÈVE

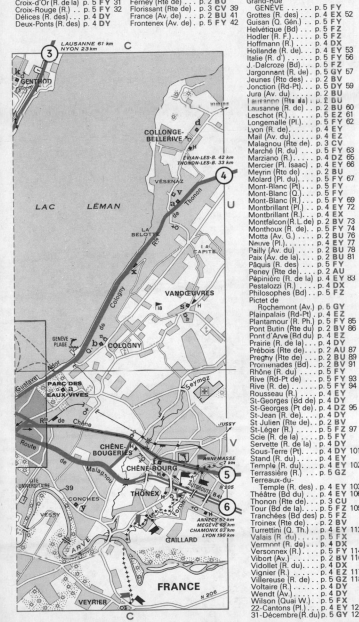

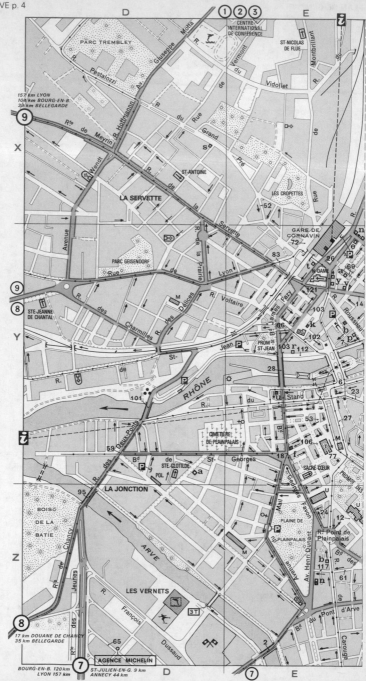

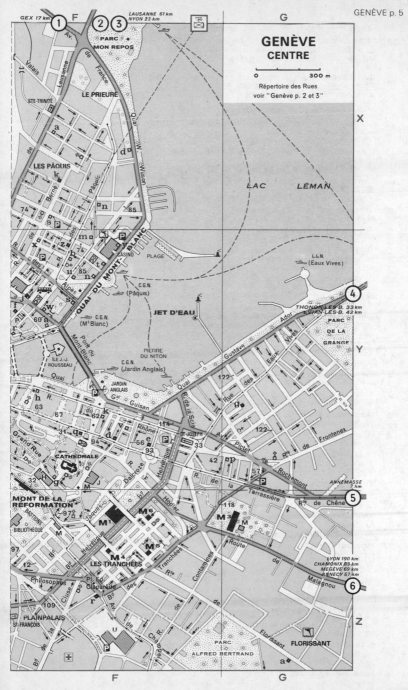

2ᵉ - Au Nord (Palais des Nations, Servette) :

🏨🏨 **Intercontinental** Ⓜ ⚎, 7 petit Saconnex, ⊠ 1211, Genève 19 ℡ 34.60.91, Télex 23130, ≤,
🍴 – 🛗 🗐 rest 🖲 ☎ ⇄ – 🛖 25 à 750. 🖭 ⓘ Ⓔ 𝘝𝘐𝘚𝘈. ℅ rest   BU **d**
Les Continents (1ᵉʳ étage) *(fermé dim.)* **R** carte 65 à 85 – ⊏⊐ 10 – **400 ch** 150/210, 31 appartements.

🏨 **Grand Pré** sans rest, 35 r. Gd-Pré, ⊠ 1211, Genève 16 ℡ 33.91.50, Télex 23284 – 🛗 cuisinette
🖲 ⎚wc 🖩wc ☜. 🖙 🖭 ⓘ Ⓔ 𝘝𝘐𝘚𝘈   DX **s**
SC : **100 ch** ⊏⊐ 68/135, 4 appartements 160.

3ᵉ - Rive gauche (Centre des affaires) :

🏨🏨 **Armures** Ⓜ ⚎, 1 r. Puits-Saint-Pierre ⊠ 1204 ℡ 28.91.72, Télex 421129 – 🛗 🗐 rest 🖲 ☎
🖧 🖭 ⓘ Ⓔ 𝘝𝘐𝘚𝘈   FY **g**
SC : **R** carte environ 35 ⚖ – **24 ch** ⊏⊐ 110/210, 4 appartements 260.

🏨🏨 **L'Arbalète** Ⓜ, 3 r. Tour-Maîtresse, ⊠ 1204, ℡ 28.41.55, Télex 427293 – 🛗 🗐 🖲 🖧 – 🛖 30.
🖭 ⓘ Ⓔ 𝘝𝘐𝘚𝘈   FY **v**
SC : **R** carte environ 35 ⚖ – **32 ch** ⊏⊐ 110/210.

🏨🏨 **Century** sans rest, 24 av. Frontenex ⊠ 1207 ℡ 36.80.95, Télex 23223 – 🛗 cuisinette Ⓟ – 🛖
35. 🖭 ⓘ Ⓔ 𝘝𝘐𝘚𝘈   GY **p**
SC : **125 ch** ⊏⊐ 45/145, 15 appartements 150/210.

🏨 **Lutetia** Ⓜ sans rest, 12 r. Carouge, ⊠ 1205, ℡ 20.42.22, Télex 28845 – 🛗 cuisinette ⎚wc ☜
30 ch.   EZ **b**

🏨 **Plaine** sans rest, 11 av. H.-Dunant, ⊠ 1205, ℡ 20.92.88, Télex 28845 – 🛗 ⎚wc 🖩 ☜   EZ **n**
47 ch.

🏨 **Touring Balance**, 13 pl. Longemalle, ⊠ 1204, ℡ 28.71.22, Télex 27634 – 🛗 🖲 ⎚wc 🖩wc
☜ – 🛖 40. 🖧☜ 🖭 ⓘ 𝘝𝘐𝘚𝘈 ℅ rest   FY **k**
SC : **R** 24/30 ⚖ – **56 ch** ⊏⊐ 45/120 – P 90/120.

🏨 **Le Grenil**, 7 av. Ste-Clotilde, ⊠ 1205, ℡ 28.30.55, Télex 429307 – 🛗 🖩wc ☜ – 🛖 220. 🖧☜
🖭 ⓘ Ⓔ 𝘝𝘐𝘚𝘈   DY **a**
SC : **R** *(fermé lundi)* carte environ 40 ⚖ – **50 ch** ⊏⊐ 38/78 – P 64/81.

XXXX ✿ **Parc des Eaux-Vives**, 82 quai Gustave-Ador, ⊠ 1207, ℡ 35.41.40, « Agréable situation
dans un grand parc, belle vue » – Ⓟ. 🖭 ⓘ Ⓔ 𝘝𝘐𝘚𝘈   CV **a**
fermé 1ᵉʳ janv. au 15 fév. et lundi – SC : **R** carte 60 à 85
Spéc. Gratin de cuisses de grenouilles (saison), Filet de féra aux groseilles (saison), Sabayon glacé à la ''Williamine''. **Vins** Clos-du-Roussillon, Yvorne.

XXX **Aub. de l'Or du Rhône**, 19 bd G. Favon, ⊠ 1204, ℡ 28.25.21 – 🗐. 🖭 ⓘ Ⓔ 𝘝𝘐𝘚𝘈   EY **f**
fermé 30 juil. au 24 août, sam. midi et dim. – SC : **R** carte 65 à 85 ⚖.

XXX **Via Veneto**, 10 r. Tour Maitresse ⊠ 1204 ℡ 21.65.93 – 🗐. 🖭 ⓘ 𝘝𝘐𝘚𝘈   FY **d**
fermé 15 juil. au 15 août, dim. et fériés – SC : **R** carte 60 à 80 ⚖.

XXX **Roberto**, 10 r. P.-Fatio, ⊠ 1204, ℡ 21.80.33, Spécialités italiennes – 🗐   FY **e**
fermé sam. soir et dim. – SC : **R** carte 50 à 70 ⚖.

XX **Mövenpick Fusterie**, 40 r. Rhône ⊠ 1204 ℡ 21.88.55 – 🗐. 🖭 ⓘ Ⓔ 𝘝𝘐𝘚𝘈   FY **h**
SC : **R** Baron de la Mouette (sous-sol) carte 45 à 65 ⚖.

XX **Laurent**, 13 r. Madeleine, ⊠ 1204, ℡ 21.24.22 – 🖭 ⓘ Ⓔ 𝘝𝘐𝘚𝘈   FY **q**
fermé dim. – SC : **R** carte 50 à 65 ⚖.

XX ✿ **Béarn** (Godard), 4 quai Poste, ⊠ 1204, ℡ 21.00.28 – 🖭 Ⓔ 𝘝𝘐𝘚𝘈   EY **u**
fermé 15 juil. au 15 août, sam. midi et dim. – SC : **R** 65/90
Spéc. Terrine d'écrevisses, Suprême de loup au gingembre, Aiguillette de pigeon. **Vins** Dardagny, Satigny.

XX **Sénat**, 1 r. E.-Yung, ⊠ 1205, ℡ 46.58.10 – 🖭 ⓘ Ⓔ 𝘝𝘐𝘚𝘈   FZ **r**
fermé dim. – SC : **R** 27/55 ⚖.

XX **La Pescaille**, 15 av. H.-Dunant, ⊠ 1205, ℡ 29.71.60 – 🗐. 🖭 ⓘ Ⓔ 𝘝𝘐𝘚𝘈   EZ **n**
fermé sam. midi et dim. midi – SC : **R** carte 70 à 105.

XX **Al Cavalieri**, 7 r. Cherbuliez, ⊠ 1207, ℡ 35.09.56 – 🗐. 🖭 ⓘ Ⓔ 𝘝𝘐𝘚𝘈   GY **g**
fermé août et lundi – SC : **R** 30/40 ⚖.

XX **Parc Bertrand**, 62 rte Florissant, ⊠ 1206, ℡ 47.59.57 – 🗐. 🖭 ⓘ Ⓔ 𝘝𝘐𝘚𝘈   GZ **a**
fermé Pâques, 23 déc. au 5 janv. et dim. – SC : **R** 20/50 ⚖.

Environs

Route de Lausanne au bord du lac - BCU :

à Bellevue : 6 km - BU – ⊠ 1293 Bellevue :

🏨🏨 **La Réserve** Ⓜ ⚎, 301 rte de Lausanne ℡ 74.17.41, Télex 23822, ≤, « Bel ensemble dans un
parc près du lac, port aménagé », 🍴, ℅ – 🛗 🖲 🖧 Ⓟ – 🛖 80. 🖭 ⓘ Ⓔ 𝘝𝘐𝘚𝘈. ℅ rest BU **u**
SC : **R** carte 60 à 80 – **65 ch** ⊏⊐ 150/275, 4 appartements – P 500.

XXX ✿ **Tsé Fung**, 4 chemin des Romelles ℡ 74.17.41 – Ⓟ. 🖭 ⓘ Ⓔ 𝘝𝘐𝘚𝘈   BU **u**
SC : **R** 50/85
Spéc. Canard à la Pékinoise, Marmite Mongole ''Genghis-Khan'', Poulet farçi à 8 trésors. **Vins** Dézaley, Yvorne.

X **Lacustre**, ℡ 74.10.02, ≤, Plein air   CU **t**
fermé merc. soir et jeudi d'oct. au 28 fév. – SC : **R** carte 40 à 60 ⚖.

à Genthod : 7 km – ⊠ 1294 Genthod :

XX **Rest. du Château de Genthod,** 1 rte Rennex ☎ 74.19.72 – AE ⓪ E VISA   CU **k**
fermé 20 déc. au 10 janv., dim. soir et lundi – SC : **R** 35/60.

vers la Savoie et bord du lac - CU :

à Cologny : 3,5 km - CU – ⊠ 1223 Cologny :

XXX ❀ **Aub. du Lion d'or** (Large), au Village ☎ 36.44.32, ≤, « Situation dominant le lac et
Genève, terrasse » – ℗. AE ⓪ VISA   CU **b**
fermé 20 déc. au 20 janv., merc. midi et mardi – SC : **R** carte 70 à 100
Spéc. Saumon mariné, Filets de rouget à l'orange, Aiguillettes de caneton aux poires et vieux Bordeaux. **Vins**
Villeneuve, Yvorne.

X **Pavillon de Ruth,** 86 quai Cologny ☎ 52.14.38, ≤ – ℗   CU **x**
fermé janv., fév. et jeudi – SC : **R** carte environ 45.

à Vandoeuvres : 5,5 km - CU – ⊠ 1253 Vandoeuvres :

XX **Cheval Blanc,** ☎ 50.14.01, cuisine italienne – AE E ❀   CU **s**
fermé 1er au 21 juil., mardi midi et lundi – SC : **R** carte 50 à 75 ♨.

à Vésenaz : 6 km par rte de Thonon - CU – ⊠ 1222 Vésenaz :

🏠 **La Tourelle** sans rest, 26 rte Hermance ☎ 52.16.28, ♠ – 🛏wc 🛁 🕾 ℗. 🚗 AE ⓪ E VISA
❀   CU **v**
fermé 1er déc. au 15 fév. – SC : **24 ch** ⊃ 40/98.

XXX **Chez Valentino,** 63 rte Thonon ☎ 52.14.40, Cuisine italienne, ♠ – ℗. AE VISA. ❀   CU **a**
fermé août, mardi midi et lundi – SC : **R** carte 45 à 70 ♨.

à Collonges : 8 km - CU – ⊠ 1245 Collonges :

XXX **Le Chambord,** ☎ 52.25.85 – AE ⓪   CU **d**
fermé 1er au 21 juil., sam. midi et merc. – SC : **R** 55/75.

par route de Chêne - CV :

à Chêne-Bourg : 4,5 km - CV – ⊠ 1225 Chêne-Bourg :

X **Le Leonardo,** 48 r. Genève ☎ 48.51.73 – ℗. ⓪ E VISA   CV **f**
fermé mardi midi et lundi – SC : **R** carte environ 35 ♨.

à Jussy : 11 km - CV – ⊠ 1254 Jussy :

X **Aub. Vieux Jussy,** ☎ 59.11.10 – ⓪
fermé fév., mardi soir et merc. – SC : **R** carte 40 à 60.

route de Florissant - CV :

à Conches : 2,5 km - CV – ⊠ 1231 Conches :

X **Le Catalan,** 175 rte Florisant ☎ 47.06.23, cuisine espagnole   ℗. AE ⓪ E VISA   CV **y**
fermé 20 déc. au 20 janv. et dim. – SC : **R** (dîner seul.) carte environ 60.

à Carouge : 3 km par r. Carouge - BV – ⊠ 1227 Carouge :

XX **Olivier de Provence,** 13 r. J.-Dalphin ☎ 42.04.50 – AE ⓪   BV **p**
fermé dim. – SC : **R** carte 50 à 70.

XX **Aub. Communale** avec ch, 39 r. Ancienne ☎ 42.22.88 – 🚗
SC : **R** (fermé mardi) carte 35 à 55 ♨ – **9 ch** ⊃ 30/45 – P 60/70.   BV **s**

à Troinex : 5 km - BV – ⊠ 1256 Troinex :

XXX ❀❀ **Vieux Moulin** (Bouilloux), 89 rte Drize ☎ 42.29.56 – ℗. AE VISA   BV **a**
fermé 1er au 15 avril, 1er au 15 sept. dim. soir et lundi – SC : **R** 70/100 et carte
Spéc. St Jacques au curry (nov. à mars), Bavarois d'écrevisses (mai à oct.), Cuisse de Bresse farcie aux chanterelles
(août à oct.). **Vins** Lully, Petit Arvine.

XX **La Chaumière,** r. Fondelle ☎ 84.30.66, ♠ – ℗. AE ⓪ E
fermé dim. soir et lundi en hiver – SC : **R** carte 50 à 80.

par route de St-Julien - BV :

au Grand-Lancy : 3 km - BV – ⊠ 1212 Lancy :

XXX ❀ **Marignac** (Pelletier), 32 av. E.-Lance ☎ 94.04.24, parc – ▤ ℗. VISA   BV **v**
fermé 16 au 29 août, 20 déc. au 2 janv., sam. midi et dim. – SC : **R** carte 65 à 90
Spéc. Escalopes de foie gras de canard poêlées, Cassolette de queues de langoustines et de filets de sole, Ris et
mignon de veau à la crème de basilic.

au Petit Lancy : 3 km - BV – ⊠ 1213 Petit Lancy :

🏨 ✿ **Host. de la Vendée et rest. Pont Rouge** M, 28 chemin Vendée ☎ 92.04.11, Télex
421304 – 🛗 📺 ℗ – 🔬 50. AE ⓪ E VISA   BV **q**
fermé 24 déc. au 6 janv. – SC : **R** (fermé Pâques, Pentecôte et dim.) 40/68 ♨ – **30 ch** ⊃ 70/125
Spéc. Foie gras d'oie frais, Poissons, Suprême de Bresse au blanc de blanc. **Vins** Pinot gris, Gamay.

X ❀ **Le Curling,** chemin du Fief-de-Chapitre ☎ 93.62.44, ≤   BV **r**
fermé 31 juil. au 24 août, 23 déc. au 4 janv., lundi midi et dim. – SC : **R** 40/70
Spéc. Salade gourmande, Mille feuille au foie de canard, Sole vapeur à l'aneth. **Vins** Pinot noir, Gamay.

au Plan-les-Ouates : 5 km - BV – ⊠ **1228** Plan-les-Ouates :

🏨 **Plan-les-Ouates** Ⓜ sans rest, 135 rte St-Julien ☎ 94.92.44 – |🛗| 🛁wc 🏧. ◻⊟ 🝞 ⑩ **E**
VISA BV **e**
SC : ⇌ 6 – **24 ch** 35/65.

par route de Chancy - ABV :

à Confignon : 6 km - AV – ⊠ **1232** Confignon :

XX Aub. de Confignon, 6 pl. Église ☎ 57.19.44, 🍴 AV **n**

à Cartigny par ⑧ *:* 12 km – ⊠ **1236** Cartigny :

XX ❀ **L'Escapade** (Studhalter), 31 r. Trably ☎ 56.12.07 – 🅿. ⑩
fermé 1ᵉʳ au 10 sept., 22 déc. au 2 fév., lundi et mardi – SC : **R** carte 70 à 90
Spéc. Filets de rougets aux tomates, Foie de canard poêlé, Râble d'agneau rôti.

vers le Jura - AUV :

à Cointrin : par route de Meyrin : 4 km - ABU – ⊠ **1216** Cointrin :

🏨 **Hôtel 33**, 82 av. L.-Casai ☎ 98.02.00 – |🛗| 🛁wc 🏧 🅿. ◻⊟ 🝞 ⑩ **E** *VISA* AU **b**
SC : **R** *(fermé dim.)* carte environ 45 ⅃ – **33 ch** ⇌ 70/100.

à l'Aéroport de Cointrin : 4 km - AU – ⊠ **1215** Genève :

XX **Rôt. Plein Ciel**, ☎ 98.22.88, < – ▤. 🝞 ⑩ **E** *VISA* AU
SC : **R** carte 45 à 70.

à Meyrin : 5 km – ⊠ **1217** Meyrin :

X **Levant**, 43 r. Cardinal Journet ⊠ 1217 ☎ 82.51.14 AU **d**
fermé 10 au 31 juil., sam. et dim. – SC : **R** carte 40 à 60 ⅃.

à Peney-Dessus O : 10 km par rte de Peney - AUV – ⊠ **1242** Satigny :

XX **Aub. de Châteauvieux** ⑤ avec ch, ☎ 53.14.45, < – 📺 🛁wc 🏧 🅿. ◻⊟ 🝞 ⑩ **E** *VISA*
fermé 20 déc. au 10 janv. – SC : **R** *(fermé dim. soir et lundi)* 30/60 – **12 ch** ⇌ 60/90.

à La Plaine par ⑧ *:* 17 km – ⊠ **1249** La Plaine :

XX Buffet Gare, à la Gare ☎ 54.12.16.

ZÜRICH

ZÜRICH 8001 427 ⑥. 21 ⑱ G. Schweiz – 422 640 Ew. Höhe 441 m – ۞ 01.

Sehenswert : Die Quais★★ BYZ – Alter Kreuzgang★ des Frauenmünsters BZ – Stadtansichten★ vom Zürichhornpark aus V – Kirche St. Felix und Regula★ UE – Protestantische Kirche in Zürich -Altstetten★ UF – Zoo Dolder★ UK – Museen : Schweizerisches Landesmuseum★★★ BX, Kunst haus★★ CZ, Museum Rietberg★★ V M2.

✈ Kloten (② : 10 km) ☏ 812 71 11.

🛈 Offizielles Verkehrsbüro, Bahnhofplatz 15 ⊠ 8023 ☏ 211 40 40, Telex 813744 - A.C.S. Furchstrasse 95 ⊠ 8032 ☏ 55 15 00 - T.C.S. Escher-Strasse 38 ⊠ 8002 ☏ 201 25 36.

Basel 84 ⑦ – Bern 124 ⑦ – Genève 276 ⑦ – Innsbruck 286 ② – Milano 344 ⑤.

Rechtes Limmat-Ufer (Universität, Kunsthaus)

🏨 ۞ **Dolder Grand Hotel et rest. La Rotonde** ৯, Kurhausstr. 65 ⊠ 8032 ☏ 251 62 21, Telex 53449, ← Zürich und See, Park, ☚, ⌚, ℁ – ▮ ⊟ Rest ⊡ ☎ ⇔ Ⓟ – 🔬 200. 🝤 E VISA ⌘ Rest
Karte 50/80 – **200 Z** ⌸ 130/290
Spez. Gratin d'écrevisses (Juli.-Sept.), Filets de sole au Dézaley, Dodine de poularde Talleyrand.

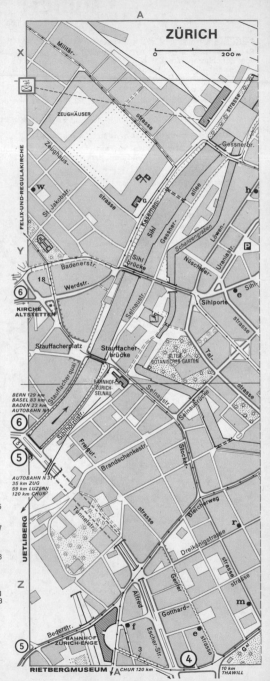

ZÜRICH

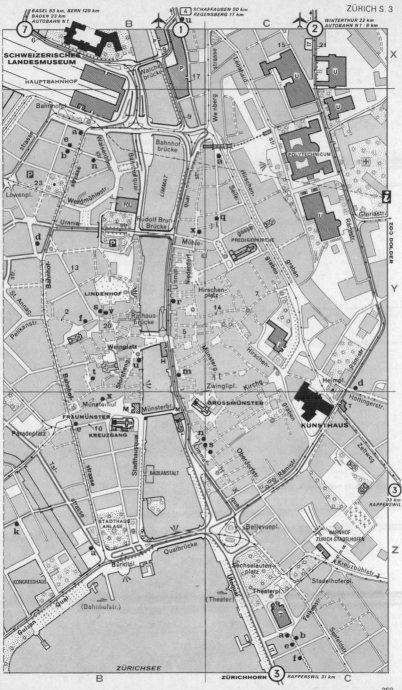

BASEL 83 km, BERN 129 km
BADEN 23 km
AUTOBAHN N 1

SCHAFFAUSEN 50 km
REGENSBERG 17 km

WINTERTHUR 22 km
AUTOBAHN N 1 : 8 km

SCHWEIZERISCHES
LANDESMUSEUM

HAUPTBAHNHOF

Bahnhofpl.

Walchebrücke

P

Wenberg strasse

Leonhard str.

POLYTECHNICUM

X

Löwenpl.

Bahnhof brücke

Bahnhof brücke

LIMMAT

Waisenhaus str.

Werdmühlestr.

POL.

Rudolf Brun Brücke

PREDIGERKIRCHE

Gloriastr.

ZOO DOLDER

Urania

Mühle-

Niederdorf

Seiler

gasse

graben

graben

Rämistr.

St. Annastr.

Bahnhof str.

LINDENHOF

Rathaus brücke

Hirschen platz

Y

Pelikanstr.

Weinplatz

Storchengasse

H

Münsterg.

Hirschen-

Heimpl.

Hottingerstr.

Zwinglipl.

Kirchg.

FRAUMÜNSTER

Paradeplatz

Tal str.

Münsterhof

KREUZGANG

Münsterbr.

GROSSMÜNSTER

KUNSTHAUS

Zeltweg

Bahnhof strasse

Stadthausquai

BADEANSTALT

Limmat

Oberdorfstr.

Rämistr.

33 km
RAPPERSWIL

STADTHAUS ANLAGE

BAHNHOF
ZÜRICH-STADELHOFEN

Z

KONGRESSHAUS

Qualbrücke

Bürklipl.

Bellevuepl.

Kreuzbühlstr.

Stadelhoferpl.

General Guisan Quai

(Bahnhofstr.)

Sechseläutenplatz

Theaterpl.

Seefeldstr.

Utoquai

(Theater)

Falkenstr.

ZÜRICHSEE

B

ZÜRICHHORN

RAPPERSWIL 31 km

C

🏨 **Eden au Lac,** Utoquai 45 ⊠ 8023 ℱ 47 94 04, Telex 52440, ≤, « Elegant Inneneinrichtung »,
⇔ – 🛗 ▤ ▥ ☎ 🅿 – ₰ 25. AE ① E VISA. 🍴 Rest   V a
Karte 36/72 – **54 Z** ☐ 125/260.

🏨 **Zürich** M, Neumühlequai 42 ⊠ 8001 ℱ 363 63 63, Telex 56809, ≤, ⇔, ▨ – 🛗 ▤ ▥ ☎ ර
⇔ – ₰ 400. AE ① E VISA. 🍴 Rest   U b
Karte 29,50/61 – ☐ 7 – **221 Z** 120/250.

🏨 **International** M Am Marktplatz ⊠ 8050 ℱ 311 43 41, Telex 55681, ≤, ⇔, ▨ – 🛗 ▤ ▥ ☎ –
₰ 800   U s
350 Z.

🏨 **Waldaus Dolder** M ﹩, Kurhausstr. 20 ⊠ 8030 ℱ 251 93 60, Telex 52277, ≤, Park, ⇔, ▨,
🌳, 🎾 – 🛗 kleine Küche ▥ ☎ 🚗 🅿 – ₰ 50. AE ① E VISA   V r
Karte 27,50/43 – ☐ 8 – **100 Z** 100/220.

🏨 **Bellerive au Lac,** Utoquai 47 ⊠ 8008 ℱ 251 70 10, Telex 53292, ≤ – 🛗 ▥ – ₰ 100   V a
57 Z.

🏨 **Excelsior,** Dufourstr. 24 ⊠ 8008 ℱ 225 25 00, Telex 59295 – 🛗 ▤ Zim ▥ ☎ – ₰ 25. AE E
VISA   CZ f
Karte 24/50 – **50 Z** ☐ 102/184.

🏨 **Zürich Continental H.,** Stampfenbachstr. 60 ⊠ 55393 ℱ 363 33 63 – 🛗 ▤ ▥ ☎ 🚗 –
₰ 80. AE ① E VISA   U a
Karte 25/48 – ☐ 8 – **134 Z** 88/197.

🏨 **Zürcherhof,** Zähringerstr. 21 ⊠ 8025 ℱ 47.10.40, Telex 54477 – 🛗 ▥ 🚽wc 🕾 – ₰ 30. AE
① E VISA   CY q
Karte *(Sonntag 17 Uhr. Montag geschl.)* 25/43 – **35 Z** ☐ 76,50/133.

🏨 **Europe,** Dufourstr. 4 ⊠ 8008 ℱ 47 10 30, Telex 54186, Alkoholfrei, « Geschmackvolle Einrichtung » – 🛗 ▤ Zim ▥ 🚽wc 🕾. AE ① E VISA   CZ e
Karte ca. 16 – **42 Z** ☐ 85/290.

🏨 **Ambassador,** Falkenstr. 6 ⊠ 8008 ℱ 47 76 00, Telex 54671 – 🛗 ▤ Zim ▥ 🚽wc 🕾.
AE ① E VISA   CZ a
Karte 21.50/49 – ☐ 7 – **45 Z** 70/144.

🏨 **Opéra** garni, Dufourstr. 5 ⊠ 8008 ℱ 251 90 90, Telex 54414 – 🛗 ▤ ▥ 🚽wc 🕾. AE ①
E VISA   CZ b
☐ 7 – **67 Z** 70/144.

🏨 **Schifflände,** Schifflände 18 ⊠ 8001 ℱ 69 40 50 – 🛗 ▤ Zim ▥ 🚽wc 🕾   CZ s
17 Z.

🏨 **Chesa Rustica,** Limmatquai 70 ⊠ 8001 ℱ 251 92 91, Telex 57380, ≤ – 🛗 ▤ ▥ 🚽wc 🚽wc
🕾. AE ① E VISA   BY r
Karte 23 /62,50 – **23 Z** ☐ 80/150.

🏨 **Ammann** M garni, Kirchgasse 4 ⊠ 8001 ℱ 252 72 40, Telex 56208 – 🛗 ▤ ▥ 🚽wc 🚽wc
₰ 30. AE ① E VISA   BCZ n
19 Z ☐ 80/150.

🏨 **Alexander** garni, Niederdorfstr. 40 ⊠ 8025 ℱ 251 82 03, Telex 57735 – 🛗 🚽wc 🚽wc 🕾. AE
① E VISA   BY x
61 Z ☐ 60/130.

🏨 **Théâtre** garni, Seilergraben 69 ⊠ 8023 ℱ 252 60 62, Telex 56853 – 🛗 ▥ 🚽wc 🚽wc 🕾. AE
① E VISA   CY a
60 Z ☐ 60/108.

🏨 **Helmhaus** garni, Schiffländeplatz 30 ⊠ 8001 ℱ 251 88 10, Telex 55101 – 🛗 🚽wc 🚽wc 🕾.
AE ① E VISA   BCZ s
25 Z ☐ 75/120.

XXXX ❀ **Agnès Amberg** Hottingerstr. 5 ⊠ 8032 ℱ 251 26 26, Elegante Inneneinrichtung – AE ①
E VISA   CY d
26.Juli-9 Aug., Samstag Mittag und Sonntag geschl. – **Karte** 64/90
Spez. Galette de pommes de terre à la truite marinée, Foie gras frais poêlé sur poireaux, Lapin de l'Oberland
zurichois.

XX **Haus Zum Rüden,** Limmatquai 41 ⊠ 8001 ℱ 47 95 90, Zunfthaus – AE ① E VISA. 🍴
Karte 38/82.   BY m

XX ❀ Riesbächli (Frau Tshudi), Zollikerstr. 157 ⊠ 8008 ℱ 55 23 24   V s

XX **Jacky's Stapferstube,** Culmannstr. 45 ⊠ 8006 ℱ 361 37 48, Spez. überwiegend Fleisch-
gerichte – 🅿. AE E VISA   U r
3.Juli-2.Aug., Sonntag u. Montag bis 17 Uhr geschl. – Karte 32/61.

XX **Casa Ferlin,** Stampfenbachstr. 38 ⊠ 8006 ℱ 362 35 23, Ital. Küche – AE ① E   BX u
15.Juli-15.Aug., Sonntag geschl., Samstag nur Abendessen – Karte 36/53.

XX **Bolognese,** Seegartenstr. 14 ⊠ 8008 ℱ 252.37.37, Ital. Küche   V u
23.Dez.-14.Jan. ,Samstag und Sonntag geschl. – Karte 18/50.50.

X **Wolfbach,** Wolfbachstr. 35 ⊠ 8032 ℱ 252 51 80, Spez. Süsswasserfische – AE ① E
1.-22.Aug., 24.Dez.-2.Jan. und Sonntag geschl. – Karte Tischbestellung ratsam. 33/55.   V b

Linkes Limmat-Ufer (Bahnhof, Geschäftsviertel)

🏨 **Baur au Lac,** Talstr. 1 ⊠ 8001 ℱ 221 16 50, « Lage am See, Park » – 📶 🍴 📺 ☎ 🚗 🅿 –
🔥 80. 🅰🅴. 🎖 Rest   BZ **a**
Karte 42/48 – **153 Z** ⌷ 140/300.

🏨 **Savoy Hotel Baur en Ville** Ⓜ, Poststr. 12 ⊠ 8022 ℱ 211 53 60, Telex 812845 – 📶 🍴 📺 ☎
🔥 – 🔥 200. 🅰🅴 ⓪ 🄴 *VISA* 🎖 Rest   BZ **e**
Karte Grill 38/60 – **112 Z** ⌷ 120/280.

🏨 **Schweizerhof** Ⓜ, Bahnhofplatz 7 ⊠ 8023 ℱ 211 86 40, Telex 813754 – 📶 🍴 Zim 📺 ☎ –
🔥 25. 🅰🅴 ⓪ 🄴 *VISA*   BY **a**
Karte 32/60 – **115 Z** ⌷ 105/250.

🏨 **Atlantis Sheraton** Ⓜ 🍃 Döltschiweg 234 ⊠ 8055 Zürich ℱ 35 00 00, Telex 813338, ≼, 🈂, 🔲,
🎿 – 📶 kleine Küche 🍴 Rest 📺 ☎ 🚗 – 🔥 200   V **z**
173 Z.

🏨 **Zum Storchen** Weinplatz 2 ⊠ 8022 ℱ 211 55 10, Telex 813354, ≼, « Am Limmat-Ufer » –
📶 📺 🍴 – 🔥 50. 🅰🅴 ⓪ 🄴 *VISA* 🎖 Rest   BY **u**
Karte 22/00 – **77 Ⲙ** ⌷ 102/254.

🏨 **St. Gotthard,** Bahnhofstr. 87 ⊠ 8023 ℱ 211 55 00, Telex 812420 – 📶 🍴 📺 ☎ – 🔥 50. 🅰🅴
⓪ 🄴   BY **b**
Rest. **Hummer und Austernbar** Karte 40/72, **La Bouillabaisse** Karte 38/55 – **140 Z** 123/306.

🏨 **Nova Park** Ⓜ, Badenerstr. 420 ⊠ 8040 ℱ, 🈂, 🔲, – 📶 🍴 📺 ☎ 🅿 – 🔥 250   U **n**
376 Z.

🏨 **Carlton Elite** 🍃, Bahnhofstr. 41 ⊠ 8023 ℱ 211.65.60, Telex 812781 – 📶 🍴 Rest 📺 ☎ 🔥 🅿
– 🔥 250. 🅰🅴 ⓪ 🄴 *VISA*   BY **d**
Locanda Karte 30/55 – ⌷ 10 – **72 Z** 105/220.

🏨 **Ascot,** Lavaterstr. 15 ⊠ 8027 ℱ 201 18 00, Telex 52783 – 📶 🍴 📺 ☎ 🅿. 🅰🅴 ⓪ 🄴 *VISA*
Jockey Club *(Samstag Mittag geschl.)* Karte 16/50 – **60 Z** ⌷ 98/165.   AZ **f**

🏨 **Glärnischhof,** Claridenstr. 30 ⊠ 8002 ℱ 202 47 47, Telex 52536 – 📶 📺 ☎ 🅿 – 🔥 50. 🅰🅴
⓪ 🄴 *VISA*   BZ **k**
La Rôtisserie Karte 30/52 – **70 Z** ⌷ 105/120.

🏨 **Splügenschloss,** Splügenstr. 2 ⊠ 8002 ℱ 201 08 00, Telex 53956 – 📶 🍴 Rest 📺 ☎ 🅿 –
🔥 35. 🅰🅴 ⓪ 🄴 *VISA* 🎖 Rest   AZ **e**
Karte 25/50 – **55 Z** ⌷ 100/200.

🏨 **Glockenhof,** Sihlstr. 31 ⊠ 8001 ℱ 211 56 50, Telex 812466 – 📶 🅰🅴 ⓪ 🄴 *VISA*   AY **e**
Karte 23.50/45 – **106 Z** ⌷ 82/138.

🏨 **Engematthof,** Engimattstr. 14 ⊠ 8002 ℱ 201 25 04, Telex 56327, 🎿, 🍽 – 📶 🍴 Rest 🛁wc
🛁wc ☎ 🅿 – 🔥 30   V **e**
Karte 26.50/42 – ⌷ 8.50 – **80 Z** 62/110.

🏨 **Trümpy,** Sihlquai 9 ⊠ 8005 ℱ 42 54 00, Telex 56416 – 📶 🍴 Rest 🛁wc 🛁wc ☎ – 🔥 35. 🅰🅴
⓪ 🄴 *VISA*   U **v**
Karte 13.50/35 – **78 Z** ⌷ 75/138.

🏨 **City,** Loewenstr. 34 ⊠ 8001 ℱ 211 20 55, Telex 812437 – 📶 🍴 📺 🛁wc 🛁wc 🅰🅴 ⓪ 🄴 *VISA*
Karte *(Sonntag geschl.)* 12 /36.50 – **74 Z** ⌷ 62/144.   AY **h**

🏨 **Stoller,** Badenerstr. 357 ⊠ 8040 ℱ 52 65 00, Telex 53381 – 📶 📺 🛁wc 🛁wc 🚗 🚗 🅰🅴 ⓪
🄴 *VISA*   V **x**
Karte 34/66 – **101 Z** ⌷ 70/135.

🏨 **Simplon** garni, Schützengasse 16 ⊠ 8023 ℱ 211 61 11 – 📶 🛁wc 🚗 – 🔥 25. 🅰🅴 ⓪ 🄴 *VISA*
74 Z ⌷ 59/140.   BY **e**

🏨 **Neues Schloss,** Stockerstr. 17 ⊠ 8022 ℱ 201 65 50, Telex 54121 – 📶 📺 🛁wc 🛁wc ☎. 🅰🅴
⓪ 🄴   AZ **m**
Karte *(Samstag ab 14 Uhr u. Sonntag geschl.)* 18/40 – ⌷ 7 – **60 Z** 100/150.

🏨 **Kindli** garni, Pfalzgasse 1 ⊠ 8001 ℱ 211 59 17, Telex 812426 – 📶 📺 🛁wc 🛁wc 🚗. 🅰🅴 ⓪
🄴 *VISA* 🎖   BY **s**
22 Z ⌷ 58/150.

🏨 **Limmathaus,** Limmatstr. 118 ⊠ 8031 ℱ 42 52 40 – 📶 🛁wc 🚗 🅿 – 🔥 700. 🅰🅴 ⓪ 🄴 *VISA*
Karte *(Sonn- und Feiertage geschl.)* 9/13 – **64 Z** ⌷ 42/95.   U **y**

XXX ❀ **Rebe** (Witschi), Schützengasse 5 ⊠ 8001 ℱ 221 10 65 – 🍴. 🅰🅴 ⓪ 🄴 *VISA*. 🎖   BY **n**
Sonntag geschl. – Karte 45/83
Spez. Cabri des Grisons à la moutarde (1. April-30. Juni), Filet de chevreuil aux fleurs des bois (1. Okt.-15. Nov.).

XXX **Baron de la Mouette** (Mövenpick Dreikönighaus), Beethovenstr. 32 ⊠ 8002 ℱ 202 09 10
– 🍴. 🅰🅴 ⓪ 🄴 *VISA*   AZ **r**
5 . 25 Juli geschl. – Karte 26.50/61.

XXX **Accademia-Piccoli,** Rotwandstr. 48 ⊠ 8004 ℱ 241.42.02, Ital. Küche – 🅰🅴 ⓪ 🄴 *VISA*
Samstag, Sonntag Mittag und Juli geschl.   Karte 32 /62.50.   AY **w**

XXX **Rôtisserie Lindenhofkeller,** Pfalzgasse 4 ⊠ 8001 ℱ 211 70 71 – 🅰🅴 ⓪ 🄴   BY **v**
31. Juli-22. Aug., Samstag u. Sonntag geschl. – Karte 32/64.

XX **Veltlinerkeller** Schlüsselgasse 8 ⊠ 8001 ℱ 221 32 28, « Haus a. d. 16. Jh. ». 🅰🅴 ⓪ 🄴 *VISA*
25. Juli-15. Aug. u. Sonntag geschl. – Karte 28/45.   BY **t**

XX **Zunfthaus zur Waag,** Münsterhof 8 ⊠ 8001 ℱ 211 07 30 – 🅰🅴 ⓪ 🄴 *VISA*   BZ **x**
Karte 30/60.

XX **Osteria Da Primo,** Wetlibergstr. 166 ⊠ 8045 ☎ 35 30 22, Ital Küche. 𝖠𝖤 ⓞ 𝖤 𝘝𝘐𝘚𝘈   V **k**
24. Dez.-3. Jan., Sonntag geschl.-Samstag nur Abendessen – Karte 85.

XX **Nouvelle,** Erlachstr. 46 ⊠ 8003 ☎ 462,63 63 – ⓟ. 𝖠𝖤 ⓞ 𝖤 𝘝𝘐𝘚𝘈   V **y**
Samstag Mittag, Sonntag und Feb. geschl. – Karte 34,50/59.50.

XX **Widder,** Widdergasse 6 ⊠ 8001 ☎ 211 31 50 – 𝖠𝖤 ⓞ 𝖤 𝘝𝘐𝘚𝘈   BY **f**
2.Juli-2. Aug. geschl. – Karte 34 /68,50.

In der Umgebung

über ① Richtung Affoltern

in Regensdorf : 12 km – ⊠ **8105** Regensdorf :

🏨 **Moevenpick Holiday Inn** Ⓜ, im Zentrum ☎ 840 25 20, Telex 53658, 🔲 – 🛗 🖃 ℡ ☎ ᕖ
🚗 – ᵹᴬ 1 000. 𝖠𝖤 ⓞ 𝖤 𝘝𝘐𝘚𝘈
Karte Grillroom 27/52 – 🍴 11 – **153 Z** 94/129.

in Dielsdorf : 15,5 km – ⊠ **8157** Dielsdorf :

XX **Bienengarten,** Regensbergerstr. 9 ☎ 853 12 17 – ⓟ. 𝖠𝖤 ⓞ 𝖤
Ostern, 1.-20.Okt. und Samstag Mittag geschl. – Karte 19 /46,50.

in Regensberg : 17 km – ⊠ **8158** Regensberg :

XXX **Krone,** ☎ 853 11 35, ≤ Züricher Berge. 𝖠𝖤 ⓞ
20. Dez.-20. Jan und Sonntag 15 Uhr - Montag geschl. – Karte 55/140.

über ② Richtung Schaffhausen

in Zürich-Kloten (Flughafen) 10 km :

🏨 **Hilton International** Ⓜ, Hohenbühlstr. 10 ⊠ 8058 Zürich ☎ 810 31 31, Telex 55135, ≤, ⇔,
🔲, 🐎 – 🛗 🖃 ℡ ☎ ⓟ – ᵹᴬ 180. 𝖠𝖤 ⓞ 𝖤 ⅏ Rest
Sutter'Grill Karte 43/51, **Coffee Shop** Karte 16,50 – ⌸ 10,50 – **287 Z** 102/171.

🏨 **Mövenpick Hotel Zürich Airport** Ⓜ, Walter Mittelholzerstr. 8 ⊠ 8152 Glattbrugg ☎ 810
11 11, Telex 57979, 🔲 – 🛗 🖃 ℡ ☎ ᕖ ⓟ – ᵹᴬ 160. 𝖠𝖤 ⓞ 𝖤 𝘝𝘐𝘚𝘈
Karte 12/37 – 🍴 12 – **335 Z** 100/150.

🏨 **Airport** Ⓜ Glattbrugg ⊠ 8152 Glattbrugg ☎ 810 44 44, Telex 53287 – 🛗 ℡ ⌷wc 🛁wc ☎
ⓟ – ᵹᴬ 20. 𝖠𝖤 ⓞ 𝖤 𝘝𝘐𝘚𝘈
Karte 25/54 – **47 Z** ⌸ 70/130.

🏨 **Welcome Inn,** Holbergstr. 1 in Kloten ⊠ 8302 Kloten ☎ 814 07 27, Telex 54653 – 🛗 🛁wc ☎
🚗 – ᵹᴬ 15
91 Z.

XXX **Top Air,** ⊠ 8058 Zürich ☎ 814 33 00
Karte 22/56.

über ③ Nordufer

in Zollikon : 5 km – ⊠ **8702** Zollikon

XXXX ❀ **Chez Max** (Kehl), Seestr. 53 ☎ 391 88 77, ≤ – 𝖠𝖤 ⓞ 𝖤   V **n**
9.-19. April, 19. Juli-2. Aug., Sonntag und Montag Mittag geschl. – Karte 65/140
Spez. La crêpe de riz sauvage au balik et caviar, les aiguillettes de cailles, crêpes soufflées.

XX **Wirtschaft zur Höhe,** Höhestr. 73 ☎ 391 59 59 – 𝖠𝖤 𝖤
5.- 27. Juli, 7.-15. Feb. u. Dienstag geschl. – Karte 24/50.

in Küsnacht : 6 km – ⊠ **8700** Küsnacht

🏨 **Ermitage du Lac,** Sustr. 80 ☎ 910 52 22, Telex 53036, ≤, « Schöne Lage am Seeufer,
Garten, Terrasse » – 🛗 🖃 Rest ⌷wc ⓟ. 𝖠𝖤 ⓞ 𝖤 𝘝𝘐𝘚𝘈
11. Jan.-10. Febr. geschl. – Karte 30/56 – **27 Z** ⌸ 55/160.

über ④ Richtung Chur-Südufer

in Rüschlikon : 9 km – ⊠ **8803** Rüschlikon :

🏨 **Belvoir** Ⓜ Ⳣ, Sa umerstr. 37 ☎ 724 02 02, Telex 59447, ≤ See – 🛗 ℡ ⌷wc 🛁wc ☎ 🚗
ⓟ – ᵹᴬ 300. 𝖠𝖤 ⓞ 𝘝𝘐𝘚𝘈 ⅏ Rest
Karte 27.50 /46,50 – **20 Z** ⌸ 70/120.

in Gattikon : 13,5 km – ⊠ **8136** Gattikon-Thalwil :

XX ❀ **Sihlhalde,** Sihlhaldenstr. 70 ☎ 720 09 27 – ⓞ 𝘝𝘐𝘚𝘈
20.Juli-15. Aug., Montag ab 14 Uhr und Dienstag geschl. – Karte 22/55.

in Wädenswil : 22 km – ⊠ **8820** Wädenswil

XXX ❀ **Eichmühle** (Wannenwetsch), Neugutstr. 933 ☎ 780 34 44 – ⓟ. 𝖠𝖤 ⓞ 𝖤
22. Aug.-12. Sept. und Dienstag geschl. – Karte 47/75
Spez. Truffe en surprise, Blanquette de homard à la crème de ciboulette, Mignonette d'agneau au thym et ail.

XXX **Wirtschaft Zum Letten,** Neudorfstr. 30 ☎ 780 86 55 – ⓟ. 𝖠𝖤 ⓞ 𝖤 𝘝𝘐𝘚𝘈
Samstag Mittag geschl. – Karte 26/52.

INDICATIFS TÉLÉPHONIQUES EUROPÉENS

EUROPEAN DIALLING CODES

TELEFON-VORWAHLNUMMERN EUROPÄISCHER LÄNDER

INDICATIVOS TELEFÒNICOS DE PAISES EUROPEOS

INDICATIVI TELEFONICI DEI PAESI EUROPEI

(A)	Österreich, Autriche, Austria	43	(I)	Italia, Italie	39
(B)	Belgique, België, Belgium	32	(IRL)	Ireland, Irlande	353
(CH)	Schweiz, Suisse, Svizzera, Switzerland	41	(L)	Luxembourg	352
			(MC)	Monaco	33
(D)	Bundesrepublik Deutschland, RFA, West Germany	49	(N)	Norge, Norvège, Norway	47
(DK)	Danmark, Danemark, Denmark	45	(NL)	Nederland, Pays-Bas, Netherlands	31
(E)	España, Espagne, Spain	34	(P)	Portugal	351
(F)	France	33	(S)	Sverige, Suède, Sweden	46
(GB)	Great Britain, Grande-Bretagne	44	(SF)	Suomi, Finland	358
(GR)	Hellás, Grèce, Greece	30	(YU)	Jugoslavija, Yougoslavie	38

Entre certains pays limitrophes, il existe des indicatifs spéciaux. S'informer.

Between certain neighbouring countries the dialling code may vary. Make enquiries.

Zwischen bestimmten benachbarten Ländern gibt es spezielle Vorwahlnummern. Informieren Sie sich.

Entre ciertos paises limítrofes, existen indicativos especiales. Informarse.

Fra alcuni paesi limitrofi esistono dei prefissi telefonici speciali. Informarsi preventivamente.

VITESSE

Comment déterminer la vitesse à laquelle on roule :
Chronométrer le temps employé pour parcourir un kilomètre à vitesse constante ; lire ensuite dans le tableau ci-dessous, en face du temps relevé, la vitesse correspondante en kilomètres ou en miles par heure. (Cette vitesse est calculée avec une approximation pratiquement négligeable).

SPEED

To determine the speed at which you are travelling :
Check the time you take to cover a kilometre at constant speed ; in the table below, you will find the corresponding speed in kilometres or miles per hour. (The figures have been rounded to the nearest m.p.h.).

GESCHWINDIGKEIT

Wie man die Geschwindigkeit bestimmt, mit der man fährt :
Messen Sie genau die Zeit, die Sie brauchen, um einen Kilometer bei gleichbleibender Geschwindigkeit zurückzulegen. Auf der untenstehenden Tabelle können Sie dann Ihre Geschwindigkeit in Kilometern oder Meilen pro Stunde ablesen. (Diese Werte weisen eine nur geringfügige Ungenauigkeit auf).

VELOCIDAD

Cómo determinar la velocidad a la que se rueda :
Cronometrar el tiempo empleado en recorrer un kilómetro a velocidad constante. Después, leer en el cuadro siguiente frente al tiempo anotado, la velocidad correspondiente en kilómetros o en millas por hora. (Esta velocidad ha sido calculada con un minimo margen de error).

VELOCITÀ

Come determinare a quale velocità si sta correndo :
Cronometrare il tempo impiegato per percorrere un km a velocità costante ; leggere quindi nella tabella che segue, a fianco del tempo determinato, la velocità corrispondente, calcolata in km o miglia orari. (Questa velocità è calcolata con un'approssimazione praticamente trascurabile).

	km	miles		km	miles		km	miles
0mn18s	.200	.124	0mn49s	.73	.45	1mn30s	.40	.25
19	.189	.117	50s	.72	.44,5	33	.39	.24
20s	.180	.112	51	.70	.43,5	35	.38	.23,5
21	.171	.106	52	.69	.43	37	.37	.23
22	.164	.102	53	.68	.42	40s	.36	.22,5
23	.157	.97	54	.67	.41,5	43	.35	.21,5
24	.150	.93	55	.66	.41	46	.34	.21
25	.144	.89	56	.64	.39,5	50s	.33	.20,5
26	.138	.86	57	.63	.39	53	.32	.20
27	.133	.82	58	.62	.38,5	56	.31	.19
28	.129	.80	59	.61	.38	2mn00	.30	.18,5
29	.124	.77	1mn00	.60	.37	5	.29	.18
30s	.120	.74	1	.59	.36,5	10	.28	.17,5
31	.116	.72	2	.58	.36	15	.27	.16,5
32	.113	.70	3	.57	.35,5	20	.26	.16
33	.109	.68	4	.56	.34,5	24	.25	.15,5
34	.106	.66	6	.55	.34	30s	.24	.15
35	.103	.64	7	.54	.33,5	35	.23	.14,5
36	.100	.62	8	.53	.33	45	.22	.13,5
37	.97	.60	9	.52	.32	55	.21	.13
38	.95	.59	10s	.51	.31,5	3mn00	.20	.12,5
39	.92	.57	12	.50	.31	15	.19	.12
40s	.90	.56	14	.49	.30,5	20	.18	.11
41	.88	.55	15	.48	.30	30s	.17	.10,5
42	.86	.53	17	.47	.29	45	.16	.10
43	.84	.52	19	.46	.28,5	4mn00	.15	.9,5
44	.82	.51	20s	.45	.28	15	.14	.8,5
45	.80	.50	22	.44	.27,5	30	.13	.8
46	.78	.49	24	.43	.26,5	5mn00	.12	.7,5
47	.77	.48	26	.42	.26	30	.11	.7
48	.75	.46	28	.41	.25,5	6mn00	.10	.6

Notes

Notizen

Apuntes

MANUFACTURE FRANÇAISE DES PNEUMATIQUES MICHELIN

Société en commandite par actions au capital de 700 millions de francs

Place des Carmes-Déchaux - 63 Clermont-Ferrand (France)

R.C.S. Clermont-Fd B 855 200 507

© Michelin et Cie, Propriétaires-Éditeurs

Dépôt légal 5-82 - ISBN 2 06 007 022 - 8 - ISSN en attente

———————

Printed in France 3-82-90

Photocomposition : Imprimerie S.C.I.A. La Chapelle d'Armentières

Impression Kapp et Lahure n° 336

Les cartes et les guides Michelin sont complémentaires, utilisez-les ensemble.

Michelin maps and guides are complementary publications. Use them together.

Die Michelin-Karten und Führer ergänzen sich. Benutzen Sie diese zusammen.

Le carte e le guide Michelin sono complementari : utilizzatele insieme.

De Michelin kaarten en gidsen vullen elkaar aan. Gebruik ze samen.

France
Benelux
Deutschland
España   Portugal
Great Britain and Ireland
Italia